T0317433

Rival Partners

HARVARD-YENCHING INSTITUTE MONOGRAPH SERIES 133

Rival Partners

How Taiwanese Entrepreneurs and Guangdong Officials Forged the China Development Model

By Wu Jieh-min
Translated by Stacy Mosher

Published by the Harvard University Asia Center
Distributed by Harvard University Press
Cambridge (Massachusetts) and London 2022

The Harvard University Asia Center publishes a monograph series and, in coordination with the Fairbank Center for Chinese Studies, the Korea Institute, the Reischauer Institute of Japanese Studies, and other faculties and institutes, administers research projects designed to further scholarly understanding of China, Japan, Vietnam, Korea, and other Asian countries. The Center also sponsors projects addressing multidisciplinary and regional issues in Asia.

The Harvard-Yenching Institute, founded in 1928, is an independent foundation dedicated to the advancement of higher education in the humanities and social sciences in Asia. Headquartered on the campus of Harvard University, the Institute provides fellowships for advanced research, training, and graduate studies at Harvard by competitively selected faculty and graduate students from Asia. The Institute also supports a range of academic activities at its fifty partner universities and research institutes across Asia. At Harvard, the Institute promotes East Asian studies through annual contributions to the Harvard-Yenching Library and publication of the *Harvard Journal of Asiatic Studies* and the Harvard-Yenching Institute Monograph Series.

Library of Congress Cataloging-in-Publication Data

Names: Wu, Jiemin, 1962– author. | Mosher, Stacy, translator.
Title: Rival partners : how Taiwanese entrepreneurs and Guangdong officials forged the China development model / Wu Jieh-min ; translated by Stacy Mosher.
Other titles: Xun zu Zhongguo. English | Harvard-Yenching Institute monograph series ; 133.
Description: Cambridge, Massachusetts : Harvard University Asia Center, 2022. | Series: Harvard-Yenching Institute monograph series; 133 | Includes bibliographical references and index. |
Identifiers: LCCN 2022020657 | ISBN 9780674278226 (hardcover)
Subjects: LCSH: Investments, Taiwan—China—Guangdong Sheng. | Corporations, Taiwan—China—Guangdong Sheng. | Rent seeking—China—Guangdong Sheng—History. | Guangdong Sheng (China)—Economic conditions. | China—Economic policy—1949–
Classification: LCC HF1606.Z4 C684713 2022 | DDC 337.512490512/7—dc23/eng/20220602
LC record available at https://lccn.loc.gov/2022020657

Index by Do Mi Stauber
♾ Printed on acid-free paper

Last figure below indicates year of this printing
30   29   28   27   26   25   24   23   22

I dedicate this book to my mother, 蔡靜子 Tshuà Tsīng-tsú.

Contents

List of Tables   xi

List of Figures   xiv

Map   xvi

Foreword by Elizabeth J. Perry   xvii

Preface to the English Edition   xxiii

Preface   xxvii

Abbreviations   xxxi

Introduction: Taishang, China, and the World   1
    1. The Taishang Enigma   2
    2. Exploitation with Chinese Characteristics   5
    3. The Neomercantilist Policy   7
    4. The United States Challenges China's Industrial Strategy   10
    5. The Taishang Perspective   14
    6. How This Book Is Organized   21

1   Forging the Factory of the World   27
    1. Analytical Focus   31
    2. The March toward Becoming the Factory of the World   35
    3. An Examination of Existing Theoretical Propositions   44
    4. The GVC and Local Growth Alliances   58
    5. Cases, Methods, and Data   71

2   The Origins, Performance, and Evolution of the
    Guangdong Model   80
    1. One Step Ahead: Opportunity and Risk   81
    2. The Origins of the Guangdong Model   88
    3. Guangdong's Economic Performance   102
    4. Changing Trends in Guangdong's Macro Environment   130

3   Taiyang Company, 1979–94   144
    1. A Brief History of Taiyang Company   145
    2. The Business Model at the Taiwan Stage   148
    3. Proceeding to Guangdong: The Shifting of GVCs   151
    4. Faux Joint Ventures and the Head Tax   163
    5. Guanqiang and the Head-Counting Game   169
    6. The 1994 Foreign Exchange Reform   176
    7. Building a New Factory in Nafu Village   179
    8. The Institutional Emergence of the Head Tax   183

4   Taiyang Company, 1995–2010   187
    1. Nafu Village: The Grassroots Unit of the EOI Growth
       Model   188
    2. The Second Generation Takes Over   194
    3. Changes in Government-Business Relations   198
    4. The Localization of Cadres and Increasing Social Insurance
       Fees   206
    5. Closing the Factory   212
    6. The Disappearance of the Head Tax and the Emergence
       of Social Insurance Fees   216

5   The Migrant Worker Class: Differential Citizenship,
    Double Exploitation, and the Labor Regime   221
    1. The State Creates the Migrant Worker Class   222
    2. The Figuration of the Migrant Worker Class   232
    3. The Dual Labor Market: The Myth of Low Wages and
       Overtime   245
    4. Differential Citizenship and Double Exploitation   257
    5. New Urban Protectionism: Discrimination in Education
       and Social Insurance   267
    6. Reexploring the Labor Regime   285

6   Taiwanese- and Chinese-Owned Companies under the
    Transformation of the Guangdong Model   302
    1. State Policy and Changes in Government-Business Relations   303
    2. Smiles Shoes Company: A Taishang Transforms on
       the Ground   321
    3. Taishin Shoe Manufacturing Group: The Diversified
       Transformation of a Taiwanese Company   330
    4. The Changing Ecosystems of Taiwanese and Chinese
       Companies   351
    5. Industrial and Social Upgrading   368

7   The GVC and the Rent-Seeking Developmental State   374
    1. Changes in the GVC and Reorganization of the
       Growth Alliances   375
    2. A Theory of the Rent-Seeking Developmental State   381
    3. Comparing the Development Experiences of China and the
       Rest of East Asia   394
    4. A Preliminary Evaluation of the Semiconductor Industrial
       Upgrading Blueprint of Made in China 2025   413

Conclusion: Pitfalls and Challenges   425
    1. The Pitfalls of China's Development   425
    2. The United States Challenges Made in China 2025   429
    3. China and Globalization Theory   439

    Glossary   447
    Index of Interview Codes   451
    Works Cited   455
    Index   479

List of Tables

2.1.   Comparison of Dongguan's fiscal revenue and
        processing fee earnings in selected years, 1979–2003.   121

2.2.   Average urban-work-unit employees' wages and minimum
        wages in Guangdong Province, the Shenzhen SEZ, and
        Shenzhen outer districts, 1992–2014 (yuan per month).   124

2.3.   Minimum wages and average urban-work-unit employees'
        wagess in Shanghai, Suzhou, and the Shenzhen SEZ,
        selected years 1993–2013 (yuan per month).   126

2.4.   The launch of the Guangdong model and its two
        transformations.   131

2.5.   Guangdong's export trade amount and export
        composition, selected years, 1990–2013.   137

2.6A.   Foreign exchange earnings by Guangdong's various
        ownership sectors, selected years, 1990–2013
        (US$100 million).   141

2.6B.   Foreign exchange contribution by Guangdong's various
        ownership sectors, selected years, 1990– 2013 (% of foreign
        trade surplus).   142

3.1.   Various taxes and related fees paid by Taiyang in 1993.   172

3.2.   The annual fees Taiyang's new factory paid to
        Nafu Village.   181

4.1.   Taiyang's social insurance costs per employee
in 2006–7 (yuan per month).   210

4.2.   Number of staff members employed by Taiyang and
social insurance participation rates, selected periods
in 1994–2009.   211

4.3.   Taiyang's formula for calculating severance pay.   213

5.1A.   China's floating population in censuses and sampling
surveys, selected years, 1982–2010 (thousands of people).   234

5.1B.   Gender ratio of China's floating population in the 2000
and 2010 census (thousands of people).   236

5.2A.   Ratio of nonnatives to natives in the local
urban-work-unit employed population, 2008
(thousands of people).   239

5.2B.   Ratio of nonnatives to natives in the local
urban-work-unit employed population, 2013
(thousands of people).   239

5.3.   Proportion of nonnative residents in Shenzhen and
Dongguan, 2005–13 (tens of thousands of people).   240

5.4A.   Number of workers employed in China's urban industries
by ownership category, 2006 (thousands of people).   242

5.4B.   Number of workers employed in China's urban industries
by ownership category, 2011 (thousands of people).   243

5.5A.   Minimum wage and the average wage of urban
employed staff, 2008 (yuan per month).   246

5.5B.   Minimum wage and the average wage of urban
employed staff, 2012 (yuan per month).   247

5.6.   Differentiated payment rates for three types of
insurance plans in Shanghai, 2008 (%).   272

5.7.   Survey of social insurance in six Shanghai factories,
2007.   275

5.8.   Differentiated payment rates for Shanghai's social
insurance during the transition period (2011–16) under
the 2011 plan (%).   277

5.9.   Social insurance payment rates for migrant workers
        in four southeastern coastal cities, 2008 (%).   280

5.10.   Social insurance payment rates in three major cities
        of the Pearl River Delta, 2008 (%).   284

7.1.   Categories of rent-seeking behavior from the
        organizational standpoint.   386

7.2.   The developmental states of China (Guangdong),
        Taiwan, and South Korea.   396

List of Figures

1.1. Dynamic links between global capital and the
    local polity.   32

1.2. G-D-L links: the three domains in the revised
    global-local analysis framework.   60

1.3. G-D-L analysis: the value chain governance domain
    and locally embedded governance domain.   62

1.4. Analytical framework for a local growth alliance
    oriented to a global value or commodity chain.   69

2.1. Shenzhen's first agreement for processing shipped
    materials, 1978.   93

2.2. FDI's contribution to capital formation in Guangdong,
    Jiangsu, and China as a whole, 1985–2013.   107

2.3. Guangdong's FDI in billions of US dollars and as a
    percent of the national total, 1985–2014.   108

2.4. Taiwan's direct investment in China, 1992–2013
    (US$1 billion).   112

2.5. Taiwan's direct investment in Guangdong, 1991–2013,
    (US$1 billion).   114

2.6. Foreign trade dependence in Guangdong, Jiangsu,
    and nationwide, 1978–2013 (%).   115

2.7.   Guangdong's trade surplus as a percentage of the
       national trade surplus, 1990–2013.   118

2.8.   Trends in China's foreign trade balance and foreign
       exchange reserves, 1981–2013 (US$1 billion).   119

2.9.   Minimum wages in Shenzhen, Shanghai, and Suzhou,
       1992–2013 (yuan).   127

2.10. The ratio of China's total labor remuneration to GDP,
      1994–2012 (yuan).   128

2.11. Guangdong's processing trade surplus and its
      contribution to total trade surplus (EP/T ratio),
      1995–2013.   139

3.1.   Taiyang Company's supply chain structure, 1979–88.   151

3.2.   Taiyang Company's supply chain structure, 1998–2010.   158

3.3.   The foreign exchange earning mechanism of local
       Chinese foreign trade companies, using Taiyang
       as an example.   167

3.4.   The institutional origins of the head tax.   184

3.5.   The floating significance of the head tax.   185

4.1.   The differential citizenship framework in Nafu Village.   190

4.2.   Taiyang's reduction in head tax and increase in social
       insurance fees, selected years in 1998–2008.   217

4.3.   Institutional emergence of social insurance fees and
       the housing fund.   219

5.1.   Foxconn pay slip, April 2008.   256

6.1.   Taishin's GVC position in relation to its
       internal organization.   352

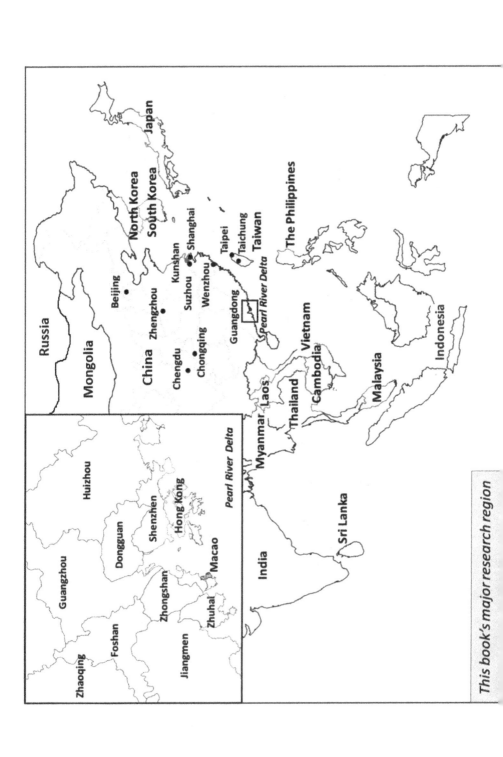

This book's major research region

Foreword by Elizabeth J. Perry

In this illuminating book, Wu Jieh-min tackles one of the most pressing challenges of our day: explaining the rise of China. His answer draws intelligently and inventively upon previous theoretical and empirical scholarship, while also introducing a wealth of new information and insight based on twenty-five years of pioneering fieldwork and painstaking documentary research.

Like Ezra Vogel's classic *One Step ahead in China: Guangdong under Reform*, Wu's book points to the catalytic role of Guangdong's post-Mao economic experiments in paving the way for a new national growth strategy. But whereas Vogel's study was based primarily on interviews with Chinese provincial officials responsible for economic reforms, Wu's key informants are the Taiwanese entrepreneurs (Taishang) and managers (Taigan) who provided much of the essential capital and expertise that allowed the reforms to work. Fueling the Guangdong model as it took shape in industrial hubs like Dongguan and Shenzhen was the significant financial investment and manufacturing know-how of numerous Taiwanese businessmen and technicians. A Taiwanese himself, Wu elicits from his interlocutors the inside story of how the crucial connections between overseas investors and local governments originated and operated.

Why did profit-oriented Taiwanese entrepreneurs and a rent-seeking Chinese state find it in their common interest to cooperate? Wu explains that the mutually advantageous relationship was built on the backs of poorly paid migrant workers from the countryside whose dual exploitation by state and capital was enabled by a restrictive household registration (*hukou*) system that denied people of rural origin the benefits of urban residency. Low wages allowed Taiwanese capitalists to employ high-quality labor at globally competitive prices, while migrants' exclusion from the privileged status of urban citizenship also spared the Chinese state from having to provide expensive welfare benefits. The arrangement was sufficiently lucrative for both state and capital to allow local governments to charge Taiwanese investors hefty rents in the form of so-called processing fees, management fees, fictive ownership contractual schemes, and the like.

Previous scholars have examined the place of the *hukou* system in relegating migrants to second-class citizenship, as well as the role of local governments in serving simultaneously as engines of both rent seeking and rural industrialization, but Wu's original investigation of Taiwanese involvement connects the dots between these well-known phenomena and the wider global value chain in which they functioned and from which they derived profits. The global networks that Taiwanese entrepreneurs introduced to Guangdong, he shows, became embedded in a developmental governance structure sustained by rent seeking.

While the Chinese state, at both the central and local levels, played a major part in shaping the rural industrialization process, its role differed substantially from that of other authoritarian states as delineated in the East Asian development model of an earlier era. Not only was the People's Republic of China (PRC) much more welcoming to foreign direct investment, but its discriminatory policy of differential citizenship kept migrant workers from realizing a fair return on their labor. Thus, unlike in Taiwan and South Korea, where industrialization brought impressive gains in income equality and social welfare, in China the process was accompanied by increasing socioeconomic inequality. Village cadres and factory heads constituted a privileged rentier class that collected factory rent, land rent, management fees, migrant labor agency fees, and more.

The financial advantages of these arrangements for the Chinese state were substantial, leading to a rapid diffusion of the Guangdong model. Wu traces its spread from the Pearl River Delta to the Yangtze Delta's industrial hubs of Shanghai and Suzhou. The forms of Taiwanese embedment in local governance differed to some degree across regions, but the cumulative impact was nonetheless considerable. In 2010, some 85 percent of Taiwan's total overseas investment went to the PRC, although Chinese official records played down Taiwan's contribution. Wu puts it starkly: "It is hard to imagine the Guangdong model without Taiwanese investment; and without the Guangdong model, the rise of China would not have occurred."

The rise of China required more than local rent seeking, of course. As Wu notes, this was "rent seeking behavior with Chinese characteristics." Driven by a developmental agenda of economic nationalism, the PRC leveraged the infusion of foreign capital strategically to protect and promote the growth of domestic industry. Wu traces how the central government's gradual adoption of new industrial policies to move beyond low-end manufacturing and upgrade its emerging high-tech sector ultimately undermined the Guangdong model, based as it was on an equilibrium of formal and informal rules governing local processing fees. A spectacularly successful thirty-year effort to build the world's factory was superseded by an attempt (whose success is as yet uncertain) to construct a Chinese-controlled global value chain geared to the knowledge economy of the twenty-first century. The result has been a mass exodus of Taiwanese investors and advisors. By 2018, the PRC's share of Taiwan's overseas investment had dropped to 40 percent, less than half of what it had been only a few years earlier.

Today, China's combination of concentrated investment in infrastructure, tight control over state-owned enterprises, and command-style regulation of industrial policy have put the PRC on a development path that many find concerning if not threatening. As Wu observes, however, there is nothing inevitable about its continued success: "China may well descend into developmental slowdown or stagnation." Under Xi Jinping's "Made in China 2025" program, the ambitious bid to construct a self-controlled high-tech supply chain to replace the global value chain could certainly backfire. China's rent-seeking developmental trajectory has to date defied conventional theories of economic development, and its future direction is impossible to predict with confidence.

Regardless of how the future unfolds, Wu's insightful analysis of the past forty years of Chinese economic progress will stand as a major contribution to explaining China's historic rise. Combining rich ethnographic detail with a comprehensive theoretical framework that links international connections to local governance networks, Wu offers a convincing account of one of the most important and least expected stories of our time.

Anyone seeking to understand how China defied the best predictions of Western social science to advance in less than two generations from one of the poorest countries in the world to one of the most prosperous and powerful, while eschewing fundamental political reform, should read Wu's fascinating book. But those hoping to find here a replicable recipe or transferrable China model for rapid economic growth will be disappointed. Very few other countries can expect to attract the levels of capital and capability that Taiwanese entrepreneurs and managers provided the PRC. And fewer still can exert the degree of government control over their populations that in the case of China has allowed state and capital alike to prosper so abundantly at the expense of labor.

The PRC's stratified and unequal system of differentiated citizenship, Wu concludes, is the most important example of authoritarian citizenship since Nazi Germany and wartime Japan. Marginal reforms (to improve the treatment of migrants and expand educational opportunities for their children) have done little to redress the fundamental injustice of a discriminatory system that continues to serve the common interests of state and capital.

It is common for observers of contemporary China to point out that despite the rapid growth of a business class in the post-Mao period, the PRC shows no sign of bourgeois-driven democratization along the lines that modernization theory might predict. However, rather than dismiss Barrington Moore's *Social Origins of Dictatorship and Democracy* as irrelevant—inasmuch as China is not following the bourgeois revolutionary path of modernization forged by England, France, and America—we might be better advised to ponder Moore's sobering discussion of an alternative aristocratic revolutionary path: the repressive coalition of state and capital that allowed fascist Germany and militaristic Japan to industrialize rapidly on the backs of their enserfed peasantry. Although China lacks a landed aristocracy like the Prussian Junkers or Japanese samurai, its so-called red aristocracy (composed of the descendants of Communist revolutionaries) has participated in a disturbingly similar consolidation of state and capital at the expense of rural labor. Even as the PRC moves beyond the alliance of Taiwanese investors and local officials that characterized the Guangdong model, the intertwining of capital and state interests persists.

Marked by calls for the "great rejuvenation of the Chinese nation," together with the brutal treatment of ethnic minority groups at home and an increasingly muscular stance abroad, the current expression of China's economic rise generates understandable anxiety around the world. However it may evolve, its foundations demand serious scholarly analysis. Toward that end, Wu's thoughtful and thought-provoking book on the origins and iterations of China's rent-seeking development state is an indispensable guide.

Preface to the English Edition

Taiwan has been both a beneficiary and a victim of China's rise. This duality highlights the tangled relationship between the world and China today. When the Chinese edition of this book was finalized in late 2018,[1] the US-China trade war was less than a year old, and the technology war had just begun. In December of that year, Meng Wanzhou, the deputy chair and chief financial officer (CFO) of China's pride and joy, Huawei Technologies (and daughter of Huawei's founder and chief executive officer [CEO], Ren Zhengfei), was arrested in Canada on charges of shipping sensitive technology to Iran and North Korea in violation of US export controls. Hundreds of Chinese companies, including Huawei, are now on the US government's list of entities requiring export control of high-tech products on the grounds of national security and human rights violations. In the administrations of both President Donald Trump and President Joe Biden, China has been treated as a strategic competitor, and US-China confrontation has replaced the mutual engagement of the previous era. The geopolitical conditions that enabled China's rapid development no longer exist. Meng was released in September 2021, but this didn't mean the end of the technology war.

---

1. The Chinese edition (*Xunzu Zhongguo: Taishang, Guangdong Moshi yu Quanqiu Zibenzhuyi* [Rent-Seeking Developmental State in China: Taishang, Guangdong Model and Global Capitalism]) was published as the National Taiwan University Press–Harvard-Yenching Institute Book Series 07 by the NTU Press in 2019.

This book offers a Taiwanese perspective on the rise of China's economy and uses the eyes of Taiwanese businesspeople to analyze China's unique but globally influential citizenship system, institutional rent seeking, and development model. My hope is that the Taiwanese perspective can provide readers with a fresh perspective, as the world closely watches the political and economic direction that China is taking. During the years of China's opening reform, Taiwanese businesses and entrepreneurs commuted in and out of China under a special and flexible status, helping initiate China's global links and introducing the capitalist system to China. In the process, however, China also demonstrated the resilience of its institutions and its ambition to compete for technological hegemony and geopolitical supremacy. This book suggests that the fundamental way for China to defy US regional and global dominance was to challenge US hegemony at the economic level. The China model's explosive achievements have unexpectedly become a stumbling block to its own sustainability. I'm gratified to see this point of view, which runs through this book, becoming more distinct and prominent as the international situation has evolved over the past few years.

I'm particularly grateful to Elizabeth Perry for inviting me to have the book translated, arranging for the Harvard-Yenching Institute to sponsor most of the translation costs, introducing me to the Harvard University Asia Center book series, and writing the foreword. My colleagues, Shieh Gwo-Shyong and Chih-Jou Jay Chen, former and current director, respectively, of the Institute of Sociology at Academia Sinica in Taiwan, also facilitated the project and arranged for the institute to sponsor a portion of the funding.

Stacy Mosher was the best translator I could have found. As soon as Sebastian Veg recommended Stacy to me, I wrote an effusive late-night invitation and heard back from her before dawn. With professionalism and efficiency, Stacy has produced an informative, accurate, and reader-friendly translation, and she has provided translator's notes to help readers who are not China specialists better understand the context. The original Chinese text inevitably carried the conceptual structure of Chinese syntax, while my Taiwanese perspective legitimately made use of Taiwanese idioms and scholarly research. Furthermore, there is no ready English equivalent for many Chinese terms. I'm grateful to Stacy for working closely and collaboratively with me to present difficult text using the most precise and accessible vocabulary possible. I have proofread the manuscript several times and have discussed it with Stacy repeatedly, so if there are any errors in the English version, of course I take responsibility for them.

Because of space limitations, I have slightly condensed the original text to streamline some of the literature review, fieldwork quotes, tables, charts, and footnotes. These edits should not detract from the logic and argumentation of the original text. In addition, where necessary, I have added footnotes that begin "Author's Postscript" to explain a few special terms and events and research findings that have cropped up since the publication of the Chinese edition.

I would like to thank Ching Kwan Lee, who anonymously reviewed an earlier draft of the manuscript for the Harvard University Asia Center, for suggested changes to the translation. Andrew Nathan and Michelle Fei-yu Hsieh gave me valuable advice on preparing the English manuscript and submitting it for review. My research assistant Lin Cheng-yu assisted with locating references and checking statistical figures for this edition. I extend further thanks to Robert Graham, director of publications for the Harvard University Asia Center, and Kristen Wanner, editor at the center, for their professional and enthusiastic assistance. Thanks also to Angela Piliouras for handling the production process and to Jeanne Ferris for her copyediting assistance. The process of double-checking the URLs for the Chinese references had me exhausted and even indignant. Many posts I cited either disappeared or were deleted due to censorship or other mysterious reasons, and some of them were no longer traceable. The Kafkaesque specter loomed large as I struggled with digital Leninism. But when I finally overcame these difficulties, I felt empowered and treasured this round of virtual fieldwork. After months of revising the copyedited manuscript and proofreading the typeset pages, I realized how rigorous the production process can be. I genuinely appreciate Kristen, Jeanne, and Angela's support, and I thank Lin Cheng-yu and Liao Mei for their help with the final stage of proofreading and Do Mi Stauber for providing an excellent index for the book.

Preface

The conception of this book can be traced back to my youthful dream of directing films. In the early 1990s, some friends and I established the Lanes and Alleys Workshop to produce documentary films. One of those films was *Taiwan Compatriots* (*Taibao*), which described the experience of the first generation of Taiwan entrepreneurs (Taishang) and Taiwanese managers (Taigan) in China. At that time, this topic was controversial, and because of that and our technical limitations, the film bombed at its premiere at National Taiwan University. I confronted doubts by issuing this bold promise: "I will spend five or ten years finding the answers." I never guessed that doing so would take me so far and so long. My parents viewed the film, and my mother said, "How shocking! Is that criticism?" I said, "It's an academic discussion." This book's publication can be considered my effort to help my mother get over her shock.

After the Mao era ended, China earned its first bucket of money from the Guangdong model in US dollars. Earning US dollars showed that China had become linked to global capitalism. This bucket of money served as primitive accumulation, and years later, in a roundabout way, it facilitated China's rise. The Guangdong model seems to have faded from memory over time, but its importance resurfaces whenever China encounters external or internal crises. Taishang have also left an indelible mark on Guangdong and the growth of China's export-oriented economy. The time is ripe for a systematic summary of the relationship between Taishang, the Guangdong model, and China's development. My intensive scrutiny of this topic over the course of twenty-five years proposes an overall analysis of the Guangdong model and assesses the role of Taishang. I predict that viewpoints currently ignored for political reasons, such as seeing the Taiwan factor as a driving force in China's contemporary economic development, will become more distinct and explicit in the decades to come.

In early summer 1994, I took a train from Guangzhou to Henan with a migrant worker couple on their way home to visit family members. When we got off the train at Zhumadian, my field of vision was overwhelmed by a mass of blue-clad people. As the wave of humanity poured from the train compartments and flooded the station platform for some fifteen minutes with no letup, my understanding of the developmental economist Arthur Lewis's concept of "unlimited supply of labor" (1954) went from abstract to concrete in the almost suffocating turbulence. Being in the presence of an enormous mass of Chinese was both a realistic and a surrealistic experience. Twenty-five years have passed, and a sense of the Chinese presence has agitated people around the world and triggered a heated global debate. This book is a response to people's concern about the current situation in China, but even more importantly, I have chosen core issues in social science as my point of departure, and I adhere to my theoretical interests in answering these questions. As to how the sense of the Chinese presence has been constructed by the Chinese themselves and by others in recent years, this book also provides a politico-economic approach.

The starting point of my research is inquiring into Taiwan's entanglement with China. I have chosen the entry points of economics rather than culture and contemporary times rather than history. Fumbling about for twenty-five years has brought me back to the initial question: what is Taiwan's future? This question has no easy answers, but this book provides tools for solving the puzzle. I propose using the rent-seeking developmental state to dissect the fundamental questions of China's development. A thorough study of the Guangdong model, together with a clear look at the advantages and weakness in China's development, enables us to make a more confident and balanced evaluation of the status quo and the way forward for Taiwan's economy. At this time, China has reached a critical stage, and both Taiwan and China need to take a long view in calmly pondering their respective ways forward, their linkages with the world, and their relationship with each other.

At multiple points in the research process, I seemed to encounter the legendary Sphinx who blocks the way and demands the answer to an intimidating riddle. The writing process extended endlessly, as fieldwork recollections poured in. Deeply held convictions and the good will of teachers and friends in my research journey sustained me as I shuttled back and forth across borders, leading me to savor the risks, setbacks, and joys of field history. I must first thank my many interviewees, who provided me with valuable data as well as information about their working and living experiences. Academic norms require that I maintain your anonymity, but without your help, this book could never have come about. I especially thank "Mr. Lee" and "Senior Hsu" for their early guidance of my research. In the later stage of research, "WSF," Lo Ming-ling, Freedom Huang, and Cheng Chih-peng shared precious specialized knowledge and research findings. Liao Chinghua and Lin Cheng-yu gave me enormous help in the data collection, creation of tables, and tedious proofreading. My colleagues, students, and assistants at National Tsing Hua University contributed all kinds of intellectual stimulation and assistance. I thank especially my field study partners, whose contributions have merged into the spaces between the lines. At the manuscript drafting stage, my colleagues at the Academia Sinica Institute of Sociology and other academic peers did not hesitate to provide comments. I especially thank Nan Lin, Michelle F. Hsieh, and Shieh Gwo-Shyong for reading my rough draft and writing detailed suggestions, and making the analysis more focused. Andrew Nathan, Dorothy Solinger, Mark Selden, Ho-fung Hung, Ching-Kwan Lee, Yingfang Chen, Tsai Hung-Jeng, Chih-Jou Jay Chen, Hu Shu-wen, and Chang Kuei-min proposed revisions at every stage, from research to finalizing the manuscript. I especially thank Liao Mei for repeatedly copyediting the manuscript and pointing out errors. I thank the anonymous readers at National Taiwan University Press, who required exacting revisions and stimulated my ability to respond to questions. I am also grateful for the assistance of Chen Jo-shui, the convener of the editorial committee of the National Taiwan University Harvard-Yenching Academic Series, and Jih Shu-ling, an editor at National Taiwan University Press. Finally, this book benefited from the support of a specialist book project grant from the Ministry of Science and Technology (Grant No. 102-2410-H-001-051-MY2, for 2013–2015). I also spent months gathering material at the Universities Service Centre for China Studies at the Chinese University of Hong Kong, and I extend my thanks to Jean Hung, Gao Qi, and others there for their assistance.

Abbreviations

BDCC	Buyer-driven commodity chain
CCP	Chinese Communist Party
CEO	Chief executive officer
CFO	Chief financial officer
CIDM	Commune integrated device manufacturer
CSR	Corporate social responsibility
DUP	Directly unproductive profit-seeking activities
EOI	Export-oriented industrialization
EP/T	Export processing/trade
FDI	Foreign direct investment
FIE	Foreign-invested enterprise
GCC	Global commodity chain
G-D-L	Global capital–domestic industrial district–local polity link
GDP	Gross domestic product
G-L	Global-local link
GSC	Global supply chain
GVC	Global value chain
HK	Hong Kong
HR	Human resources
IC	Integrated circuit
ICT	Information and communication technology
IMS	IP [internet protocol] Multimedia Subsystem
ISI	Import-substitution industrialization

IT	Information technology
NGO	Nongovernmental organization
NT$	New Taiwan Dollar
ODM	Original design manufacturing
OEM	Original equipment manufacturing
PDCC	Producer-driven commodity chain
PLA	People's Liberation Army
PRC	People's Republic of China
R&D	Research and development
SEZ	Special economic zones
SOE	State-owned enterprise
TSMC	Taiwan Semiconductor Manufacturing Company
TVEs	Township and village enterprises
UMC	United Microelectronics Corporation
VAT	Value-added tax
WTO	World Trade Organization

INTRODUCTION

Taishang, China, and the World

Talking about China's development model must begin with Guangdong, and talking about the processing trade growth model that rose to fame in Guangdong means starting with Taiwanese entrepreneurs, or Taishang.[1] Yet the contribution of Taishang to China's economy touches not only on the course of history and identity politics on either side of the Taiwan Strait but also on value judgments regarding development and distribution. For this reason, this contribution has long been treated as unclear or even unmentionable.

From the Chinese government's perspective, excessively commending the contribution that Taishang have made to China's economy would cause a loss of face. From Taiwan's perspective, those who criticize authoritarian developmentalism ignore this contribution in favor of emphasizing distribution and exploitation. For Taiwan, the political effect of Taishang is even more difficult to analyze. After all, the collective noun "Taishang" is overly weighted with significance, and companies such as Chi Mei, Want Want, Ting Hsin, Taiwan Semiconductor Manufacturing Company (TSMC), United Microelectronics, and Hon Hai (Foxconn) are each freighted with a different political imagination.[2] The

---

1. What this book refers to as "Taishang" includes Taiwanese businesses operating in China as well as Taiwanese-owned businesses that operate on both sides of the Taiwan Strait; Taishang also refers to the proprietors of these businesses. For a detailed definition of the term, see chapter 1, section 5.

2. Foxconn, a major manufacturer for Apple products, is the trade name of the Taiwanese-owned Hon Hai Precision Industry Co, which has its headquarters in Taiwan.

westward-moving Taishang are given different labels of industrial value such as "traditional industry" or "high-tech industry," but so-called traditional industry has experienced obvious upgrading and transformation over the past thirty years.

1. The Taishang Enigma

At the high-profile annual Boao Forum for Asia held on April 10, 2018, Xi Jinping, China's leader, complacently declared: "Today, China has become the world's second-largest economy, its top industrial nation, its top trading country, and its top holder of foreign exchange reserves. . . . Today, the Chinese people can proudly say that China's second revolution of opening reform has not only profoundly changed China but has also profoundly influenced the entire world!"[3] Despite his full schedule, Xi managed to find ten minutes to receive Taishang representatives. According to a report in *China Times*, he flattered them by saying that the development of China's forty years of opening reform "has to be chalked up to our Taiwan compatriots and Taiwan companies." But he also required Taiwan's industrial and commercial sector to take a clear stand by upholding the "1992 Consensus" and opposing "Taiwan independence," as well as by staunchly promoting the peaceful development of cross-strait relations.[4] By affirming the contribution of Taishang to China's economic development and at the same time warning Taiwan's capitalists to take Beijing's side by upholding the consensus and opposing Taiwan independence, Xi was sending the message that Taishang still have considerable utilitarian value as China pursues global hegemony. But this subtext could not be openly expressed.

---

3. Xi Jinping's speech at the 2018 Boao Forum. "Kaifang gongchuang fanrong, chuangxin yinling weilai (Openness creates prosperity, innovation leads the future)," Xinhuanet, April 10, 2018, http://www.xinhuanet.com/politics/2018-04/10/c_1122660064 .htm.

4. Quoted in Chen Po-ting, "Xi Jinping zan Taishang, gonglaobu ji yibi" (Xi Jinping praises Taishang and records their merits), *China Times*, April 11, 2018, http:// www.chinatimes.com/newspapers/20180411000558-260108.

The Sunflower Movement that erupted in Taiwan in March 2014 targeted the Cross-Strait Service Trade Agreement that resulted from the cooperation of the Chinese Communist Party (CCP) and the Kuomintang and disrupted Beijing's road map for Taiwan. In the previous month, an American scholar of international relations, John Mearsheimer, published "Say Goodbye to Taiwan," in which he took a realist's viewpoint in projecting that a rising China would ultimately achieve hegemony in East Asia and eliminate American influence in the region and would then proceed to annex Taiwan. Mearsheimer wrote that although this wouldn't be accomplished today, next year, or in the coming few years, it would occur within the next few decades. Why was China able to achieve its economic rise in such a short time? Mearsheimer identified a key factor: "By trading with China and helping it grow into an economic powerhouse, Taiwan has helped create a burgeoning Goliath with revisionist goals that include ending Taiwan's independence and making it an integral part of China. In sum, a powerful China isn't just a problem for Taiwan. It is a nightmare" (Mearsheimer 2014).

Xi Jinping and Mearsheimer's views on Taiwan may be diametrically opposite, but the two men reach startlingly similar conclusions about Taiwan's economic role: Both feel that Taiwan played an important role in China's economic rise. In the process of China's opening reform, Taishang helped China develop capitalism and greatly strengthened China's ability to annex Taiwan. For Beijing, this is a giant step toward what Xi refers to as the "great rejuvenation of the Chinese nation," (Xinhuanet 2012), but for many Taiwanese, China's rise and its plans to annex Taiwan are a source of increasing anxiety.

How did Taishang facilitate China's rapid economic growth?

Forty years ago, when China was groping its way along the path of opening up to the outside world, it targeted Taiwan for emulation and imitation, putting particular emphasis on the ability of Taiwanese business to earn foreign exchange through exports. The foreign exchange targets that China's policy makers initially set for Guangdong now look like a modest beginning, and they were achieved well ahead of schedule. Before the early 1990s, however, China barely achieved a trade balance and remained short of foreign exchange. Then, in just ten years, China achieved an overwhelming trade surplus and its foreign exchange reserves increased dramatically, so Taiwan was relegated to the back burner. Yet, the true story is far more complicated than this narrative would suggest.

In this book I analyze how in the course of China's development, Taishang served as a bridge between China and global capitalism and helped China link up with the world. I also show that the Chinese government firmly grasped this opportunity to enter into global value chains (GVCs) and make China into the factory of the world, from which it derived an abundant economic surplus, accumulated foreign exchange reserves, and pushed forward its economic and military modernization. This book focuses its analysis on the historical phase of China's economic transformation from state socialism to capitalism, the development phase lasting from the late 1970s until the mid-2000s. After establishing this foundation, I extend the discussion to China's industrial transformation policy that began in the late 2000s and the effect this had on foreign investment and Taishang.

At the early stage, traditional industrial Taishang followed Hong Kong businesses into China. Hong Kong and Taiwanese businesses introduced capital, technology, and markets, while China provided plentiful low-cost labor. Relatively high-quality labor was an important legacy of the Mao era. Labor-intensive traditional industries such as apparel, footwear, toys, luggage, and other products for everyday use seem insignificant compared with China's development achievements today, but they played a crucial role in allowing China to obtain its first pot of gold after opening reform, and an immense pot of gold that was. This is the first story this book tells, and it is also the starting point of China's economic rise.

Investment by Taishang and Hong Kong businesses in Guangdong's Pearl River Delta, especially in Shenzhen and Dongguan, triggered the takeoff of China's export-oriented economy. In the manufacturing sphere, the importance of Taishang rapidly eclipsed that of Hong Kong investment. Until China joined the World Trade Organization (WTO) in 2001, Taiwanese capital served as a go-between, linking China with the world market. It helped create the Guangdong model that soon set an example for other regions: the urgent catch-up efforts in the mid-1990s of the Yangtze Delta region (Shanghai, southern Jiangsu, and norther Zhejiang), whether through the Suzhou model or the Kunshan model, were all variations of the Guangdong model. Had Guangdong not taken the first step, there would have been no export-oriented development in other regions of China.

After the 1989 Tiananmen Incident, the economic sanctions that Western democracies imposed on China created serious difficulties and stalled opening reform. To break through the Western blockades, China ardently courted overseas Chinese capital, using special incentives and preferential treatment. In this difficult time for China, many Taishang shifted into reverse and upped the stakes in their westward march, creating a so-called mainland fever in Taiwan. This upsurge in investment reflected not only the opportunistic thinking of those Taishang, but also the thrust of Taiwan's own industrial restructuring at that time. Another mainland fever occurred in the late 1990s when the information and communication technology (ICT) industry moved its assembly lines to China's coastal region, mostly concentrated in the Yangtze Delta. Taiwanese capital helped China lay the foundation for its processing trade and prepared it to become the factory of the world.

After China joined the WTO, global foreign capital poured into the country, and booming exports greatly increased China's foreign exchange reserves. The role of Taiwanese capital in China faded during this stage. As China felt pressure to upgrade its industries, labor costs rose, demands for environmental protection increased, Taishang faced the choice of staying or leaving, and the 2008 global financial crisis catalyzed a major Taishang exodus.[5] Over the next ten years, the features of Taishang in China rapidly changed.

2. Exploitation with Chinese Characteristics

Both the Guangdong model and the China model look bright and beautiful in official propaganda, but the underlying exploitation is usually covered up. The GVC is actually an exploitation chain that straddles national borders, penetrates classes and genders, and destroys the natural

---

5. Lu Kuo-chen and You Tzu-yan, "Zhongguo bianle, Taishang da taowang" (China has changed, and Taiwanese businessmen flee), *Shangye Zhoukan* (Business Weekly), May 29, 2008, https://www.businessweekly.com.tw/Archive/Article?StrId=33244.

environment. The price paid by humans and the environment is shifted downward layer by layer in the chain. In a documentary film describing the industry chain for high-heeled shoes,[6] a designer says: "People always think that fashion design is a charmed profession, but in fact it is only 5 percent glamour, while 95 percent is sheer hard work." A Taishang out-sourcing factory owner grumbles, "If the international buyer wants you to crawl, you crawl." Meanwhile, the Chinese migrant workers draw such scanty wages that it's not clear how they could ever wear the beautiful products they make with their own hands. The extravagant, dazzling glow obscures a cold, cruel chain of exploitation.

Exploitation is a key element of all capitalist economies, but the spe-cific form of exploitation differs across times and places. The special char-acteristic of the China model is that by creating the migrant worker class, the state competes with capital in the exploitation of migrant work-ers. Taiwanese capital, like all foreign capital and Chinese capital, has also become part of this capitalism with Chinese characteristics. How-ever, neither the state nor investors are willing to face the truth about the exploitation of migrant workers. As the Chinese scholar Qin Hui (2007) has said, China's competitiveness depends on "low wages, low welfare, and low human rights," using an institutional logic of political repres-sion to create a "freak efficiency." Because Chinese workers receive such low pay and so few benefits, they have to work overtime to make a liv-ing, and after-hours work is typically justified with statements such as "workers like working overtime." A series of suicides among Foxconn workers in Guangdong in 2010 exposed this myth.

In the classic scenario of capitalistic exploitation, the state takes a hands-off attitude toward the squeeze that capital puts on labor. In China, however, the state does not adopt a laissez-faire policy toward labor-capital relations. Rather, the state has actively intervened in the use of migrant labor from the outset, and its intervention has actually ensured a high degree of exploitation of labor by capital. To explore the logic of Chinese-style capitalistic exploitation, I propose a theory of differential citizen-ship: China's state system creates differentiations between different groups of citizens, and around this differential citizenship, the state has con-

---

6. He Zhaoti, director, *Wo Ai Gaogenxie* (I love high heels), created and distributed by Taiwan Public Television, 2010.

structed a dual labor market, with varying minimal wages and a graded social insurance program and other institutional plans. As a result, migrant workers face a situation of dual exploitation. On one side is the classic exploitation of the working class by capital, which is class exploitation according to traditional political economy. On the other side is the state's designation and definition of migrant worker status, which allows enterprises hiring migrant workers to lawfully apply labor conditions for second-class citizens, which is exploitation based on status guided by the state system.

In China, globalization forces and the country's differential citizenship have engendered a symbiotic relationship that allows capital to carry out twofold exploitation on migrant workers. As a result, globalization has not mitigated existing economic and social inequality but rather has fortified yet another unequal system by creating the new social class of migrant worker. Under this logical sequence, pondering the effects of capital (both foreign and domestic) on China's development requires including the angles of surplus extraction and economic distribution, and at the same time considering the pervasiveness of capitalist exploitation and the uniqueness of an exploitation mechanism with Chinese characteristics. Only this analytical perspective will allow us to clearly perceive the interrelation between Taishang (as a form of foreign capital), the Guangdong model, and China's development.

3. The Neomercantilist Policy

As the vanguard of global capital, Taishang linked China with the world market and helped China carry out capital accumulation in the first stage after opening reform. With foreign capital helping it develop its export economy, China rapidly became a major manufacturing nation. In the previous East Asian development model, foreign capital (foreign direct investment) was not crucial in South Korea and Taiwan. In retrospect, foreign capital played an important role in China. Yet unlike what the past dependency theory would have predicted—that is, foreign investment leading to underdevelopment—China did not fall into underdevelopment but rapidly consolidated a semiperipheral status and even demonstrated an intense ambition to challenge core countries. Why was China able to resist dependency? First, when China began opening itself to the outside world in the late 1970s, the CCP was already a regime with highly centralized power, strong controls on the economy and society, and the capacity to guide policies. Furthermore, China enjoyed an obvious influence in regional politics. The state apparatus already had a high degree of autonomy and dynamism, so when China reestablished its links with capitalism, its local polity could cut into the GVCs with rather strong state capacity and give free rein to its dynamism. In addition, local governments were able to seize economic surplus where they intersected with the chains and pursue industrial upgrading that allowed them to climb up the chain. Second, China's strategy of opening itself up to foreign investment differentiated between internal and external: China was very open to the export processing form of foreign investment, but it was very cautious about foreign investment aimed at the domestic market—especially strategic industries. It protected the domestic market, strictly limited the proportion of foreign ownership, and demanded joint ventures, technical transfers, and so on.

Once labor-intensive traditional industries began accumulating national wealth, the Chinese government invested part of it in infrastructure and in fostering strategic target industries. In just a few decades, China's industrial structure and the appearance of its cities were completely transformed. China's own ICT brands and industry chains have grown rapidly since the 2000s. The enormous domestic market, the state's targeted policy support, and jump-starting strategies have all been important contributing factors. Why was the ICT industry able to spring up in such a short time? Most noteworthy is the emergence of a new ICT ecosystem in Guangdong's Pearl River Delta region. This system depends on the vast domestic market and has gained the key support of state policy makers. In the research area, it has adopted a human wave strategy and employee poaching (including from Taiwan), first breaking through a certain number of key industrial sectors and rapidly enhancing its manufacturing capacity through jump-starting, then taking over international mid- and low-range markets with low pricing, and later cutting into the markets of developed countries. Telecommunications companies targeted by the state for focused cultivation, such as Huawei (China's top telecommunications equipment company) and ZTE, have all followed this trajectory. In their start-up phase, the Chinese government used the allocation of domestic consumption markets and various preferential subsidies to drive the so-called latecomer's advantage. We can see that Huawei, Xiaomi, and OPPO all adopted the same tactics to seize the global cell-phone market share.

Observing the expansion of China's global telecom and internet empires and state behavior, we discover that it qualifies as a neomercantilist state policy. For example, the American economist Dani Rodrik (2013) adopts this approach in analyzing China's economic strategy. Neomercantilism uses state power to consolidate capital, with economic nationalism as the driving force behind it (don't forget, Xi Jinping frequently emphasizes "the great rejuvenation of the Chinese nation"). One viewpoint holds that China is following the course of neoliberalism, but this judgment remains moot. In fact, China hitchhiked through the globalized free trade environment using a neomercantilist strategy. China's so-called state-leftists once warned against China taking the road of neoliberalism, but that was a smoke screen: their real concern was that China's embarking on Western-style market democracy would be a harbinger of what they referred to as a color revolution.

Based on a similar logic of supporting national industry, the Chinese government has used the domestic market to foster the emerging online video, internet, and social media industries, with companies such as Tudou, Youku, Baidu, Alibaba, and Tencent (WeChat)—the latter three referred to as BAT—as counterparts to YouTube, Google, Amazon, and Facebook. The rapid development of China's e-commerce and sharing economy in recent years is also closely related to national industrial policy. The strategic matrix of this industrial policy includes the interlinked state-surveillance society, domestic market protectionism, and escape from the Western technological monopoly. The Chinese government brings about a commercialization of social control by combining the motivations of the state-surveillance-society" and businesses seeking profit. An example is the symbiotic relationship between business and the state in e-commerce, in which businesses provide data on commercial trading activity to help the state carry out social surveillance and investigations, and the state grants the businesses privileges as monopolies or oligopolies. The inevitable tendency of this internal social control model is to construct a closed political and economic system. Western countries have recently woken up to China's control methods, but in fact this grand strategy has been used for years, and it already operates at a high level of proficiency.

4. The United States Challenges China's Industrial Strategy

The story of China's economic rise has to be observed against the historical trajectory of East Asia's development, but it exceeds the framework of the East Asian model. The East Asian model component of China's development process is following the GVCs to create the factory of the world. The Chinese characteristics of China's development process are as follows: China created a path of rent-seeking developmentalism in which rent seeking coexists with development. Furthermore, after accumulating a vast amount of capital, China has demonstrated its ambition to challenge the technological hegemony of Western countries and attempt to use an illiberal approach to break the rules of the game set by core nations, set its own standards, and create its own sphere of influence.

China's industrial upgrading involves capital, markets, and technology. The upgrading of the first two has already been preliminarily resolved, but technological development has encountered a bottleneck. China is heavily dependent on importing semiconductor (integrated circuit) products from core countries and is anxious for breakthroughs in this domain. Consequently, the State Council in 2014 established the China National Integrated Circuit Industry Investment Fund (known as the Big Fund) to heavily subsidize the semiconductor industry. In 2015, China formulated a "Made in China 2025" strategy and listed ten key sectors, the first of which was the semiconductor industry.[7] As the Made in China 2025 has been executed over the past few years, China has been buying

---

7. The ten sectors included: semiconductors, artificial intelligence manufacturing and robotics, aviation and aerospace, high-tech maritime vessels, advanced rail equipment, new energy vehicles, electrical equipment, agricultural equipment, new materials, and biopharmaceuticals (The Strategy Advisory Committee for National Manufacturing and Strong Nation 2015).

out high-tech companies overseas and gaining technology. This has caused alarm in Western countries, whose businesses have found their intellectual property rights infringed on through the theft of trade secrets—which is turn has created constant disputes.[8]

China's behavior has caused Western countries to worry that China wants to destroy the existing order and is even plotting to dominate the world. The current world order is composed of the two core elements of market capitalism and free and democratic government, but China has taken its own direction in development. Consequently, the world-dominating United States has begun to be concerned about a power transition and has become increasingly on guard against this rising revisionist country. In fact, even before the 2016 presidential election, the American pro-establishment political camp and academic community had already been moving toward abandoning the engagement policy toward China. "The National Security Strategy of the United States of America," issued by President Donald Trump (White House 2017), listed China as a strategic competitor. America's March 2018 trade report stated that the Made in China 2025 strategy constituted a challenge to America's technological lead (Office of the United States Trade Representative, Executive Office of the President 2018). According to this viewpoint, if China implements its current program of action, it may become a world-dominating superpower. This rising power, with the party-state apparatus comprehensively controlling economic resources (in other words, practicing state capitalism), has formulated a general strategy (Made in China 2025) for industrial upgrading to overtake Western countries. The state apparatus uses the latest technology to control society (practicing digital totalitarianism),

8. For example, TSMC sued SMIC for infringing on its intellectual property rights, as a result of which SMIC paid compensation to TSMC to settle the case (see chapter 7, section 4). A recent famous case was the suing by Micron Technology (an American company) of China's state-owned Fujian Jinhua Integrated Circuit Company and Taiwan's United Microelectronics Corporation (UMC) for stealing its intellectual property. See Paul Mozur, "Inside a Heist of American Chip Designs, as China Bids for Tech Power," *New York Times*, June 22, 2018, https://www.nytimes.com/2018/06/22/technology/china-micron-chips-theft.html. UMC filed a successful lawsuit against Micron Technology for patent infringement in the Chinese courts. See Su Chia-wei, "Meiguang yi zhan bihe weihe ti dao tieban?" (Why did Micron achieve nothing in the stalemate?), *Gongshang Shibao* (Commercial Times), July 4, 2018, http://www.chinatimes.com/newspapers/20180704000257-260202.

export surplus capital (via the Belt and Road Initiative and the Asian Infrastructure Investment Bank), and manipulate the political and social order of other countries (practicing sharp power). This new species of regime is quite unfamiliar to Western countries.

Some people believe that the empire posture that China is currently presenting to the world is just a paper tiger, a form of psychological warfare aimed at cowing the enemy into submission. As Sun Tzu put it, the most effective military tactic for a general is "to conquer without fighting." In fact, Beijing has been carrying out a Great External Propaganda (*da wai xuan*) campaign. The sharp power it has been applying to many countries is little more than psychological warfare, and the scale and influence of its foreign investment is often inflated and unsubstantial. A detailed look at China's industrial prowess shows that although the country is referred to as the factory of the world, the foundation of its manufacturing industry still appears fragile: it is still striving to climb the ladder of industrial upgrading and remains heavily dependent on Western technology. Even so, China is creating an image of itself as a new empire, whether in regional politics or in the diplomatic sphere. The Chinese People's Liberation Army (PLA) is building long-range projectile capabilities, and the navy and air force engage in concentrated operations in the East China Sea, the Taiwan Strait, and especially in the South China Sea, causing a continual escalation of tensions in the region. On the ideological front, the widespread use of the expression "doing business with a sword in hand" has inflamed China's economic nationalism. As one blogger noted, "In the face of China's increasingly immense capital and exports, the PLA must protect China's overseas interests and shatter the global hegemonic system with the United States at its core, 'strike down the champion fighter, smash the boxing world,' and build a new world system and order with China at its center."[9] The desire to restore the Chinese empire resounds in populist discourse. Here we discover the same emphasis on having a strong and prosperous country that has been

9. Ling Dao, "Duihua Wang Hui: 'Yidai yilu' heyi chengwei dui 'shijie lishi lujing de chongxin xiuzheng'" (Conversation with Wang Hui: How One Belt One Road can become "a new correction on the path of world history"), *Potu* (*Groundbreaking*), April 3, 2015, https://www.inmediahk.net/node/1033026.

deeply branded into China's ruling elite and intelligentsia over the past two centuries. And when Chinese believe themselves to be encountering resistance from Western empires, a collective mood of grief and indignation fills the land. The Chinese people's image of China as an empire seems to be a self-fulfilling prophecy, and it is setting off warning bells against China throughout the world.

In April 2018, the US Department of Commerce announced that it was placing a seven-year trade embargo on ZTE, citing its illegal shipment of American-made semiconductor chips to Iran. This sanction, which prevented China's second-largest communications equipment company from obtaining key chips and technology, dealt a harsh blow to the development of its 5G communication network. In June, ZTE promised to pay a heavy fine and dismiss its top executives in exchange for a partial lifting of the US sanctions. It is hardly coincidental that the ZTE Incident occurred just as a Sino-US trade war was brewing. Over the years, Huawei has been unable to crack the US market. Even after spending large amounts of money on political lobbying, it has failed to quell the US government's suspicions about the relationship between Huawei and the Chinese military (and government). US government reports years ago posited the threat that Huawei's products might pose to America's national security. When the Sino-US trade war was officially launched on July 6, the technology war led the first round of economic sanctions, which targeted the Made in China 2025 strategy. By exposing China's vulnerability if it could not have access to advanced chip technology and revealing the fault line in China's technological prowess, the ZTE Incident gives us the opportunity to observe the true situation of China's economic development.

In any case, the Sino-US trade war must be analyzed in terms of the geopolitical and geoeconomic structure. An empire's adjustment of strategy is usually considered in tandem with economic trade, and sometimes trade even takes precedence over strategy. In light of the history of American global strategy, the US government was fully prepared to address this major issue and had shrewdly calculated its options. For example, when Sino-US relations began to thaw in the early 1970s, Secretary of State Henry Kissinger and other policy makers had already included a preliminary lifting of trade sanction among the items to be negotiated with China.[10] At that time, the formation of an alliance between the United States and China against the Soviet Union in the Cold War already foreshadowed China's eventual return to the capitalist world.

America's current grand strategy of challenging China's industrial upgrading is not aimed at preventing China's businesses from upgrading or causing China to suffer crushing economic failure because that would compromise America's own economic interests. Rather, the American objective is to protect the leading position of its own technology, continue to seize massive profits from the GVCs, and deter China's expansion overseas.

This book proposes a new theory of the state: the rent-seeking developmental state (*xunzu fazhanxing guojia*). This kind of state is adept at cutting into the governance structure of foreign capital's value chains and extracting economic surplus from them. That is, the state has an especially prominent function in value capture. But does a rent-seeking developmental state have the capacity to engage in a catch-up form of industrial upgrading? Under the rule of Mao Zedong, China at one point attempted a self-regenerative policy, the Great Leap Forward (1958–60), which was intended to rapidly "overtake England and catch up with the US." The result was a crushing failure that brought about the Great Famine. Now that the domestic and external situations have undergone great changes, is the Chinese Communist regime likely to take this same disastrous route? Does it hope to break history's curse in one stroke?

5. The Taishang Perspective

In the late 1970s, as China gradually emerged from the autarkic policies of the Mao era and in an attempt to forge an escape route for its moribund economy, the government decided to create special economic zones (SEZs) in the Pearl River Delta and learn from the experience of Hong Kong and Taiwan in acquiring foreign exchange through export pro-

---

10. Henry A. Kissinger, "National Security Decision Memorandum 105," April 13, 1971, US Department of State, Office of the Historian, https://history.state.gov /historicaldocuments/frus1969-76v17/d116#fn:1.5.4.2.16.40.8.2.

cessing. In the 1980s, capital from Hong Kong and Taiwan flowed into Guangdong and was channeled into labor-intensive processing GVCs, spurring the growth of export-oriented processing of shipped materials (*lailiao jiagong*). Local governments gradually accumulated foreign exchange by recruiting migrant labor and charging foreign businesses processing fees. This development base point doesn't look too impressive today and is seldom mentioned by the government. Yet this apparently negligible base point had a butterfly effect that triggered China's cyclone of capitalist development decades later. In expounding on this process, this book aims to show how the turbulence of the butterfly wings set off a chain reaction that combined with other factors to create this cyclone.

Without the Guangdong model, China's rise would not have occurred, nor would today's so-called China model exist. Taishang were a key factor at the earliest stage of this development. By tracking the arrival of Taishang in Guangdong and their spreading throughout China, we can see the development process of the Guangdong model, its diffusion and transformation, and the difficulties it faced. By hiring millions of migrant laborers, Taishang became part of the ingenious, complex, and crude apparatus that exploited the differential citizenship system. By embedding themselves in the local polity and engaging in all kinds of transactions with local governments, Taishang became well versed in China's informal institutional arrangements (otherwise known as unspoken rules), fictive ownership arrangements (defined in chapter 2), and sham contractual relationships. The intensive interaction between Taishang and Taigan (Taiwanese management) and Chinese officials and cadres help us understand their state of mind and statecraft. The Taishang perspective provides us with a way to record the development and evolution of the Guangdong model. Furthermore, it helps us unearth the intentions, apprehensions, and setbacks in China's catch-up development at that time.

Made in China 2025 aims to pull China rapidly up the GVCs and even allow it to bypass chains dominated by core countries and attempt to establish its own value chains—that is, the so-called red supply chains promoted in the Chinese and Taiwanese media. The Chinese government has set a self-sufficiency rate for semiconductors, with the ultimate aim of building an autonomous high-end industrial chain that no longer relies on Western technology for key components. The opinions of Western experts are still split, however: many don't see good prospects for China's grand objective and consider it excessively ambitious because China's technological prowess will remain unequal to the West's in the short term. While still lacking key technology, what China can do today is: (1) use its abundant foreign reserves to buy out high-tech companies and technology all over the world; (2) offer good pay to poach talent from enterprises in South Korea, Taiwan, and the West;[11] and (3) engage in industrial espionage wars over intellectual property—or, to put it bluntly, engage in borderline behavior that includes theft, infringement, imitation, and pirating.

By way of contrast, Taiwan's development route since the 1960s has involved step-by-step industrial upgrading following the GVCs of Western countries. Although Taiwanese manufacturing technology has continuously become more advanced, it stalls the moment it touches the leading Western high-end brands (the dominant lead firms in the GVCs), and it has encountered unsurpassable obstacles.[12] Half a century into Taiwan's economic rise, only a tiny number of manufacturers (e.g., TSMC) have been able to achieve the status of lead firm in the GVC and develop a comprehensive semiconductor manufacturing ecosystem. In addition, this route has basically followed the development model of Western core technology and market supremacy. Taiwan's geostrategy has relied on American support, and the country's economy is medium-size—as a result of which the strategy has evolved into a follow-up one that takes the conventional path of climbing the global supply chains (GSCs), with sensitive responses to the market demands of core countries, and of keeping the entire industry highly integrated with those chains. As a result, the outward movement of Taiwanese capital is closely linked with international brands (buyers) in the GVCs.

Since Taiwanese businesses began their western march into China in the late 1980s, the economic landscapes of the world, Taiwan, and China have all undergone dramatic change. Over the past thirty years,

11. This intention is expressed in one item of China's "31 Preferential Measures for Taiwan" unveiled in February 2018. See "Guowuyuan Taiban 31 tiao huitai cuoshi quanwen" (The full text of the 31 Preferential Measures for Taiwan by the Taiwan Affairs Office of the State Council), March 1, 2018, *Commercial Times*, https://www.chinatimes.com/newspapers/20180301000200-260210?chdtv.

12. The shoe industry is one example. See the case of the Taishin Shoe Manufacturing Group in chapter 6.

Taiwan's foreign investment has been highly concentrated in China, and so-called globalization has led to an effective Sinicization. Yet the fundamental structural dynamic of this form of globalization is the restructuring and redivision of labor in the capitalist world system, which also reflects the shifting vectors of the GVCs. The westward march of Taishang has had multiple consequences, including driving Taiwan's industrial upgrading, and it has raised apprehensions of hollowing out Taiwan. With the further shift of the GVC since the late 2000s, Taishang have developed new arrangements, and the concentration of investment in China has decreased in recent years.[13] One reason is sinking profit margins in China. Others reflect an increasing consciousness among some Taishang of the risk of doing business in China.

Over the past ten years, Taishang in Guangdong encountering dual pressure from the GVCs and the Chinese government's industrial upgrading have adopted various exit strategies: closing factories, moving further inland, pulling out of China, and transformation on the ground (some manufacturers have used multiple options at once). This has greatly changed the situation of Taishang in the Pearl River Delta region, especially Shenzhen and Dongguan. The escalating trade and technology wars between China and the United States have provided even more impetus for Taishang to expedite their exit from China.

At the same time, China's export-oriented economy also began to show signs of change: During the first thirty years of opening reform, China's development route was mainly forging the factory of the world. Over the past ten years, the Chinese government has attempted to use China's lure as an international market to forge its own value chains, but it has encountered a forceful challenge from the United States. A US-dominated geopolitical situation prone to containing China is also forming. Positioned in the midst of two storms, can the Taishang referred to by Xi Jinping as deserving a record of merit still provide Beijing with utilitarian value? I believe that Taishang still have two types of value in China's desire to pursue global hegemony: the value of their political identity and their value in industrial upgrading.

13. China still receives the largest share of Taiwan's export capital. But Taiwanese investment in China made up 39.8 percent of its total overseas investment in 2018, in contrast to 85.2 percent in 2010.

In terms of political identity, Taiwanese investment has been an important medium for China's Taiwan strategy all along, first and foremost for its propaganda value in Taiwan. As busy as Xi Jinping was at the Boao Forum for Asia, he found ten minutes to receive Taiwanese business representatives. For decades, the Chinese government has granted Taiwanese investors preferential treatment for the sake of the united front strategy toward Taiwan, and this preferential treatment is rent value derived from political status. Consequently, apart from standard commercial operations, some Taishang have also devoted themselves to rent-seeking activities based on their identities (especially in terms of real estate interests). For Beijing, establishing cross-strait political and commercial relations through the Taishang network, and thereby cultivating local collaborators in Taiwan, is not a high-cost transaction. However, the collective identity capital of Taishang depreciated at the height of cooperation between the CCP and the Kuomintang. In 2011, a long-time China-based Taigan observed: "Now that the governments [on either side] are holding their own talks, you're cut loose, so we've come to think that [the political-commercial environment] has deteriorated. . . . The two associations [Taiwan's Straits Exchange Foundation and China's Association for Relations across the Taiwan Straits] are talking to each other so they don't need you."[14] Conversely, when cross-strait relations are strained, this identity capital appreciates in value. During the Taiwan Strait Crisis in 1995–96, one Taishang said: "When there are tensions on both sides and the risk of war, the CCP treats us even better and even fawns on us!"[15] In the current situation, when both Sino-US relations and cross-strait relations are strained, and the Democratic Progressive Party is Taiwan's ruling party, China desperately needs to strengthen its united front. That's why it issued its "31 Preferential Measures for Taiwan," which was tantamount to increasing the value of Taiwanese identity capital. Although the redeemability of that capital in China has been called into question, it is played up in Taiwanese media as a symbolic code, creating publicity beneficial to Beijing. Based on observations of past experience, the political-commercial relationship Beijing most needs is the cross-strait capital that can navigate high-level party and government networks on both sides of

14. Interview: ZJC201211.
15. Interview: Leegm199508.

the strait, and this type of political-commercial relationship remains influential even as Taiwanese political parties regularly alternate in controlling the government. When regional geopolitical relations become strained, there is an opportunity for observing changes in cross-strait political-business relations. As long as China maintains its objective of annexing Taiwan, Beijing's "business model as united front" toward Taiwan will not change (Wu Jieh-min 2017b).

In terms of industrial upgrading, when China's strategy for such upgrading met with resistance from the West, the value of Taiwanese investment increased correspondingly. Soon after the United States imposed sanctions on ZTE, MediaTek filed an application with Taiwan's Ministry of Economic Affairs to sell chips to ZTE. The ministry granted permission after a brief investigation. In this way, under the dark clouds of the Sino-US trade and technology wars, some Taishang profited from this window of opportunity by quickly meeting China's overwhelmingly urgent need to obtain chips. However, the technological level of Taiwan's chip design houses is still lower than that of America's firms such as Qualcomm, so their long-term role remains in doubt. The "31 Preferential Measures for Taiwan" also has implications of poaching Taiwanese talent. China is making a great push to develop its semiconductor industry, and Taiwan has accumulated plentiful experience in chip manufacturing. Since it began building advanced wafer foundries in 2000, China has adopted the method of luring employees from Taiwan. Some of the large number of wafer foundries that have been established are joint ventures with Taiwanese firms that have no lack of Taiwanese high-level managers and engineers. China has used massive amounts of cash to attract talent from Taiwan as well as other advanced countries. However, the results are still hard to predict because technical learning requires time and accumulated experience, and technology transfer involves the issue of intellectual property rights—and it is not easy for the Chinese side to bypass these obstructions. TSMC's solely owned high-grade wafer fab in Nanjing has been fully operational since 2018. The significance of this company, a global pure-play foundry giant, as an indicator of Taiwan's industrial technology, is self-evident and also highly symbolic in terms of Taiwan's industrial development. TSMC's recently retired founder, Morris Chang, gave the following assessment: "Although China's semiconductor industry is breathing down our necks and continues to make progress, TSMC will also continue to advance during this time. Whether in terms of technology or efficiency, it has at least a five-year lead over its competitors. But this lead time will last for about ten years. In ten years' time, China will gradually catch up, so we shouldn't take anything for granted."[16] Chang's optimistic but cautious predictions for Taiwan's semi-conductor industry reflect China's eagerness to catch up with and over-take its competitors.

Semiconductors are a key section in Taiwan's industry, but not the entirety. Taiwan's overall industrial capabilities have been accumulating over the long term, including the craftsmanship and managerial resilience forged in traditional industry. Today, quite a few companies in traditional industries have managed through upgrading and advancing their manu-facturing technology to qualify as hidden champions and have even neared the pinnacle of the GVC. But Taiwan's discourse arena is so of-ten overwhelmed by China's hegemonic (propaganda) terms such as "strong nation," "empire," "strive for supremacy," "One Belt One Road," "Big Fund," and "red supply chain" that the importance of so-called tra-ditional industries and small and medium-size companies has been woe-fully underestimated, and the facts that they have already entered the high-tech ranks and are engaged in diversified development that hedges risk are often overlooked.[17]

I have tracked and interviewed Taishang over an extended period, exploring the interactive relationship between Taishang, the Guangdong model, and China's development. One of my main objectives has been to demonstrate the long-term collective and cumulative role of countless large- and small-scale Taishang and their enormous effect on con-temporary China and Taiwan-China relations. Taishang introduced the

16. Atkinson, "Zhang Zhongmou: Taiwan bandaoti lingxian Zhongguo haiyou shi nian shejian, zhihou que buneng dayi" (Morris Chang: Taiwan semiconductors have a ten-year lead on China, but after that it can't be taken for granted), *Keji xinbao* (Tech-News), June 11, 2018, https://technews.tw/2018/06/11/taiwan-semiconductor-3/.

17. For example, the head of Taiwan's leading bicycle manufacturer, Giant, says: "Giant is a high-tech company, not an everyday traditional industry." Quoted in Tseng Li-fang, "Du Xiuzhen chenggong dazao dier pinpai cuisheng Liv quanqiu zixingche weiyi jiaodian" (Bonnie Tu successfully creates a second brand, Liv, the only bicycle in the world designed by and for women), *China Times*, October 2, 2017, www.chinatimes .com/newspapers/20171002000044-260202.

modern manufacturing industry into China, and China drew Taishang into its development model. We continue to live in the eye of this cyclone to this day.

6. How This Book Is Organized

Chapter 1 states the main questions of this book: How did the factory of the world come into being? How did the global level link up with the local level in the process of China's transition to capitalism? What role did Taiwanese capital play in this? The chapter then recounts the path Guangdong took in becoming the factory of the world and lists the theoretical topics for discussion. The existing literature discussing China's developmental dynamics is mainly approached from three angles: market transition theory, state-centered theory, and export-oriented development theory. Drawing on the literature, the chapter examines the global commodity chain (GCC) theory derived from world-systems theory, and the GVC theory developed from that. I propose a local growth alliance as the analytical framework. In this alliance, the local polity has autonomy and dynamism and involves itself in GVC governance to carry out value capture, while foreign capital gains the low labor costs, other essential factors of production, and bureaucratic protection provided by the state. Finally, this chapter describes my case selection, research methods, and the sources and structure of the data.

Chapter 2 provides an overview of the origins and development of the Guangdong model. By taking the first step, Guangdong soon became the core region of the factory of the world, but the period from the late 1970s to the early 1980s was filled with uncertainty, opportunity, and risk. This chapter first deals with the main controversies in the process of Guangdong's opening to the world—including those having to do with relations between the central government and Guangdong and with the origins of the processing trade model. Based on memoirs and policy and historical documents, we learn from remarks by Deng Xiaoping, Xi Zhongxun, Ren Zhongyi, Gu Mu, and other central and provincial leaders, as well as from the reminiscences of cadres actually carrying out the SEZ policies, what the policy implications were of terms such as "take one step ahead," "special policies and flexible measures," "processing of shipped materials," "learning from the experience of Hong Kong and Taiwan," "earning foreign exchange," and "three-plus-one trading." The chapter then analyzes Guangdong's economic performance, looking at various economic indicators and development trends and comparing Guangdong with China at large and other key regions within the country. At the same time, it analyzes Guangdong's labor cost competitiveness, comparing migrant labor wages and growth trends over time and Guangdong's social insurance with that in other places, as well as analyzing high accumulation rates. Finally, it analyzes two phases of institutional and policy changes in Guangdong over the past thirty years and the evolving Guangdong model. The processing trade continued to play an important role in Guangdong's industrial structure until recent years.

Chapter 3 and chapter 4 describe in depth a Taiwanese leather goods manufacturer, Taiyang,[18] as the microscopic foundation for this book's macroscopic framework of local growth coalitions. Taiyang's business activities in Taiwan and its history in China provide the book's main illustrative data. Taiyang has experienced three stages of development: first as a Taiwanese trading company (1979–88); second in renting a building and establishing a factory in Dongguan, Guangdong (1989–94); and third in building its own factory, enhancing product quality and production capacity, and being taken over by the second generation of management until it stopped doing business in China (1995–2010). These two chapters use the GVC/GCC analytical framework to illustrate Taiyang's strategic decisions and migration through Hong Kong to China, as well as the related changes in its production organization and technical links. Starting out in Taiwan as a trading firm, Taiyang used an outsourcing and network production model, but in Dongguan it became a vertically integrated factory, and it achieved enormous growth in terms of scale and production capacity.

Taiyang serves as a small but complete and self-contained example of presenting a macroscopic phenomenon in miniature: how Taishang moved their production bases, capital, technology, and access to Western markets into China; how Taishang, as foreign investors, interacted with local structures, institutions, and behaviors; how through a process of locally embedded governance they formed special political-business re-

18. Taiyang is a pseudonym.

lationships with local governments and officials (for example, interest allocation mechanisms such as the head tax, sharing of foreign exchange earnings, and management fees); how Taishang adapted to the corrupt and chaotic environment in China during its economic transformation, surmounted the problem of rent seeking, and achieved relatively stable property rights arrangements; with institutions and policies as a manufacturing cost, how changes in institutions and policies obliged factory owners to change partners or adjust their relationships with present partners and influenced the decisions of factory owners about whether to continue investing or to withdraw their investment. The year 1994 is the watershed between these two chapters. In that year, China's central government reformed its foreign exchange system, substantially devalued the renminbi, and reformed its tax system. These new policies altered the relative price of essential factors of production and institutional conditions for factory owners and therefore altered the ability of local governments to negotiate with factory owners. Changes in central government policies and their implementation at the local level influenced the behavioral model of factory owners and were consequently reflected in Taiyang's business activities. Taiyang's decision to terminate its business operations in 2010 reflected rising labor costs in China and the decline of the labor-intensive export processing model, which at the same time spurred the disappearance of the head tax and the emergence of social insurance fees. This stage was the tipping point for Guangdong's industrial transformation, as well as the moment when Taishang and foreign investment began pulling out of China.

Chapter 5 proposes an institutional logic of Chinese-style exploitation. It first analyzes how the state created the migrant worker class and then describes the form of that class. Providing relatively high-quality and low-cost labor, the class allowed the GVCs, ever in search of cheap labor, to extend into China, rapidly embed themselves in the local institutional structure of China's coastal regions, and link China into global production system. The dual labor market's economic and social exploitation of migrant workers remains a key engine of China's capital accumulation. Situated in a system of differential citizenship, the migrant worker class suffers the double exploitation of the state and capital. Finally, in discussing the nature of China's migrant labor system and analyzing the debate in the existing literature on whether China is a despotic or a hegemonic system, I return to the role of the state. The theory of Michael Burawoy presupposes the conditions of a presumed market capitalist state. But in China, the base point is the party-state capitalist state. The state has always coercively intervened in labor-capital relations, but the main objective of its intervention is to derive financial income. Although the state power is ubiquitous, it is frequently absent on the issue of protecting labor. It is because the state sustains the differential citizenship system that capital could have been able to exploit labor so ruthlessly in China. The overtime and rush work phenomenon in the export processing industry in China's coastal regions is dominated by sham contractual arrangements: ostensibly progressive working hour policies, suppressed minimum wages, and flexible enforcement at the local level join together to create a three-sided tacit agreement between labor, capital, and the government. Under this tacit agreement, overtime pay becomes the main incentive to workers that enables the capital to squeeze labor output, and its use has become a routinized discursive practice.

Chapter 6 discusses the transformation of the Guangdong model. During the global financial crisis in 2007–8, Dongguan experienced a Taishang exodus. This crisis also affected other foreign investment, with many Hong Kong investors also making emergency exits from the mainland market. The global financial crisis was an external shock, but the more deep-seated cause of the exodus was long-term transformation pressures on the Chinese economy. These factors included rising costs in the factors of production, increasing mass protests by workers, changes in the policy and institutional environment and in relations between government and business, increasing pressure from industrial upgrading policies, and so on. These internal and external factors converged in an enormous force that impelled a further shift in the GVCs and GSCs, putting the Guangdong growth model under pressure to reorganize. This chapter starts by analyzing state policies, Guangdong's industrial upgrading, and changes in the relationship between government and businesses. As Guangdong's labor-intensive growth momentum slowed, Taishang had to respond by altering their profit model. Responding to transformation pressure, Pearl River Delta Taishang who did not shut down their factories had the options of moving further inland, relocating their factories outside of China, or upgrading on site. Individual factory owners might combine all three options. Using the Smiles Shoe Company as a case study of a small to medium-size Taishang, I focus on its core factory strategy and note the increasing competitiveness of Chinese-invested factories. The Taishin Shoe Manufacturing Group, as a representative case of a large original equipment manufacturing company undergoing a transformation, employed strategies that included a diversified response of redeployment of overseas production bases (relocation overseas), redeployment of inland Chinese production bases (moving inland), and developing a domestic sales department.[19] At the same time, the succession of Taishin's second generation also brought the multiple processes of corporate organizational reform, risk management, and group restructuring. As a transnational company focusing on manufacturing, Taishin had been climbing the GVC and attempting to reach its pinnacle, but it was unable to shake off the hegemonic domination logic of the GVC and encountered the limits of catching up. Finally, this chapter analyzes the emergent ecosystem of the Chinese-invested enterprises. In the transformation of the Guangdong model up to now, certain indications of upgrading have emerged. One of these is the rise of Chinese-invested factories in traditional manufacturing, such as a local supply chain in the shoe industry, that carries the genetic code of Taiwanese factories. A second indication is the emergence of a Chinese-investment-led ICT industrial chain, which has brought about a competitive relationship with Taiwanese capital.

The transformation of the Guangdong model has caused a development result: Although the processing trade's momentum has suffered from saturation in the global market and catching up by developing countries, it still is fairly sustainable because the Pearl River Delta's export economy has been deeply infiltrated by the GVC. Buyers for international brands still need the Pearl River Delta as a high-end manufacturing base, and they also need Taishang to integrate the components of the supply chain. As Taiwanese investment has pulled out, Chinese-invested factories have promptly entered the supply chains, allowing the Pearl River Delta export processing system to maintain its integrity to a certain degree. Furthermore, local governments have long drawn fiscal revenue from the export processing sector and have become heavily reliant on the sector's revenue due to path dependence.

Chapter 7 discusses the theoretical implications of this book by treating the Guangdong model as a prototype for the Chinese model.

19. Taishin Shoe Manufacturing Group is a pseudonym.

The book uses the theoretical perspective of the GVC or GCC, along with the concept of locally embedded governance, to analyze how China utilized the historic opportunity of GVC expansion to adopt a policy of export-oriented industrialization; in only thirty years, accumulated vast amounts of foreign exchange reserves and gained production technology and corporate organizational capacity; and (after accumulating a certain degree of manufacturing prowess) used its powerful state capacity to try to break through the hegemonic domination in the value chain governance structure. In the process of China's development, Taishang played the roles of "semiperipheral elbows" and executing arrangements on behalf of the GVC hegemons. At the same time, they brought diffusion of technology and industrial upgrading and collaborated with China in resisting the hegemony of the GVC.

This book adopts the viewpoint of locally embedded governance to position the intervention of China's local governments—the nodule of profit distribution in the value chains—and explain the phenomenon of economic growth coexisting with institutional rent seeking (*jigouhua xunzu*). I sum up Guangdong's development experience and institutional rent seeking, along with the value-capturing behavior of local officials in the value chains, to propose the concept of a rent-seeking developmental state. China is unique among East Asian and world economies, but its scale and influence give it a distinctiveness and theoretical importance surpassing that of the typical country. Analyzing China's rent-seeking developmental state helps us review the theoretical proposition of the East Asian developmental state and carry out historical comparisons. Finally, China is anxious to break through the constraints of the current rent-seeking developmental model and has proposed Made in China 2025. This chapter places a preliminary assessment of China's semiconductor industrial upgrading under this development blueprint.

The conclusion summarizes three questions: Will China fall into the development trap? Why are the United States and other Western countries becoming wary of the China threat and resisting the industrial upgrading of Made in China 2025? Finally, what theoretical challenges will China's return to the capitalist world bring? The conclusion synthesizes the book's arguments to answer these questions and propose a possible theoretical contribution.

CHAPTER ONE

Forging the Factory of the World

China started its export-oriented industrialization (EOI) in the 1980s, becoming the factory of the world in a little more than a decade and sustaining rapid growth for thirty years. This allowed China, once a country lacking in foreign exchange, to accumulate more foreign reserves than any other in the world. It also transformed China's closed-off state-socialist economic system into a capitalist economic system linked to the rest of the world. A great deal of research has attempted to explain the so-called China miracle, but a series of riddles remain regarding the structural characteristics and institutional momentum of the country's rapid growth: How exactly was the factory of the world forged? How did the global level become linked with the local level in the process of China's transformation toward capitalism? What role did Taiwanese investment play at this time? Why was the Guangdong model the key? How is the government-business relationship one of both collusion and contestation?

The existing literature on China's rapid economic growth proposes three competing explanations. First, market theory emphasizes the economic growth momentum released with China's reform of the public ownership system, focusing on individual spontaneity, structural changes in property rights, and the process of privatization. But this standpoint of bottom-up capitalism overlooks capital's enormous gray area and the transactional relationship between government and business, and it can only partially explain the development of Chinese capitalism. Second, state-centered theory proposes that the government played the leading role in promoting economic growth. This standpoint of top-down capitalism supplements market theory, laying particular emphasis on state capacity, policies, and institutions. But it is still unable to explain the impetus for China to link up with global capitalism or the relationship between external links and China's regional disparities. Third, export-oriented development theory states that foreign capital and exports promoted China's economic growth, and it explains the growth impetus for China carrying on the East Asian development model. But this standpoint of capitalism from outside is often excessively macroscopic and fails to explain the mutual engagement of China's economy and global capitalism (or the embeddedness of the former in the latter) at the institutional and corporate level. Furthermore, this theoretical orientation is unable to explain the puzzling coexistence of rent seeking and growth.

This book handles China's linkages with global capitalism by revising the GVC or GCC theory to analyze how China used the critical turning point of the extension and shift of the traditional industry value chains in the 1980s (from the Four Little Dragons of East Asia—Taiwan, South Korea, Hong Kong, and Singapore—to China's southeastern coastal region) to seamlessly forge the factory of the world. Taiwanese investment was at the front line in extending GVCs to Guangdong. Without that investment, it would have been impossible to establish the Guangdong EOI development model, and China's economic rise would not have occurred without the Guangdong model. Although the Guangdong model is not the entirety of China's development experience, it is the most important component of the first stage of China's development, and it served as a learning tool for subsequent models (for example, the Suzhou model). Even now, elements and influences of the Guangdong model remain deeply embedded in China's developmental trajectory.

The specific process of China's linking up with capitalism at the outset of opening reform was driven by the GVC, with foreign direct investment (FDI) in manufacturing as the vanguard. From the 1980s until the early 2000s, China used its plentiful labor force to break into the capitalist world economy, enter the labor-intensive traditional manufacturing sphere, earn processing fees, and accumulate foreign exchange and capital. In the early 2000s, China entered a new phase, using the latent energy of its enormous domestic market to develop domestic sales, deepen its manufacturing technology, and create its own brands with the intention of seizing the global market. It is commonly believed that China is transforming itself from the factory of the world into the market of the world. Even if that is the case, however, the effects of previous EOI policies on the country's development path are still distinct: China remains heavily reliant on the export market, capturing foreign exchange, and labor-intensive traditional industries.

Behind China's miraculous transformation into the factory of the world is yet another puzzling issue: the coexistence of rampant bureaucratic rent seeking with economic growth. This phenomenon violates the standard explanations of neoclassical economics and has perplexed many scholars who have carefully considered it. This book uses the concept of institutional rent seeking to explain this theoretical puzzle. It shows how local governments and officials use institutionalized, collectivized rent-seeking activities to extract economic surplus from China's development toward capitalism. Previous literature on the phenomenon of rent seeking's leading to low or stagnant economic growth has largely focused on the import-substitution industrialization sector. What's interesting about the China conundrum, however, is that rent seeking also occurred in the EOI sector. As China's economy became drawn into the globalization process, local bureaucrats were also rolled into the management structure of the GVCs, and institutional rent seeking flourished in tandem with the rapid growth of China's economy driven by the GVCs. The chief motivation for local officials (cadres) to become involved in the management structure of value chains was to seize economic surplus, and the main incentives driving this economic motivation were local fiscal needs and the collective and individual interests of officials. China's incorporation into the GVC therefore resulted in the simultaneous escalation of both economic growth and rent-seeking activity. From a historical standpoint, China's traditional economic structure easily induced rent-seeking activity, but when driven by globalization on a massive scale, rent seeking by cadres became institutionalized, organized, and normalized.

Extracting, controlling, and distributing economic surplus is a major impetus of the capitalist mode of production. A semiopen secret in the narrative of China's economic miracle is the exploitation of the economic surplus produced by the legions of migrant workers. The main form of exploitation is suppressing wages to provide cheap labor for domestic and foreign investment, attract large amounts of labor-intensive foreign investment into China, and make products manufactured in China competitive in the global market. In this process, foreign investors have gained enormous profits, China's central government has gained enormous foreign exchange reserves and tax revenues, and local governments and officials have gained enormous rent.[1] Although the migrant labor force created important economic surplus under globalized production, the vast majority of this surplus was divided up among capital and various levels of government. One portion of this surplus was seized and distributed in the form of rent—a pattern that is highly characteristic of China's system. Under globalized production, the capacity for value capture determines the main results of development, so we need to regard the state as an actor in value capture. From the analytical angle of the GVC, the method the Chinese government uses to extract economic surplus is to engage in value capture through participation in the value chain structure. How is economic surplus extracted and distributed? That is, during China's more than thirty years of economic growth, how did the economic surplus distribution mechanism work in the labor-intensive export-oriented sector? Through what sociohistorical process did it develop? And through what kind institutional structure did it specifically emerge? This book proposes an explanation from the approach of historical institutionalism.

The initial stage of China's export-oriented economic development relied primarily on manufacturing FDIs importing GVCs to China. For a GVC to function in a specific national environment, it has to interact with the local institutional structure. Consequently, a key theme of this book is to analyze what kind of embedded relationship was engendered between the GVC and rent-seeking behavior with Chinese characteristics. Drawing on GVC theory, I propose a concept of locally embedded governance, and from this analytical angle I propose a framework of local growth alliance to explain the dynamics of and distribution structures used in China's rapid growth. Based on empirical findings in this book, chapter 7 proposes a theory of the rent-seeking developmental state and

---

1. Economic rent typically refers to the excess income obtained through monopoly and regulation. For the empirical applications and theoretical implications of the concepts of rent and rent seeking in the case of China, see chapter 7, section 2.

compares the similarities and differences between the Chinese and East Asian developmental states (Japan, South Korea, and Taiwan).

1. Analytical Focus

The analytical core of this book is the dynamic link between global capital and the local polity. I adopt the methodological pathway of historical institutionalism, commencing with the prototype of China's EOI (the Guangdong model), to explain the role that foreign-invested manufacturers—especially Taishang (see below for a fuller definition)—played in the economic growth process and to tell how, at the historical juncture of the extension of the GVC, Taishang played a semiperipheral role (Cheng Lu-lin 1999) in bringing capitalist modes of production, capital, and technology, as well as the international market, to China's coastal region and allowing Guangdong to quickly become a world-class manufacturing base. Taishang (only slightly later than Gangshang—i.e., Hong Kong investors) were the most important foreign investors to enter China's coastal region at this early stage, and Taishang and local governments therefore occupied pivotal positions in the local government's mechanism for distributing economic surplus. In the Guangdong model, in addition to the capture and distribution of economic surplus through the production process, surplus is distributed to various levels of the government in the form of rent, as an incentive for government officials to attract business and investment in this process. The local growth alliance is the political arrangement of this distribution mechanism. The main actors in the alliance include foreign investors, local governments, and cadres, while the central government and lead firms in the GVC are invisible allies as well as extractors of economic surplus. Figure 1.1 shows the dynamic links between various actors at the global and local levels that initiate globalized production, organization, and mobilization of the labor force; distribution; and surplus capture. The local level (the local polity) includes the two strata of the national state (central government) and subnational state (local government). Due to its vast territory, China's administrative strata are numerous and complex. In simple terms, the local government (which is below the central government) includes

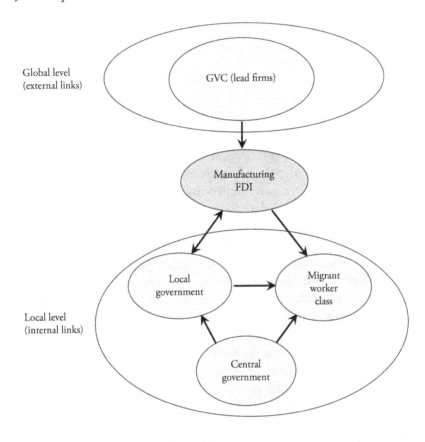

FIGURE I.I. Dynamic links between global capital and the local polity.

the governments of provinces (and municipalities directly under the central government), prefecture-level cities, counties and county-level cities, and townships and villages.[2] In this book's analysis, the local government includes the abovementioned levels of local government, all of which are potential members of the local growth alliance. Among this book's

2. The primary level of village (or administrative village) is a self-governing unit and strictly speaking does not qualify as a government unit, but village cadres are generally classified as local cadres.

empirical cases, the alliance relationships to which the company Taiyang belonged included provincial, prefectural, township, and village units and cadres (see chapters 3 and 4 for details). Other cases are similar.

As organizers of economic activity, foreign companies must form links with local society to mobilize local resources and channel them into the production system. The embedded relationship between foreign investors and the local institutional structure is therefore the focal point of this research. When we explore the institutional arrangements of China's EOI process, we use manufacturing FDI as the analytical axis to describe a threefold interaction. From the angle of institutional analysis, these three relationships have a high degree of Chinese characteristics.

The first relationship is between FDI and the lead firms in the GVCs. When GVCs first entered China, it was mainly through manufacturers in newly industrialized countries, and not through direct investment by lead firms in core countries; global production links were introduced into China's coastal regions through Taiwan, Hong Kong, South Korea, Singapore, and other "semiperipheral elbows" (Cheng Lu-lin 1999). Because these manufacturing foreign-invested enterprises (FIEs) were characterized by a network-style production organization (see Shieh Gwo-Shyong 1989 and 1992; Chen Chieh-Hsuan 1994; Sabel 1994; Scott and Davis 2007), they had extremely concentrated geographical distribution upon entering China, and they manifested certain traits of an enclave economy in outward appearance. The FIEs formed special embedded relationships with local governments and local society and therefore became nodes that linked the global level (global capital) with the local level (local polity).

The second relationship is between FDI and the local government, which involves the subject of governance. Research using the GVC or GCC theory places governance in a pivotal position, yet the vast majority of the analysis in the literature is devoted to governance issues within the commodity chains and emphasizes the power of lead firms (Gereffi and Korzeniewicz 1994; Gereffi and Lee 2012). This is certainly important, but another key topic that is routinely overlooked is the governance evoked by the embedding of the commodity (or value) chain in local society. When a global production system descends on a specific place, it inevitably forms an embedded relationship with the local network—otherwise it would be impossible to launch the operations of the commodity chain. The governance issues in this link therefore urgently require painstaking research to explain. Because of the particularities of China's political structure, FIEs must rely on the local government to provide protection and services, therefore giving rise to numerous institutional arrangements. This institutional matrix includes formal and informal rules, with the formal rules including national laws and policies and the informal rules including interpersonal networks, tacit understanding, local culture, customs, and so on. When the state extracts financial income from the FDI production and circulation process apart from formal taxes and fee revenues, unofficial financial extraction also deserves attention. Clientelist networks (Wank 1996; Wu Jieh-min 1997) form between local government, FIEs, and domestic private capital, and local governments and officials acquire additional rent as repayment in this exchange relationship. A portion of this rent is paid through foreign exchange earnings, sharing of foreign-currency earnings, and management fee mechanisms, and another portion comes through fees and gratuities listed under various names.

The third relationship is between FDI and labor. The enormous rural labor force from China's inland provinces (migrant workers) provides manufacturing FIEs with the cheap labor they need. The provision of labor and the suppression of wages (due to China's unique mechanism of status exploitation) guarantee that FIEs will reap enormous economic surpluses, which gives the labor market a dual structural feature. Because of China's household registration (*hukou*) system, migrant laborers do not have permanent resident status in the industrial cities and towns where they work and are not employees in the formal system. Therefore, not only do migrant workers receive lower wages, but they are also deprived of social insurance benefits or enjoy them at a lower level (Solinger 1999; Wu Jieh-min 2010). Furthermore, migrant laborers are unable to enjoy collective village benefits when they work in rural areas according to the household registration system. The second-class citizenship of the migrant workers causes them to suffer double exploitation by both capital and the status system. Therefore, when analyzing China's labor-capital relations, the role of state policies and systems cannot be overlooked. In other words, it is necessary to simultaneously analyze the relationships among capital, the state, and labor. That is the focal point of this book's analysis. In the next section, I present a concise historical narrative of Guangdong's march toward becoming the factory of the world and use that narrative to explain the theoretical topic for discussion.

2. The March toward Becoming the Factory of the World

The external conditions driving China's export-oriented development model originated in a dual transformation of geopolitics and the world capitalist division of labor, while the internal conditions originated with the launch of the opening reform policy in the post-Mao era. The 1970s were the starting point of this historical capitalist movement. Beginning in the early 1970s, the United States decided to improve its political relationship with China and draw China over to its side against its Cold War opponent, the Soviet Union. The warming of Sino-US relations made political and economic change possible in China. However, because radical Maoists still held political power, changes in economic policy had to wait until Mao died, the Gang of Four was purged, and Deng Xiaoping and other reformers grasped power, which conjointly provided the critical juncture for opening reform to emerge. After 1978, China gradually relaxed its strict controls on the agricultural sector and allowed the contracting of collectively owned farmland to individual households, which ultimately led to the official disbanding of the people's commune system in 1984. Individual entrepreneurs and some privately run enterprises also gained development opportunities, and governmental control over industry was gradually loosened.

Changes in transnational economic relations, including trading policies and the extension and relocation of the GVC, were usually closely connected to geopolitical changes, which were also a major driving force for industrialization. For example, after World War II, the formulators of American diplomatic and security policies at the end of 1949 won President Harry Truman's approval of National Security Council Report No. 48, which combined security considerations with economic targets. According to research by Bruce Cumings, the original American plans for East Asia "would have yielded 'a unified Asian region,'" but the Cold War introduced divisions to the region, and the Korean War (1950–53) intensified them (Cumings 1999a, 20). The Korean War accelerated changes to American plans regarding the East Asian political situation. It also altered the political relationship between the United States and Japan, which in turn influenced America's position on Japan's economic role, turning Japan into an economic animal supported by the United States. The United States also drove South Korea and Taiwan to establish powerful militaries, and those two countries gained opportunities for economic growth. This political and economic setup in East Asia continued until the Vietnam War ended in the 1970s. Only then did China slowly become integrated into the world economy (Cumings 1999a and 1999b).

US-Taiwan relations were also influenced by the regional configuration. The Korean War changed the US attitude toward Chiang Kai-shek's Kuomintang regime from practicing noninterference in the Taiwan Strait situation to forming an alliance with the Kuomintang and granting it large amounts of military and economic aid. In the late 1950s, the United States announced that it would gradually cease providing aid to Taiwan. Under this political pressure, the Nationalist government implemented a nineteen-point economic reform program in 1960, which included establishing a single exchange rate, relaxing trade restrictions, and encouraging both exports and privately run businesses (Wen Hsien-shen 1984; Li Kwoh-ting and Chen Mu-tsai 1987; Li Kwoh-ting 2005; Wang Tso-jung 2014), and it established several export-processing zones in 1966 (Li Kwoh-ting 1999). One key to the Taiwanese economy's shift from import substitution to export-oriented industrialization was the opening of the US domestic market to products made in Taiwan. Consequently, Taiwan turned into an (American market) demand-responsive economy (Hamilton and Kao 2018). Likewise, an important economic consequence of the change in US policies toward China was the opening of the US market to products manufactured in China. For example, China was granted most-favored-nation status in customs tariffs for the first time in 1979, by the administration of President Jimmy Carter. This provided China with the conditions to push forward EOI under the US political and economic hegemony of that time.

After the United States and Japan signed the Plaza Accord in 1985, the Japanese yen rapidly appreciated and spurred currency appreciation in other newly industrialized Asian countries. Changes in the relative cost of factors of production—including currency or capital, labor, environmental protection, and so on—triggered a reorganization of the international economic division of labor in the Asia-Pacific region.[3] The traditional industries that originally flourished in the Four Little Dragons (the labor-intensive export processing manufacturing of such items as textiles, garments, shoes, luggage, and toys) became sunset industries under these altered macro conditions.

In their search for lower costs, these industries began relocating in great numbers to China's coastal regions and to Southeast Asian countries starting in the late 1980s. This wave of industrial relocation reflected both a geographical shifting of global value and supply chains and the convergence of pushing and pulling forces. The pushing force came from the increasing cost of factors of production in the Four Little Dragons, and the pulling force originated in China's cheap and disciplined workforce. At this juncture, China energetically promoted its opening reform policy and welcomed manufacturing FDI, with Hong Kong and Taiwanese investment playing a vanguard role in the initial stage. Against the backdrop of these historical impetuses, buyers in the global market pushed the migration of Taiwanese and other foreign investment into Guangdong, bringing their capital, technology, and markets into China and extending GVCs into coastal China. Taishang followed their buyers by shifting their manufacturing to China's coastal regions and acquired the

---

3. Gary Hamilton and Cheng-shu Kao take the same viewpoint as this book toward the role of the Plaza Agreement. Their viewpoint is very enlightening regarding the enlarged scale of operations of Taishang in China. However, their historical narrative holds that the Plaza Accord directly but unintentionally encouraged the government to open Taiwan's borders and made it easier for people to leave the country for travel. The government even allowed army veterans to return to mainland China to visit family members (Hamilton and Kao 2018, 147). This latter argument may overlook the fact that the policy to allow veterans to return to China was one round of Taiwan's political liberalization and was closely related to Taiwan's democracy movement. The authors focus only on Chiang Ching-kuo's reforms and do not mention the democracy movement's contribution (see, for example, 133) or the support for the movement among owners of small and medium-size businesses during the crucial stage from when the movement was launched in the 1970s until the early 1990s. These topics go beyond the scope of this book, but if we want to discuss the relationship between political transformation and economic development, we cannot overlook the links between the democracy movement and small and medium-size enterprises.

capacity to engage in large-scale output (Hamilton and Kao 2018). Thus, FDI brought the value chain to Guangdong and rapidly turned its economy into a demand-responsive economy.

As GVCs shifted, coastal China formed export processing production network clusters. These clusters were initially exogenous rather than endogenous—originating with the extension and shift of the GVCs and the introduction of Taiwanese and other FDI into China's local society and economy—and they therefore initially had strong FDI enclave qualities. The interfirm networks of these enclaves were composed of numerous small and medium-size foreign-invested factories. Using Taiwanese FIEs as an example, these business clusters and production networks originally had internal social trust relations, which constituted the social foundation for the high efficiency and outstanding productivity of the Taishang community. At the early stage of Taiwan FIEs' migrating from Taiwan to coastal China, changes at the organizational level included expanding the scope of production and the large-scale hiring of cheap migrant labor, as well as internalizing some of the outsourced work procedures originally adopted in Taiwan and becoming vertically integrated assembly line factories. When we investigate these changes in depth, however, we discover that so-called FDI enclaves were only a surface phenomenon, and that FDI manufacturing clusters (or industrial areas) actually became gradually embedded in local society, rather than being the enclave economies presupposed in the literature.

At this point, how the global linked with the local is a theoretically significant problematic. In their research on the classic case of Torreon in Mexico, Bair and Gereffi (2001) emphasize that it was essential for Torreon's original local manufacturing clusters to link up with GVCs. The nature of these links was external, and the linkage was buyer-driven. Yet when we compare Guangdong's process of global-local linkage, it was likewise buyer-driven. However, the integration of Guangdong's burgeoning industrial clusters with the world market did not in itself become a focus because this integration occurred in tandem with the relocation of FIEs, which merely carried out a spatial redeployment of existing networks between international buyers and foreign manufacturers. From this angle, although the problematic that Bair and Gereffi propose based on the Mexican case is enlightening, is doesn't necessarily lead us to a deeper understanding of the theoretical significance of the Chinese case.

What requires explanation in the Chinese case is how the so-called enclaves of manufacturing FIEs that entered China under the extension of the GVC managed within such a short time to make Guangdong's agricultural region, which did not originally have an industrial foundation, into the factory of the world. Explaining this requires first solving another group of puzzles: How did capital shifting at the global level link up with a demand for industrialization at the local level? What was the role of manufacturing FDI? How were China's migrant workers mobilized as a cheap and disciplined labor force? How did this labor force enter the FDI sector? How were land and other resources mobilized? What role did local governments play in this? What benefits were gained or shared in the cooperation between FIEs and local governments and officials? What kind of interest distribution formula existed between the two?

Chapters 2, 3, and 4 of this book offer supporting empirical data on a formula for the cooperation between local officials and FIEs. For now, I will explain that it was the existence of such a benefit distribution formula that led to the institutionalization of rent-seeking activity, reducing uncertainty and providing a degree of predictability. A portion of the distributed economic surplus was collected in the form of rent. The collection method was through a series of institutionalized rules and informal unspoken rules, the former including mechanisms such as processing fees and foreign exchange retention, and the latter including such things as gratuities and bribes. This book argues that the operational mechanism of economic rent was the economic incentive that motivated local governments and officials to actively attract outside investment and led their cooperation with FIEs to develop on a basis of mutual agreement or tacit approval.

In the day-to-day operations of local growth alliances, local governments and cadres provided protection and services to foreign businesses, approved the leasing of land, and organized migrant workers from other regions to enter the local labor market (for which they collected "commissions), while simultaneously using coercive social control methods to deploy and manage the migrant worker class. Foreign businesses reciprocated with paying rent, gratuities, and bribes and incurring other expenses. The nature of this exchange relationship was that of a clientelist network on a foundation of government-business relations. For this reason, the political foundation of this alliance was an authoritarian-style local relationship network, a government-business relationship with deep-seated Chinese characteristics. However, manufacturers in export-oriented local growth alliances had to link up with the world market, their end products competed on the global level, and their prices were set by lead firms in the value chains—which imposed structural limits on the rent-seeking behavior of local governments (the ceiling effect). Excessively rampant rent-seeking activity by local governments would make it difficult for the manufacturers to do business and would cause them to shut down or relocate, so rent-seeking activity had to be curbed to a certain extent.

It is worth noting that FIEs and local governments were the main actors in day-to-day interactions within the local growth alliance, while the central government and lead firms in the GVCs were invisible partners in this control syndicate. Although the silhouettes of the latter two were concealed and not obvious, they likewise benefited from this production system, especially given the steep profits earned by lead firms. Furthermore, although the central government was an invisible member and beneficiary of the local growth alliance, that didn't mean that the central government's interests were the same as those of local governments. In fact, conflicts often arose between the central and local governments on topics such as tax incentives for investors, social insurance, land development, and local debts. Generally speaking, however, the central and local governments were fundamentally of one mind in terms of the grand objectives of spurring economic development and attracting outside investment.[4]

In the course of thirty years, China's EOI brought several major benefits and development results. First, the Chinese economy rapidly merged into the globalized capitalist production system. On the whole, the gist of the Guangdong experience was following the GVCs to forge the factory of the world. Coastal China seized this historic opportunity and very quickly put China on a trajectory of rapid growth. This FDI-driven path

---

4. In economic analyses, we cannot assume that the state or government is a homogeneous entity. Likewise, different levels of local government cannot be regarded as a homogeneous entity. In other words, conflicts occur between the central and local governments, and also between local governments (in the same or different levels or sectors). In the course of analyzing actual cases, I distinguish between the integration and conflict of interests between the various different government units.

of labor-intensive EOI began heading toward saturation in the mid-2000s. Apart from entering Guangdong's traditional industries, ICT-sector Tai-shang and other FIEs began moving their production chains to eastern China's Yangtze Delta region in the mid-1990s, with Taiwanese investment mainly concentrated in Suzhou's Kunshan region. During this round of extension of the value chains, the manufacturing classification was different from that in the traditional industries in the previous round in Guangdong in that it was primarily the processing of relatively capital-intensive ICT products. Even though capital investment was relatively high, this processing still required a large number of assembly line workers. For that reason, cheap labor and factory costs were still the main draws for foreign companies. This migration of ICT manufacturing chains to China was mainly concentrated in the Yangtze Delta region, but some firms also migrated to the Pearl River Delta. The most notable of these was Foxconn, which established a factory in Shenzhen and became the main contractor for Apple products. In addition, cell-phone chip modules supplied by MediaTek facilitated the rise of the Pearl River Delta's copycat cell-phone system.

Second, export-oriented development allowed China to rapidly become a trade surplus country: From the mid-1990s onward, it accumulated vast foreign reserves and shook off its previous foreign exchange deficit. Its enormous reserves of foreign exchange established the Chinese government's financial capacity to engage in rapid modernization and laid the foundation for China's rise. Apart from bringing in foreign exchange, export-oriented industry also allowed the Chinese government to increase its tax revenues and rapidly accumulate capital. The state's formidable fiscal capacity allowed it to launch large-scale infrastructure projects such as expressways, high-speed railways, and urban renewal, as well as in the purchase of raw materials and technology overseas—including investing in and buying out companies in developed countries and gaining advanced technology and markets. This export-oriented development model led to even greater leaps after China joined the WTO at the end of 2001. Right before the WTO opportunity arrived, China's coastal processing trade and industry had laid the groundwork for rapid export growth by establishing stable links with the global economy through the GVCs. Thus, after joining the WTO China already had mature manufacturing capacity to gain even more substantial growth opportunities.

Having taken one step ahead long ago, Guangdong led the country in foreign exchange earnings.

Third, Chinese-invested suppliers gradually grew out of the FIE-dominated traditional industry value chains in Guangdong's Pearl River Delta region. Beginning in the early 2000s, the enclave-type manufacturing spaces and production networks that Taishang had originally established in Guangdong underwent a change in quality. Enhanced technical competence and staff turnover among Chinese managers and foremen in Taiwanese-invested businesses had a spillover effect on the region's production technology and management styles. Many Chinese workers who had served as foremen in Taishang factories set up their own workshops and began competing with FIEs on orders for medium- or low-grade products, gradually threatening the existence of these FIEs. Another portion of mainland-owned factories served as contractors for FIEs, resulting in the emergence in traditional industries of mainland-owned factories under a Taiwanese system, or Taiwanese-acculturated mainland-owned factories (*taizixi luzichang*). The cultural models and behavioral habits of these factories were deeply influenced by Taishang (Cheng Chih-peng 2014 and 2016).[5] In other words, the networked production system that Taishang supply chains introduced to Guangdong initially operated only in Taiwan-invested community networks, but they gradually became embedded in the local economic structure. This led to the rise of local suppliers and caused a qualitative change to the original embedded relationship of the enclave economy with local society.

Fourth, the GVCs relocated again. From the mid-2000s onward, labor-intensive EOI tended toward saturation, and purchasing power in the world market stagnated. The relative price of China's local factors of production (especially labor costs) also changed with increasing speed, and collective protests by workers increased, accompanied by pressure for industrial upgrading. In Guangdong, the government promoted a policy of *tenglong huanniao* (emptying cages and replacing birds, or eliminating traditional industries and promoting industrial upgrading) in an attempt to bring in high-tech FDI. These new policies put the original local growth

5. Cheng Chih-peng (2016) first coined the term Taizixi qiye (a mainland-owned enterprise under a Taiwanese system), which I have rephrased as Taizixi luzichang.

alliances under heavy attack, and they faced pressure to dismantle or reorganize. As a result, the traditional industry GVCs migrated once again. One direction was relocation to China's inland regions in pursuit of relatively cheap labor, land, and factory costs. Another direction was migration to Southeast Asian countries, and the motivation was again considerations of labor costs. The ICT industrial chain also experienced a similar trend of heading inland or to other countries. At the same time, however, a portion of FIEs were transformed or upgraded on the spot in the Pearl River Delta region, which prolonged their survival capacity.

Fifth, the red supply chain emerged. This term refers to China's self-cultivated and controlled indigenous supply chain system, which does not belong to the existing FDI-dominated global supply chain (GSC) setup. The Chinese government invested capital and selectively nurtured designated ICT industries to develop in parallel with the FDI-dominated value chains. After many years of operation, a portion of local Chinese capital has gradually matured and gained a space in the world market—for example, in telecommunications equipment (Huawei, ZTE, and other companies) and cell phones (Huawei, Xiaomi, OPPO, and other brands). These products, relying on the massive Chinese consumer market, first gained a share of the low- to mid-price market and then began competing in the international market. Chinese manufacturers gradually obtained some key technology, and with autonomous research and development capabilities they gradually formed industrial chains and ecosystems: the development of Shenzhen's ICT industrial cluster is one example. For some products and items in this type of industry, the technical capacity and market occupancy rate of China-invested enterprises has already surpassed that of Taiwanese-invested companies, and the former enterprises are attempting to compete in the world market and capitalist core countries.

Going a step further, Made in China 2025 emphasized the need to "master core technologies, perfect the industrial supply chain, and form our own development capabilities. Deploy an innovation chain revolving around industry, and deploy a resource chain revolving around the innovation chain. . . . Strengthen key core technologies to tackle key problems, accelerate the industrialization of technical achievements, enhance the innovative capacity of key links and focal domains" (State

Council of the People's Republic of China 2015). Correspondingly, forging the red supply chain is an extension of the Twelfth Five-Year Plan[6] to emphasize the domestic market as a basis for developing the external market. In terms of strategic significance for national development, Made in China 2025 attempts to shake off the hegemony of the GVC controlled by the lead firms of core countries. The Xi Jinping administration has promoted the Belt and Road Initiative to export China's domestic production surplus and expand its geoeconomic influence. Although its main investment is in infrastructure, it can also be seen as China's attempt to shake off the technical dominance of Western core countries. Yet what should be especially noted here is that Made in China 2025 is the subjective vision of China's industrial strategy and cannot be considered fact, because it is as yet uncertain whether China will be able to achieve these strategic objectives. In recent years, Western core countries (especially the United States and Germany) have become uneasy about China's expansionist ambitions. These countries have begun sounding the alarm and formulating policies in response to China's incessant scheming to buy Western technology to enhance its industrial capacity in an attempt to shake off technical dependency. Viewed from this angle, the fight for hegemony brought about by China's rapid growth and economic rise will continue to attract international attention.

3. An Examination of Existing Theoretical Propositions

The existing literature explaining the dynamics of China's rapid growth mainly falls into three trains of thought. The first combines market transition theory and privatization theory; the second uses state-centered theory, including local state corporatism theory and developmental state theory; and the third uses export-oriented development theory. All three

---

6. Beginning in 1953, China has proposed a five-year plan for economic and social development every five years. The Twelfth Five-Year Plan served as the guiding principles for China's development in 2011–15.

can explain China's development at certain stages or can partly explain China's developmental dynamics.

1) Market Transition Theory

Market transition theory holds that China's growth momentum developed alongside its socialist, public-owned economy (Nee 1989; Sachs and Woo 1994; Naughton 1995). This theoretical framework in particular can explain the privatization process following the dismantling of China's rural communes and how the nonpublic sector developed outside of the socialist planned economy. This bottom-up capitalist development viewpoint particularly emphasizes the incentives and spontaneity of the private economy. Yet from the mid-1990s onward, China's rural areas experienced a wave of recollectivization, in which rural cadres and local officials took control of publicly owned assets and the rights to collective property (Liu Yia-ling 2003 and 2009), leading to the emergence of various hybrid property rights, flexible arrangements, and fictive ownership (Nee 1992; Yusuf 1994; Wu 1998). In the Guangdong model, the institution of fictive ownership played an important role in the cooperative relationship between local governments and FIEs and embodied a special institutional form. Fictive ownership arrangements are closely related to informal institutions. In a state lacking democracy and the rule of law, informal institutions provide a protective umbrella to the private sector (Wu 1997; Tsai 2007). Furthermore, as the CCP continued to control political power while gradually opening up the private sector, China produced a group of red capitalists who had close relationships with the party (Dickson 2003). This series of issues related to fictive ownership challenges the market transition theory standpoint.

Nee and Opper (2012) have proposed "capitalism from below" to explain how China's private sector gained opportunities for growth in a macro environment of state socialism. They have adopted a new-institutionalist perspective emphasizing how informal norms and institutions helped China's private entrepreneurs work around the unfavorable formal institutional environment. This is a refinement of market transition theory. Yet in addition to the private sector, an ambiguous gray capital space exists in China, and some of the capital in this space has quasi-state (half-official, half-private) characteristics, while some relies on special relationships with the state bureaucracy to develop. In addition, the Chinese government still controls a large portion of state-owned enterprises, which include strategic industries that the state controls, monopolizes, or franchises. Accordingly, China's overall economy forms a kind of state capitalism with a nationalistic connotation (Tsai and Naughton 2015). The market reform and privatization standpoint can provide only a partial explanation of the growth of capitalism in the private sector.

2) State-Centered Theory

State-centered theory emphasizes the leading role of the government in economic growth—that is, the top-down forging of a capitalist system. This theory is part of an immense theoretical genealogy (Johnson 1982 and 1999; Evans et al. 1985; Öniş 1991) that has occupied a key position in explanations of the development of the East Asian region (Gold 1986; Deyo 1987; Johnson 1987; Woo-Cumings 1999; Amsden 1989; Wade 1990; So and Chiu 1995; Amsden and Chu 2003; Weiss 2003; Wang Jenn-hwan 2010). After China's rapid economic growth, the state-centered theory standpoint was applied to China (So 2003a). Local state theory (defined below) and developmental state theory were mainly used to explain China's development.

I start with local state theory. Initially, Oi (1992; see also 1996 and 1999) proposed "local state corporatism," and Nan Lin (1995) proposed "local market socialism," both emphasizing the active role of cadres in economic development. Oi stressed how the local government surmounted the difficulty of what the Hungarian economist Kornai (1986; see also 1992) referred to as "soft budget constraint."[7] Nan Lin stressed the importance of local horizontal coordination networks to differentiate be-

---

7. When state-owned enterprises (SOEs) suffered financial deficits, the government usually helped them out with price subsidies and injections of funds, and as a result these enterprises lacked fiscal discipline. These are what Kornai refers to as soft budget constraints. As opposed to the strict and rigid budget constraints that the typical corporation faces in capitalist market economics, soft budget constraints are regarded as the main factor that created inefficiency in socialist SOEs.

tween market coordination and bureaucratic coordination. He especially emphasized that the coordinating role of cadres in economic activities can fill gaps in market coordination. Both Oi's and Lin's theories were able to explain the growth of township enterprises at that time. Unger and Chan (1995) also used the concept of corporatism to analyze the East Asian and Chinese development models. Subsequently, Walder (1995) extended Oi's proposition and added the property rights perspective of new-institutional economics. He stated that as long as ownership rights can be clearly delineated, public enterprises can be as efficient as private enterprises. I call this theoretical genealogy "local state theory."

Local state theory was very popular in the 1990s because it explained China's political and economic situation at that time. Yet the theory has several limitations. First, the Oi-Walder proposition overlooks cadres' personal interests as an important incentive for local industrialization. In a campaign to usher in a market economy, cadres seek personal benefit for themselves, their relatives, and members of their retinues. When the private incentives of officials are aligned with the public interests of economic development, official conduct is positive and active. However, if there is a conflict between personal incentives and public interests, official conduct is negative, characterized by corruption and plundering. Oi (1992, 113, note 44) assumes that cadres are "non-corrupt," overlooking their personal economic motivations. In fact, China's central government actually used those motivations to induce cadres to spare no effort in attracting outside investment. The same kind of bureaucratic economic activity produces a different sense of legitimacy at different stages of economic development—related to changes in the relative cost of using a specific system, among other factors. A core aim of this book is to explain the role of bureaucratic institutional rent seeking in the local economy, as well as the factors creating changing feelings of legitimacy toward rent-seeking behavior.

Second, regional differences highlighted variations in the role of cadres. Local state theory has a compelling explanatory power when applied to southern Jiangsu Province, Shandong Province, and other such places. However, it has little explanatory power when applied to individually and privately owned enterprises in Zhejiang Province or to the export-oriented development in Guangdong because local companies in those cases have actual ownership rights and are not under direct control of cadres. The role of government officials in local state theory is comparable to that of an entrepreneur who is involved in a company's production activities, and the role is therefore easily associated with the transition from commune and brigade enterprises under the commune system to township and village enterprises (TVEs) after the dismantling of communes in the southern Jiangsu region from the 1970s onward. By way of contrast, the role of cadres in the abovementioned market transition theory is akin to that of patrons who are not involved in the enterprise's internal decision making but provide the enterprise with various institutional umbrellas such as redcap affiliations,[8] for which they collect protection fees—a kind of official role that typically arises in government-business relationships under the Wenzhou model. In the foreign investment–driven growth model of the Pearl River Delta and the Yangtze Delta in the 1990s, cadres link globalization with the local level in a role akin to that of broker, providing FIEs with cheap labor and land and covering other production costs.

Third, as the overall economic environment changed, TVEs began closing down and dissolving in the mid-1990s. The Chinese postsocialist transitional economy was already gradually transforming into an economy that combined state-led capitalism with foreign and private investment. Local state theory was able to explain the rise of TVEs, but it was clearly unable to explain their fall. At the same time, after the 1994 taxation reforms, the central government gradually gained control of tax revenues; property rights to rural land showed a trend toward reconcentration; and the decline of TVEs and the fall of many model villages made local state theory quiet.

Recently, there has been a revival of interest in the role of local governments. Chunyu Wang, Jingzhong Ye, and Jennifer Franco (2014) have proposed "neo-guanxilism" to replace Oi's local state corporatism theory. They emphasize the exchange of interests between local political and economic elites due to the resources they respectively control. Looking back at local state developmentalism, Schubert and Heberer (2015) hold that local governments still control private sector development and entrepreneurial agency, but their role has been transformed from that of bu-

---

8. "Redcap affiliation" means that a private enterprise bears the title of the public or collective enterprise offered by local authorities.

reaucratic patron, cadre entrepreneur, and corporate agent to that of a private enterprise's interested facilitator.

The second type of state-centered theory is developmental state theory. It is typically assumed that the developmental state has the capacity to use state resources to guide the direction of industrial development and spur industrial upgrading. There are two main strategies: import-substitution industrialization (ISI) and EOI. During the Mao era, China adopted the Soviet-style industrialization model, which emphasized autarky and could be considered a fairly extreme ISI strategy. The opening reform strategy launched in the late 1970s was a classic EOI strategy. However, when we more closely analyze China's industrialization policies, we discover that they were in fact a mixture of EOI and ISI strategies, and that different regions had different policy matrixes: ISI and market protectionism were adopted to target the domestic market and strategic industries, and measures encouraging EOI were adopted to target the export sector. ISI policies commonly included customs barriers, import restrictions, subsidies, bank loans, joint ventures, local content rates, and other such methods. Common EOI policies included export tax rebates, preferential tax rates and fees, low-cost leases for state-owned and collective land, facilitating the provision of cheap labor (through suppressed wages, the repression of labor unions, and other means), and providing infrastructure. All of these typical policies could be found in China. In comparison, the main East Asian–style developmental states emphasized their own qualities: Japan had an outstanding and highly efficient economic bureaucracy to push its economic development strategy forward (Johnson 1982); South Korea was able to make full use of its advantages of scale, giving rise to close relationships between the government and private industrial conglomerates (chaebols) (Amsden 1989); and in Taiwan it was the state that had the capacity to guide new technology research and development and industrial policy (Wade 1990; Wang Jenn-hwan 2010; Hsieh 2015).

So if China is regarded as a postsocialist developmental state, what characteristics does it have? First of all, Marc Blecher (1991, 267–68) argues that in postsocialist transitional China, because state bureaucrats controlled enormous resources and often had an "entrepreneurial status" in economic activities, the situation in China was that of a "developmental state" coexisting with an "entrepreneurial state," the former aimed at developing state policy and the latter having "profit" motives. According to Blecher, the entrepreneurial state's control of companies is therefore even deeper than that of the developmental state, and its planning and coordination is also more extensive. The entrepreneurial state more easily compels officials to promote economic development for the sake of personal motivations. Jane Duckett (2001) proposed the concept of "state entrepreneurialism" to explain that state bureaucrats were willing to accept market reform because they were becoming business managers and enjoying personal benefits. Tsai and Naughton (2015) examined the similarities and differences between China's state capitalism and East Asian developmentalism. The authors discovered that the similarity between the development trajectories of China and the East Asian developmental states was the growth miracle, which had very similar stages and speeds of development in all the countries. But China had differed from the other states in two basic ways. The first difference was one of scale: China's enormous size meant that it had to rely even more than the other countries on central directives, and a larger area of the economy escaped government control. The second difference was that China adopted a more open attitude toward FDI and did not follow the path of East Asian countries, which limited FDI to a certain extent and promoted the development of the domestic private sector.

China's second characteristic is a high degree of regional variation. The country's vast expanse results in immense differences among various places in terms of natural resources and structural and institutional conditions. Although as a whole China is a developmental state, it is very difficult to apply uniform systematic concepts to describe the different conditions in various places. From 1978 on, part of China's regional developmental disparity could be attributed to links with global capitalism. In his research on the role of FDI in China's automotive industry, Eric Thun (2006) discovered obvious typological differences between different regions. Regional disparities highlighted the theoretical potential of the abovementioned local state theory. By placing the local states within the comparative institutional framework, we can explain the developmental disparities across China's various regions.

China's third characteristic is that Hong Kong and Taiwanese capital left a major mark on China's economic structure. In the early stage of opening reform, the Chinese government intentionally mobilized Chinese diaspora capital (mainly Taiwanese and Hong Kong capital), seeking to have it returned to China and invested there (So and Chiu 1995; So 2003a; Hsiao 2003). You-tien Hsing (1998) has also used ethnic and cultural ties to analyze how early Taiwanese investment and the collaboration of cadres hastened the birth of transnational capital networks and launched China's capitalistic development. Some hold that China's developmental state shared many features with Taiwan's developmental state (Baek 2005). The model of Taishang profoundly influenced the behavior and culture of a portion of privately owned factories in China's coastal areas (Cheng Chih-peng 2015). One scholar argues that in Guangdong, the low wages and low workers' rights provided by Gangshang and Taishang influenced the behavior of China's local capital. As a result, although the influence of Taishang has gradually decreased, path dependence has led local capital to adopt low-wage practices like those of Taishang.[9] Another scholar holds that although Guangdong has undergone industrial upgrading in recent years, its labor conditions and hiring patterns have not greatly improved (Butollo 2014). This statement requires scrutiny, however (see chapter 6, section 5). Even so, we cannot overlook one fact: in the Chinese-style labor exploitation, class relations and the migrant worker status system both affect labor conditions, and the system deprives workers of local household registration and social welfare and other rights to lower the enterprise's labor costs. China's state apparatus and local institutions play a key role in this status system. This puts Taishang in a collusive or allied relationship with the state. In fact, a repressive labor regime is a characteristic common in East Asian developmental states, from the Four Little Dragons to China and Southeast Asian countries, although each country has its own particular institutional configuration (Deyo 1987; Ching Kwan Lee 1998; Selden and Wu 2011; Wu Jieh-min 2011; A. Chan 2011 and 2015).

The influence of Hong Kong and Taiwanese capital on China's development indicates the importance of external links and therefore highlights the limitations of the state-centered theory. Both local state theory and developmental state theory make the state their analytical focus and tend to emphasize endogenous variables, while overlooking the dynamic of globalization. China's opening reform and rapid growth from 1978

9. Interview: BL201506.

onward must be analyzed within the larger historical space of the East Asia region.

3) Export-Oriented Development Theory: The World System, Globalization, and the Commodity/Value Chain

The main standpoint of export-oriented development theory is "capitalism from outside": according to the theory, China's opening reform resulted from an external capitalist dynamic (Lardy 1992; Huang Yasheng 2003; Liu Yia-ling 2003; Ho-fung Hung 2016). The introduction of FDI and links with the global economy also have an "contagious" effect on institutional reform (Gallagher 2005). How did the Chinese economy link up with the global economy? What competitively advantageous factors did China enjoy in its links with the global economy? And what are the points in time and the patterns of China's links with the world economy? World-systems theory and commodity chain analysis provide a powerful way to answer these questions.

Giovanni Arrighi borrows the industrious revolution viewpoint from the Japanese scholars Hayami Akira and Kaoru Sugihara and integrates it with world-systems theory, providing a unified historical narrative to explain the rapid growth of East Asia and China after World War II: From the 1880s onward, East Asia developed a labor-intensive industrialization that differed from the Western model, and East Asia was less reliant than the West on replacing the labor force with automation and capital. Beginning in the 1950s, East Asia began to combine its labor-intensive model with the Western capital-intensive model and quickly began catching up with Western countries in terms of levels of gross domestic product (GDP) (Arrighi 2007, chapter 1). China's rapid growth from the 1980s onward is part of this East Asian development model, and it has the following characteristics: (1) It used its enormous, educated, healthy, and high-quality labor force to rapidly expand production (this was partly a legacy of the Mao era), and it did not abandon labor-intensive industries in the process of developing capital- and knowledge-intensive industries. (2) The preliminary stage of this wave of industrialization attracted large amounts of capital from the Chinese diaspora, especially from Hong Kong and Taiwan. (3) Although using the development concept of the market as a foundation, the growth did not follow neoliberalist doctrine; rather, the state maintained control of the banking system, strategic industries, and state-owned enterprises (Arrighi 2007, chapter 12).

Arrighi's theory is based on world-systems theory but resembles the hypothesis of the East Asian developmental state's growth miracle and mainly relies on state policies and high-quality human capital. His theory can explain how in the 1980s and 1990s China relied on a cheap and relatively high-quality labor force to grasp the historical opportunity of the capitalist world system's redivision of labor to embark on rapid growth. But the theory has some serious flaws. First, Arrighi underestimates the deprivation and devastation this wave of industrialization wreaked on rural land and communities, and he overlooks the exploitation of the enormous migrant labor class outside of the formal sector (P. Huang 2017). Although he acknowledges the social conflicts and resistance that development brought, he still defines China's development model as one of "accumulation without dispossession (of farmers' land)" (Arrighi 2007, 361–67). Second, his analytical perspective is too structural and does not account for dynamic human agency. His framework cannot explain the place of China's migrant labor class in relations among the state, capital, and labor—that is, he cannot explain how the channeling of China's state policies and local institutions into the world capitalist system molded labor-capital relations and the exploitative apparatus. In general, Arrighi's theory is excessively macroscopic, and like all world-systems theories, it has difficulty explaining changes at the institutional level and the behavior of firms. It also cannot explain the specific mode that links China's modern industrialization with the global economy. On this point, the commodity or value chain approach provides us with a theoretical basis for constructing an analytical framework.

The concept of commodity chains comes from the world-systems theorists Hopkins and Wallerstein (1977). This concept implies the global division of labor and integration of labor into the world economy, unequal trade, and the spatial and social configurations of commodity chains linked to cyclical shifts in the world economy (Bair 2009b, 7–8). Under this conceptual stimulus, Gary Gereffi and coauthors created the neologism "global commodity chain": "A GCC consists of sets of interorganizational networks clustered around one commodity or product, linking households, enterprises, and states to one another within the world-economy. These networks are situationally specific, socially constructed, and locally integrated, underscoring the social embeddedness of economic organization" (Gereffi, Korzeniewicz, and Korzeniewicz 1994, 2).

Gereffi also points out that commodity chain analysis includes three dimensions: an input-output structure, a territoriality (spatial dispersion or the concentration of production and distribution networks), and a governance structure (with authority and power relationships) (Gereffi 1994). GCC theory brings several new orientations to empirical analysis: (1) It introduces the concept of globalization, to be distinguished from world-systems theory's viewpoint of a world economy. World-systems theory has only one analytical unit (the systemic level), but the globalization perspective accommodates a relatively multivariant understanding of the world economy. (2) Commodity chain analysis in world-systems theory puts greater emphasis on the analysis of primary commodities, while GCC theory focuses on an analysis of manufacturing—in particular, the networks among manufacturers (i.e., how export manufacturers in developing countries link up with the world market). (3) By placing chain governance at the meso level, GCC theory can explain manufacturers' behavior at the micro level (see Bair 2009a) and analyze the effect on the national economy of extending the commodity chain to the macro level (Hamilton and Gereffi 2009).

GCC theory provided a new theoretical perspective and empirical analysis, especially in terms of the conceptual differentiation between a buyer-driven commodity chain (BDCC) and a producer-driven commodity chain (PDCC) developed by Gereffi—which was pathbreaking and guided and stimulated a great deal of empirical research. Using this research as a foundation, in the early 2000s, a group of scholars carried out a series of interdisciplinary discussions based on their respective in-depth and on-the-spot observations of cross-border production, and they proposed the concept of GVCs. The dichotomy between BDCCs and PDCCs originally proposed by Gereffi was too static, and the new concept was meant to develop a more comprehensive theory of governance. The substitution of the word "value" for "commodity" was based on two rationales: (1) The term "commodity" is easily associated with primary products such as crude oil and bulk agricultural products; (2) the term "value" captures the concept of "value added" and focuses on the main source of economic development—that is, the return on invested capital generated by human effort (Sturgeon 2009, 112 and 117). Thus, the concept of the

GVC can explain a full range of possible chain activities and end products (Bair 2009b, 12), and it has a greater potential for analyzing the value-production process of chain activities and the problem of value distribution.

After the concept of the GVC was proposed, Gereffi, Humphrey, and Sturgeon (2005, 83–84) proposed an even more dynamic five-part governance structure, including: (1) markets, mainly defined by cost (that is, the relative price of essential factors); (2) modular value chains, which provide turnkey services that facilitate the diffusion of knowledge and technology between firms; (3) relational value chains, in which the interaction between firms creates mutual dependence and trust, as well as spatial clusters and networks; (4) captive value chains, in which lead firms control small suppliers, and the power relationship between the two sides is fairly asymmetrical; and (5) hierarchy, characterized by an individual firm's vertical integration. The first and fifth parts were developed from Ronald Coase's (1988) theory on transaction costs and the market or firm, while the middle three belong to the network structure analysis developed from economic sociology theory.

The GCC theory developed from world-systems theory expanded analyses of GSC and gradually gave rise to GVC analysis. This theoretical lineage lowers analysis to the levels of the institution and firm and can minutely dissect both the actors in the export-oriented development process and the interaction between the actors. It can therefore produce more detailed analyses than Hopkins and Wallerstein's initial skeletal perspective.

The GCC and GVC theories inspired a great deal of empirical research, and studies on the Asia-Pacific region, East Asia region, and China flourished. These included research on the relationship between the value chain and EOI, regional economic ties, specific industrial commodity chains and industrial upgrading strategies of East Asian countries, and the role played by specific brand-name firms. In terms of export-oriented strategies, some studies focused on the key role of lead firms in the value chain. By placing orders, signing contracts, establishing links, and sometimes also outsourcing product design to companies on the ground in East Asia, these lead firms were able to expand their roles beyond limited specializations, causing the GVC to form multilateral, transnational, and transregional production networks and proceed into high value-added activity (Borrus, Ernst, and Haggard 2000; Ernst and Guerrieri 1998; Sturgeon and Lester 2004; Yeung, Liu, and Dicken 2006). In terms of the regional economy, research has focused on how commodity chains drove industrial restructuring of the garment trade and manufacturing in the Pacific Rim (Applebaum, Smith, and Christerson 1994); how the social and cultural affinities, kinship networks, and geographical proximity of the South China region, Hong Kong, and Taiwan introduced GCCs to South China (Chen Xiangming 1994); and how value chains have driven the dynamics of local learning and industrial upgrading (Kawakami and Sturgeon 2011). In terms of the commodity chains of individual industries, research on the footwear and garment industries is plentiful (Gereffi and Korzeniewicz 1990; Taplin 1994; Korzeniewicz 1994; Gereffi and Pan 1994), and of the research on footwear brands, that on Nike is most notable (Korzeniewicz 1994; Cheng Lu-lin 1999). With the rise of cell-phone manufacturing in China, researchers have observed how local Chinese companies create domestic value chains, use technology introduced by foreign businesses to transform themselves, and use the enormous and diverse domestic market to establish business opportunities (Imai and Shiu 2011).

Hamilton and Gereffi (2009) challenge the role of the developmental state emphasized in state-centered theory by examining the leading role the GCC played in East Asia's economic rise. They emphasize the urgent need to find theoretical links between macroscopic structural analysis and GCC analysis at the organizational level, to effectively explain the historic dynamics of globalization. They argue that the revolutionary development in the scale of the American retail market, along with the seeking of suppliers overseas by brand- and retailer-dominated commodity chains, has caused constant iterative matching between international buyers and manufacturers and has spurred East Asian countries to develop demand-responsive economies (Feenstra and Hamilton 2006)—the result at the macroscopic level of the expansion of the GCC. Hamilton and Gereffi (2009, 143) criticize the excessive emphasis in existing research on the linkage between manufacturers in the commodity chain, pointing out that the industrial policies pushed by the state have their limits, even though they are not completely without function. It is worth noting that the activities by the state and officials that the authors presuppose are mainly in formulating and executing industrial policies, legal decrees, and standards (2009, 159–61), and the authors do not include the state's fiscal extraction activities and entrepreneurial behavior in their analysis. According to this book's approach, the basic problem with existing research is its underpoliticized analysis of global commodity or value chains, along with its lack of political analysis of the local polity in which value chains become embedded. An underpoliticized approach cannot grasp the nature of the interaction between value chains on the one hand and local politics and society on the other hand. Such an approach underestimates the role of the state, especially in value capture. The role of state as a value capturer is exceedingly understated in current GVC literature.

Furthermore, although Gereffi's early work stated that GCC analysis emphasizes elements such as local integration and social embedding, neither GCC nor GVC theory have led to in-depth study of these phenomena, and there are no analytical tools for local embedding and government-business relationships. The majority of existing research on chain activity is too narrowly demarcated, and analyses of spatial organization are mainly focused on industrial clusters. Although the value distribution produced by chain activity has attracted interest, there is still a lack of research into the role of the local government in the distribution mechanism. As the case studies in this book show, the local government not only provides infrastructure and an institutional system for chain activities but also takes part in value distribution activities. Therefore, in terms of problematics, we need to return to the dimensions of economic surplus (surplus value) distribution and labor input, which were first emphasized in the commodity chain analysis of world-systems theory (Hopkins and Wallerstein 1977). Arrighi and Drangel proposed to further explore the "unequal distribution of reward among the various activities" in world-systems division of labor relationships (requoted from Bair 2009b, 8).

This book proposes an integrated approach that provides a relatively complete picture of China's export-oriented economic transformation process, sorting out the political processes and institutional arrangements that link the global and local levels and analyzing the interactive patterns of FDI and the local political, economic, and social systems. Based on a critical revision of the abovementioned theories, the next section will construct the core theory of this book step by step.

4. The GVC and Local Growth Alliances

Taking the GVC or GCC as a point of departure, this analysis explains how the external forces of global capital combined with the internal forces of the local polity, and as a result local growth alliances formed to join the value distribution game.

1) The Limits of GVC Governance Analysis

How do the various actors in the value chain create and capture value (profit) in the production and distribution segments of the chain? Gereffi (1994 and 1995) refers to the governance structure, focusing on how chain drivers control the distribution of value. But dissecting the distribution of interests among the various firms in the commodity chain solely in terms of the chain's governance structure is too simplistic. Local government organs as well as firms have roles in the operation of the value or supply chain. As components of the commodity chain, government organs may take part in the creation of value and distribution of profit. In the interactions within the buyer-driven commodity chain, the buyer plays the dominant role toward small suppliers, but manufacturers of significant scale may enjoy some leeway in negotiating prices with buyers. Taking this argument a step further, when we consider the political geography of the chess game between the buyer and the manufacturer (this is not the territoriality that Gereffi speaks of, although the two have a degree of overlap), it is essential to look at the role of local governments and officials in the political geography where the suppliers operate. As economic sociologists often remind us, the state and the economy are mutually constituting spheres of activity (Block and Evans 2005). We should not assume that local governments have no role to play in this game of interest distribution. In fact, their role is critical, not only as rule makers but also often as game players. In China, the local government captures the historic opportunity of manufacturing FDI flowing into China and enters the negotiating arena with foreign-invested manufacturers. From this perspective, local governments and officials are also actors in the relationships in this commodity chain. Although international buyers have an overwhelming influence on price setting and the distribution of profit, local governments can still benefit from the price negotiation process, and in some industries, they even gain a substantial share of the profit. Local governments have thus formed alliances with foreign investors in the game process.

Accordingly, the governance structure analysis developed by Gereffi and colleagues is really just an explanatory framework that lacks a local viewpoint. We need to take the analysis a step further and ask: What kind of embedded relationship do the recipients of capital flow (i.e., local governments and actors) form with FIEs? What institutional adjustments do local governments make as a result? What effect do these adjustments have on FDI?

GVC theory's global-local links basically refer to the links between the GVCs and domestic industrial clusters. For that reason, links between global capital and domestic districts are often analyzed with a focus on the internal governance structure of the GVCs. For example, both the abovementioned case analysis by Bair and Gereffi (2001) regarding a Mexican industrial zone and the analysis by De Propris, Menghinello, and Sugden (2008) of an Italian industrial zone contracting for transnational businesses focus on the ties between internationalized production and local industrial zones. Although Bair and Gereffi (2001) point out that GCC links shaped local development and brought opportunities for industrial upgrading, their analysis overlooks the embedding of the GCC in local politics and society. Lee Joonkoo's (2010) review of GCC and GVC literature points out that the strategies of buyers and suppliers are embedded in and shaped by the supplier's local polity, including state policies, regulations, social conventions, and public opinion. However, most of these topics have not been discussed in detail or in terms of specific case studies.

2) From G-L to G-D-L Analysis

GVC or GCC theory provides a road sign for mapping the entrance of FDI into China, but the theory lacks a mechanism to explain the mutual embeddedness of the value chain and the local polity. Therefore, it overlooks the institutional basis upon which various actors interact (including cooperating and competing) and the behavioral consequences of their interactions. For this reason, I add the dimension of local polity to

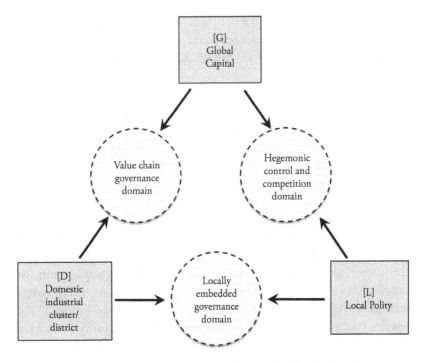

FIGURE 1.2. G-D-L links: the three domains in the revised global-local analysis framework.

the original global-local link (G-L) framework and expand the analysis to cover the global capital–domestic industrial district–local polity link (G-D-L). The local polity is both a spatial and a power concept: it is a social construct under the jurisdiction of the sovereign nation-state that includes government, institutions, and culture. Global capital is embedded not only in the network space of domestic industrial clusters, but also in the local polity.

Figure 1.2 shows a simplified model of this framework. I differentiate among three blocks of actors: global capital, domestic industrial districts, and the local polity. The three blocks produce three interactive domains: the value chain governance domain, between global capital and domestic industrial districts (the domain emphasized in the existing literature); the locally embedded governance domain, between the local polity and domestic industrial districts (which has not been analyzed in the existing literature and is the main analytical focal point and theoretical contribution of this book); and the hegemonic control and competition domain, between global capital and the local polity. The forces of global capital carry out domination and surplus extraction on the local polity through the value chain, while the local state forms a cooperative or competitive relationship with global capital. Based on a calculation of its own interests, the local state may cooperate with and yield to global capital on industrial policy at a specific time but then develop a competitive relationship with global capital at a later time. For example, China's industrial upgrading and fostering of native supply chains in recent years has created conflicts with global capital hegemons. In this regard, the state contends for global capitalist hegemony. Using the foundation of chain analysis, this book focuses its analysis on the second domain. I return to the third domain in chapter 7 and the conclusion.

3) *The State as Capturer of Value*

Under globalized production, an important indicator for evaluating the results of development is whether or not local economic entities can achieve value capture. However, in the existing literature, analysis of value capture in both GVC theory and the global production network (Coe and Yeung 2015) still centers on the manufacturer (using firm-specific analysis) and focuses on governance within the value chain, therefore overlooking the role of state actors in directly capturing value.[10] The concept of locally embedded governance proposed above attempts to amend this theory. We need to bring the state into GVC and global production network analysis and to regard the state as an actor in value capture.

Figure 1.3 is a more complex version of figure 1.2. Using a buyer-driven value chain as an example, I have divided the value chain into five links: design, raw materials, semifinished product, assembly, and brand

---

10. *Author's Postscript*: After the Chinese edition of the book was published, I found several pertinent chapters in Ponte, Gereffi, and Raj-Reichert's edited volume (2019): on policy rents, Kaplinsky 2019; on redistributive rents, Havice and Pickels 2019; and on the neglected role of the state as a producer by controlling SOEs, Horner and Alford 2019. Yet, these studies do not address the role of the state as a capturer of value in its participation in the GVC and the agency of the state in fostering native supply chains to compete with global capital, as treated in this book.

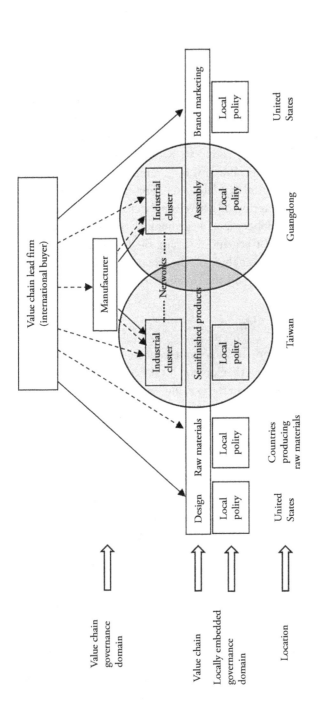

FIGURE I.3. G-D-L analysis: the value chain governance domain and locally embedded governance domain.

marketing. Imagine that the international buyer or lead firm in this example has its headquarters in the United States, the raw materials are produced in multiple countries, the semifinished product is produced in Taiwan, the assembly is carried out in Guangdong, and the brand marketing is done in the United States. Of course, this is a highly simplified conceptualization of the value chain links and spatial locations for analytical purposes.

In the value chain governance domain, the international buyer, as the lead firm in that value chain, controls the key segments of design and brand marketing, which are also the links where the creative industry is believed to capture the most added value. The international buyer controls those two segments through ownership or equity. In addition, the buyer controls the raw materials, semifinished products, and assembly process links through selection and purchase, specifications, quality control, manufacturing standards, and so on. The buyer can therefore achieve control over the semifinished product and assembly process through outsourcing to the manufacturer—that is, through placing an order. Likewise, a manufacturer that accepts an order from the buyer can manufacture the semifinished product and assemble the final product through its own factories in Taiwan and Guangdong or can complete the order by outsourcing a portion of the processing. In this analysis, the internationalization or globalization of production, spatial reconfiguration, and networks between manufacturers facilitates the emergence of industrial clustering. This kind of industrial cluster exists in both Taiwan and China. Going a step further, the relationships between manufacturers and within business conglomerates allow us to also observe the emergence of interactive and networked relationships between industrial clusters in Taiwan and Guangdong. The two shaded circles in figure 1.3 indicate the dense interaction of the industrial clusters.

Most of the analysis of commodity chains and industrial clusters has focused on this interaction and has gone no further. But if we stop here, we miss a major empirical phenomenon—namely, the embedding of industrial clusters in the local polity. For example, in Guangdong, since extension of the GCC has developed industrial clusters, what roles do local government and cadres play in global capital's local links? In typical commodity chain analysis, an analysis of state policy does not explain local embeddedness but only describes the general local laws and institutions or the local society's economic structural features (for example, Gereffi 1994; Bair and Gereffi 2001). At the same time, this research usually assumes that the local government is merely the formulator of a portion of the rules of the game (with the main portion coming from laws and regulations) and is not a player in the game. However, this assumption is inaccurate in the case of China. For this reason, we need to include an analysis of the locally embedded governance domain.

Peter Evans (1995) has proposed the term "embedded autonomy" to explain what kind of developmental state is conducive to industrial upgrading policies. This book's concept of locally embedded governance has parallels with Evans's theory, but I particularly emphasize the mutual embeddedness between the developmental state and the GVC and the role played by the capturers of value. My question is therefore closer to the core concern: What kind of developmental state is conducive to the state's capturing economic surplus? Given its formidable capacity and autonomy, the Chinese state (including the local state) is able to extract economic surplus by embedding itself in the value chain governance domain. Regarding the state as a capturer of value therefore leads to a deeper understanding of the role of state autonomy.

In locally embedded governance relations, it is particularly important to note the role that local governments play in promoting, controlling, standardizing, and arbitrating economic activity, paying special attention to what kind of institutional mechanism they adopt to extract financial gain in the value chain segment. In GVC theory, this is one of the domains in which value capture occurs—that is, local state forces intervene in the distribution of economic surplus in this interactive domain of the value chain. The behavior of China's local governments and officials therefore interacts with value chain activities and chain governance and leads to the formation of a G-D-L linkage. After a Taishang or Gangshang takes an order from an international buyer to assemble a product in Guangdong, it can employ ownership control by establishing its own directly run factory on the spot, or it can employ nonownership control by providing the semifinished product and outsourcing the finishing and assembly. According to the type of governance structure depicted in the abovementioned value chain theory of Gereffi and colleagues, adopting the ownership-control manufacturing method falls under the internal hierarchical governance of a business conglomerate (i.e., a single manufacturer's vertically integrated relationships), and adopting the outsourcing method is closer to the networked value chain governance structure (which can employ any one or a combination of the multiple types defined by Gereffi and colleagues).

However, China's transition from socialism to market economy, with its particular institutional legacies, state policies, and the intervention of local governments, causes this kind of analysis to lose focus and become divorced from reality. My research found that local governments usually gained rent and benefit from participating in value chain activity through arranging fictive ownership among foreign-invested manufacturers. For example, a contract for processing shipped materials (*lailiao jiagong*) in Guangdong fell under this kind of ownership arrangement: the foreign corporation arranged a processing contract with the local government or township enterprise, the local processing plant was responsible for assembly and earned processing fees, and the local government earned an additional economic rent income (in the form of processing-management fees, management fees, etc.). In terms of the type of contract, the local processing plant's ownership was in the hands of a local enterprise or government unit, but in reality, it was a foreign-controlled plant and was solely responsible for the entire process, from hiring workers and production and assembly processes to exporting, so its control resembled the equity control of a wholly foreign-owned enterprise. How can we explain why anyone would go to the trouble of arranging fictive ownership? Only from the standpoint of G-D-L can we clearly see the actual operations of the GVC in China's local polity. The local government, acting out of financial motivations, intervened in the governance structure of the value chain under the state's two-tier exchange rate policy (which was annulled in 1994) and in that way derived rent income and achieved value capture through fictive ownership contract arrangements. Essentially, it was extracting economic surplus (value) in the production process. However, through the use of fictive ownership, local government units gained legal profit as fictive firms and covered up the role of financial extraction in this process. We can therefore observe that local governments adopted the contractual arrangement of processing contracts to carry out their multiple political and fiscal functions, including increasing the GDP growth rate and meeting quotas for attracting outside investment, foreign exchange earnings, additional taxes and levies, and so on. To access the cheap essential factors of production at that time (mainly labor and land rent), foreign companies entering China had to reach a meeting of minds with the local government and accept that special form of contract, thus becoming embedded in the local polity. Under that particular temporal and spatial configuration, globalization and the local polity hastened the birth of local industrial clusters and at the same time gave rise to the locally embedded governance domain.

The G-D-L analytical framework allows us to observe the local polity interacting with industrial clusters and forming a larger operational domain on a value chain link, such as the semifinished product or assembly process; and to see semifinished products and the assembly process each creating overlapping relationships through the spread and influence of networks and behavioral models, in particular spatial and temporal operational domains. Analyzing these complex interactions and intersections gives us a new standpoint for observing value chain movement and industrial upgrading. For example, the phenomenon of enterprises under a Taiwanese system discovered by Cheng Chih-peng (2016) can help provide a more complete theoretical understanding under this analytical framework. Likewise, the wave of labor strikes in Taiwan-invested companies from the early 2010s onward is closely related to the shifting of the GSC. Even more noteworthy is the fact that the role played by local governments and the local polity in this wave of strikes needs to be analyzed from the G-D-L standpoint to be appropriately interpreted.

4) Local Government-Business Relationships, Distribution of Profit, and the Extension of the Value Chain

In the locally embedded governance domain, government-business relationships especially deserve in-depth research. Local government-businesses relationships play an extremely important role in the extraction of economic surplus from GVCs. In the labor-intensive processing export industries of China's coastal regions, the labor force constitutes a key link in the creation of value in value chain activities. Financial benefit is a major motivation for cadres to intervene in the production activities of value chains (i.e., intervening in the distribution of the value chain's economic surplus and playing a role in the chain's production segment), even though most officials are not involved directly in production activities. The Chinese government therefore joins the alliance with international buyers and FIEs that exploits the surplus value of Chinese labor, just as the local government has an important role in the growth alliance formed by international buyers and foreign companies, and the central government is the policy maker behind the scenes. This book expounds on the following points in detail. First, the exploitative system on which this growth alliance relies is composed of a political system with Chinese characteristics: China's dual labor system painstakingly suppresses the labor cost of using migrant workers. Propping up this dual labor market is a set of institutional arrangements created through the system of differential citizenship. Apart from its nationwide features, this system is also highly localized. The migrant worker community is at the lowest level of this hierarchical system of differential citizenship.

Second, in addition to local governments and officials, China's central government shares in the extraction of economic surplus (in the form of taxes, levies, and foreign exchange), and distribution of the surplus is the result of negotiations between the government and business. The types of contracts adopted and the distribution provisions in them all have the quality of particularistic contracting, including contractual arrangements between government and business and between different levels of government. For this reason, we can regard rent-seeking behavior as institutional rent seeking. This book differentiates between various types of rent seeking. Institutional rent seeking refers to the possession by governments, officials, and cadres of extensive executive power and discretionary power in the economic sphere and to the fact that in addition to being regulators of the rules of the game, they are also players involved in rent-seeking activity.

Third, in the case of China, we must regard bureaucratic protection as an essential factor of production, even though that protection is hard to quantify. China's official business interactions reflect a clientelist relationship. Officials provide manufacturers with affiliations and protection, and the benefit they obtain in return is a kind of protection fee. Discriminating between protection and extortion depends primarily on the sense of legitimacy of the protection fee. Fluctuations in the sense of legitimacy are closely related to changes in the relative price of bureaucratic protection as a factor of production.

Fourth, the spatial extension and outward shift of value or commodity chains are correlated with the reduction, stagnation, or exhaustion of extracted economic surplus. Fluctuations in the extraction rate of economic surplus are linked to changes in the world market, the prices of factors of production, state policies and local adjustments, and the ability of the working class to negotiate pay and other such factors. The industrial upgrading that started in Guangdong in the late 2000s was reflected in a new wave of GVC extension. The extension and shift of value chains will seriously affect government-business relationships in existing growth alliances.

5) Local Growth Alliances

The export-oriented economic development model used in the early stage of China's opening reform (the 1980s to the early 2000s) was designed to grasp the historical opportunity brought by the shift of GVCs by industrializing export processing. The primary operational mechanism of this Chinese development model was creating a local growth alliance with a GVC as its central pivot.

Figure 1.4 shows an analytical framework for a local growth alliance guided by a GVC or GCC. The main actors in this alliance include the manufacturing FIE and the local government (including local officials and township and village cadres). The local government, officials, and cadres provide the FIE with a protective relationship, and in addition to paying the taxes required by the state, the FIE needs to pay additional rent and fees to the local government and officials. The local growth alliance also has a group of actors that belong to an invisible alliance, including lead firms in GVCs and China's central government. Lead firms drive the shift of value chains and indirectly take part in this growth alliance by outsourcing (i.e., placing orders to manufacturing FIEs). In addition, through non-ownership control lead firms also set the manufacturing process and standards and bring about the extraction of economic surplus. The central government regulates the macro economy and provides local governments with flexible policies, and it becomes an invisible member of the alliance through the extraction of economic surplus in the form of taxes and levies. In other words, these two entities are not superficially evident on the local scene, but they play key roles. Situated between the forces of global capital and the local political system, FIEs link the value chain's key nodes of lead firms and local governments (see figure 1.1). They are the pivot of this economic surplus distribution,

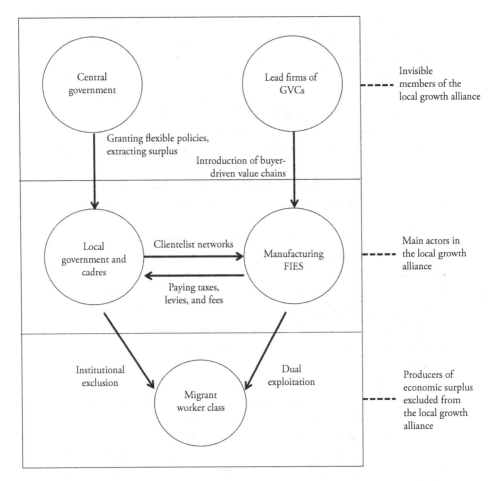

FIGURE 1.4. Analytical framework for a local growth alliance oriented to a global value or commodity chain.

and they are also situated in the transition zone between value chain governance and locally embedded governance (see figure 1.2.; FIEs are located in the domestic industrial cluster/district). Through a case study of Taiyang, chapters 3 and 4 of this book explain in detail this group of complicated socioeconomic relationships.

The migrant worker class at the bottom of figure 1.4 is the main producer of economic surplus in labor-intensive industrialization but is excluded from the distribution in this growth alliance. China's labor market is a dual labor market: employees (*zhigong*), who typically have local household registration status and belong to the formal sector, enjoy better wages and working conditions and full social insurance benefits; and migrant workers (*mingong*) have generally poorer working conditions, long working hours, more overtime, low wages, and poorer social insurance benefits. The vast majority of workers hired by non-state-owned enterprises and FIEs belong to the migrant worker class.[11] The dual labor market is embedded in the differential citizenship system. The citizenship status of migrant workers is separate from the citizenship system of their place of temporary residence, so they do not have local household registration and therefore are deprived of or limited in their freedom to change their domicile, seek employment, obtain education for their children, and receive social welfare benefits. Through systematic exclusion, the state deprives migrant workers (and their family members) of their rights as citizens. Migrant workers are therefore in a situation of dual exploitation: on the one hand is the classic form of exploitation of the working class by capital, and on the other hand is the state's designation of migrant worker status, which allows companies to lawfully treat their hired migrant workers as second-class citizens.

Furthermore, researchers using global production network theory call for focusing not only on workers' roles inside the factory but also on labor's spatial strategies from the standpoint of labor geography, including labor migration and human agency (Coe, Dicken, and Hess 2008). Chapter 5 explains how FIEs, as a link in GVCs, interact with and are embedded in the local migrant labor system, as well as explaining the structural limitations and dynamics of migrant labor actions. Chapter 6 discusses how strike activity by migrant workers excluded from the local growth alliance affects value chain governance when the growth alliance faces reorganization.

State intervention is usually part of a relationship of both cooperation and competition with the lead firms in the GVC. China drives industrial upgrading by relying on its formidable state capacity, including macroeconomic regulation and financial capacity, and its vast market potential. Therefore, the manufacturing prowess cultivated in the course of thirty years is testing its strength against the existing forces that domi-

11. Many state-owned companies also hire a large number of migrant workers.

nate GVCs in the world market. Chapter 6 analyzes the rise of Chinese-capital-led ecosystems in the transformation of the Guangdong model as an attempt to bypass or challenge the GVC.

5. Cases, Methods, and Data

In terms of analytical strategy, this book combines macro (structural), meso (institutional), and micro (firm and individual) levels of systematic analysis. Following is a description of the book's empirical case selection, research methods, and data structure.

1) Case Selection: The Guangdong Model and Taiwanese Investment

This book takes Guangdong's development experience as its case, with a research timeframe extending from the late 1970s to the late 2010s. Guangdong was the region that first linked up with global capitalism in China's post-Mao opening reform. The Guangdong model was China's keynote development model during its thirty years of development from the 1980s to the 2000s, which makes the Guangdong model the prototype for the China model.[12] In the Guangdong model, the government used FDI to import manufacturing capital, technology, and gain access to international markets, and Taishang played a decisive role in this process.

---

12. This book uses both the China model and the Guangdong model as a reference for empirical analysis. This does not involve normative meaning—that is, the objective is not to prove or refute the desirability of the China model as a practical norm but rather to describe and explain its characteristics as a component of an analytical model for China's development experience. The topic of the China model has engendered considerable debate, and interested readers can refer to Ding Xueliang (2014) for an analysis of the debate. Qin Hui's (2007) summarization of the China model as "low wages, low welfare benefits, low human rights" supports this book's standpoint. But very few of the many articles in Chinese focusing on the China model address in detail the circumstances and process of economic growth, let alone combine macro, meso, and micro levels of analysis. The topics of many English-language monographs and papers (the most important of which are discussed in the previous section of this chapter) come close to that of this book, but those works still have shortcomings.

Here it is necessary to define the term "Taishang": a business initially established in Taiwan, or the proprietor of which is a citizen of Taiwan, and whose place of operation was eventually concentrated in China or spanned Taiwan and China (but is not limited to China and Taiwan and may also operate throughout the Asia-Pacific region or worldwide). Accordingly, Taishang in this study can be divided into two main types: First, "Taishang" in the narrow sense refers to China Taishang: firms whose operations and activities are concentrated in China and firms whose proprietors or upper-level managers are Taiwanese, but that basically no longer do business in Taiwan, or whose proportion of revenues that come from Taiwan is relatively low. Second, "Taishang" in the broader sense includes cross-strait capital: business operations that span both sides of the strait, or global transnational Taiwan-invested companies. The operating environment for this type of capital is situated in the context of globalization, but upon close examination, the majority of these transnational companies (primarily small or medium-size) operate only in Taiwan and China and their production bases are mainly located in both places. However, they have established holding companies to control their finances—mostly in tax havens such as the Virgin Islands, the Cayman Islands, and Bermuda—so this kind of globalization is in fact bound to the two sides of the strait. In other words, it is a globalization only in the greater China region. China Taishang arrived in China before cross-strait capital did. In addition to referring to the abovementioned companies and capital, in the everyday context the term "Taishang" also includes those companies' owners and top managers. The term "Taigan" refers to Taiwanese agents or managers who work in Taishang companies.

Ever since opening reform began in the late 1970s, Guangdong, having taken one step ahead, has always stood on the front line of China's exploratory development model. The story of China's rise begins in Guangdong's rapid growth since the 1980s. A sequence of historical events that developed in a specific time and place was related to the restructuring of the international division of labor, the movement of global capital, and the integration of the regional economy. From the theoretical angle, China grasped the historic opportunity of the shift of GVCs, and through the medium of foreign investment—in which Taiwanese investment played a key role—jumped onto the express train of rapid growth. This allowed China to quickly become the factory of the world and accumulate large amounts of capital and foreign reserves, creating the century-defining rise of China.

Guangdong's Pearl River Delta began linking up with the world economy in the late 1970s, when it adopted the processing trade original equipment manufacturing (OEM) models (referred to in China as the processing of shipped materials). At this stage, Hong Kong manufacturing capital played the role of bridge builder. But the most substantial development began after the currencies of East Asian industrialized countries steeply increased in value following the Plaza Accord, and Taiwan-invested manufacturers gradually entered Guangdong through Hong Kong from the mid-1980s onward. At the same time, China's coastal region attracted the attention of lead firms in labor-intensive GVCs and became a new paradise for pursuing low-cost labor. Analyzing Guangdong's development process is doubly meaningful for GVC theory. First, a key starting point of the Guangdong model is the spatial extension and reorganization of GVCs. Value chain theory can explain how, beginning in the 1980s, Guangdong was selected by brand-name companies because of its low labor costs and became a base for OEM or original design manufacturing (ODM) production (i.e., assembly). Cheng Lu-lin's (1999) research shows how the policy decisions of Nike (a commodity chain driver) forced the Taiwanese footwear industry to shift to China. As the prototype for export processing industrialization, Guangdong conforms to Gereffi's definition of a BDCC, especially in the case of industries such as footwear, garments, toys, luggage, bicycles, and consumer electronics. Second, this book innovates this theory by focusing on Guangdong's government-business relationships and locally embedded governance.

Commencing with Guangdong, this book analyzes the specific mechanisms that facilitated China's rapid growth under the EOI model. This development prototype profoundly influenced China's development model in the 1990s, as well as its subsequent development experience. The Guangdong model also brought China an enormous trade surplus, eliminating the country's foreign exchange shortage in the 1990s. The accumulation of vast amounts of foreign reserves established the fiscal and financial foundation for China's rise. Without the foreign exchange earning function of Guangdong's processing trade model, the economic foundation for China's rise—not to mention the China model—would have been inconceivable. The Guangdong model is the key for understanding the origin, dynamics, and current predicament of China's rapid growth.

In the comparative perspective of China's overall growth, Guangdong performed outstandingly not only in terms of growth and foreign exchange earnings, but also in the experimental and novel qualities of its institutional figuration. These qualities influenced subsequent localized development models to a greater or lesser extent. Starting with the Guangdong model is therefore an advantageous way to compare China's various development models. At the same time, the Guangdong model provides a benchmark for comparison in institutional analyses because of its classic qualities, and it was both an important component of China's subsequent development and a standard for reference and comparison for the Wenzhou, Suzhou (Kunshan), Zhengzhou, Chengdu, Chongqing, and other models.[13]

In terms of methods, this book does not presuppose there is an a priori China model. Therefore, I do not inductively sort out the various subtypes under the China development model, propose typologies among them, and then contrast them with the China model in general. Rather, the method I adopted is as follows: When I traced the historical antecedents, I discovered that the Guangdong model was the prototype for China's subsequent models (such as the Suzhou model) or a reference for them (as in the case of the Wenzhou model, for example), and realized that only after more than twenty years of development did there gradually emerge a concept that summarized the overall China development experience—the so-called China model. In terms of chronological order, therefore, the China model is a labeling concept that came into being only after China joined the WTO, its exports quickly increased, it rapidly accumulated

13. The Wenzhou model was proposed in the late 1980s and early 1990s as a way to explain the development of household private businesses (Liu Ya-Ling 1992; Parris 1993). The Suzhou (Kunshan) model sprang up in the 1990s, mainly as a processing industrialization model driven by the Yangtze Delta region's openness to foreign investment (Po Lan-chih and Pun Ngai 2003; Liu Yia-ling 2003). The Zhengzhou, Chengdu, and Chongqing models are all new models from the 2000s, produced to explain the migration of export-oriented FDI to the interior regions of China, which drove a shift of global value and supply chains. Comparisons of the Chongqing model (which was a focus of attention in China for a time) and the Guangdong model triggered considerable discussion (Mulvad 2015; Lim and Horesh 2017).

foreign reserves, and it experienced its economic rise. From the outset, the term "China model" carried strong normative overtones, referring for example to the formulation of the so-called Beijing consensus in contrast to the Washington consensus (Ramo 2004; Halper 2010). This book starts by using historical facts to excavate the origins of the Guangdong model. The Guangdong model (and other regional models) existed first, and only later did the overall concept of the China model gradually emerge. Consequently, when chapter 7 of this book compares China with other East Asian developmental states, this is anchored in a comparison of historical experiences.

In short, the Guangdong model has two functions: it is both the prototype of the China model and a typical example of China's various main regional development models. According to the concept of the Guangdong model, different regions diverge to varying degrees. For example, industrial upgrading in Shenzhen and Dongguan began to present relatively evident differences in the 2010s, with Shenzhen's upgrading related to the ICT industry constituting a new ecosystem, while Dongguan faced difficulties and had to make strategic choices in upgrading traditional industries. Fang and Hung (2019) explain the rise and fall of Dongguan's local developmental state, arguing that in the past ten years Dongguan has been unable to upgrade its industrial sector mainly because of obstructions caused by the inertia of the development model set by local groups with vested interest in development. Meanwhile, Shenzhen provided high-tech manufacturers with more incentives for innovation and therefore performed outstandingly well in its industrial upgrading. But Fang and Hung also note that Shenzhen's development was not without obstacles, as surging real estate prices caused many companies to relocate. For example, Huawei moved a portion of its factories to Dongguan in 2014–15 and became Dongguan's largest corporate taxpayer. This book argues that although its performance has been outshone by that of Shenzhen, Dongguan has experienced a degree of industrial upgrading over the past ten years, such as the rise of Chinese-invested supply chains in traditional industries (see chapter 6).

Overall, although various cities in the region each have their own development features, they still share a set of key characteristics of the Guangdong model (for details, see chapter 2). Guangdong's export-oriented development model was revised in the 1990s, and it was imitated by other coastal regions (which adapted its methods to local conditions). In the 2000s it spread further, reaching inland provinces. This process produced the factory of the world in the new century, as cheap industrial products processed in China were sold on the global marketplace. But at the time when purchasing power in the global market trended toward saturation, China's export growth model was brutally tested, causing nearly thirty years of double-digit growth to decline to growth of only 7 percent in 2015. This is because the bulging economy could no longer only rely on the export sector for GDP growth. Although China's exports continued to grow in absolute value, the share of exports to GDP declined from the peak 36 percent in 2006 to 19 percent in 2018.[14] At the same time, the momentum of growth in the use of Guangdong's EOI model as the prototype for China's rapid growth began slowing from the mid-2010s onward, just as the China model faced enormous pressure to transform itself. Is the factory of the world facing a crisis of decline? Can the factory of the world successfully undergo industrial upgrading and transform itself into a market of the world? In short, Guangdong's labor-intensive EOI development model has run its course: the period from its initiation to its takeoff and rapid growth, combined with the period of its slowing growth and pursuit of industrial upgrading, form a complete development cycle.

Accompanying a key moment of systemic adjustment in the capitalist world and in pursuit of low-cost factors of production (mainly labor costs), East Asia's newly developed nations (the Four Little Dragons) extended GVCs to China's southeastern coastal region, incorporating China into the capitalist world economy and facilitating triangular manufacturing trade. In this restructuring process, Taiwanese investment played an important bridging role. Guangdong's Pearl River Delta was the main region where Taishang first entered China, as well as the largest region for early Taiwanese investment.[15] In this new GSC node, Taishang played the role of semiperipheral elbow or "hidden dragon" (Fuller 2016).

14. The data are generated from World Bank Open Data, https://data.worldbank .org/indicator/NE.EXP.GNFS.ZS?locations=CN.

15. The regions for foreign investment in China's first round of reforms included Guangdong and Fujian, but the scale of foreign investment in Fujian was smaller than that in Guangdong. A portion of the Taishang also entered Fujian, but in smaller numbers than in Guangdong.

This book carries out multiple analyses: changes in the economic structure; aggregate data; institutional arrangements; and in-depth interviews, using the life history of Taiyang as a Taiwanese-invested factory to examine value chain operations, locally embedded governance, and government-business relationships in the Guangdong model. Carrying out research on Taiyang from the early 1990s, I discovered that the relationship between this Taishang and the local government was one of rival partners, involving both cooperation and conflict. I continued to follow the development of Taiyang until it ended its business operations in China in 2010. Afterward, I continued to collect material on the Guangdong model. For more than twenty years, I focused my field research on other Taiwan-invested, China-invested, and foreign-invested companies. Two of the Taiwan-invested companies, Taishin Shoe Manufacturing Group and Smiles Shoes Company (see chapter 6), provide rich material on industrial upgrading, transformation, and diversified development.

2) Research Methods and Data Structure

This book employs a macro historical perspective as its approach to institutional analysis and micro-level behavior; in its analysis of the Guangdong model; and, on the theoretical level, to explain the complicated relationships between the extension of GVCs and economic growth and between rent seeking and rent sharing. The existing literature does not report institutional research with similar historical depth on Guangdong's manufacturing Taishang (and other FIEs).

This book's research methods include analyzing official Chinese documents as well as conducting archival research on opening-reform institutions, field observations and interviews relating to opening reform, and an analysis of the aggregate data. Documentary archives have been analyzed on the three topics. First is a clarification of the disputes during the formulation of policies to encourage exports during Guangdong's initial opening to the outside world. I consulted government documents and relevant memoirs of participants in China's central government and in Guangdong, as well as other related documents, to analyze the origins of and controversies concerning (among other items) shared foreign-currency earnings, the processing trade, the so-called three-plus-one trading mix (*sanlai yibu*),[16] the processing of shipped materials, and processing management fees. Second is the evolution of China's urban-rural dual system, the institutional origins of differential citizenship, the migrant worker citizenship system, and the special multitrack social insurance system. The large majority of this material, apart from research on the literature, required sorting the documents according to relevant local government policies. Third is case studies of various grassroots units, which involved the use of village-level data.

I carried out field research and interviews from 1994 to 2015 in Guangdong as well as in the Yangtze Delta region, the southern Zhejiang Wenzhou region, Zhengzhou City in Henan Province, Beijing, Sichuan, and other places. Based on years of observation and investigation, I realized that changes in the development of various regions confirmed the influence of the Guangdong model on China's overall development. In Shanghai, southern Jiangsu (Suzhou, Kushan, and Wuxi), and other localities I collected data on wages, labor conditions, social insurance, and government-business relations as well as individual Taishang, FIEs, and domestic factories. These data provide an important basis for this book's comparison of development in Guangdong and other regions.

In Guangdong's Pearl River Delta region, my interviewees included Taishang, Taigan, proprietors of Chinese-invested factories, Lugan (mainlander managers and staff members employed in Taiwanese-invested enterprises or mainland-owned factories), migrant workers, family members of migrant workers, government officials, employees of labor nongovernmental organizations (NGOs), and scholars. Hong Kong and Taiwan were also important data collection points. Data for the cases this book analyzes—including information on Taiyang, Smiles, Taishin, and other manufacturers—were all obtained through on-the-ground field research and interviews. The interviews were carried out from 1993 to 2018 in locations ranging from China to Hong Kong and Taiwan. For code names

16. According to the official Chinese definition, the "three-plus-one trading mix" consists of the processing of shipped materials, the processing of shipped samples, the assembly of shipped components, and compensation trade (i.e., a form of countertrade in which an incoming investment is repaid from the revenues generated by that investment).

and background information on the interviewees, please refer to the index of interview codes in the backmatter.

The aggregate economic data include information on the overall economy, population, import and export trade, investment, FDI, fiscal revenue and expenditure, and foreign exchange. I also used other data at the national, provincial or municipal, prefectural, county, and township levels. Most of this data, as well as population census data, is accessible in published works such as statistical yearbooks. Taiwan's university and research institutions have collected a portion of this material. For some more specialized or earlier yearbooks, I had to consult the Chinese University of Hong Kong's Universities Service Centre for China Studies or seek them on location in China. A portion was collected through the internet.

CHAPTER TWO

The Origins, Performance, and Evolution of the Guangdong Model

Guangdong was the vanguard of China's opening reform in the post-Mao era. The central government designated Guangdong and Fujian Provinces as open regions at the end of 1978 and established SEZs. Given its geographical proximity to Hong Kong, Guangdong Province (especially Shenzhen and Dongguan in the Pearl River Delta) rapidly grasped the opportunity to be one step ahead (Vogel 1989). Yet being one step ahead was not entirely a result of rational or advanced planning. Rather, it resulted from a confluence of central policy decisions, institutional paths, and local structural endowments. Among the ranks of those "feeling for rocks while crossing the river" (in the words of Deng Xiaoping), the Guangdong government was given the first opportunity to test the water, but that opportunity was filled with peril. In terms of this book's argument, the main questions are how the early growth model was initiated and what obstacles it encountered. Early reformers had to remove obstacles to reform, especially resistance from the central planning bureaucracy. At the local level, however, it was not a struggle between socialism and capitalism that presented the main obstacles: rather, it was a matter of reversing the socialist behavioral characteristics of local officials. Therefore, the key lay in creating incentives for enthusiastic competition among local officials in attracting business and investment.

Guangdong took the road of export processing during opening reform in the late 1970s, and it has continued to grope its way along this road over the past forty years, achieving impressive economic results but also paying massive social costs. This chapter describes the initial decision to grant Guangdong special policies, traces the origins of Guangdong's labor-intensive industrialization model, and then analyzes the changing economic conditions following the launch of the Guangdong model. The chapter examines the advantageous conditions the Guangdong model created for local government and capital in the competition to attract FDI, including suppressed wages and social insurance rates—which provided conditions conducive to embracing the extension and shift of GVCs to Guangdong. Finally, the chapter analyzes the significance of two important policy changes (in 1994 and starting in the late 2000s) and the recent performance of Guangdong's processing trade. In the process of analyzing Guangdong's economic conditions and performance, the chapter also compares Guangdong to all of China and to other key regions in the country, to simultaneously survey the overall situation of China's development.

1. One Step Ahead: Opportunity and Risk

In the early stage of opening reform, Guangdong groped its way along the road toward a market economy in a political and institutional environment of state socialism. In experimenting with a type of capitalism and feeling out ways to link up with the capitalist world market, Guangdong faced the risk of rectification at any moment.

1) The Socialism versus Capitalism Debate

Ren Zhongyi, the first party secretary of Guangdong Province in the initial stage of opening reform, recalls:

> From the outset there were always people who were very anxious about implementing special policies in the two provinces: There was fear of sliding onto the capitalist road, of creating chaos in the overall national economy, and of committing errors. . . . Many documents issued by State Council ministries and commissions added the sentence "Guangdong and Fujian are no exception." . . . These departments were unwilling to delegate their power. As a result, the special policies in the

two provinces were not special, the flexible measures were not flexible, and going one step ahead did not go ahead (quoted in CCP Guangdong Party Committee 2008, 20).

At that time, opening to the outside world entangled the CCP in an internal debate on socialism versus capitalism. Local cadres were wary of being labeled capitalists. In Wenzhou, famous for privatization, the Cultural Revolution had brought multiple purges to—in the words of a traditional proverb—chop off the tail end of capitalism (Liu Ya-Ling 1992; Parris 1993). For this reason, officials implementing opening reform in Guangdong needed clear-cut policies and documents and constantly requested reassurance from the central leaders, even if only in the form of verbal conversations or directives. When Zhao Ziyang made an inspection visit to Guangdong in August 1981, soon after being appointed premier, he asked Ren Zhongyi: "In Beijing people are always asking me if the special economic zones are socialist or capitalist, and I myself am always considering this question. What do you say?" Ren replied: "[I] browsed through a large number of classic works by the 'old ancestors'[1] in search of the answer. . . . In my view, the term state capitalism can be applied to an enterprise, whether it's a joint venture or a wholly foreign-invested enterprise; but in terms of the entire SEZ, it can't be said to be state capitalism because the SEZ is led by a socialist country, implementing special policies and flexible measures, so it's a socialist special economic zone" (quoted in CCP Guangdong Party Committee 2008, 22).

According to Ren, Zhao nodded to express his agreement with this view. In this conversation, although Ren used the highly sensitive term "capitalism," he added the word "state" in front of it. He also said that this designation applied only at the level of individual enterprises; at the level of an entire SEZ, socialism still prevailed. Most important, while Ren mentioned that the SEZ was under the leadership of a socialist state, he didn't forget to emphasize that the "special policies and flexible measures" were a central policy, to gain the affirmation of an upper-level leader.

---

1. *Translator's Note*: A typical way of referring to Karl Marx and Vladimir Lenin in the CCP.

The special policies that Guangdong sought permission from the central government to use included fiscal contracting, the granting of foreign trade rights, foreign exchange retention, commodity price management, project approval authority, and personnel control. As early as April 1979, when Xi Zhongxun (Ren Zhongyi's predecessor as first party secretary of Guangdong Province) attended an economic conference convened by the CCP's Central Committee, he said: "I hope the Central Committee will give us a little authority and allow Guangdong to move a step ahead and let it go."[2]

In July of that year, the Central Committee handed down Document No. 50 (CCP Central Committee 1979), which granted Guangdong advantageous special policies: "Foreign exchange income and fiscal administration will implement fixed revenue quotas that will remain unchanged for five years. Beginning in 1980, foreign exchange income over and above the 1978 baseline amount will be divided between the Center and the Province by a proportion of three to seven. For fiscal revenue, using 1979 as a baseline, 1.2 billion [yuan, subsequently changed to 1.0 billion yuan] must be handed over to the state [the central government] each year, and the remainder can be retained by the Province for allocation" (quoted in CCP Guangdong Party Committee 2008, 101). Guangdong subsequently also acquired other documents to ensure that the opening reform policy would not change.

While Deng Xiaoping was celebrating the Spring Festival in Guangdong at the beginning of 1982 (January 20–February 7), Ren Zhongyi reported to him on the results of Guangdong's implementation of the special policies and flexible measures. Deng responded: "This shows that the policies decided by the Center are still correct. If you think they're good, continue carrying them out" (quoted in CCP Guangdong Party Committee 2008, 24). Deng did not say "if the higher-ups think they're good," but rather "if you think they're good." Ren understood this to indicate that Deng was tactfully expressing his trust and support for the Guangdong Party Committee. One year later, Guangdong completely

2. Quoted in Zhang Hanqing, "Xi Zhongxun ruhe dailing Guangdong gaigekaifang 'xianzou yibu'?" (How Xi Zhongxun led Guangdong's opening reform into 'one step ahead'), People Net, October 12, 2015, http://dangshi.people.com.cn/BIG5/n/2015/1011/c85037-27684510.html.

opened up commodity price management for agricultural and aquatic products, which was tantamount to eliminating the state monopoly for purchasing and marketing. This was a huge step.

2) "Some People Will Have to Be Killed . . . That Is Inevitable"

During that period, implementing opening reform policies was very risky. Smuggling became a serious problem in Guangdong's coastal region in 1980 and 1981, involving many local cadres, and this was a severe test for the continuation of opening reform in 1982 and 1983. At the same time that Deng Xiaoping had the abovementioned conversation with Ren Zhongyi, the elder statesman of the party's faction in favor of a planned economy, Chen Yun (at that time first secretary of the Central Commission for Discipline Inspection) commented on a report: "Regarding those who commit serious economic crimes, I advocate dealing severely with some, sentencing some to prison, and even killing some of those guilty of the most heinous crimes. And it should be published in the newspapers. Otherwise, the work styles of Party members cannot be rectified." On January 11, 1982, the Central Committee had issued an "Urgent Notice" to the entire country to crack down on economic crimes and elevated the seriousness of the problem to "the life or death of our party"—pointing to Guangdong and Fujian, the provinces implementing the SEZ policy; and targeting problems such as smuggling, illegal foreign exchange dealing, profiteering, corruption and the acceptance of bribes, and "economic liberalization tendencies." In mid-February, the Central Committee Secretariat called leading cadres from Guangdong and Fujian to Beijing to attend a symposium, presided over by Party General Secretary Hu Yaobang. Hu, Zhao Ziyang, Gu Mu, and other members of the reformist faction took Guangdong's side, but the opposition faction vociferously criticized the SEZs, holding that Guangdong was "getting ahead of itself" and "letting things go," that the provincial Party committee was unable to control the county Party committees and grassroots cadres, and that some provincial-level cadres were personally involved. At that symposium, someone stated: "The greater the openness, the stricter the requirements toward cadres and within the party. There should be a regulation punishing corruption and accepting bribes. We should be prepared to dismiss a certain number of people and kill a certain number of people.

Some people will have to be killed in Guangdong and Fujian; that is inevitable" (quoted in CCP Guangdong Party Committee 2008, 25–30).

A few days after the symposium ended, Hu Yaobang once again called Ren Zhongyi (accompanied by Liu Tianfu, at that time vice-governor of Guangdong Province) to Beijing (in Guangdong's policy circles, this was jokingly referred to by the name of a traditional play, *Jailed for a Second Offense*) and told him that there was still great uneasiness regarding Guangdong within the Politburo Standing Committee. Hu said that he had undergone self-criticism, and he required Ren to personally take charge of rectification work after returning to Guangdong. Hu also required Ren to write a self-criticism taking responsibility for Guangdong's getting ahead of itself and letting things go. These demands were actually Hu's way of showing the central leaders that he was doing something. After Ren returned to Guangdong, he immediately convened a "democratic life meeting"[3] for local cadres. Ren gave a speech at the meeting: "It is necessary to seriously address the trend of capitalistic corruption and bourgeois liberalization in Guangdong; we need to deal severely with criminal activity in the economic sphere and rectify liberalizing tendencies, seize on investigating and prosecuting major cases, and not be irresolute or lenient. Economic work must be both invigorating and strict, keeping it dynamic but orderly, managed but not stifled" (quoted in CCP Guangdong Party Committee 2008, 36).

The result of the rectification was that during 1982–83, Guangdong investigated more than eight thousand cases of economic crimes involving nearly ten thousand state cadres, and more than one thousand people were sentenced. But Ren Zhongyi's memoirs state that he decided not to engage in mass debate because he was afraid that it would evolve into a political movement in which people would be "arbitrarily accused and labeled." With Hu Yaobang's permission, he took pains not to inform local cadres of the harshly critical language that some people in the Center had employed against Guangdong, such as the abovementioned quote that "some people will have to be killed," for fear of creating the impression that the opening policies were changing (CCP Guangdong Party

---

3. *Translator's Note*: A term for periodic meetings at which party cadres would engage in criticism and self-criticism.

Committee 2008, 36–37).[4] Guangdong spared no effort in performing in that political drama to cope with pressure from the Center, and in fact this was no mere acting because the human costs were very high. This purge often blurred the boundary between criminals and innocent victims, and political criteria were used to make many decisions. The memoirs of local leaders provide a handful of statistics regarding the numerous arrests and sentencings and an unknown number of executions, but there is no telling how many constituted cases of injustice.

After the abovementioned two-province symposium, the deputy secretary of the Central Commission for Discipline Inspection, Zhang Yun, went to Guangdong to inspect the economic crime situation, and after reading her investigation report, Deng Xiaoping had it circulated within the Politburo Standing Committee. In February 1983, Hu Yaobang paid an inspection visit to Shenzhen and expressed his endorsement of reform in Guangdong. On June 25, Gu Mu (at that time vice-premier of the State Council in charge of foreign trade) communicated Deng's directive: The SEZs "were now being run quite well, and it is recognized in China and abroad that there is no question of wiping [them] out" (CCP Guangdong Party Committee 2008, 41). In this way, Guangdong pulled through this nerve-wracking crisis and passed the test. The alliance of reformists in the Central Committee and at the local level successfully resisted pressure from the opposition faction to wipe the SEZs out. Yet criticism of liberalization periodically cast a cloud over the 1980s. The debate of socialism versus capitalism gradually subsided only after Deng's famous pronouncements during his southern tour in 1992, resulting in the opening up of the coastal regions.

3) Special Policies, Flexible Measures

The historical incidents discussed above show the tenuousness of the early policies of opening reform. Executing reform policies entailed political

4. The words "some people will have to be killed" might have made CCP officials recall the purging methods of Mao-era political campaigns, such as the method of executing criminals according to a per capita quota during the campaign to suppress counterrevolutionaries in the early 1950s (Chen Yung-fa 2001; Yang Kuisong 2006; Dikötter 2013).

risk and therefore required constant requests for affirmation by central leaders. At first glance, the expression "special policies, flexible measures" looks like a stereotypical political slogan, but it was by no means trivial. The "special policies" referred to the central government's policy of delegating power and yielding profit to local governments; and the "flexible measures" referred to the way that local governments applied central policies at the local level and attempted to maximize their use. It was an ingenious counterpoint to the usual practice of policies from above, counterpolicies from below. That phrase referred to the passive evasion and perfunctory lip service with which local cadres met state policies, whereas in "special policies, flexible measures," the state provided policy space for local cadres to be more proactive and ingeniously interpret that space. Ren Zhongyi interpreted policies circumstantially in this way: First, policy stipulations included many clauses, so if one didn't work, another was applied instead. Second, policy stipulations had a certain scope, so they were flexibly executed to stimulate the economy to the greatest extent possible. Third, if the basis for existing documents could not be found, it was possible to "experiment with" breaking through existing stipulations (quoted in CCP Guangdong Party Committee 2008, 125). Once a flexible measure was widely implemented, convention and unspoken (i.e., informal) rules were implemented, which then made any attempt by the central government to wipe the measure out excessively costly or even insupportable. As the benefits of letting Guangdong take the first step—chief among them, the foreign exchange-earning capacity—were gradually acknowledged by the central government, the Guangdong growth model firmly established its status.

During the two-province symposium in February 1982, another controversy touched on the so-called little coffers, or collective slush funds maintained by officials: "Someone says that the sum of money a work unit raises from smuggling and trafficking doesn't go into private purses. It is so his small work unit can do this or that. In fact, this kind of behavior is extremely dangerous, even more dangerous than individual smuggling and trafficking, or profiteering" (CCP Guangdong Party Committee 2008, 29).

Ren Zhongyi and Liu Tianfu felt that little coffers should be treated differently from private purses, and they won the support of Zhao Ziyang and Gu Mu. This controversy shows that the reformist faction tended to adopt a permissive or tacitly consensual attitude toward rent seeking by work units. This controversy provides collateral evidence for this book's argument that rent-seeking activity by government organs was conducive to creating the momentum for local cadres to attract outside investment and business, and that China's leaders clearly recognized this fact.

2. The Origins of the Guangdong Model

In 1978, in yuan Guangdong's GDP was 18.47 billion, its fiscal revenues 3.95 billion, and its foreign trade exports 1.39 billion, with annual per capita wages averaging 615. In 1979, Guangdong's per capita industrial and agricultural output value was 526 yuan, lower than the national average of 636 yuan. Guangdong was included in the first round of opening reform, and Shenzhen and Zhuhai in the estuary of the Pearl River Delta established SEZs in 1980. At that time, the Pearl River Delta was still an agricultural region and had a weak industrial foundation.[5] Lacking capital and technology, how was the local government to use its advantages to take the first step? Guangdong made use of its cheap factors of production (low wages, low factory rentals, etc.) to attract FDI and develop a processing and assembly industry that became an export-processing industrial model with Chinese characteristics. Guangdong's FDI was mainly concentrated in the Pearl River Delta, in particular in the Shenzhen, Dongguan, and Guangzhou regions. The Guangdong model that this book refers to is therefore interchangeable with the Pearl River Delta model.

At the outset of opening reform, this model mainly involved the three-plus-one trading mix, with the model of processing of shipped materials (*lailiao jiagong*) most prominent. The operational model of local governments was to earn processing fees or management fees (*guanli fei*) for renting land and factory buildings and bringing in workers. Rapid growth soon outstripped the local labor force, so large numbers of rural migrant workers were imported from inland provinces to sustain the sup-

---

5. The scope of the Pearl River Delta was vast, including the cities of Guangzhou and Shenzhen below the provincial level and seven prefectural-level cities: Zhuhai, Foshan, Huizhou, Zhaoqing, Jiangmen, Zhongshan, and Dongguan.

ply of cheap labor. In the early 1980s, most of the FIEs coming to the Pearl River Delta to engage in export processing were from Hong Kong, but in the latter part of the 1980s, Taishang and other foreign companies were increasingly involved. This industrialization model rapidly brought prosperity to local industry and commerce and earned considerable foreign exchange (which China was short on at that time) for the state. The economic benefits of the Guangdong model rapidly gained fame in China and attracted the attention of the international community (Vogel 1989).

1) Learning from the Experience of Hong Kong and Taiwan

Several pieces of historical evidence indicate that China referred to the experience of East Asia's Four Little Dragons, especially Hong Kong and Taiwan, while planning its SEZ and reform policies. The first piece of evidence comes from a conference convened by the Central Committee in November 1978, at which four reports were distributed, including one titled "How Did the Economies of Hong Kong, Singapore, South Korea, and Taiwan Rapidly Develop?" (CCP Guangdong Party Committee 2008, 240–42). The second piece of evidence comes from Wu Nansheng, who at that time was chairman of the Guangdong Province SEZ Management Committee and first party secretary of Shenzhen. He recalls the preparations to establish the SEZ in 1979: "A friend said to me, do you dare to run an export processing zone like they have in Taiwan? Do you dare to operate something like a free port? If you dare to do it, it would be a piece of cake. He said, 'Look at Singapore and Hong Kong. . . . That's how their economies developed!' That brought a sudden realization to me" (CCP Guangdong Party Committee 2008, 214). Wu bluntly spoke of imitating the Hong Kong and Taiwan models, and through his own overseas (Hong Kong) connections, he collected material on export processing and free trade areas all over the world.

The third piece of evidence is a speech that Gu Mu gave to provincial-level cadres in Guangzhou in May 1979, in which he said: "There's a great future for Guangdong in introducing technology from Hong Kong, processing raw materials, and using our cheap labor force. In sum, we need to liberate our thinking a little and fight our way out in order to gain experience." He proposed three objectives: "The first is to strive to exceed the quota of US$5 billion in foreign exchange earnings; the second is to recapture the Hong Kong market that Japan and Taiwan stole from us; the third is to overtake Hong Kong" (CCP Guangdong Party Committee 2008, 14).

The above quotes deserve special attention. First, it specifies Hong Kong as an intermediary for introducing technology and foreign investment. Second, it openly proposes using China's cheap labor force to engage in processing shipped materials. Third, the goal is to earn foreign exchange, and Gu Mu even set a quota for Guangdong's foreign exchange earnings. In 1978, China's foreign reserves totaled only US$167 million; in 1979 they totaled US$840 million. According to an interview with Liu Tianfu, Central Committee Document No. 50 in 1979 stipulated that Guangdong had to bring in US$10 billion in foreign exchange earnings by 1990. This was an ambitious goal at that time, so to mobilize local governments and officials, Guangdong decided to reform its system of sharing foreign exchange earnings and allowed local governments to retain a share of them (CCP Guangdong Party Committee 2008, 102). Guangdong remitted US$1 billion in foreign exchange to the central government every year from 1981 to 1983 (CCP Guangdong Party Committee 2008, 117). Fourth, the objective was to surpass Hong Kong, and the rivals were Taiwan and Japan. At that time, Chinese leaders were still cautious and were in a completely different category from those of the ascendant China forty years later. Looking back with today's perspective, the parameters and scope of China's opening reforms at that time were still very limited, but this kind of reform attempt nonetheless required central leaders to urge Guangdong officials to liberate their thinking a little and fight their way out. This shows that walking out of a planned economy system and linking up with the capitalist world economy was extremely difficult, and the constant attacks that the reformist faction encountered from the planned economy faction in the initial period of the reforms explains the reformers' fear and trepidation. In September 1980, the CCP Central Committee Secretariat convened a meeting specifically to discuss work in Guangdong. At the meeting, Liu Tianfu gave a speech calling for the Central Committee to allow Guangdong to "make reference to the successful experience of foreign countries and the Four Little Dragons of Asia and try operating special export zones." The opposition faction immediately said: "If Guangdong does this, we'll need to build a 7,000-kilometer barbed wire fence to isolate Guangdong from neighboring provinces" (quoted in CCP Guangdong Party Committee 2008, 123).

Chinese politics has traditionally emphasized "name and title" (*ming-fen*). How did Guangdong come up with the right name for the policy of taking the first step? Given that opening reform was a sensitive political issue, Guangdong needed to create its own exclusive and appropriate terminology. It couldn't use Taiwan's term of "export processing zone" (*chukou jiagong qu*),[6] nor could it use "free trade zone" for fear of being accused of engaging in capitalism. In April 1979, the Guangdong provincial Party committee temporarily used the term "trade cooperation zone" when reporting to the Center (CCP Guangdong Party Committee 2008, 215–16). A little later, Deng Xiaoping rapped his gavel and settled on "special zone." This was later called a "special export zone," and in 1980 it began to be called a "special economic zone," with the land use period for the zones set at fifty years. The rent for land to FIEs wasn't called "land rent" but rather "land usage fee." However, the meaning was the same, as those early policy makers understood clearly without putting the fact into words (CCP Guangdong Party Committee 2008, 220–22). The discrepancy between name and reality is ubiquitous in institutions such as the various fictive ownership arrangements during the reform era.

2) Processing Shipped Materials and Earning Foreign Exchange

How was the road of processing for export hewed out? And how exactly did it work?

The Taiping Handbag Factory (in Dongguan's Humen Town) and the Dajin Garment Factory (in Rongqi Town, Shunde City)[7] have long competed for the title of China's first enterprise to use the three-plus-one trading mix. Both were established during July–August 1978 (Wu Zhe 2008; Bin Hongxia 2021). The story of the handbag factory is very vivid:

> On July 30, a nearly bankrupt Hong Kong businessman named Cheung Tzi-mei, carrying several handbags and some material samples, drove through Guangdong's vast green fields and arrived in Humen. The agreement he reached with the Taiping Handbag Factory[8] included the following provisions: Cheung would provide the raw materials and

6. In fact, in Taiwan it was called a "processing export zone" (*jiagong chukou qu*).
7. Rongqi Town is now part of Shunde District, in Foshan City.
8. The original text says "Garment Factory," but this is probably an error.

equipment, and the Dongguan side would provide a factory and workers and collect a processing fee, and every month, 20 percent of the processing fee would be refunded to Cheung to pay for equipment. Taiping charged a processing fee of 12 yuan for handbags costing an average of 20 yuan per dozen. This is how the first license issued by China's State Administration for Industry and Commerce for a "three-plus-one" enterprise, "Yue 001," officially came into being. (Wu Zhe 2008)

Shenzhen has its own share of legendary tales, which include even greater detail. On December 18, 1978, the same day as the historic Third Plenum of the Eleventh CCP Central Committee, Shenzhen signed its first agreement with a Hong Kong business for processing shipped materials. Available documents indicate that three parties signed this document: the Shenzhen Light Industry Handicrafts Import and Export Branch Company, the Bao'an County Shiyan Commune Shangwu Brigade Processing Factory, and Hong Kong Eagle Industrial Ltd., which together established the Shangwu Production Brigade Thermal Coil Factory. The first two parties were on the Chinese side, and the third was from Hong Kong, while the fourth was a processing factory that was run and controlled by the Hong Kong company. Because the Shangwu Production Brigade Thermal Coil Factory was not a corporate legal entity, it had no import or export rights and therefore needed to use the Shenzhen Light Industry Handicrafts Import and Export Branch Company as an intermediary. The agreement also laid out the rights and responsibilities of the respective parties, along with the spoilage rate and processing fee. Terms for the latter were as follows: "In the first three months, 'the processing fee' is set at 90 percent of what Party B [i.e., the Hong Kong company] pays in Hong Kong for processing similar products (see Attached Table 2). After three months, the two sides can again confer and reach an agreement; if the Hong Kong processing fee rises during that time, the 'processing-management fee' that Party A [i.e., the two local units on the Chinese side] receives should also increase"[9] (see figure 2.1).

9. In practice, the processing fee (*jiagong fei*) and processing-management fee (*gongjiao fei*) are often interchangeable, but in this contract, they appear to be distinct items. The processing fee is the fee needed to pay the costs of labor, factory rent, and so on, while the processing-management fee is a kind of service charge that FIEs pay to

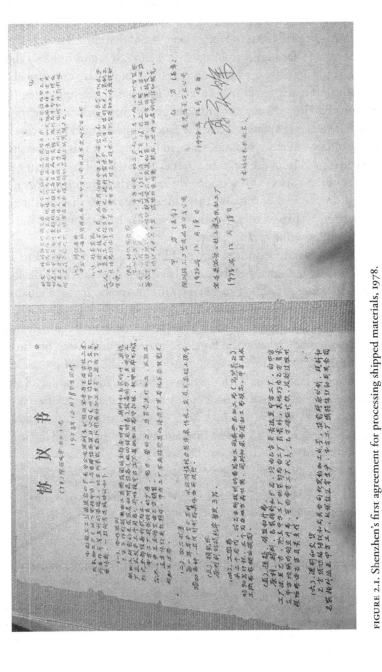

FIGURE 2.1. Shenzhen's first agreement for processing shipped materials, 1978.
Source: Photographed by Liao Chinghua, the author's research assistant.

This clause is worth deeper study. According to this agreement, the Chinese party collected a processing fee equivalent to 90 percent of that for processing similar goods in Hong Kong, but at that time, Hong Kong's salary levels were far higher than those in China. It seems unlikely that an order would actually be placed on that basis, but I have not been able to find the "Attached Table 2," so it is not possible to ascertain what information the Hong Kong side provided about the processing fee. Furthermore, this clause stipulated that the processing fee could be discussed and renegotiated in three months' time, indicating that this partnership was experimental in nature, and the parties were wary of committing to a fixed fee at the outset. Furthermore, the text of the agreement does not indicate how the two entities on the Chinese side were sharing the retained foreign exchange; there may have been another internal document stipulating the sharing arrangement.

The abovementioned ostensibly pathbreaking processing plants in Dongguan, Shunde, and Shenzhen may have been only the tip of the iceberg at that time. According to Liu Tianfu's memoirs, by 1978 Guangdong had already attracted a number of three-plus-one enterprises (CCP Guangdong Party Committee 2008, 90). The State Council promulgated "Trial Measures to Develop the Foreign Processing and Assembly Business" on July 15, 1978, and it is quite possible that the rise of processing factories in the Pearl River Delta region had attracted the notice of the central government, which worked out methods to manage them.

In 2009, *China Resources Magazine*—the official publication of the China Resources Group, a Chinese-invested company established in Hong Kong—disclosed in an article on the history of the company that the three-plus-one trading mix had been created by China Resources in 1975:

> In order to solve the problem of unstable supplies and lack of quality assurance for raw materials for Chinese goods marketed overseas,

---

the cooperative unit (or affiliated unit) on the Chinese side. Fees in this category are collected on the rationale that three-plus-one enterprises are not corporate legal entities as defined by Chinese law and therefore need the cooperation of local units to carry out their business. Thus, the local units charge fees for the affiliation service. It should be noted that the processing fee or processing-management fee has to be paid in the form of foreign currency transfer, the purpose of which is to secure foreign exchange earnings on the Chinese side.

China Resources launched the processing industry in the Shenzhen area starting in 1975 with the participation of Hong Kong businesses. This trading method gradually flourished in 1977, with the development of various businesses during this time: Ng Fung Hong imported mung beans from Thailand and transported them to the mainland for processing into Longkou brand vermicelli, which was then exported to the Hong Kong market; China Resources Textiles organized the processing of cotton-polyester fiber, cotton-polyester yarn, and cotton belts; Hua Yuan processed leather shoes, radio recorders, electronic watches, calculators, electric water heaters, stainless steel tableware, and other light industrial products on the mainland. Through building bridges, paving roads, and establishing links, the China Resources processing business gradually expanded in both China and Hong Kong.[10]

This account requires further study. In 1975, Mao Zedong was still alive, the Cultural Revolution had not yet ended, and the Gang of Four was still in power. China Resources was established in Hong Kong in 1938. It had a close relationship with the Hong Kong office of the Eighth Route Army and always served as an important window between Hong Kong and China.[11] The authorities concerned may have endowed it with special power to carry out innovative businesses. It is therefore not impossible that as early as the mid-1970s, China Resources, in its capacity as a Hong Kong company, launched the processing of imported goods in the Shenzhen area. However, it should be noted that the company claimed that the original purpose of processing shipped materials was "to solve the problem of unstable supplies and lack of quality assurance for raw materials for Chinese goods marketed overseas"—that is, to solve the problem of product quality and sourcing for goods made in China for sale overseas, which is different from the subsequent motivation of attracting FDI. Moreover, the "Hong Kong businesses" that China Resources organized (Ng Fung Hong, China Resources Textiles, and Hua Yuan) were all its subsidiaries and were under the supervision of the Chinese government. Ng Fung Hong, established in 1951, had an administrative

10. Zhu Hongbo, "Huarun, yu zuguo fengyu tonglu" (China Resources, with the motherland through thick and thin), *Huarun zazhi* (*China Resources Magazine*), September 2009, http://crchat.crc.com.cn/2009/200909/06.htm.

11. When the company was established in 1938, it was called Liow and Company. It changed its name to China Resources in 1947.

hierarchal relationship with China Resources, and in 1961 it became the Hong Kong agent for China National Cereals, Oils, and Foodstuffs Import and Export Company. When China Resources was reorganized into a group company in 1983 and changed its subsidiary organizations into companies linked by shareholding rights, Ng Fung Hong formally became part of the China Resources Group. Hua Yuan was also a company owned by the China Resources Group, and at one point it became the sole agency authorized by China's Ministry of Foreign Economic Relations and Trade to export toilet paper to Hong Kong.[12]

China Resources Magazine also states:

> In 1978, Duan Yun, vice-chairman of the State Planning Commission, led a team to Hong Kong to investigate and research the processing and assembly of imported materials. China Resources explained to the inspection group its own processing and assembly businesses, hoping that the state would popularize this trading method. The State Planning Commission took China Resources' description of the situation very seriously and asked China Resources to draft a policy document on its behalf. Based on the document drafted by China Resources, the State Planning Commission tabled "Trial Measures to Develop the Foreign Processing and Assembly Business" (also known as the "Twenty-two Articles"), and reported it to the State Council; the State Council approved and promulgated it in July. From then on, the "three-plus-one trading method" unfolded on the mainland on a spectacular scale and became an important form in the early stage of opening reform.[13]

According to this version of events, China Resources, as a Hong Kong China-invested organization, not only introduced the three-plus-one trading method but also designed the entire processing trade system. China Resources had established this processing method several years before the

---

12. "Duiwai Jingji Maoyibu guangyu jinyibu jiaqiang weishengzhi dui Gang-Ao diqu chukou guangli de tongzhi" (Notice by the Ministry of Foreign Economics and Trade regarding further reinforcing management of the export of toilet paper to the Hong Kong and Macau region), 1991, Ministry of Foreign Economics and Trade Document No. 190.

13. Zhu Hongbo, "Huarun, yu zuguo fengyu tonglu" (China Resources, with the motherland through thick and thin), *Huarun zazhi* (*China Resources Magazine*), September 2009, http://crchat.crc.com.cn/2009/200909/06.htm.

three-plus-one trading method was comprehensively launched, and it recommended this business to the State Planning Commission in 1978 and drafted a policy document on the commission's behalf, after which the state officially stipulated implementation methods. This account is very different from the previous one describing the Pearl River Delta region's spontaneous and bottom-up development of the three-plus-one trading method. It also diverges from Gu Mu's description of proposing that Guangdong "fight our way out in order to gain experience" in 1979. The China Resources Group's version falls under a narrative of state-centered rationalized planning: state organs and a China-funded offshore company collaborated to artfully design the processing trade development model.

Perhaps China's State Planning Commission and the Hong Kong–based mainland-invested company did initially come up with the development channel they had in mind, but the road that was actually taken was not the one designed by the planners. As this book will prove, the alliance that formed the Guangdong growth model consisted of FIEs, local governments, village cadres, and local state-owned capital, with the central government as an invisible partner. Under special circumstances, central government policies provided local actors with institutional incentives and pressured them to transform themselves, while local state-owned capital consisted of foreign trade enterprises with import-export rights that joined in the rent-seeking and rent-sharing game. As for the large Hong Kong–based mainland-owned corporate groups, ascertaining whether they played a crucial role in this growth will require the unearthing of more historical and economic evidence.

In September 1979, the central government issued "State Council Measures Regarding Developing Foreign Processing and Assembly and Medium-Size and Small Compensatory Trade" (State Council Document No. 220) to replace "Trial Measures to Develop the Foreign Processing and Assembly Business" of the previous year. The new document was called the "New Twenty-Two Articles," and its main points included:

(1) A definition of "processing and assembly industry": The industry was divided into three types: (a) The foreign company provided certain raw materials, components, and parts, as well as certain equipment when necessary; the Chinese factory carried out processing or assembly according to the other party's requirements; and the finished product was handed over to the other party to be sold, with the Chinese side collecting a processing fee.

The cost of the equipment provided by the foreign company was repaid by the Chinese side out of the processing fee. (b) The imported raw products and exported final products each had a price, with contracts signed for each separately, and the Chinese side earned its profit from the price difference (i.e., the processing fee), which was used to repay the cost of the equipment. (c) The foreign trade departments of a local government signed agreements with foreign companies to undertake processing and assembly and then organized factories for production; the departments and factories treated the agreements as constituting a purchasing and selling relationship.

(2) A statement of the main objective: "earning foreign exchange." Developing export commodity production and increasing foreign exchange income had to be the main objectives of export-oriented development of the processing and assembly business and medium-size and small compensatory trade.

(3) The method of sharing foreign currency earnings: In addition to being used to defray the cost of equipment provided by the FIE, 15 percent of the processing and assembly income, in the form of foreign currency, was retained by the enterprise. An additional 15 percent was shared with the provincial, municipal, and autonomous region governments where the enterprise was located, and a portion of this was to be appropriately shared with the prefectures and counties (if the enterprises were subsidiaries of the State Council's ministries, this portion was equally divided among local governments and supervisory departments of the enterprises).

(4) The tax reduction method: For the first three years, the net income of enterprises undertaking processing and assembly was exempt from commercial tax and profit remittance in the case of SOEs, and from commercial and income tax in the case of collective enterprises.

These points roughly delimited a contour of activity for processing and assembly (the processing of shipped materials). The business units on the Chinese side included processing plants and foreign trade departments, which respectively engaged in processing and assembly and organizing factory production. However, the reality in most cases was that the factory's actual production and management was the responsibility of the FIE. This resulted in the phenomenon of processing in name, FDI in reality (Wu Jieh-min 1997; Cheng Lu-lin 1999). This situation was carried out virtually in the open, as I discovered during my field research in the mid-1990s. An economic development bureau official in Longgang, Shenzhen, confirmed this: "The actual situation in my district is that the foreign company takes on all of the management and operations of the processing enterprise, and the enterprise takes part in market economy activities as something like the economic organization of an independent legal entity. The Chinese side never participates in the enterprise's economic activities, and as a result it is difficult to define civil liabilities versus civil rights and interests" (quoted in Zhang Xuguang 2001, 47). Why did FIEs tend to invest in China in the form of the processing of shipped materials in the early stage of development of China's processing trade? It was because the central government stipulated tax exemptions for processing and assembly businesses. According to the provisions in the policy documents mentioned above, the enterprises that nominally enjoyed tax reductions were SOEs and collective enterprises that undertook processing and assembly, but because FIEs actually managed the businesses, it was FIEs that enjoyed the tax exemptions.

The government's objective in expanding processing and assembly was to earn foreign exchange, so it stipulated that processing fees should be remitted to China in the form of foreign currency. To encourage local governments and rural cadres to attract business and investment, the central government also stipulated a quota for sharing foreign exchange, with the enterprise receiving 15 percent and the local government where the enterprise was located getting another 15 percent (divided among the various levels of government). Here "the enterprise" refers to the Chinese enterprises that nominally undertook the processing and assembly, including SOEs and collective enterprises. The stipulations on dividing and retaining a share of foreign exchange constituted the institutional root of collective institutional rent seeking by government work units in the early stage of China's opening reform. Because the processing of shipped materials was still in its start-up phase, the 1979 policy document did not create detailed and specific stipulations on how the processing fee was to be calculated and collected, and it therefore left room for local governments to operate flexibly.

Once the basic rules of the game were set, it was up to local governments to wield their respective magic powers.[14] The key to the growth

14. On July 18, 1981, the State Import and Export Commission issued "Several Regulations Regarding the Implementation of 'Methods for Developing Export-Oriented Processing and Assembly and Medium-Size and Small Compensatory Trade.'"

model for Guangdong's labor-intensive industries was the emergence of the system for processing shipped materials. In the late 1970s and early 1980s, before the central government finalized its policies regarding special economic zones, cooperation between local cadres and Hong Kong businesses was already in full swing. Available official statistical yearbooks began including statistics relating to the three-plus-one trading mix in Dongguan and other places in 1979. Dongguan's local government included three-plus-one export amounts and earned fees for processing shipped materials settled by foreign exchange transfer in its official statistics. According to the *Dongguan Statistical Yearbook 1995* (Dongguan Municipal Statistics Bureau, 1995), in 1979, Dongguan's three-plus-one enterprises exported goods valued at US$2.34 million, which accounted for 4.6 percent of total foreign trade exports that year. The numbers were US$18.15 million and 23.5 percent for 1980 and 28.9 percent, 30.7 percent, and 38.6 percent for 1981, 1982, and 1983, respectively. In 1984, three-plus-one exports totaled US$61.11 million, or 47.1 percent of total exports. In comparison, exports by *sanzi qiye* (FIEs)[15] were only US$2 million in 1984, or 1.6 percent of total exports. It was not until 1992 that FIEs surpassed three-plus-one enterprises: in that year, the exports of foreign, private, and joint-venture enterprises totaled US$405.33 million (41.2 percent of total exports), while three-plus one enterprises exported US$359.37 million worth of products (36.6 percent of total exports). This shows that the model of processing shipped materials had a critical status in Guangdong in the early stage of opening reform.

In fact, localities that engaged in the three-plus-one trading mix included not only Guangdong but also other coastal provinces, only on a lesser scale. For example, although Shanghai's formal opening to outside investment was delayed until 1992, it began cooperating with Japanese, South Korean, and Hong Kong businesses in the 1980s, carrying out processing and assembly in labor-intensive industries and collecting processing fees. From 1978 to 1990, Shanghai collected a total of US$260 million in processing fees (Shanghai Financial Gazetteer Compilation Committee 2003, 619–20). In comparison, Guangdong collected US$1.5

15. TRANSLATOR'S NOTE: The term "*sanzi qiye*" refers to Sino-foreign joint ventures, cooperative businesses, and wholly foreign-owned enterprises. For the sake of brevity, the translation will use the umbrella term "foreign-invested enterprises" (FIEs).

billion in remittances from three-plus-one businesses from 1980 to 1987 (Guangdong Province Regional Historical Gazetteer Compilation Committee 1999, 525). In addition, the foreign exchange earnings of FIEs at the township level throughout Guangdong totaled nearly US$1.2 billion for 1982–87 and US$22 billion for 1982–2000 (Guangdong Province Regional Historical Gazetteer Compilation Committee 2006, 185). Shanghai's figures were clearly lower than Guangdong's. Shanghai and the Yangtze Delta region were latecomers, only opening up to foreign investment after 1992, and by then the Chinese government was encouraging foreign investors to establish FIEs and replace the processing of shipped materials (*lailiao jiagong*) with the processing of imported materials (*jinliao jiagong*). For this reason, foreign investment in the processing and assembly industries of the greater Shanghai–Yangtze Delta region mainly took the form of sole ownership by foreign investors, basically leapfrogging over the stage of processing shipped materials in the Guangdong model.

The distinction between the processing of shipped materials and the processing of imported materials is explained in greater detail below. It suffices here to note that a factory that undertakes the processing of shipped materials is not a corporate legal entity according to Chinese laws and policies, and it does not have import or export rights. Therefore, it needs to be affiliated with an official entity or state-owned enterprise to engage in such processing. This initially created the opportunity for local governments and officials to collect extra charges (rent seeking) by proving the needed affiliation service. In contrast, a factory undertaking the processing of imported materials is registered with the government as a foreign-invested legal entity that enjoys the right to import and export items. An enterprise for processing shipped materials is exempt from a variety of taxes and duties, while an enterprise for processing imported materials is not. Ostensibly, an enterprise for processing shipped materials is a Chinese-run unit, but in reality, most of these enterprises (particularly in Guangdong) are invested in and directly run by foreign capital to take advantage of tax exemptions and other flexible treatment. This form of corporate organization is what this book calls "fictive ownership." Section 4 of this chapter describes the government's motivation in replacing enterprises for processing shipped materials with enterprises for processing imported materials.

3. Guangdong's Economic Performance

From 1979 (when the opening reforms began) to 2017, China's per capita GDP grew at an average annual rate of 8.5 percent. During the same period, Guangdong's GDP grew by 10.4 percent, outpacing the national growth rate. During 2007–8, China's economy suffered the effects of the global financial crisis, and weakening export momentum hit Guangdong especially hard. In 2012, China's economic growth began to slow. Using 2011 as a cutoff point, from 1979 to 2011, China's per capita GDP grew by an annual average of 8.8 percent, while Guangdong's grew by 11.0 percent. From 2012 to 2017, the growth rates were 6.8 percent for China and 7.1 percent for Guangdong.[16] Generally speaking, Guangdong's economic performance continued to lead China's. This section first analyzes the economic conditions of Guangdong's initial launch of EOI and the province's economic performance after the launch. It then analyzes Guangdong's industrial structure and urban and rural income, its proportion of FDI and foreign trade dependence, foreign trade performance and foreign exchange earning capacity, and wages and other indicators, comparing Guangdong with the entire country and other major regions.

1) Industrial Structure and Urban and Rural Incomes

On the eve of opening reforms, Guangdong's economic structure in terms of the three-sector model was very close to the national average. Guangdong's secondary sector (manufacturing and construction) amounted to 46.6 percent, compared to the national average of 47.7 percent. Overall, China's degree of industrialization was substantial by then, and the primary sector (agriculture and fisheries) maintained a proportion of 27.7 percent, but the tertiary (service) sector was relatively undeveloped, at 24.6 percent.[17]

16. Calculated from "Indices of Gross Domestic Product of China (1978 = 100)," All China Data Center, https://www.china-data-online.com/member/macroy/macroyt show.asp?code=A0102, for national data; "Indices of Gross Domestic Products (Preceding Year=100)," All China Data Center, https://www.china-data-online.com/member /macroyr/macroyradvshow.asp, for Guangdong data.

17. Calculated from "Gross Domestic Product of China," All China Data Center, https://www.china-data-online.com/member/macroy/macroytshow.asp?code=A0101,

Jiangsu's structure was slightly different. The proportion for the primary sector (27.6 percent) was close to the national average, while the tertiary sector (19.8 percent) was nearly 5 percent lower than the national average, and the secondary sector (52.6 percent), was nearly 5 percent higher than the national average.[18] In the 1970s, the Pearl River Delta region was predominantly agricultural, and its industrial base was relatively weak. Comparatively speaking, the rural areas in southern Jiangsu had a relatively developed rural industrial base (at that time referred to as commune- and brigade-run enterprises) and a plentiful supply of skilled industrial workers. As early as the Cultural Revolution, southern Jiangsu gained an opportunity to develop its rural industries as a hinterland for production outsourced by Shanghai's manufacturing sector. Although Jiangsu opened up to foreign investment later than Guangdong did, its industrial foundation was stronger than Guangdong's on the eve of their respective openings. As a result, once the Yangtze Delta region embarked on opening reform in 1992, southern Jiangsu enjoyed a certain latecomer's advantage and attracted FDI at a relatively higher technical level—for example, in ICT. In 1978, the proportion of Zhejiang's economy held by the agricultural sector was 10 percent higher than the national average. The province's service sector proportion was not only lower than the national average but also lower than that of Jiangsu, and its industrialization was also lower than that of China as a whole.

By 2000, the proportion held by Guangdong's agricultural sector had declined to 9.1 percent, compared with the national average of 14.7 percent, while Jiangsu's had declined to 12.3 percent and Zhejiang's to 10.2 percent (the greatest decrease, indicating the rapid industrialization of the province's rural areas). The industrial sector accounted for 46.6 percent of the economy in Guangdong, 51.9 percent in Jiangsu, 53.3 percent in Zhejiang, and 45.4 percent in China overall. While Guangdong was energetically developing its processing trade during the 1990s, Jiangsu's TVEs were flourishing, and household enterprises (self-employed people or small, single-owner companies) and privately owned enterprises proliferated in Zhejiang. There was a notable increase in the size of the service

---

for national data; "Guangdong Gross Domestic Product," All China Data Center, https://www.china-data-online.com/member/macroyr/macroyrtshow.asp, for Guangdong data.

18. "Jiangsu Gross Domestic Product," All China Data Center, https://www.china-data-online.com/member/macroyr/macroyrtshow.asp.

sector both in Guangdong and Jiangsu, but the proportion of the service sector in Jiangsu (35.9 percent) was smaller than that of Guangdong (44.2 percent).[19] From 2000 until the present, the trend in the economic structure across China has been a steady decline in the agricultural sector, accelerating growth in the service sector, and a slight decrease in the industrial sector.

Since the reforms, whether in Guangdong, Jiangsu, Zhejiang, or as a national average, the proportional contribution of the industrial sector to GDP has not changed noticeably (growth of the sector in Zhejiang has been slightly greater than elsewhere). What has changed is the content of industrialization: one of the main impetuses for growth until the mid-2000s has been the transition from a domestic-oriented industrialization strategy (the Mao era's autarky) to an EOI strategy. We therefore need to measure industrialization by other statistical indicators.

I focus on per capita income in Guangdong and other coastal provinces since opening reform. Guangdong's urban per capita income in yuan (412) at the initial stage in 1978 was higher than the national average (343) and also higher than in Shandong (392), Fujian (371), Zhejiang (332) and Jiangsu (288).[20] Guangdong pulled away from the other provinces in the 1990s, the golden era for Guangdong's three-plus-one processing trade. By 2000, in yuan Guangdong's urban per capita income (9,762) was about one third higher than the national average (6,280), but Zhejiang was rapidly catching up (9,279). Since the start of the new century, other provinces in the southeastern coastal region have also been catching up. By 2010, urban per capita income in yuan in Zhejiang (27,359), with its household units and privately run companies, had long surpassed Guangdong's (23,898). Zhejiang continued to maintain its lead at 37,851 yuan in 2013, while Jiangsu (32,538) was nearing Guangdong's level (33,090) (Wu 2019, 94).

Guangdong's rural incomes present even more dramatic change. In 1978, in yuan Guangdong's rural per capita income (182) was higher than

19. Calculated from "Guangdong Gross Domestic Product," "Jiangsu Gross Domestic Product," "Zhejiang Gross Domestic Product," All China Data Center, https://www.china-data-online.com/member/macroyr/macroyrtshow.asp.

20. "Urban per capita income" refers to the absolute disposable income of residents of cities and towns.

the national average (134) and higher than in Zhejiang (165), Jiangsu (152), Fujian (135), and Shandong (101).[21] In 1990, Zhejiang (1,099) caught up with Guangdong (1,043), and Jiangsu (959) was not far behind. From then on, the other coastal provinces experienced rapid growth, and in the 2000s, Zhejiang drew ahead of Guangdong. By 2013, Guangdong's rural per capita income in yuan (11,669) was barely higher than that of Fujian (11,184) and Shandong (10,620) and had fallen behind that of Zhejiang (16,106) and Jiangsu (13,598) (Wu 2019, 95). This set of data shows that the Guangdong model's economic performance in rural areas, especially outside the Pearl River Delta, did not stand out compared to the rapid economic growth in other coastal provinces. It also shows Guangdong's urban-rural divide to be greater than that of Zhejiang and Jiangsu. The FDI-dependent processing trade's hiring large numbers of migrant workers from other provinces has not brought obvious benefit to Guangdong's rural per capita income. In recent years, the Guangdong growth model has experienced a bottleneck and been assessed more negatively, and the great disparity between rural and urban incomes in the province is a major reason for this.

2) FDI and Processing for Export

Holding the advantage in the first round of opening to outside investment, Guangdong quickly grasped the critical turning point of development and delegated authority to the lower level to attract FDI (which initially was mainly from Hong Kong but gradually expanded to include investment from Taiwan and elsewhere), and this rapidly turned the Pearl River Delta's rural areas into a constellation of industrial towns. The processing and assembly model soon became renowned throughout China. This Guangdong model was dependent on foreign capital, technology, and management as well as on export markets, but the model also gave China an opportunity for development. It can be called a kind of dependent development model, and I present its characteristics through data analysis.

---

21. "Rural per capita income" refers to the absolute net income of rural residents.

(A) DOMESTIC FIXED CAPITAL FORMATION

Starting in 1978, the original momentum for China's export industrialization came from FDI, which occupied an important position in domestic fixed capital formation in the first stage of opening reform. Figure 2.2 shows historical trends in the contribution of FDI to China's domestic fixed capital formation, measured as fixed asset investment.[22] Guangdong's reliance on FDI has always been greater than the national average. In 1990, when three-plus-one trading was developing vigorously in Guangdong, FDI accounted for 14.9 percent of fixed asset investment in the province, compared with only 6.3 percent for China as a whole. FDI's share of China's capital formation hit its peak in the mid-1990s, reaching 21.6 percent in Guangdong in 1994, 17.7 percent in Jiangsu in 1997, and 11.8 percent for the whole country in 1996. From then on the share gradually dropped: In 2000, it was 10.5 percent in Guangdong, 9.4 percent in Jiangsu and 5.1 percent in China as a whole. By 2009 (after the global financial crisis), it had dropped to 4.3 percent in Guangdong, 4.9 percent in Jiangsu, and 1.8 percent in China as a whole. In 2013, it declined further, to 2.5 percent in Guangdong, 2.6 percent in Jiangsu, and 0.9 percent nationwide. Jiangsu and Guangdong followed a very similar trend from 1997 onward.

Figure 2.2 also shows that the proportion of FDI in Guangdong's capital formation can be roughly divided into three stages. The first stage maintained a high level prior to the Asian financial crisis (1997–98), averaging up to 16.7 percent. It took a step down after that crisis, averaging 9.9 percent from 1999 to 2007. It continued to fall after the global financial crisis (2007–8), averaging 3.7 percent from 2008 to 2013. The nationwide trend was similar, averaging 5.0 percent from 1981 to 1992. In 1992, the Chinese government decided on its coastal development strategy and allowed foreign investment in the coastal provinces outside of Guangdong and Fujian, as a result of which the average level reached 10.0 percent from

22. The term domestic fixed asset investment is defined in National Bureau of Statistics of the People's Republic of China (2014) as total investment in the fixed assets of the whole society, with the sources of assets including the national budget, domestic credit, use of foreign funding, independently raised funds, and other capital. The foreign funding referred to here is used in the broad sense, including foreign loans, direct foreign direct investment, and other kinds of foreign investment.

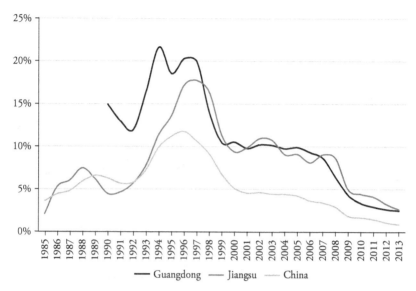

FIGURE 2.2. FDI's contribution to capital formation in Guangdong, Jiangsu, and China as a whole, 1985–2013.
Source: Compiled and calculated from National Bureau of Statistics of the People's Republic of China (2014); Guangdong Provincial Statistics Bureau (2014); and Jiangsu Provincial Statistics Bureau (2014).

1993 to 1998. But following the Asian financial crisis and up to the present, the level continued to decline, averaging 3.4 percent from 1999 to 2013. From this trend we can observe that China's reliance on FDI has continued to drop in this century, indicating plentiful domestic capital and enhanced autonomous investment capacity. China's capital and technological accumulation, along with its vast accumulation of foreign reserves, has led to the emergence of overcapacity, and China has become a capital-exporting country instead.

(B) FOREIGN DIRECT INVESTMENT

I turn now to trends in FDI. Figure 2.3 shows Guangdong's FDI as a share of China's FDI.[23] Guangdong has all along been a major province for drawing foreign investment. In 1990 it acquired US$1.5 billion in FDI,

23. Here FDI refers to actually utilized FDI.

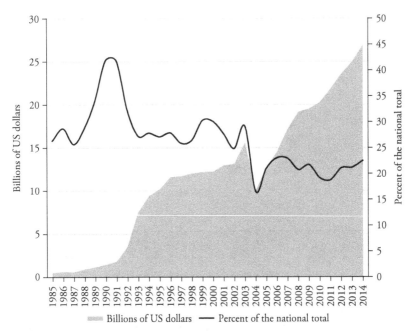

FIGURE 2.3. Guangdong's FDI in billions of US dollars and as a percent of the national total, 1985–2014.
Source: Compiled and calculated from National Bureau of Statistics of the People's Republic of China (1999 and 2017); Guangdong Provincial Statistics Bureau (2014); and (for Guangdong's 2005 data) Guangdong Statistical Information Network, http://stats .gd.gov.cn/sjlywz/content/post_1424267.html.

41.9 percent of the national total. The numbers in 1991 were US$1.8 billion, or 41.8 percent. Proportionately, this was the historical peak, but at that time the total amount of FDI was still small. In succeeding years, Guangdong's FDI increased rapidly, but at a lower rate than the national average—so its proportionate contribution presented a smooth downward trend.

In 2003, Guangdong attracted US$15.6 billion in FDI, or 29.1 percent of the total for the whole country. The amount declined in 2004 but continued to rise from then on, reaching US$17.1 billion in 2007. However, that was only 22.9 percent of the national total. In absolute numbers, Guangdong's foreign investment has continued to increase in recent years, reaching a new high of US$26.9 billion in 2014. But during the same period, the Yangtze Delta and other coastal regions experienced upsurges in FDI, so Guangdong's proportionate share dropped. In 2007–12, Jiangsu attracted more than one-fourth of China's FDI, overtaking Guangdong.

Overall, Guangdong, a hot spot for FDI throughout the reform era, has gradually shared its halo with other provinces such as Jiangsu, Shanghai, and Shandong since the 1990s, and more recently with burgeoning inland manufacturing bases such as Henan, Sichuan, and Chongqing. But from the perspective of foreign investment, Guangdong remains an important production center. New foreign investment in recent years has also gradually shifted from traditional manufacturing to ICT and other high-tech sectors. Yet the question is what proportion of the foreign investment in recent years is actually Chinese capital circling back into China from overseas. Limited data make it impossible to answer this question accurately, but the weight of Hong Kong's investment in China may provide us with a clue (for a further analysis, see section 2(c) below).

(c) source countries for foreign investment

China's early statistics on actually utilized foreign investment included external loans, FDI, and other investment. From 2000 onward, the government no longer published data on outside loans and based its calculations mainly on FDI. According to China's official statistics, the total amount of actually utilized foreign investment for 1986–96 was US$262.2 billion.[24] For 1997–2007 it was US$625.9 billion,[25] and for 2008–13 it was US$645.6 billion.[26]

Observe the proportion of foreign investment from various countries in China's total accumulated foreign investment in 1986–96: Hong Kong and Macau (the vast majority coming from Hong Kong) accounted for 40.4, Japan 15.0, Europe 12.5 percent, the United States 6.5 percent, Taiwan 5.6 percent, Singapore 2.6 percent, and South Korea 1.5 percent. In contrast, in 1997–2007 (roughly, the period between the two international financial crises), the proportions changed: Hong Kong and Macau

24. Calculated from the National Bureau of Statistics of the People's Republic of China (1991, 1992, 1993, and 1997).

25. Calculated from the National Bureau of Statistics of the People's Republic of China (1999, 2001, 2003, 2005, 2007, and 2009).

26. Calculated from National Bureau of Statistics of the People's Republic of China (2009, 2011, and 2014).

accounted for 36.7 percent, Latin America 14.4 percent (of which the British Virgin Islands made up 90 percent of the total, the most notable increase compared with the previous period), Europe 8.3 percent, Japan 7.8 percent, the United States 6.9 percent, South Korea 5.6 percent, Taiwan 5.3 percent, and Singapore 4.3 percent. In 2008–13 (i.e., after the global financial crisis), there was further change: Hong Kong and Macau accounted for 56.8 percent, Latin America 12.5 percent (90 per of which came from the British Virgin Islands), Europe 5.6 percent, Japan 5.4 percent, Singapore 5.1 percent, South Korea 2.7 percent, the United States 2.5 percent, and Taiwan 2.2. Compared with the previous period, the proportion of investment by Hong Kong increased greatly, while Taiwan made up only 2.2 percent, but the proportion from the British Virgin Islands was substantial. Based on these official Chinese statistics, especially noteworthy sources in 1986–2013 are Hong Kong (placing first), the British Virgin Islands (placing second), and Taiwan (placing sixth). Due to certain factors, Taiwan's share of foreign investment in China has always been underestimated. In fact, a great deal of Taiwanese capital has entered China through third-country registration, with the British Virgin Islands being a key capital transit point.[27] However, it is difficult to accurately estimate how much of the investment in China from the British Virgin Islands is made up of Taiwanese capital.

Guangdong used US$64 billion in foreign investment in the years 1986–1996, or 24.4 percent of China's total foreign investment for that period. Investment in the province from Hong Kong and Macau totaled US$47.5 billion, or 74.1 of the total for China.[28] Compared with the national trend, this more clearly displays Hong Kong's status and the influence of its capital on Guangdong. Taiwanese investment made up only 2.9 percent during this stage according to official figures, but these are clearly underestimates. Especially noteworthy is that in 1997–2007, investment by Latin America (including the British Virgin Islands) and Samoa made up 17.4 percent and 1.9 percent of the total, respectively.[29] In

27. Capital transit points with smaller shares include Samoa and, in recent years, the Cayman Islands.

28. Calculated from National Bureau of Statistics of the People's Republic of China (1993, 1995, and 1997).

29. Calculated from National Bureau of Statistics of the People's Republic of China (1999, 2001, 2002, 2004, and 2006).

2008–2013, Latin America and Samoa made up 14.6 percent and 2.3 percent, respectively.[30] The British Virgin Islands placed second in total foreign investment in Guangdong in 1997–2013.

(D) THE WEIGHT OF TAIWANESE INVESTMENT, UNDERESTIMATED BY CHINESE STATISTICS

Now I focus on Taiwan's direct investment in China, also using data from Taiwan. The available data include no clear-cut figures on Taiwan's direct investment in China until the early 1990s. According to official Chinese statistics (see figure 2.4), direct investment by Taishang in China increased substantially in 1993, reaching its peak (close to US$4 billion) in 2002. In the mid-2000s it leveled off, at a point even lower than that in the 1990s. But after the two sides signed the Economic Cooperation Framework Agreement in June 2010, Taishang investment began trending higher again. In 2013 it was US$2.1 billion.

However, the data from Taiwan present a very different picture. Taiwan's official statistics are based on the figures on approved investment in the mainland from the Ministry of Economic Affairs and the cumulative totals should be more accurate than the official Chinese figures. From 1992 to 2013, the cumulative total reached US$133.5 billion, more than double the total of US$58.2 billion from the Chinese figures.[31] Taiwanese FDI reached a historical high of US$14.6 billion in 2010.[32] The approved total amount of capital is lower than the actual amount that reached its destination. Compared with the analysis of source countries for foreign investment in China above, tax havens such as the British Virgin Islands (which also serve as hedges for risk management) accounted for a substantial proportion of foreign investment in China, and a good deal

---

30. Calculated from National Bureau of Statistics of the People's Republic of China (2010, 2012, and 2014).

31. The investment ban on China began to be officially lifted by the Taiwanese government in 1990. In 1993, the Ministry of Economic Affairs opened supplementary registrations for the Taishang who have invested in China over the previous years, so the Taiwanese figures are substantially higher for that year than for 1992.

32. *AUTHOR'S POSTSCRIPT:* China received 85.2 percent of Taiwan's total global FDI (US$17.4 billion) in 2010. Since that year, the share has steadily decreased, falling in 2020 to 38.5 percent (US$6.8 billion). This trend reflects the shifting of supply chains from China to other regions, such as countries in the Association of Southeast Asian Nations, and Taishang reshoring their investments to Taiwan (see chapter 6).

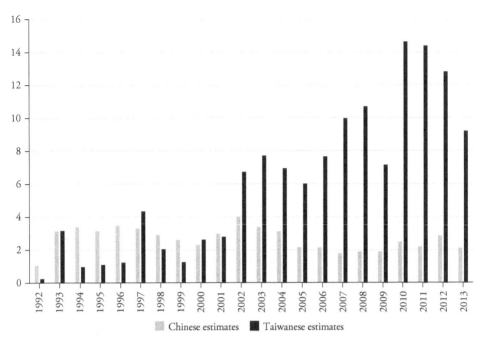

FIGURE 2.4. Taiwan's direct investment in China, 1992–2013 (US$1 billion).
Source: The Chinese data come from National Bureau of Statistics of the People's Republic of China (1991–93 and 1995–2014). The Taiwanese data was downloaded from the Ministry of Economic Affairs Investment Review Board, December 20, 2022, "110 nian 12 yuefen Hezhun qiaowai touzi, luzi laitai touzi, guowai touzi, dui zhongguodalu touzi tongji yuebao" (Monthly statistical reports of approved overseas Chinese, mainland and foreign investments to Taiwan, and Taiwan's investment in mainland, December, year 110), Table 16. https://www.moeaic.gov.tw/news.view?do=data&id=1596&lang=ch &type=business_ann.

of that capital came from Taiwan. Furthermore, a report by the Taiwan Institute of Economic Research points out that total initial capitalization by Taishang in China was calculated at US$133.7–297.9 billion, with the former figure not including increased capitalization and the latter based on Taishang continuing to invest their profits on site (Kung Minghsin 2014). Judging from these figures, it is highly probable that Taiwan's contribution to direct investment in China has been grossly underestimated by the Chinese government.

Guangdong's Pearl River Delta region is where Taishang first entered China, and it has therefore accumulated a considerable amount of investment. According to official Chinese figures, the direct investment by

Taiwan in Guangdong for 1988–2013 totaled about US$8.2 billion. But on-site observation and study of the activity level and actual influence of Taiwan-invested factories in Dongguan, Shenzhen, and other places indicate that this number underestimates the scale of Taiwanese investment. In 1994, the head of the Office of Taiwan Affairs in Shenzhen wrote:

> The absolute majority of investment by Taishang in Shenzhen is indirect investment that comes through third regions or other countries. For years, the Shenzhen Municipal Taiwan Affairs Office has identified and registered Taiwan-invested enterprises and has issued certificates to enterprises in Guangdong Province in which Taiwan compatriots have invested, has implemented the State Council's relevant preferential policies for encouraging investment by Taiwan compatriots, and along with the public security department has examined, approved, signed, and issued multi-entry visas for Taishang to facilitate Taishang crossing the border. (Huang Yaonan 1994, 213)

This historical testimony provides supporting evidence for this book's argument. Moreover, according to figures from Taiwan's Investment Board, the registered total of Taishang investment in Guangdong approved by the Taiwanese government from 1991 to 2013 was US$27 billion, which is 3.3 times the Chinese side's estimate (see figure 2.5). Taken together, these figures indicate that due to factors such as risk avoidance or tax avoidance, a great deal of Taiwanese investment nominally entered China through other places. Based on this estimate, the share of investment in Guangdong from Taiwan should be second only to that from Hong Kong.

Taiwan's investment in China spurred a growth in trade across the strait and at the same time expanded into multilateral trade relations. Many Taiwan-invested companies in China imported raw materials and semifinished products from Taiwan and, after processing and assembly in China, shipped the finished products to the United States, Japan, Europe, and elsewhere. The United States had long been Taiwan's biggest trading partner, but in 2005, according to statistics from the Bureau of Foreign Trade in Taiwan's Ministry of Economic Affairs, Taiwan's trade with China reached US$60.8 billion—for the first time surpassing trade with the United States (US$49.5 billion) and Japan (US$60.4 billion). China became Taiwan's biggest trading partner. According to Chinese statistics, China's total trade in 2008 amounted to US$2.5633 trillion and cross-strait trade totaled US$129.2 billion, making Taiwan China's fifth

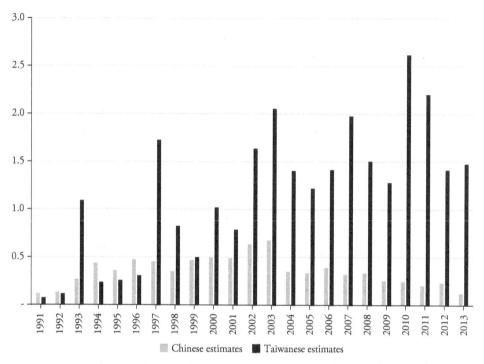

FIGURE 2.5. Taiwan's direct investment in Guangdong, 1991–2013 (US$1 billion). Source: The Chinese data come from Guangdong Provincial Statistics Bureau (1993, 1999, 2008, and 2012–4). The Taiwanese data come from the Ministry of Economic Affairs Investment Review Board, Monthly statistical reports of approved overseas Chinese, mainland and foreign investments to Taiwan, and Taiwan's investment in mainland, Table 16.

largest trading partner.[33] This structural change brought about by triangular trade reflects the shift of GVCs.

(E) FOREIGN TRADE DEPENDENCE

Processing for export is Guangdong's forte, so the province is heavily dependent on foreign trade.[34] Figure 2.6 shows that on the eve of opening reform, Guangdong's foreign trade dependence was 7.2 percent, while the

33. Taiwan was behind the United States, Japan, Hong Kong, and South Korea (National Bureau of Statistics of the People's Republic of Chin 2009, tables 17–1 and 17–8).

34. Here foreign trade dependence is defined as the ratio of trade*1/2 to GDP—that is, the ratio of the total value of the import and export trade divided by two to a country's GDP during the same period.

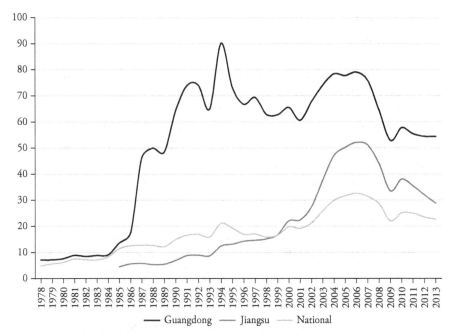

FIGURE 2.6. Foreign trade dependence in Guangdong, Jiangsu, and nationwide, 1978–2013 (%).
Source: Guangdong Provincial Statistics Bureau (2014); Jiangsu Provincial Statistics Bureau (2014); National Bureau of Statistics of the People's Republic of China (1996 and 2014).

figure for the entire country was only 4.9 percent. After Guangdong opened to foreign investment, its foreign trade dependence continued to climb in the 1980s, reaching 50.0 percent in 1988 (compared with 12.7 percent nationwide). At this time, the Guangdong model outshone others in its foreign trade performance. In 1994, Guangdong's foreign trade dependence was 90.2 percent (in that year, the renminbi's exchange rate with the US dollar depreciated by 50 percent), while it was 21.1 percent nationwide. In the same year, Guangdong's foreign trade dependence reached its highest point for the entire period of opening reform, and during the same period, the foreign trade dependence of other coastal open provinces and cities also gradually climbed. Over the next few years, Guangdong's foreign trade dependence showed a downward trend until it hit another high point of 79.0 percent in 2006. In that year, foreign trade dependence at the national level also reached its peak, at 32.6 percent. In 2009, under the influence of the global financial crisis, Guangdong's trade dependence dropped to 52.9 percent (roughly the same level as in 1988), while the nationwide figure was 22.1 percent (around the same level as in 1994). In 2010, the figure for Guangdong recovered slightly, reaching 57.7 percent. However, it gradually dropped again starting in 2011, and it was 54.4 percent in 2013 (compared with 22.7 percent nationwide).

Now let's look at the pace of Jiangsu's foreign trade dependence. Jiangsu opened to foreign investment in the early 1990s. Its foreign trade dependence was lower than the national level until 1999, when it climbed to 16.8 percent and surpassed the national level (16.7 percent) for the first time. Jiangsu was beginning to show the effects of the promotion of EOI. The province's foreign trade dependence increased substantially in the new century, hitting a peak of 52.1 percent in 2006. However, from then it decreased, falling to 28.8 in 2013 (close to the national level). Figure 2.6 shows that Jiangsu's curved trend from 2002 onward is very close to the trends for Guangdong and the entire country, which indicates the effect of China's entry in the WTO in 2001. The patterns of Jiangsu's and Guangdong's upturn and downturn in foreign trade dependency after that are identical, differing only in proportion. Figure 2.6 clearly shows the trajectory of Guangdong's one step ahead in China's open-door sequence and demonstrates that, in terms of the EOI development model, Jiangsu has nearly paralleled Guangdong.

Based on an observation of overall trends, the Guangdong model is undergoing a structural change. Mainly, foreign trade-oriented momentum has slowed, and foreign trade dependence has returned to its level at the beginning of the twenty-first century. This reflects the rapid growth of China's GDP and the considerable effectiveness of the Chinese government's encouragement of regional parity and the development of manufacturing for domestic markets over the past ten-plus years. Yet overall, the Guangdong economy's reliance on foreign trade stands out in comparison to that of the country as a whole. Guangdong is still the most outwardly directed province in the Chinese economy.

3) Foreign Exchange Earning Capacity

Foreign exchange earnings were the main motivation for China to formulate its open policy. Guangdong's flourishing manufacturing and exports allowed the province to earn large amounts of foreign exchange, which became one of the main characteristics of the Guangdong model. In the 1980s, China was still a country operating with limited foreign exchange: it had a trade deficit of 24.4 billion yuan in 1989 and did not start showing a stable trade surplus until the 1990s. Apart from a trade deficit in 1993, China has enjoyed generous trade surpluses for more than twenty years, allowing it to rapidly accumulate foreign reserves and strengthening its government's financial operations domestically and abroad. Guangdong played the most crucial role in this accumulation.

Guangdong still had a small foreign trade deficit in 1987 and 1988, but in 1989 it enjoyed a trade surplus of 2.4 billion yuan. In 1993, the province's trade deficit was 20.5 billion yuan and the national trade deficit was 70.1 billion, mainly because of the importation of large amounts of machinery and equipment that year. From 1994 onward, Guangdong had a stable trade surplus, which grew rapidly: in 2003 its trade surplus was 183.5 billion yuan, accounting for 87.7 percent of the country's trade surplus (see figure 2.7). From then on, with the rise of export processing industrialization in other coastal areas, Guangdong's share of foreign exchange earnings dropped slightly, but the actual amount remained enormous. In 2008 it reached 867.3 billion yuan, composing 41.6 percent of China's entire trade surplus. In 2009, under the influence of the global financial crisis, Guangdong's trade surplus dropped slightly (to 729.5 billion yuan), but that year the entire country's total trade surplus was much lower than in previous years, so Guangdong made up 54.4 percent of the national trade surplus. In 2011, Guangdong's trade surplus reached 970.6 billion yuan, composing 96.3 percent of the national trade surplus. In 2012, Guangdong's trade surplus was 1.04 trillion yuan, composing 71.2 percent of the national trade surplus. In 2013 it increased to 1.12 trillion, making up 69.6 percent of the national trade surplus.

As mentioned above, FDI gradually began entering the Yangtze Delta region in the early 1990s, and the Guangdong model began to seem less alluring. Yet from the perspective of foreign exchange earnings, the Guangdong model retains a key status in China to this day. Figure 2.8 shows trends in China's foreign trade balance and foreign reserve growth. It can be said that without the foreign exchange–earning capabilities of Guangdong's processing trade model, China could not have earned such enormous amounts of foreign exchange in the twenty-first century and established the economic foundation for its rise as a world power. In the

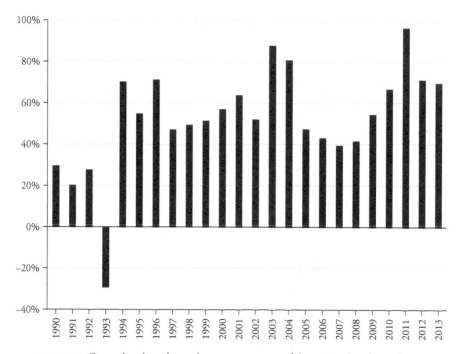

FIGURE 2.7. Guangdong's trade surplus as a percentage of the national trade surplus, 1990–2013.
Source: The data were compiled and calculated from Guangdong Provincial Statistics Bureau (2010 and 2014); National Bureau of Statistics of the People's Republic of China (1996, 2010, and 2014).

period that China rapidly accumulated foreign exchange, all levels of the Guangdong government earned vast amounts of capital and wealth from mechanisms such as the retention of foreign exchange and the exchange-rate differential or exchange-rate spread (*huicha*)[35] in processing fee remittances or management fees. Here, exchange-rate spread refers to the difference between the official exchange rate and the swap market exchange rate for a foreign currency implemented in China's financial system before 1994. A foreign exchange swap center was set up in Shenzhen,

35. *AUTHOR'S POSTSCRIPT*: Exchange-rate differential means the difference between the official exchange rate and the adjusted (market) exchange rate for a foreign currency in a double-track exchange rate system. In general business writing, "exchange-rate differential" has the approximate meaning of "exchange-rate spread." For the sake of easier reading, this latter term is used from now on throughout the book.

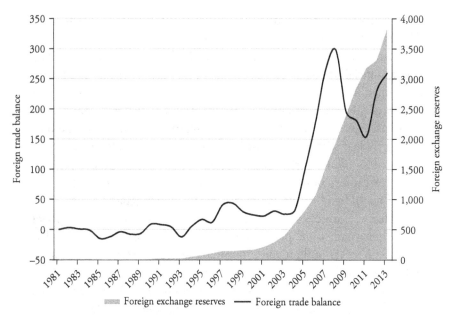

FIGURE 2.8. Trends in China's foreign trade balance and foreign exchange reserves, 1981–2013 (US$1 billion).
Source: Ministry of Commerce Commercial Figures Center, PRC, "Huowu jin-chukou niandu tongji" (Annual statistics of import and export of goods), http://data .mofcom.gov.cn/hwmy/imexyear.shtml; State Administration of Foreign Exchange, PRC, "Guojia waihui chubei guimo (1950 nian-2015 nian)" (National foreign exchange reserves [1950–2015]), January 12, 2018, http://www.safe.gov.cn/safe/whcb/index.html.

and then other centers were established in other cities. See below and chapter 3 for more details.

4) Processing Fee Earnings

The processing fees earned by three-plus-one enterprises have been a ma-jor source of income for local governments. Three-plus-one enterprises are also known as "both ends outside" enterprises because the raw material sources and the export markets are both outside of China. Taishang, how-ever, refer to these enterprises as "three ends outside," including the doc-umentary bills. The entire process—from the import of raw materials to processing, assembly, and export—is basically under the control of the

FIE, which also assumes all responsibility for profit and loss, while the Chinese side merely earns a specified processing fee.

Statistics on processing fees are usually difficult to identify among China's official statistics. On the one hand, they involve the various above-mentioned flexible measures and preferential treatment and the rebates that local governments grant manufacturers. On the other hand, processing fees symbolize the stigmatized sweatshop money that the processing trade is still earning. The Guangdong model has frequently been criticized for allowing the processing trade to earn only processing fees. Yet the fiscal function of these fees in local governments cannot be dismissed out of hand. Using statistical data from Dongguan as an example (see table 2.1), we can see that Dongguan's fiscal revenue in 1979 was 66 million yuan, while processing fees were a negligible 4 million. The numbers were 111 million and 176 million in 1985, 1.156 billion and 4.319 billion in 1995, and 6.745 billion and 15.495 billion in 2003.

This enormous amount of processing fees is what Dongguan earned through foreign exchange quotas on processing and assembly. A portion of the processing fee remittance spread (*gongjia fei huicha*)[36] was a source of extrabudgetary revenue for the various levels of government. If the income that local governments earned from the remittance spread is estimated to be 30 percent of the processing fees, it surpassed these governments' formal fiscal revenues in 1992. In 1997, the income is estimated to have surpassed 1.8 billion yuan, amounting to 163.4 percent of tax revenues. In comparison with fiscal revenue, processing fee income reached its peak in 1997 and gradually dropped from then on, but in 2003, it was still equivalent to 68.9 percent of tax revenue. Even if we use a relatively conservative proportion (20 percent) to calculate the remittance spread on processing fees, the amounts are still considerable.

From the figures in table 2.1, we can see the processing fees and their significance in the financial structure of the localities where they're retained. They bolster local fiscal revenues as an unofficial or concealed form

36. *AUTHOR'S POSTSCRIPT*: The processing fee remittance spread means the amount derived from the exchange-rate differential in processing fee remittance. As in the case of the exchange-rate differential or spread, remittance differential can also be translated as remittance spread, and this latter term is used throughout the remainder of the book.

Table 2.1. Comparison of Dongguan's fiscal revenue and processing fee earnings in selected years, 1979–2003

	(A) Fiscal revenue	(B) Processing fees (100 million yuan)	(C) 30% of processing fees (100 million yuan)	(D) 30% of processing fees, or (C)/(A) (% of fiscal revenue)	(E) 20% of processing fees (100 million yuan)	(F) 20% of processing fees, or (C)/(E) (% of fiscal revenue)
1979	0.66	0.04	0.0	1.6	0.0	1.1
1980	0.67	0.27	0.1	12.2	0.1	8.1
1985	1.11	1.76	0.5	47.5	0.4	31.7
1990	3.57	7.18	2.2	60.3	1.4	40.2
1994	7.69	40.94	12.3	159.6	8.2	106.4
1995	11.56	43.19	13.0	112.1	8.6	74.7
1996	9.65	51.22	15.4	159.2	10.2	106.1
1997	11.41	62.12	18.6	163.4	12.4	108.9
2000	30.47	118.57	35.6	116.7	23.7	77.8
2003	67.45	154.95	46.5	68.9	31.0	45.9

Source: The fiscal revenues come from Dongguan Municipal Statistics Bureau (2008, Table 10-3, 313). The processing fees come from Dongguan Municipal Statistics Bureau (1993, 1995, 1997, 1998, and 2000–2004).

Notes: Fiscal revenue for 1979–94 is calculated according to the old specifications and show revenue excluding customs duty. Fiscal revenue for 1995–2003 is calculated according to the new specifications and show revenue excluding extrabudgetary revenue.

of tax revenue, while at the same time they increase the income and spending capacity of local cadres and residents. This allows us to infer why the economy of the Pearl River Delta began to prosper in the 1980s; why the region's restaurant, tourism, financial, and other service sectors flourished; and why the various informal sectors serving the industries related to the processing trade also blossomed. Yet it is worth noting that since the beginning of the twenty-first century, the share of processing fee income in local government finance has steadily declined. This is the result of reform of the government taxation system, which has greatly increased commercial taxes, and because governments have gradually pushed for industrial organizational transformation, reregistering the factories that process shipped materials as FIEs. Note that this reregistration is basically an alteration of the ostensible form of enterprise ownership and does not affect the actual ownership and management.

Processing factories enjoy relatively generous tax rebates, and the fees sustaining local government are chiefly management fees or remittance spreads on processing fees. FIEs are now comparatively standard according to the new policy and are required to pay relatively higher formal taxes. In other words, this is an institutional transformation from collecting processing fees to formal taxation, but we cannot overlook the weight of processing fees.

5) Suppressed Wages and Social Insurance Coverage

In a local growth alliance, the Chinese side earns processing fees and collects various kinds of economic rent. What does it give the FIE in return? Primarily, the local government and local cooperative unit provide a low-cost and docile labor force, cheap factory space and land, and *guanxi* services. *Guanxi* here refers to personal ties or patron-client relationships between officials and businesspeople.

The Pearl River Delta region began drawing migrant workers from inland provinces very early. On the eve of China's opening reform, inland villages had a great deal of surplus labor, which flowed into coastal provinces via domestic migration. Shenzhen, Dongguan, and other coastal areas in Guangdong were the destinations of the first wave of migrant workers. The processing and assembly labor force was primarily composed of migrants, and most of them performed nontechnical (unskilled) labor on production lines. Local residents (including urban residents of cities and towns as well as rural residents of industrialized villages) mainly served as clerical staff members, accountants, customs clerks, drivers, and so on.

The government sedulously suppressed migrant workers' wages over the long term to speed up the pace of industrialization. Generally speaking, migrant workers' base pay was the minimum wage. The minimum wage was the wage criterion that the Chinese government originally set to guarantee a minimum level of income for workers, but in practice it became the ceiling for migrant workers' salaries. Usually, companies hiring migrant workers set the minimum wage as the starting wage, which was used to calculate daily and hourly wages. All of China's provinces and cities were authorized to set a minimum wage, and the minimum wage that the various localities applied to migrant workers was generally several magnitudes lower than the average wage for permanent workers and staff members who had local urban *hukou*. Table 2.2 shows the situation in Guangdong. In 1992, the difference between the monthly minimum wage in yuan in the Shenzhen SEZ (245) and the average full-time salary in Guangdong's urban work units (336) was still fairly small, but after that, urban wages greatly increased and became far higher than the minimum wage.[37] In 1999, in yuan the average urban employee's wage was 942, while the minimum wages inside the Shenzhen SEZ and in the outer districts were 547 and 419, respectively.[38] Wages in other less-developed areas of Guangdong Province ranged from 250 to 450 yuan. In 2009, the average urban full-time wage in yuan had reached 3,030, while the minimum wages in the Shenzhen SEZ and outer districts were only 1,000 and 900, respectively; wages in other parts of Guangdong ranged from 530 to 860. The wage disparity between urban employees and migrant workers continued to grow. From 2010 onward, the Shenzhen government eliminated the minimum wage difference between inside and outside the SEZ. In 2012, the minimum wage in yuan in Shenzhen rose to 1,500, while in other parts of Guangdong it ranged from 850 to 1,300, and the average monthly wage for urban workers was 4,215. In 2014, Shenzhen's minimum wage was raised to 1,808 yuan, while other areas' minimum ranged from 1,010 to 1,550, and the average urban wage was 4,986. The wage disparity between urban workers and migrant workers continued to widen.

37. Here urban work units do not include private enterprises, the self-employed, or flexible employees (National Bureau of Statistics Population and Employment Statistics Division, 2009). The category of urban work unit employees may include a portion of migrant workers (if they sign labor contracts with employers and are fully covered by social insurance); migrant workers are not shown as a separate category in the statistics. The migrants' average real wage is somewhat higher than the minimum wage because most of them have to work lengthy overtime and earn overtime pay (see chapter 5), but this comparison still indicates the wage differential in general.

38. *TRANSLATOR'S NOTE:* Originally, the Shenzhen SEZ included the Luohu, Futian, Nanshan, and Yantian Districts, while the rest of the city of Shenzhen was considered to be outside of the SEZ. Eventually this distinction was eliminated.

Table 2.2. Average urban-work-unit employees' wages and minimum wages in Guangdong Province, the Shenzhen SEZ, and Shenzhen outer districts, 1992–2014 (yuan per month)

	Average urban-work-unit employee wage	Guangdong minimum wage	Shenzhen SEZ minimum wage	Shenzhen outer district minimum wage
1992	336	NA	245	245
1993	444	NA	286	286
1994	593	NA	338	300
1995	688	NA	380	300
1996	761	NA	380	300
1997	808	NA	420	320
1998	853	NA	430	330
1999	942	250–450	547	419
2000	1,152	250–450	547	419
2001	1,307	270–480	574	440
2002	1,485	280–510	595	460
2003	1,666	280–510	600	465
2004	1,843	352–684	610	480
2005	1,997	352–684	690	580
2006	2,182	450–780	810	700
2007	2,454	450–780	850	750
2008	2,759	530–860	1,000	900
2009	3,030	530–860	1,000	900
2010	3,363	660–1,030	1,100	
2011	3,763	850–1,300	1,320	
2012	4,215	850–1,300	1,500	
2013	4,468	1,010–1,550	1,600	
2014	4,986	1,010–1,550	1,808	

Source: The data are from Guangdong Provincial Statistics Bureau (2015).

Notes: Guangdong minimum wages range from 1,010 to 1,550 in 2014. NA is not available.

Table 2.3 compares real wage levels in Shenzhen, Shanghai, and Suzhou. Overall, Shenzhen's minimum wage was slightly higher than wages in Suzhou and Shanghai. But in these three regions, there is a fairly sizable difference between the minimum wage and the average urban employee's wage.

In Shanghai in 1993, the average urban salary was 2.2 times the minimum wage. The numbers were 3.2 times in 1999, 3.7 times in 2009, and 3.1 times in 2013. From 2000 to 2013, the actual annual growth rate for the average monthly salary was 8.7 percent, while the growth rate for the minimum wage was 8.9 percent.

In Suzhou, the average urban salary was 2.5 times the minimum wage in 2000, rising to 4.0 times in 2010 and then dropping back to 3.5 times in 2013. During this period, the average urban salary grew by 10.9 percent annually in real terms, while the minimum wage grew by 8.3 percent.

In Shenzhen in 1993, the average urban wage was 2.4 times the minimum wage; by 2004 the gap had increased to 4.4 times. From then on, the minimum wage began to increase a little more quickly, so the disparity dropped to 3.3 times in 2013. From 2000 to 2013, the average urban wage increased in real terms by 5.9 percent annually, while the minimum wage grew by 5.8 percent.

Overall, in Shanghai and Suzhou, the income disparity between urban employees and migrant workers was at its greatest in 2009–10, while in Shenzhen, the wage gap did not begin to shrink until the late 2000s. What is worth noting is that although the wage gap lessened in all three cities, the actual wage disparity continued to grow.

Figure 2.9 compares growth trends in the actual minimum wage in Shenzhen, Shanghai, and Suzhou (with 1990 as the price baseline year). Shenzhen's actual minimum wage was higher than Shanghai's and Suzhou's throughout this period. Specifically, Shenzhen's minimum wage trend can be divided into three phases: First, from 1992 to 1998, wages stagnated, averaging only 215 yuan. Second, in 1999 the minimum wage was adjusted upward by 28 percent, but after that it showed stagnation again, averaging only 294 yuan from 1999 to 2004. And third, starting in 2005, the minimum wage rose for several years in a row, but wages did not substantially increase in 2007 or 2009 (around the time of the global financial crisis). After that, wages were adjusted upward several years in a row, reaching 612 yuan in 2013. In Shanghai, the actual minimum

Table 2.3. Minimum wages and average urban-work-unit employees' wages in Shanghai, Suzhou, and Shenzhen SEZ, selected years 1993–2013 (yuan per month)

	Shanghai			Suzhou			Shenzhen SEZ		
	Urban-work-unit wage	Minimum wage	Ratio	Urban-work-unit wage	Minimum wage	Ratio	Urban-work-unit wage	Minimum wage	Ratio
1993	322	144	2.2	241	NA	NA	511	215	2.4
1999	482	151	3.2	376	NA	NA	892	283	3.2
2000	512	170	2.9	419	166	2.5	965	275	3.5
2004	789	246	3.2	757	250	3.0	1,325	304	4.4
2009	1,245	335	3.7	1,188	301	3.9	1,716	441	3.9
2010	1,320	379	3.5	1,301	329	4.0	1,791	469	3.8
2011	1,395	412	3.4	1,403	372	3.8	1,857	533	3.5
2012	1,470	454	3.2	1,524	419	3.6	1,933	590	3.3
2013	1,542	496	3.1	1,591	460	3.5	1,986	612	3.3
Annual growth rate, 2000–2013 (%)	8.7	8.9		10.9	8.3		5.9	5.8	

Source: The data were compiled and calculated from Shanghai Municipal Statistics Bureau (2014); Suzhou Municipal Statistics Bureau (2014); and Shenzhen Municipal Statistics Bureau (2014).

Notes: Consumer price base period 1990 = 100. NA is not available.

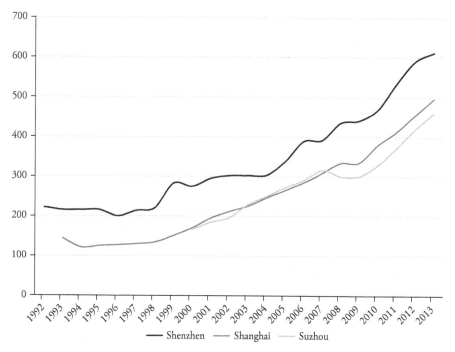

FIGURE 2.9. Minimum wages in Shenzhen, Shanghai, and Suzhou, 1992–2013 (yuan; CPI: 1990 = 100).
Source: The data were compiled and calculated from the Shanghai Municipal Statistics Bureau (2014), Suzhou Municipal Statistics Bureau (2014), Municipal Statistics Bureau (2014).

wage remained stagnant in the 1990s and then began slowly climbing, from 170 yuan in 2000 to 496 in 2013. In Suzhou, the minimum wage climbed from 166 yuan in 2000 to 316 in 2007 (it was 309 yuan in Shanghai in 2007, a year in which the trend in Suzhou was very similar to that in Shanghai), then stagnated for two years at the time of the global financial crisis, and began to rise in 2010. It reached 460 yuan in 2013, although that was still the lowest among the three cities. Comparatively speaking, Shenzhen had the highest wages among these three cities, but it should be noted that although Shenzhen paid the highest migrant worker wages in the Pearl River Delta (and in the country generally), wage levels in other parts of the delta, such as Dongguan, were close to those in Suzhou and lower than in Shanghai.

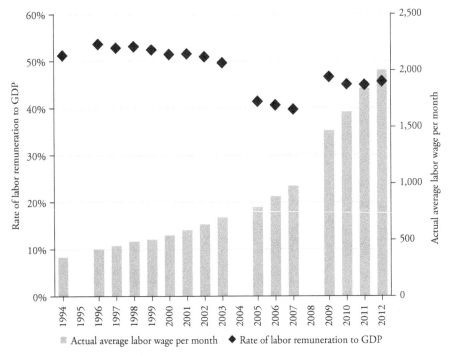

FIGURE 2.10. The ratio of China's total labor remuneration to GDP, 1994–2012 (yuan; CPI: 1994 = 100*).
* Calculated as the average of all employed persons. Source: Compiled from National Bureau of Statistics of the People's Republic of China (1995–2014).

Overall, the actual wage levels of China's migrant workers did not begin to gradually improve until the mid-2000s. I next show how much the wages of basic laborers changed proportionate to GDP during the previous twenty years.

Figure 2.10 shows total actual monthly wages for China's workers as a percentage of GDP. In 1994, labor remuneration composed 51.2 percent of GDP, increasing to 53.6 percent in 1996. It dropped steadily from then on, hitting 49.6 percent in 2003 and averaging 51.8 percent for this period. The proportion dropped sharply from the previous stage during the period 2005–7, averaging 40.6 percent. It has rebounded since 2009, averaging 45.5 percent during 2009–12, but in that period it was still 6.3 percentage points lower than the average for 1994–2003. It should be noted that total national worker remuneration includes both the permanent employee (*zhigong*) and migrant worker (*mingong*) sectors. From the above analysis, we know that the actual earnings of migrant workers were much lower than those of permanent employees, so we can infer that the proportionate income of the migrant worker class, as the lowest grade of worker, was even lower.

Wage suppression has resulted in China's broad working class having insufficient purchasing power, which prevents China from developing domestic consumption markets. Even more critically, the benefits of rapid economic growth since opening reform have mostly been distributed to the SOE sector and the population that enjoys urban *hukou*, while rural residents and migrant workers are deprived of similar wage and social welfare benefits.

Suppressing the wages of migrant workers was the main factor that allowed coastal regions to attract labor-intensive foreign-invested manufacturers, and Guangdong is a classic example of this. In addition to low wages, the Guangdong government tolerated flexible measures in terms of requiring manufacturers to take part in social insurance, being even more lenient than the governments of Jiangsu, Shanghai, and other places. The Guangdong government generally required FIEs to cover a certain proportion of workers but didn't require high or complete coverage. It is hard to obtain actual figures about coverage because these transactions were secretly negotiated. However, some investigative reports state that there was a phenomenon of buying numbers. For example, in terms of employment injury insurance, a company needed to buy only a certain amount of insurance to meet the requirement and didn't need to insure all of its workers (Liu Kaiming 2004, 56 and 214). According to my years of field research, the number buying phenomenon also applied to other types of insurance (pension, medical, maternity, etc.). In 2007, I investigated the social insurance coverage rates of seven foreign-invested factories in the Pearl River Delta region. I found that coverage for old-age (pension) insurance, which is the most expensive type of social insurance required by the government, ranged from zero percent to 35 percent among the factories, and rates were the same for other types of insurance. This number buying operation required the tacit consent or cooperation of local officials. It operated in the manner of discounted processing fees, requiring reliable relations and cooperation between government and business. The massive discounting of social insurance participation rates gave manufacturers huge savings on labor costs and created the conditions for local governments' engagement in institutional rent seeking. Chapter 5 further compares the social insurance situation in different regions.

Local government officials helped enterprises save on labor costs and externalize various kinds of social costs (for example, environmental pollution controls), while the government collected hidden taxes from the enterprises, and officials gained all kinds of additional benefits (free entertainment, gifts, bribes, etc.). In this kind of government-business relationship, the role of local officials (especially those in foreign trade units and village- and township-level cadres) was very much that of a broker, for which they earned processing fee remittance spreads, land and factory rents, and other types of economic rent. They acted just like a rentier class (see Wu Jieh-min 2000; Liu Yia-ling 2009).

4. Changing Trends in Guangdong's Macro Environment

According to the data analyses above, the golden period of the Guangdong growth model was from the 1990s until the mid-2000s. Starting in 1978, Guangdong launched primary (early stage) EOI. From the structural perspective, the Guangdong model underwent two major institutional transformations. The first began in 1994, and the second started around the late 2000s. The main impetus for the first transformation was the Chinese government's pursuing the strategy of opening up the entire coastal region, along with exchange rate reform (including merging the double-track foreign exchange system and substantially devaluating the renminbi to promote foreign trade) and tax reform (including differentiating between national and local taxes and providing an export tax rebate). The impetus for the second transformation was mainly pressure to adjust the international and domestic industrial structure, along with the global financial crisis (see table 2.4).

The prototype of the Guangdong model was to push EOI forward through the processing trade. The late 1970s to the early 1990s was the age when three-plus-one trading (mainly in processing shipped materi-

Table 2.4. The launch of the Guangdong model and its two transformations

	Launch	First transformation	Second transformation
Starting point	1978	1994	Late 2000s
Impetus for change	Opening reform policy pilot projects in Guangdong and Fujian; central government granting localities special policies, flexible measures; establishing foreign exchange swap centers	Foreign exchange rate reform, depreciating the renminbi; canceling dual foreign exchange rates, tax reform, export tax rebates	Adjustment of the domestic and foreign industrial structure, global financial crisis, gradual appreciation of the renminbi; reduced export tax rebates, gradual emergence of overcapacity
State industrial policy keynote	Encouraging foreign exchange earnings, using cheap labor to engage in labor-intensive primary EOI	Central and local governments' encouraging secondary EOI and introducing advanced technology	Central government's promoting of domestic demand industries and domestic consumption power, Guangdong government's pushing the policy of "empty the cage and change birds" industrial upgrading, central government's promoting Made in China 2025
Changes in the processing trade	Launch of three-plus-one (mainly shipped materials) processing and assembly	Shift from processing shipped materials to processing imported materials	Gradual increases in ordinary trade, though processing trade still holds a key position
Changes in corporate structure	Mainly three-plus-one enterprises; local state-run foreign trade companies and industrial companies play the role of intermediaries	Shift from three-plus-one enterprises to FIEs	Some labor-intensive FIEs move inland or overseas or close down; some transform on site
State social policies	Releasing inland rural laborers to work in coastal regions, suppressing wages, strictly controlling the personal freedom of migrant workers	Continued suppression of migrant worker wages, scant social insurance for migrant workers	Incremental increases in minimum wages, progressive strengthening of labor security legislation, implementation of the Labor Contract Law (2008) and Social Insurance Law (2011)

Source: Author's analysis.

als) flourished. For example, in June 1978 Dongguan, where Taiyang Company was located, established a Processing and Assembly for Export Office. At that time, the county had more than 140 three-plus-one enterprises, and income from processing fees totaled US$2.34 million (Yang Ming 1994, 76–77). In 1979, Dongguan signed 184 three-plus-one trading contracts, and it did not sign its first two contracts with FIEs until 1981. By 1988, the number of three-plus-one contracts had climbed to 1,839, while there were only 209 FIE contracts (Dongguan Municipal Statistics Bureau 2003, 337). At that time, manufacturers investing in Dongguan were primarily from Taiwan and Hong Kong; the first Taishang enterprise was established in Dongguan in 1985. By 2006–7, Dongguan had nearly five thousand Taiwan-invested enterprises (accounting for one-tenth of the number of Taishang investing in all of China), with a total contracted investment of US$4.85 billion, around one-third of the Taiwanese investment in all of Guangdong. Most of the Taiwanese-invested enterprises in Dongguan were small or medium-size, and the majority were in traditional industries. Apart from the information technology (IT) industry, industries such as footwear, plastics, toys, and lamps operated on a considerable scale, creating complete industry chains (Wu Jiehmin et al. 2007).

From the late 1970s until the mid-1990s, the state pushed its labor-intensive processing EOI strategy by allowing migrant workers from inland areas to move to coastal regions, suppressing the wages of migrant workers, and strictly controlling their personal freedom. Apart from earning the minimum wage and overtime pay, migrant workers had no coverage under the social insurance system.

The Guangdong model began facing its first major pressure for change in the early 1990s. First came the central government's opening up of other coastal regions in 1992: Jiangsu and Shanghai began attracting foreign investment, and their export industries grew rapidly, putting competitive pressure on Guangdong. The state forcefully promoted its EOI strategy, and in 1994 it devalued the renminbi by around 50 percent (the average exchange rates were 5.76 yuan to one US dollar in 1993 and 8.62 yuan to the dollar in 1994), pegging it to the US dollar to sustain the competitiveness of China's exports.[39] It also engaged in currency exchange reform,

---

39. This exchange rate policy continued until 2005, when the renminbi gradually appreciated against the US dollar.

eliminating the double-track foreign exchange system and adopting unitary pricing. At the same time, the foreign exchange retention system was also canceled.

China also carried out tax reform in 1994. In the 1980s, the central government had delegated power and yielded profit to local governments, adopting various kinds of fiscal responsibility arrangements (a contracting system for tax collection). The national tax structure tilted toward the local level, bringing the central government lower tax revenues than local governments and triggering a sense of governance crisis in the central government. The central government therefore launched tax reform, the main content of which included separating national tax from local tax, levying value-added tax (VAT), and adopting export tax rebates to encourage the expansion of the export sector. Tax reform soon reversed the national tax revenue distribution structure, and from then on, the central government had the advantage in terms of tax revenue.

A shift in processing trade patterns from the processing of shipped materials to the processing of imported materials could be observed during this period. Correspondingly, the organization of enterprise ownership changed from three-plus-one factories to FIEs in legal terms. Three-plus-one factories enjoyed advantageous treatment in tax and customs duty in the original design, while FIEs would enable the government to increase tax revenues. During this stage, the industrial policy that China promoted could be called secondary EOI, with an emphasis on introducing foreign investment in advanced technology and enhancing the value added to export goods. The state's keynote social policy was to continue suppressing the wages of migrant workers. Starting in 1988, local governments began requiring foreign companies to pay social insurance fees for workers. But as mentioned above, with the local government's tacit consent or collusion, manufacturers were often able to get away with merely buying numbers. The actual social insurance that migrant workers gained was very limited.

From the perspective of the enterprises, the most important change in this round of transformation was in the reorganization of exporting enterprises from the form of three-plus-one enterprises to that of FIEs (mainly wholly foreign-owned enterprises). This transformation affected the payment methods and amounts of processing fees. The processing factories under the three-plus-one umbrella were not independent legal entities in law. The relationship between the exporting enterprise and FIE was nominally a contracting relationship, so processing fees were paid by remitting a certain sum of foreign exchange. This amount, as mentioned above, was subject to negotiation and was often calculated by the number of workers. Thus, foreign companies referred to it as a head tax.[40] When the processing factories were reorganized into FIEs, they also became legal corporate entities, and their operational model changed from processing shipped materials to processing imported materials.

At this point, the government began implementing a new method called *cha'e huiru*, effectively a "customs spread." The amount of foreign currency that an FIE was required to remit to China for a particular processing contract was the difference between the import customs declaration and the export customs declaration. This remittance of foreign exchange was used to pay the enterprise's various production costs. In principle, the new operational method could extricate enterprises from the head tax, and after the merger of the double-track foreign exchange system in 1994, there was no longer any exchange-rate spread. The Chinese partnering units still collected hidden local taxes under various names such as "management fees," but the enforcement and amount of the head tax was greatly reduced (this transformation trend is reflected in Taiyang Company's partnership arrangements; see chapters 3 and 4).

From the mid-2000s onward, the Guangdong model gradually faced pressure for a second structural transformation. China's capital accumulation and foreign exchange reserves had reached a fairly high level, and massive foreign trade surpluses caused the renminbi to gradually appreciate. The government had also cut the export tax rebate, and the entire Chinese economic system was gradually showing production overcapacity— which put pressure on the industrial structure to transform. The Guangdong government tried promoting an industrial upgrading policy. However, the sharp drop in orders from Europe and the Americas due to the global economic crisis in 2007–8 caused Guangdong to suffer an enormous economic shock.

40. Head tax (*rentou shui*) is a nickname for a form of processing management fees paid to a Chinese sponsoring unit for business cooperation, collected through foreign exchange remittances or another mechanism. For a detailed origin of the term, see chapter 3, section 4.

China's long-term suppression of wages had left the broad working class with inadequate purchasing power, and the coastal development strategy had also created a serious developmental imbalance between China's eastern and western regions. The state began promoting the Great Western Development Policy, attempting to reverse the regional imbalance and encourage production for domestic consumption and enhance domestic consumption power. It also adopted stricter environmental protection standards. During this phase, labor costs began to increase, and the coastal areas began to experience unprecedented migrant worker shortages, which led to a gradual upward adjustment of migrant workers' wages. In 2008, the central government enacted a Labor Contract Law, which required enterprises to sign labor contracts with workers. Signing a contract meant enrolling workers in social insurance, which greatly increased labor costs for enterprises. In 2011, the central government implemented the Social Insurance Law, which required manufacturers to provide workers with complete social insurance coverage. These policies and laws put further pressure on the Guangdong model to change.

Consequently, some labor-intensive industries began moving to other countries or China's inland provinces. The shock of the global financial crisis also caused a wave of closures of foreign companies in Guangdong. During this phase, the proportionate contribution of Guangdong's processing trade began sliding from a high of 80 percent of gross export value in 2001 to only 62 percent in 2009. During the same period, the percentage of ordinary trade increased from 18 percent to 31 percent. The state's industrial adjustment policy was also reflected in the appreciation of the renminbi as well as in the decline in trade's share of GDP. The renminbi's exchange rate with the US dollar began gradually increasing in 2005, from 8.19 yuan to the dollar (the average value in 2005) to 6.77 yuan to the dollar (the average value in 2010), with an overall increase in value of 17.4 percent. The greatest annual increase was 8.7 percent, in 2008. In 2007–8, under pressure from these changing macro policies and structural conditions, the Guangdong government began encouraging industrial upgrading, referred to as "empty the cage and change birds."[41] Starting in the early 2010s, the Chinese government began emphasizing the

---

41. Regarding the difficulties encountered by the Pearl River Delta model, see Zhu Weiping (2008).

construction of indigenous supply chains, enhancing the domestic production of components, attempting to establish vertically integrated supply chains in the advanced technology sphere, and accelerating development by purchasing companies and technology overseas. In 2015, the central government rolled out its Made in China 2025 to enhance indigenous manufacturing capacity and reduce technological reliance on core Western countries.

Changes in trade figures allow us to observe several trends in the transformation of Guangdong's export-oriented economy.

1) The Processing Trade Slips Proportionately but Still Has a Key Status

Although the proportion of the processing trade (including the two main items of processing of shipped materials and processing of imported materials) in Guangdong's trade structure decreased, the trade still occupied a key position. The processing trade made up 70–80 percent of total exports from 1990 to 2005, but the substance of the processing changed. In 1990, the processing of shipped materials (three-plus-one enterprises) composed 41.2 percent of exports, while the processing of imported materials composed 30.8 percent. The share of the processing of shipped materials dropped sharply in the early 1990s, falling to 16.9 percent of exports in 2005 and only 5.6 percent in 2013. Conversely, the proportion of trade composed of the processing of imported materials by FIEs greatly increased: it reached a high of 56.6 percent in 2005, dropped to 48.9 percent in 2009, rebounded slightly to 49.3 percent in 2012, and then dropped to 45.2 percent in 2013 (see table 2.5). The proportion of total exports made up by the ordinary trade ranged from 19 percent to 30 percent before the mid-2000s. However, it rose steadily after that, exceeding 30 percent in 2009 and reaching 33.7 percent in 2013.

Under the impact of the global financial crisis, Guangdong's total exports in 2009 fell by 11.2 percent compared with the previous year, the first decline in two decades. In 2009, the processing of imported materials declined to an even greater extent than ordinary trade, which shows the reduction in the structural ratio of the processing trade and the continued increase in ordinary trade.

The proportion of Guangdong's processing trade overall averaged 75.6 percent in the 1990s. It reached a peak of 80.2 percent in 2001 but

Table 2.5. Guangdong's export trade amount and export composition, selected years, 1990–2013

	Export trade amount (US$100 million)					Export composition (% of trade)			
	Total exports	Ordinary trade	Processing of shipped materials	Processing of imported materials	Other	Ordinary trade	Processing of shipped materials	Processing of imported materials	Other
1990	222.2	59.5	91.7	68.4	2.6	26.8	41.2	30.8	1.2
1995	565.9	136.0	159.4	263.4	7.1	24.0	28.2	46.5	1.3
2000	919.2	174.4	265.8	452.0	27.0	19.0	28.9	49.2	2.9
2005	2,381.7	533.2	402.7	1,348.0	97.8	22.4	16.9	56.6	4.1
2008	4,041.9	1,163.0	577.8	2,035.8	265.3	28.8	14.3	50.4	6.6
2009	3,589.6	1,098.2	475.5	1,755.8	260.1	30.6	13.2	48.9	7.2
2010	4,531.9	1,492.2	513.9	2,241.8	284.0	32.9	11.3	49.5	6.3
2011	5,317.9	1,836.9	499.2	2,616.0	365.9	34.5	9.4	49.2	6.9
2012	5,740.6	1,903.3	417.2	2,831.6	588.5	33.2	7.3	49.3	10.3
2013	6,363.6	2,145.7	358.8	2,875.4	983.7	33.7	5.6	45.2	15.5

Source: The data were compiled from Guangdong Provincial Statistics Bureau (2001, 2006, 2010, and 2014).

then began to slide, falling to 73.5 percent in 2005 and 62.1 percent in 2009. In that year, because of the reverberations of the global financial crisis, the processing trade export value dropped from US$261.4 billion to US$223.1 billion, equivalent to a 14.6-percentage-point decrease. Although the processing trade's value rebounded to the 2008 level in 2010, its proportion of total exports continued to decline. In 2013, the value of processing trade exports totaled US$323.4 billion, a 0.4-percentage-point decrease over the previous year, and the processing trade accounted for 50.8 percent of exports. Along with the relative stagnation of the processing trade, Guangdong's overall exports performed less well than before, and the province's export growth rate has been much lower since the global financial crisis. This is another indication of the transformation of the Guangdong model. The processing trade still props up half of Guangdong's foreign trade economy, but its future direction will require close observation.

2) The Contribution of Foreign Exchange Earnings from the Processing Trade Shrinks but Is Still Notable

Guangdong is one of China's major foreign exchange earning provinces, and the processing trade's foreign exchange earning capacity is the most notable. In 1993 and 1994, the processing trade's contribution to foreign exchange earnings was negative, mainly because of the great amount of foreign investment attracted in 1993–97. The amount of processing equipment imported by foreign companies was larger than the amount of processing trade exports, so 1993 and 1994 came out in the red, but in 1995 (the year after foreign exchange reforms), the processing trade began showing a balance surplus that increased substantially from then on. The enormous foreign exchange surplus generated by the processing trade in Guangdong alone shows the importance of that trade to the trading structure of Guangdong and the entire country.

I have coined the term "EP/T ratio" to measure the contribution of the surplus from the export processing trade to the total trade surplus.[42]

---

42. The formula for the EP/T ratio is as follows: (processing trade exports − processing trade imports) / (total foreign trade exports − total foreign trade imports). Here "processing trade" refers to total trade minus ordinary trade, donations, and other income.

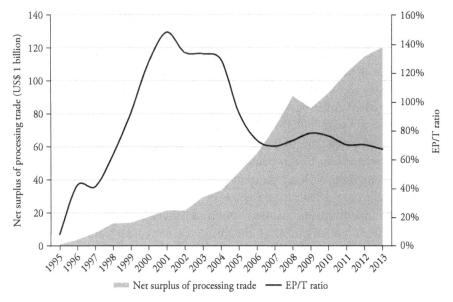

FIGURE 2.11. Guangdong's processing trade surplus and its contribution to total trade surplus (EP/T ratio), 1995–2013.
Source: Calculated from Guangdong Provincial Statistics Bureau (2001, 2006, 2010, 2013, and 2014).

Figure 2.11 shows the EP/T ratio trends in Guangdong during 1995–2013. In 1995, Guangdong produced a processing trade surplus of US$729 million, and its EP/T ratio was only 8 percent. The numbers were US$7.7 billion and 41 percent in 1997. In 2000–2004, the EP/T ratio was over 100 percent: in other words, if there had been no processing trade, Guangdong's total trade balance would have been negative. In 2003, the EP/T ratio reached a peak of 133 percent (a surplus of US$29.5 billion), and from then on the ratio trended downward but the net processing trade surplus continued to increase. In 2009 (a year when exports declined as a result of the aftershocks of the global financial crisis), the EP/T ratio was still 78 percent (US$83.4 billion). The absolute value of foreign exchange

---

It includes the processing of shipped materials, processing of imported materials, compensatory trade, processing equipment, equipment as foreign investment, barter, and bonded warehouses.

earnings reached US$120.45 billion in 2013, although the EP/T ratio dropped to 67 percent in that year.

The EP/T ratio plunged in 2005 and 2006. This shows that the Guangdong model was undergoing a major structural change, since from then on the figure stabilized around 70 percent. Overall, the Guangdong model had an excellent report card for the foreign exchange earnings assignment the state had given it, but its most glorious page had turned, and it is now in a stage of flattened (though still quite notable) contribution. Over the past fifteen years or so, other localities have joined forces with Guangdong to develop export processing, and the Chinese government has accumulated a large amount of foreign reserves, so Guangdong's performance has been eclipsed correspondingly. However, as long as China needs foreign exchange, the role that Guangdong plays cannot be ignored.

3) Foreign Investment Still Has an Important Place in the Export Economy

Foreign companies have always occupied a leading position in Guangdong's foreign exchange earnings performance. Since 2000, the contribution of foreign companies to the province's foreign exchange earnings has held steady at over 50 percent. Even as the Guangdong model has faced crisis and transformation in recent years, the role of foreign companies has increased rather than declined (see tables 2.6A and 2.6B). In 2013, foreign exchange earnings by foreign companies reached US$122.5 billion, contributing 68 percent to the earnings.

By contrast, the state-owned sector's foreign exchange contribution in those years shrank radically: it was the main contributor in the 1990s but dropped to 10 percent in 2005 and to 6 percent in 2013. The collective economy has performed modestly in the twenty-first century, but it has been unable to grow. Thus, its importance is far less than that of foreign companies and the private sector of the economy. The domestic private sector reached a historical high of 40 percent in 2012 and held at 39 percent in 2013. The manufacturing and export capacity of Guangdong's private sector has already increased substantially. From the angle of the export-oriented economic sector, Guangdong's state-owned enter-

Table 2.6A. Foreign exchange earnings by Guangdong's various ownership sectors, selected years, 1990–2013 (US$100 million)

	State-owned economy	Collective economy	Private economy	Foreign-invested economy	Other economy	Total foreign trade surplus
1990	42.3	NA	NA	−16.1	−0.8	25.4
1995	115.6	1.0	−0.0	−16.9	−7.6	92.1
2000	72.1	−0.3	0.6	69.8	−4.9	137.3
2005	49.2	41.0	90.1	306.7	−3.6	483.4
2006	60.3	53.2	214.3	426.0	13.1	766.9
2007	70.0	80.2	327.1	559.9	7.3	1,044.4
2008	103.4	92.4	332.8	724.7	−4.5	1,248.8
2009	80.0	78.6	274.3	651.9	−16.8	1,067.9
2010	73.9	95.0	312.7	792.0	−58.8	1,214.9
2011	96.8	115.6	471.9	996.7	−178.5	1,502.5
2012	102.9	103.3	652.6	1,098.8	−315.9	1,641.7
2013	103.2	106.0	711.2	1,225.1	−336.5	1,809.1

Source: The data were compiled and calculated from Guangdong Provincial Statistics Bureau (2001, 2006, 2010, and 2014).

Note: NA is not available.

prises are retreating and its private sector is advancing, exactly the opposite of the recent trend in the overall national economy of the state sector advancing and private sector retreating (*guojin mintui*). FIEs and private enterprises still play a key role in Guangdong's EOI development.

Guangdong has experienced enormous economic changes over the past four decades. It initially groped its way toward creating a channel for the processing of shipped materials, used low migrant worker wages to push EOI forward, and was entrusted by the state with the mission of earning foreign exchange. Not long after opening reform, the province encountered a political crisis and became embroiled in the debate between socialism and capitalism, facing the threat of a political purge. But shielded by the central government's reformist faction, Guangdong continued to take the road of the market economy and swiftly integrated into the global capitalist production system, allowing China to become the factory of the

Table 2.6B. Foreign exchange contribution by Guangdong's various ownership sectors, selected years, 1990–2013 (% of foreign trade surplus)

	State-owned economy	Collective economy	Private economy	Foreign-invested economy	Other economy
1990	166	0	0	−63	−3
1995	126	1	0	−18	−8
2000	53	0	0	51	−4
2005	10	8	19	63	−1
2006	8	7	28	56	2
2007	7	8	31	54	1
2008	8	7	27	58	0
2009	7	7	26	61	−2
2010	6	8	26	65	−5
2011	6	8	31	66	−12
2012	6	6	40	67	−19
2013	6	6	39	68	−19

Source: The data were compiled and calculated from Guangdong Provincial Statistics Bureau (2001, 2006, 2010, and 2014).

world. In retrospect, it seems that in the words of a traditional proverb, the skiff has already passed ten thousand mountains. Yet the Guangdong model has exacted a heavy price at different development stages—for example, the purge of smuggling in the early 1980s and the squeezing of workers and the destruction of the environment throughout the opening reform era. Beginning in the late 2000s, policies pushing industrial upgrading were aimed in part at improving working conditions and reducing environmental pollution. Wage levels for migrant workers have increased at a faster pace in recent years, but the wages are still not enough to allow migrant workers and their families to enjoy a decent living. The increase in wages and levies imposed for social insurance fees raised labor costs, causing enterprises that had long relied on cheap labor to experience several waves of closures. Under the major trend of industrial transformation, foreign-invested companies faced the choice of either closing down, moving overseas, moving inland, or transforming their local operations.

As the Guangdong development model has endured intense transformation over the past decade, what changes have occurred in the cooperation and mutual relationships within the growth alliances? What kind of collective action has been taken by the migrant workers, whose working conditions and pay levels have improved in recent years? How have Taishang adjusted their behavioral patterns? What form has industrial upgrading taken? These questions are discussed in chapter 6.

CHAPTER THREE

Taiyang Company, 1979–94

The life history of Taiyang Company,[1] including its move from Taiwan to China, provides this book with a microscopic foundation for its macroscopic argument. Taiyang experienced three stages of development: as a trading company in Taiwan (1979–88), when it leased a building and established a factory in China (1989–94), and when it built its own factory and improved its product quality and production capacity (1995–2010). In this chapter and the next, I use Taiyang Company to illustrate how the migration of global value or commodity chains led Taishang to move their manufacturing bases, capital, technology, and markets into China; how the interaction of Taishang (as foreign-invested companies) with local structures, institutions, and actors generated special embedded relationships; how Taishang adapted to the environment of this corruption- and chaos-filled period of China's transforming economy to surmount the problem of rent seeking and achieve relatively stable ownership arrangements; and how institutional and policy changes and their costs caused manufacturers to adjust their collaborative partnerships and influenced their decisions about whether to continue investing or withdraw their investments.

The year 1994 marks the dividing line between this chapter and the next. As described in chapter 2, it was in this year that China's central

1. In Wu 1997, I discuss the first stage of Taiyang's development in China. This chapter contains some updated information based on data I collected since that publication appeared.

government carried out a reform of the country's foreign exchange system, a major devaluation of the renminbi, and a reform of the tax system. This changed the relative cost of manufacturers' factors of production and institutional conditions, and therefore also altered the relative negotiating power of local governments and manufacturers. The central government's policy changes, along with the implementation of those policies by local governments, affected the behavioral patterns of manufacturers, as reflected in Taiyang's business activities. The crucial year of 1994 therefore demarcates two distinct developmental stages in Taiyang's history in Guangdong.

1. A Brief History of Taiyang Company

The parent company of Taiyang's Dongguan factory was established in Taipei in 1979 as an import-export trading company. This was the period in which Taiwan's economy took off, and EOI advanced at a rapid pace. Taiyang's main business was the sale of leather goods overseas. Acting as a trading company, Taiyang took orders from international buyers and then outsourced the orders to Taiwanese manufacturers, most of which were located in central and southern Taiwan. Taiyang's first generation of top-level managers regularly rushed between factories along the Vertical Line, inspecting goods and carrying out other tasks.[2] As a result, by the time Taiyang established a factory in China, its proprietors and managers were old hands at manufacturing, quality control, and estimating costs for their products.

By the mid-1980s, Taiwan's first stage of EOI was approaching saturation and exhaustion. Pressure was building to reshape the international division of labor, while domestic labor costs were increasing, environmental protection requirements were being enhanced, and factory space was becoming more expensive and harder to obtain. In addition, the 1985 Plaza

2. The Vertical Line is a popular term for Taiwan's Provincial Highway 1. Before the construction of the national superhighway networks, the Vertical Line was the main road running from northern to southern Taiwan on the west side of the island, and many export processing factories were clustered along it.

Accord caused a major appreciation of the Japanese yen and the New Taiwan dollar, weakening the competitiveness of local products abroad. These factors led small and medium-size Taiwanese export manufacturers to look for new manufacturing bases overseas. At that time, the first choices for these small and medium-size Taishang were China (specifically, Guangdong and Fujian) and Southeast Asia. Taiyang was part of that wave of industrial redeployment, and in 1988 it decided to invest in Guangdong. As a result, Taiyang changed its role from trading company and became both a trader and a manufacturer.

Taiyang headed west to the mainland via Hong Kong. It was first registered in Hong Kong as a trading company, and a Hong Kong company (or Gangshang) then helped Taiyang identify several original equipment manufacturers near Dongguan. Taiyang tried giving small orders of goods to the contracting factories for the processing of shipped materials. Eventually, because of quality control problems, Taiyang decided to set up its own factory. It first rented an existing factory and staff quarters in Xishui Town, in Dongguan City, and it found a Chinese partner (*guakao danwei*).[3] This Chinese partner was an SOE called Guanqiang Import-Export Company, located in Dongguan City. Taiyang established a joint-venture enterprise with its new partner called Taiyang Dongguan Company (hereafter Taiyang).[4] Taiyang quickly set up its factory and began production in 1989 under half a dozen Taiwanese managers who had transferred from its Taipei headquarters. These managers included financial affairs and sampling staff members, a mold master, a workshop supervisor, and other such personnel, and the CEO (Mr. Lee) made regular trips between Taipei and Dongguan. At this stage, like many other westward-shifting Taishang, Taiyang kept part of its operations (in this case, its sample department) in Taiwan. As Taiyang's mainland management became increasingly localized, the number of Taigan residing in China was reduced to three or four in the early 2000s. And in 2001, Tai-

---

3. *Guakao danwei* is a sponsoring unit, usually a government branch or state-owned enterprise that offers affiliation to a private enterprise, NGO, or quasi-governmental entity.

4. Xishui Town and Guanqiang Import-Export Company (hereafter Guanqiang) are pseudonyms.

yang eliminated the sample department at its Taipei headquarters and ran that department's operations directly from its Dongguan factory.

Due to a series of macroscopic reforms implemented by the Chinese government in 1994, Taiyang decided to terminate its partnership arrangement with Guanqiang and reached an agreement with Nafu Village,[5] in Xishui Town, to buy land and build its own factory. The reason for this relocation was mainly because Nafu Village was willing to charge a lower sponsorship fee than Guanqiang. Taiyang began using its new factory in 1995.

As the twenty-first century began, Taiyang experienced a major change in its internal management. Because its first generation of proprietors and senior managers had gradually reached retirement age, the company needed to identify their successors. The son of the chairman of the board came back from abroad to take over managing the factory in the early 2000s, and Taiyang modernized its business management after that. From the mid-1990s until around 2006–7, Taiyang constantly enhanced its product quality, and it began receiving orders from a number of European and American brand-name manufacturers, while also promoting domestic sales. This stage marked the high point of Taiyang's revenue. In 2008–9, Taishang in Guangdong encountered multiple business problems. For example, the Chinese government's new Labor Contract Law improved protections for migrant workers, which greatly increased labor costs for Taishang. At the same time, the Guangdong provincial government began implementing its new industrial upgrading policy. Furthermore, export manufacturers experienced a major decline in orders following the global financial crisis, and Taiyang's 2009 orders were 70 percent lower than those in the previous year. In 2008, Taiyang experienced labor strikes and demands by workers for the payment of docked wages. Under enormous pressure, Taiyang accepted most of the demands of its employees. At this stage, many foreign investors (mainly Taishang and Gangshang) opted for a midnight run, closing their factories without making good on their outstanding obligations.

The business slump and labor strikes led Taiyang to decide to close its Dongguan factory. The factory ended its business operations at the end

---

5. Nafu Village is a pseudonym.

of 2010, but the practical procedures for closing the factory took another few years as the company faced the issues of paying severance to its staff members and transferring its lease of the factory's land to another company.

2. The Business Model at the Taiwan Stage

Before analyzing Taiyang's history of operating a factory in China, I expand the timeframe to first describe Taiyang's business as a trading company in Taiwan. This will help explain the company's subsequent development. Like most of Taiwan's small and medium-size companies, Taiyang was a family-owned business, and its top managers were all members of the same family. After Taiyang was established, it mainly exported synthetic leather goods. From 1979 to 1988, 90 percent of the buyers of its exported products were in the United States, with the remainder in Japan, Europe, and elsewhere. According to Lee's recollections, at their peak (in terms of sales volume), exports reached an average of New Taiwan (NT)$1 billion per year. Since the exports were considered low-grade mass consumer products at a low unit price, the average free on board was only US$3.0–4.0, or only US$1.5 for lower-grade shopping bags, and profit margins were slim. At that time, Taiwan had two or three leather goods trading companies similar in scale to Taiyang, and twenty to thirty such companies of various sizes.[6]

1) Operational Model

Taiyang mainly used two models for accepting orders from international buyers. In the first model (known as the OEM model), the international buyer would give Taiyang a sample drawing, sometimes enclosing a sample as a reference. Taiyang would make a prototype, and after gaining the buyer's approval, Taiyang would accept the order. Under the other model (the ODM model), Taiyang would develop its own new sample

---

6. Interview: Leegm201510.

and offer it to clients as a reference for sending orders. For this reason, although Taiyang was a trading company, it had quite a large sample department. During the late 1980s, Taiyang's Taipei office had around a hundred employees, half of whom were in the sample department.

After Taiyang received an international order, it followed one of two kinds of manufacturing models:

(1) It transferred the order to a manufacturer. At that time around seven or eight manufacturers (typically employing 300–500 people) took orders from Taiyang. Most of these manufacturers took orders exclusively from Taiyang, but a small number also took orders from other trading companies. These manufacturers procured the raw materials and outsourced some processes to lower-level contracting factories. This business model earned Taiyang a gross profit of around 4 percent.

(2) Taiyang procured the main materials (including leather, linings, hardware, etc.) and commissioned a contracting factory to produce the goods. The contractor had to procure the secondary materials (e.g., wire) and provide its own sewing machines and other equipment. At that time, around three or four factories (each with around one hundred workers) took contracting work from Taiyang. These factories accepted orders exclusively from Taiyang. Under this model, Taiyang earned a gross profit of 8 percent.

In the first model, the manufacturer that accepted an order from Taiyang made a profit on the raw materials but had to provide more working capital than manufacturers in the second model. The main raw material was synthetic leather, and at that time almost all of it was purchased in Taiwan, with a small amount coming from Germany or Japan. Taiwan's leather goods production had a complete supply chain and outsourcing system. In Taiyang's transfer order or OEM process, the most important link was quality control, so the company had a quality control department. Its personnel had to make regular trips to the various factories in central and southern Taiwan to inspect the production conditions and monitor the quality of the goods.

2) Relations with International Buyers

Taiyang's buyers could be divided into two types. The first type was what Lee called "stores" (retail chains), including Kmart, Sears, JCPenney, and other chain stores, which were retailers that dealt directly with customers in the US market. The second type was what Lee called "importers," which were on a smaller scale than stores. After these importers purchased merchandise from Taiyang, they would sell it to stores. Most of these small-scale importers had offices in Taipei, which facilitated their contacting Taiwanese trading companies and factories.

Both types of buyers had staff members to control quality, and with Taiyang's cooperation these people would enter the factories where Taiyang had placed orders to carry out quality inspections. Was it necessary to wine and dine the American clients?[7] Lee said: "It wasn't necessary. Many of these buyers and clients were importers themselves, so they didn't need you to look after them. In any case, Americans didn't enjoy that kind of thing. The Japanese liked it more."[8]

Taiyang usually developed its own samples for chain retailers like Kmart, but importers tended to bring their own new product designs to Taiyang to create a prototype. The time from placing an order to delivering the goods was typically two months for importers and three to four months for chain retailers. Why was there a difference? The lead time was shortened for importers since they were more sensitive to fashion trends and still had to sell the items to stores after receiving the goods.

Both stores and importers had to pay for transportation costs (because the goods were priced free on board), the packing tissue inside the leather goods, and the delivery costs. Compared with the Taiwanese exporter's slim profit margin, how much profit did the international buyer make? Lee estimated that it was 35 percent, but duty had to be subtracted from that.

At this stage, Taiyang already had the capacity to design its own new products, so it could be said that Taiyang grew from a trading company engaged in OEM production to one also engaged in ODM production. Using GVC analysis, figure 3.1 shows Taiyang's production network with its buyers and contracting manufacturers and its relationship with raw material suppliers at this stage.

---

7. To wine and dine (*he huajiu*) meant treating clients to lavish banquets as well as sexual entertainment.

8. Interview: Leegm201510.

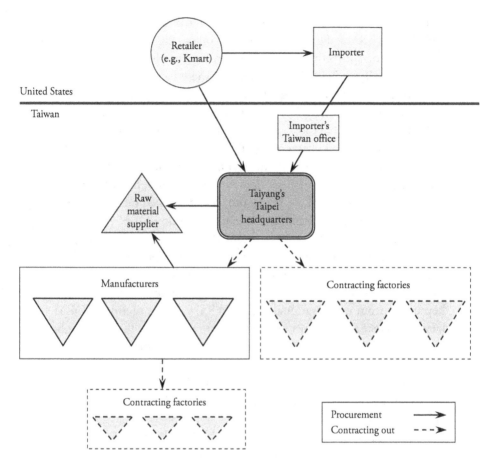

FIGURE 3.1. Taiyang Company's supply chain structure, 1979–88.

3. Proceeding to Guangdong: The Shifting of GVCs

When Taiyang decided to establish a factory in China in 1988, other Taiwanese leather goods manufacturers were also moving west, extending GVCs to Guangdong.

At the outset, Taiyang transferred its orders to a Hong Kong manufacturer. By then, some Hong Kong companies had been moving their manufacturing to Guangdong, so Taiyang's orders were in fact being fulfilled in Guangdong. Because of this relationship, Taiyang's Lee had to go to the factory in Guangdong to inspect the manufacturing conditions, and thus he became familiar with the mainland environment. Taiyang then sent orders directly to three factories (one in Huizhou and two in Dongguan, all operated by mainlanders). These factories had been recommended by a "Hong Kong friend," the term Lee used for the Hong Kong company to which Taiyang initially transferred its orders. The mainland factories that took Taiyang's orders employed around 500–800 people and specialized in accepting OEM orders from overseas. How did these mainland factories acquire the technology needed for leather goods production? According to Lee, "it was initially brought in by Hongkongers." When Guangdong began processing shipped materials in the late 1970s, Hong Kong businesses began contracting OEM production to Chinese factories and in that way trained the first batch of local export-oriented factories. Leather goods are not high-tech products, but there were still quality control problems at these factories.

The orders that Taiyang sent to mainland factories differed in one key aspect from its operational model in Taiwan: the mainland OEM factories were required to buy raw materials from Taiyang. Taiyang bought the raw materials in Taiwan and sold them to the mainland factory through its Hong Kong branch specifically to produce Taiyang's order. This operational method allowed Taiyang to gain more profit at the stage of reselling the raw materials, which increased its gross profit to 15–20 percent.

Its operations required Taiyang to establish a Hong Kong branch office, although this kind of OEM model violated the Taiwan government's prohibitions against "three exchanges" (air traffic, postal communications, and trade) at that time. This was the first-generation triangular trade model that Taishang used in China. Taiyang continued this transfer production model until 1990 and then ended it for two reasons: First, Taiyang was already running its own factory in Dongguan in 1989. Second, there were constant problems with production quality in Chinese factories, and Taiyang was afraid this would cause compensation disputes and discourage international buyers from placing orders.

1) Establishing a Factory in Dongguan

In 1988, while Taiyang was sending orders to Guangdong, it also began preparing its own factory. Taiyang settled on Dongguan for the location.

Through its Hong Kong friend, Taiyang found a state-owned factory that could be managed through the rental model, as well as a joint-venture partner: Guanqiang Company. Lee said, "Initially, the main reason for running our own factory was for the sake of quality control." In 1989, Taiyang's Dongguan factory began production, and from then on Taiyang was a manufacturer as well as a trading company. At that time, Taiyang employed more than a thousand people and provided them with room and board. The investor had to cover half the cost of the meals, while the housing was free. Lee said: "It was impossible not to provide housing, because all of the workers were migrants from other provinces, and the rent outside was too expensive. . . . At that time it was really easy to hire people; you could get as many as you wanted. Back then, the mainland salaries of 150 yuan per month were about NT$5,000 less than [salaries] in Taiwan, so the wage difference alone was enormous. At Dongguan, a certain large factory hired fifty thousand people and saved NT$3 billion per year on wages."[9]

Taiyang's output value (sales volume) from 1989 to 1994 was 70–80 percent of the value when it was a trading company in Taiwan, but its gross profit was 20 percent, much higher than in Taiwan. The main profit came from low labor costs.

Among Taiyang's first batch of Taigan (six people) at the Dongguan factory, several (including the assistant general manager, manager, mold master, etc.) came from its Taiwan OEM factories, and the others were transferred from the Taipei headquarters. Their salaries were doubled, with the assistant general manager's pay increasing from NT$60,000 to NT$120,000, and the mold master's from NT$40,000 to NT$80,000. Taiyang had never carried out its own factory production in Taiwan, but its Dongguan factory was fully integrated, with only a tiny number of procedures outsourced. Direct production on the mainland inevitably encountered problems, mainly in terms of production flow, technology, and quality control. However, because the technology involved in producing leather goods was not very advanced and Taiyang's top management was already quite familiar with the production process and quality control, the problems were surmounted within one or two years.

Did American buyers ever directly place orders with mainland factories at that time? As far as Lee knows, that didn't happen with any of

9. Interview: Leegm201510.

Taiyang's American clients. The situation was different from the time when Nike tried to find an OEM factory in China but gave up because of poor quality and then asked its Taiwan manufacturer to relocate to China (see Cheng Lu-lin 1999). But generally speaking, the GVCs for leather goods, sports shoes, ready-to-wear fashions, and bicycles shifted at similar times through similar methods and used similar operational models.

In 1995, after Taiyang bought its own land, built a factory, and expanded its production capacity, the quality of its products also improved, and its unit prices and gross profits increased. All the Taishang in Guangdong knew how to avoid and reduce taxes. At that time, although Taiyang had established a joint venture with Guanqiang, it was basically exempt from income tax (or paid very little, as I discuss below). Thus, it largely followed the operational model of processing shipped materials that was prevalent at that time. The earnings were deposited in Hong Kong, and China's local governments gave preferential tax rates to FIEs. Even more important was the triangular trade accounting method. Taiwan would accept an order and export raw materials to its Hong Kong branch under an inflated price that gave the Taiwanese company a higher profit. The Hong Kong branch didn't show profits in its accounting because it reported higher than actual wages at the mainland factory. This narrative is consistent with the intra-firm trading method of multinational corporations commonly seen in international political economics.

2) Changes in the Procurement of Raw Materials

In the early 1990s, the main materials and components needed by Taiyang's Dongguan factory were almost all imported from Taiwan, with only a small portion (such as packaging material, including cardboard boxes, polyethylene bags, etc.) purchased in Guangdong. But sometime around 1995, Taiwan's raw material factories began establishing factories on the mainland, including factories that produced synthetic leather materials (polyurethane, polyvinyl chloride), hardware, and zippers. Taiyang, like many Taiwan-invested factories, then turned toward local purchasing. Leather manufacturers—including the main ones, Nan Ya Plastics and San Fang Chemical Industrial Co. Ltd.—established factories on the mainland. Nan Ya established one in Nantong, in Jiangsu

Province, in 1995–96 and others in Guangzhou and Huizhou in 2000. These leather factories were suppliers to the manufacturers of leather goods, sport shoes, furniture, and automobiles. Guangdong's local supply chains gradually formed beginning in the mid-1990s, but at this stage, most of the raw material suppliers were still Taiwanese-invested factories. Manufacturers referred to synthetic leather production as secondary processing and to the manufacturing of leather goods, sports shoes, and furniture as tertiary processing. The westward movement of tertiary processing drove the arrival of the secondary processing industries only a few years later.

Like other Taiwanese-invested companies, Taiyang's main method for procuring materials in Guangdong was the interplant transfer method. The payment didn't need to be made on the ground in China but could be paid in Hong Kong so it wouldn't affect profit. The internal leather materials, hardware, and zippers that Taiyang used were bought on the mainland, but exterior leather materials (considered relatively high-level materials in the technical sense) were still procured in Taiwan. Taiyang eventually produced genuine leather goods, and the genuine leather was procured from South Korea, Taiwan, or mainland Taishang.

Brand-name firms and raw material suppliers would develop a cooperative relationship of mutual development and establishing standards. The development departments of raw material suppliers geared themselves toward brand firms' department of new products and designers, developed forward-looking products jointly with the brands, and became involved in research and development for manufacturers (such as Pou Chen). This production model generally emerged in Taiwan's OEM industry, including both traditional industries and the ICT industry. For example, Nan Ya's development and promotion staff members would develop shoe materials jointly with Nike and Adidas. It often took a year to develop new materials, and in the last stage of this process Nan Ya would share information with Pou Chen, Feng Tay, and other leading shoe manufacturers. After new footwear material was successfully developed, the brand-name firm would require these shoe manufacturers to buy their raw materials from Nan Ya.[10] Taiyang's Lee said that this kind of cooperation

10. Interview: LTM201510.

also appeared in leather goods, luggage, and other manufacturing industries.[11]

3) Developing High-Unit-Price Products

As Taiyang diversified its products and improved its product quality from 1995 onward, it was able to gain OEM orders from European and American name brands. Taiyang's buyers had previously been concentrated in the United States, but now the European and Japanese markets made up nearly half of its business. Buyers included the European brands Le Coq Sportif and Victorinox Swiss Army and the American brands Samsonite and Ghurka. These brand name products had a high unit price of up to US$40–50, and gross profit was as high as 35 percent. But the size of each order was small, so arranging production for these orders required even greater precision and flexibility. In the late 1990s, factories in Dongguan and the surrounding region that could match Taiyang's production quality were OEM factories from Taiwan (there were around ten of these), Hong Kong, or South Korea. A local South Korean factory could produce on an even larger scale than Taiyang. At this stage, Taiyang added buyers from European, American, and Japanese brands, but the chain retailers and importers that originally placed orders with Taiyang in Taiwan were still important customers.

4) The Extension of the Global Leather Goods Value Chains

The lead firms that bought leather goods produced by Taiyang were American chain retailers and name brands. As with goods such as ready-to-wear garments and sports shoes, the products these firms bought had initially been mainly produced in the United States. Around 1965, leather goods supply chains shifted to Japan, but they quickly became a sunset industry there. In the 1970s, supply chains shifted from Japan to Taiwan, South Korea, and Hong Kong. Beginning in the late 1980s, these supply chains extended and shifted to China's coastal regions. In this process we can clearly observe the stratified power relations of GVCs dominated

11. Interview: Leegm201511.

mainly by core countries, all pursuing lower labor costs. Fluctuations in the relative price of other essential factors (exchange rates, environmental protection, social insurance costs, etc.) served as an additional impetus to shift value chains.

The period from the mid-1970s until the late 1980s was a time when Taiwanese synthetic leather goods manufacturers flourished, and Taiyang sprang up at this time. At this stage the production chain shifted from Japan to Taiwan, and Taiyang took orders and contracted out production as a trading company. Leather goods producers in Taiwan formed production networks as well as complete production chains (see figure 3.1). Taiyang moved to the mainland through Hong Kong in 1988 and changed its corporate business model after establishing its own factory for direct production in 1989. Taiyang's cross-strait business operations concretely illustrate the shift and extension of the GVC, which drew capital, manufacturing and management techniques, and markets into the Pearl River Delta region. Taiyang experienced industrial upgrading and witnessed the gradual establishment in Guangdong of the supply chain system brought over by Taiwanese investment. In the westward movement, Taiyang also set up a holding (shell) company in a Caribbean tax haven for financial manipulation—which was almost standard operating procedure for emerging Taishang multinational corporations, regardless of their size. From an organizational standpoint, this change was enormous and comprehensive, and Taiyang was a classic case rather than an exception in this historical trend (see figure 3.2).

5) The Results of the Extension of Value Chains and the Transnationalization of Taiwanese Small and Medium-Size Companies

The shift of leather goods value chains described above was not an exception. During the same period (late 1980s to 1990s), the shifting of value chains from the newly industrialized countries of East Asia (Taiwan, South Korea, Hong Kong, and Singapore) to China was a synchronized trend, with traditional industries moving first, followed by the ICT industry. Taiwanese companies rapidly completed their redeployment along the China coast, consolidating mass production in spatially concentrated manufacturing bases. One key driver was the American retail revolution

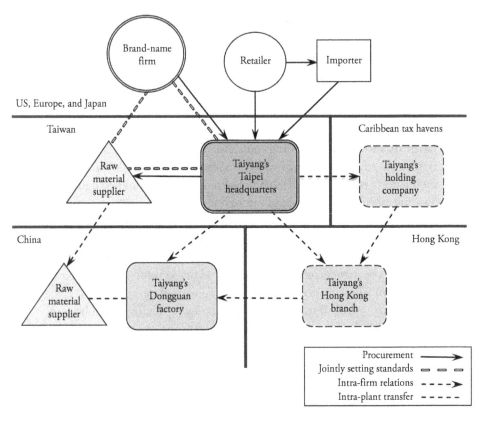

FIGURE 3.2. Taiyang Company's supply chain structure, 1998–2010.

(Hamilton, Petrovic, and Senauer 2011). Gary Hamilton and Kao Cheng-shu believe that the retail revolution spurred a concentration of global production and that the entire process was a "rationalization of demand-led capitalism" (2018, 184). Beginning in the 1990s, the retailers and brand-name manufacturers that served as lead firms in the GCC began using the lean inventory technique to systematize the GSC and became titans of globalization. One such example is the American retailing giant Walmart, which moved its global purchasing hub to Shenzhen in 2001. By 2004, Walmart was buying US$18 billion worth of goods from China annually, which accounted for 10 percent of the total imports to the United States (Hamilton and Kao 2018, 42–52 and 184–85). This shows the power of the lead firm. By emulating the redeployment of global production space, Taishang gained the opportunity for mass production.

In terms of Taiwan, we can see the significant effects that shifting GVCs had on exporters:

First is the transformation from trading companies to manufacturers, or from small or medium-size manufactures to large manufacturers. The former change was one of business content, as happened with Taiyang. The latter change was the expansion of organizational scale and the emulation and updating of organizational techniques, as happened in the cases of Pou Chen Corporation (and its subsidiary Yue Yuen Industrial Limited, listed in Hong Kong, the largest footwear maker in the world) and the Hon Hai Precision Industry Co., Ltd. (trading as Foxconn Technology Group).

Second are the changes in the organization of production. Many Taishang that established factories in China or moved their factories to China early on had mainly applied the networking model to their production in Taiwan. But when they first established factories in China, especially in the Pearl River Delta region, they lacked a set of subcontracting firms, so many manufacturers internalized the outsourcing procedure, integrating production and expanding their production capacity. For example, the production capacity of Taiyang's single Dongguan factory was nearly as great as that of all of the factories to which it subcontracted production in Taiwan. From the perspective of new institutional economics, this internalization could reduce transaction costs in a new manufacturing environment and with new production conditions, and it could facilitate quality control. But this kind of integrated production is also flexible: as Taishang networks emerged locally, hub factories also began outsourcing certain working procedures. Furthermore, organizational change was related to the nature of the product. For example, when Taiwan's computer assembly industry began establishing factories in Suzhou and Kunshan in the mid-1990s, Taiwanese firms also required their subcontracting factories to establish factories there at the same time. As a result, the westward movement of the entire computer industry duplicated and shifted Taiwan's production chains and collaborative networks.

Third is mass production. With the redeployment of global production space, output was closely related to two factors: the abovementioned organizational changes and expanded production capacity and the massive increase in the employed labor force. The latter was determined by China's abundant and low-cost labor supply. In the early 1990s, a single Taishang shoe manufacturer employed up to 30,000 employees in Dongguan. From 2000 onward, some manufacturers (such as Yue Yuen) employed upward of 100,000 people, and Foxconn, which subsequently moved into Shenzhen, employed 100,000 people in a single plant. This scale of production was unimaginable in Taiwan. Taiyang's Dongguan factory employed 2,400 people at its height, making Taiyang what would have been considered a large-scale business at that time in Taiwan, but a business of that size in the Pearl River Delta would be considered only a medium-size enterprise.

Fourth are changes in profit margins. Expanded production and low labor costs generally increased Taishang profits to a considerable degree. For example, although Taiyang's products were in a relatively low-tech traditional industry, its profits increased markedly after it established its factory in Dongguan. This was mainly because of low wages, but it was also because Taiyang put effort into industrial upgrading. As a result, Taiyang began receiving orders from brand-name firms soon after it entered China, which elevated its unit prices and gross profits. But changes in profit margins depended on the industrial category and the nature of individual products. Companies in the ICT industry's computer and cellphone assembly sectors (such as Foxconn) relied on output to increase business volume, but their profit margins were much lower than those in many traditional industries.

Fifth is the triangular trade and transnationalization of small and medium-size companies. Taishang that moved west to the mainland launched an export manufacturing model of taking orders in Taiwan and producing in China. At the same time, due to geopolitical factors and political considerations at the early stage, Taishang usually went in and out of China via Hong Kong, and gradually they developed a model of overseas capital management and shell companies in tax havens. Previous literature on international political economics has focused on large-scale transnational companies, but while this round of migration of GVCs hastened the birth of corporate giants such as Foxconn and Pou Chen, it also created countless small and medium-size Taiwanese transnationals. Compared with the classic transnational corporation, these smaller companies had a different transnationalization experience: one that mainly involved restructuring the division of labor in East Asia. And this regionalization, or perhaps a transnationalization within the so-called Greater China region, is even considered Sinicization. If we focus our observations on Taiwan's major corporate groups, their transnationalization was highly concentrated in the dependency structure of the triangular manufacturing trade formed by their relations with China's processing trade. In 2012, for example, about 30 percent of the total revenues of Taiwan's top three hundred businesses came from China.[12] Among the top thirty-two corporate groups (ranked by global total revenue, and excluding financial holding groups and banks), eighteen received more than 30 percent of their global net revenues from China. Nine of the eighteen earned higher revenue from China than from Taiwan. Six of these (Foxconn, Quanta, Kinpo, Inventec, Lite-On, and Delta Electronics) were in the ICT industry; one was the footwear manufacturer Pou Chen; and one was the diversified manufacturer Walsin Lihwa (Wu Jieh-min 2016).[13] Given the transnationalization of large export manufacturers, the degree of reliance on China (especially its labor supply) of small and medium-size manufacturing Taishang goes without saying.

6) The Position of Hong Kong in the Extension of GVCs

Taiyang and many other Taiwanese companies that entered China used Hong Kong as a bridgehead. We can observe that Hong Kong played a key intermediary role for certain types of products in the shift of value chains.

Information and social trust played important roles. Until the 1980s, Chinese society had been closed to the outside world for a long time but had maintained ties with Hong Kong. Consequently, Hongkongers were more familiar with China (especially Guangdong) than people in other

---

12. Calculated from "Ranking of mainland investment's contribution to the enterprise (top 300) using the total sum method" (data for 2013–2014), China Credit Information Service, 2014, Taipei.

13. The ninth was Ruentex, which was engaged in the distribution industry and drew 51.5 percent of its business revenue from China. It is heavily reliant on China's domestic market, but its industrial type is not a focus of this book's analysis.

countries were, and their human ties and social relations with Chinese were also plentiful. Furthermore, once China embarked on opening reforms, Hongkongers were the first to enter China, especially Guangdong. Using Gangshang connections therefore saved Taiwanese companies substantial transaction costs when they began migrating to China in the late 1980s.

Moreover, at that time cross-strait relations were just beginning to thaw, and the Taiwanese government still did not allow Taishang to invest in China. This meant that they had to take a circuitous route by establishing branch offices in Hong Kong and engaging in triangular trade outside of China's borders. In the early 1990s, the Taiwanese government allowed Taishang investing in China to register retroactively, and it gradually became more open about investment in China. However, a *jieji yongren* (go-slow policy) in the mid- and late 1990s attempted to limit this investment. From 2000 onward, the administration of President Chen Shui-bian, a member of the ruling Democratic Progressive Party, adopted a policy of proactive liberalization, and Taiwanese investment in China increased dramatically, as did the use of the model of taking orders in Taiwan and manufacturing in China. Even so, Hong Kong retained a valuable intermediary role for Taishang investing in Guangdong, because the processing trade model that prevailed in Guangdong still required Hong Kong to handle imports and exports and documentary bills offshore. Handling financial affairs (such as documentary bills) in Hong Kong also allowed Taishang to retain a large amount of their profits overseas. Even when Taiwanese companies were eventually allowed to invest in China, it remained common for them to use Hong Kong as an intermediary for offshore operations.[14]

Hong Kong's status as an intermediate stop in the westward movement of Taiwanese investment shows that Hong Kong was a node in the reorganization of the regional division of labor, and it also highlights Hong Kong's importance to China's linking up with the global capitalist

14. The example of Taiyang shows that when Taishang selected Hong Kong as a middle ground when they first invested in China, it was due to political considerations, geographical factors (Hong Kong was contiguous to Guangdong, and at that time many Gangshang had already established OEM networks in the Pearl River Delta), and so on. These factors facilitated the capital remittance operations of Taishang and helped them avoid legal problems. See also Hamilton and Kao, 2018, 144.

system (Chiu and Lui 2009). Until recently, Hong Kong continued to have the largest proportion of FIEs in China, and China's offshore investment is also concentrated in Hong Kong. Hong Kong plays an irreplaceable role in China as it deepens its links to the global marketplace.

4. Faux Joint Ventures and the Head Tax

From the stages of Taiyang's development, we can observe the capital migration and diffusion of technology resulting from the shift and extension of GVCs. When value chains extended to China's coastal regions, how did global-local linkages occur? How did FIEs create interactive relationships with local institutions and structural endowments? Specifically, how did Taiyang interact with the local government? How did it arrange the ownership of its factory? How did it surmount problems such as rent seeking, corruption, and the solicitation of bribes? With what government units did Taiyang seek to cooperate? What were the organizational characteristics of this cooperation? What was its institutional foundation? What institutional results did it produce?

Taiyang's Dongguan factory was a classic labor-intensive export processing factory. The registration certificate hung on the wall of the factory office stated that it was a Chinese-foreign joint-venture enterprise, and its partner was the plastic products department of Guanqiang Import and Export Company. It was therefore a joint-venture company in the nominal legal sense.

In fact, the factory was a wholly foreign owned enterprise. Several key pieces of evidence show that Taiyang was a single-venture foreign company: First, according to the cooperation agreement between the two parties, Taiyang had invested 70 percent of the total capital, and Guanqiang had invested 30 percent. But in fact, Guanqiang did not invest any capital. Second, the chair of Taiyang's board of directors and the factory's deputy general manager were appointed by the Chinese side, while the vice-chair and the general manager were appointed by the Taiwanese side. But Guanqiang did not send anyone to Taiyang to take charge of production management. Third, Guanqiang did not take on any business risk, nor did it share in the company's profits. Taiyang's success or failure was the complete responsibility of the Taiwanese side: the amount of Taiyang's profits or losses would not affect the profit that Guanqiang gained from the cooperative relationship (as I will explain in detail below). Put plainly, Taiyang was a faux joint-venture enterprise. In this kind of relationship, the cooperating partners had a tacit agreement under which each took what it needed and neither exposed the other, and the relationship was therefore able to operate smoothly.

At that time, Taiyang and Guanqiang's faux joint-venture relationship was the norm rather than the exception in China. Because of the laws and implementation methods left over from China's state-socialist system—especially the extensive economic controls, the approval authority enjoyed by executive units, and the lack of safeguards for private property rights—all kinds of fictive ownership arrangements were extremely popular, including private enterprises wearing a red cap and fake collective enterprises (Wu Jieh-min 1998). These kinds of flexible ownership rights became a key feature of government-business relations in China from the 1980s to the 1990s, benefiting private enterprises and FIEs but also planting the seeds of commercial disputes. They were the concrete manifestation of the dependence on institutional evolution, a residue that affected subsequent government-business relations.

In 1986–87, when the NT dollar appreciated sharply (with the exchange rate for the US dollar falling from NT$38 to NT$26), Taiwan's labor costs and other expenses also increased, and labor-intensive export processing factories began moving out in large numbers. At that time, geographical proximity and shared language made China the best choice for Taishang. Adding in the cheap labor force led many Taishang to believe that investing in China would be more productive than investing elsewhere in Southeast Asia. Additionally, in the mid-1980s, the Chinese government began implementing a series of preferential measures to encourage investment by so-called compatriots in Hong Kong, Taiwan, and Macau and by overseas Chinese.

Taiyang was not exceptional in arriving in China in the first mainland rush. What is interesting is why it would choose to cooperate with Guanqiang. As mentioned above, this was mainly because of the relationship between Taiyang and a Hong Kong company (Hong Kong Star).[15]

15. Hong Kong Star is a pseudonym.

Hong Kong Star had transferred Taiyang's orders in 1988 for manufacturing products in the Pearl River Delta region. Hong Kong Star recommended that Taiyang go to Dongguan City, and it represented Taiyang in arranging the initial business negotiations. The key to this consultation process was Taiyang's trust in Hong Kong Star. Some people may wonder why Taiyang didn't go to Shenzhen, which had a better infrastructural standard at that time. "Of course, under normal conditions Shenzhen looked better," Taiyang's Lee said. "But right because it was an SEZ, there were more constraints. Its labor policies were stricter, its wages higher, and its land prices more expensive, while Dongguan was more flexible in all of these things." He added, "The Special Economic Zone was not special!"[16]

The bureaucratic protective umbrella that Guanqiang provided allowed Taiyang to quickly build its factory and put it into production. Guanqiang provided Taiyang with many services. For example, it helped Taiyang obtain liberal tax reductions, handled complicated bureaucratic paperwork on Taiyang's behalf, and coordinated with government departments. It also delivered certain special benefits, such as providing a portion of its export quotas at no cost (at that time some of the products that Taiyang exported to the United States were still subject to quotas). Most important, China was notorious for its three arbitraries (local governments arbitrarily collected fees, levied fines, and imposed the apportioning of extrabudgetary funds), and when other government units would come to Taiyang demanding various miscellaneous fees, Guanqiang would step in to smooth the way. Taiyang's assistant manager, Mr. Su, who was from Taiwan, says: "They had units as numerous as buffalo hair, and they wanted money for everything! The number of times they came extorting payments was unbearable. . . . They were always bringing along a photocopy of some decree or other that made no sense to me. It made it impossible for me to manage the factory. . . . What could I do? I telephoned Guanqiang and asked them to handle it. They were almost always able to take care of things very quickly. You know, we gave them a lot of money. If we didn't ask for their help, what were we paying them for?"[17]

16. Interview: Leegm199404.
17. Interview: Su199405.

Su said this complacently and laughed. What he said had rich implications and revealed a great deal of information: local officials frequently solicited fees and engaged in rent-seeking activities, and the greatest benefit to Taiyang of its partnership was to have Guanqiang help eliminate this annoyance. The relationship between Taiyang and Guanqiang seems to have been very friendly at this stage. Guanqiang's helping Taiyang address the three arbitraries, quarantining it from the harmful outside environment, and creating relatively stable production conditions could be considered an isolation effect. Doing business in an environment of socialism with Chinese characteristics seemed to make an official protector essential. There's an old Chinese saying that "he who lacks a mother-in-law wishes he had one." Guanqiang was Taiyang's mother-in-law in dealing with Chinese officialdom. The relationship between Guanqiang and Taiyang was a clientelist transactional relationship between government and business.

Some people may wonder if the large fee that Guanqiang collected from Taiyang wasn't a source of the three arbitraries. For Taiyang this was a relative question, and it was closely related to the course of China's opening reform. At this stage, at a reasonable price Guanqiang provided FIEs with convenience in entering the government-business network of the local market (the market for factors of production such as labor and factory space). Because of the functionality of this government-business network, paying a fee to solve problems had a degree of legitimacy in the perception of foreign investors. Below I analyze how the fee demanded by Guanqiang was not entirely like the standard three arbitraries or corrupt conduct, and I show that instead it was relatively stable rent-seeking behavior with a high degree of predictability. What did Guanqiang gain from this cooperative relationship? Taiyang's Lee says: "They gained a head tax (*rentou shui*) of more than one million yuan every year."[18]

What is a head tax? In the early 1990s, when Lee blurted out the term, it could not be found in the academic literature and had not even appeared in news reports. I investigated the term for a time, carrying out multiple interviews and consulting books and periodicals relating to China's foreign exchange management system until I was finally able to clarify its meaning. The trick lies in the institutional design of the double-

18. Interview: Leegm199401.

Taiyang remitted Hong Kong (HK) dollars from Hong Kong every month to Guanqiang's Bank of China account in Dongguan.

→   The bank converted HK$ into renminbi according to the official exchange rate.

→   Taiyang obtained that amount of renminbi.

→   Guanqiang obtained foreign exchange use rights for that foreign exchange retention quota (20 percent).

→   Pearl's Light in Guangdong Province obtained a portion of Guanqiang's foreign exchange use rights for a portion of Guanqiang's transferred quota.

→   Guanqiang and Pearl's Light were allowed to purchase their shares of foreign exchange at the official exchange rate, or sell their foreign exchange use rights at the foreign exchange swap center at an adjusted exchange rate.

FIGURE 3.3. The foreign exchange earning mechanism of local Chinese foreign trade companies, using Taiyang as an example.
Source: Collected and compiled by the author.

track exchange rate. The abridged version here of this complex research process describes the results of my investigation.

The head tax in the foreign trade and economic relations in Guangdong at that time referred to the processing fee remittance spread. Chapter 2 described in general the nature and payment method of the processing fee. The remittance spread refers to the price differential between the official exchange rate and the market exchange rate applied to the remittance of foreign currency to China. The head tax was therefore not really a tax: referring to it jokingly in this way had satirical implications. Digging deep into this satirical term can help us understand the institutional mechanism of the processing trade in Guangdong at that time.

In terms of its financial character, the processing fee remittance spread was something like a management fee. But it was not collected directly from the FIE by the partnering unit on the Chinese side. Instead, it was collected through a complicated foreign exchange earning process in which the FIE paid its sponsoring Chinese unit and the local government through an indirect and circuitous method. How was the remittance spread created and levied? The mechanism is summarized in figure 3.3.

According to this set of rules, Taiyang remitted HK$270,000 every month to the Bank of China in Dongguan. This amount was specified in the cooperation agreement that Taiyang and Guanqiang signed. According to Taiyang's calculations, it lost the exchange rate differential between the HK dollar black-market price and the official price.[19] This remittance spread was the "head tax" that Lee referred to. In the fourth quarter of 1993, the official exchange rate was 0.76 yuan to one HK dollar, while the black-market exchange rate was around 1.15 yuan to the HK dollar. The exchange rate differential was therefore 0.39 yuan.

How were the heads of the "head tax" calculated? Lee said, "It was calculated as the total number of 'heads' [workers] that Taiyang employed." This was the origin of the expression. According to the processing contract between the two sides, Taiyang anticipated hiring six hundred workers, with each paid an estimated monthly salary of 340 yuan, equivalent to HK$450 (according to the official exchange rate at that time). Because Taiyang was basically a processing and assembly enterprise and did not earn renminbi in China, it had to use renminbi to pay the processing fee. According to the agreement, each worker was paid a monthly processing fee of HK$450, and HK$270,000 was remitted every month to Guanqiang's Bank of China account. So according to the above formula and exchange rate, how much did Taiyang pay Guanqiang each year? The amount was around 1.26 million yuan:

0.39 (exchange rate differential) × 450 (HK$, for each month's wage)
   × 600 (workers) × 12 (months) = 1,263,600 yuan

Why did FIEs regard this processing remittance spread as a loss or extra encumbrance? Lee explained: "When we needed renminbi, we could always buy it on the black market in Dongguan or Hong Kong. Why should we use the official exchange rate with them?"[20] To cooperate with Chinese work units, FIEs had to do as the Romans do—that is, abide by the local rules of the game and buy renminbi at the official exchange rate. Accordingly, Lee asserted, the loss on the remittance exchange rate was a tax or political insurance fee paid to the Chinese government. "Tax" in

19. The black-market price referred to here was close to the adjusted exchange rate at the foreign exchange swap center.
20. Interview: Leegm199401.

this context has a negative implication. In fact, the head tax was an operational cost, and Taiyang used it to pay for the services that Guanqiang provided. The head tax implied a specific exchange relationship, and essentially it was the price the manufacturer paid for official protection. In short, the price paid for dealing with the Chinese side was not cheap, but relative to the profits that the FIE earned, it was worth the price, because at that time the wages of migrant workers and other production costs were kept very low.

5. Guanqiang and the Head-Counting Game

Guanqiang Import and Export Company emerged in the early stage of opening reform in 1979. It was a Dongguan subordinate unit of Pearl's Light Import and Export Company in Guangdong Province.[21] Institutionally, provincial-level Pearl's Light led and supervised prefectural-level Guanqiang, which was accountable to Pearl's Light both administratively and financially. Guanqiang was divided into many specialized departments, of which plastic products was one. Guanqiang had around four hundred employees in 1994.

When Guanqiang was first established, apart from its ordinary foreign trading business, it also drew in FIEs to invest in the processing of shipped materials and in processing and assembly, and it sought opportunities to cooperate with FIEs. The plastics department launched its first joint-venture business with Hong Kong Star in 1985–86. Headquartered in Hong Kong, Hong Kong Star moved most of its labor-intensive assembly plants to Dongguan, where labor was cheap. Later, Hong Kong Star acted as a go-between in recommending that Taiyang establish a factory in Dongguan.

Guanqiang signed hundreds of processing contracts with FIEs that came to China to engage in the processing of shipped materials, and it opened joint-venture enterprises with around ten FIEs (all Gangshang or Taishang). Most of these were only faux joint ventures for which Guanqiang served as the sponsoring unit. The main operational model was as

---

21. Pearl's Light Import and Export Company is a pseudonym.

follows: The joint-venture company signed a processing contract with a certain Chinese processing plant for shipped materials (which did not qualify as a legal entity), and it was the contracting unit in name only. The Chinese side collected rent for the factory and appointed a factory head, accountant, and other staff members to be stationed at the factory, but in fact the FIE had all of the factory's administrative power. Like Taiyang, these companies remitted HK$300–500 every month for each worker, with the amount of head tax set according to specific investment agreements. As Ms. Zheng, the deputy director of Guanqiang's plastics department, said, "We were very flexible when discussing business with foreign companies."[22] The term "flexible" inevitably brings to mind the advantageous policies that the central government granted to Guangdong, which were also special and flexible and which the provincial government passed down to lower-level governments.

The processing fees remitted by FIEs helped Guanqiang accomplish two fiscal tasks. First, according to the remittance formula mentioned above, every year Guanqiang had around HK$3.36 million in foreign exchange remitted by Taiyang. According to Guanqiang's agreement with its provincial-level import-export company in Guangdong, it was to earn US$20 million in foreign exchange in the 1993 financial year. Guanqiang therefore needed to cooperate with only fifty FIEs of Taiyang's scale to achieve its yearly foreign exchange quota. In this way, remittances by FIEs helped Guanqiang accomplish its foreign exchange earning assignment. What if Guanqiang was unable to realize its contracted foreign exchange earnings in a certain year? Zheng said, "We could also buy it [the required currency] on the black market!" But that situation never arose.

Moreover, Guanqiang relied on the remittance spread to pay a large portion of its expenses. Guanqiang was rewarded for earning foreign exchange by acquiring foreign exchange use rights (commonly referred to as foreign exchange retention) on 20 percent of that foreign exchange income, as well as a sum for special compensation, while 80 percent of the foreign exchange use rights were designated for the provincial-level Pearl's Light. Guanqiang and Pearl's Light, like other Chinese companies with foreign exchange use rights, could purchase the foreign exchange they required at the official price within that quota, or they could sell their

22. Interview: GQ_Cheng199405.

foreign exchange use rights at an adjusted exchange rate at the foreign exchange swap center.[23] Complicated formulas existed for the distribution of profit from foreign exchange among the various levels of work units. Assuming that the foreign exchange earnings created in Dongguan could be converted into renminbi, the formula would be something like this:

HK\$1 = {0.8 × official exchange rate + 0.2 × adjusted exchange rate
+ 0.8 × 1/2 [adjusted exchange rate - official exchange rate]} yuan

Using the abovementioned fourth quarter of 1993 as an example, the official exchange rate for the HK dollar was 0.76 yuan, while the black-market rate was 1.15, and the adjusted exchange rate was close to the black-market rate, at around 1.05. Based on this conversion, each remittance of HK\$1 produced by Guanqiang was worth around 0.934 yuan, or 0.174 above the official value, and this difference was the gross profit that Guanqiang gained for each HK dollar remitted by FIEs. However, from the perspective of the foreign company, for each HK dollar that Taiyang remitted, it lost 0.39 yuan, because it could obtain 0.76 yuan only under the official exchange rate. So where did the difference go? The answer could not be clearer: it went to Guanqiang, and into the coffers of the government units at the provincial and other levels. Driven by this incentive structure created by the double-track exchange rate, Guanqiang provided

23. In October 1980, the Bank of China opened foreign exchange swap branches in Beijing and eleven other cities. According to the market quote for renminbi, US\$1 could be exchanged for 1.5 yuan. In 1981 China began implementing an internal trading settlement exchange rate of US\$1 for 2.8 yuan. The basis for this calculation was the actual conversion cost plus a reasonable profit. This price was not changed until 1984. For this reason, three foreign exchange prices coexisted during this period (the official price, the internal settlement price, and the black-market price). In 1985, the internal settlement price was abolished, and a single exchange rate was restored. However, the official price and the adjusted exchange rate coexisted in a double-track pricing system. China referred to the difference between the official price and the adjusted price as the quota price (see Yin Yanlin 1993). When Li Hao was appointed vice-governor of Guangdong Province and mayor of Shenzhen in 1985 (he later also became party secretary of Shenzhen), part of his mission was to establish a foreign exchange swap center. His interviews also mention the coexistence at that time of an official price, internal settlement price, and black-market price for foreign exchange and the inevitable phenomenon of speculation in foreign exchange (Guangdong Party Committee 2008, 347–48).

Table 3.1. Various taxes and related fees paid by Taiyang in 1993

Item	Department paid	Calculation method
(1) Labor management fee	Labor Bureau	8 yuan per month × 1,000 people
(2) Application for temporary residence permit	Public Security Bureau	30 yuan × 1,000 people
(3) Extension of temporary residence permit	Public Security Bureau	4 yuan per month × 1,000 people
(4) Staff dormitory rent	Alfa Plastics Factory	30 yuan per month × 900 people
(5) Security guards	Coastguard local unit	700 yuan per month × 15 people
(6) Corporate income tax	Tax Bureau	200,000 yuan × 12%
(7) Head tax (processing fee remittance spread)	Guanqiang	$0.39 \times 450 \times 600 \times 12$ (or 1,263,600 yuan)

Source: Author's analysis based on the information collected in the fieldwork.

sponsoring services (under the name of a joint venture) to FIEs. Apart from closely tracking whether or not Taiyang remitted funds on time every month, Guanqiang paid no attention whatsoever to Taiyang's business. In fact, this hands-off approach was exactly what FIEs hoped for.

The head tax was merely the most important fee that Taiyang paid to the Chinese side. It also had to pay a multitude of other fees. Table 3.1 lists some of the more notable items. This table reveals a great deal of important information that can explain the detailed mechanism of the head-counting game and the operational model of the informal institutions.

First, head counting was a method commonly used by the Chinese side for levying various fees. What is interesting is that the various work units Taiyang dealt with used different calculation methods. How many workers did this factory actually employ: 600 (according to the agreement between Taiyang and Guanqiang), 900 (according to the rent paid to Alfa Plastics Factory) or 1,000 (according to the fees paid to Labor Bureau and Public Security bureau)? Mr. Chang, the manager of the factory service department, revealed that it actually employed 1,500 people. This seems to indicate that Taiyang concealed 900 people from Guanqiang, 600 from the plastics factory that rented out its dormitory, and 500 from the Labor Bureau. At first glance, this is a story of an FIE cheating a local government, but the situation is not actually that simple. The crux of the problem is that "in calculating the head count, we had to see whom we were paying and the outcome of the negotiations and then finally decide. If we had somewhat better relations with them, we could report fewer [employees]," as Chang said. "They didn't actually come into the factory and count exactly how many people were there! Once we'd reached an agreement, they would come for a look around and then report the number."[24] In other words, head counting could be an empty gesture or could proceed strictly according to regulations.

The head count could be agreed upon and discounted, and individual agreements could be reached with different government departments, in the manner of separate fiefdoms and approaching what is called particularistic bargaining (Shirk 1993). Here, what local bureaucratic organs cared about was protecting their own interests, and they decided on reductions to the head count based on whether they had friendly or poor relationships with individual manufacturers. The shortfall in a head count was therefore not a deception but rather collusion between the government and business. In China, especially in Guangdong at this stage, all kinds of taxes and fees could be discounted: Taiyang's case was the rule rather than the exception. One study of Shenzhen at that time noted that according to government regulations, in Shenzhen City's Bao'an County, the processing fee remittance was 600 yuan per worker, while inside the Shenzhen SEZ it was 700–800 yuan. However, FIEs in these places generally enjoyed a 20 percent "discount" (Shao Mingjun 1992, 550).

Second, the discrepancy in the head counts that Taiyang reported shows a lack of communication and coordination between various departments regarding the business situations of FIEs, or perhaps that these departments simply did not care about the horizontal flow of information. If various government units could supervise the accounting of enterprises by way of interdepartment information networks, they would very easily have been able to grasp the true situation. Upper-level governments—especially the central government—should have an intense interest in clarifying the detailed situation of foreign companies.

24. Interview: Chang199405.

However, at this stage, because the monitoring tools of the Chinese government were still inadequate and the institutional structure was incomplete, the government lacked infrastructural power. Furthermore, at that time the government desperately needed to attract capital, technology, and export markets through foreign companies, so it turned a blind eye to the collusive activities at the local level and even tacitly consented to them.

Third, the formal tax that Taiyang paid to the Chinese government (table 3.1, item 6) was very small—only about 14 percent of the total that Taiyang paid in labor management and temporary residence fees (items 1–3) and only 1.9 percent of what Taiyang paid in head tax. Taiyang had US$20 million, or approximately 116.6 million yuan (according to the official exchange rate), in total sales in 1993. If profit is calculated at 10 percent, Taiyang's taxable profit would have been 11.7 million yuan. With the help of Guanqiang, Taiyang gained the preferential treatment of "three exempt and four reduced" on income tax.[25] Because Dongguan City was included among the coastal open economic regions, the income tax rate was 24 percent, so half of the rate was 12 percent. Nineteen ninety-three was the fifth year of Taiyang's official operations and the fifth year that it posted a profit. According to the official standards, Taiyang would need to pay 1.4 million yuan in income tax.

Because Taiyang was a standard "three ends outside" FIE (with its raw material supply, product export market, and letter of credit documentary drafts all outside of China), it was very easy to manipulate the accounts and very difficult for the Chinese side to vet the company's financial reports. In 1993 Taiyang reported a small portion of its profits to the Chinese side and paid a small amount of tax. Guanqiang accepted at face value the operating conditions that Taiyang reported because Guanqiang was the greatest beneficiary of this cooperative relationship. It is no accident that with Guanqiang's help, Taiyang never experienced any problems when it came to taxes.

Fourth, the head tax was the largest fee that Taiyang paid to the Chinese side (1.26 million yuan). Curiously, this fee was very close to the Chinese government's lost tax revenue (1.40 million yuan). In any case,

25. "Three exempt and four reduced" refers to the exemption from income tax for the first three years in which a company posted a profit and the taxation at only half of the usual rate for the next four years.

that money still went into the Chinese side's pockets, just to a different government unit—and the collection method was also different. The head tax was a fixed and unchangeable contracted amount and would fluctuate only according to differences in the exchange rate, rather than reflecting the enterprise's actual profits or losses. In terms of fiscal function, the head tax used the foreign exchange earning process to pay the local state-owned enterprise, and the enterprise's income tax was paid directly to the state tax organ: the former was informal, extrabudgetary income; and the latter was formal tax revenue.

The significance of this difference was that the taxes and levies that the Chinese side acquired from the FIE were diverted from government finances to the local government or local state-owned enterprise. This financial diversion is evidence of the operational model called delegating power and yielding profit to the local level in the market reforms of China's opening to the outside world. This method effectively drove local officials' economic incentives and led them to enthusiastically compete for outside investment. Ostensibly, Guanqiang took money by inserting itself between the FIE and the taxation unit. In fact, this was according to the government's plan, which allowed local officials and state-owned enterprises to join in the rent-sharing game.

Fifth, we see that the local coast guard unit in Dongguan also squeezed Taiyang. The unit's commanding officer sent fifteen soldiers to serve as security guards for Taiyang's factory. They wore military uniforms but were not armed, and they became associate staff members of Taiyang: they lived and ate at the factory, punched its time clock, and submitted to the factory management's work directives. Taiyang paid the soldiers a liberal salary (compared to what general staff members received). However, Taiyang paid these salaries to the commander of the coast guard unit, while the soldiers drew their ordinary military pay from the unit. For Taiyang's managers, this sum of money was a public relations fee that had to be paid and was worth paying. At that time, law and order was rather limited in the Pearl River Delta, and the managers acknowledged that "having troops stationed at the factory gave a sense of security." It was by no means an unusual scenario for "troops to run over to guard a factory."[26] In Guangdong, all kinds of local work units were seeking rent

26. Interview: Chang199405.

from foreign companies in the name of apportionments and donations, as I often observed in my field investigations.

Finally, we do not see an item in table 3.1 relating to social insurance. Taiyang was required to pay a social insurance fee to the Labor Bureau at one point in the mid-1990s, but the amount was very low, and the government did not go out of its way to collect it. Only in the late 1990s, when the relevant laws were gradually implemented and the government increased its collection enforcement, did the social insurance fee become an important topic. This issue is discussed in detail in chapter 4.

What is clear is that in this transactional game between government and business, migrant workers were subject to elimination and trading and became abstract numbers without individual faces. It wasn't until after the mid-2000s—a time of saturation in the labor-intensive industries, gradual increases in the minimum wage for migrant workers, stronger social insurance laws, and other factors—that the collective and individual faces of workers gradually came into focus, and workers began to challenge this highly exclusionary alliance through collective petitions, reports to the authorities, lawsuits, and strikes. This topic is explored in depth in chapter 6.

6. The 1994 Foreign Exchange Reform

In the final analysis, the abovementioned complex mechanism of rent creating and rent sharing was the outgrowth of the double-track exchange rate and foreign exchange retention systems, which were designed by the central government. In fact, this design was not original: many newly industrializing countries, including Taiwan, have adopted policies such as binary exchange rates in the past. Imitation may therefore be a more appropriate description of what happened in China. The head tax game was the local government's flexible application of central government policies, and driven by the central policies, it emerged under favorable local conditions. During my field investigations in Guangdong, I often found that local cadres mentioned that they flexibly applied policies or maximized their use. Although when the central government established the rules of the game, it could not have foreseen exactly how flexibly local governments would apply these policies, it certainly crafted the incentive structure in such a way as to spur local officials to attract investment. In the first stage of the reforms, the central government created institutional rent-seeking opportunities for local governments. So if the central government changed the rules of the game, how would the local governments react? And how would foreign investors react?

The rules were finally changed. Starting with Deng Xiaoping's southern tour in 1992, China's arrangements for its opening reforms underwent a structural transformation. The Pudong New District Development Plan in Shanghai was presented, the strategy of developing the Yangtze River Basin region to drive the economic development of eastern China gradually took shape, and many cities in the interior were added to the list of cities to be opened to foreign investment. In early 1994, the central government launched a new round of institutional reforms, which (especially the substantial depreciation of the renminbi and the unification of the exchange rate) had a serious effect on local governments, as well as administrative decoupling (reforms that broke administrative links between different administrative levels of foreign trade SOEs). All of these reforms sent the existing informal financial arrangements between local work units and FIEs into flux.

"Unification of the exchange rate" refers to the elimination of the double-track foreign exchange pricing system and allowing the price of the renminbi to fluctuate within a small range. In 1994, at the same time that unification of the exchange rate was carried out, the exchange rate for the renminbi was depreciated to near the market price, so that its value compared to the US dollar fell from 5.76 yuan to 8.62 yuan. Next came relaxation of foreign exchange controls within a small range and the cancellation of the foreign exchange retention system. "Administrative decoupling" meant that prefectural-level foreign trading companies were no longer administratively subordinate to the higher-level provincial foreign trading companies and now were local SOEs of the prefectural governments. Consequently, Guanqiang now reported to the Dongguan prefectural government. At the same time, this meant that the central government had extended the downward delegation of foreign trade rights and further relaxed the foreign trade management system.

For foreign businesses, once the exchange rate was unified, it was clearly no longer legitimate to pay processing fees through the remittance of foreign currency and have a high fee extracted in the process. FIEs could now easily obtain the yuan they needed at an official exchange rate close to the market rate, so why should they go to the expense and trouble of using the abovementioned complex remittance procedure?

The problem was the effect on the interests of local government units. According to the arrangements in the era of the double-track system, in 1993 Guanqiang made a gross profit of about 0.17 yuan for every HK dollar remitted for the processing fee. With the processing fee remittance spread eliminated, Guanqiang would suddenly lose a large amount of money. After the exchange rate was unified, there was no longer such a thing as a remittance spread, which is why the Chinese government declared that "unification of the exchange rate in itself is a new advantage for foreign businesses."[27]

Guanqiang announced that to compensate it for its losses under the unified exchange rate, all of the enterprises for which it was the sponsoring organ, including joint ventures, would still have to remit a monthly processing fee in renminbi, and Guanqiang would extract a 25 percent management fee from that. This move naturally drew opposition from FIEs, but Guanqiang's method was quite pervasive in the Pearl River Delta.[28]

What could be observed on the ground in the Pearl River Delta at that time was that many FIEs temporarily halted remittances and adopted

27. Interview: GQ_Cheng199405.

28. The following observation is consistent with the results of my field research: "Many Guangdong towns took at least 20 percent of the processing fees that were remitted to the banks as a municipal support fees or fees under different names. This was mainly before the end of 1993, when the official exchange rate and adjusted exchange rate hadn't yet been unified, and the wages for processing shipped materials had to be remitted to the local government in renminbi, and the local government would gain the differential. When the exchange rates were unified in 1994, the local government still didn't give up its vested interests and continued the same as before, merely extracting its fee under another name. Out of fear that foreign companies would underreport the processing fee, some local governments calculated the processing fee to be remitted based on the weight of exports. But it wasn't like that everywhere in Guangdong: for instance, Huizhou didn't 'levy a percentage of the processing fee' and didn't care if the processing fee was underreported. . . . In terms of foreign exchange, although some localities took a percentage of the processing fee for processing shipped materials, they were also often somewhat hostile to wholly foreign-owned companies and would charge them a higher management fee (head tax)" (Hsu He-jung 2005, 627).

a wait-and-see attitude. Taiyang held several talks with Guanqiang on this issue, which wasn't resolved until 1995.

Following the administrative decoupling of Guanqiang, the prefectural government now had a legitimate reason to share in the profits of subordinate state-owned trading companies. The new reforms also complicated the game of rent sharing. In March 1994, the Dongguan government issued a new formula for remittance allocation. The government wanted to take 5.5 percent of the remitted funds as a service charge, and it allowed the sponsoring work unit to take 24.5–29.5 percent, while the FIE could take the remaining 65–70 percent. This indicates that the fee that the FIE now had to pay was not lower than under the former dual exchange rate system. Needless to say, the Dongguan government's announcement immediately created an uproar among foreign companies. It also exacerbated the friction between Guanqiang and its clients. An increasing number of FIEs stopped remitting funds. Mr. Yen, the manager of a local shoe factory, said: "This hand had to be played. We temporarily held back to see their next move!"[29]

7. Building a New Factory in Nafu Village

In fact, Taiyang had quietly begun taking action to change its mother-in-law much earlier. In early 1994, Taiyang gave notice that it would be terminating its cooperative relationship with Guanqiang at the end of the year. At that time, a new Taiyang factory was being constructed with a sense of urgency in Nafu Village.

"Village" was not an administrative term in Guangdong, and the proper name was "Nafu Administrative District," but people still used the word "village." "Administrative district" was a term used only in Guangdong to refer to what other provinces called an "administrative village." It was the lowest level of administrative unit and usually encompassed multiple natural villages. But the extent of a Guangdong administrative district was typically much larger than that of an administrative village in other provinces, and the term was mainly an institutional

29. Interview: Yen199405.

remnant of the people's commune era. During that era, the commune in a typical province was around the scale of a township, but in Guangdong the scale of communes was very large (in some areas, a commune was the equivalent of a county), so production brigades in Guangdong were also very large. After the people's communes were dismantled, production brigades were changed into administrative districts. The Nafu Administrative District was subordinate to Xishui Town and was located a little over ten kilometers from the town center. Nafu included seven natural villages. In January 1994, it had around four thousand native village residents (registered permanent residents) and around three thousand migrant workers and their dependents (who made up the non-native population), most of them from other provinces. The administrative district office owned five collective enterprises, and all of them contracted work out. The district had around fifteen FIEs (all small-scale factories) that paid head taxes to the district office. In the 1993 financial year, the district office's budgeted revenue was around three million yuan, which included 1.25 million yuan from subcontracting fees. The district office employed around fifteen people (including full-time cadres and temporary employees). According to the cadres, they shared a bonus totaling five thousand yuan that year.

Taiyang's Lee was quite well informed about changes in the Chinese central government's policies. It should not be surprising that Taiyang's decision to move to a new factory was timed to match the implementation of the new round of macroeconomic reforms launched by Zhu Rongji, vice-premier of the State Council. It is significant that FIEs started looking for new partners at the same time as the central government's new reform plan was implemented. As described above, the combination of the unification of the exchange rate and other decoupling measures changed the original interactive environment between local cadres and foreign businesses, and it also changed their respective incentive structures. Furthermore, Taiyang's "three exempt and four reduced" tax incentives were about to end. For Lee, what was most important at this time was to find a new partner that was cheaper and more reliable. Psychological factors also played a role. Lee had come to what he called a "chaotic society" and had done business there for seven years. Now he had the self-confidence to make sense of the rules of the game. He had his own information network as well as relationships with people outside of

Table 3.2. The annual fees Taiyang's new factory paid to Nafu Village

Item	Cost
(1) Head tax (management fee)	10 yuan ×1,700 people ×12 months (204,000 yuan)
(2) Special fee	200,000 yuan
Total	404,000 yuan

Source: Author's analysis.

Guanqiang. In this new situation, he "no longer wanted to mess around with mainlanders and engage in fake joint ventures."[30] Put simply, he hoped to have a more transparent and simpler cooperative relationship with local people. He was planning a new operational model for Taiyang: Taiyang wanted a new mah-jongg table, new mah-jongg partners, and a completely new relationship with them.

Taiyang was investing even more money in China. For example, the new factory in Nafu cost US$9 million. Plans for the company's move began to be carried out in 1993, including finding a new location for the factory and a new cooperation partner, as well as buying machinery and other equipment. Taiyang finally chose Nafu and signed a contract with the cadres there as a wholly foreign-owned company. The new factory would hire 1,700–2,500 workers, and its estimated maximum annual production capacity would reach US$40 million.

Taiyang leased a piece of land measuring 30,000 square meters at a cost of 140 yuan per square meter, paid to the Nafu Administrative District office. Taiyang began operating its new factory in Nafu in January 1995. It paid the administrative office a management fee of 204,000 yuan per year. Once again, the management fee was calculated on the basis of a head count: 10 yuan per worker per month, with the number of workers fixed at 1,700 (see table 3.2). This payment to the local partner was now called a management fee, but Lee was still accustomed to calling it a head tax. Apart from the head tax, Taiyang promised to pay another sum of 200,000 yuan as a special fee each year.

The conditions that Taiyang gained from its move to Nafu were all much more liberal than those under Taiyang's relationship with

30. Interview: Leegm199508.

Guanqiang. The new company also gained the "three exempt and four reduced" tax incentive. Apart from the export quota, Nafu gave Taiyang almost the same services as Dongguan had provided, but the total fees were only one-third of what Taiyang had paid to Guanqiang. The new company also had a much higher production capacity than the old one. In calculating the actual head tax for each worker, Guanqiang had demanded sixty-four yuan, while Nafu required only sixteen yuan. Furthermore, the method for paying the management fee no longer required the tortuous foreign exchange-earning process: instead, the company paid renminbi directly to the Nafu Administrative District office. At first glance, the fee required by Nafu was much lower than Guanqiang's, but Taiyang had already spent more than four million yuan on the land lease.

The reason for choosing to become Nafu's son-in-law was very simple: Many nearby administrative districts were competing to provide the most advantageous conditions, and Taiyang found Nafu's conditions most advantageous. The main consideration was that this new partner's asking price was much lower. In fact, compared with neighboring villages, Nafu was rather remote and had developed later as an administrative district, so it was willing to offer better terms to attract investors. When Taiyang was preparing to build its new factory, Guanqiang's manager came to talk to Lee several times (although by then it would have been hard to change Taiyang's plans), demanding that Taiyang give Guanqiang a stake in the new company. Lee refused for this reason: "There was no benefit to having an extra mother-in-law!" Taiyang worried that continuing to cooperate with Guanqiang would only increase its outlay without bringing any actual benefit.

This policy change caused Guanqiang to lose some very profitable business, and the relationship between the two companies began to sour. Reportedly, when Guanqiang's manager saw that persuasion was ineffective, he threatened to create problems for Taiyang. What kind of problems? Lee wasn't willing to disclose the details, but he repeatedly complained that the manager used "despicable methods." According to regulations, one of the conditions for Taiyang to enjoy tax reductions was that the business had to continue operating for at least ten years. If Taiyang terminated its cooperative relationship with Guanqiang (i.e., closed down its business), it would have to pay back its previous tax breaks. This suggests that Guanqiang was not without bargaining chips. Furthermore, the dispute over the unpaid processing fee and service charge (the fee required by the prefectural government) had not yet been resolved. By taking on a new mother-in-law, Taiyang ended the increasingly acrimonious relationship of rival partners. In Lee's eyes, Guanqiang had changed from a protector into a plunderer. The long-drawn-out drama finally ended in 1995, as Taiyang ended its relationship with Guanqiang through the negotiation method. In the transitional period of this institutional environment, we can observe the state (the central government) carrying out a new policy that caused the relative price of the deal between a local government and a foreign company to change and then impelled changes to the interactive model between the two sides. Government-business relationship networks are embedded in a specific policy and structural environment, and as soon as the external institutional environment changes, the cooperation or collusion between government and business is bound to be affected and then adjusted.

8. The Institutional Emergence of the Head Tax

Taiyang's story shows that the function of head tax is an element in the Guangdong growth model. Starting with the head tax phenomenon, I have painstakingly examined and traced the institutional figuration of the Guangdong model. This includes formal and informal rules, as well as the rent-seeking behavior of the bureaucratic collective. Head tax as a medium of dealings between local government and business led Guangdong's labor-intensive industrialization to take off like wildfire under the dominance of foreign investment. Observed from the perspective of new institutional economics, the head tax can be said to reflect the institutional equilibrium of the Guangdong growth model.

Why did the head tax emerge in Guangdong? And how did it emerge? Figure 3.4 is a schematic diagram of the institutional origins of the head tax. First, the dual-track foreign exchange system in state policy encouraged exports to earn foreign exchange, and implementing a system of foreign exchange retention spurred local officials to attract outside investment. We cannot forget that in the early 1990s, China was still in desperate need of foreign exchange, and the lack of foreign exchange was

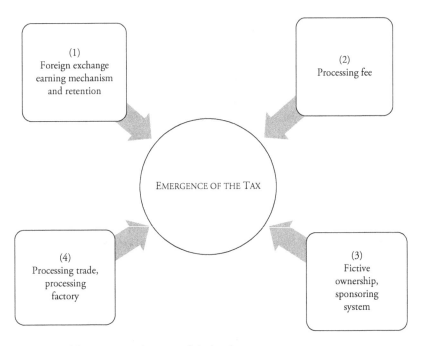

FIGURE 3.4. The institutional origins of the head tax.

the structural force that activated the mechanism to earn that exchange. At that time, engaging in foreign trade and using foreign exchange were both administrative privileges. In Guangdong, the right to engage in foreign trade was delegated down to grassroots government units, and each unit was tasked with earning a certain quota of foreign exchange. Each unit therefore explored all possible means of meeting its quota. But what actual benefit did local cadres gain from taking on these quotas? The answer is foreign exchange retention, which provided cadres with an incentive to put great amounts of effort into earning foreign exchange.

The second fountainhead for the head tax was the processing fee, which was closely linked to the mechanism of earning foreign exchange. The remittance procedure for processing fees was a mechanism for creating extrabudgetary fees. This procedure for earning foreign exchange was a bureaucratically collectivized institutional rent-seeking mechanism. The exchange relationship between Guanqiang and the FIEs it sponsored distinctly displays this quality. The processing fee then connected to the third fountainhead: The government work unit or state-owned enterprise could provide arrangements and protection for fictive ownership. The various elastic or flexible ownership relations pervasive in China at that time all point to the pervasiveness of the sponsorship system. A new form of local government–business relationship thereupon emerged, under which a work unit that accepted a company for sponsorship would collect a sponsorship or management fee from it.

These mutually linked institutional factors point to the fourth fountainhead: the processing trade. These ostensibly complicated and intertwined institutions allowed the smooth operation of factories for processing shipped materials, the main corporate organizational model at that time. Taiyang was ostensibly a joint-venture company, but its production

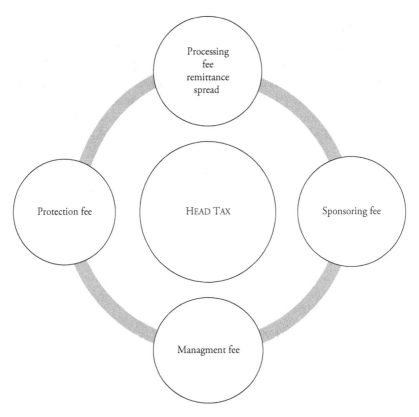

FIGURE 3.5. The floating significance of head tax.

methods, corporate operations, and sponsoring model were identical to those of the typical wholly foreign-owned factory processing shipped materials.

By granting sponsoring services for fictive ownership and gaining rent-seeking privileges from the companies they served, local cadres made these companies into their sphere of influence, with the companies both accepting the cadres' protection and having to pay a protection fee. At a certain stage in history, when the companies accepting sponsorship services felt that paying the management fee was reasonable, this fee was seen as legitimate by those companies. But after the policy environment had changed, companies felt that this fee was not justified, its legitimacy eroded, and the government units providing sponsorship became plunderers who forcibly extracted protection fees like gangsters. For this reason, the same fee charged to a different actor, at a different time, and in a different institutional relationship, acquired a different signifier and a completely different subjective affect (see figure 3.5). The variety of terms— "head tax," "processing fee remittance spread," "sponsorship fee," "management fee," and "protection fee"—all meant the transaction cost for government-business relations. In this study, I treat this transaction cost as institutional rent seeking. Like fluid semantic symbols accompanying changes in actors, the passage of time, and changes in the environment, different names call up diametrically opposite images and value judgments. The fluidity does not imply that there is no pattern to be grasped. Rather, the researcher must seize the historical moment within the flow and observe how an institution emerges in the structural interstices and then how it vanishes.

CHAPTER FOUR

Taiyang Company, 1995–2010

Nineteen ninety-four was a key year for reforms. During this year the Chinese government carried out a series of macroscopic reforms that altered the incentive structure and interactive model between local governments and manufacturers, creating a wave of change in government-business relations at the local level.

In terms of tax reform, the central government established local state tax bureaus to collect taxes, whereas the previous method had required local governments to collect taxes and turn them over to higher-level governments. Now, a local government was empowered to grant manufacturers tax reductions only on tax revenues that belonged to the local government, such as the revenues from the business income tax. Taxes belonging to the central government (for example, the majority of VATs) could not be reduced. Tax reform put the central government in control of dividing up tax revenues. Originally the central government received 40 percent and local governments received 60 percent, but those shares were quickly reversed. The central government's fiscal capacity was greatly enhanced, giving it the advantage in tax revenue from then on.

In terms of foreign exchange reform, the substantial depreciation of the renminbi powerfully enhanced the price competitiveness of export processing businesses. Abolishing the dual-track exchange rates dismantled the legal foundation for local governments to collect the exchange rate spread on foreign remittances. This changed the relative price to FIEs of using local institutions and increased FIEs' negotiating capacity relative to local government. Generally speaking, this wave of reforms was a set of measures accompanying China's strategy of comprehensively opening its coastal regions. From then on, Guangdong no longer outshone the rest of China: the Yangtze Delta region soon began catching up and attracting large amounts of FDI.

State policy changes affected Taiyang's cooperative relationship with Guanqiang. As related in chapter 3, after exchange rates were unified, Guanqiang lost its ability to use exchange spreads in rent seeking, but did this mean it was going to provide services free of charge to Taiyang? That was impossible. Instead, Guanqiang demanded that Taiyang maintain its payments in different forms (such as management fees). But Taiyang felt the cost was too high, so the relationship between the two evolved from the happy cooperation of the early years into disputes and then a parting of ways.

1. Nafu Village: The Grassroots Unit of the EOI Growth Model

Once Taiyang decided to build its own factory, the first step was to lease land. Taiyang settled on a piece of agricultural land in Nafu Village. The enthusiastic efforts of village cadres smoothed the way for Taiyang to procure this piece of land, which was categorized as collectively owned, and go through a two-step certification process. Taiyang first obtained a township and village enterprise land use certificate, after which it applied for a state-owned land use certificate and repaid a land requisition fee to the state, in that way greatly reducing the cost of land compared with the officially mandated one-step process.[1] In short, Nafu Village leased land at low cost to FIEs in exchange for stable income from management fees.

---

1. Following China's legal stipulations and using the official one-step procedure to obtain a state-owned land use certificate for agricultural land would have required paying a higher requisition fee. But because the village cadres effectively controlled land use rights, they were able to divide the procedure into separate parts, which helped businesses reduce the cost of obtaining land.

Grassroots administrative organizations like Nafu Village represented the basic unit that sustained China's labor-intensive processing trade development model, and Nafu is a typical example of China's newly industrialized villages. Let's first look at the situation of this village. In 2006–7, the Nafu Administrative District had more than one thousand locally registered households that collectively contained more than five thousand people. The nonnative population consisted mainly of migrant workers, who numbered more than forty thousand. When Taiyang began building its new factory in Nafu in 1994, there were only three thousand nonnative residents, which shows how rapidly that number increased.

1) The Pyramid of Status Power

In 2006–7, the Nafu Administrative District had an authorized staff of eight cadres, who all served concurrently as members of the village committee. Each cadre earned a salary of 5,000–10,000 yuan per month. For example, the chairman of the processing section earned more than 8,000 yuan per month. And this was merely what they were paid on the books: they enjoyed a number of supplementary benefits, as well as many opportunities for expenditure in their official capacity. Because the collective" was well-off, ordinary villagers also enjoyed many benefits. The village had a kindergarten that was free to local village children. Older children went to the junior high school in the nearest town, with a village bus taking them there and back at no charge. When village women reached the age of fifty and men the age of sixty, they could apply for a pension of 200 yuan per month subsidized by the administrative district, and the social insurance fund paid an additional 150 yuan per month. All villagers were enrolled in rural health insurance under the New Cooperative Medical Scheme if they paid a premium of 20 yuan per month, with the remainder subsidized by the administrative district or the local government. In addition, all adult villagers received an annual bonus that was determined by the amount of management fees paid by enterprises, with each person typically getting 3,000–5,000 yuan.

These benefits could be enjoyed only by the village's indigenous residents, however. The 40,000-plus migrant workers did not have local *hukou*, which meant that they didn't have the status of local villagers and therefore were excluded from the welfare system. The village committee

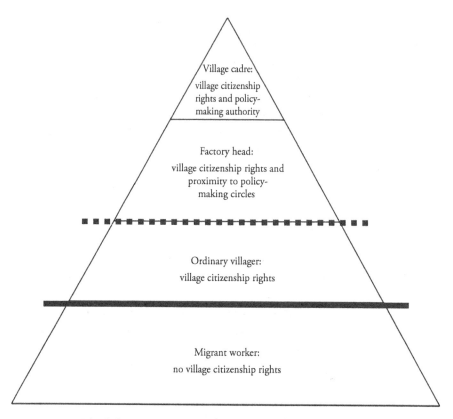

FIGURE 4.1. The differential citizenship framework in Nafu Village.

was elected by local residents, and migrant workers did not have voting rights in local village elections. This was a quasi-apartheid differential citizenship system (see figure 4.1). Nonnative residents were second-class citizens, and as long as they continued living in this village, they had no upward mobility in the social pyramid. There was an unbridgeable status gap between migrant workers and indigenous residents.

In terms of labor earnings, migrant laborers received the minimum wage along with overtime pay. According to stipulations in 2006–7, Guangdong Province's minimum wage was divided into five grades (of 780, 690, 600, 500, and 450 yuan per month, respectively), and Dongguan fell into the 690-yuan grade. Under the labor conditions at that time, an ordinary worker (such as a worker on a production line) with more than a hundred hours of overtime would draw a maximum salary of around 1,400 yuan. If an enterprise actually paid the social insurance fees it declared that it paid, the cost of each worker would be around 1,800 yuan, which was still much lower than the 5,000–10,000 yuan that village cadres earned.

In addition to the status differential between local and nonlocal residents, there was also a stratification in terms of power among local residents. Village cadres enjoyed the greatest amount of special power and economic gain. The factory heads (*changzhang*)[2] that the administrative district posted at the various companies also enjoyed a relatively substantial economic benefit: in 2007, these factory heads drew salaries of around 3,000 yuan. Sources of income for ordinary villagers included renting rooms to migrant workers, running grocery stores, and offering motorcycle taxi services.[3] Village cadres' power to approve land leases greatly increased their opportunities to earn gray income. Taiyang committed to paying Nafu 200,000 yuan as a special fee every year, and whose pockets this money went into remains a mystery. Since the early 1990s in Guangdong's economically developed regions, there have been countless incidents of villagers protesting the unauthorized approval of land leases by village cadres who diverted the village's collective profits (Wu Jieh-min 2000). The 2011 Wukan Incident, in which violent protests broke out among villagers in Lufeng, in Guangdong Province, involved conflicts over the allocation of benefits from the village's collective land (Zhang Jieping 2016). Nafu Village never experienced this kind of protest. In 1995, I saw a financial affairs notice board in the lobby of the Nafu Administrative District office building, which posted the village's financial situation for each month.

The dividing line between native and nonnative residents is structural and unbridgeable. The line between local cadres and ordinary local villagers is relative, and an unequal power relation exists between them.

2. Factory heads, posted by the administrative district (village) at FIEs and other factories, did not actually manage the factories.

3. After economic conditions improved, villagers no longer offered motorcycle taxi services, which were taken over by migrant workers. In 2008, Dongguan imposed a ban on riding motorcycles, so in principle such services were no longer available. However, villagers still rode motorcycles by themselves to and from work within the village. This shows that local villagers with village citizenship rights enjoyed small privileges.

However, ordinary villagers can still lodge a complaint or protest against cadres.

2) *The System of the Fictive Factory Head*

A business's factory head served as the bridge for contact and everyday communication between the administrative district and the business. In 2006–7, Nafu had more than a hundred enterprises, more than sixty of which were foreign owned (the rest were run by local people). In every business the administrative district posted a factory head who was appointed by the village committee secretary or the head of the processing section. If the business was established by a local villager, one of the villager's relatives could be appointed factory head. The factory head that the village posted at Taiyang was a woman called Ah-Xiu, who was in her forties in 2007. She had been serving as factory head for village businesses since 1992, and she was first posted at Taiyang in 1999. Taiyang was considered a large factory in the village (there were only a few other factories there on an equivalent scale), and its salaries and benefits were relatively good. Thus, Ah-Xiu could consider her assignment there to be a promotion. What work did Taiyang assign to Ah-Xiu? She was to handle public relations with the village. Why was this role referred to as factory head? It was continuing the system of factories processing shipped materials under the "three-plus-one trading mix" system. The original meaning of processing shipped materials was that the foreign business would transport raw materials into China, and after these materials were processed and assembled in China, the finished products were exported. Under this arrangement, the Chinese side earned merely a processing fee. The Chinese side needed someone in charge at the processing plant, and that person was the factory head. But in practice, so-called processing factories were managed by the FIEs themselves, and the factory head was just a placeholder, who typically knew nothing about production or management. The factory head's functions therefore became to manage public relations and to relay and exchange information. In principle, Taiyang was a wholly foreign-owned factory and not a factory that processed shipped materials, and the administrative district had no authority to post a factory head there. Yet like the thousand other local FIEs, Taiyang accepted this system, doing in Rome as the Romans do. In any case, the personnel cost was not great.

Furthermore, according to government policy, Taiyang was required to establish a labor union, but the union existed in name only, and Ah-Xiu served as its president. Basically, it did not function in terms of collective discussion or rights protection. An experienced head of the migrant worker section confirmed this: "Taiyang established a union, but it didn't hold regular or frequent meetings. The union president was the factory head. . . . Foreign-invested factories seldom conform to the Labor Law. It [the union] was required, so we set one up, but it wasn't done very thoroughly with regular meetings and so on."[4]

3) The Rentier Class and Double Exploitation

There were many places in Guangdong, where, as in Nafu, the entire village's economic activities revolved around FIEs. Nafu's economy relied on foreign investment, and through foreign investment the village was linked to the global capitalist economy. Village cadres and the factory heads were integrated with FIEs in this politico-economic system, serving as elements of the local growth alliance. The role they played wasn't directly productive in nature. Instead, they were like land brokers or employees at a labor agency or public relations company, and they collected rent for their work. Moreover, an important task for village cadres was ensuring social control within the village. Generally speaking, they weren't involved in social control inside a business, apart from tasks required by the state such as implementing family planning and pregnancy tests among female workers. In a social system with rapid economic growth and such a high proportion of nonnative residents, as well as high population density, coercive political control was inevitable, whether this involved targeting migrant workers or ordinary villagers dissatisfied with village cadres. The cadres had a militia and contracted public security that constituted a village-level apparatus of state repression. Generally speaking, village cadres and factory heads formed a rentier class, with the rent including the management fees, factory rent, land rent, and migrant labor force agency fees that businesses had to pay. Thus, the entire village was like a mini rentier state.

This structure embodied the institutional particularity of the Chinese-style capitalist system—that is, its double exploitation of migrant workers.

4. Interview: ZJY200603.

The first layer of exploitation was the relatively familiar class exploitation under Marxist analysis; the second layer was the status exploitation resulting from the status of migrant workers. As nonnatives, migrant workers could not enjoy socioeconomic rights in the village, reflected in the village's collective benefits, social insurance and social welfare, employment opportunities, and the right of residents' children to education. For factory owners (not only foreign businesses), the painstakingly suppressed wages and reduced social insurance fees for migrant workers greatly reduced capital's labor costs. In China, this kind of double exploitation was closely entwined with the differential citizenship system. Although the Chinese government began to take steps in the twenty-first century to improve the treatment of migrant workers and issued new laws (the Labor Contract Law, Social Insurance Law, etc.), this did not solve the fundamental structural problem of differential citizenship.

Nafu Village, as a basic politico-economic unit of China's labor-intensive EOI growth model, was the social space where Taiyang's new factory was located. In fact, Taiyang's Lee and the factory's Taigan were not unfamiliar with this environment: they needed to adapt only to new interpersonal relationships in the village. When the factory moved, it retained all of its old employees, and since production expanded after the move, it hired even more workers. Below I show how it adjusted to the new macro-level changes, as well as to changes in the company's internal personnel and strategies, by focusing on the company's leadership power succession and product upgrading, changes to the government-business relationship, the role of stricter social insurance policies in increasing costs and labor strikes, and the factory's ultimately closing.

2. The Second Generation Takes Over

Taiyang was a classic family-owned business. The first generation established the company's success as a trading company in Taiwan, beginning in the late 1970s by taking orders and then sending them to OEM factories in the south of Taiwan. At that time, the company's first-generation leaders were in their thirties. In the late 1980s, Taiyang established its factory in Dongguan and joined the manufacturing industry. By the beginning of the twenty-first century, members of the first generation were nearing retirement age. In 2000, the first-generation managers were still regularly working at the factory, which employed around ten Taigan, but their sample department remained in Taiwan. At this stage, half of Taiyang's orders came from the United States, with the other half coming mainly from Japan and Europe, and the products were mainly of medium price.

In the early 2000s, Taiyang began shifting its internal leadership from the first to the second generation. The second-generation general manager, Ben,[5] had received standard business management training in the United States and had earned an MBA, and he had plentiful work experience in Europe and America. He could have continued developing his career overseas, but he was willing to come back and take over the family business out of a sense of mission. What kind of mission? Put simply, he wanted to modernize the family business, upgrade its product line, and create its own brand. Second-generation Taishang with Ben's qualifications and experience are not rare in China. Over the past decade or so, my research team and I interviewed many second-generation Taishang with similar backgrounds in China's coastal regions with high concentrations of Taishang. After Ben took over the factory, he went through a breaking-in period with the company's veteran managers. Lee remained behind to help out during the transition, but he eventually retired. At that point, Ben had to take charge, though he was only in his early thirties.

1) The Apprenticeship Culture of Taigan

Some of Taiyang's veteran managers were classic cases of "*oo-tshiú*-turned-Taigan."[6] They had acquired strong skills (for example, as mold makers or production line managers) in Taiwan, but they were relatively unfamiliar with modernized management methods. I carried out interviews at a Taiwanese-owned luggage factory whose workshop (production site)

5. Ben is a pseudonym.

6. AUTHOR'S POSTSCRIPT: The Taiwanese Hokkien term *oo-tshiú* (*heishou* in Chinese; black hand) refers to technicians and mechanics, who were typically trained through an apprenticeship system, and it signifies the rise of these employees from blue-collar dirty work to management or factory bosses.

manager, Mr. Chen, had originally been a section manager at a factory in Taiwan. Chen's special assistant was the production line team leader. Both had been trained in Taiwan as apprentices and were gradually promoted to the management level. During their years in Taiwan, labor-intensive factories hiring hundreds of workers were considered quite large. Once the company had arrived in Guangdong, everything from production capacity to the numbers of production lines and workers far surpassed the scale in Taiwan, and the positions and salaries of the Taigan likewise typically jumped three grades. These men were among the vanguard of managers who came from Taiwan to manage Chinese workers at Chinese labor sites, and the vast majority of the workers that these Taigan dealt with were members of the first generation of migrant workers who came to the coast from inland rural areas. The knowledge gaps and conflicts between these two groups can only be imagined. The first generation of Taigan had grown up in Taiwan under anticommunist authoritarianism, and they often emphasized that they had come to what they called bandit territory. They did not trust the people they referred to dismissively as "a-la̍k-á" (sixers),[7] and they demonstrated an undisguised superiority complex.

The members of this older generation of Taigan enforced stern management and discipline referred to as militarized management. Militarized management was a fusion of the management experience in Japanese-owned companies in Taiwan in the 1960s and 1970s (which involved strict working procedures, submission to command, an emphasis on order, the performance of calisthenic exercises, etc.) with Taiwan's exclusive army culture, which emphasized masculine qualities. In a workshop of this factory in 1995, I watched a Taigan reprimand a production line worker for an operational error in a foul-mouthed harangue that lasted ten minutes. That Taigan subsequently told me: "If I don't curse them this way, they'll never learn."[8] In the early years, public order in Dongguan was rather poor, and there were numerous carjackings and robberies. Chen told me: "The first few years I was here, there was a lot of tension on payday every month for fear of holdups. We were afraid that if we distributed pay on the same day every month, word would leak out.

---

7. *TRANSLATOR'S NOTE*: In Taiwanese Hokkien, the word for "six" sounds similar to a syllable in the term for "mainlander."

8. Interview: CY199506.

We kept handguns on us just in case." The handguns Chen refers to weren't loaded but were to be used only as a threat. He said: "One time when the kitchen cooked food too slowly, the workers just grabbed rice out of the cooker. They almost started a riot."[9] During my early field-work, when I went out at night with Taigan to chat over tea or liquor, the conversations often revolved around their negative experiences in deal-ing with mainlanders.

Going out for drinks or other socializing was part of everyday life for the first generation of Taigan. I once interviewed a Taigan, a director named Chiu, who went to work in China back in 1989 (and subsequently formed his own company with friends). Mr. Chiu told me in 2004: "In the early days, we'd go to karaoke bars seven days a week. Back in Dong-guan, a large proportion of the top managers who were sent over early on, like me, died when they were around forty or fifty years old. They drank themselves to death. In the early days, as soon as there was a phone call, you had to go, and there was pub crawling as well. Besides, most of those who came early on were from the older generation, and they'd also been drinking in Taiwan for a long time. It was required for socializing, and they weren't going to change that culture after coming over to the mainland."[10]

This interview describes the pervasiveness of the drinking culture among the old Taigan as not just for socializing with mainland officials: drinking was a deeply entrenched habit among them. According to many veteran Taigan, if you didn't invite a client for drinks, it was impossible to talk business or resolve issues, and they made it sound compulsory. However, this socializing was largely avoidable. Chiu's comparison of changes over the course of fifteen years shows that the drinking culture was also changing.

2) Differences in Management Style between the Two Generations

For a time after Ben took over Taiyang, he energetically set about mak-ing new arrangements, hiring highly educated professional financial staff members, computerizing production management information, and in-creasing investment. Taiyang invested in a new production line that

9. Interview: Chen199506.
10. Interview: Chiu200404.

specialized in products with high prices. This high-priced branch shifted from the Japanese market to the American brand-name market, and one of the strategies for grabbing the latter market was to buy shares in international brands. Consequently, Taiyang's production scale and revenue both reached their peak in 2006–8. During this period, Taiyang also tried developing the domestic market, but it soon ended that experiment. The main difficulty was that the company was used to engaging in OEM production in China, and shifting its market orientation to China would be a completely new challenge that would result in financial losses for a considerable period of time.

It can be imagined that Ben's business style and plans might create friction between him with older cadres. The conflict arose from differences between two sets of business concepts and management philosophies. When the older generation went from Taiwan to China, its members endured all kinds of hardships but were able to survive, and therefore they had bragging rights. Ben's insistence on reform looked unworkable in the eyes of the older managers. One year before the Spring Festival, I took my research team to a karaoke party that Taiyang hosted for Nafu cadres, which was eagerly attended by the village's young cadres. Ben didn't attend, but Jerry, the financial affairs manager, was present. Jerry didn't like drinking and had a low tolerance for liquor. With everyone flushed with alcohol, an old Taigan pointed at Jerry, sitting far away, and said, "If you're like that one . . . that work style won't get you anywhere. . . . He doesn't know how to drink."[11] In the view of this old Taigan, it was very important to hang out with local Chinese officials, and drinking was a way of nurturing relationships. In the eyes of the veteran cadres, the youngsters hadn't been put to the test.

3. Changes in Government-Business Relations

Changes in the government-business relationship between Taiyang and local government cadres were mainly reflected in evolving macroscopic conditions and a shift to new cooperative partners, as well as upgrading in the quality of Chinese officials.

11. Interview: Lin200701.

Starting in 1995, Taiyang established a wholly owned company; moved to Nafu Village; leased land and built a factory; and, through a two-stage process, obtained a state-owned land use certificate. The benefit of such a certificate was that the holder could freely sell or transfer this right to use land during the fifty years that the certificate was valid. In terms of the company's organization, Taiyang no longer had to sign a processing contract with a factory processing shipped materials, as its wholly owned status exempted it from this formality. Furthermore, the foreign exchange rate had been unified by then, and the company's Chinese partner had no legal basis for collecting the processing fee remittance spread. However, because local governments had long relied on that enormous remittance spread, they devised every possible means to collect additional cooperation fees. Thus, the agreement between Taiyang and Nafu Village still committed Taiyang to paying a substantial management fee.

1) From Processing Shipped Materials to Processing Imported Materials

In the new cooperative relationship, Taiyang's model changed from processing shipped materials to processing imported materials. The company still needed to remit a processing fee from Hong Kong to Guangdong, but now this was done through the method of a customs spread. How did this spread work? Jerry explained: "Customs spread meant that the foreign company remitted the difference between the import value and the export value, and this spread had to be remitted in foreign currency. This method was particular to Guangdong. It didn't exist in other regions, and it was an extension of the special three-plus-one trading mix operation."[12]

Compare this with the definition of this operational model by a business consultant: "For wholly owned companies, calculation of the processing fee came under the model of processing imported materials, and the foreign remittance for processing imported materials could be transacted as setting off receipts against expenditure; it was acceptable to calculate the differential remittance between the import customs declaration

12. Interview: Jerry200909.

and export customs declaration, and therefore required the remitted capital to approximately tally with the fixed monthly expenditure" (Chang Tsung-teh 2004).

The two accounts verify the earlier analysis. Guangdong's processing trade model had a consistent logic for earning foreign exchange: even if the macroscopic system changed, its operational method retained vestiges of path dependence. It is worth noting that in the processing of imported materials, the calculation of the processing fee became uncoupled from the head count. Furthermore, a remittance spread was no longer withheld from the remitted foreign exchange converted into renminbi.

Even though central government's policy changes spurred the transformation of local macroeconomic conditions, the rent-seeking behavior of Guangdong's local cadres continued as before. Foreign investors and local governments still had plenty of bargaining room over issues such as management fees and social insurance. FIEs still had to pay many other kinds of fees in addition to processing fees. For example, one veteran Taiyang cadre said that when the local government disseminated news of a food supply shortage in the mid-1990s, the company had to pay a food insurance fee to ensure that the company's food supply would not be interrupted.[13] In the mid-2000s, there were electrical supply shortages in China's coastal regions, and I heard of companies being charged an electrical insurance fee. My field research interviews from 2007 show that the Dongguan Public Security Bureau alone charged the following fees to manufacturers: fire prevention facility fee, public order joint defense fee, industrial and commercial security management fee, security patrol fee, security management fee, security training fee, and temporary residential permit fee (some of these items were paid through the village committee). The temporary residential permit fee was abolished following reform of the nonnative resident management system. In recent years, after management of FIEs became stricter, the bizarre assortment of fees decreased, but there are still many kinds of institutionalized rent that must be paid.

Observing Taiyang's interaction with the local government in these years, we see several indications that institutional change caused changes to the functioning of relationships (*guanxi*): First, business dinners were

13. Interview: Su199508.

fewer, and the topics of discussion changed. Second, brazen greasing of the palms of local officials decreased, but the institutional rent-seeking and rent-sharing games continued. Third, the management fee that Taiyang paid Nafu Village decreased each year. Fourth, the factory head system became more transparent.

2) The Taiwan Merchants' Association as a "Watering Hole"

For the older generation of Taishang managers, socializing with Chinese personnel was unavoidable. But the new generation of managers typically considered it a burden and avoided it whenever possible. Regarding socializing, Ben said:

> They're making progress. You see, the younger mainland cadres are better educated: not all of them love going out drinking and singing karaoke, and when you have dinner with them, the conversation is quite sophisticated. Like the current party secretary of Nafu Village—he served as a deputy bureau head in the township government, and he's only thirty-plus years old. Because we're all young, we have more to talk about, and we feel closer. The young party secretaries aren't willing to go out drinking with the old people; they look down on each other. Added to that, a lot of sons and daughters of party secretaries and officials have studied overseas, so my experience in England and America gives us a lot to talk about.[14]

Regarding relations with the social insurance bureau, Ben said:

> That's where the *guanxi* never stops. You can become very involved with them or keep your distance. There's no definite standard for how far you should go. Our current so-called mainlander factory head's family has a 500-tree lychee orchard. Our factory took out a contract for four lychee trees, around 400 catties [approximately 200 kilos], and let the social insurance bureau staff go pick lychees there. That's also *guanxi*. After they picked the lychees yesterday, we invited them to dinner at the restaurant in Nafu. I stay for about five minutes on this kind of occasion and then leave. Where I actually appear [in negotiations] is

14. Interview: Ben200504.

on necessary occasions when I privately arrange to meet someone in a coffee shop.[15]

Ben's comment on the Dongguan's Taiwan Merchants' Association was very direct: he said that it was just a "watering hole" that brought no business benefit to companies.[16] In fact, the many Taiwan Merchants' Associations all over China still have a definite economic and social function, as they circulate information and provide a social space for fostering government-business relations. Ben's remark reflects his own preferences and his loathing of the drinking culture in Taishang circles. In any case, his subjective appraisal shows that the operational methods of *guanxi* are slowly and subtly changing. One of the indications of these changes is that officials are taking a more gracious attitude, and rude, direct bribe-seeking behavior is waning.

However, *guanxi* and *kau-puê* (cultivating officials to foster a deeper friendship and trust) are still important. Ben said: "In fact, all of the fees and taxes can be avoided: it's a matter of whether or not you want to use *guanxi* and shoulder the risk, and whether it's worth the cost." Using *guanxi* means taking on risk. The formula followed is determining whether the gain of evading taxes and fees is greater than the costs of *guanxi* and risk. The logic of utility, rather than sentimental factors, decides the calculations of *guanxi* politics. Over the past decade or so, corporate social responsibility has become more stringently enforced, and the brand-name companies that place orders all send people to inspect factories. There are tricks here as well, however. Ben said that during factory inspections, "foreign firms usually send a pair of representatives from different regions to avoid the problem of corruption, but someone will still stuff a *hong bao* (red envelope, meaning bribes) in their pocket. . . . During inspections, as long as we conform to local laws, we're fine. Through *guanxi* we get a paper that says, 'This factory pays social insurance for a certain number of people in compliance with labor bureau regulations.' . . . Then they put a big stamp on it and we're okay."[17]

15. Interview: Ben200406.
16. Interview: Ben200504.
17. Interview: Ben200406.

3) Rent-Seeking Games Continue

The Chinese government stipulates that businesses must hire a certain percentage of handicapped people. Nafu Village cadres taught Taiyang a way to deal with this:

> The stipulation was for 1.5 percent of total staff hired, but the discounted number of people reported for social insurance purposes could be used, so we had to hire around twelve people. But after talking with the village secretary, we thought of a way: This money was given to the administrative district to facilitate public relations. That way money could be deducted for meals, utilities, etc., and it wasn't necessary to apply the minimum wage. It was all right to pay around 400 yuan for each person. According to government regulations, if we didn't hire them, that sum of money had to be paid to the labor bureau.[18]

This method allows us to observe several things: First, the government policy that required looking after handicapped persons became a channel for rent seeking once it reached the local level. Second, a regular policy became an irregular rent-seeking activity, and various local government units took part in this game to compete for and divide up the rent. Third, because it was a rent-sharing game, the payment could be discounted through negotiation: a discount on the head count (which was the preferred discount) or on the minimum wage, or the deduction of expenses that weren't actually paid (meals and utilities). Fourth, the money was given to the village where the factory was located, rather than to the labor bureau.

As observed in the above examples, it was essential for FIEs to maintain friendly relations with local cadres. The importance of *guanxi* was even greater than Ben was willing to acknowledge. In any case, Ben attempted to maintain this government-business relationship using the methods of the new generation.

4) The Gradually Decreasing Management Fee

As mentioned above, the key to Taiyang's cooperation with Nafu Village was the payment of a substantial management fee every month. According

18. Interview: Ben200406.

to the initial agreement, Taiyang had to pay the village around 40,000 yuan each month, but this fee gradually decreased over the course of more than ten years: by 2008 it had dropped to around 15,000 yuan per month, or less than half of the original amount. From Taiyang's perspective, the reduction of the head tax showed that the local institutions had gotten on the right track, and this was progress. Reducing the management fee indicated that in the labor-intensive processing trade that sustained the local economy, the Chinese side's bargaining power was eroding. The reasons were complex, but they included competition (to attract foreign investment) among the villages of the Pearl River Delta; the gradual erosion of the Pearl River Delta's advantages, with an increasing number of manufacturers opting to move out or further inland and newly arriving manufacturers no longer giving top priority to Guangdong; and China's economic system's becoming more formal and transparent. The reduced management fee also indicated a drop in the average profits of businesses engaged in the processing trade in Guangdong, which had led them to demand a reduction of payments to local cadres. The downward slide in the percentage weight of processing fee remittance spreads in local finance in the twenty-first century serves to validate the analysis in chapter 2.

For Nafu Village, although the management fees paid by individual manufacturers decreased, the substantial increase in the number of manufacturers moving in over the years kept the total amount of payments at an impressive level.

5) Ah-Xiu's Awkward Role as Factory Head

Nafu Village's one hundred or so factory heads were tasked not with involving themselves directly in production, but with serving as the administrative district's public relations people or liaisons at the factories. At the same time, the position created well-paying jobs for villagers. As an intermediary between the administrative district and the manufacturer, the factory head had a role worth analyzing. In a dinner gathering, my research team and I listened to a discussion between Taiyang's factory head, Ah-Xiu, and Jerry that is worth repeating here. I asked Ah-Xiu how the factory head was selected. Ah-Xiu said she wasn't sure, and Jerry impatiently jumped in and answered for her:

The factory head is chosen by the head of the Foreign Economic Co-operation Office [also called the Processing Office], and the factory can decide whether or not to accept [that person]. Of course, the villagers hope to go to a large factory, because large factories have better salaries and benefits. When the village wants to station a factory head, it first notifies the boss [manufacturer] . . . After Ah-Xiu came over, Taiyang gave her lots of work, like "fighting for us on the outside." . . . For the villagers, if the factory they're sent to is lousy, they also lose face [prestige], so they'll help the factory gain face. . . . She helps me, and I help her. For example, sometimes the administrative district wants to host an activity, and she'll come back and tell us, and we'll immediately support it.[19]

Ah-Xiu found an opportunity to interject and said, "The factory head is a link of mutual cooperation between the locality and the enterprise." Jerry quickly added, "and for monitoring [the enterprise]!" When Ah-Xiu heard this, she smiled and explained: "That's never happened. . . . I protect our factory much more." Jerry indicated that he agreed. Ah-Xiu went on: "The Chinese side's factory head represents the Nafu Administrative District's image and also helps the enterprise develop. This link safeguards the factory's interests and protects the image of the Nafu Administrative District: the two are inseparable." I asked, "Does the factory head need to have regular meetings with the processing office?" Ah-Xiu said: "Not necessarily. It's the village teams' meetings or factory heads' conferences that we go to." She gave an example of a meeting regarding a safety campaign, including the living environment in the factories and safety in production.[20]

This conversation (including interjections, interruptions, and arguments) shows: First, the factory head had become an institutionalized role in the Pearl River Delta. The head was a representative of the village who had been stationed at the factory and who helped the factory handle external dealings (limited to less important affairs), but was not allowed to inquire into the factory's internal business. Second, the factory head was a public relations person linking the village and the manufacturer. Third, the factory head also played the role of monitoring the factory's situation and had to provide information to the village's assembly, committee, and processing office—for example, on the factory's environmental impact and safety. Fourth, serving as a factory head was a good job for local villagers, and it was an especially lucrative posting for villagers stationed at a foreign-invested factory of substantial scale.

At this dinner, there was a clear sense that Jerry, the Taishang manager, was in a stronger position and Ah-Xiu, the factory head, was in a defensive position. This could be explained by Ah-Xiu's cautious, bashful personality, but it also revealed the awkward role of the factory head. Ah-Xiu drew a salary from Taiyang, but at the same time she helped handle matters for both the company and the administrative district. Taiyang had a cooperative partnership with the administrative district, but the factory head was assigned to help the administrative district monitor the factory. The relationship between the FIE and the local government was one of both cooperation and mutual wariness, and the factory head was situated at the nexus of exchange between and mutual monitoring of the local government and business. The relationship of rival partners between the FIE and the Chinese side is fully revealed here.

4. The Localization of Cadres and Increasing Social Insurance Fees

In the early years when FIEs began to move into China, local people with management skills were in relatively short supply, and most manufacturers sent a substantial number of managers from the parent company. For Taishang, the cost of bringing in Taigan had become quite high by the late 1990s. Staff members sent to the mainland initially received double the salaries of their counterparts in Taiwan, and these Taigan were also provided with housing, air fare (they traveled back and forth on average every two or three months), and other benefits. But with an increase in management talent in China, a growing familiarity with the operation models of capitalist manufacturers, a glut of Taigan, and steadily increasing pressure to lower costs among manufacturers, salaries in China and Taiwan had become identical by the late 2000s. Similarly, as Taishang became increasingly familiar with China's business environment and talent market, a general trend of management localization developed, and Taiyang was no exception. As early as the mid-1990s, Taiyang had begun gradually shifting its Taiwan-based samples department (which at that time employed dozens of people) to its Dongguan factory, where it hired mostly mainland Chinese staff. Finally, the samples department in Taiwan was dissolved, and the remaining few experienced Taiwanese staff members were stationed in Dongguan, allowing Taiyang to save a large amount in payroll expenses.

1) The Localization of Management

Localization of the factory's management was carried out at the same time. In the 1990s, I observed that on Taiyang's production line, the highest mainland manager was only a section head. By the mid-2000s, mainland staff members were serving at the level of department head. Above the department head was the assistant manager, who was the highest level of manager at Taiyang's factory. In other words, mainlanders were already serving as the top managers in charge of production lines. Taiyang's two mainland department heads were in charge of quality control and production, respectively, and in 2006–7, their salaries were close to 4,000 yuan per month.

Ben said: "How far they're [mainland staff are] able to get promoted depends on the person. Our company has never had a rule that if you're a mainlander, you don't have opportunity for advancement. It's just that their previous educational backgrounds didn't prepare them for management positions, so over the last few years we've been sending them to classes."[21] It is worth noting Ben's response when I asked him to compare the quality of labor on the two sides of the strait:

> I've been extremely disappointed with our staff from Taiwan. They're extremely unmotivated. I don't dare use graduates from Taiwanese universities; I only use people with mainland experience. [Graduates of Taiwanese universities] all think that any Taiwanese staff brought over here will be put in charge of things, but they're basically neophytes.

21. Interview: Ben200701.

We have a mainland manager who's been working over here for twenty years, while there are basically no Taiwanese managers who have been working for twenty years—not to mention that you have no experience whatsoever, and you still want to be put in charge over others. In Taiwan, working inside a large company, it takes more than ten years to reach the position of section head. You come to the mainland, and because you're Taiwanese, I'm supposed to give you a title?[22]

At that time, Taiyang had been operating its factory in Dongguan for nearly twenty years, and some of its mainland staff members had been working for the company from the outset. In fact, a few of the Taiwanese managers stationed in Dongguan had also been there all along. Ben's remarks expressed his disappointment with young Taiwanese staff members, and similar comments could often be heard in informal conversations among Taishang. They generally felt that the competitiveness of young Taiwanese was deteriorating and that they lacked the fighting spirit of young mainlanders. In fact, Ben's assessment of young workers on either side of the strait reflects the different stages of industrial development in the two places. However, his comparison did not bring in this difference, focusing instead on personnel costs.

At the same time that management was becoming localized, the business costs of Taishang were rising, especially in terms of labor. This situation pertained to all foreign-invested companies, but the effect was especially great in the labor-intensive industries. The processing export industries under the Guangdong model had always called for low salaries for migrant workers, but as the migrant worker shortage emerged in the mid-2000s (Chen Huirong 2006), the minimum wage for migrant workers gradually rose (although it remained lower than wages for domestic permanent workers or international salaries). In 2008, Dongguan's minimum wage (Taiyang managers referred to it as the "basic wage") was 770 yuan per month, and this was the starting wage that Taiyang paid its staff. Adding in overtime pay, the average wage of all workshop staff members was 1,450 yuan. Comparatively speaking, average take-home pay in the local textile industry was 1,800 yuan, because of more overtime. From the perspective of labor-intensive industries, rising labor costs gradually ate into profits.

22. Interview: Ben200701.

2) *Increasing Social Insurance Fees*

For factories in labor-intensive industries producing for export, the social insurance fees stipulated by Chinese government were high compared with salary levels—assuming that manufacturers paid social insurance fees in full compliance with legal stipulations, and that local governments fully enforced the laws. Social insurance regulations were not uniform throughout China, however, and different localities had their own policies. Comparing the social insurance fees in the industrialized coastal regions of Shanghai, Suzhou, Shenzhen, and Dongguan, we find that Dongguan and Shenzhen provided the worst social insurance safeguards for migrant workers (Wu Jieh-min 2011, 80–81). For this reason, the social insurance costs of manufacturers in Dongguan were quite low. In addition, the Dongguan government adopted a relaxed policy toward social insurance coverage rates and required manufacturers to insure only a certain percentage of their employees. I carried out research on five foreign-invested manufacturers in Dongguan in 2007 and found that their coverage rates for pension insurance ranged from 10 percent to 30 percent. Furthermore, the Dongguan government allowed pension insurance to be paid separately from the other types of insurance, referred to as the "three golds."[23] Because pension insurance was the most expensive, most companies balked at paying for it on behalf of their employees (see table 4.1). Using Taiyang's social insurance expenses for 2006–7 as an example, the social insurance cost for each employee was 175.6 yuan per month, of which pension insurance was 140.4 yuan, or 80 percent of the total. Staff members who worried that they would be unable to draw pensions in that location after leaving their employment also tended to be unwilling to comply with paying the fee. Staff unwillingness to pay for pension insurance also gave the employer a pretext for not including pension insurance for staff. These factors combined to make pension insurance coverage rates relatively low.

---

23. Generally speaking, social insurance includes five types of insurance: old-age (pension), medical, occupational injury, unemployment, and maternity insurance. Dongguan did not require maternity insurance, so Taishang referred to social insurance as the "four golds." When pension insurance was omitted, this became the "three golds."

Table 4.1. Taiyang's social insurance
costs per employee in 2006–7
(yuan per month)

Type of insurance	Cost
Pension	140.4
Medical	15.6
Unemployment	11.8
Occupational injury	7.8
Total	175.6

Source: Author's analysis.

In 2011 the Chinese government implemented the Social Insurance Law along with the off-site transfer of social insurance accounts (i.e., allowing accounts to be transferred between geographical locations). The new policy has had the clear effect of increasing social insurance coverage, and off-site transfers are being carried out.

The fees enumerated in table 4.1 were not what Taiyang actually paid, but what it should have paid. Table 4.2 shows the number of staff members Taiyang employed in 1994–2009 and their social insurance participation rates. In 1994, Taiyang employed an average of 1,500 people, but the number for head tax purposes was 600, or about 40 percent of its actual staff (i.e., a discount of 60 percent). This was a very common practice at that time. My field research found that the number of people covered by social insurance "golds" was very low: just the minimum to get by. In the late 1990s, the Chinese government began relatively strict enforcement of social insurance fee collection from FIEs. Clear data from Taiyang appear first in 2005. In April of that year, Taiyang employed 2,000 people, but its pension insurance coverage rate was only 16 percent, and coverage for the other "three golds" (medical, occupational injury, and unemployment insurance) was only 33 percent. Over the next few years, increasing pressure from the central government for better social insurance coverage by FIEs resulted in enhanced enforcement by the Dongguan government. In January 2007, Taiyang employed 2,300 people, and its pension insurance coverage rate increased to 23 percent, while coverage for the other "three golds" rose to 46 percent. In the next two

Table 4.2. Number of staff members employed by Taiyang and social insurance participation rates, selected periods in 1994–2009

	Staff members	People with:		Coverage rate	
		Pension insurance	Other "three golds"	Pension insurance	Other "three golds"
1994 average	1,500	NA	NA	NA	NA
April 2005	2,000	320	660	16%	33%
January 2007	2,300	530	1,060	23%	46%
2008 average	2,400	720	2,400	30%	100%
Early 2009	1,200	360	1,200	30%	100%
2009 average	900	270	900	30%	100%

Source: Author's analysis.
Note: NA is not available.

years, the pension insurance rate rose to 30 percent, and the other "three golds" had complete coverage. Here we can see that the pension insurance coverage rate of 30 percent was the maximum limit and probably the lowest level that the local government would tolerate. We can also see that the discounting of social insurance fees saved Taiyang a great deal of money. Social insurance fees gradually increased each year, and business costs rose with them. Table 4.2 also shows another interesting numerical relationship: in several surveys before 2008 (the year that the Labor Contract Law came into effect), the ratio of coverage for pension insurance versus the other "three golds" was 1:2.[24] This indicates a tacit rule in the Dongguan area regarding social insurance coverage. After the Labor Contract Law was implemented, complete coverage of the "three golds" became imperative.

Among the "three golds," occupational injury insurance is especially worth mentioning. The very low social insurance coverage rates for migrant workers in Guangdong was an open secret. Occupational injury insurance, related to worker safety, was long subject to the phenomenon of number buying (Liu Kaiming 2004), so there was great risk if a worker who was not enrolled in social insurance was injured on the job. Taiyang's

24. Chu Yintzu (2011) has an identical finding.

risk-avoidance method was to enroll a certain percentage of its staff in occupational injury insurance (one of the "three golds") and to purchase occupational injury insurance from a commercial insurance company, just in case.

5. Closing the Factory

The global financial crisis began in 2008, and in the next year China experienced a sharp drop in overseas orders. During the 2009 export recession, Taiyang, like many other Taishang, decided to close its factory. Table 4.2 shows that the number of people employed by Taiyang reached a peak in 2007–8 and then rapidly shrank. In early 2009 there were still 1,200 staff members, but by the end of the year only a few hundred were left, and the average number of staff for that that year was only 900, less than half of the number at its peak. In 2009, Taiyang received 70 percent fewer orders than in 2008. In the first half of 2009, Ben went to the United States to observe market conditions, and after finding America a dead zone, he decided to close the factory.

1) Labor Strikes

As mentioned above, for more than ten years, Taiyang adopted numerous methods to save on costs, including shrinking the scale of the Taiwan headquarters and reducing expenses at the Hong Kong branch. In addition to the financial crisis, 2008 brought immense pressure from implementation of the Labor Contract Law. In that year, Taiyang experienced labor strikes prompted by demands for pay increases. In 2008, Dongguan's minimum monthly wage was adjusted upward from 690 yuan to 770 yuan. Taiyang's pay slips ostensibly showed a pay adjustment. However, after the deduction of certain fees, there was no actual pay increase, and this caused discontent among the workers. After a strike, Taiyang quickly compromised and agreed to the majority of the workers' demands. According to Jerry's recollection, the strike occurred suddenly, with workers occupying the national highway and obstructing traffic. The local government was very anxious and put pressure on the

Table 4.3. Taiyang's formula for calculating severance pay

Years of service	Less than 4	4–8	More than 8 and up to 12
Months of severance pay	2	4	6

Source: Author's analysis.

company. That was just when deliveries were at their peak, causing a sense of urgency in Taiyang and among local officials, "so there was no choice but to compromise." At that time, "several old Taigan went into hiding and refused to make an appearance, as if just watching the show."[25] This expression brings to mind the friction between the veteran Taigan and the company's second generation of managers. At that time, there were many labor strikes in the Dongguan and Shenzhen area, sparked by adjustment of the minimum wage and disputes concerning overtime pay.

The strike was one reason for Taiyang's decision to shut down. Yet legally closing the factory (rather than shutting down and skipping town in the middle of the night, as some other companies did) involved a great many final tasks. The greatest issue was the enormous amount of severance pay. According to the old method, length of service was capped at twelve years for calculation purposes. When the Labor Contract Law came into effect in January 2008, a new method was implemented. Calculation of monthly wages was based on each worker's take-home pay of base salary plus overtime pay. For example, if a worker had been employed at Taiyang for eighteen years, sixteen of those years were calculated under the old system, which capped the length of employment at twelve years, and two years were calculated under the new system, which allowed the worker to collect severance pay for a total of fourteen months. However, the amount of severance pay that Taiyang was willing to pay was lower than the legally stipulated amount, and "that point was subject to agreement with the staff. The agreement method was individual and not collective. If the worker accepted this severance method, she had to sign a letter of agreement to avoid future legal disputes."[26] Table 4.3 shows the formula that Taiyang used to calculate severance pay for its employees.

25. Interview: Jerry200902.
26. Interview: Jerry200909.

Taiyang thought of every way possible to reduce its amount of severance pay. First, because of the drop in orders, the company had been lowering the number of employees from the end of 2008 onward, which made things easier. Second, it decreased overtime, or made workers follow an overtime schedule of two days on followed by three days off, which reduced take-home pay and caused some staff members to resign (when they did so, they were required to sign a resignation letter). Third, the factory shut down for a long period, and employees who didn't report for work afterward were written off. The following quote vividly describes the company's tactics before shutting down the factory: "We couldn't [at this point] dismiss workers with severance pay, so we went for natural attrition. We put them on furlough and didn't add overtime at night, so that naturally decreased their pay, and may people felt they couldn't make a living and preferred to earn money elsewhere. [Furthermore,] we began enforcing our factory regulations very strictly. Before, the penalty for fighting was ninety *kuai* [yuan], but now we made [the punishment] heavier, and anyone else involved was also penalized."[27]

Many employees resigned without knowing that the factory was about to close, so when Taiyang shut down in 2010, the total amount of severance pay was only a few million yuan, instead of more than ten million originally projected.

2) Lights Out

At that time, many Hong Kong and Taiwanese manufacturers closed their factories, and many of them skipped town. A Taiwanese magazine referred to it as "the great Taishang exodus." Why run off? Jerry said it was "hard to clean up the mess," so it made more sense to "do a runner and abandon everything, which made everything easier."[28] When closing a factory, a company had to deal not only with severance pay but also with taxes (state, local, and customs) and accounts payable. In Guangdong, due to the history of the three-plus-one trading mix, writing off accounts payable used the method of "balance write-off" (*cha'e hexiao*) rather than the "full write-off" (*quan'e hexiao*) used in the Yangtze Delta region. As

27. Interview: Jerry200909.
28. Interview: Jerry200902.

a rule, the balance write-off was around 20 percent—that is, the portion used to pay the processing fee.[29] But manufacturers usually bought material within China, which spoiled the account book balance. The category of inventory was empty, and the accounts didn't hang together. All of these problems had to be dealt with when a factory was closed.[30] These problems were specific to Guangdong and were the classic institutional consequences of path dependence.

There was a fundamental reason for Taiyang's prudent handling of the closure of its factory and its decision not to act rashly and irresponsibly: Taiyang was a wholly owned factory rather than a three-in-one trading factory, and the company held a state-owned land use certificate for the land and the factory building on it. This was an enormous asset that had to be gradually disposed of. Years later, Taiyang finally sold off its rights to the land and factory and brought its business in Dongguan to a close.

Taiyang's decision to close its factory appeared sudden, but in fact it was predictable: The company came to an end under the external and internal pressures of an unfavorable macroenvironment and the second-generation managers' efforts to promote industrial upgrading (specifically, to develop domestic sales and build the company's own brand). The end of Taiyang's more than twenty years of business in China was a setback for the modernizing efforts of this family company's second generation. For the Taishang manufacturing sector, it was a warning that traditional labor-intensive export production was in a difficult transition, and for China's relations with foreign investors, it signified a crisis in Guangdong's processing trade growth model. The government-business relationship between China and foreign investors also faced a critical turning point. It was no accident that the Guangdong government encountered major obstacles in pushing its industrial upgrading policy of emptying the cage and changing birds at this stage.

The considerable overlap of the life history of Taiyang with the rise and fall of the foreign investment dominated labor-intensive EOI growth model is no coincidence. The withdrawal of Hong Kong and Taiwanese

---

29. "Balance write-off" is a concept paired with "customs spread" (see above).
30. Interview: Jerry200902.

capital reflected the transformation and reorganization of the local growth alliance over the past thirty years.

6. The Disappearance of the Head Tax and the Emergence of Social Insurance Fees

With the gradual dissolution of the labor-intensive growth alliance in the late 2000s, we see a clear sequence of institutional change involving the disappearance of the head tax and its replacement with social insurance fees.

1) The Disappearance of the Head Tax

The head tax originated with the processing fee in the processing trade process. At one point, the processing fee constituted a major form of revenue for local governments in Guangdong (especially in Shenzhen, Dongguan, and other localities in the Pearl River Delta). But with institutional change, the importance of the processing fee gradually waned, and it was replaced with social insurance fees. The institutional and structural conditions that initially gave rise to the head tax have now disappeared, been abolished, or faded away. For example, the dual-track foreign exchange system was abolished in 1994, the processing of shipped materials in Guangdong's processing trade was replaced with the processing of imported materials, and faux joint ventures and other fictive ownership arrangements in the sponsoring system were rapidly being transformed. As a result, the processing fee's contribution to local finance was greatly reduced. Yet path dependence made the disappearance of the head tax slow and gradual. In financial terms, the head tax was extrabudgetary income for local governments, and its collection mechanism reflected rent sharing among government organs. The disappearance of the head tax shows that rent-seeking behavior by local government organs became somewhat restrained, but it continued to exist in an evolved form.

Furthermore, China's social insurance system didn't start developing until the late 1990s. Under pressure from central government policies, local governments began collecting social insurance fees in 1998, and

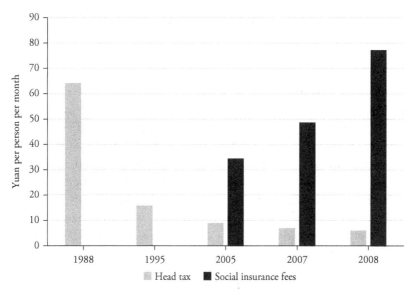

FIGURE 4.2. Taiyang's reduction in head tax and increase in social insurance fees, selected years in 1998–2008.

they began enhancing their collection efforts in the mid-2000s. With the passage of the Labor Contract Law (which took effect in 2008) and the Social Insurance Law (implemented in 2011), FIEs in the export-oriented processing trade in developed coastal regions gradually achieved 100 percent coverage rates. In this gradual process of institutionalization, we can see the emergence of social insurance fees. For manufacturers in Guangdong, social insurance fees replaced the head tax and became the largest surcharge in purchasing a labor force.

A comparison of the decline and growth of the two fees over the course of twenty years that uses Taiyang as an example verifies this trend (figure 4.2). The calculation method here uses the actual average payments. When Taiyang first established its factory in Dongguan in 1988, for each worker it hired, it had to pay its cooperative partner (Guanqiang) an average of 64.2 yuan per worker per month. In 1995, after Taiyang switched to a new cooperative partner (Nafu Village), it had to pay only 15.9 yuan, and the amount continued to decline, falling to 6.0 yuan in 2008. Conversely, the social insurance fee in 2005 averaged 34.4 yuan per worker, which was already higher than the head tax. In 2007 it was

48.6 yuan, and by 2008 it was 77.3. This fee was already greatly minimized because Taiyang enjoyed a 30 percent discount on its pension insurance payment. If the company had completely complied with the law, it would have had to pay 175.6 yuan for each worker in 2008. These costs are not adjusted for inflation. If the price index is taken into consideration, the social insurance fees that Taiyang paid in 2008 (along with a small amount of head tax) were still much lower than what it paid in head tax in 1988.

Due to pressure from the central government, enhanced legal consciousness among migrant workers, and increasingly frequent strikes, local governments in Guangdong began making a genuine effort to collect the fee for the housing provident fund. According to law, this fee was no lower than the social insurance fee. During the waves of strikes in 2014–15, one of the demands of workers was that businesses pay the social insurance fee (mainly pension insurance) and housing provident fund fee. This enormous fee caused many manufacturers to flee or close down even faster. The housing provident fund fee was calculated as 5–20 percent of the salary, and both employer and employee had to pay it. Most employers were willing to pay only an amount equivalent to 5 percent of the minimum wage. For pension insurance, companies shouldered the cost at a rate around 12 percent, and workers paid 8 percent. If a worker had been employed for ten years, the company had to retroactively pay thousands or even tens of thousands of yuan in housing provident fund and pension insurance costs on his or her behalf. That enormous fee had previously been exempted under the cooperative framework of the local growth alliance (an example of collusion). However, as soon as central government policies changed and workers began to take collective action, local governments came under pressure and demanded that companies retroactively pay in full the costs of social insurance and provident funds. The formerly harmonious relationship began to sour. Taiyang closed its factory in 2010. If it had remained in operation in recent years, it would have come under the onslaught of this wave of retroactive social insurance and provident fund payments.

2) The Emergence of Social Insurance Fees

The emergence of the social insurance fee system (including the housing provident fund) was of major significance. First, China's central government strengthened its efforts to enhance workers' wages and labor protections. Labor and social insurance legislation compelled enforcement by local governments, even if in a perfunctory manner and at a discount. Second, policy pressure for industrial upgrading, from the central government down to the local level, made local governments begin driving out industries that produced a great deal of pollution, consumed large amounts of energy, and were labor-intensive. Strictly auditing companies to make sure that they were paying social insurance fees in accordance with the law was another method that governments used. Third, workers' rights awareness and legal awareness gradually increased, which was also related to the government's labor legislation. In recent years, collective action by workers using strikes to demand wage arrears, overtime pay, social insurance fees, and provident fund payments has become increasingly both common and effective. This is partially attributable to local governments' tacit consent to labor resistance. This can clearly be seen in the case of the Yue Yuen footwear factory in Dongguan in 2014. Finally, the local alliances that were the impetus for rapid growth in labor-intensive

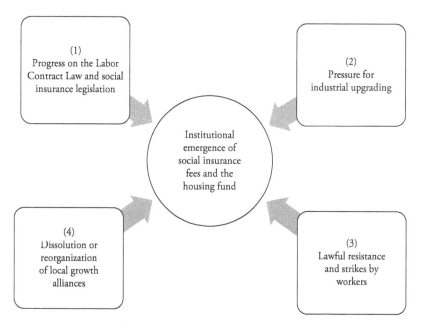

FIGURE 4.3. Institutional emergence of social insurance fees and the housing fund.

industries dissolved. The most important functions of this growth alliance from the 1980s until the 2000s were to suppress worker wages, strengthen international competitiveness through low wages, and share in the fruits of growth. With the gradual exhaustion of low-cost labor-dependent EOI, this alliance faced immense pressure to dissolve. The emergence of social insurance fees and the housing provident fund points to the historical reorganization of this alliance (see figure 4.3).

It is worth noting that institutional change always follows the characteristics of path dependence. The emergence of a social insurance system for migrant workers went through a slow formation process all over China. The operational model for businesses paying social insurance fees was initially developed based on prices negotiated between government and business, and particularistic transactions between officials and businesses played an important role in this process. Yet different regions had their own operational mechanisms. Guangdong still proceeded according to the path dependence on counting heads, discounting, and buying numbers, and collusion between local governments and businesses in this process allowed businesses to amass enormous outstanding debt on social insurance fees and housing provident fund payments. This historical debt is still being cleared.

CHAPTER FIVE

The Migrant Worker Class

Differential Citizenship, Double Exploitation,

and the Labor Regime

The migrant worker class created the most economic surplus for China during the opening reform era. China's export-oriented growth model essentially relied on exploiting rural migrant workers to achieve a high accumulation of capital and constrained the purchasing power of rural migrant workers so the state could gain enormous amounts of funds to develop infrastructure. But how did this growth and exploitation model operate on the institutional level? This chapter provides a comprehensive explanation.

China has been a country with massive domestic migration that has made rapid growth possible. After opening reform, capital accumulation relied mainly on the labor provided by migrant workers, who moved from the countryside to the cities. The state stipulated that migrant workers had the *hukou* status of peasant, but in terms of occupation they were laborers. The work sites of these migrant workers in the coastal regions were located far from their primary social groups in the inland provinces, and as a result they lived an uprooted existence. The term "uprooted" implies migration, floating, roaming, and the inability to find a stable footing from which to set down roots. In the localities where the migrants worked, they were situated at the bottom of the social structure, unmoored from their hometown social ties while also lacking protection from the local government. The institutions, organizations, and labor regimes centered on the migrant worker community all created this uprooted situation. Many migrant workers have been living for decades in the cities where they work, and their children have been born there, but they still live a nonnative existence. Migrant workers are the most important surplus producers of the labor-intensive industries, but for a long time they were excluded from the growth alliances where they lived and worked, fully experiencing what it means to be exploited.

This chapter has six sections, in which it describes how the state created the new migrant worker class, analyzes the structure of China's migrant worker class, describes the myth of low wages and overtime in the dual labor market, proposes a theory of differential citizenship and explains the logic of double exploitation, analyzes the discriminatory treatment of migrant workers under differential citizenship, and summarizes the problems of China's migrant worker labor regime.

1. The State Creates the Migrant Worker Class

Over the past forty years, China's market economy flourished, but the country would not have become the factory of the world without the enormous low-priced and docile labor force provided by the migrant worker community. Migrant workers have become the most important component of China's blue-collar working class and have made a huge contribution to the Chinese economy. However, the migrant worker class has long been excluded from local growth alliances, which prevents migrant workers from enjoying their fair share of the fruits of economic growth. In fact, the so-called miracle of China's export-oriented labor-intensive industrialization was built on the exploitation of migrant workers. The success of the Guangdong growth model—the prototype of the Chinese growth model—depends on whether or not a local growth alliance is able to ensure the supply of a large, efficient, docile, low-cost labor force. For this reason, introducing migrant workers from other provinces, organizing and managing migrant workers, suppressing wages and reducing the level of real wages, and improving the productivity of migrant workers became the core concerns of growth alliances. Because of the special qualities of China's migrant worker class, the GVC, ever in search of cheap labor, shifted to China and rapidly embedded itself in the structure and institutions of China's coastal regions, integrating China into the global capitalist production system.

1) Rural Migrant Workers Become an Official Category

How did the state create the migrant worker class? Migrant workers as a population and a social phenomenon emerged as far back as the 1950s. However, migrant workers as a class under China's special form of capitalism are a product of opening reform from the late 1970s onward.

In China's current political and economic system, the concept of the migrant worker is different from that of the worker, as defined in the classic socialist system. Migrant workers do not have the status of permanent worker, and therefore they are unable to enjoy the benefits of employees with urban *hukou*. As a special class, migrant workers are a product of the combination of post-Mao era's liberalized internal population flow and China's being integrated into globalized production. As a status, migrant workers originated in the strict household registration differentiation under the rural-urban dualism of the Mao era. Under the *hukou* system, residents of rural areas were stipulated as having an agricultural household status and were tied to the land. The state stipulated making grain the key link, so farmers were tasked with agricultural production, and for a period of time even agricultural sidelines (the handicraft industry) were strictly controlled or banned (Fei Xiaotong 1957). Industrial production was limited to urban areas, and residents of cities and towns (who lived in nonagricultural households) were mostly employees, with formal worker status. This spatial and status dichotomy between urban worker and rural farmer was an institutional marker of China's state socialism at its peak.[1]

---

1. Rural-urban dualism was seriously impacted by the Great Leap Forward. Later, there were frequent attempts to industrialize rural regions. For example, the underground factories in the Wenzhou region during the Cultural Revolution and the commune- and brigade-managed enterprises (*shedui qiye*) in the southern Jiangsu region in the late 1960s to the 1970s were developed in the 1980s into flourishing TVEs.

The concept of the rural migrant worker is self-contradictory because a rural migrant worker is both a peasant and a worker in fact but simultaneously neither a peasant nor a worker in the formal sense. After opening reform, the migration of rural migrant workers to cities and towns (or newly industrialized villages) where they did not have local *hukou* gave rise to all kinds of exploitation and control based on household status, which affected migration and employment rights, social welfare, education for their children, and access to public goods. From the perspective of capital, the special status of migrant workers lowered labor costs, including wages, overtime pay, and social insurance fees.

As a status, migrant workers initially had a dubious existence, and the term was seldom seen in early official documents. From the 1990s onward, however, *nongmingong* (rural migrant worker), *mingong* (migrant worker), and other such terms gradually became official categories and appeared frequently in government documents. Terms related to migrant worker status—such as "floating children," "left-behind children," and "left-behind elders"—also emerged. Consequently, discourse related to migrant workers was reproduced in the political and social domains. The children of migrant workers were labeled "peasants" in something like a "hereditary status system" (Chen Yingfang 2005, 131). These official categories rationalized discriminatory policies toward migrant workers by the state and capital. As a result, socioeconomic inequality was replicated through official categories (Tilly 1998).

How did the state qualify the oxymoronic term of "rural migrant worker?" In 2006, an investigative research report organized by a research organ related to the State Council stated: "'Rural migrant worker' is a special concept of China's economic and social transition period. It indicates a person whose *hukou* status is still that of a peasant and who is contracted to cultivate the land, but whose main occupation is nonagricultural, and whose main source of income is wages" (Chinese Rural Migrant Worker Issues Research Report Drafting Committee 2006).

In the same year, an important document, titled "State Council Opinions Regarding Solving the Problem of Rural Migrant Workers" included the following statement:

> Rural migrant workers are a new type of labor contingent emerging in the process of our country's opening reform and industrialization and

urbanization. Their *hukou* is still in the villages, but they mainly engage in nonagricultural industries. . . . They have become an important component of [the] industrial worker [class]. A large number of peasants have entered the cities to engage in industrial activity, or have taken jobs in township and village enterprises, and have made an enormous contribution to our country's modernization construction. . . . The phenomenon of a large number of rural migrant workers flowing between the cities and the countryside has existed in our country for a long time. . . . Gradually and conditionally the *hukou* problems of rural migrant workers living and working long-term in the cities have been solved . . . protecting the land contract rights and interests of rural migrant workers. . . . The land is not only the means of production for peasants but also ensures their livelihood.[2]

These official documents both point to a deep-seated contradiction in state policy. On the one hand, the state acknowledges both that migrant workers have contributed to economic development and that they are "a new type of labor contingent" and "have become an important component of [the] industrial worker [class]" in a period of social transition. In other words, they are working class in the modern sense. On the other hand, the state is still unwilling to grant them worker status: they still have peasant *hukou* status, retain a piece of contracted land in their native place, and shuttle back and forth between city and countryside for work over the long term. Under this state policy, migrant workers have the awkward status of being both workers and peasants, but neither industrial nor agricultural.

The state's original intention in reaffirming and protecting the rights of migrant workers to contracted land was to protect the workers and prevent them from suffering the predicament of becoming proletarian (people without property). But the assumption behind that intention was that migrant workers who left their native villages would return there after they retired, so the land became the final safeguard of their livelihood. This state policy undoubtedly contributed to capital accumulation in the initial stage of China's market economic development—that is, China

---

2. The State Council of the PRC, "Guowuyuan guanyu jiejue nongmingong wenti de ruogan yijian" (State Council Opinions Regarding Solving the Problem of Rural Migrant Workers), State Council Bulletin, January 31, 2006, http://www.gov.cn /gongbao/content/2006/content_244909.htm.

rapidly accumulated capital by exploiting migrant workers. The state formed an alliance with capital to transfer labor force reproduction costs to the native places and primary families of migrant workers. Investigative reports have shown that many migrant workers have become delanded peasants. In any case, how could a small piece of contracted land (which in some cases doesn't even exist now) ensure the retirement livelihood of second- and even third-generation migrant workers with no agricultural experience? How could such land become a social safety net during times of economic recession and unemployment? The status of migrant workers—neither industrial nor agricultural, but simultaneously both industrial and agricultural—leaves them suspended in a semiproletarian state that makes them even more exploitable by capital (Huang Te-pei 2006; Pun Ngai and Lu Huilin 2010; Selden and Wu 2011).

In addition to benefiting capital, the exploitation of migrant workers conforms to the strategy of China's rapid development and its economic growth targets. The *hukou* system plays a key role in the process. A scholar of social development in Shanghai makes the following argument:

> China's cheap labor force is mainly rural migrant workers, so if China didn't have a *hukou* system, and if rural migrant workers could enjoy all of the same remuneration as urban workers, then China would not have been able to maintain such low labor costs over the course of twenty years, and China would not have been able to build itself into the factory of the world over the past twenty years. Of course, the prerequisite for this accomplishment is: the people making the sacrifices are China's rural migrant workers, and in a certain sense, China's rural migrant workers have used their blood and sweat and their low pay to drive forward China's economic reforms over the past twenty or thirty years; and an important precondition for the rural migrant worker sweatshop system is the urban-rural dualism created by the *hukou* system. (Wei Cheng 2007, 112–13).

This argument lays bare the hard truth of China's path toward capitalist development: Rapid economic growth has relied on the merciless exploitation of migrant workers. The foundation of this exploitation is a corresponding system of differential citizenship, and the axis of this system is the *hukou* system. Under this system, migrant workers are counted as a floating population, and at the localities of their employment, they are regarded by the local government as a *wailai renkou* (a nonnative population with no local *hukou*).

2) From Unbinding the Rights of Migrant Workers to the New Urban Protectionism

Since the late 1970s, urban-rural dualism has become more flexible, and a large share of the vast rural population has left the countryside in search of employment in more developed regions. However, they do not have *hukou* in the cities where they reside. Therefore, the nonnative population is excluded from the citizenship status, rights, and social welfare system of the place to which they have migrated (Solinger 1999; Wang Fei-ling 2005). The inequality experienced by migrant workers began attracting increased attention in the late 1990s. The case of a college graduate named Sun Zhigang, who died from torture in Guangdong in 2003, shocked the nation. Subsequently, the Chinese government adopted measures such as abolishing the Custody and Repatriation Methods (an ordinance issued by the State Council)[3] and facilitating a wave of reforms to the temporary residence permit and temporary residence system (Wu Jieh-min 2010).

Beginning in the late 1990s, as the system of urban-rural dualism was relaxed, state policies related to the social and economic status of migrant workers were adjusted from harsh control of an unchecked population flow to maintenance of an orderly population flow. Tan Shen (2004) notes: "In the late 1990s, the focus of the government's work was still on 'management.' The local governments of the intake localities put the focus on local economic development and social stability, public security departments concentrated on public order and crime governance, while labor departments were devoted to 'orderly population flow' under government control; social insurance for the nonnative population was gradually channeled into the social insurance systems of the intake locations."

The state began requiring the governments of intake locations to bear a portion of the welfare provisions for the floating population, but in fact, the majority of local governments employed countermeasures to deal with these requirements. For example, many large cities designed dual- or multitrack social insurance systems and provided low-grade comprehensive insurance to rural migrant workers. This was the case with the Migrant Worker Social Insurance System in Shanghai and Chengdu (Hu Wu

---

3. The full name of the ordinance is "Custody and Repatriation Methods for Urban Vagrants and Beggars." It was issued in 1982 and repealed in August 2003.

2006) and the discounted pension insurance implemented by the governments of Kunshan and Wenzhou (Chiu Mingtze 2007; Wu Jieh-min 2017a). The strategy is in fact one of urban protectionism, involving incorporation with discrimination. Many large cities have reorganized migrant worker schools and channeled the children of those workers into public schools, but providing them with diluted resources or second-class treatment is the concrete manifestation of this policy (Lee Shang-lin 2008).

At this stage, urban housing, medical treatment, and education were all becoming greatly commercialized, and this not only affected the welfare of urban residents in general but had an even more serious impact on the survival of migrant workers, who lacked an urban status. In the early 2000s, some large cities expanded residential rights, for example through a "blue stamp" system (Liu Ying-feng 2008), a "residential permit system," and so on.[4] But it is extremely difficult for the average migrant worker to obtain such residential rights in a large city or metropolis (referred to as tier 1 or tier 2 cities), especially where the blue stamp system has been abolished. Countless migrant workers therefore continue to live with the status of nonnative population.

Since the late 2000s, some cities have annulled temporary residential permits and replaced them with a residential permit system. For example, Shenzhen began implementing such a system in 2008.[5] This is a relatively advanced policy, centered on working rights: the work units of nonnative people with stable employment can apply for residential permits on the workers' behalf, which can be used for ten years and are therefore quite convenient. However, the new system still has very strong path dependence in that the residential permit is divided into two grades: The lesser grade is called a "provisional residential permit," under which

4. The "blue stamp" is believed to have come from public security organs' use of a blue stamp for documents relating to migrant workers, as opposed to the red stamp used on other official government documents. People who possess a blue stamp *hukou* do not have the status of a temporary resident or that of a formal permanent resident of the relevant locality. Having a residence permit is similar to having a blue stamp *hukou*. Regarding the origins and evolution of China's blue stamp residential status, see Liu Ying-feng (2008).

5. An ordinance titled "Temporary Measures for Shenzhen City Residence Permit" took effect on August 1, 2008.

the rights enjoyed are effective for only six months (such permits can be renewed) and are hardly better than those under the original temporary residential permit. The crux is in the convertibility of a residential permit into the provisional residential permit. If the nonnative person loses his or her job and is unable to find new employment within sixty days and no longer meets the other requirements for a residential permit, the residential permit will be converted into a provisional residential permit.[6] The residential permit system is still a comprehensive method of control applied to the floating population, and the government uses advanced electronic technology to tie the residential permit to labor, social insurance, childbearing, and public security, thereby effectively eliminating the possibility of people who are not working and not economically viable living in the cities. Overall, the residential status designed under this system is at first glance similar to the denizenship in international immigration theory, but in fact there are still substantial differences.[7] In Shenzhen, possessing a residential permit can guarantee the right to long-term residence, but the holder is still not a genuine Shenzhen resident: becoming a permanent resident requires settling down (*luohu*). Like Shanghai and other large cities, Shenzhen has very strict vetting for settling down that involves a credit system with a high threshold. For instance, a person might meet certain standards for education, licenses, ownership of residential property, payment of social insurance fees for a certain number of years, and so on. It is quite difficult for the average blue-collar migrant worker to meet these requirements. Generally speaking, a residential permit is a relatively progressive reform of the residential system for the nonnative population, but it still eliminates the citizenship rights of migrant workers in the cities where they reside, and an ingenious and concealed binary status is still deeply embedded in the new urban citizenship rights system. Migrant workers can live in a city like Shenzhen only as second-class citizens.

Shenzhen's experiment gradually spread. In January 2010, the entire province of Guangdong launched a residential permit system, affecting

6. Within fifteen days after a nonnative person has left a job, the original work unit must report this to the government or face a penalty.

7. Regarding denizenship, see Hammar (1989).

the rights of thirty million people in the floating population.[8] The new system stipulates that the children of nonnative residents who have paid for social insurance for five years can receive the same schooling as the children of people with local *hukou*, and after seven years of residence, nonnatives can apply for a local *hukou*. In practical terms, however, nonnative residents who attempt to settle down still encounter the thresholds of the credit system and annual quotas. Beijing, Shanghai, and other large cities all use various kinds of residential permit systems. Beijing implemented a work residential permit in 2014 and has discussed using the residential permit to replace the temporary residential permit and upgrading public services for the nonnative population based on length of residence and employment.[9] Shanghai stipulates that anyone holding a residential permit for seven years can apply for settled down status, but the conditions are quite strict. One of them is that the person must have midlevel or above specialized technical skills.[10] It is hard for the average migrant worker to meet this standard.

In December 2014, China's State Council issued a document titled "Residential Permit Management Methods (Draft for Soliciting Opinions)." Article 6 stipulates that "the people's government at the county level and above shall provide holders of residential permits with basic public services and facilitated channeling into the national economy and social development plan and improve the financial transfer payment sys-

8. "Guangdong quan sheng jin qiyong juzhuzheng, 7 nian hou ke shenqing changzhu *hukou*" (All of Guangdong Province starts using residential permits, permanent *hukou* can be applied for after seven years), *Guangzhou ribao* (*Guangzhou Daily*), January 1, 2010.

9. "'Beijing gongzuo juzhuzheng' banli tiaojian ji daiyu" ("Beijing work residential permit" conditions and treatment), Wangyi, January 15, 2014, http://news.163.com/14 /0115/09/9IKCEVoOoo01124J.html; Wu Tingting, "Beijing yankong renkou guimo, juzhuzheng zhidu jiang tidai zhanzhuzheng" (Beijing strictly controls scale of population, residential permit will replace temporary residential permit), *Beijing chenbao*, January 15, 2014.

10. Paragraph 4 of article 5 of the ordinance "Ways for Holders of 'Shanghai City Residential Permit' to Apply for a Local Permanent *Hukou*" stipulates that a person must have been "evaluated and employed as a specialist technician at the middle rank or above or have professional qualifications at the level of technician (at or above the level of national second-class professional credentials) or above, and have a specialization and type of work corresponding to the employment position."

tem, and the funding required for basic public services and facilitation will be channeled into the fiscal budget."[11] Article 14 stipulates:

> The relevant ministries of the State Council, the local people's governments at all levels, and their relevant agencies shall actively create conditions allowing holders of residential permits to enjoy the same entitlements as local permanent residents to midlevel vocational education subsidies, support in obtaining employment, housing security, old-age (pension) services, social welfare benefits, social assistance, residential committee elections, selection of people's mediators, qualification of their children to take the local high school and college entrance exams, and other privileges, and in their place of residence to enjoy convenience in exchanging and renewing residential identity cards, registering marriages, etc.[12]

These stipulations are aimed at breaking down domicile management barriers and requiring local governments to prepare budgets that provide domestic migrants with social, educational, and political rights (such as participating in residents' committee elections) in their place of actual domicile. However, the more progressive recommendations in this document are still at the stage of "soliciting opinions."

In March 2014, the State Council had promulgated the "National New Urbanization Plan," which called for a hundred million rural *hukou* holders and members of the floating population to be settled in the cities in which they permanently reside by 2020. At the same time, a document titled "Opinions Regarding Further Moving Forward Reform of the Household Registration System" proposed comprehensively lifting restrictions on settlement in towns and small cities, orderly settlement in medium-size cities, and strict control on the population size of extra-large cities (Kam Wing Chan 2014). These plans affect the rights of rural migrant workers, but on close analysis, their focus is still on resolving the problem of settlement in small and medium-size cities so as to drive the

---

11. Legislative Affairs Office of the State Council, "Juzhuzheng guanli banfa gongkai zhengqiu yijian" (Residential Permit Management Methods [Draft for Soliciting Opinions]), PRC Central Government Portal, December 4, 2014, http://www.gov.cn/wenzheng/2014-12/04/content_2786681.htm.

12. Legislative Affairs Office of the State Council, "Juzhuzheng guanli banfa gongkai zhengqiu yijian."

growth of the domestic market. Solutions for the large coastal cities where many migrant workers are concentrated have yet to be proposed. In tandem with the new urbanization plan, many of the provincial cities within its scope are gradually breaking down the urban-rural dualism and promoting urbanization and are marching toward the ultimate goal of eliminating the difference between urban and rural *hukou* (Kam Wing Chan 2010b).

Long-distance transprovincial migration still makes up a large proportion of rural migration to the cities. The crucial step in China's household registration reforms is whether members of the nonnative transprovincial population will be able to obtain *hukou* in the cities where they reside. On this question, the reforms have wavered, and some policies have even become harsher. In 2015, the State Council promulgated an administrative order titled "Provisional Regulations on Residential Permits,"[13] which designates the conditions and categories of public services available to nonnative residents in their cities of domicile.

This new order continues the reforms carried out under the new urbanization mind-set by relaxing provisions for nonnative settlement in small and medium-size cities. However, for large cities (those with a population of three million or more) it establishes a settlement credit system and allows the cities to establish thresholds such as lawful stable employment, lawful stable residence, years of participation in social urban insurance, and years of continuous domicile that make it difficult for members of nonnative populations to attain their goal of permanent settlement—especially laborers with only basic skills and low levels of education.

2. The Figuration of the Migrant Worker Class

In terms of demographic structure, what are the features of the migrant worker class? Generally speaking, from the 1980s onward, the migration pattern of migrant workers went from mostly short-term and within their

---

13. This is Zhonghua Renmin Gongheguo Guowuyuan ling di 663 hao (State Council of the People's Republic of China Order No. 663), which took effect on January 1, 2016.

own province to long-term and long-distance (including transprovincial). At the same time, the southeastern coastal EOI belt attracted a large number of migrant workers from inland provinces.

1) The Flow, Distribution, and Gender Ratio of Migrant Workers

Based on China's census statistics, in 1982 the floating population numbered only 0.6 percent of China's total population, and 10.5 percent of this floating population was in the coastal regions.[14] By 1990 the floating population had increased to 1.8 percent of the total population, and the coastal regions accounted for 42.5 percent of the floating population. By 2000 the floating population stood at 11.6 percent of the total population; transprovincial flow accounted for 29.4 percent of the floating population, and 51.6 percent of it was in the coastal regions. A sample survey in 2005 showed that the floating population made up 11.5 percent of the total population; transprovincial flow accounted for 34.0 percent of the floating population; and 57.1 percent of it was in the coastal regions. According to the sixth census in 2010, China's total floating population stood at 19.6 percent of the total population; the transprovincial floating population made up 32.9 percent of the total floating population, and 52.9 percent of the transprovincial floating population had flowed into the eastern coastal regions (see table 5.1A).

14. *AUTHOR'S POSTSCRIPT*: Here floating population is defined as the population of people whose "place of domicile is not the same as the township or neighborhood of the household registration, and [who had] left the registered location for half a year or more." This statistical caliber (measurement method) is also called *renhu fenli* (separation of people's domicile from their household registration). China used a stricter definition of floating population for the seventh census, 2020: total *renhu fenli* population minus those whose domicile do not move out of the prefecture (or municipal city's district) within which they register the household. According to the seventh census, China had a total population of 1.412 billion, a *renhu fenli* population of 492.76 million, a floating population of 375.82 million, and a transprovincial floating population of 124.84 million. See National Bureau of Statistics, "Diqici quanguo renkou pucha gongbao (dierhao, diqihao)" (Seventh census bulletin [No 2, No. 7]), May 11, 2021, http://www.stats.gov.cn/tjsj/tjgb/rkpcgb/qgrkpcgb/202106/t20210628_1818821.html; http://bigs.www.gov.cn/gate/bigs/www.gov.cn/shuju/2021-05/11/content_5605791.htm. If using the most recent measurement, the proportion of floating population will be slightly smaller than the figures in Table 5.1A and Table 5.1B, but it wouldn't affect the current analysis.

Table 5.1A. China's floating population in censuses and sampling surveys, selected years, 1982–2010 (thousands of people)

	(A) Floating population	(B) Total population	(C) Floating population share of total population, or (A)/(B)	(D) Transprovincial floating population	(E) Trans-provincial population share of floating population, or (D)/(A)	(F) Trans-provincial Floating population entering coastal regions	(G) Share of transprovincial floating population entering coastal regions, or (F)/(D)	(H) Floating population of coastal regions	(I) Share of total floating population in coastal regions, or (H)/(A)
1982	6,575	1,031,883	0.6%	NA	NA	NA	NA	2,245	10.5%
1990	21,354	1,160,017	1.8%	NA	NA	NA	NA	9,083	42.5%
2000	144,391	1,242,612	11.6%	42,419	29.4%	32,114	75.7%	74,446	51.6%
2005	NA	NA	11.5%	NA	34.0%	NA	82.4%	NA	57.1%
2010	260,938	1,332,811	19.6%	85,876	32.9%	68,136	79.3%	137,983	52.9%

Source: The data were calculated from: (1) the third census, in 1982 ("Household registration of permanent residents," National Bureau of Statistics of the People's Republic of China [1990, 45]); (2) the fourth census, in 1990 ("Household registration of resident population," National Bureau of Statistics of the People's Republic of China [1990, 65]); (3) State Council data from the fifth census, in 2000 (http://www.stats.gov.cn/tjsj/pcsj/rkpc/5rp/index.htm); (4) the State Council's 2005 sampling survey of 1.31 percent of the population (http://www.stats.gov.cn/tjsj/ndsj/renkou/2005/renkou.htm); and (5) the State Council's sixth census, in 2010 (http://www.stats.gov.cn/tjsj/pcsj/rkpc/6rp/lefre.htm).

Note: NA is not available.

The geographical distribution and employment sectors of migrant workers are roughly apparent in another official survey. According to this survey, the transprovincial portion of the floating population reached 51 percent in 2005. This figure is different from the data from the population sampling of the same year, but it is still a worthwhile reference: Eighty-two percent of the entire transprovincial floating population was in the eastern coastal regions (four provinces and three municipalities under the direct jurisdiction of the central government), and more than 60 percent of these people were in large cities. The main employment sectors of migrant workers were manufacturing (30.3 percent), construction (22.9 percent), services (10.4 percent), restaurants and hotels (6.7 percent), and the wholesale and retail sector (4.6 percent) (Chinese Rural Migrant Worker Issues Research Report Drafting Committee 2006). Manufacturing accounted for nearly one-third of the workers in these sectors, which shows the contribution that migrant workers made to China's rapid industrial growth.

From the above data we can observe several trends. First, although the scale of the floating population was still quite small and the proportion of workers in the transprovincial flow was modest until 1990, the coastal regions drew a large proportion of migrant workers before that year. Second, from 1990 onward, the trend toward transprovincial migration from the inland provinces to the coast continued to grow, with the proportion hitting a peak around 2005 (Fan 2005). Third, the 2010 census data show that the floating population had increased substantially in the previous ten years, and the transprovincial floating population had doubled. The transprovincial population's proportion of the whole floating population (32.9 percent) was slightly lower than in the 2005 sampling survey, which shows that a large portion of the floating population moved within provinces. Therefore, although the floating population entering the coastal regions reached 138 million, which was an increase of 185 percent (nearly double) over 2000, the percentage of the entire floating population located in the coastal areas was 52.9 percent, which was 4.2 percent lower than in 2005. This set of figures shows that the flow of the floating population from the inland provinces to the coastal regions was easing by the end of the 2000s.

What about the gender ratio in China's floating population? According to the 2000 census, the country's total floating population was 144.39

million, of which men made up 75.92 million, or 52.6 percent, and women made up 68.47 million, or 47.4 percent. In the 2010 census, the floating population had increased to 261 million, of which men made up 137 million, or 52.5 percent, and women made up 124 million or 47.5 percent (table 5.1B). In ten years, the floating population had increased by 80 percent, but the gender ratio remained nearly constant. From these

Table 5.1B. Gender ratio of China's floating population in the 2000 and 2010 census (thousands of people)

		2000 census		2010 census	
		Number	*%*	*Number*	*%*
China		144,391	100.0	260,938	100.0
	Male	75,920	52.6	136,975	52.5
	Female	68,471	47.4	123,963	47.5
Beijing		4,638	100.0	10,499	100.0
	Male	2,552	55.0	5,532	52.7
	Female	2,085	45.0	4,966	47.3
Shanghai		5,385	100.0	12,685	100.0
	Male	2,888	53.6	6,684	52.7
	Female	2,496	46.4	6,001	47.3
Jiangsu		9,100	100.0	18,227	100.0
	Male	4,721	51.9	9,581	52.6
	Female	4,379	48.1	8,646	47.4
Zhejiang		8,599	100.0	19,901	100.0
	Male	4,564	53.1	10,631	53.4
	Female	4,034	46.9	9,270	46.6
Fujian		5,911	100.0	11,075	100.0
	Male	3,177	53.7	5,909	53.4
	Female	2,735	46.3	5,166	46.6
Guangdong		25,304	100.0	36,807	100.0
	Male	12,683	50.1	19,940	54.2
	Female	12,622	49.9	16,867	45.8

Source: The data were calculated from (1) State Council data from the fifth census, 2000 (http://www.stats.gov.cn/tjsj/pcsj/rkpc/5rp/index.htm); and (2) the State Council's sixth census, 2010 (http://www.stats.gov.cn/tjsj/pcsj/rkpc/6rp/lefte.htm).

data we know that China's female floating population made up nearly one-half of the total, which also shows their importance in the labor force. A look at the situation in the six key highly industrialized provinces and cities of the coastal regions shows that apart from Guangdong, the gender ratio there was very close to the national ratio.

In Guangdong in 2000, men made up 50.1 percent of the floating population (which is 2.5 percent lower than the national average), and women made up 49.9 percent (which is 2.5 percent higher than the national average). What is interesting is that by the time of the 2010 census, men made up 54.2 percent of Guangdong's floating population (1.7 percent higher than the national average), and women made up 45.8% percent (1.7 percent lower than the national average). This reversal in the shares of the male and female floating populations brought Guangdong closer to the average for the coastal regions.

The 2000 census shows that the transprovincial floating population made up 29.4 percent of the entire floating population. Guangdong Province absorbed 25.3 million people, or 17.5 percent of the entire floating population. Furthermore, Guangdong had a transprovincial floating population of 15.1 million, or 35.5 percent of China's total transprovincial floating population. This set of data proves that when the labor-intensive processing trade industry was at its peak, Guangdong absorbed the largest share of the country's floating population, providing the export sector and FIEs with plentiful labor. Women accounted for 7.7 million, or 51.5 percent, of this transprovincial floating population. Guangdong's female proportion of this population was 5.7 percent higher than that for the entire country, which further shows the importance of the female migrant workforce in the Guangdong model.

By the time of the 2010 census, the transprovincial floating population made up 32.9 percent of the total floating population. Guangdong accounted for 36.81 million of these people, an increase of 11.50 million in the previous ten years, but its proportion of the total dropped from 17.5 percent to 14.1 percent. Guangdong's 21.49 million members of the transprovincial floating population represented an increase of 6.43 million from ten years before, but the proportion dropped to 25 percent. This shows that although Guangdong remained a major destination for the transprovincial floating population, the comparative attractiveness of other coastal regions had greatly increased.

Finally, let's look again at changes in the gender structure. In 2010, Guangdong's transprovincial floating population included 9.53 million women. Although this was an increase of 1.83 million over the decade before, the proportion dropped to 44.3 percent, a decrease of 6.8 percent during the decade that brought the share close to the national average. This might indicate that changes in Guangdong's industrial structure had resulted in a lower proportion of labor-intensive traditional industries, which decreased the demand for female laborers.

2) Migrant Workers' Heavy Concentration in the Southeastern Coastal Region

The southeastern coastal region is China's export processing base and the area with the heaviest concentration of Taishang. It therefore goes without saying that the migrant workers who have flowed into this region have been important to China's industrial growth and to the labor supply of Taiwanese-invested companies. Table 5.2A shows that in 2008, the nonnative population made up an enormous proportion of the resident population of the southeastern coastal region and occupied an important position in the local labor force. Beijing's proportion of nonnatives in the total population was 41 percent, and Shanghai's was 31 percent; the respective ratios of nonnatives to local urban-work-unit employed population were 1.21 and 1.55. This ratio is mainly used to compare the share of the local workforce made up of nonnatives in the various provinces and municipalities. In Guangdong, nonnatives accounted for 25 percent of the total population, and the ratio of nonnatives employed in urban work units was 2.36. The figures for Jiangsu, Zhejiang, and Fujian are relatively low, but these provinces, along with Guangdong, have relatively large agricultural belts and agricultural populations, while their nonnative populations are concentrated in the urbanized industrial zones. For example, the ratio of nonnative residents in Shenzhen, Dongguan, Guangzhou, and other cities in Guangdong Province was very high. Table 5.2B shows that the nonnative populations of various cities had increased significantly across the board in 2013, both in absolute numbers and proportionately. In terms of the ratio of nonnatives to local urban-work-unit employed population, Shanghai, Zhejiang, and Fujian experienced significant increases, while the ratios dropped in Jiangsu and Guangdong.

Table 5.2A. Ratio of nonnatives to natives in the local urban-work-unit employed population, 2008 (thousands of people)

	(A) Population	(B) Urban employed population	(C) Estimated nonnative population	Nonnative share of total population, or (C)/(A)	Ratio of nonnative population to the local urban-work-unit employed population, or (C)/(B)
Beijing	16,950	5,703	6,883	41%	1.21
Shanghai	18,800	3,772	5,844	31%	1.55
Jiangsu	76,770	7,076	8,267	11%	1.17
Zhejiang	51,200	7,412	8,437	16%	1.14
Fujian	35,350	4,587	5,643	16%	1.23
Guangdong	95,440	10,079	23,833	25%	2.36

Source: Calculated from National Bureau of Statistics of the People's Republic of China (2009).

Table 5.2B. Ratio of nonnatives to natives in the local urban-work-unit employed population, 2013 (thousands of people)

	(A) Population	(B) Urban employed population	(C) Estimated nonnative population	Nonnative share of total population, or (C)/(A)	Ratio of nonnative population to the local urban-work-unit employed population, or (C)/(B)
Beijing	21,148	7,423	11,154	53%	1.50
Shanghai	24,152	6,188	14,523	60%	2.35
Jiangsu	79,395	15,033	14,305	18%	0.95
Zhejiang	54,980	10,716	22,173	40%	2.07
Fujian	37,710	6,440	13,794	37%	2.14
Guangdong	106,440	19,670	36,428	34%	1.85

Source: Calculated from National Bureau of Statistics of the People's Republic of China (2014).

Table 5.3. Proportion of nonnative residents in Shenzhen and Dongguan, 2005–13 (tens of thousands of people)

	Shenzhen		Dongguan	
	Long-term residents	Share of long-term residents with no local hukou	Long-term residents	Share of long-term residents with no local hukou
2005	827.8	78.0%	656.1	74.8%
2006	871.1	77.4%	674.9	75.1%
2007	912.4	76.7%	694.7	75.3%
2008	954.3	76.1%	695.0	74.8%
2009	995.0	75.7%	786.1	77.3%
2010	1,037.2	75.8%	822.5	77.9%
2011	1,046.7	74.4%	825.5	77.6%
2012	1,054.7	72.7%	829.2	77.4%
2013	1,062.9	70.8%	831.7	77.3%

Source: Shenzhen Municipal Statistics Bureau (2014), Dongguan Municipal Statistics Bureau (2014).

The migrant worker flow was largely concentrated in the coastal regions, and Guangdong's Pearl River Delta region attracted migrant workers the earliest, and in the greatest concentration. Table 5.3 shows the proportion of the nonnative population in Shenzhen and Dongguan, the most important processing trade cities of the region. Because China's officially published statistical data are often adjusted in terms of statistical caliber, in recent years many statistical yearbooks have not included statistics on the nonnative population. Furthermore, the statistical calibers and items vary from place to place, which creates difficulties for making comparisons. Using Shenzhen and Dongguan as examples, it is impossible to obtain successive longitudinal data on temporary residents or the nonnative population, so it is possible only to estimate the share of the nonnative population from the category of proportion of long-term residents (*changzhu renkou*) with no local *hukou* (i.e., people residing there for six months or more), and data allowing relatively systematic comparisons can be calculated only from 2005 onward. We can observe that the proportion of the nonnative population in the two cities is very high. Shenzhen reached 78.0 percent in 2005. Although that proportion subsequently declined, the decrease has been very small, and the percentage remained as high as 70.8 percent in 2013. The proportion in Dongguan was 74.8 percent in 2005 and rose gradually after that, reaching a peak of 77.9 percent in 2010 and falling only slightly to 77.3 percent in 2013. It should be noted that this is probably an underestimate of the nonnative population, because these statistics don't include nonnative residents living in those cities for less than six months. These figures show that the scale of the nonnative population has decreased in recent years, which is related to adjustments to the industrial structure of the Pearl River Delta: industrial upgrading has put pressure on labor-intensive manufacturing to move inland or overseas, leading to a reduction in the number of migrant workers. Even so, the nonnative population still constitutes the majority of the local population, and the continued reluctance of local governments to grant them permanent resident status is colored by regional protectionism (as I show in detail below).

3) FIEs Employ Large Numbers of Migrant Workers

Next I analyze the proportion of the Chinese workforce employed by FIEs. Tables 5.4A and 5.4B show the shares of the urban industrial workforce occupied by different ownership sectors (publicly and privately owned enterprises and FIEs). On a nationwide basis, in 2006, privately owned enterprises accounted for 23.4 percent of the urban workforce, and FIEs for 25.1 percent; the two combined employed up nearly half of the workforce. In the coastal industrial provinces and cities that were strategic locations for export processing, apart from Beijing, private companies and FIEs had the greatest share and mainly hired migrant workers. In Guangdong, FIEs employed 7.81 million workers, or 63.3 percent of all urban industrial employees. For Taiwanese-owned companies, even more important is that because Taishang manufacturers made up a large share of FIEs, they also hired a large proportion of migrant workers. For example, Guangdong's companies owned by Taiwan, Hong Kong, or Macau organizations made up 68.5 percent of the workforce hired by FIEs, and the shares were 60.2 percent in Fujian, 47.7 percent in Zhejiang, and 36.1 percent in Jiangsu. Since migrant workers make up such a large

Table 5.4A. Number of workers employed in China's urban industries by ownership category, 2006 (thousands of people).

	Publicly owned enterprises		Privately owned enterprises		FIEs		Taiwan-, HK-, and Macau-owned companies as share of FIEs	Total workers employed
China	43,499	(51.5%)	19,710	(23.4%)	21,181	(25.1%)	48.7%	84,390
Beijing	1,035	(67.9%)	149	(9.8%)	341	(22.4%)	25.8%	1,525
Shanghai	1,075	(34.8%)	554	(17.9%)	1,464	(47.3%)	27.8%	3,093
Jiangsu	2,481	(30.4%)	2,768	(33.9%)	2,922	(35.8%)	36.1%	8,171
Zhejiang	2,094	(28.1%)	3,470	(46.5%)	1,892	(25.4%)	47.7%	7,456
Fujian	758	(22.3%)	755	(22.2%)	1,882	(55.4%)	60.2%	3,395
Guangdong	2,366	(19.2%)	2,157	(17.5%)	7,810	(63.3%)	68.5%	12,333

Source: Author's calculations from data in National Bureau of Statistics Industrial and Transportation Statistics Division (2007).

Note: Numbers in parentheses are the shares of total workers employed. HK is Hong Kong.

Table 5.4B. Number of workers employed in China's urban industries by ownership category, 2011 (thousands of people)

	Publicly owned enterprises		Privately owned enterprises		FIEs		Taiwan-, HK-, and Macau-owned companies as share of FIEs	Total workers employed
China	47,518	(46.2%)	29,564	(28.8%)	25,741	(25.0%)	46.8%	102,823
Beijing	1,085	(67.2%)	138	(8.5%)	393	(24.3%)	24.8%	1,616
Shanghai	913	(29.7%)	551	(17.9%)	1,610	(52.4%)	27.7%	3,075
Jiangsu	2,433	(21.5%)	4,339	(33.9%)	4,550	(40.2%)	35.7%	11,322
Zhejiang	1,767	(23.9%)	3,595	(48.7%)	2,024	(27.4%)	48.9%	7,386
Fujian	948	(22.7%)	1,270	(30.5%)	1,949	(46.8%)	61.7%	4,167
Guangdong	3,499	(23.5%)	2,864	(19.3%)	8,512	(57.2%)	61.8%	14,875

Source: Author's calculations from data in National Bureau of Statistics Industrial and Transportation Statistics Division (2012).

Note: Numbers in parentheses are the shares of total workers employed. HK is Hong Kong.

proportion of the manufacturing workforce, the supply of migrant workers to Taishang enterprises and the effect of wage levels on the competitiveness of Taishang exports affected the interests of Taishang. For example, in 2004 and 2005, when the labor shortage in the coastal areas led to discussions of a migrant worker famine, the Taishang community followed the issue with great interest. After the Spring Festival in 2010, the coastal areas experienced a second migrant worker famine. These two labor shortages were related to the Chinese government's new agricultural policy and rising wages in the western provinces (Chen Huirong 2006; Li Boping and Tian Yanping 2011). Analyzing the second migrant worker famine involves arguing about whether China's labor supply is already facing the Lewis turning point (Hamlin 2010; Zhang Xiaobo, Jin Yang, and Shenglin Wang 2010). Kam Wing Chan (2010a) believes that factors such as the obstruction of internal migration created by the *hukou* system, the preference for hiring young workers in labor-intensive industries, and cyclical fluctuations in the international economy might be even more critical than the Lewis turning point in creating shortages of migrant workers.

Table 5.4B shows the labor force distribution in various cities in 2011, which allows us to observe changes since 2006. The number of workers employed in China's urban industries rose from more than 84 million to more than 103 million. The share of workers employed by publicly owned enterprises dropped from 51.5 percent to 46.2 percent; the share employed by privately owned companies rose from 23.4 percent to 28.8 percent; and the share employed by FIEs remained largely unchanged, falling from 25.1 percent only to 25.0 percent. But the total share of FIEs made up of Taiwan-, Hong Kong–, or Macau-owned companies dropped slightly, from 48.7 percent to 46.8 percent. The decrease in Guangdong was greatest, from 68.5 percent to 61.8 percent. This declining trend reflects the effect of the global financial crisis on Guangdong's export processing sector, as well as some of the results of industrial upgrading. Although the importance of Taiwanese investment declined slightly, it retained a key position in Guangdong's manufacturing sector. It is worth contrasting these changes with those in the share of workers employed by Guangdong's publicly owned enterprises, which did not drop but increased from 19.2 percent to 23.5 percent. To a certain extent, this reflects the expansion of Guangdong's SOEs in the industrial sector.

3. The Dual Labor Market: The Myth of Low Wages and Overtime

Salaries and working hours are the core of the migrant worker's daily working experience. Following opening reform, China's capitalist development model produced a dual labor market: differences between the labor force sectors of permanent employees and migrant workers became extremely prominent, and the salary gap between the two was enormous.

1) Wages and Working Hours

The minimum wage system became the keystone of the migrant worker labor market in practice. The Chinese government set the standard minimum wage, which was originally meant to serve as the base for ensuring workers' incomes. However, in practice, it became the ceiling for starting salaries for migrant workers, with businesses treating it as the workers' base pay. Usually, businesses hiring migrant workers would take the minimum wage as a starting salary and use it to calculate daily and hourly wages. As a rule, the monthly take-home pay of migrant workers, without taking overtime into account, was calculated based on the 21.75 working days per month stipulated by China's Ministry of Human Resources and Social Security.[15]

Chapter 2 discussed how the average urban-work-unit employee wage was two to three times higher than the minimum wage set for a migrant worker (see table 2.3). The difference between the average wage for

---

15. Before 2008 there were two methods of calculating the number of working days per month: basing the calculation on the officially published 20.92 working days per month and basing it on 26.00 working days per month (the typical method, according to my field interviews). The second method relied on chapter 4, article 38, of the Labor Law (enacted in 1994 and effective in 1995), which states that "the employing unit shall guarantee that its employees have at least one day off in a week." After 2008, the Ministry of Human Resources and Social Security announced that salaries should be calculated based on 21.75 working days per month, using this calculation method: (365–104 [days off]) / 12 = 21.75.

Table 5.5A. Minimum wage and the average wage of urban employed staff, 2008 (yuan per month)

	Urban employed staff wage	Minimum wage	Wage gap	Urban employed staff wage as a multiple of the minimum wage
China (national average)	2,408	NA	NA	NA
Beijing	4,654	800	3,854	5.8
Shanghai	4,344	960	3,384	4.5
Jiangsu	2,608	590–850	1,758–2,018	3.1–4.4
Zhejiang	2,802	690–960	1,842–2,112	2.9–4.1
Fujian	2,130	480–750	1,380–1,650	2.8–4.4
Guangdong	2,774	530–860	1,914–2,244	3.2–5.2
Shenzhen	3,700	900–1000	2,700–2,800	3.7–4.1

Source: The data were calculated from National Bureau of Statistics Population and Employment Statistics Division (2013, table 1–28) and Shenzhen Municipal Statistics Bureau (2009, table 13–5).

Notes: Minimum wages are based on data published by local governments and local departments of human resources and social security. Jiangsu and Fujian did not adjust their minimum wages in 2008, so the data for them use 2007 minimum wages. NA is not available.

urban employed staff members (on-the-job employees)[16] and the migrant worker's minimum wage was even greater. Table 5.5A shows that in 2008, the minimum wage in six coastal provinces and municipalities ranged from 480–750 yuan (Fujian Province) to 900–1,000 yuan (Shenzhen, in Guangdong Province). In the same year, an urban employee's wage ranged from 2,130 yuan (Fujian Province) to 4,654 yuan (Beijing). The wage gap between these two labor markets ranged from 2.8 times (Fujian) to 5.8 times (Beijing). Table 5.5B shows the situation in 2012. The wage differentials have not changed much: they grew slightly in Zhejiang

16. The employees used to calculate the average urban employed staff wage are on-the-job employees (*zaigang zhigong*). Not included are employees who have left the work unit but retain their labor relations (*laodong guanxi*) with the work unit or workers hired through labor dispatch (the practice of hiring workers through third-party employment agencies) (National Bureau of Statistics of the People's Republic of China 2017, 12).

Table 5.5B. Minimum wage and the average wage of urban employed staff, 2012 (yuan per month)

	Urban employed staff wage	Minimum wage	Wage gap	Urban employed staff wage as a multiple of the minimum wage
China (national average)	3,897	NA	NA	NA
Beijing	7,062	1,260	5,802	5.6
Shanghai	6,556	1,450	5,106	4.5
Jiangsu	4,220	950–1,320	2,900–3,270	3.2–4.4
Zhejiang	4,183	950–1,310	2,873–3,233	3.2–4.4
Fujian	3,710	830–1,200	2,510–2,880	3.1–4.5
Guangdong	4,190	850–1,300	2,890–3,340	3.2–4.9
Shenzhen	4,963	1,500	3,463	3.3

Source: The data were calculated from National Bureau of Statistics Population and Employment Statistics Division (2013, table 1–28) and Shenzhen Municipal Statistics Bureau (2009, table 14–6).

Notes: Minimum wages are based on data published by local governments and local departments of human resources and social security. Zhejiang and Guangdong did not adjust their minimum wages in 2012, so the data for them use 2011 minimum wages. NA is not available.

and shrank in Shenzhen. Shenzhen also unified the separate minimum wages for inside and outside of the SEZ into a single wage, as was the case in Beijing and Shanghai.

Given their rather meager minimum wage, migrant workers might find it difficult to support a family. As a result, they rely on large amounts of overtime work to boost their take-home pay. China's statutory working hour policy is quite strict: statutory working hours are eight hours per day; average working hours per week cannot exceed forty-four hours; and overtime is limited to three hours per day and thirty-six hours per month. Overtime pay is calculated as 1.5 times the minimum wage on weekdays, 2.0 times the minimum wage on weekends (Saturday and Sunday), and 3.0 times the minimum wage on holidays.

It is evident that someone working only the statutory working hours and drawing the minimum wage would earn very little. Working overtime to earn money was forced self-exploitation, but in fieldwork surveys, my research team and I often found that the business owners said that workers voluntarily work overtime, vie for it, and demand it. This paradoxical phenomenon is because workers had no way to increase their earnings if they didn't work overtime. As a result, China's ostensibly quite progressive policy for working hours ingeniously conceals the true face of exploitation. In reality, the minimum wage is painstakingly minimized so that excessive overtime becomes necessary.

2) Excessive Overtime: Collusion between Capital and Government

In China's processing trade industry, excessive overtime is normal and results from the collusion of capital and government. To a certain extent, workers also tacitly approve of the game rules of excessive overtime. In 2004 my research team and I interviewed the deputy manager of a Taiwanese-owned wooden furniture factory. When we began talking about the requirements of corporate social responsibility, we immediately touched on the sensitive subject of overtime. The interview included the following questions and answers:

Q (the author and research team): What is the relationship between you [Taiwanese-owned factory] and them [international buyers]?

A (deputy manager): When they're preparing to place an order with us to manufacture, he [the buyer] will come to the factory first. . . . Some of the problems he lists are where we don't meet his standards. . . . For example, on overtime hours, he requires us to comply with the stipulations in China's Labor Law. . . .

Q: So if you don't comply, do you tell him that honestly?

A: Right, that's an area where we have to put effort into improving. Of course, we hope to comply in all areas of China's labor regulations.

Q: If Coca Cola (the international buyer) doesn't require it, do you have leeway to do things that don't comply with the local labor regulations?

A: In fact, as far as the local labor bureau is concerned, they turn a blind eye, but in terms of the development of our company, of course we don't hope for that. We'll adjust our working conditions as much as possible to comply with the labor regulations. But sometimes there will be differences between peak season and low season, and to get orders out on time, sometimes we arrange a little more overtime, in consultation with the workers.

Q: How do you consult the workers?

A: Our statutory overtime cannot exceed forty-four hours per month,[17] so before we add overtime, we'll notify the workers. According to the stipulations in China's Labor Law, one rest day is required in every seven days, and we will also adopt a system of rotating days off.

Q: The wages portion—can you tell us a little about that?

A: On our side the current wage system is calculated using the daily salary method. The wage portion is approximately the average wage of each worker, and for a newcomer it's around eighteen *kuai* (yuan). That doesn't include other benefits: it's his direct wages.

Q: What are the other benefits?

A: For example, housing is free . . . the company has to pay 40 percent of the cost of meals, and then the company has a lot of other benefit activities and systems, like distributing work uniforms, which they don't have to pay anything for.

Q: If one day is eighteen *kuai*, that's only five hundred *kuai* per month.

A: Then you add overtime. Right now, the average monthly salary is around 1,050 *kuai* per month.

Q: In Dongguan, is the pay in the furniture industry high or low?

A: It's lower-middle. Most [workers] rely on overtime.

Q: In the average wood item or furniture factory, do Taishang in Dongguan generally implement a daily wage system?

A: The vast majority do.

Q: You said before that according to government regulations, overtime pay can't exceed forty-four hours per month. But do you actually exceed it when you're rushing an order?

A: It's possible, it's possible. But that has to be discussed with the workers. But generally, the workers also hope to earn a little more overtime pay, so they're happy to cooperate. . . . [Mr. Hsu, a manager at another Taiwanese-owned furniture factory, interjected:] Another thing is that in mainland regulations, very similar to Taiwan, there's what's called a "flexible synthesized work hours system." During slack periods, your regulations have to be adjusted from the peak periods. . . . The flexible work hours system means, for example, you can't exceed thirty-six hours of overtime in one month, but you can apply

17. This should be thirty-six hours.

for forty-four hours. It's possible that this month you'll definitely surpass it, but you go through the workers, inform them to get their agreement, and then it doesn't matter; we go to city hall and apply for what's called a flexible work hour system. That means you calculate your peak time hours, so for example during the peak period in September, you went over by a total of twenty-five hours, then it's very possible that in [a] low-season month there's no overtime at all, because there are no orders and there's time off. So if you average it over the entire year, it won't exceed thirty-six hours.

Q: Of the foreign buyers' CSR [corporate social responsibility] requirements, which are the biggest headache[s] and most troublesome for you?

A: The biggest problem is that they require us to fully comply with China's Labor Law stipulations, and on this point the companies here find it very hard to manage completely, because it will increase your costs a lot.

Q: Have you calculated how much more it would cost?

A: We haven't calculated it in detail, but if your overtime pay complies completely with the Labor Law provisions, it would probably increase wages by 60 percent or even more.

Q: You just talked about overtime pay. What else do you find very difficult?

A: Overtime hours, overtime pay—those are the main things. The other things—like worker benefits, work site safety, fire regulations, human rights, and things like that—we find very easy to put up with.[18]

We can sum up the above interview in a few points. First, wages make up the largest share of direct costs in labor-intensive manufacturing, so maintaining low wages is the area that the manufacturer cares most about and is least able to compromise on. Compared with low wages, the benefits and subsidies that manufacturers provide to workers are just spare change.

Second, although international buyers demand that manufacturers comply with China's labor laws and regulations, these demands are mainly for the buyer's protection to cope with pressure from the international consumers' movement. As long as the manufacturer can pull out a document saying that he's complying with regulations and the manufacturer can get a green light from the local government, that will pass muster with the buyer.

18. Interview: XFL200410.

Third, local governments "turn a blind eye" in their enforcement of labor regulations. They effectively allow manufacturers to impose excessive overtime by approving a "flexible work hours system" and by being flexible in executing policy. But local governments cannot guarantee that they will adopt flexible policies forever. If central policies fluctuate or macroscopic conditions change, they might end their flexible concessions and demand repayment of unpaid overtime. For this reason, Taishang who were able to take advantage for a time and became used to flexible work hours and accumulated considerable historical debt became ticking time bombs, and if they were reported and the local government decided to investigate, the manufacturer would face a crisis.

This is where the self-protective measures of local officials come in. The manager of the wooden furniture factory said, "Of course, we hope to comply in all areas of China's labor regulations." "Of course, we hope" is the secret of the story. In fact, it was impossible to abide by the law completely, and Chinese officials knew this. However, they didn't set things in stone or reveal secrets, and by allowing a gray area to exist, they facilitated capital's squeeze on the workforce as well as their own rent-seeking space (gray income). Hsu, the manager who interjected his comment into the interview above, later explained to us:

> Regarding the Labor Bureau, you see this example, the furniture factory, shows the attitude of mainland officials, how they protect themselves, how their thinking isn't much like ours. The officials know very well that a lot of factories can't manage the legal working hours and go into excessive overtime and extra shifts, but they say: "You should abide by the law, you shouldn't impose excessive overtime. If no one reports you, I assume you don't have any problems. But if you're reported, I'll make trouble for you, and I may need to close down your factory." On tax reductions, how would I dare promise you anything against the Constitution? I'm just a bureau head. How would I dare stick my neck out? Even Wen Jiabao[19] wouldn't dare say that if you pay 60 percent of your taxes it's all right, you don't have to pay 100 percent. No one's going to actually say that. But he'll say, "I believe that what you're reporting is true," and this sentence is very artful. [It means:] "But if someone reports you, or if someone inside your organization

---

19. *Translator's Note*: Premier of China from 2003 to 2013.

reports you, it's your problem, not my problem. It's you who wasn't honest and didn't abide by the law." Among Dongguan's five or six thousand Taishang, merely a handful follow the law on overtime. It forces us to sometimes go against our conscience and write some false numbers that don't show overtime. You examine yourself. Self-examination is prevalent on the mainland. You examine yourself over whether you've evaded taxes. The officials ask you to write in the amount you've evaded. That's a skill.[20]

The collusion between local officials and manufacturers regarding overtime and extra shifts is not written in black and white but is a tacit agreement and an operational skill. Both sides understand that overtime, and relatively high overtime wages, are an inducement that stimulates the willingness of workers to work. And when factory owners calculate costs, they include overtime pay in the calculation. This cost formula is pervasive at the management level of Taiwanese-owned factories in China's coastal regions.[21]

From our interviews with migrant workers, my research team and I can also verify that excessive overtime and extra shifts are widespread phenomena. A factory section head responsible for arranging work shifts in Taiyang's Dongguan factory told us in 2005: "Our factory has one rest day per week, and overtime is until around 8:00. Occasionally we have an overtime shift on Sunday, and also overtime until 10:00 at night. The time that exceeds what's in the Labor Law is also considered overtime pay. According to the Labor Law, none of the factories can adhere to overtime regulations, apart from their management staff."[22]

Another Taiyang employee had a son working at another factory in Dongguan. In 2007 the employee told me: "My son's salary is around 1,000 *kuai*; his factory is quite small, around one thousand people. It's run by people from Hong Kong. The pay is lower than at Taiyang, and there's no social insurance. Payday isn't at a set time; sometimes when the capital turnover isn't good, the time for workers to collect their salaries is delayed. There's also more overtime, sometimes lasting all night."[23]

20. Interview: XZS200410.
21. Interviews: ZJC200701 and ZJQ200707.
22. Interview: TY_Zhu200504.
23. Interview: TY_Cheng200701.

Here, the 1,000 yuan salary includes overtime: in 2007, the minimum monthly wage in Dongguan was 690 yuan. From these two interviews we can see that excessive overtime and extra shifts were very common at that time, and that workers also knew that their overtime hours exceeded the stipulations in the Labor Law.

3) The Foxconn Incident and the Overtime Myth

Foxconn is a very large Taishang enterprise engaged in the manufacture of computer and cell-phone components. It's part of the ICT industry, and at one time it employed a million workers in the Shenzhen area. The ICT industry is generally classified as a high-tech industry, but in fact, Foxconn's labor patterns qualify as labor-intensive, and its labor intensity is actually even higher than that of some traditional industries.

Let's first look at the situation my research team and I observed in our fieldwork in Guangdong. It was very common for workers to put in ninety to one hundred hours of overtime per month, and sometimes even more. Although this amount of overtime was clearly illegal, the businesses and the workers had a tacit agreement. For example, at F Factory in Shenzhen in the first half of 2010,[24] the minimum wage of an ordinary worker (a production line operator) was only 950 yuan per month. However, if he or she worked ninety-eight hours of overtime (sixty-six hours on normal workdays and thirty-two hours on weekends), the take-home pay was around 1,840 yuan. For the workers, the base pay was almost the same as the overtime pay. No wonder that in my team's field interviews, managers often said: "Mainland workers love to work overtime. If you don't let them work overtime, they'll be really unhappy!" These words imply that the employer has no choice, but what sounds true is false. It's only because workers are paid so little that they are eager to work overtime. If their base pay was a living wage, there would certainly be much less demand to work overtime.

Another field survey drew these words from a Foxconn worker: "Excessive overtime is Foxconn's greatest incentive to [the workers]."

---

24. F Factory is a pseudonym.

However, another worker said: "If you gave me a decent salary, I wouldn't mind if you cut back on my overtime hours" (quoted in Tseng Wei-ling 2012, 67). According to an "undercover investigative report," "Chinese workers demand overtime from the capitalists. They even toady to line foremen and section heads to accomplish this" (*Nanfang zhoumo* 2010). Because basic working hours are set so low, businesses demand overtime for the sake of productivity; and because the minimum wage is so low, workers are compelled to work as much overtime as possible. This inevitably gives rise to excessive overtime. This system design has given rise to the myth of workers' voluntary overtime.

However, even if a Shenzhen worker works a hundred hours of overtime, his take-home pay is still much lower than that of a local permanent employee. Tables 5.5A and 5.5B, which show the gap between the minimum wage and the wages of permanent employees in urban areas, verify this simple calculation.

The series of suicides among Foxconn employees exposed the myth that workers enjoyed working overtime. Not long after the incident, Shenzhen's labor oversight unit stated that Foxconn hadn't forced workers to work overtime. But in fact, the overtime required during rush periods often surpassed what workers were willing to perform as well as what they could physically and mentally bear. One former employee posted this text on the internet:

> The Shenzhen Federation of Trade Unions also stated in a report that it had not found that Foxconn forced overtime, engaged in excessive overtime, or violated the Labor Law in other ways. . . . I won't say more here, but I'm posting my pay slip for everyone to see. . . . Every month I worked more than 100 hours of overtime and only rested two days in one month. . . . At the end of every month, we all had to sign a paper explicitly stating that we were willing to work overtime, but that was really just for show. If you didn't sign it, the line foreman and section head would be afraid that they couldn't complete the job and would sign it for you! And if you didn't sign, you'd be scolded. You didn't want to offend the higher-ups, otherwise you'd lose out when it came to work, and it was all on you! So for the most part we would all sign it without even reading it, out of force of habit! In fact, it was exhausting. If you wanted to rest or take a day off it was impossible, what were you going to do? We'd usually run off to the factory health care center and find a doctor to write up a medical record for sick leave, but there

were only fifteen days a year for that privilege, so we'd be very economical about using those fifteen sick days![25]

According to the April 2008 pay slip, the worker received standard pay of 950 yuan per month (equivalent to the minimum wage), 636 yuan for 65.5 hours of normal overtime hours, and 877 yuan for 62.0 hours of weekend overtime (figure 5.1). The overtime pay exceeded the standard wage. Because they worked overtime, workers had to sign a voluntary overtime confirmation. This was for the factory owner to use during government labor inspections. If the worker didn't sign, the supervisor would sign on his or her behalf, a process referred to as "being signed, being voluntarily overtimed." And even taking sick leave was very difficult.

Originally, China's Labor Law had very strict stipulations on overtime: generally, it could not exceed one hour per day, under special circumstances it could not exceed three hours per day, and it could not exceed thirty-six hours per month. How did factory owners make workers work excessive overtime during rush periods? There were different rules to the game in Guangdong.

According to the law, in addition to the standard working hours system, there was a comprehensive working hours system and an irregular working hours system. Many manufacturers used the comprehensive working hours system to evade limitations on overtime. This system was based on the normal working day (eight hours) and working week (forty hours), with one day of rest each week, and allowed flexibility in calculating overtime. But Guangdong's factory owners applied this stipulation to overtime:

> During the off season in July and August, orders are only 75 percent, while during the peak period we have to rush orders, so we use the "comprehensive overtime system," also called the "full-year flexible working hours system." According to regulations, overtime is a maximum of thirty-six hours per month, or 432 hours for twelve months. These [hours] can be concentrated in the months of the peak period, and in those months we can exceed the originally stipulated overtime limit of thirty-six hours per month. . . . But working hours still can't exceed sixty hours per week or eleven hours per day. This is an "unwritten rule" that the buyer also agrees to, and [it] conforms to CSR standards.[26]

25. "Did Foxconn Break the Law on Overtime? Netizen's Pay Slip Shows the Truth," Aboluo xinwenwang, May 26, 2010, https://goo.gl/P2baHJ.

26. Interview: L201504.

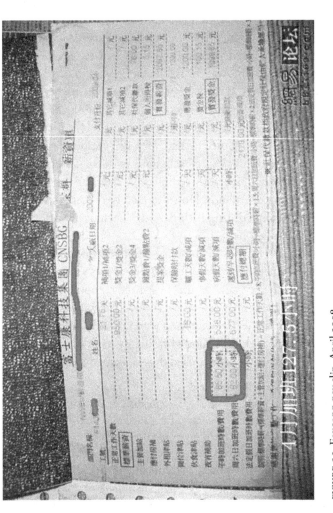

FIGURE 5.1. Foxconn pay slip, April 2008.

Source: "Did Foxconn Break the Law on Overtime? Netizen's Pay Slip Shows the Truth," Aboluo xinwenwang, May 26, 2010, https://goo.gl/P2baHJ.

According to the government's laws, before implementing this "full-year flexible working hours system," the factory owner must obtain approval from the labor administrative department and announce it. However, it is unclear whether manufacturers generally comply with this announcement process. According to this method, workers can be made to work a maximum of eighty-odd hours of overtime per month. The pay slip posted by the former Foxconn employee quoted above shows that he regularly worked more than a hundred hours of overtime, which clearly exceeds the scope of this system.

Generally, foreign-invested factories are better than factories run by local people at complying with labor regulations. Conditions in Hong Kong—and Taiwanese-invested factories fall between those in European, American, and Japanese foreign factories and those in locally run factories. Migrant workers at locally owned factories, especially the smaller ones, enjoy very little protection from the labor administrative department.

4. Differential Citizenship and Double Exploitation

I have described how the state created the migrant worker class, the form of that class, and the empirical phenomenon and evidence of low wages and excessive overtime under the dual labor market. This section proposes a theory of differential citizenship and explains the mechanism that creates double exploitation.

1) The Origin and Definition of the Concept of Differential Citizenship

In the ideal traditional democratic state, citizenship presupposes equal rights among citizens. In 1949, the sociologist T. H. Marshall published a classic treatise that elaborated on the development of modern citizenship. He asked a profoundly meaningful question: In modern times, could the popularization and deepening of citizenship rights continue to alleviate inequality among the social classes? Marshall argued that in the early stage of development of modern citizenship rights, the single uniform status of citizenship "was clearly an aid, and not a menace, to capitalism and the free-market economy, because it was dominated by civil rights, which confer the legal capacity to strive for the things one would like to possess but do not guarantee the possession of any of them" (1994, 20). He observed that there was an "affinity" between the right to freedom and early capitalism. Since World War II, social rights and social welfare have become common practice in Western Europe. Marshall maintained that endowing social rights could enhance the exercise of freedom, especially for resource-deprived lower-class workers. But could social rights solve the problem of class inequality? Marshall gave a qualified negative answer. Although historical experience suggests that social rights cannot completely solve the problem of inequality, logically speaking, they can alleviate inequality. At least social rights should not exacerbate inequality, as long as they are granted under the principle of a single uniform status of citizenship.

Using Marshall's theoretical proposition as the foundation for our analysis, we can clearly see divergences between the progress of contemporary Chinese citizenship and the ideal type of citizenship developed by Marshall. First, in Western European society, the citizen is the subject of rights and obligations, but in China, citizenship is closely bound to the household registration system, which uses the household as the unit of rights and obligations. In legal terms, the *hukou* system restricts people's right to various freedoms, including the freedom of migration and the freedom of employment. According to the PRC's constitution, all citizens enjoy equal rights, but the constitution does not state explicitly that people have the freedom of migration. The *hukou* system is also bound up with social and economic rights. The system therefore strips migrant workers of both their civil rights and their social and economic rights.

Second, the *hukou* system and urban-rural dualism are interwoven. The *hukou* system divides Chinese citizens into rural residents and urban residents, and population and household registration employ the doctrine of territorial jurisdiction (*shudi guanli*). Someone with rural residential status has difficulty obtaining a local *hukou* in the migration destination (especially if it's a large city). This urban-rural dual *hukou* system, which took shape in the Mao era, has been greatly relaxed since the

1980s, allowing peasants to go to the cities to work or conduct business, but the institutional path dependence created by the binary system still limits the freedom of rural migrant workers.

Third, in granting citizenship, the Chinese government does not abide by the principle of a single uniform status of citizenship. On the contrary, since the founding of the PRC, the state has deprived many individuals and social groups of their civil rights based on political grounds (political status such as belonging to one of the black five categories[27]), social status (such as peasant status under urban-rural dualism), administrative jurisdiction (such as territorial jurisdiction, according to the location of the household registration), and ethnicity (such as belonging to an ethnic minority group). There is therefore a great discrepancy in both degree and typology between China's actual situation and Marshall's citizenship paradigm. In China, the citizenship system is a stratified, hierarchical one loaded with functional discrimination and bias.

This book has proposed the concept of differential citizenship, referring to the Chinese sociologist Fei Xiaotong's theory of *chaxu geju* (differential mode of association)[28] and the Western sociological tradition's theory of citizenship. The book uses the following definition of "differential citizenship": An institutional figuration woven from a set of formal and informal regulations of the state (including the central and local state); the entire citizenry within this system is incorporated into divided, hierarchical, differentiated status and rights groups, giving rise to a phenomenon of inequality between different groups of citizens in terms of economic status, social welfare, and political rights.

While working out this concept, I alternately referred to the Chinese term *"gongmin shenfen chaxu"* (literally "citizenship status hierarchy") and the English term "differential citizenship," and I translated "universal citizenship" into the Chinese term *"putong gongmin shenfen."* For the sake of parallelism and succinctness, I retranslate "differential citizenship"

27. *TRANSLATOR'S NOTE:* During the Mao era, people in one of the "black five categories"—landlord, rich peasant, counterrevolutionary, bad element, and rightist—were considered members of a political underclass that was subject to discriminatory treatment and persecution.

28. Gary Hamilton and Wang Zheng (1992) first rendered Fei's *chaxu geju* as "differential mode of association" in their translation of Fei's *From the Soil*.

as *"gongmin shenfen chaxu."* I first read about the concept of differential status in Marshall's text (1949), and I translated that term into Chinese as *"shenfen chaxu"* in analyzing the stratification of Shewei Village[29] in the Pearl River Delta (an administrative village with a large number of migrant workers) (Wu Jieh-min 2000). The article I wrote about that village began my dialogue with Fei Xiaotong's differential mode of association. From differential status I developed the concept of "differential citizenship" (*"gongmin shenfen chaxu"*), and I traced the influence of the Soviet Union's *propiska* system of internal passports on China's urban-rural dualism (Wu Jieh-min 2010).

A core conceptual element of differential citizenship is *chaxu* (differentiation). This term can be theoretically linked to the phrase differential mode of association, which Fei Xiaotong applied to traditional Chinese rural society. Fei (1991) used the phrase in contrast to the "organizational mode of association" (*tuanti geju*)[30] in the conceptual framework of Western society. Traditional Chinese society emphasized differentiated human relationships, and these are still quite evident in contemporary China's social structure (e.g., in administrative rankings, interpersonal relationships, and state-owned enterprises and government work units). Yet the differential citizenship defined here not only has the traits of traditional Chinese society, but it also indicates that after the Communist revolution in 1949, the Chinese state used its immense despotic power and infrastructural power to transform the country's social structure[31] and enmeshed traditional Chinese society with urban-rural dualism. As a result, differential citizenship was not only influenced by the traditional cultural structure, but it was also created by state policy and is related to the CCP's distinctive modernization strategy and the characteristics of its rule. The CCP party-state system played a key role in creating unequal citizenship rights. The concept of differential citizenship therefore has a twofold compulsory quality: it is endogenous to society and exogenous to the state.

Under this system, migrant workers are subjected to systematic deprivation of their civil rights. Differential citizenship has become a key

29. Shewei Village is a pseudonym.
30. This translation of *tuanti geju* is also by Hamilton and Zheng (1992).
31. Regarding this pair of state power concepts, see Mann (1986).

component of China's system of government, permeating the political, economic, social, and cultural spheres. Like the ideal type of democratic citizenship mentioned above, this is also an ideal type, and in the world of practical experience, it varies according to locality and temporality.

2) The Institutional Characteristics of Differential Citizenship

The most important effect of differential citizenship is the institutional exclusion of migrant workers. Although unequal citizenship status will also exist in a classic democratic state, the distinguishing features of China's system are built on the institutional evolution of urban-rural dualism, the features of which are mutually linked as follows:

First, double-track status: The urban-rural, worker-peasant status dichotomy of the Mao era continued after opening reform. This institutional legacy is manifested in the double- or multitrack urban citizenship status that arose in the market transformation process. Its operational logic is similar to the double-track pricing system in the early state of market reform. Urban residents have a privileged status. Members of the nonnative population become noncitizens in the cities to which they migrate, and therefore second-class citizens. Many large cities, especially first-tier (Beijing, Shanghai, Guangzhou, Shenzhen, etc.) and second-tier cities (mainly provincial capitals), prioritize safeguarding the interests of their own residents and use the *hukou* system as a tool to exclude nonnatives from the urban social benefit system.

Second, the doctrine of territorial jurisdiction: From the Mao era to the present, this doctrine has had a major effect on citizenship status in relation to institutional arrangements for financial and administrative governance (Zhou Hong 2003). In terms of population governance, territorial jurisdiction means that the local governments of the floating population's places of origin are responsible for managing the population outflow.[32]

---

32. According to Wu Jinglian, territorial jurisdiction originated in 1956 with Mao Zedong's "On the Ten Major Relationships," and after the Great Leap Forward it became a policy of transferring administrative functions to the lower levels. The 1958 "CCP Central Committee and State Council Stipulations Regarding Improving the Planning Management System" (Zhonggong zhongyang Guowuyuan guanyu gaijin

But territorial jurisdiction combined with the *hukou* system turned the governance of migrant workers and the provision of related public welfare benefits into an administrative no-man's-land. According to the principles of territorial jurisdiction, the local government at the place of origin is in charge of migrant workers. However, migrant workers in distant provinces were usually out of range of their home governments, for instance in terms of educating their children and administering family planning (Chang Kuei-min 2007). At the same time, the government of the destination city could use territorial jurisdiction as a pretext for refusing to provide welfare benefits to the nonnative population. The central government has tried to deal with the problems generated by territorial jurisdiction through various reforms (e.g., by promoting the use of residential permits and allowing nonnative populations to settle in small and medium-sized cities, as described above), but it has never been able to solve the problem of migrants' establishing permanent residency in large cities.

Third, reproduction of labor power: Because migrant workers had a noncitizenship status in their destination cities, the local government didn't need to provide them and their families with many public goods, which reduced the local government's financial burden. Businesses hiring migrant workers could save a great deal on labor costs, for example by not providing social insurance or providing it only at an inferior grade. For this reason, businesses and the governments of destination cities shifted the reproduction of labor power to the migrant workers' places of origin and their families, giving rise to phenomena such as left-behind children and left-behind elders. The effect was similar to the exploitative mechanism of South Africa during the apartheid era (Burawoy 1976) and the caste system for labor in South Asia (e.g., in the Bengal region) prior to independence (Chakrabarty 1989), but it was accomplished through the characteristically Chinese elements of the *hukou* system and urban-rural dualism.

---

jihua guanli tizhi de guiding) changed the planning management system—originally centrally balanced by the State Planning Commission and then gradually transmitted to the lower levels—into a planning management system based on overall balance in the regions and integrating specialized departments with the regions (Wu Jinglian 2005, 82–86).

Fourth, the *hukou* system: Urban governments reconstituted the system as a tool for excluding migrant workers. The system limited people's freedom of movement and employment options and stripped members of the nonnative population of their civil rights as citizens. Without local *hukou*, migrant workers and their families were also segregated from local citizens in terms of social and economic rights. The *hukou* system also became a rent-seeking tool for local governments. In the 1980s and 1990s, some industrialized coastal cities collected fees for temporary residential permits from rural migrant workers, which constituted a sizable rent that became an additional burden on migrant workers. Furthermore, the high gold content of urban citizenship, especially in the large coastal cities, made such status an artificially scarce good as well as a tool for seeking and competing for rent. Possessing permanent residential status in a major city was like having a social welfare voucher. As a result, this voucher also had a price and engendered a corresponding status market (Wu Jiehmin 2011). This status market was further institutionalized, run as a monopoly by the government to control people's social mobility, and charged fees for buying rank status and privilege qualifications from the government (Chen Yingfang 2014).

3) *The Logic of Double Exploitation*

The differential citizenship system has created double exploitation of migrant workers. Classic capitalist exploitation is the state's noninterference in capital's squeezing of labor, such as the low pay, long working hours, and poor working conditions in the early stage of England's Industrial Revolution. After that, the state gradually improved the treatment of workers through administrative intervention and labor laws. In China, the state has not adopted a laissez-faire policy toward labor-capital relations but has intervened in the migrant worker sector from the outset. However, the state's intervention has ensured a high level of exploitation of workers by capital. The main reason for this is that the state has institutionalized differential citizenship, giving rise to a dual labor market (permanent employees versus migrant workers) and a graduated social insurance scheme that greatly reduces labor costs.

Migrant workers therefore face a situation of double exploitation. One aspect is the classic form of exploitation imposed by capital on the working class (collecting surplus value from the labor process), which is class exploitation in the sense of traditional political economy. The other aspect stems from the state's demarcation of the migrant worker status, which allows companies to legitimately treat the migrant workers they employ as second-class citizens in terms of wages, working hours, social insurance, working conditions, and so on. This is status-based exploitation guided by the state system. The dormitory labor regime in the Guangdong model (described in detail in section 6 of this chapter) helps capital enhance production efficiency to squeeze out surplus. Two major reasons for the formation of the dormitory regime are the dual labor market and the *hukou* system. Double exploitation allows capital and the state to more easily extract economic surplus.

In forging the migrant worker class, the state provided capital with a system that facilitated extracting surplus and reducing labor costs. What did the state gain in return? First of all, in China's current party-state capitalist system, the state has the status of capitalist and hires large numbers of migrant workers, thereby becoming a direct exploiter. Even more important, the state provides cheap migrant labor to take its cut of value capture in the GVCs. The government's participation in local growth alliances ensures that it shares in the capture and distribution of economic surplus, and in that way the state becomes an indirect exploiter. The state's active participation in the globalization process causes the local polity and domestic industrial clusters to become closely embedded (see figures 1.2 and 1.3). This is the state's docking point in the GVC.

Consequently, the state effectively joins local growth alliances, and from that exploitative apparatus it captures rich economic surplus, facilitating the formation of the rent-seeking development state. The distinguishing feature of China's rent-seeking development state is the pervasive rent-seeking activity in the economic development process. This system creates a variety of rent-seeking opportunities, including the government's institutional rent seeking, collective rent seeking by officials, and individual rent seeking by officials and cadres. The targets of rent seeking include capitalist enterprises and migrant workers. Institutional rent seeking in this book's context particularly points to the capture of economic surplus through collecting rent from companies, including processing fees, management fees, land lease permit fees, social insurance fees, and so on (as described in detail in chapter 7). Migrant workers are also targets of rent seeking by the local government and officials, as in the case the abovementioned fee for processing a temporary residence permit and the fee-collecting behavior in the custody and repatriation process (both of which have been abolished). On an even larger scale, the pension insurance fee is a target of rent seeking. Because China has not yet implemented nationwide integrated management of social insurance funds, each level of local government uses those funds and regularly shirks the restraints of the central government's laws and directives. Behind these cases are complex rent-seeking chains. In 2006, a case came to light in Shanghai of top officials who were unlawfully diverting and seizing social insurance funds on a scale of ten billion yuan. The case involved dozens of people, including the municipal party secretary, district heads, the director of the social insurance bureau, and heads of privately-run and state-owned enterprises. Similar cases of diversion of social insurance funds have also erupted in Guangzhou, Shenzhen, and other places.[33]

This exploitative apparatus in China constitutes a symbiotically integrated institutional network. Everything from differential citizenship, the dual labor market, the graduated social insurance plan, local growth alliances, GVC management, and local governance to the rent-seeking development state is mutually linked. The state has a powerful incentive to maintain differential citizenship, and fundamental reforms to the *hukou* system will be very difficult. Over the past twenty years, there have been occasional rumors that the Chinese government will completely reform the *hukou* system, but every instance turned out to be a great deal of thunder with little rain. Deeper examination shows that although urban-rural dualism and the *hukou* system were formed prior to marketization, both played a historical role in the emergence of differential

---

33. See Lee (2012); Hua Shiming, "Guangzhou shebao jijin bei nuoyong xiangguan zerenren yi bei chachu" (Investigation of those responsible for diversion of Guangzhou's social insurance fund), *Nanfang ribao*, April 5, 2007, https://reurl.cc/r8YW1E; Hu Jiali, "Shenzhen shebao jijin 17 yi zaonuoyong" (1.7 billion of Shenzhen social insurance fund was misappropriated), *Zhonghua gongshang shibao*, May 3, 2013, http://finance.people .com.cn/fund/n/2013/0503/c201329-21350757.html.

citizenship after opening reform. Rather than being eliminated, urban-rural dualism has been bundled into the new urban status system, though it is concealed by layer upon layer of exclusionary mechanisms. This differential citizenship system is an ingenious, complex, and brutally exploitative apparatus, an institutional matrix that has been implemented for decades and constantly revised and mended—and it has a self-reproducing institutional circular logic that disincentivizes its destruction by vested interests.

As a result, an equal and universal citizenship system has not emerged in the course of China's capitalist development. The state's forceful intervention has caused global capitalism to become interwoven with the migrant worker status system, and the two work together. China's road to globalization has consolidated a new form of dualism, constituting a capitalist exploitative apparatus with Chinese characteristics.

During the Mao era, China carried out an economic policy of self-sufficiency. At that time, the state used the unequal exchange of agricultural and industrial products to reap large amounts of rural surplus, and it used that in turn to irrigate the urban industrial sector, forming the price scissors that facilitated original accumulation (Ka and Selden 1986). From 1978 onward, China rejoined the global capitalist system, and peasants entered the cities to become migrant workers, drawing wages while preserving their peasant status. Because this status glossed over the fact that migrant workers were workers, the unequal structure originating in the Mao era of urban-rural and peasant-worker duality was not eliminated; rather, it was transformed and built into the urban industrial system. In the current context, the term "price scissors" not only refers to the unequal exchange of agricultural and industrial products but also includes the dual labor market of permanent employees and migrant workers. From a historical perspective, the current exploitation of rural migrant workers is effectively the historical and spatial shift of price scissors. We can see amazing continuity on this axis of class exploitation in the postsocialist transformation from the Mao era to the Deng Xiaoping era. The enormous surplus squeezed from the bodies of migrant workers is divided between the state and capital. This model of distribution of surplus and capital accumulation has also created a highly unequal society.

5. New Urban Protectionism: Discrimination in Education and Social Insurance

In the Chinese government's exclusionary treatment of migrant workers, the provisions of social insurance and of education for the workers' children stand out. I turn first to the biased and discriminatory treatment of the children of migrant workers in education.

1) Educating the Children of Migrant Workers

The inequitable educational opportunities available to children of migrant workers (so-called floating children) were not thoroughly addressed for a long time. Up until the mid-2000s, public primary and secondary schools in economically developed regions often denied admission to the children of migrant workers, and even if some children were allowed to attend the schools, all kinds of extra fees (e.g., temporary schooling fees and support fees) were imposed. In 2003, a central government document required local governments to grant equal treatment to the children of migrant workers, but according to reports and on-the-ground field investigations, there was no fundamental improvement in the range of pretexts for discriminating against those children. Under pressure from the central government, many metropolises with large influxes of migrant workers adopted relatively lenient policies for admitting the children of migrant workers to local primary and secondary schools. According to field interviews that I conducted in 2006 and 2007 in Shanghai, Suzhou (the Kunshan region), Beijing, and other places, local public elementary schools have admitted a relatively large number of nonnative children. But this new policy acts as a double-edged sword: On the one hand, the dependents of migrant workers have more opportunities to study in local schools rather than in migrant worker schools, which tend to be shabby and lack skilled teaching personnel. However, on the other hand, local governments have taken harsh measures to suppress and rectify migrant schools and expel them from their administrative jurisdictions, as has happened in Shanghai and in several districts of Beijing. Furthermore, these governments also subsidize some reasonably well-run migrant schools and have integrated them into the local educational sector in a process known as normalizing migrant worker schools, but their subsidies are far less than those for regular public schools (Lee Shang-lin 2008). Overall, in terms of educational resources, the children of migrant workers receive much lower subsidies than students with local *hukou*s. Differential status is also clearly reflected in the elementary and secondary education system. Until recently, Shanghai's policy of allowing the children of migrant workers to attend public schools was still only partially implemented under segmented incorporation (Lan Pei-chia 2014).

Until recently, in Pearl River Delta localities such as Dongguan, education for the children of migrant workers still lags behind that in Kunshan. One Taishang said: "Dongguan really doesn't look after its nonnative population very well. At a large foreign-owned factory on the scale of B Factory, the local government is only willing to provide four high school placements per year to the children of mainland managers."[34] If even mainland managers, who tend to be well educated and have higher incomes, are treated this way, it goes without saying how ordinary migrant workers serving as assembly line operators or team leaders must be treated.

Discrimination against migrant workers applies to their rights in terms of migration, permanent residence (the attainment of local *hukou*), wages, social insurance, and children's education. In the past ten years or so, local governments have had to find ways to deal with the central government's new policies, which has resulted in the emergence of a new urban protectionism. From the perspective of a city's vested interests, a large influx of nonnatives has a serious effect on social resource allocation, budgetary expenses, infrastructure, cultural differences, and population governance. Furthermore, in the Chinese tradition, urban residents have maintained an attitude of exclusion and disdain toward peasants coming to town, and all of that forms the background that creates urban protectionism. In the new urban citizenship rights regime, people with local *hukou* are prioritized when it comes to the financial resources of local governments, and while the nonnative population has been partially absorbed into the urban regime, various institutional thresholds have rel-

---

34. Interview: Xu201504. B Factory is a pseudonym.

egated them to second-class citizenship status. For example, they have lower-grade social insurance, are subject to a credit system of screening for establishing permanent residence, and must pay temporary schooling fees. Beijing, Shanghai, and other major metropolises, which experience budgetary pressure from their own populations, have in recent years imposed even harsher controls on the nonnative population, and it has become increasingly difficult for the children of migrant workers to attend public schools. In recent years, Beijing has required nonnatives to provide five proofs before their children are allowed to attend school. Assembling all five proofs is an extremely harsh demand to place on the floating population, and as a result, this has become a method used to drive out the children in order to drive out the parents and thereby expel the nonnative population (Zhou Hualei 2016).

More recently, household registration and social welfare reforms in Shenzhen, Shanghai, and Beijing have guided a new form of urban protectionism. The old type of protectionism directly eliminated the rights and interests of migrant workers or ignored their existence. The new type of protectionism has taken the discriminatory treatment implied by the original urban-rural dual structure and incorporated it into the urban institutional structure, which has resulted in a new dual system to replace the old type of protectionism while continuing to discriminate against the nonnative population (Wu Jieh-min 2017a). No matter how it is whitewashed, there is no way to conceal the fundamentally exclusionary nature of discrimination against migrant workers in the cities. The most recent case occurred in the cold of November 2017, when the Beijing government forcibly drove out the low-end population—that is, migrant workers. This cleansing process thoroughly revealed the despotic control unleashed by powerful political authority on grassroots society.

In the course of China's capitalist transformation, the state has retreated from the social welfare sphere to a great extent, and cities distribute their limited social and financial resources in a graduated fashion to the various population groups under their jurisdictions. When the state retreated from the welfare sphere, all citizens were affected, but not everyone was affected equally or in the same way. Compared with migrant workers, residents with urban *hukou* enjoy more policy safeguards and protectionist measures, while migrant workers suffer systematic deprivation due to their second-class citizenship.[35] Next I use the differentiated so-cial insurance system to examine the institutionalization of discrimina-tion and deprivation against migrant workers.

2) Discrimination in Social Insurance

Migrant workers and permanent employees belong to different graduated social insurance benefit payment plans. As a result, the differential citi-zenship system is starkly manifested in unequal social insurance bene-fits. The worker social insurance system that China currently uses began in the late 1990s. However, it was not strictly applied to FIEs until the early 2000s, and the typical private mainland-owned company avoided it whenever possible under the flexible enforcement of local officials. As a result, overall social insurance coverage of migrant workers is very low. According to an official report, in 2006 the coverage rate of migrant work-ers for the four main types of social insurance (pension, medical, unem-ployment, and occupational injury) was only 26.6 percent, 26.2 percent, 15.3 percent, and 32.5 percent, respectively.[36] In 2004 the coverage rate for these four types of insurance for the entire urban working popula-tion was estimated to be 36.7 percent, 27.8 percent, 23.7 percent, and 15.3 percent, respectively.[37] At first glance, there doesn't seem to be a large difference between the social insurance coverage rates of migrant work-ers and ordinary urban residents, and in terms of occupational injury, the insurance rate for migrant workers is higher. However, on closer analysis we can see that this is not the case. First, many migrant workers have not

35. Of course, we cannot overlook the impoverished lower class with urban *hukou* that has emerged in the cities because of market reforms (Solinger 2006; Lin Thung-Hong 2007), but that topic falls outside the scope of this book.

36. These figures were calculated from National Bureau of Statistics Service Sector Survey Center, "Nongmingong shenghuo zhiliang diaocha zhiyi: laodong jiuye he she-hui baozhang" (Rural migrant worker living quality survey no. 1: Labor employment and social insurance), Zhongguo tongji xinxiwang, October 19, 2006, http://www.stats .gov.cn/ztjc/ztfx/fxbg/200610/t20061011_16082.html.

37. These figures were calculated from the National Bureau of Statistics of the People's Republic of China (2007 and 2009) and National Bureau of Statistics Popula-tion and Employment Statistics Division and Ministry of Labor and Social Security Planning and Finance Division (2007).

signed contracts with their employers, and this makes the social insurance coverage rate for migrant workers appear higher than it actually is. Second, what these data show is the average situation: the FIEs, which the government monitors more closely than other businesses, typically have higher social insurance rates, while privately owned mainland-invested factories usually have very low social insurance rates. Third, in many large cities, migrant workers enroll in lower-quality social insurance plans specifically designed for them (an example is Shanghai's non-native employee comprehensive insurance). This low-grade social insurance greatly reduces the burden on companies, while the social insurance benefits that the migrant workers enjoy are much lower than what workers with local *hukou* enjoy under urban employee insurance plans. Fourth, a large number of migrant workers are employed in construction and manufacturing, both of which have high occupational injury rates, so employers have a stronger incentive to provide insurance for migrant workers—and the occupational injury insurance payment rate is very low. After the Labor Contract Law and the Social Insurance Law took effect, local governments came under greater pressure to increase social insurance coverage rates. In 2011, local governments also began to more rigorously collect housing provident fund payments. The payment rate for this fund is second only to that for pension insurance.

The graduated social welfare provision in different regions and cities displays different institutional forms and degrees of discrimination due to regional variations. Through regional comparisons, we can highlight the distinguishing features of the Guangdong model.

3) Shanghai

The stratified and differentiated social insurance system that Shanghai designed in the early 2000s embodies classic urban protectionism. Shanghai divided its social insurance recipients into four categories: urban permanent employees, residents of small towns, nonnative employees (migrant workers), and local rural residents. Each of these four categories participated in different schemes of insurance: urban social insurance (*chengbao*), small-town social insurance (*zhenbao*), nonnative employee comprehensive insurance (*zonghe baoxian*), and rural social insurance (*nongbao*). Table 5.6 compares the differential benefits under urban, town,

Table 5.6. Differentiated payment rates for three types of insurance plans in Shanghai, 2008 (%)

	Urban plan		Small-town plan		Nonnative comprehensive plan	
	Company	Individual	Company	Individual	Company	Individual
Pension	22	8	17	Voluntary	7	Voluntary
Medical, maternity, unemployment, and occupational injury	15–17.5	3	7.5–10		5.5	
All insurance	37–39.5	11	24.5–27	Voluntary	12.5	Voluntary
Payment base	Fluctuated as a share (60–300%) of the previous year's average urban monthly wage, calculated at 1,735–8,676 yuan		Set at 60% of the previous year's average urban monthly wage, around 1,735 yuan		Set at 60% of the previous year's average urban monthly wage, around 1,735 yuan	

Source: The data were compiled from relevant laws and regulations in Shanghai and field surveys.

Note: To simplify the analysis, medical, maternity, unemployment, and occupational injury insurance were combined.

and nonnative comprehensive insurance, manifested in payment rates and payment bases. Taking pension insurance as an example, employers have to pay 22 percent of the insurance fee on behalf of employees with urban social insurance, while the individual has to cover 8 percent of the cost. In the case of small-town social insurance, the employer has to pay only 17 percent, and for comprehensive insurance, the employer has to pay only 7 percent. Furthermore, the payment bases for small-town and comprehensive insurance are both set at the minimum base number, while the payment base for urban social insurance fluctuates between 60 percent and 300 percent of the average monthly wage of all employed persons in the municipality in the previous year.

For participants in urban social insurance, the amount shouldered by the individual is mandatory; but in the case of small-town and comprehensive social insurance, the individual's payment for pension insurance is voluntary. The so-called voluntary payment means that workers can decide whether or not to contribute the portion that is their responsibility. Whether or not workers pay the individual portion, the employer has to insure them. Under these conditions, workers do not have a personal account. Why was this plan adopted? The explanation by local government officials is that if migrant workers aren't forced to pay for pension insurance, the business cannot use the migrant worker's unwillingness to be insured as an excuse for not providing workers with insurance.[38] Because migrant workers have no way of obtaining *hukou* in Shanghai, and at that time personal social insurance accounts could not be transferred across provinces, most migrant workers chose not to pay the personal portion of the insurance fee. This was quite a shrewd design on the part of Shanghai. In fact, it was common in other regions for a company's management to use the worker's unwillingness to pay for social insurance as a pretext for evading social insurance fees. In Shanghai, the employer still had to pay that fee to the local government, regardless of whether workers were willing to pay. The differences in payment rates and payment bases for different insurance plans allowed different types of insured people to receive unequal benefits.

According to Table 5.6, we can calculate the different social insurance fees that a company has to pay when hiring workers with different status types. Take, for example, a worker with monthly earnings of 1,800 yuan in 2008. If the worker had a Shanghai urban *hukou*, the company had to pay a social insurance premium of 711 yuan (1,800 × 39.5 percent = 711); if the employee had a small-town *hukou*, the employer had to pay 468 yuan (1,735 × 27.0 percent = 468.45); and if the employee didn't have a Shanghai *hukou* (i.e., was a migrant worker), the company had to pay only 217 yuan (1,735 × 12.5 percent = 216.875). It is no wonder that the vast majority of factory production lines in China's export processing regions had no workers with local *hukou*. Based on a similar logic, the Shanghai municipal government's expenditure on social benefits for migrant workers was also far less than on benefits for people with a local *hukou*.

In terms of the payment base, for people with small-town insurance and nonnative employees, a set amount of 1,735 yuan was adopted. As a result, even if a worker's monthly earnings did not reach that amount,

38. Interview: SHPD_LB_200701.

the insurance fee still had to be calculated on that set amount. In other words, no matter how much the workers earned, their employers still had to pay 217 yuan as a social insurance fee on their behalf.

Table 5.7 presents the social insurance situations at six Shanghai factories that I surveyed in 2007. Regardless of whether the factories were foreign- or locally owned, their workers all had a variety of social insurance statuses. For example, the SH-Y-ks factory was a labor-intensive processing plant on the outskirts of Shanghai, and although it was registered in the British Virgin Islands, it was in fact a Taiwanese-invested company. In July 2007, this factory employed 3,224 workers, among whom 2 percent had local urban *hukou*s and 10 percent had small-town *hukou*s; both of these categories were mainly composed of clerical workers. The remaining 88 percent had *hukou*s outside of Shanghai, and most of these workers were production line operators.[39] In this factory, the insurance enrollment of these workers with three different *hukou* statuses revealed that a single factory had three systems, and three different government units handled the three insurance types. Macroscopic differential citizenship operated on a scaled-down level within one factory.

Shanghai's meticulous planning can be observed in this multilevel social insurance plan: at the same time that migrant workers are channeled into the insurance system, they are placed in a relatively low socioeconomic status to avoid eroding the interests of Shanghai's permanent residents. It is worth noting that in addition to discriminating against migrant workers, Shanghai's system also discriminates against local small-town residents. Many residents of the small towns in Shanghai's suburbs originally had rural (peasant) status, but because their land was appropriated, they were referred to as delanded peasants, and their household registrations were switched to nonagricultural *hukou*—a type of urban household, but inferior to the normal urban *hukou* in the city proper.

After the central government enacted the Social Insurance Law in 2011, the Shanghai government gradually reformed its social insurance system. The new system stipulated a transition period designed to ultimately merge the different types of insurance. We can observe the system's

39. Interview: SH-Y-ks2007.

Table 5.7. Survey of social insurance in six Shanghai factories, 2007

Factory code	Nationality	Product	Export ratio	Employees	Urban plan	Small-town plan	Comprehensive plan
SH-Y-ks	Taiwan (BVI)	Leisure equipment	100%	3,224	2%	10%	88%
SH-WN	Taiwan	Semiconductor testing and packaging	90%	1,800	22%	22%	56%
SH-FJ	Japan	Printers	50%	48	10%	11%	79%
SH-Y-6	United States	Inkjet printers and ink	0%	6	0%	83%	17%
SH-Y-7	Germany	Automobile assembly line	0%	150	70%	10%	20%
SH-B	China	Air compressors	10%	350	11%	69%	20%

Source: Author's field survey.

Note: BVI (British Virgin Islands) is where SH-Y-ks is registered.

changes and continuations under the new plan (see table 5.8). The first change is the elimination of the voluntary individual payment. The second is that in the transition period, a five-year transitional plan is applied for nonnative employees with rural *hukou* (i.e., the typical rural migrant worker). During this period, fees are paid on only three types of insurance (pension, medical, and occupational injury, called the "three insurances"), which is the same as the original comprehensive insurance type; maternity and unemployment insurance are not included. The third change is that nonnative employees with urban *hukou* (i.e., those who are not rural migrant workers) are compelled to enroll in standard urban social insurance, but the fee they pay is exactly the same as that for employees with small-town *hukou*. In terms of continuations, this reform still has path-dependent characteristics, and the transition period continues to use the original status differentiation (urban, small-town, and nonnative *hukou*), as well as differentiated fees and benefits.

It should be noted that the payment rates listed in table 5.8 are what was stipulated when the new plan was implemented in 2011. In 2015, the Shanghai government lowered the employer's shares of payments for pension insurance (from 22 percent to 21 percent), medical insurance (from 12 percent to 11 percent), and unemployment insurance (from 2 percent to 1.5 percent). These new payment rates slightly reduced the burden on employers.

The new plan thus eliminated the comprehensive insurance for nonnative employees that had been implemented for ten years. Ostensibly, urban social insurance channeled migrant workers into a unified social insurance system, but under the stipulations of the transition period, discriminatory treatment continued. According to the new formula, the social insurance fees (i.e., fees for the three insurances) that the employer had to pay on behalf of migrant workers were still only around half as much as the lowest amount they had to pay for urban social insurance (five insurances). The Shanghai government announced that employees covered by small-town insurance during the three-year transition period would be merged into the urban social insurance program in 2015. The merger actually took place in 2017, and the stipulated standard was not met, which triggered protests among the delanded peasants covered by small-town social insurance.

According to an official journal, this reform of Shanghai's system affected 200,000 employing units (enterprises) and 3.6 million employees.

Table 5.8. Differentiated payment rates for Shanghai's social insurance during the transition period (2011–16) under the 2011 plan (%)

	Urban (five insurances)		Suburban small-town households (five insurances, three-year transition period)		Nonurban nonnative workers (rural migrant workers) (three insurances, five-year transition period)	
	Company	Individual	Company	Individual	Company	Individual
Pension	22	8	17, 19, 22	5, 8, 8	22	8
Medical	12	2	7, 9, 12	1, 2, 2	6	1
Occupational injury	0.5	0	0.5	0	0.5	0
Maternity	0.5	0	0.8	0	NA	NA
Unemployment	2	1	1.7	1	NA	NA
All insurance	37	11	27, 31, 37	7, 11, 11	28.5	9
Payment base	Fluctuated as a share (60–300%) of the previous year's average urban monthly wage. In 2011 the payment base was calculated at 2,338–11,688 yuan.		Set at 60% of the previous year's average urban monthly wage. In 2011 the fee base was 2,338 yuan.		For the first four years, set at 40%, 45% 50%, and 55%, respectively, of the previous year's average urban monthly wage. In the fifth year, set at the worker's average monthly wage for the previous year. In 2011 the payment base was 1,558 yuan.	

Source: The data were compiled from relevant laws and regulations in Shanghai and field surveys.

Notes: Where more than one number is given in a single cell, the first number represents the first year, the second number the second year, and so on. NA is not available.

One of the people in charge said in 2012: "The characteristics of the groups insured under comprehensive insurance and small-town insurance were clearly different from people insured under urban insurance. Their mobility was much greater than for those under urban insurance. And the reporting, enrollment, continuation, transfer, and other pressures resulting from the merger would come one after another. . . . Before the merger, comprehensive and small-town insurance had no personal accounts, but now we have to establish an account for each individual. After the personal accounts are established, the record of rights and entitlements, remittance of benefits, remittance to other locations, and other pressures will also gradually increase" (quoted in Guo Jian 2012). This quote shows the immensity of the process of transforming social insurance as well as the pressure on the relevant work units. It also reveals that prior to the merger, there were no personal accounts for comprehensive and small-town insurance, so the original voluntary payments to individual accounts were only pro forma.

Furthermore, first-tier cities such as Shanghai had an immense number of nonnatives serving as domestic workers. This group never fell into the scope of insurance coverage, even under the new regulations in 2011. The Shanghai municipal government in 2013 issued additional stipulations under the flexible employment methods that enrolled these workers in insurance.[40]

The design of Shanghai's social insurance system and its evolution embodies the ideal type of the differential citizenship system. Before the implementation of the Social Insurance Law in 2011, first- and second-tier cities such as Beijing, Chengdu, Chongqing, Hangzhou, and Guangzhou implemented similar multilevel and discriminatory social insurance systems.

4) A Comparison of Four Coastal Cities

Shanghai's differentiated social insurance is a formal institutional plan. In the other main industrialized eastern coastal cities, there is no obvious discriminatory treatment, but there are many invisible exclusionary mechanisms. For example, the local Dongguan government allows fac-

---

40. Shanghai Department of Human Resources and Social Security (2013).

tory owners to get away with enrolling only a percentage of their employees in social insurance. According to my field surveys, in 2006 and 2007, five foreign-owned manufacturers in Dongguan had pension insurance coverage rates ranging from 10 percent to 30 percent—much lower than in Shanghai and Suzhou. In Suzhou, manufacturers pervasively used labor dispatch to evade formal labor contracts and social insurance fees.[41] In the Yangtze Delta region, discriminatory social welfare benefits still exist, but they are applied using concealed or roundabout methods. A Taigan who had been posted for a long time in the Yangtze Delta region said:

> In order to attract business, the local governments would all promise or tacitly consent to newly established enterprises' reporting more social insurance than they actually used. In order to save on costs, businesses would make this item a focal point of evaluation for investment. It had an even greater effect on overall labor costs in labor-intensive industries. For this reason, this phenomenon was not at all unusual in most mainland regions like Kunshan or northern Jiangsu; companies and governments had tacit agreements. . . . This is the main reason that most companies liked using nonnative workers—the social insurance costs were lower.[42]

Table 5.9 compares the social insurance systems of four key industrial cities in the southeastern coastal region in 2008. As mentioned above, Shanghai implemented a multilevel differentiated social insurance system with specially designed comprehensive insurance for migrant workers. Dongguan and Shenzhen also had social insurance plans designed specifically for migrant workers, but Suzhou did not adopt a differentiated system. Comparing the social insurance fees of these four cities, we can roughly sum them up as follows:

First, Dongguan and Shenzhen had the worst social insurance safeguards for migrant workers. This is reflected not only in payment rates, but also in the payment base numbers. In Dongguan, for example, businesses paid 15.0–16.0 percent of the insurance fees for workers, which on the surface seems higher than Shanghai's 12.5 percent. However, Shanghai's

41. See Chiu Mingtze's (2007) analysis of pension insurance in Kunshan (which is under the jurisdiction of Suzhou Prefecture).
42. Interview: SH-Yeh200707.

Table 5.9. Social insurance payment rates for migrant workers in four southeastern coastal cities, 2008 (%)

	Shanghai (nonnative comprehensive insurance)		Suzhou (same as urban insurance)		Shenzhen (nonnative social insurance)		Dongguan (nonnative social insurance)	
	Company	Individual	Company	Individual	Company	Individual	Company	Individual
Pension	7	voluntary	20	8	10	8	10	8
Medical	5.5	voluntary	10	2	1	0	2	0
Other			4	1	0.5–1.5	0	3–4	0
All insurance	12.5	voluntary	34	11	11.5–12.5	8	15–16	8
Payment base	Set at 1,735 yuan		Fluctuating: 1,369–6,844 yuan		Fluctuating: 900–9,699 yuan		Fluctuating: 770–7,362 yuan	

Source: The data were compiled from the relevant social insurance documents of the various cities and field surveys.

Notes: To simplify the analysis, occupational injury, unemployment, and maternity insurance are combined into "other." Fluctuating amounts in the SEZ range from 1,000–9,699; fluctuating amounts outside the SEZ range from 900–9,699.

payment base was set at 1,735 yuan, and while Dongguan's base number fluctuated between 770 and 7,362 yuan, the vast majority of businesses calculated their insurance fees based on the lowest base number, even if their employees earned higher wages. Furthermore, the Dongguan government allowed pension insurance to be paid separately from other kinds of insurance, and as a result, the majority of businesses were very reluctant to pay for pension insurance (which had the highest premiums) on behalf of their workers. Because workers worried that they would be unable to collect their pensions after they left the locality of their employment, they tended to be unwilling to cooperate in paying for it, and as a result, the coverage rates for pension insurance were generally very low. As discussed in chapter 4, Taiyang Company employed 2,000 people in April 2005 (the vast majority of whom were migrant workers), and its pension insurance coverage rate was only 16 percent, while its coverage rates for the other three insurances were 33 percent. In subsequent years, under pressure from the central government, Dongguan required businesses to increase their insurance coverage rates, and in January 2007 Taiyang's pension insurance coverage rate increased to 23 percent of the 2,300 people it then employed, while coverage rates for the other three types of insurance rose to 46 percent. In 2008, its pension insurance coverage rate rose to 30 percent, and it finally achieved 100 percent coverage for the other three types of insurance. Taiyang's social insurance coverage rate was already above average for the Dongguan region, which shows how low the social insurance levels were there in general. The payment rates for social insurance fees among Shenzhen businesses were 11.5–12.5 percent, even lower than in Dongguan, but the payment base numbers were higher than in Dongguan. Overall, Shenzhen's social insurance coverage rates for migrant workers were higher than Dongguan's, but the two cities provided only a bare minimum of medical insurance to migrant workers.

Second, comparatively speaking, the Suzhou region had a relatively complete social insurance system. According to table 5.9, businesses had to pay 34 percent of social insurance fees for their workers, and the lowest payment base number was higher than Dongguan's or Shenzhen's. This payment rate was applied to both workers with local *hukou* and migrant workers. Furthermore, the central government has publicized Suzhou (especially Kunshan City, which falls under the jurisdiction of

Suzhou) as a model city, and it is renowned for a social insurance coverage rate of 100 percent. However, according to my field interviews, foreign-invested companies there pervasively play the labor dispatch game with the tacit consent or under cover of government officials. Wherever workers are hired through the labor dispatch method, businesses, with the assistance of dispatch companies, will provide social insurance fees for these workers under the rural insurance scheme and in that way save hundreds of yuan in social insurance fees for each worker every month. I surveyed local Taiwanese-owned factories and found that one covered only 26.8 percent of the 280 employees it had in January 2007 under the regular social insurance plan, while the remaining 73.2 percent were covered using the labor dispatch method. In the official statistics, however, this factory's social insurance rate was calculated at 100 percent.[43] Another Taiwanese-owned factory employed 1,750 workers in July 2007, 86 percent of whom were covered by social insurance and the remaining 14 percent of whom were dispatch workers. This factory can be considered to be on the upper track in terms of local conditions.[44] Another Chinese-owned factory, which was registered as a Canadian-owned company (which is referred to as a fake foreign-devil enterprise), employed 300 workers, 30 percent of whom were dispatch labor. The dispatch workers were all covered under the cheap rural insurance, which was paid for by the dispatch company on behalf of the employing enterprise. These three factories generally reflected the lower and upper limits of social insurance coverage by FIEs in the Kunshan region. Although flexible measures arose in Suzhou's coverage rates, generally speaking, the social insurance benefits that Suzhou migrant workers enjoyed were better than those enjoyed by migrant workers in Dongguan. The principal difference was that at that time, Suzhou enterprises had to pay 10 percent of the medical insurance fees for migrant workers, which was much higher than the shares in Shenzhen (1 percent) and Dongguan (2 percent). As long as an enterprise was enrolled in the locally administered social insurance plan, Suzhou's migrant workers enjoyed the same medical benefits as workers with local *hukou*.

43. Interview: KS-KY2007.
44. Interview: KS-HG2007.

5) Similarities and Differences within the Pearl River Delta

As shown above, the benefits for migrant workers in the Pearl River Delta were generally lower than for those in the Yangtze Delta. I will now discuss differential treatment within the Pearl River Delta, including between cities and within cities. Table 5.10 compares the social insurance conditions in Guangzhou, Shenzhen, and Dongguan in 2008. Guangzhou and Shenzhen both had social insurance plans designed specifically for the nonnative population. Guangzhou's companies had to pay 31.7 percent of the social insurance fees for workers with local *hukou* and 22.5 percent for nonnative workers. Shenzhen companies had to pay 18.5–19.5 percent of the fees for workers with local *hukou* and only 11.5–12.5 percent for nonnative workers. The difference was not in the pension insurance fees but in medical insurance fees: the Guangzhou municipal government did not provide medical insurance for migrant workers; the Shenzhen government provided only pro forma medical insurance for migrant workers—the 1 percent payment rate by companies was inadequate to guarantee the provision of that insurance. The nonnative populations of Guangzhou and Shenzhen did not have maternity insurance, and Shenzhen's nonnative population did not have unemployment insurance.

Dongguan's institutional design was very special: it divided companies into two grades, those that fell under the jurisdiction of the prefecture level (*shishu*) and those that fell under the jurisdiction of a town or district level (*zhenqushu*). Prefecture-level enterprises had to pay 20.5–21.5 percent of the fees on behalf of their workers, while town- or district-level enterprises had to pay 15–16 percent. On the surface, this does not discriminate against the nonnative population, but in practice, the vast majority of foreign-invested companies and local privately owned companies that employed migrant workers were town-level enterprises, as a result of which the companies paid lower insurance rates. As in Guangzhou and Shenzhen, Dongguan's migrant workers basically enjoyed no medical insurance because their employers paid only 2 percent of the medical insurance rate. The differences in fee payment rates and fee base numbers highlight the discriminatory treatment suffered by migrant workers. Guangzhou's nonnative population enjoyed better pension insurance benefits, while migrant workers' situations in Shenzhen and Dongguan were almost equally inferior.

Table 5.10. Social insurance payment rates in three major cities of the Pearl River Delta, 2008 (%)

| | Guangzhou | | | | Shenzhen | | | | Dongguan | | | |
| | Local hukou | | Nonnative | | Local hukou | | Nonnative | | Prefecture-level enterprise | | Town-level enterprise | |
	Com.	Ind.	Com.	Ind.	Com.	Ind.	Com.	Ind.	Com.	Ind.	Com.	Ind.
Pension	20	8	20	8	10	8	10	8	10	8	10	8
Medical	8.5	2	NA	NA	6.5	2	1	0	7.5	2	2	0
Occupational injury	0.5	0	0.5	0	0.5–1.5	0	0.5–1.5	0	0.5–1.5	0	0.5–1.5	0
Maternity	0.7	0	NA	NA	0.5	0	NA	NA	0.5	0	0.5	0
Unemployment	2	1	2	1	1	0	NA	NA	2	1	(2)	(1)
All insurance	31.7	11	22.5	9	18.5–19.5	10	11.5–12.5	8	20.5–21.5	11	13–14 (15–16)	8 (9)
Payment base (yuan)	1,472–7,361		900–9,699		1,940–9,699		900–9,699		770–7,362			

Source: The data were compiled from the relevant social insurance documents of the various cities and field surveys.

Notes: Figures in parentheses indicate that Dongguan hukou holders are required to pay. All payment bases are fluctuating amounts (explained in table 5.9). Com. is company. Ind. is individual. NA means that a type of insurance is not applicable.

In 2009, Guangzhou implemented a basic medical insurance program for migrant workers, with compulsory enrollment. Businesses had to pay 1.2 percent of the insurance premium for migrant workers every month, but the payment rate for urban permanent workers (those in locally registered households) was raised to 10 percent that year. According to a news report, "in terms of benefits, the minimum payment standard for admission to hospital and specific procedures at clinics for rural migrant workers is 50 percent lower than that of medical insurance for urban permanent workers, which to a great extent reduces the burden on the insured."[45] Low insurance premiums mean low benefits. Guangzhou's new medical insurance measures for migrant workers were aimed at reducing the burden of the insured, but here the insured meant the companies, because the workers weren't required to pay for medical insurance. Thus, the medical benefits that Guangzhou gave migrant workers were only at the level of those in Shenzhen and Dongguan and not that at the level of those in Shanghai, much less Suzhou.

In short, the geographical variations among insurance plans are a microcosm of differential citizenship in China. The institutional evolution of new urban protectionism has had different content in various places due to regional differences: it has not developed uniformly throughout the country. Different regions run things their own way, which is why off-site transfer of social insurance accounts and provincial-level coordination have still not been fully achieved after so many years. Migrant workers are therefore uninterested in paying for pension insurance, and it is only in recent years that there has been gradual improvement in this area.

6. Reexploring the Labor Regime

Starting from a historical perspective and macrostructure, I have shown how the state created the migrant worker class, described the features of that class and the dual labor market, proposed a theory of differential

---

45. Yang xia, " Guangzhou wei nongmingong 'liangshen dingzhi' shehui yiliao baoxian" (Guangzhou "custom makes" social medical insurance for rural migrant workers), Xinhuashe, March 18, 2009, http://www.gov.cn/govweb/fwxx/jk/2009-03/18 /content_1261734.htm.

citizenship and its exploitative mechanism, and analyzed the institution-alization of discriminatory treatment toward migrant workers. Now I narrow the focus to the worksite, to observe the factories and dormito-ries where migrant workers spend their daily lives—that is, the places where control and resistance occur.

1) *The Dormitory Labor Regime*

Researchers of China's modern industrialization have easily discovered that labor-intensive foreign-invested factories have a high degree of spa-tial proximity or overlap with the living quarters for the migrant workers they employ. The residential spaces of migrant workers come in several types. The first type is the workers' dormitory constructed by the propri-etor within or near the factory compound, where housing may be rented by or is provided gratis to the workers. In the second type, the factory proprietor cooperates with the landlord of the residential quarters (which could be state-owned, collectively owned, or privately owned) to lease the quarters and rent them to the workers. In the third type, the factory pro-prietor does not provide accommodation, and the workers rent rooms from residents of the village where the factory is located or in an urban village or migrant worker village near the factory.

The first type is commonly seen in Guangdong: most workers live in quarters that the factory owners have constructed in or near the factory compound. In one typical example, Taiyang built three dormitories in-side its factory compound, which could accommodate roughly 90 percent of its employees. Ren Yan and Pun Ngai (2006) refer to this arrangement as the "dormitory labor regime." Under it, labor has a high degree of over-lap with living, consumption, and rest spaces. Other researchers have also provided detailed descriptions of this kind of space (Peng Fang 2007a; Ip Iam-chong 2007).

Within Guangdong, however, there are also regional differences. For example, in Zhongshan, on the western bank of the Pearl River, fewer factories provide dormitories (this is also the case in the Yangtze Delta and Xiamen). In Dongguan and Shenzhen, on the eastern side of the Pearl River, where there is a high concentration of Taiwanese- and Hong Kong–invested factories, the classic dormitory labor regime appears. A Taiwan-ese entrepreneur told me: "In the 1990s, if Taishang [in the Shenzhen-

Dongguan region] didn't provide dormitories, they weren't able to hire workers. Rural migrant workers imagined dormitories like a 'work unit system'—that is, factories were responsible for looking after their workers in terms of their living, old age, illness, death, education, and entertainment."[46] In recent years, the situation has gradually changed, and some foreign-invested factories do not provide dormitories or have reduced the amount of residential space that they provide. As migrant workers live and work longer in a particular place, they come to prefer renting quarters away from the factory.

My research team and I came across the second and third type of residential quarters more often in our fieldwork and interviews outside of Guangdong. A Taiwanese manager in Kunshan said: "The local government here doesn't allow factories to build dormitories, so workers have to rent rooms outside on their own. Our factory at one point thought about 'secretly building' a dormitory next to the factory."[47] Another Taigan said something similar: "Officials at the investment promotion bureau told me that they restricted companies with fewer than two thousand employees from building a dormitory on site, and there was a reason: The vacancy rate was too high."[48] A village party secretary in a suburb of Xiamen, in Fujian Province, said: "Here we don't allow foreign companies to build dormitories for nonnative workers to live in. Nonnative workers have to rent rooms outside of the factory so the villagers can earn rental income; this is a benefit to the villagers."[49] These interviews show that many local governments don't allow or don't encourage foreign-invested companies to provide dormitories for their workers because they want to look after the economic needs of local residents and allow them to rent rooms to earn money and invigorate the local real estate market and economy.

In contrast to the case in other regions, the Guangdong government allows FIEs to build workers' dormitories because the dormitory labor regime has become the main type in the Shenzhen-Dongguan region. But why did this kind of dormitory system take shape in this region? There

46. Interview: KL201507.
47. Interview: HG200707.
48. Interview: KS_RT200810.
49. Interview: XM200406.

are two main reasons: First, Shenzhen and Dongguan were the earliest outposts of China's export-oriented economy, and when opening reform began, the factory areas that FIEs entered and established had the characteristics of enclave economies. Furthermore, at this initial stage, the migrant workers who came to these areas without local social networks and ties were in greater need of dormitories provided by the factories. Second, in the early stage, once it became common for factories to provide dormitories, migrant workers were more likely to expect it. As the interviewee above said, if factories "didn't provide dormitories, they weren't able to hire workers." This is clearly the result of institutional path dependence.

Foxconn, most of whose factories are in Shenzhen, is an outstanding case of Guangdong's dormitory labor regime. Foxconn is a manufacturer of electronic services for Apple cell phones and other high-end electronic consumer products, and its factories feature high capital investment and high labor intensity. At the peak of its operations in Shenzhen, it employed around a million workers. Before Foxconn experienced a series of employee suicides in 2010, it provided dormitories basically at no charge to its workers in a system referred to as "food and lodging included." After the suicides, Foxconn increased salaries, but at that point, according to a graduate student who carried out a field survey in Shenzhen, "the method for some business groups was to no longer provide housing or most of the cost of meals. What were originally provided as 'benefits' became cash given to workers, and as a result, workers who needed housing had to pay for it, and the price of food in the dining halls increased."[50] In other words, after salaries increased, room and board were no longer free. Foxconn's dormitory system in the inland regions (for example, at the Chongqing factory that began formally operating in 2010) was different from that in Guangdong. According to local workers, at least a large portion of Foxconn dormitories were "public rental units provided by the government."[51]

The above information confirms that the form of factory regime varies in different regions. The main characteristic of the dormitory labor regime under the Guangdong model is the overlap between working and living space, which creates the conditions for control and exploitation. Ren Yan and Pun Ngai (2006, 23) point out that "the dormitory labor regime signifies the day-to-day reproduction of factory-centered labor and the infiltration of management power into workers' lives, and the arbitrary extension and elastic control of working days and working hours." As an ideal type of labor control, this kind of system presents the following characteristics:

First, the overlap of working and living space facilitates management's adoption of excessive overtime, flexible working hours, double shifts, and other working hour plans that make the movement, assignment, notification, and reshuffling of workers more efficient and flexible.

Second, it reinforces control over the personal freedom of workers and the domestication of their bodies. Migrant workers are severely deprived of freedom of migration and labor rights under the *hukou* system, and an additional layer of surveillance is applied to reproductive control of the female floating population. These external institutional conditions increase the likelihood of migrant workers' being locked into the dormitory system. Once workers join the dormitory labor regime, management's everyday surveillance of their eating, clothing, shelter, and movement is even more detailed and often takes place in areas that outsiders cannot easily observe (e.g., canteens, dormitories, entrance checkpoints, and the places where workers use and manage of personal items). In these cases, management's "material and spatial deployment powers" within the factory compound will reveal even more dominance over workers; this is dominance through material deployment (Peng Fang 2007a, 146).

Third, the dormitory system reinforces the segregation of the nonnative population from local society and further highlights the uprootedness of migrant workers. In Guangdong, industrialized villages are often seen as enclaves, and the migrant workers who are restricted to that production site are also restricted to working and living within a limited spatial parameter. Because migrant workers do not have citizenship status in the local village, they are unable to enjoy the village's social benefits, and their children are generally unable to attend kindergartens or elementary schools provided by the village collective. Even if they obtain permission for their children to attend these schools, they have to pay expensive school fees (Nafu Village, where Taiyang was located, was a classic example). The other side of social segregation is that the reproductive cost of the migrant labor force is shifted to the family and government in the migrant worker's home village. The dormitory labor regime can be considered an enclave within an enclave.

Yet this labor regime space cannot a priori be assumed to be an airtight total institution (Goffman 1961). Below I describe in detail how under certain circumstances, this kind of labor regime can become a sociospatial carrier of resistance that promotes solidarity among workers.

Some factory managers are fond of using *hukou* status to manage workers—for example, by putting workers from the same hometown into the same workshop or dormitory. Others take a diametrically opposite approach (see Ching Kwan Lee 1998). The grouping strategy can promote emotional ties and trusting relationships among workers. The density of the living space also encourages more efficient communication networks, which facilitates contact among workers for group activities such as labor strikes.

An interesting comparison is provided by mainland-owned factories in Guangdong. As the supply chains in Guangdong's export processing sector matured, local mainland-owned factories gradually formed networks. According to the observations of one researcher, mainland-owned factories in the Shenzhen-Dongguan region are predominantly privately owned, and many of the proprietors once worked or served as managers in Taiwanese-owned factories. As a result, these mainland-owned factories exhibit a Taiwanese style in their management, corporate culture, and production, and like Taiwanese-owned factories, they provide their workers with dormitories. However, their management "doesn't adopt 'militarized management' to the extent of Taiwanese-owned factories, and they're more relaxed; generally speaking, they are much more humane than Taishang."[52]

2) Control and Resistance

The dormitory labor regime's sociospatial linkages also increase opportunities for migrant workers to engage in the informal sector and become small proprietors and operators of their own businesses that provide ser-

---

52. Interview: CCP201507.

vices to the migrant worker community. I once interviewed small retailers across the street from Taiyang's factory compound, and I found that the relatives of these shopkeepers worked at Taiyang. Ip Iam-chong (2007, 108–11) observed that in Guangdong, many migrant workers fled from the factory system (the formal sector) and set up their own small shops. In the labor-intensive factories of the Pearl River Delta region, workers leave their jobs at a very high rate, often going back to their villages for the long holidays and then not returning to work afterwards delaying returning to work, or changing to a new factory (switching to a better job). Shuttling back and forth between the coastal regions and their home villages can become a disguised form of freedom. In spring 1994, I accompanied two migrant workers (Dong and Qin), who were also romantic partners, when they returned to their home village in Henan from their factory in Dongguan. I stayed with Qin's family and learned that Qin's younger sister had worked at the same factory in the past. She had returned home to rest for a while and was enjoying a leisurely existence in the countryside. I asked when she planned to return to work, and she said, "I'll go back out once I've rested long enough." During our conversation, she showed little interest in the question of whether or not to go back to work. In any case, she said that she would "go back out when she felt like it."[53]

Migrant workers lack the conditions for collective public resistance, and their resistance often emerges in individual form. Thus, incidents that look trivial or minor in fact have far-reaching implications. One example is Peng Fang's observation of the way workers at the Hengfa factory in Dongguan stood up to management's water-saving measures:[54] The factory management installed water faucets that would save water at fixed times and reduce the amount of water available to the workers for bathing, with the expectation that this would achieve the factory's goal of saving on water costs. This installation caused great inconvenience during the times that workers bathed. The workers' resistance method was not to express their dissatisfaction to the management individually or in groups, but rather to constantly dismantle the water-saving faucet heads so that the factory management had to constantly keep installing them.

53. Interview: SP199405.
54. Hengfa is a pseudonym.

As a result, the factory not only did not save on water, but it had to spend more on maintenance costs, and ultimately the factory management was forced to compromise (Peng Fang 2007a). The workers didn't reach an agreement to adopt this strategy. Instead, they disseminated and imitated the method spontaneously, with tacit coordination and rapid action.

I witnessed similar resistance scenarios. When I was at the Taiyang factory in 1994, I unintentionally observed an eye-catching scene. Early one morning, around 7:30, I walked in a narrow passageway through the dormitory compound to the workshop. Along the passageway was a drainage ditch about one foot wide. Hundreds of staff members filed past me in an orderly group and at a rapid pace. Most of them were young women, and as I was pondering their ages and places of origin, I glimpsed someone nimbly toss a white object into the drainage ditch. When I tried to see clearly what the object was, I saw several more white objects being tossed into the ditch. A few minutes later, after the long line of workers had entered the workshop, I leaned down toward the ditch for a closer inspection and saw that the objects were steamed buns, dozens of which had simply been tossed away. Some had a bite taken out of them, but others were completely intact.

The scene made me immediately think of the "weapons of the weak" that James Scott (1985) wrote about: the behavior of the workers could be considered an alternative, wordless form of protest. This discarding of buns might very well have been a synchronized performance of individual acts without prior agreement, but it constituted a symbolic collective protest: The workers were complaining about the poor quality of their breakfast. I don't know if the factory management discovered this conduct by the workers, but I believe that it was not an isolated incident.

Dormitories can also serve as venues for workers to stand up to the state. The Chinese government strictly controls the reproductive rights of migrant workers, and the surveillance apparatus extends from the worker's home village to the coastal town where she works. Female workers regularly encounter the interference and vexation of pregnancy inspections. Chang Kuei-min (2007) observed that because of the closed-off nature of foreign-invested factories in Guangdong, female workers used the factories to evade the state's family planning controls. When female workers were pregnant, they took refuge in the factories, never leaving the factory compound and thus never stepping into the territory pervaded by state authority. Dormitories are also venues where workers can share their consumer experiences and their dreams and engage in emotional exchanges (Pun Ngai 2006).

Beginning in the late 2000s, an increasing number of migrant workers (especially second-generation migrant workers) were enjoying more choices and were able to rent rooms outside of the factory compound and escape the controls of the dormitory labor regime. Based on his field research in an industrial village of Shenzhen in 2010, Siu (2015) found that the second generation of migrant workers who rented their own rooms experienced an enormous change in living conditions compared with the first generation. The second-generation workers all enjoyed greater freedom in their housing, food, time arrangements, life imagination, and maintaining social relations. Siu's comparison of the life patterns of the two generations of migrant workers once again verifies the intensity of the controls that the dormitory labor regime imposed on the first generation of migrant workers.

3) The Dialectic of Chaos and Security

In newly industrialized cities and towns such as Dongguan, public order problems sometimes become prominent. Complaints regarding poor public order typically represent the viewpoint of business owners (foreign investors). For example, in 1995, Mr. Chen (a Taigan who was an assistant manager) talked about "carrying a gun while distributing paychecks." Chen's handgun wasn't loaded with bullets and was used only for intimidation.[55] I don't have quantitative evidence to measure the relative quality of public order in the Dongguan-Shenzhen regions. According to my fieldwork observations, in those years Dongguan's public order problems were not bad enough to require being armed and prepared to take the law into one's own hands while handing out paychecks. However, at that time, the assemblage of foreign investors, the inundation of large numbers of people from other provinces, the large-scale construction going on everywhere, the motorcycles zooming along the roadways and through narrow lanes, the random honking of horns by large and small vehicles,

---

55. Interview: Chen199506. This incident is mentioned in chapter 4.

and occasional rumors of highway robberies did create a sense of *luan* (chaos) in the Pearl River Delta. Chinese detest *luan*, and the Pearl River Delta was truly chaotic at that time. However, during our fieldwork in the Pearl River Delta, my research team and I also observed that there was order in the midst of chaos in the industrial jungle.

Peng Fang's field investigation at the Hengfa factory discovered that migrant workers referred to the interior and exterior of the factory compound as "inside" and "outside," with the latter being a danger zone full of "gangsters" while the former was comparatively safe (Peng Fang 2007a, 62–66). The sense of security inside came from the management's and workers' social construct of the outside as chaotic. This discovery has echoes of the abovementioned discovery by Chang Kuei-min that factory dormitories were being used to evade pregnancy examinations, reclaiming the private space of reproductive rights from the state. We cannot forget that allowing local law enforcement officers to arbitrarily arrest and fine members of the nonnative population under the Custody and Repatriation Methods system was not abolished until after the 2003 Sun Zhigang Incident. At that time, the terror of the incident still lingered; furthermore, the power of family planning units to impose fines also made migrant workers avoid the units at all costs. For ordinary people, the government's unfettered public power was also a source of chaos.

The chaos and danger outside were constantly reconstructed through various incidents and rumors and caused migrant workers to voluntarily stay in the factory compound, as if it was the factory that provided workers with safety and protection and not allowing the chaos outside to flow into the factory compound was a driving force. There was also a pulling force that led workers to voluntarily remain in the factory compound: the benefits and facilities that the factory management provided, such as the facilities in the Foxconn factory compound that made workers feel that "even if they spent all day within Foxconn and didn't leave the factory, they could live very well" (Tseng Wei-ling and Lin Thung-Hong 2012, 27). Because of its especially large scale, Foxconn was an extreme example of this image of a miniature paternalistic welfare enclave, but similar situations are not hard to find in the Pearl River Delta. The Hengfa factory was such a welfare enclave on a smaller scale than Foxconn, providing a canteen, dormitory, medical clinic, relatively cheap medicines, a kindergarten, and so on. The manager said that the company's relationship to its workers was one of "their family, their shelter" (quoted in Peng Fang 2007a, 108).

But we cannot exaggerate the benefits described here. The provision of benefits in this factory system combined the intentions of squeezing out productive efficiency and enhancing safety management. These paternalistic welfare enclaves cannot be compared to the welfare concepts of a Western-style welfare state. Rather, they represent the overall harsh macro management of migrant workers and a deficiency of social welfare, along with the state's painstaking noninterference, that highlight the benefits of a dormitory factory. Even if migrant workers use the factory space to flee or skirt the margins of state control, it is ultimately hard to escape the external and even greater authoritarian control apparatus, and this apparatus's institutional foundation is the omnipresent differential citizenship. Observed from this angle, the dormitory labor regime can be considered the embodiment of differential citizenship in the sociospatial order of the work site.

4) Despotism or Hegemony

The miniature paternalistic welfare enclaves scattered in large numbers all over the Pearl River Delta can give some workers a feeling of sanctuary, but even though we cannot regard them as total institutions, their fundamental nature is still that of a spatial mechanism for controlling the labor force. This question leads to another theoretical debate: based on Burawoy's (1979) classic study we can ask, does the labor system of FIEs in the Pearl River Delta qualify as despotism or hegemony?

In the 1990s Ching Kwan Lee researched and compared two garment factories in Hong Kong and Shenzhen. Both were of small to medium size and run by the same proprietor, and the production line operators were mainly women, but the two locations presented different labor regimes. Lee referred to the Hong Kong plant as "familial hegemony" and the Shenzhen plant as "localistic despotism" (1998, 9). Shenzhen's localistic despotism is a subtype of Burawoy's despotic labor regime. Lee discovered that China's despotic system was not only due to the absence of the state and constraints on autonomous trade unions that allow capital to arbitrarily control and coercively discipline labor. She observed that localistic networks and genderism played an even deeper role in the politics of production. Localism and genderism not only organized the labor market but also channeled labor to Shenzhen from all over China, and they were then integrated into the factory system and used to legitimate the management class's control of workers. In this Shenzhen factory, managers (most of whom were male) controlled workers on the production line (most of whom were female), using de facto gendered localistic authority to disguise class domination and make it more effective (Ching Kwan Lee 1998, 135). The epistemological feature of this groundbreaking study of Chinese labor is in its foregrounding of localism and genderism to present the interlocked hierarchies of class, gender, and localism in the same labor space. On the level of empirical phenomena, Anita Chan's (2001) research findings are aligned with Lee's argument.

In the mid-2000s Peng Fang (2007a and 2007b) carried out research on the Hengfa factory in Dongguan, a medium-size enterprise that adopted a timekeeping system for its production line wages, instead of calculating wages by piecework. Although this factory had a paternalistic authoritarian management style, the workers still willingly engaged in the rush-work game, or what Burawoy refers to as the "making-out game" (1979, 80). Why was that so? Peng proposed a multidimensional institutional explanation: Hengfa's timekeeping wage system was in fact a disguised form of the piecework system. Examining the arrangements of the production line at the work site, he discovered that management's use of a covert piecework system, coupled with stipulations on when shifts ended, entrance controls, and so on, led to a spontaneously organized and to some degree consensual making-out game, which then shaped a hegemonic system. This study's findings were different from Ching Kwan Lee's findings ten years earlier and constitute a potential theoretical revision to Burawoy's proposition. Lee brought gender and localism into class analysis. Peng's analysis of the labor regime brought living space (dormitory, canteen, etc.) into the politics of production and likewise expanded the focus to extend beyond class dominance relations within the workshop, pointing out the existence of a resistance space in the dormitory labor regime.

The series of suicides at Foxconn in 2010 shocked the world and reignited interest in China's labor system. A major manufacturer of electronic services for Apple systems, Foxconn operates on an enormous scale: its factory compound is composed of supersize plants, and its production bases throughout China often employ hundreds of thousands of workers. According to research by Tseng Wei-ling (2012) and Tseng and Lin Thung-Hong (2012), Foxconn is a key link in Apple's value chain, and it is under Apple's direction and intervention in terms of manufacturing and personnel matters. Foxconn's production divisions are independent of each other and compete with each other for orders. In terms of labor management, Foxconn exhibits arbitrary management authority at the work site, leading to despotization of management. Lin Thung-hong and others have referred to Foxconn's labor system as "global fragmented despotism" and use this concept to explain the chain of suicides at Foxconn: Under this enormous factory system, workers led atomized lives and suffered under the pressure of excessive overtime and social isolation (Tseng Wei-ling and Lin Thung-Hong 2012; Lin Thung-hong, Yi-ling Lin, and Wei-ling Tseng 2016; see also J. Chan, Pun, and Selden 2013).

The studies by Ching Kwan Lee (1998), Peng Fang (2007a), and Tseng and Lin Thung-Hong (2012), spanning a period of twenty years, are individual case studies, so we cannot use them to fully determine whether the labor regime of the Pearl River Delta qualifies as despotic or hegemonic. But the methodology of these three case studies falls under the "extended case method" (Burawoy 2009): the data saturation in each study is very high, is based on solid field investigations, and has had its theoretical proposition examined, which makes them authoritative. Therefore, using these three ideal-typical cases combined with the field data analysis in this book, I move from the theoretical angle of Burawoy's proposition to expound on the theoretical nature of the labor regime under the Guangdong model.

First, we can affirm the view of Ching Kwan Lee, Anita Chan, and others that the local labor regime, space, and conditions are despotic. Peng Fang's definition of his research subject as a hegemonic system challenges the viewpoints of Lee and Chan, but is this challenge particularized or generalized? Before working through this puzzle, we must note the different points in time represented by Peng's observations relative to those of Lee and Chan. Peng was observing the Hengfa factory in the mid-2000s. At that time, labor conditions in the Pearl River Delta had improved to a certain degree over the 1990s, reflecting the stricter CSR demands of international buyers—which were also reflected in management methods. Behind the improvement of labor conditions were the enhancement of the relative price of China's labor force and the strengthening, to a certain extent, of the Chinese government's protection of workers. According to my field investigations from the 1990s to the 2010s, these improvements were generally evident. Of course, the despotic management model can still be discovered at work sites in the Pearl River Delta even now, but generally speaking the arbitrariness and dominance of management behavior has come under a degree of constraint. This trend can be seen in the gradual increase of labor strikes, state intervention, and management concessions starting in the late 2000s. Furthermore, Peng's finding of workers' living space being channeled into the politics of production is not limited to class domination in the workshop, which enlarges the scope of research. His research reminds us that we cannot ascertain the nature of a system from the work site alone, because social relations in living spaces beyond the work site also affect social relations at the work site. Using this enlarged perspective, he analyzed the Hengfa factory as a hegemonic system. An analysis of workers' living space is an important supplement to Burawoy's classic proposition, and it enriches our understanding of China's labor system.

Second, on further reflection, the making-out game is a core explanatory mechanism for Burawoy's proposition. In Burawoy's primary train of thought, the reason workers are willing to engage in "making out"— that is, voluntarily making out in the sense of the hegemonic system—is because doing so becomes a kind of game (play). This proposition of Burawoy's, does not pertain to the vast majority of China's migrant worker factory regimes. In China, so-called making out is usually the result of management pressure and coercion and is an involuntary submission. The piecework system (or covert piecework system) easily leads to rush work, but the rush-work phenomenon does not necessarily mean that it is a Burawoyian game. For this reason, the focus of analysis must return to the problem of excessive overtime emphasized above in this book. Migrant workers desire overtime because their base pay (the minimum wage) is too low and forces them to work overtime. And under the piecework system, overtime inevitably is presented as the rush-work phenomenon, because only through rush work can wages be increased and the proprietor, during peak delivery periods, demands that workers do rush work. The rush-work behavior of workers under the low-wage regime cannot be simply equated with a Burawoyian game. That is, the making-out image that workers present in their behavior cannot serve as proof that they consent to making out and excessive overtime.

Burawoy's despotic-hegemonic dichotomy is predicated on the state's role in tempering capital's power. The state's intervention in labor-capital relations—for example, through labor laws or social insurance that provides workers with resources outside of the market—allows workers to not be fully dependent on wage income. Workers gained negotiating power granted by state institutions and were able to contend with capital, and as a result capital was obliged to obtain the consent of labor. When we view the situation from this angle, we must return to the role of the state to discuss the nature of the labor regime. According to Burawoy's theory, state intervention in the labor regime presupposes that such intervention improves labor conditions (only in this way will production be transformed from a despotic to a hegemonic regime). However, what we see of the state's role in China is just the opposite: For a time, the state intervened in labor-capital relations and participated in the competition to exploit labor, as a result of which poor working conditions for migrant workers were retained and the differential citizenship of laborers rigidified.

Furthermore, Somers (2008) points out that under the pressure of neoliberal globalization, the state often abdicates the role it should play as protector (safeguarding rights) and allows this role to be taken over by the profit-oriented market economy, resulting in the contractualization and marketization of citizenship. But the situation is different in China. A major characteristic of China's state capitalism is the integration of the work unit system and bureaucratic capital, which results in the state's major withdrawal from the social welfare sphere. The permanent employees working in the government and state-owned enterprises enjoy relatively generous remuneration from the government, state-run institutions, and state-owned enterprises. But privately owned and foreign-owned enterprises that employ blue-collar migrant workers cannot possibly give them that kind of remuneration. The state therefore needed to intervene in the labor market, which resulted in a new form of dual labor market. This deprived migrant workers of the support of the state system and benefits and subjected them to the negative results of the marketization of citizenship rights.

5) The Role of the State and Pseudo-Contractual Relations

When we observe the influence that China's state apparatus has on labor-capital relations in the process of capitalist development, we must especially take note of the variable of the nature of the state. In the theories of Burawoy and Somers outlined above, their propositions proceed from the presupposition of a market capitalistic state. Yet in China, the point of departure is the party-state capitalist state: the state has always forcefully intervened in labor-capital relations, but the most important objective of its intervention is to extract fiscal revenue. Although the state is present, it is often absent from the question of protecting labor. In China, the state's institutional fostering of differential citizenship has exacerbated capital's exploitation of labor, and this is a major characteristic of China's rent-seeking development state.

Under the differential citizenship system for migrant workers, we often observe behavior such as migrant workers willingly working overtime or striving for overtime and signing agreements with management for voluntary nonenrollment in social insurance, all of which occur under the asymmetrical power structure of labor and capital. In the class relations of Europe and America, workers use trade unions to negotiate with management, reach agreements (for instance, on pay increases), and suspend fighting between labor and capital. But in China, because labor has access to only a tiny amount of resources, it is unable to organize autonomous trade unions, and as a result the contractual relations or tacit agreements it reaches with management are dominated by management.[56] These pseudo-contractual relations, under which equal negotiation relations do not exist between labor and capital, have the following characteristics:

First, this kind of pseudo-contractual arrangement, from the perspective of state law, is illegal or extralegal behavior, and strictly speaking it should be null and void. However, these arrangements are tacitly agreed to or surreptitiously encouraged by local government, and they constitute hidden rules or unofficial local rules—a concrete manifestation of so-called flexible policies.

---

56. Here I am discussing contractual relations from the angle of new institutional economics.

Second, individual migrant workers tacitly endorse this kind of contractual arrangement, and they show submission by working overtime to rush orders and make as much money as they can. Migrant workers temporarily accept this kind of control, not due to the effects of their false consciousness, but rather because they have no better alternative under the existing system. This kind of class control model can help capital prevent workers from adopting collective resistance, and as a result, the resistance of workers can be expressed only as individual, uncoordinated resistance until the point at which the external equilibrium is shattered, or the resistance actions of labor gain the government's tacit consent.

Third, the stability of the flexible rules that local governments permit is influenced by external conditions, including the continuity of state policies, the stability of the relative price of essential production factors and of the industrial structure, and so on. As soon as state policy changes (such as with the implementation of the Labor Contract Law and Social Insurance Law) the price of factors of production change (e.g., when real wages increase), or industry faces pressure to upgrade (as when Guangdong implemented its policy of empty the cage and change birds), the equilibrium of local regulations decreases, leading the original control model to malfunction. From 2008 onward, Guangdong's gradual increase in collective resistance actions by labor—demanding pay increases, the payment of wages in arrears, social insurance payments by management, etc.—was because the former equilibrium had broken down, crippling the control model over the migrant worker class.

In short, behind the overtime and the making-out phenomenon in China's coastal export processing industries is a mandatory everyday discourse: superficially progressive working hour policies, suppressed minimum wages, and elastic local law enforcement have combined to construct a tacit agreement between labor, capital, and the government. Under this tacit agreement, overtime wages become the main incentive driving labor aspirations and squeezing labor productivity, and they become a routine practice. Here we see that the phenomenon of Chinese migrant workers' voluntarily working overtime is comparable to the "pure labor" consciousness in Shieh Gwo-Shyong's (1997) study of Taiwanese workers and small labor contractors in 1970–80. Although there are differences in the structural and social factors in these two situations, the similarities deserve further exploration.

CHAPTER SIX

Taiwanese- and Chinese-Owned Companies under the Transformation of the Guangdong Model

The global financial crisis triggered a great Taishang exodus in Dongguan, Guangdong Province, in 2008. Many Taishang that were experiencing financial difficulties shut down without warning and even skipped town under the cover of night. Why did Taishang leave in such haste? One Taigan who spent a long time in the Pearl River Delta insightfully described the Taishang exodus: "They ran off because it was too difficult to do the right thing. Just leaving it all behind was actually a relief, because conscientiously dealing with years of accumulated 'debt' would have wasted too much time, without even knowing when it might end."[1] The economic crisis affected other foreign-owned companies as well, and many Hong Kong–invested companies joined the exodus.

The emergence of this crisis put foreign investors and local governments under enormous pressure. Yet the external shock of the global financial crisis was only a catalyst for the exodus: the deeper cause was pressure from the long-term transformation of China's economy. The factors involved in this pressure included an upsurge in production costs in China (for labor, land, and environmental protection), changes in China's pol-

---

1. Interview: Jerry200902.

icy environment and relations between government and business, and the promotion of the industrial upgrading policy. The enormous force of these internal and external factors, coupled with the attraction of lower labor costs in peripheral countries, caused new changes in the regional division of labor and impelled another shift of GVCs and GCCs. This shift included simultaneously moving further inland and migrating outward. The ways that FIEs responded to this crisis revealed characteristics of path dependence and ultimately resulted in the dismantling and reorganization of the Guangdong growth model. This was a long-term restructuring process that had been fermenting before the crisis, and the adjustment to it continues to this day.

Yet the withdrawal or redeployment of FIEs is not a simple story of dis-embedding. FIEs' entering China and forming embedded relationships with local society entailed a long-term breaking-in process, and their withdrawal also involved a complex transformation. In other words, FIEs withdrew under a range of models, the choice of which reflected the path dependence of individual manufacturers in their prior interactions with local society.

1. State Policy and Changes in Government-Business Relations

Guangdong's export-oriented economy came under a new wave of transformational pressure from the mid-2000s onward. The first topic of discussion here is the rising labor costs. For labor-intensive factories long accustomed to high profit margins guaranteed by low wages, increasing labor costs inevitably threatened their profitability and even their survival. The effect of this nationwide problem was heightened in the Pearl River Delta, with its concentration of low-capitalized, labor-intensive industries. The search for cheap labor was the main incentive for Taishang to enter China in the first place, and rising labor costs brought the Guangdong EOI growth model to the brink of dissolution.

1) New State Policies, Worker Protests, and Rising Labor Costs

Two reasons for rising wages were the relative decline in the size of the rural labor force entering the industrial sector of coastal cities and the central government's response to this demographic trend by increasing wages and enforcing labor protections. From the mid-2000s onward, the minimum wage rose noticeably in all coastal regions. In the Pearl River Delta from 2006 to 2017, the minimum wages in Shenzhen and Dongguan rose from 810 yuan to 2,130 yuan and from 690 yuan to 1,510 yuan, respectively. In 2010, a strike broke out at the Japanese-owned Honda automotive plant in Guangzhou, prompting the company to promise wage increases. The same thing happened to Foxconn, after a string of suicides occurred among its staff members. The Guangdong government seized this opportunity to substantially increase the minimum wage.

During this same period, the Chinese government also reinforced its collection of social insurance fees from FIEs and began collecting fees for the housing provident fund. The central government's policy of collecting social insurance fees from companies began in 1997, but it was not formally legislated until 2011. For a long time, Guangdong's local governments had adopted flexible measures to address the social insurance issue and had granted companies large discounts on the social insurance fees they were meant to pay: following the logic of discounting the number of employees for the head tax, they reduced both the number of people enrolled in social insurance and coverage rates, especially for the relatively costly pension insurance. Although discounts to social insurance fees were illegal or extralegal under the Labor Contract Law and Social Insurance Law, they were a major prop for the Guangdong growth model and pervasive throughout China. Local officials and businesses were initially in tacit agreement on this issue, but as the macroenvironment of central government policy changed, social insurance became a point of dispute between government and business and triggered waves of labor unrest. Guangdong's problem was especially troublesome, as labor began demanding repayment of the social insurance debt that had accumulated, along with worker grievances, under the flexible policies adopted during the era of rapid economic growth.

The Social Insurance Law stipulates that social insurance accounts are geographically transferrable: "Article 19: The basic old-age [i.e., pension] insurance relationship of a member who has worked across different pooling districts shall transfer together with the member, and the member's lengths of contribution payment shall be cumulative."[2] This new safeguard gives migrant workers a stronger incentive to participate in pension insurance. In the Pearl River Delta region, worker demands that companies pay what was owed on social insurance fees became the focus of frequent collective protest starting in 2012. Migrant workers at foreign-invested factories generally do not have labor unions, and even the few labor unions that have been organized are mostly pro forma and have no collective consultation function. The government has never encouraged protest by migrant workers, especially during the stable operation of Guangdong's growth alliances.

The new government policies and laws empowered worker protests and put pressure on local governments and FIEs. But collective action requires a trigger point and external support, such as NGOs engaged in labor movements and lawyers defending workers' rights. Although the Chinese government is extremely wary of civil society organizations, it reserves a certain space for these rights-defending organizations and individuals and maintains contact with them. The trigger point for worker resistance was demanding payment of social insurance fees and housing provident fund fees. Current laws retain a measure of fuzzy space that allows workers two years to press for payment, and this has led workers to press for concessions from management through strikes and other actions. The intervention and assistance of labor NGOs are often evident in these collective actions by workers—for example, in the strike at Yue Yuen, the largest Taiwanese-owned factory in Dongguan, in 2014. This wave of labor protests was followed by increasing labor costs. During this process, the interactive relationships among government, foreign investors, the workers' movement, and its outside supporters became more intricate and complex (see Lo Chao-Kuang 2014).

It is worth examining a review of these incidents by NGO workers who have been involved in labor protests in recent years. Dadong is the

---

2. *Translator's Note:* The quote is from the official translation by the Ministry of Human Resources and Social Security, posted on the website of the Congressional-Executive Commission on China, December 2, 2016, https://www.cecc.gov/resources /legal-provisions/social-insurance-law-of-the-peoples-republic-of-china.

head of a labor NGO in the Pearl River Delta and has years of experience in defending labor rights;[3] he is circumspect about his sources of funding. Because he has successfully supported many appeals and strikes by workers, foreign NGOs have been willing to provide him with funding, but he feels that this could complicate his relationships and attract the attention of "domestic security," so he has refused financial assistance from NGOs outside of China.[4] Given that the central government has imposed harsher controls on rights defenders since 2012, why is this kind of organization still able to take part in labor movements? In August 2015 I asked Dadong whether his organization's work had been affected by the recent clampdown by Beijing authorities. Dadong said: "We're managing. We've maintained good relations with the government, and domestic security isn't that fearsome. The nastiest people here in Guangdong are Labor Supervision.[5] They nitpick and demand bribes."[6]

Dadong maintains regular contact with the local government and domestic security. He knows that government surveillance is ubiquitous and that it is impossible to conceal his labor support activities, so he feels it's better to maintain channels of communication. In this wave of labor unrest, labor NGOs' contact with domestic security police gives us an opportunity to observe the interactions between them.

2) The Yue Yuen Strike

In April 2014, a strike broke out at the Yue Yuen shoe factory in Gaobu Town, in Dongguan City. More than forty thousand workers demanded that management make up for its lack of payments for pension social insurance and to the housing provident fund. With the participation and assistance of ten labor NGOs, the strike was the largest labor protest in recent history in Guangdong. Why did it happen in 2014? The Chinese government began requiring foreign companies to pay into social insur-

3. Dadong is a pseudonym.
4. "Domestic security" refers to domestic security detachments or brigades, which constitute the special police force under the Ministry of Public Security that is responsible for political security within China.
5. Labor supervision section staff members fall under the Department of Human Resources and Social Security and the labor bureaus.
6. Interview: DD2015.

ance programs for their workers in 1997–98, and the policy stipulated that a worker employed for fifteen years could apply for pension insurance benefits. Consequently, the first generation of workers enrolled in social insurance was able to begin applying for retirement benefits in 2013. In terms of the housing provident fund, although the government had stipulated that payments were to begin in 1999 (management and workers each had to cover 5 percent of the fee), only a tiny number of foreign-owned and privately owned factories in the Pearl River Delta had actually paid into the fund. When senior employees of foreign companies were about to retire, demands for the factories to make up for the missing provident fund payments were also put on the table. This timeframe had been built into the system, so an institutional logic of path dependence existed. The strike at Yue Yuen was not an isolated case at that time, but it attracted more media attention than other strikes because of the factory's enormous scale and broader influence.

Observing the response by local government and public security units to the Yue Yuen strike changes the standard view of the Chinese government as strongly biased in favor of the management side. Zhang Zhiru, a rights defender who was deeply involved in this strike, was impressed by the ambivalent attitude of domestic security and the local government toward this incident. A dramatic turning point in this protest movement was the workers' occupation and blockade of a crucial bridge in the urban area on April 5, but domestic security did not catch wind of this plan in advance. From the bridge incident until the beginning of the full-scale strike on April 14, "the formidable abilities of the public security intelligence apparatus did not directly intervene in checking the spread of the strike, as in the past. . . . Zhang Zhiru used QQ[7] and the Internet to direct the workers to raise new appeals, encourage workers to elect representatives, and criticize management for a lack of good faith, telling the workers not to be taken in. Zhang Zhiru wondered why public security and domestic security tolerated him for so long and didn't interfere in any way with internet chats" (Chen Chih-Jou Jay 2015, 42–43). The management side was similarly perplexed: "QQ, Weibo, and WeChat played a powerful communications role. But before the 24th [of April], Yue Yuen's

---

7. QQ is an instant messaging software service that was popular at that time among Chinese cell-phone users.

management repeatedly asked public security and domestic security to block QQ as they had done in the past, and public security and domestic security both gave the excuse that there was no legal basis, and they were unwilling to advance their operations" (2015, 43).

Just as the strike began, the company's older generation of top-level managers asked a veteran Taiwanese political figure trusted by the Chinese government to "transmit a message to Beijing" requesting assistance, but the response they received at that time was that the government was "willing but unable to help."[8] By this stage, the central government's policies had shifted toward protecting the interests of workers. Furthermore, once Xi Jinping came to power, the high-level relationships that the older generation of Yue Yuen managers had cultivated were no longer of any use. Dealing with the labor strike crisis alerted Yue Yuen's managers to the fact that the old, familiar operation model of government-business relationships had broken down.

It was only in the last stage of the strike that the local government took a hard-line attitude toward the workers' movement and became directly involved in coordinating a return to work. Why did the local government's attitude apparently change from soft to hard? It seems that after initially adopting a policy of passive inaction or limited control of the protest and allowing the labor movement to strengthen, the local government took advantage of the situation to force major concessions from management. But the response of the local Dongguan government cannot be regarded in isolation. Instead, it was a product of the entire political and economic macroenvironment. China's economy was at a stage of industrial transformation, and the policy was to improve the wages and working conditions of migrant workers to a limited extent. Furthermore, Xi Jinping's government was carrying out an anticorruption campaign and reorganizing the power structure. Local governments exerted pressure on FIEs in line with this larger trend, making their response to the Yue Yuen strike a sign of the changing situation. Ultimately, Yue Yuen's top managers agreed to settle the matter once and for all through a one-off contribution to pension insurance, taking both years of service and wage levels into account. Yue Yuen paid a total of around 400 million yuan in social insurance fees, which was calculated to add approximately

8. Interview: YYPL2015.

US$1.50 to the cost of each pair of name-brand shoes from then on. Brand-name firms were willing to shoulder US$0.70 of this cost, with Yue Yuen absorbing the remainder.

After the strike, the local government allowed the Guangdong Province Federation of Labor Unions to send officials to Yue Yuen to reorganize the labor union. According to a manager of the Taishin Shoe Manufacturing Group, "Before the incident, there were never labor union representatives at the meetings. The provincial Federation of Labor Unions came down and treated Yue Yuen's Gaobu factory as a pilot project, forcibly intervening and forming a labor union."[9] By April 2015, 27,000 workers had joined the union. That was more than ten times the membership before the strike (2,500, or only 6.3 percent of the company's 40,000 workers). At this stage, rights defense NGOs no longer had a role to play.

From the Yue Yuen labor strike, we can further observe the interactive relationship between the local government (including domestic security) and labor NGOs. The government's model for handling rights defense NGOs and labor rights defenders can be summarized as one of nurturing and control: Government units and rights defenders normally maintain contact with each other, and when a sudden incident occurs, labor rights defenders may be placed under control as necessary (including through imprisonment, forced vacations, enforced loss of contact, and disappearance). At the same time, the government allows labor rights defenders to have a basic level of activity and contact with workers. Then at the crucial moment, the government gives rights defenders a free hand to mobilize workers to fight for their rights for a period of time. Finally, the government acts as arbitrator to tidy up the situation and formulates new guidelines for labor-management relations. Of course, this government behavioral model is an ideal type, and specific behavior may deviate from it. However, decoding the government's behavioral motivations can help us understand its statecraft. At the same time, it should be noted that this statecraft is not the result of a comprehensive rational design from the outset. Rather, it shows that the government progressively gropes its way along, interacting with business and labor and evolving a response to changing government-business and labor-management relations. Both

9. Interview: YYPL2015.

domestic security's noninterference in Zhang Zhiru's participation at one stage of the Yue Yuen strike and Dadong's assessment of his relations with domestic security can be analyzed within this framework. We can temporarily name this statecraft the "nurture and control model."

The Yue Yuen strike also gives us a glimpse of a typical model of intervention by a rights defense NGO in a workers' movement. Zhang Zhiru refers to it as "case follow-up": "When a labor dispute occurs at a factory, [we] intervene to teach workers skills for negotiating with management. The Yue Yuen strike is a typical case. The workers originally raised only two demands, which were requiring management to make postpay contributions to social insurance and the housing provident fund. After I went in, they added another condition on QQ, demanding a 30 percent wage adjustment as a bargaining chip for negotiations. Ultimately management actually did agree to a monthly 'living allowance' of 230 yuan."[10]

For Yue Yuen's senior mainlander staff members (especially those at the managerial level), the social insurance and housing provident fund payments were very attractive to them, because they had many years of service (making them close to retirement) and relatively high wage levels. As a result, they tended to participate more enthusiastically than workers in the postpay contributions (both workers and management had to make up for the missed payments for pension insurance and the housing provident fund). This demand was much less attractive to younger workers, because they couldn't be sure where they would be in the future and were therefore reluctant to pay for social insurance and the housing provident fund. Zhang Zhiru thus proposed demanding that management provide a living allowance (effectively, a pay increase), which was a major incentive for younger workers. This clever strategy was not only a response to case follow-up, but it also raised the stakes, and it took advantage of the motivations of different groups of workers to support the strike.

Yue Yuen's Taiwanese managers believed that the main fuse touching off the strike was older workers' worries that they wouldn't be able to draw their full pensions after retirement. Senior Lugan mobilized a collective action for the sake of their personal interests. According to a manager of the Taishin Shoe Manufacturing Group, "they calculated that

10. Interview: ZZR2015.

based on their most recent year's wages, they could draw an extra 100,000 yuan or more when they retired."[11] An assistant manager at the same company said: "The Lugan sensed an impending crisis. They saw that Yue Yuen was gradually moving its production lines out of China, and taking their own exit strategy into account, they were in favor of a strike so they could gain more benefit."[12] According to another viewpoint from someone else at the company, "We were all facing a factor handed down from history. When social insurance first began in 1998, the government didn't raise the idea of full coverage. [Even if] you said all of the workers had to be insured, the government didn't stipulate that number for you to insure."[13] As a result, the reductions that foreign companies had enjoyed thanks to their government-business relationships now had to be dealt with as a historical problem left behind from the era of flexible and elastic policies. Small FIEs that decided it was too hard to do the right thing, closed down, and skipped town. But larger FIEs had to deal with assets and interest relationships that were complex and had deep roots, so they had no way to evade this historical debt.

The Chinese government emphasizes stability, so its support for workers' demands and collective action has been limited and dependent on the circumstances. In March 2015, Yue Yuen experienced a second labor strike, this time over a factory merger and workers' ability to draw upon housing provident funds after leaving the company. The new policy that the Dongguan government proposed at that time was that the provident fund could not be drawn upon because that would put financial pressure on the government. The government held fast to this policy because it mainly affected the interests of senior Lugan: "this strike involves less than 5 percent of the company's employees and would not substantially affect the company's operations."[14] As the workers continued to protest, however, the Dongguan government finally made a partial concession and announced that its policy excluded four foreign companies (including Yue

11. Interview: YYPL2015.

12. Interview: XX2015.

13. Interview: HTS201212.

14. "Waimei: Dongguan Yuyuan xiechang zaici bagong yaoqiu tiqu gongjijin" (Foreign media: 3,000 workers at Dongguan's Yue Yuen shoe factory again go on strike demanding to collect provident fund), Fenghuang caijing, March 19, 2015, https://finance.ifeng.com/a/20150319/13564845_0.shtml.

Yuen). This quickly ended the strike. Zhang Zhiru believes that not allowing workers to draw upon their housing provident funds when they left their jobs was a policy retrogression that benefited company management, and that the new policy covered all workers in Dongguan—so theoretically the Yue Yuen strike could spread to other foreign-owned factories. But Zhang's role in this provident fund incident was limited. Earlier, a veteran labor rights defender had warned him: "This year doesn't look good, don't get too involved." In 2014, a domestic security officer had further alerted Zhang that Shenzhen and Dongguan would be dealing with NGOs that became involved in the Yue Yuen incident.[15] As the central government intensified its crackdown on civil society, the Guangdong government launched a series of interrogations and detentions targeting labor NGO activists in December 2015. According to one news report, "This incident is to constraint an upsurge in Guangdong's collective rights defense. Shocked by the swarm of labor rights defense movements in recent years, the government needs to find a suitable 'chicken' to slaughter."[16] These suppressed NGOs were all labor rights organizations that had been active in the Pearl River Delta, and several of their leaders had been involved in the strike at Yue Yuen. The government used the labor rights NGOs to force foreign companies to pay off their historical debt in a process reminiscent of the famous saying, "When the flying birds are killed off, the fine bow is put into storage; when the cunning hare dies, the running dog is cooked."[17] By this logic, it was all but inevitable that the government's nurture and control model of governing rights defense NGOs would be ruthlessly applied.

This book takes the G-D-L analytical standpoint, in which the local government plays a major role in the GVC. The action or inaction of local governments (including public security organs) in Yue Yuen's labor strike allows us to observe the function of government intervention in the GVC's distribution of benefit. Evidently, the wave of labor strikes at

15. Interview: ZZR2015.

16. Liang Chia-wei, "Zhongguo zhenya Guangdong laotuan, Xianggang chuanlian quanqiu shengyuan" (China suppresses Guangdong labor groups, Hong Kong establishes ties to draw global support), Jiaodian shijian, December 17, 2015, https://eventsinfocus .org/news/338.

17. TRANSLATOR'S NOTE: A quote from "The Biography of Han Xin," in Sima Qian's *Historical Records*.

Taiwanese-owned companies in the early 2010s was closely related to the migration of the GVC.

3) Emptying Cages and Changing Birds: The Industrial Upgrading Policy

The Guangdong government's motivation for promoting industrial upgrading had several sources: a bottleneck in the export processing growth model, a shift in the labor-intensive manufacturing GVC, a spatial redistribution of regional manufacturing's division of labor, and pressure from the central government. Starting with the Eleventh Five-Year Plan (covering 2006–10), the Chinese government began emphasizing the development of domestic demand and pushing for industrial upgrading. The Twelfth Five-Year Plan (covering 2011–15) ramped up the push for industrial upgrading. At this stage, the processing trade began to lose its importance, and its contribution to foreign exchange earnings also declined. Against this background, the Guangdong government proposed a strategy of emptying cages and changing birds.[18] At the end of 2007, the government put forward its "dual shift" strategy, referring to a spatial shift of industry and labor from the Pearl River Delta to Guangdong's inland region.[19]

At the same time, however, the central government in 2008 implemented the Labor Contract Law. Coupled with a drastic shrinking of export orders following the global financial crisis and a wave of FIEs closing down or moving to other countries, the new law led to the industrial

18. In March 2005, the Guangdong government issued "Guanyu wo sheng shanqu ji dongxi liangyi yu Zhujiang sanjiaozhou lianshou tuijin chanye zhuanyi de yijian (shixing)" ([Trial] opinions regarding our province's mountain region and eastern and western flanks joining hands with the Pearl River Delta to push forward industrial shifts), Guangdong Government Document No. 22 (2005), http://www.gd.gov.cn/gkmlpt/content/0/136/post_136277.html#7.

19. In 2008, the Guangdong government formally put forward its "Zhonggong Guangdong shengwei guangdongsheng renmin zhengfu guanyu tuijin chanye zhuanyi he laodongli zhuanyi de jueding" (Resolution of the CCP Guangdong Provincial Party Committee and Guangdong Provincial People's Government regarding pushing forward the industrial shift and labor force shift), Guangdong Document No. 4 (2008), May 4, 2008, http://www.gd.gov.cn/zwgk/wjk/zcfgk/content/post_2521212.html.

upgrading strategy's suffering a setback. The provincial party secretary of Guangdong at that time, Wang Yang, observed: "The global financial crisis was a vivid lesson for Guangdong."[20] The problem was also clearly grasped in a formal central document:

> With the deepened development of economic globalization and regional economic integration, and especially against the background of the continued spread of the current international financial crisis and its increasing effect on the economy, the development of the Pearl River Delta region has been seriously affected. The combined effects of the international financial crisis and unresolved structural contradictions, of external demand sharply decreasing along with excess capacity in some industries, and of major fluctuations in the price of raw materials along with greater dependence on the international market, have magnified problems in economic operations, and deep-seated contradictions and problems have become more apparent (National Development and Reform Commission 2008, 7).

The financial crisis dealt a harsh blow to the export economy. In Xishui Town, where Taiyang's Dongguan factory was located, in the first half of 2009 alone, revenue from the VAT dropped by an estimated 70 percent, which indicates the extent of the pressure on the local government. According to one news report, 20,000 out of 70,000 Hong Kong–owned businesses in Guangdong were likely to shut down.[21] Chinese and Taiwanese media frequently published reports about Taishang shutting down during this period. Because the organization, production, and marketing of these business were path-dependent, many manufacturers resisted both relocation and upgrading. For example, one report reveals in detail the difficulties manufacturers faced: "'But can I just move at short notice?' . . . Not to mention that the company's clients and satellite factories are all nearby, the removal costs are also a major consideration. In the more than ten years since the factory was built here, its busi-

20. Wang, Yang, "Jinrong weiji gei Guangdong shangle shengdong yike" (Financial crisis gives Guangdong a vivid lesson). *Renmin ribao haiwaiban* (*People's Daily* overseas edition), December 10, 2008. https://news.ifeng.com/opinion/200812/1210_23 _915697.shtml.

21. Lu Yong-shan, "Guangdong liangwan jia gangzi qiye jinnian kong guanchang" (Twenty thousand Hong Kong–invested businesses in Guangdong may close their factories this year), *Ziyou shibao* (Liberty times), June 27, 2008.

ness brand has become associated with the region. 'How can I just pack up the company's sign and run around with it?' . . . Clients are used to coming here to see you, and if the factory disappears, they think you've closed down."[22]

In 2009, I interviewed the financial affairs manager of Taiyang. He brought up Wang Yang's "emptying cages and changing birds" as an industrial upgrading plan that would force out polluting and high-energy-consuming industries and that was scheduled to be implemented from June to September 2008. According to the manager, Wang's operational method was to use annual inspections, environmental protection, and other screenings. Companies that didn't pass would not be able to process customs paperwork, and without customs paperwork, the factories couldn't operate. Many metalwork factories and electroplating plants were targeted. They were left with the choice of either migrating to inland or remote regions or going underground and continuing production without a permit. Moving inland would result in increased transportation costs and destroy the production chains. The manager concluded: "Under these circumstances this upgrading policy will die a natural death."[23]

The term "destroying the production chain" indicated the special characteristics and inherent flaws of the Guangdong model: This model was highly reliant on FIEs engaged in labor-intensive and highly polluting export processing industries that had developed entire production chains on the ground. These chains would be completely disrupted by the shifting of any component, which made it difficult to adjust the industrial structure in the short term. Guangdong had been open to the outside world since 1978 and enjoyed the advantage of having taken the first step and attracting foreign investment before other regions. However, most of these foreign investors were in the low-end industry category, so from 2000 onward, Guangdong demonstrated the disadvantage of early development—the difficulty of adjusting an established structure. Furthermore, existing production chains were embedded in specific government-business relations, including benefit distribution models, so

22. Wu Chao-yi and Hsiung Yi-hsin, "Lieri zhao Taishang: 2008, Taishang guan-jian nian" (The scorching sun shines on Taishang: 2008, the key year for Taishang!) *Tianxia zazhi* (CommonWealth magazine), January 2, 2008, pp. 104–5.

23. Interview: Jerry200902.

for Taishang, destroying the production chain was tantamount to disrupting existing trust relations and tacit agreements.

Another Taishang compared the economic benefits of labor-intensive traditional industries with those of high-tech industries: The industrial upgrading policy's objectives were excellent, but they weren't very feasible. First, traditional industry was actually more beneficial to the local economy: factories paying the same amount of tax as Taishin were conventional industries that employed a hundred thousand people; but switching to high-tech industry, the company would probably need to employ only fifteen thousand. The activity of a hundred thousand people in a city or town drives commercial vitality and consumption much more than a high-tech industry does. Second, if production moved inland, many factories would suffer loss, because the inland areas were more rigid and didn't have as flexible policies as Guangdong did. As a result, even though wages might be a little lower, the social insurance fees would have to be paid in full, and there would be no real savings in labor costs. Also, workers in inland regions didn't like working overtime, but rushed production required overtime, and without overtime there would be no profit. On top of that, transportation costs were high. In the final analysis, the only attraction was free land.[24] Considered from this angle, industrial upgrading destroyed the local consumption chain and created a depressed marketplace.

Hit by a series of internal and external pressures, in February 2009, Wang Yang was compelled to relax the industrial upgrading policy he'd once so vigorously promoted:

> The image of the expression "emptying cages and changing birds" indicates the policy orientation and not the policy content. "Emptying cages and changing birds" doesn't mean emptying out all of the birds in the cage; even an idiot wouldn't do that. . . . A coercive method of emptying cages and changing birds cannot be adopted even for labor-intensive assembly industries and low-end manufacturing segments; there is no business that is being driven out at this time, and there is no business that is having its water and electricity cut off. Our method is incentive. . . . Emptying cages and changing birds is meant to allow businesses that have contributed to the Pearl River Delta to be able to

24. Interview: HTS201212.

develop over the long term and doesn't mean simply dismantling the bridge after crossing the river. If you're going to have difficulty continuing to operate here, we'll find a place for you and give you some suggestions, and if you're willing to go you can go, and if you're not willing then you won't be forced.[25]

Given the disadvantageous economic situation and manufacturers' suffering negative repercussions, the provincial party leaders made concessions, and local governments throughout Guangdong also presented compromise measures such as discounting or temporarily postponing social insurance fees and increasing various tax reductions. One Gangshang estimated that every business in Dongguan was able to save about 4 percent of its costs and expenses per year because of these concessions.[26]

Even so, "unresolved structural contradictions" continued to trouble Guangdong's economic prospects, and with the macroscopic conditions becoming increasingly disadvantageous, the Guangdong government was forced to push forward industrial structural transformation and promote the "Pearl River Delta Region Reform Development Plan Outline (2008–20)." According to reports, in March 2011, Guangdong provincial leaders led a delegation to Beijing to attract investment and signed a large number of contracts with some central-level SOE groups for a total investment of 2.5 trillion yuan. This method took advantage of the stimulus for the domestic demand economy in the Twelfth Five-Year Plan (Chen Hewu 2011) and was clearly a major divergence from the growth model Guangdong had been using for the past thirty years. Depending on SOEs to invest in the local economy might elbow out FIEs and privately owned companies and take Guangdong toward a situation of *guojin mintui*.

25. "Wang Yang: Tenglong huanniao zhishi daoxiang, bu qiangzhi qiye zhuangyi" (Wang Yang: Emptying the cage and changing the bird is an orientation, business won't be forced to move), *Zhongguo pinglun xinwenwang*, February 12, 2009, https://goo.gl/WQx1cX.

26. Xie Sijia, Wu Zhe, and Hu Nianfei, "Jinrong haixiao yinian Gangqi zhenxiang: Tenglong huanniao zeng bei wudu" (The true situation of Hong Kong businesses in the year of the financial tsunami: Emptying the cage and changing birds was misread), *Nanfang ribao*, August 17, 2009, posted by Souhuwang, November 18, 2020, https://ppfocus.com/0/he8f9666e.html.

From the perspective of labor-intensive FIEs, regardless of whether the government's advocacy of industrial upgrading was a policy error or was of limited effectiveness, the Pearl River Delta's industrial structure was not likely to stand still. Some industries that were highly reliant on a massive labor force—for example, the ICT assembly industry represented by Foxconn—had some time before begun migrating to inland regions or other countries. In terms of traditional industries, at the same time that FIEs were making their exit, local OEM factories were on the rise, creating new supply chains. In terms of the ICT industry, the Pearl River Delta also gradually formed industrial clusters dominated by Chinese-owned companies, composing alternative ecosystems to those of FIEs.

4) The Central Government Shrinks the Space for Local Government Rent Seeking

China's central government continued to promote industrial structural transformation and standardized the investment incentives that local governments gave manufacturers. Both factors affected the profit model and government-business relationships to which Taishang had become accustomed. In November 2014, the central government issued a Document No. 62,[27] which required local governments to standardize their preferential taxation policies by centralizing the authority to set taxation policies, standardizing the management of nontax revenues, and strictly managing fiscal expenditure. It also required them to clean up all the existing preferential policies on taxation. For foreign-owned companies, the crux of Document No. 62 was that the central government no longer allowed local governments to use taxes and other concessionary subsidies as a means of competing for investment.

The central government came out with these policies to impose order on chaotic local taxes and levies, and it applied the policies to all lo-

27. "Guowuyuan guanyu qingli guifan shuishou deng youhui zhengce de tongzhi (guofa [2014] 62 hao)" (State Council notice regarding clarifying and standardizing tax revenue and other preferential policies), State Council bulletin, November 27, 2014, http://big5.www.gov.cn/gate/big5/www.gov.cn/gongbao/content/2014/content _2792639.htm.

cally owned and foreign-owned businesses. Taishang stood to lose the most because they had long relied on tax concessions to increase their profits. Generally speaking, apart from formal tax reductions set in law, most of the tax concessions that Hong Kong—and Taiwanese-owned companies enjoyed were granted to them by local governments under local conditions and unofficial rules, with fiscal refunds being one trick of the trade. Taking land leases as an example, a local government could refund its share of the taxes to the FIE. And taking local tax as an example, the local government could refund a percentage of the income tax and VAT that it collected from businesses in its jurisdiction, the equivalent of transferring money from local government coffers to the enterprises. These incentives usually appeared in supplemental agreements rather than in an investment agreement.[28]

The deal between power (the local government) and money (business) underlies the tax and fee concessions and rebates. Document No. 62 makes its purpose clear from the outset: "Comprehensive standardization of taxation and other preferential policies . . . will facilitate implementation of national macroeconomic policies, break through local protectionism and industrial monopolies, and promote economic transformation and upgrading; it will facilitate strict financial discipline, prevent and combat corruption, and safeguard the normal order of income distribution."[29] In this way, the economic objectives of the document were combined with the political dimensions of the anticorruption campaign in an attempt to undermine the economic power of local officials and control institutional rent-seeking behavior at the local level. This document caused anxiety among Taishang, who expressed their deep concern through various means. They were apprehensive about whether elimination of the preferential measures would be made retroactive. In May 2015, the State Council issued a notice promising that preferential

---

28. See Liu Fangrong, "Caizheng fanhuan yingxiang Taishang shuiwu guihua" (Financial rebate affects Taishang taxation plan), *Jingji ribao*, December 16, 2009; "'62 haowen' chongji da, guomin daiyu hui Taishang" ("Document No. 62" has a serious effect, national treatment favors Taishang), *Wangbao*, April 5, 2015.

29. See State Council notice regarding clarifying and standardizing tax revenue and other preferential policies.

policies written into contracts would continue to be honored, but that new investment agreements would no longer include special privileges.[30]

In March 2015, the National People's Congress promulgated the "Decision to Revise the Legislation Law."[31] This new policy explicitly set limits on the legislative power of local governments and restricted their authority to grant tax and fee concessions. Although it granted prefectural-level cities a measure of legislative power, the central government took back the power to collect taxes and reduced the power of governments below the level of prefectural municipalities to examine, approve, and decide concessions for foreign businesses. According to the Minister of Finance, Lou Jiwei, revision of the Legislation Law was "a policy task" and meant that "arbitrary bargaining over tax concessions, including land" would no longer be permitted.[32] Document No. 62 and the revised Legislation Law were part of a series of policy changes aimed at returning financial and taxation authority to the central government and shrinking the space for local governments to engage in deals with business. This reduced opportunities for rent seeking by local governments, and the cost of rent seeking also rose substantially. The "national treatment plus benefits" (*chao guomin daiyu*) that Taishang had once enjoyed began to fade away. The assistant manager at Taishin, mentioned above, commented: "All this talk about same language and same race is bullshit. The central government wants to retake power and cut off the money stream of the local government."[33] "Cutting off the money stream of the local government" refers to the intention of Document No. 62 to "prevent and combat corruption, and safeguard the normal order of income distribution,"

---

30. Lai Hsiang-ju, "Lu Guowuyuan: 62 haowen bu suji jiwang" (Mainland State Council: Document No. 62 will not be retroactive), *Gongshang shibao* (*Commercial Times*), May 12, 2015.

31. "Quanguo renmin daibiao dahui guanyu xiugai 'zhonghua renmin gongheguo lifa fa' de jueding" (Decision of the National People's Congress on Amending the Legislation Law of the People's Republic of China), Zhongguo renda wang (China NPC Net), March 15, 2015, http://www.npc.gov.cn/zgrdw/npc/xinwen/2015-03/18/content _1930129.htm.

32. Lee Ming-hsuan, " Zhongguo dalu xiuzheng 'Lifa Fa,' Taishang 70% zushui shou chongji" (Mainland China revises "Legislation Law," Taishang 70% taxes and levies come under attack), *Tianxia zazhi*, (CommonWealth magazine), March 12, 2015, http://www.cw.com.tw/article/article.action?id=5065490.

33. Interview: TX3-2015.

and it has had far-reaching implications. The central government has shrunk the rent-seeking space of local officials, while at the same time shrinking the profit-making and rent-seeking space of Taishang.

Taken altogether, these national policy and institutional changes shook up government-business relations and labor-capital relations. The essential factors that had originally sustained the Guangdong growth model no longer pertained: wages were raised, social insurance coverage rates increased, and tax and fee concessions and rebates were reduced. The Xi Jinping administration's policy of governing in accordance with the law reshuffled the deck of government-business relations. There was little space left for the flexible tax and fee reductions that export processing–type Taishang had arranged through their government-business relationships (Yu Yi-wen, Ko-chia Yu, and Tse-chun Lin 2016). Overall data also clearly show that average net profits among Taishang have dropped substantially in recent years (Cheng Chih-peng and Lin Thung-Hong 2017).

The average Taishang engaged in traditional industry in Guangdong therefore became aware of a new situation: the macroenvironment was now unfavorable for Taishang, China had already mastered a portion of their manufacturing technology, and mainland-owned factories had begun accepting orders from second-tier international brands and competing with Taiwanese-owned factories. To save on labor costs, Taishang began localizing their management level, and some Taigan faced career change and unemployment. Furthermore, the former reliance on *guanxi* had become ineffective: "Bringing your wallet to discussions over drinks didn't work anymore."[34]

2. Smiles Shoes Company: A Taishang Transforms on the Ground

As Guangdong's labor-intensive growth model headed into decline, Taishang had to respond and change their profit model. In the Pearl River Delta, Taishang responded to pressure to transform by either closing down

---

34. Interview: YYPL2015.

(as Taiyang did) or choosing among three other options, which could be combined: moving inland, moving to another country, or upgrading where they were. The choice largely depended on the scale of the business, the preferences of international buyers, and the business's transformation strategy. Generally speaking, the limited resources of small and medium-size Taishang gave them fewer options. However, large Taishang adopted the three other options simultaneously—as the next section shows, using the Taishin Shoe Manufacturing Group as a case study. From the perspective of changes in the GVC, the transformation of small and medium-size Taishang especially deserves analysis, because the transformation process also gave rise to production links with local OEM factories (subcontractors), which in turn shaped complex and interesting relationships embedded in social networks. This section, based on my field study surveys and interviews, uses Smiles Shoe Company as an illustration, supplemented by related cases and the literature.[35]

1) The Development of Smiles Shoe Company

Smiles Shoes Company was originally a trading company located in Taichung, in Taiwan. Established in the 1980s, the company's main business was the export of women's shoes produced by local Taiwanese OEM factories. Taiwan's shoe factories gradually migrated abroad, and in the mid-1990s Smiles tried sending orders to OEM factories in Guangdong. However, when Europe imposed antidumping duty on footwear produced in China, Smiles had to transfer its orders to a Taiwanese-owned OEM factory in Vietnam. In the early 2000s, Smiles began investing in Dongguan, creating a joint venture with a local factory to produce mainly mid-price women's shoes for export. Due to significant increases in direct production costs in the late 2000s, Smiles ended its joint-venture business and changed to a mainly subcontracting business model, transforming its role into that of a trading company, as it had been in Taiwan, but with a significantly different operational mode. This difference reflects how Taishang changed positions during the shift of the GVC.

---

35. Smiles Shoe Company is a pseudonym.

Smiles currently has headquarters in both Taichung and Dongguan and a research and development (R&D) center in Dongguan. About 10 percent of its market is in Taiwan and China, with the remaining 90 percent in various other countries: at least half of that 90 percent is in the United Kingdom and Europe, and the rest is in the United States, Canada, and Australia. Its clients include Mango, Nine West, Zara, and other name brands. In 2012, its total sales volume was ten million pairs of shoes, with a turnover of US$100 million and gross profit of 10 percent. Smiles's Dongguan headquarters employs around three hundred people, of whom about 5 percent are Taiwanese managers and designers. The seven people at the middle management level or above are all Taiwanese and are responsible for R&D, sales, and supervision. The highest-ranking Lugan are all at the level of assistant manager and factory manager. In its business model, Smiles identifies itself as a GSC integrator, and its profit model is that of commission taker.

2) The Core Plant Strategy

Before 2010, Smiles had four joint-venture factories with a collective annual production capacity of more than a ten million pairs of shoes. It then changed its business model to custom manufacturing and worked with some thirty OEM factories. As the GVC shifted, international buyers at one point put pressure on Smiles to seek out OEM factories in Wenzhou, in Zhejiang Province. Smiles gave this a try but ultimately abandoned the plan because the prices at Wenzhou OEM factories were not cheap, and there were quality control issues as well as high transportation costs. Smiles finally developed a business model as a "quasi-international buyer."[36] In Dongguan it organized a network of mainland-owned OEM factories that served as its manufacturing department. It also established a factory with multiple functions under the direct management of the Dongguan headquarters. Smiles refers to this directly operated factory as its core plant.

Why did Smiles choose this business model? It was mainly because of rising labor costs, competitive pressure, and changes in the type of

36. The expression "quasi-international buyer" comes from Cheng Chih-peng (2016, 172).

orders. Smiles's OEM factories were scattered across China and Vietnam. It had two OEM factories in Vietnam, one of which ultimately took orders directly from Zara—effectively stealing business from Smiles. According to Smiles's deputy general manager, "this was an unavoidable outcome."[37] Quality control costs at the Vietnamese factories were also relatively high. Now that Smiles has adopted the core plant strategy, it takes orders in the name of the core factory and then sends these orders to the OEM factories. Smiles partners with ten OEM factories (one Taiwanese owned, and the others mainland owned) within a half-hour's drive from its Dongguan headquarters. It also has a small number of mainland-owned OEM factories in other places. Why does Smiles favor mainland-owned factories? The main consideration is cost. After the Labor Contract Law came into effect, labor costs increased, and Smiles can avoid a portion of these costs by contracting its orders to mainland-owned OEMs. Chinese-owned factories can more easily avoid social insurance and housing provident fund fees, because local governments adopt differential enforcement and stretch the rules for local privately owned companies. The government-business relationships behind this arrangement are unavailable to foreign companies (see Cheng Chih-peng 2014a).

As the technical competence of mainland-owned factories gradually increased, combined with their production costs, their competition with Taiwanese-owned factories for orders from international clients squeezed the profits of Smiles as a trading company. If Smiles had not gone beyond engaging in export in China as a trading company (a quasi-international buyer), its business would easily have been taken over. Developing its core plant strategy was its way of finding a niche in a constantly changing environment. Its directly operated factory allows to have Smiles a degree of innovation and a leading edge that has put it in an advantageous position in the global-local linkage of the GVC, so it cannot be easily replaced or eliminated by competition.

The directly operated factory has multiple functions. First, it is the R&D center for Smiles, creating five hundred samples per month. Smiles's original samples department in Taiwan cost the company NT$40 million per year, and the company felt that this cost was too high. By then Smiles had its production line in Dongguan, which also involved sub-

37. Interview: TR201212. This quote from Smiles's deputy general manager Mr. Hu.

stantial coordination and communication costs, so the company decided to move its samples department to Dongguan in 2000. As mentioned above, Taiyang Company also moved its samples department to China a few years after building its factory in Dongguan. The advantage of integrating the samples department with the manufacturing base includes client relations: "We have our own shoe last factory, which is the most important prototype for shoes. Then we have our own directly owned factory, which is also our testing center. In 2010, authentication by the inspection department allowed us to carry out physical testing in our own laboratory. This testing center helps us serve our clients faster and shortens our delivery period, and [it] also allows us to lower our costs. So this was major progress for us in 2010."[38]

There are also demands from clients: "The entire supply chain needs to be integrated. Why has Smiles moved toward having its own factory today? First is because customers hope that when you take orders you have your own production capacity and aren't merely playing the role of accepting orders and contracting them out."[39]

But in fact, the directly run factory has only two production lines with a collective production capacity of 60,000 pairs of shoes per month, employing the production method of small quantities of multiple styles. This accounts for less than 10 percent of Smiles's total export sales. As a result, the factory has become a showcase, acting as a boutique factory to show to clients.

Hu at Smiles noted how orders have changed: "Nowadays companies like us that make French lines produce around 3,000 pairs [of shoes]. If you do American lines you might have tens of thousands, maybe 30,000, 50,000, or 100,000. But now the customers are basically unwilling to deal with this stockpile of goods. Then there's the rapid changeover in fashion. In the past they might submit an order for 300,000, 500,000, or a million, but there's nothing like that now. So now you see the ecology of the factory; if you want to find a factory with three or five lines, there aren't that many."[40]

38. Interview: TR201212.
39. Interview: TR201212.
40. Interview: TR201212.

In recent years, the size of orders (the number of items in each order) has dropped, while the styles have multiplied. Even a relatively large order for an American line will be at most 100,000 pairs. In the age of on-line information, fashion has become faster: in the past there were only two fashion seasons, but now there are six. Reasonably, Smiles sends the small, boutique orders with the highest prices and strictest quality control requirements to its directly run factory. Changes in the way orders are made have also caused Smiles to change its mind-set:

> Facing these small numbers and multiple styles, your factory's entire R&D department needs the capacity for speed. Otherwise you won't be able to respond quickly enough to handle customers from so many different regions. . . . You have to develop the integrated capacity of your supply chain and demonstrate your value, so when customers come you can be a one-stop shop and keep international clients from placing orders directly with OEM factories. The customer thinks going through a trading company means additional cost, right? And the factory thinks, "I can do this myself, so why go through a trading company?" Some factories will approach clients directly, and you can't stop them even if you try. So you always have to innovate. A factory can provide OEM for a customer, but its vision, perspective, and feelers aren't as extensive as our trading company's. If the customer goes directly to this factory, at best he'll take his item there and ask the factory to produce it, and he can get the cost down, but it will narrow his options. Customers like to come here to choose and purchase goods because we handle fashion trends in the northern and southern hemispheres, and they can cover the European and American markets in one round.[41]

This is the value provided by the supply chain integration that Smiles emphasizes. The company earns a profit from its commission as a broker, and the broker's role is no longer the traditional one of a pure trading company but also has product development and manufacturing capabilities. By mastering skills through managing the directly run factory, Smiles has become a local hub of the GSC. As early as the mid-2000s, Smiles became aware of the need to cut into the supply chain and find a niche. Ms. Chen, the company's CEO, once even said that Smiles couldn't

41. Interview: TR201212.

remain a pure trading company, because "a trading company is a speculative profession."[42]

I visited Smiles's Dongguan headquarters. The factory directly run by Smiles is clean and orderly; its documentation is complete; and in addition to being a sample showcase, it is also a sample factory that customers can inspect for CSR purposes. The social insurance status and working conditions of staff members at the factory basically conform to the Chinese laws and standards and the requirements of clients, but there are still quite a few workers who aren't enrolled in pension insurance. Smiles requires workers who are not enrolled to sign a waiver.

Smiles's business model is not a special case: I came across it elsewhere during my long-term tracking studies in the Pearl River Delta and Yangtze Delta regions. One Taiwanese-owned garment factory in northern Zhejiang that specializes in mid- to upper-grade outdoor apparel also has since the late 2000s had a directly run factory that contracts out orders to mainland-owned factories in Anhui and other inland regions. This directly run factory also has a samples department that receives clients and serves as the site for their CSR inspections.

3) Mainland-Owned Companies Become More Competitive

In the late 2000s, the trend was for the Taishang shoe manufacturers that remained in the Pearl River Delta to team up with mainland-owned factories because these factories were not only becoming increasingly familiar with production technology but also enjoyed the advantage of lower costs. Why did mainland-owned factories enjoy an advantage that foreign-owned factories did not? It's because Taishang no longer had the same privileged access that mainland-owned factories enjoyed to low-cost capital, land, and subsidies. Hu observed:

> Mainland-owned factories have also gradually gained their own technology. A lot of those mainland-owned factories, like Huajian, now have their own brands. Huajian used to work with Yue Yuen, right? Yue Yuen raised Huajian up from nothing, but the advantage the mainlanders have is that they're very daring. If he has one *kuai* (yuan), he

---

42. Interview: SMR200710.

dares to do ten *kuai* worth of business, but if we Taiwanese have ten *kuai*, we only dare to do one or two *kuai* worth of business. We're relatively conservative, and we don't fight battles we aren't sure we'll win. But the mainlanders are always up for a fight. Once they get through the bottleneck, they're up there. They have their own business methods. We now have a factory in Guizhou [Smiles's collaborative OEM factory], which is run by ethnic minorities. When he [the ethnic-minority owner] built that factory, he told the government, I'll buy several hills of undeveloped land from you, for example just 10,000 or 20,000 yuan for a *mu* (Chinese acre) of land. He said he'd do a little planning and create a project plan and begin building some simple factory buildings. When he develops that place in the future, its value will increase to 50,000 or 60,000 yuan. It's like he used that loan from the government, and the government ended up giving him 40,000 yuan—because his development costs were only 10,000 yuan—but he'll ultimately have something with an estimated value of that much. Then the government also allowed him to use 40 percent as commercial land. So in a flash his 50,000 turned into 400,000 yuan. That one *mu* of land worth 400,000 yuan he can now use to borrow even more money. A lot of people on the mainland work that way. Then he went and formed a "Yangguang Enterprise," which employs some handicapped people. For each handicapped person the company hires, the government pays him a subsidy. Then when these factories manufacture products, he exports them under the name of Yangguang Enterprises and enjoys a tax exemption. So they have these privileges, and in an environment with so much competition, they have more plentiful capital than us, and they're more daring than us, right? And then they have a lot of *guanxi* that allows them to greatly reduce their costs.[43]

What Hu narrates seems to be a story of a company's primitive accumulation of capital and the sleight of hand of making something out of nothing. Behind the curtain is a series of events involving the establishment of ties and exchange of interests between government and business. Mainland-owned factories are "very daring" because of the social foundation behind them, with intricate government-business relations in-

43. Interview: TR201212.

volving profound trust relationships. The majority of Taishang have had great difficulty operating this way in recent years, though it is not impossible for them to do so (see section 3 below).

The advantages that mainland-owned factories enjoy are not limited to traditional industries such as shoe manufacturing. Field investigations also turn up evidence of this in the mainland-owned ICT assembly plants. The advantages include lower overhead than Taiwanese-owned factories, with Lugan paid lower salaries than Taigan. In addition, mainland-owned companies dare to exploit legal loopholes and play edge ball (*da cabianqiu*) with labor regulations and social insurance; have lower tax burden than Taishang (including higher tax rebates for exports and fewer VAT levies); and can apply for state subsidies (Wang Po-chi 2014). Their managers' local personal connections give mainland-owned factories additional protection. And because there are so many small and medium-size mainland-owned factories, the local government's transactional costs for strict law enforcement are high. Differential enforcement has become common, and it is easy for officials to turn a blind eye.

Of course, the above stories discuss Taishang facing the threat of competition from mainland-owned factories, but cooperation with mainland-owned factories also brings Taishang business opportunities and profit. While transforming themselves to survive, Taishang have shifted labor exploitation onto mainland-owned factories. Structural transformation of the GVC has become the driver at a deep level. Smiles provides a window for observing the on-site transformation of Taishang. From the perspective of the GVC, Taiwanese-owned factories that transfer orders also have the function of trading companies situated between international buyers (GVC lead firms—i.e., top-line brands) and mainland-owned factories. This shows that a large portion of mainland-owned factories still have no way of directly connecting with GVC lead firms and need Taishang as intermediaries to make these connections. Can this structural relationship continue indefinitely? A deciding factor in the competition between Taishang and Chinese companies is which can most rapidly climb the GVC power ladder and draw closest to the lead firms at the pinnacle. In shoe manufacturing, if Chinese companies are able to overtake Taishang, then Taishang will have to abdicate their intermediary role or even abandon this industry altogether.

3. Taishin Shoe Manufacturing Group: The Diversified Transformation of a Taiwanese Company

The Taishin Shoe Manufacturing Group is a world-class shoe empire. At the height of its business in the Pearl River Delta, it employed more than 100,000 workers. Its production base was an industrial park that occupied a large portion of the town where it was located. The taxes it paid gave the local government ample income as well as bringing consumption and prosperity to the surrounding area. At the same time, it brought the Chinese government considerable foreign exchange earnings. Taishin was originally a Taiwanese factory, but after it entered China, its production increased and the scale of its shoe manufacturing expanded. When I visited Taishin's Dongguan factory in 1994, it was already employing 30,000 workers, and the company had a dedicated construction team for building factories and dormitories to handle its rapid expansion. The manager who received me described the situation: "The factory provides room and board, and there are so many workers that they eat thirty pigs in one day, enough to support a local medium-size pig farm."[44]

Taishin was established in central Taiwan in the 1960s as a small family-owned shoe factory, but it grew rapidly after grasping the historic opportunity of the GVC shift in the footwear industry. In the 1980s it was transformed into a specialized manufacturer of sports shoes, and its business grew rapidly in OEM manufacturing for name brands: in just a few years it switched from pure OEM to ODM. In the late 1980s, under the urging of Nike (its international client), Taishin built a factory in Guangdong. The company went public on the Taiwanese stock market in the early 1990s and began building factories in Indonesia and Vietnam. As the company's scale and business expanded in the mid-2000s, the controlling corporation was transformed into an industrial holding company, and the subsidiary companies under its flag were divided into footwear and marketing divisions. In 2012 Taishin produced 400 million pairs of shoes, and by 2013 it employed nearly half a million people around

44. Interview: TH199405.

the globe. In 2014 its business volume reached US$8 billion, including $2 billion in retail revenue. Because it had reached monster proportions, Taishin became known as the Foxconn of footwear. Over the past ten years, Taishin has been under pressure to transform its structure, and it has undergone reorganization and decentralized its manufacturing bases. Among my research case studies, it is a classic example of moving overseas, moving inland, and undergoing on-site transformation.

1) The Operational Model of Processing Shipped Materials

Taishin was one of the first Taishang to enter the Pearl River Delta. Because it invested early, operated on a large scale, and bought abundant revenue to its locality, it had considerable bargaining power with the local government. At that time, Pearl River Delta officials were going all out to attract business and investment, and they offered foreign companies rather favorable conditions—including flexible enforcement of policies on land use, employment, and social insurance. As a result, Taishin enjoyed many concessions, including an agreement arranged under the model of processing shipped materials.

The advantage that foreign companies gained from this model was exemption from paying taxes, but from the perspective of the central government, this amounted to conceding benefit to foreign companies. Beginning in the mid-1990s, the central government urged Guangdong to promote the model of processing imported materials and to make FIEs register as legal entities (wholly owned foreign companies) and pay VAT and income tax (see chapter 2). As a result, official statistics show that the percentage of contracts for processing shipped materials dropped, and the percentage of contracts for processing imported materials increased. But Taishin withstood the pressure, and until recent years it continued to be registered as a factory that processed shipped materials. According to the recollections of a veteran manager at Taishin, a cadre in Dongguan responsible for foreign trade and economic cooperation was summoned to Beijing to explain to economic and trade officials there what benefit China gained from processing shipped materials. Since processing shipped materials was not altogether disadvantageous to China, the officials reported this to Zhu Rongji, then premier of China. Zhu went to Guangdong for a meeting that finally clarified what processing shipped material entailed, and he allowed the system to be retained.[45] Later, that Dongguan cadre explained to Taishin:

> The processing of shipped materials has a legal basis, and Taishin doesn't need to change into a single-venture company (processing of imported materials). Under the processing of shipped materials, you set your own price and don't have to pay tax, and at the early stage you can forgo billing accounts and aren't audited for taxes, and just need to pay the processing fees. After changing to a single-venture company, you have to face the "state," pay national taxes—VAT, income tax, and so on. If you change into a single-venture factory and run into problems, we local cadres won't be able to help you handle them. As long as the legal documents still exist, you don't need to change into a single-venture company.[46]

The administration of processing shipped materials was geared toward the local government. Taishin cooperated with a township government under the jurisdiction of Dongguan City, and if problems arose they were easily resolved. At that time, Taishin exported almost 100 percent of its products, so it had no incentive to change into a single-venture company (which would have given it the right to make domestic sales), and it maintained its registration as a town-level collective enterprise. But in fact, Taishin was a wholly foreign-owned factory sponsored by the town government and registered as a local collective enterprise engaged in the processing of shipped materials. This type of fictive ownership arrangement was part of the distinctively Chinese sponsorship system.

Taishin saved a large amount of tax under the model of processing shipped materials, but it still had to pay processing fees to the local government. This fee was what Taishang referred to as the head tax, because it was calculated based on the number of workers employed. When Taishin first built its factory in Dongguan, it employed 20,000–30,000 people, but by 2000 it employed around 100,000 people. It paid 20 million yuan in processing fees each year. The formula for calculating this was a remittance of HK$600 per person per month, with the number of workers set at 25,000. The Chinese side collected a 13 percent remittance spread under the name of a management fee (see chapter 3 on the remit-

---

45. Interview: HTS201310.
46. Requoted from the veteran manager at Taishin. Interview: HTS201310.

tance spread method through which Taiyang paid its head tax). Here we see that the Chinese side granted a very large discount on calculating heads. This was an open secret: "You know, back then, even when we had reached 100,000 people, the government leaders from the city to the town all told us, 'if anyone asks you how many people you have, you say you just have 25,000; even if they kill you, say it's 25,000 people.' You have to understand, the Communist Party isn't going to go to the dormitories and use public security police to count heads one by one."[47]

This unofficial agreement between Taishin and the local government on processing fees continued for more than ten years. But as the central government applied increasing pressure for changing enterprise ownership registration, Taishin also had to face pressure for transformation. At the same time, to gain the right to make domestic sales, Taishin gradually changed its registration status from processing factory to single-venture factory. By 2013, when the local government handed down a confidential document requiring processing plants to change into single-venture factories, Taishin had almost completed the change for all of its factories. But when the processing plant model was almost extinguished in the Dongguan region, the local government encountered reduced revenues. How did it deal with the new situation? As the saying goes in China, the upper level has its measures, and the lower level has its countermeasures. In recent years, the local government has obtained additional taxes and levies through two channels. The first is profit from land: by banning highly polluting enterprises, it has forced these enterprises to return their land use rights to the local government, and when enterprises close their factories and need to dispose of their land, the local government gains extra revenue through recording deed transfers and other such processes. The second is implementing the collection of "*xie-zuofuwu fei*" (collaboration fees). These fees are paid to the town government, and the town pays a share to the village (the administrative district). The local government can do this because it has the authority to approve a variety of licenses regarding enterprise management.[48] What is meant by "implementing the collection" and "collaboration fee?" A Taigan explained:

47. Interview: YYPL2015.
48. Interview: TX3-201703.

Before, when three-plus-one factories got cheap land, to make this acceptable to the various village committees and also to satisfy the need
for local revenue, the local Dongguan government would have stipulations such as [the payment of] "processing fees," "collaboration fees,"
"land compensation fees," and so on. The meaning of the collaboration fee was helping the factory declare goods at customs, integrated
administrative governance, and so on. This income became a slush
fund for the local government and village committee. . . . Before, when
enough tax was collected, the local government wouldn't haggle for
collaboration fees, land compensation fees. In recent years exports have
decreased and tax revenue has decreased, and GDP has also been affected, so they've enforced the collection of collaboration fees and land
compensation fees.[49]

In other words, the collaboration fee existed early on, but when tax
revenues were plentiful, local governments didn't make an effort to collect it. Once the central government required processing plants to change
into single-venture factories, foreign companies had to pay tax to the state,
which meant that local governments were unable to collect processing fees
under the model of processing shipped materials. To make up for this
financial loss, local governments enforced the collection of collaboration
fees from foreign companies. How was a collaboration fee calculated? According to the agreement between Taishin and the local government, it
was calculated based on the surface area of the land used by the factory—
for example, counting the number of workers employed per *mu* of land and
the amount paid per worker per month. Using a certain Taishin factory
as an example, it was calculated based on eight workers per *mu* of land
and seventy-eight yuan paid each month for each worker, which amounted
to a payment of 7,488 yuan per *mu* each year. This fee largely compensated
for the loss of the original processing fee. It is worth noting that the collaboration fee was a long-standing item, but when income from processing
fees was sufficient, collection of the collaboration fee was more theoretical
than actual. When processing fees faded away, local officials eagerly extended their hands to collect the collaboration fee. While the name
changed from processing fee to collaboration fee, the head tax quality re-

49. Interview: TX3-201609.

mained unchanged. Regarding the floating significance of the head tax, see figure 3.5.

On the arrangements for social insurance, local governments required Taishin to gradually expand its coverage. The Chinese government began stipulating the payment of social insurance fees by foreign companies in 1997–98. At the initial stage, Taishin insured only 5,000 employees, all (from supervisor to team leader) selected from the management level. Employees who enrolled in pension insurance had to pay their portion themselves, and at first almost none of the line operators wanted to take part in the program. In the second year, the government-required coverage increased to 7,000 people, and the number continued to rise from then on. The coverage rate was around 45 percent by 2007,[50] and it reached nearly 90 percent by around 2011. The willingness of employees to enroll in social insurance was also affected by local government policies. In 2005, the prefectural government stipulated that workers leaving their factory could draw their pension insurance, including the 4 percent they had contributed and 1 percent contributed by the company. The remaining 7 percent paid by the company became additional revenue for the local government.[51] Because of this new policy, workers were willing to enroll. When the insurance withdrawal policy was abolished in 2008, many workers were again unwilling to enroll in insurance.

The discounted social insurance coverage rates planted the seeds of subsequent disputes over makeup payments. According to the veteran manager at Taishin, "At first, the social insurance head count discounts were illegal, but when circumstances changed, who was going to take responsibility for it? How was the social insurance to be recovered? So today's problems arrived. Originally the flexible policies were advantageous to foreign companies. Likewise, the results of the flexible policies are hurting foreign companies now. Today it's costing us a lot to deal with it. There are too many unexploded bombs."[52] The flexible policies resulted in deferred payment of social insurance fees. In the new round of policy

50. Interview: HTS200704.

51. According to the pension insurance stipulations at that time, management had to pay 8 percent of the fee base (known as the social pool), and labor had to pay 4 percent (known as the individual account).

52. Interview: HTS201212.

and institutional changes, wages and labor safeguards were enhanced, factories closed or moved out, and labor-management conflicts followed. At the end of 2012, labor protests erupted at Shyang Ho Shoes, a foreign-owned company in the Nanhai District of Foshan City. Workers suspected that the factory was secretly transferring assets as a covert way to reduce workers' salaries, so they adopted the tactic of defending the factory building and made demands to management: If the company was not going to keep running, it should first pay all outstanding employee social insurance fees and then pay compensation in accordance with the Labor Law. And if the company intended to continue operating, management had to first buy out all worker "seniority" and then make new hires.[53] The Shyang Ho incident created apprehension in the Taishang community. As one manager at Taishin observed, "Today's Chinese government is not the government of twenty years ago. Now it can't just arbitrarily side with the company; it has to consider many factors and deal with workers' interests and their protests. But in general, the Chinese government is more likely to take action. Compared with the Vietnamese government, the Chinese government is more partial toward capital. In Vietnam, when there's a strike, the government doesn't intervene and just leaves the matter to be resolved by labor and management."[54] The Shyang Ho incident presaged the wave of labor-management conflicts to come, all of which revolved around social insurance and provident fund payments. Taishin also encountered strikes during this wave of protests, and it had to make up for years of missed social insurance payments. All employees, whether managers or line workers, had to be covered by pension insurance, with the payment base calculated on the basis of gross salary. In 2015, Dongguan City implemented a new policy that allowed pension insurance accounts to be sealed (i.e., suspension of the account upon leaving the company) or transferred between provinces.

After this wave of labor protests in Dongguan, Taishin's CSR department was also reorganized under the guidance of international clients.

53. "Foshan xiechang shubai ren tinggong shouchang, yi gongchang andi zhuanyi zichan" (Hundreds of workers at Foshan shoe factory stop working and stage sit-in at factory, suspect the factory is secretly transferring assets), *Nanfang Dushibao*, December 13, 2012, http://news.sohu.com/20121213/n360279983.shtml.

54. Interview: YYPL2015.

The new strategy combined CSR with human resources (HR) to create a new department—the sustainable development division—that was directly accountable to the company's top managers. The top-tier brands maintained a zero tolerance standard for overtime (in other words, documented overtime figures had to conform to statutory norms). "Only the top-tier brands Nike and Adidas actually care about CSR inspections, because prominent companies attract criticism and are often subjected to protests," one Taiwanese assistant manager said. He continued:

> Right now the slogan up above is "compliance with the law." This is a very high standard, and it includes compliance with regulations on social insurance, the provident fund, and so on. . . . Now half of the company's legal affairs staff are covering HR and spend all day running around to arbitrations. In the past, when labor-management disputes occurred, interaction with the local government relied on tacit agreement, but now streamlining under the new model emphasizes SOP [standard operating procedure] and no longer handing out *hong bao* [bribes], which makes things tough for us—handing them out *hong bao* is no use. As soon as there's a dispute, the town government immediately telephones and expresses concern, afraid that the matter will get out of hand. . . . A lot of CSR codes of conduct and so on are used for packaging the corporate image. . . . Our work, to be frank, is cleaning windows [referring to HR work] while sweeping the floor [referring to dealing with the aftermath of strikes].[55]

2) Moving Abroad: Redeploying Overseas Production Bases

Facing the trend of rising labor costs in the Pearl River Delta, Taishin's plan has included moving overseas and moving inland. Taishin began establishing factories in Southeast Asia in the early 2000s: "We were following the views of our clients."[56] In other words, under the hegemony of the GVC, as brand-name firms began sending orders to regions with lower labor costs, companies began establishing factories in those places. In recent years, as Taishang faced rising costs in China as a result of being dunned for social insurance and provident fund payments and

55. Interview: XX2016.
56. Interview: YYPL2015.

dealing with labor unrest, Taishin reported the situation to brand-name firms in the hope of being able to raise its prices:

> The result was that the clients—that is, the brand-name firms—said "sorry" and just ran off, because it's still producing Adidas, and if only Taishin says it wants to raise prices, it's at least 1.50–2.00 US dollars per pair, so you either don't think it's worth the trouble or you can't continue. You have to know that, usually, for the sales unit to negoti-ate prices and get an extra two or three cents is already a miracle. The concept of one dollar is: If your order is for ten million pairs per year, they have to pay you an extra ten million US dollars. If you're the only OEM factory asking for a price increase, the major brands like Nike and Adidas actually won't pay the whole amount. They say, "You want $1.50? I'll give you 70 cents!" A lot of other brands, when they hear you want to raise prices? "Too expensive! I'll go somewhere else." They'll say, "You have production lines in Vietnam, so why don't you send the order there?" It's a vicious circle, and the orders begin moving else-where. "You want to raise the price, I [the name brand] won't raise it. If you can't keep going without raising prices, then don't keep going." When we made up for unpaid provident funds, the brands didn't ap-plaud, they didn't praise you, they didn't support you because you com-plied with the government's regulations! From the perspective of the brand or the buyer, I'm going to buy where the prices are cheaper. The truth is, companies that really care about corporate social responsibil-ity are a tiny minority. We've seen a lot of second-tier brands run off to Fujian.[57]

With "I'm going to buy where the prices are cheaper," this interview clearly demonstrates the hegemonic status of brand-name firms in the footwear industry's GVC, as well as the impetus that drives OEM facto-ries to pursue low-price essential factors of production. The negative re-action of brand-name firms to rising costs caused Taishin to accelerate the reduction in its production capacity in the Pearl River Delta and shift its production lines overseas. The redeployment of the GSC led Taishin's China-based share of its total production to decline from 38 percent in 2012 to 24 percent in 2015 and 14 percent in 2018, and this decline was expected to continue. Taishin's production volume in Vietnam has long

---

57. Interview: YYPL2015.

surpassed that in China. The company is also expanding in Cambodia, and there are plans to enter Myanmar. The company's top managers anticipate that Taishin will have moved all of its production lines out of Guangdong within ten years. An even more shocking forecast is that "export processing factories will disappear from China's coastal regions within ten years,"[58] but this is the viewpoint of just one Taiwanese manager. In fact, mainland-owned factories are rapidly catching up with and replacing Taishang in the GSCs, and it is the Taiwanese-owned OEM factories that will disappear. In any case, Taishin was under enormous pressure on the manufacturing side. "Anticipating future trends, for large enterprises like Taishin, the most difficult brands like Adidas and Nike, the most difficult shoes, are made here in the Pearl River Delta, and the R&D departments and training bases remain here. The rest is sent to the Indochina Peninsula, Vietnam, Indonesia, or maybe Cambodia or Myanmar."[59]

Most Taishang factories in Vietnam are near Ho Chi Minh City, the effect of supply chain clustering. Taishin also established its factories in Ho Chi Minh City and adjacent provinces. Wages in Vietnam are lower than in China, and the statutory working hours are longer, allowing for a six-day workweek. According to the manager at Taishin, "There are also a lot of corrupt Vietnamese officials, and the infrastructure is poor, but public security is better than in China." Taishin's production volume in Vietnam in 2015 was more than 40 percent of its global production volume. But the Vietnam factories have also encountered some problems: Vietnam's production quality and technology are still inferior to China's, there are frequent labor strikes, and Vietnamese factories need to rely on Chinese managers. In 2012, a Taigan with experience in Vietnam noted that almost every Taiwanese-owned factory in Vietnam had experienced a strike. Even Taishin, which considered its CSR very good, has experienced strikes. When it examined the situation, the company discovered that the problem wasn't with CSR but rather with HR, and especially with mainland Chinese managers. When the Lugan were transferred from China to Vietnam, they were paid in US dollars, but the US dollar depreciated against the renminbi from an exchange rate of 1:8 to a rate

58. Interview: YYPL2015.
59. Interview: YYPL2015.

little higher than 1:6, which made the managers feel that they were being paid less. These Lugan didn't have social insurance in Vietnam or China, and when they saw that Taiwanese managers had Taiwanese health and labor insurance, they couldn't help but feel that they suffered in comparison. These Lugan had worked for Taishin for fifteen years, devoting the prime of their lives to the company, but they felt they had no security, and after seeing so many Taishang run off, they had lost trust in the company. These Lugan were skilled, while high-level Taigan had been away from the production lines for too long and were out of practice—which made the Lugan even more confident of having the upper hand. As a result, when strikes broke out in Vietnam, Lugan "incited the Vietnamese workers to strike," according to the manager at Taishin. "Afterward we asked the Lugan, 'why did you do that?' They answered: 'If we didn't, how could we fight for our rights?' We failed in the HR aspect by not addressing the concerns of the Chinese managers."[60]

In Vietnam Taishin originally had twice as many Lugan as it had Taiwanese managers, but after the wave of strikes, the company decided to minimize the number of Lugan and use Taiwanese instead. The salaries of Lugan were also raised to nearly the same level as those of Taiwanese managers.[61] The fact is that Taishin's overseas domain would not have expanded so rapidly without its Lugan. And for a short time during the strike at the Vietnam factories, orders were sent back to China.

In 2018, China made up merely 14 percent of Taishin's global production volume, while Vietnam made up 46 percent and Indonesia 37 percent. Another major Taishang shoe manufacturer, Feng Tay, established a factory in India, but surprisingly, Taishin did not. The main reason was: "The brands [brand-name firms] apply pressure through orders, distributing orders by region, and if you don't go [to a particular region], they'll give it [an order] to someone else."[62] So why did brand-name firms put pressure on Feng Tay to go to India, but not on Taishin? Or why was Taishin able to resist the pressure? The buyer of around 70 percent of Feng Tay's production volume was Nike. However, Nike made up less than 20 percent of Taishin's production volume and there-

60. Interview: YYPL2015.
61. Interview: HTS201212.
62. Interview: XX2016-b.

fore did not have as much influence over Taishin. Taishin's largest buyer was Adidas. According to the assistant manager at Tashin, "Adidas initially favored Indonesia and then Vietnam, and in the last three years it's been Myanmar."[63] Taishin has established a factory in Myanmar under the brand's recommendation. Here we can clearly see that the production base deployment strategies of footwear industry Taishang basically follow the hegemonic logic of the GVCs, and lead firms brandish the whip from the top of the value chain, directing the movement of the Taiwanese OEM behemoths.

3) Establishing Factories in the Chinese Hinterland: Redeploying Production Bases and Land Interests

Another part of Taishin's redeployment of its production space was the moving of its production lines to China's inland provinces. Around 2005–6, local Chinese processing plants began gradually replacing Taishang supply chains, and at this point, Taishin began establishing factories in the hinterland, including Hubei, Jiangxi, Henan, and Jiangsu. Taishin was then still in the "warlord era" of the company's first-generation leaders,[64] and several of its business groups established inland factories in each territory (at their peak, there were more than ten such factories), but the scale of the factories varied. In 2011–12, the company began consolidating, and by 2013 it had closed fifty of its inland production lines.

Taishin moved production to inland provinces mainly because it was attracted by cheaper land and labor. At first glance, its new inland factories were profitable. But five factors limited the company's movement inward: First, in general the local governments further inland did not dare to apply flexible policies to foreign companies the way Guangdong's local governments did. Second, inland supply chains and export transportation were less convenient and more costly. Third, the workers at inland factories were mostly local people, and unlike the migrant workers who flocked to the coastal areas, local workers didn't like working overtime;

---

63. Interview: XX2016-b.

64. The warlords, or generals, refer to several veteran top managers who established the shoe manufacturing empire with the company's first-generation founders. Each warlord oversaw one business group.

during the busy farming seasons, most of the workers had to request leave to help their families with farm work; and local community ties meant that workers needed more time to look after their family and community needs (see Deng Jian-bang 2017). These local labor conditions led the factory regime and social relations of the inland factories of FIEs to differ substantially from those in the coastal regions. Inland workers were not "uprooted" like coastal migrant workers (see chapter 5) and had stronger community ties. Fourth, new factories established in inland areas required technical training for the workers, so some Pearl River Delta Lugan were transferred inland. Many of these senior managers and experienced production line leaders had been working for the company for more than ten years, and when these inland factories faced consolidation and closure, disputes broke out between the company and these senior employees over seniority compensation and other issues.[65] Furthermore, the inland factories also faced competition from local family-owned OEM factories (see more in section 4 below). All of these factors led Taishin to trim back its inland production lines.

According to Taishin managers, the inland factories all failed, so retrenchment and mergers were required. However, failure meant not losing money but rather not earning enough: compared with factories in the Pearl River Delta and Southeast Asia, inland factories did not achieve anticipated profits. Furthermore, trimming back the inland factories didn't represent cutting losses and leaving, because when the overall accounts were calculated, investing in the inland regions was still very profitable. So where was the money made? Real estate and nonoperating income were the actual measures of the benefit to be gained from closing factories:

> What has earned Taishin the most money on the mainland, around NT$300 billion, is factories and land, because it finally wised up. It goes like this: I go to Jiangsu and I want 2,500 *mu* of your land to manufacture shoes, but I insist that you transfer an extra 500 *mu* to me through the method of "tender, auction, and listing" and put it on the market for me. The procedure is just a formality. Making the exchange in this way, the land has not yet been developed, so you make a killing. . . . When Taishin planned the land use, Taiwanese managers got involved in the planning process and put their hands in, buying 50 *mu*, 30 *mu*, and

65. Interview: ALN201304.

then selling it off. Some built on it—food stalls or whatever. Because it's a traditional manufacturing industry, once a factory is built and starts making shoes, it creates a town with a population of 100,000 to 200,000. It's easy to make business opportunities with 200,000 people—a big supermarket, whatever, it's sure to make money. So you haven't heard Taishin saying that it's painful to close its inland factories. The pain is for the workers. The boss and senior Taigan have made a killing. When the factory moves out and the factory building is empty, the local government comes to talk with them about what can be done with this piece of land after the building is knocked down.[66]

This quote reveals three tricks of the trade. First, although Taishin's inland shoe factories weren't as profitable as expected, the company made a massive amount of money on land leases. When negotiating its investment with local governments, it demanded permission to lease land not only for industrial use, but also for commercial purposes. Second, the company was not alone in making money from land transactions: senior managers also bought and developed land to make money. Third, after the factory was closed, the land that was left behind could still have its use modified, which was another piece of business, and local government officials could also participate in this real-estate financial game. The status of "commercial or residential land" worked this way: "So-called commercial-residential means, put simply, I can use it to house my managerial staff, but I can also use it in other ways. Because on the mainland, commercial-residential property has to go through 'tender, auction, and listing'—it has to be publicly sold by tender and can't be privately approved—so the government will find one or two fakes to bid against you. But it's a camouflage for you, theoretically and legally. It's very simple: I want that piece of land. So when you get a so-called commercial-residential property, it means you can sell commercial premises or you can rent it to Starbucks!"[67]

This operation can be carried out only by Taishang with powerful backers and excellent political connections, but Taishin was not an exception. Other Taishang belonging to the "cross-strait government-business network" (Wu Jieh-min 2017b, 684) often had access to these

66. Interview: YYPL2015.
67. Interview: YYPL2015.

privileges: "As a key point in the negotiation, I need 1,500 *mu* of industrial land, and how much commercial-residential land will you give me?
I'm telling you, the Taishang Mr. Kuo did this in the northeast: 'I'll give
you this industrial park, you have to give me this much commercial-
residential land.' That's the trick of the trade."[68]

This brings up a thought-provoking question: Do the land profits go
into the company's accounts or into private coffers? If these land profits
all revert to the public, then the company makes money when the accounts are tallied, but if the profits go into private pockets, the company's
investors lose out while the proprietor and top-level managers are allowed
to make massive profits.

4) The Second Generation Takes Over: Reform, Crisis, and Transformation

Although Taishin is a publicly listed company, it still has the quality of a
family business. Members of the second generation began joining the
company in the 2000s, and after years of grooming, they formally took
over around 2013. The generational handover changed the organizational
structure that had characterized the company for many years. Among the
second-generation successors, Sandy,[69] the new CEO, had graduated
with an MBA from a famous American university, and she adopted what
veteran managers considered to be an American style that from the outset was out of sync with the long-term business model.

After becoming CEO, Sandy launched new organizational and staff-
ing arrangements. The company originally had three business groups or
departments. The concept of the "group" relied on local autonomy, with
a strong tribal flavor. Each group was like an army led by a general, and
it had a corporate culture suited to its founding stage. These generals had
spent decades conquering the world under the company's first-generation
leaders, and all of them had strong backing, with the proprietors granting them both a considerable amount of authority and free rein. The proprietors also handled these generals with a soft touch, and they grew up
together. During this period, each of the business groups had enormous

---

68. Interview: YYPL2015.
69. Sandy is a pseudonym.

discretion, and each accepted and manufactured orders from international clients, giving rise to a kind of internal competition to obtain equilibrium. The business groups were like profit centers, and the company's top manager directly controlled the head office, requiring each business group to turn over a certain share of its profits every year (usually around 8–10 percent of the total sales), with the remaining profit divided among the managers of the relevant business group as bonuses. As a result, each business group became an operational hub in which five or six people (including the vice president, business associate, and production associate) formed an inner circle that had the greatest power. When profits were higher, bonuses were larger, and factory managers and other managers also got their share, according to rank. This operating method was like the contracting method in China, and it also approached the concept of residual rights in new institutional economics. The core managers of the business group controlled the residual rights, and this created an incentive for sales performance.

Although the business groups enjoyed a portion of the residual rights on sales performance, the head office controlled the company's overall money stream, which meant that it controlled financial affairs. At the same time, the head office was also the service unit that provided the company's public goods—for example, investment policies, customs servicing, public relations, land leases and construction—and was also responsible for auditing and supervision: "First, you in the business group don't have to deal with architectural design, contracting, or factory construction; second, you don't have to deal with financial affairs or feng shui, that's the head office, too. Although it's the business group that represents the boss in negotiations with the local government about investment conditions, the boss is still in control."[70]

To sum up, the first-generation team that led Taishin had quite a substantial division of power. This system provided opportunities for a "black hand," or apprentice-turned-manager, to make a name for himself. For example, an apprentice with only a primary school education but with strong abilities could be promoted to the level of vice president and lead a business group at Taishin with the competitiveness of Taiwan's early small and medium-size enterprises. But a shortcoming of this warlord

70. Interview: YYPL2015.

system arose from competition within the organization. Different business groups would fight for orders from the same client (e.g., Nike), and clients would complain that Taishin didn't have good coordination among its divisions, its standards weren't consistent, agreements on pricing were difficult to reach, business units snatched orders from each other, and there wasn't a single window for handling orders.

To address clients' demands for such a single window, Sandy's method was to reorganize the business groups into business divisions, with each responsible for a specific brand (e.g., Nike, Adidas, or Puma), while some divisions targeted several brands with smaller sales volumes. Sandy made the organization lateral and centralized, with the head office directly controlling the operations of each business division, and reforms progressed quickly. In this consolidation process, a number of veteran managers were dismissed with severance pay, which gave rise to complaints from the old guard: "The new leaders were too young and ungrounded and had never made shoes. The inland factories shut down one by one."[71] Another veteran manager said: "Hon Hai [Foxconn] established training courses led by veteran managers to pass on the company's organizational culture and knowledge, but Taishin didn't do that. At Taishin the old bosses were appeasing toward the staff and strove for their favor. Sandy had a new style, controlling assets worth hundreds of billions of NT dollars. . . . Old Simpson told me, 'If Sandy does things this way, she'll either win or lose within three to five years. If she wins, she'll be the one writing history.'"[72]

Additional objectives in the second generation's getting rid of the old managers were to reform the operational style of the first generation and track down internal malpractice, such as kickback deals between the business group generals and suppliers. The first-generation proprietors were concerned only with financial affairs and the company's overall direction. The professional managers of each business group were very powerful, and they also had opportunities to earn additional income. As long as the company made money, the top managers turned a blind eye to this behavior, but when profits were affected, they would be called to account and forced out. The methods that the veteran managers used to earn ad-

71. Interview: YYPL2015.
72. Interview: HTS201212.

ditional income included exchanging notes with Taishin's suppliers—
that is, the supplier (e.g., a factory producing material for shoes) had to
use cash to buy material for production, and when selling goods to Taishin
they would get a three-month promissory note. But the supplier was usually in urgent need of cash, so the business group head would exchange
the supplier's promissory note for cash as a kind of short-term loan and
earn 30 percent interest.

This was a traditional lending model developed in Taiwan. Early on,
Taiwan's small and medium-size companies needed revolving funds for
their operations, but it was difficult for them to borrow money from publicly owned banks. When suppliers received promissory notes from their
clients, they would exchange them in this private financial system. The
system of exchanging notes, like private loan associations, was part of a
credit system that people developed in private practice, and it formed a
link in the financial infrastructure of the flexible production networks of
Taiwan's small and medium-size enterprises. Taishang transplanted the
system in China when they moved west.

However, the second generation of top managers felt that the old-
guard business group managers wielded too much power and were making private deals with suppliers that allowed them to enjoy bonuses even
if the company lost money—and on top of everything, they were very
blatant about it. The new top managers therefore sped up the pace of restructuring under a new system that controlled personnel matters and
detected fraud. Taishin rapidly underwent reorganization, moving from
a division of power to the centralization of power—as Taiyang Company
had with the succession of its second generation. Although Taishin and
Taiyang operated on very different scales, their restructuring addressed
very similar concerns, and the education and mindsets of their second-
generation leaders were also very similar. Likewise, both of the second-
generation management teams encountered resentment and resistance
from the old guard.

After Sandy took over, the first challenge she faced was the wave of
labor strikes in the Pearl River Delta. Like many Taishang encountering
strikes at that time, Taishin sought help from its political connections,
but this was largely in vain: China was undergoing industrial restructuring, and the official standpoint had changed. Furthermore, while the
Communist Party's top leadership was in transition, the bureaucratic

apparatus at every level became extremely cautious about employing administrative discretion. In addition, some managers observed that the members of Taishin's second generation, with their American educations, didn't want to engage in the *guanxi* style of government-business contacts. In fact, the handover of power from the Jiang Zemin clique to the Xi Jinping clique rendered Taishin's political connections largely obsolete, so the idea of relying purely on *guanxi* to get out of trouble was probably wishful thinking in any case. Changes in the power structure shut out many Taishang: this was a commonly heard complaint within the Taishang community. When Taishin's workers went on strike to demand back payment of their housing provident funds, they posed a formidable threat. If an OEM manufacturer on Taishin's scale was not able to quickly resolve the crisis, the company would suffer heavy losses. The best option, therefore, was to accede to the demands of the local government and the workers and find a way to completely resolve the issue. As soon as labor disputes broke out, the government took the opportunity to increase wages and improve working conditions. These manufacturers, being held up as examples, had no real way out. After all, the law contained explicit stipulations, and it was only their implementation that had been flexible. Now that they were being strictly enforced, companies were pressed to pay their historical debt.

The methods that Taishin's top management used to deal with the strike had three consequences, all of which sped up Sandy's reform plans. First, Taishin learned what it cost to violate regulations, and it paid closer attention to labor-management relations and working conditions. As mentioned above, the strategy that brand-name firms demanded was to combine the handling of CSR and HR. Taishin put a great deal of effort into restoring its relationship with its staff and to carry out stability preservation, and it demanded strict adherence to regulations. Second, the company sped up the removal of its production bases from China, and especially from the coastal regions. Yet a manufacturer of Taishin's scale couldn't simply move when it wanted to, nor could it do a runner. Taishin still had substantial interests in China, so its departure became a drawnout process. Third, the company strengthened and developed its domestic marketing strongholds in China, and it executed a genuine policy of transformation along with China's grand strategy of becoming a world market.

5) Climbing the GVC

Taishin had advanced from OEM to ODM in Taiwan in the 1980s, but becoming a brand-name manufacturer was a long, slow process, even with its world-class manufacturing prowess and solid capitalization. Another path for the company was developing the domestic market in China. As early as the 1990s, Taishin created its own brands and made inroads into the Chinese retail market. At one point Taishin planned to offer a high price to buy a global second-tier brand, only to have Nike buy that company at the last minute. Nike tossed out these words: "If you really want to create a brand, we'll break up with you!"[73] Taishin could only retreat without a fight. Taishin encountered client opposition because creating its own brand would threaten the hegemony of the lead firms at the pinnacle of the GVC (Nike and Adidas). If brand-name firms allowed Taishin's own brand to succeed, it would challenge the oligarchic status of the lead firms in the world sports shoe market. Brand-name firms held the trump card when it came to orders, and Taishin was not the only OEM factory that could provide them with high-quality sports shoes (Feng Tay, e.g., could do the same). With the standards of China's local shoe manufacturing rapidly improving, brand-name firms also had the option of grooming mainland-owned factories to become major suppliers. In short, Taishin did not enjoy a monopoly on the ability to manufacture shoes (unlike TSMC did for most advanced chip fabrication). Even though brand-name firms had to a certain extent become reliant on Taishin's manufacturing capacity and quality, they still overwhelmingly dominated the global high-end sports shoe market.

The strategy that Taishin ultimately adopted was to maintain its partnership with brand-name firms but to gain agency rights for brands in China's domestic market to help them sell shoes. In other words, Taishin would put the brand-name firm's label on shoes that Taishin produced and then sell those shoes in the Chinese market.

In the mid-2000s, when Taishin was still led by its business groups, it invested in a company in China that specialized in marketing: Taichang, which was listed on the Hong Kong stock market in 2008. Taichang obtained agency rights for Nike, Adidas, and other top-tier brands, as well

73. Interview: HTS201310.

as exclusive franchising rights for Converse and Hush Puppies. Because of their relationship with Taishin, those brands gave Taichang a great deal of autonomy in terms of product design, pricing, supply chain management, marketing, and development.[74] Taichang used joint ventures, mergers and acquisitions, and directly operated showrooms to maintain control of financial management and administration, and within ten years it had owned more than three thousand shops, including complex stores (which combine selling shoes, training, and dining), mall shops, specialty stores, franchise shops, and so on. However, due to financial and training issues during the expansion process, "consolidated financial statements were chaotic, and it was badly managed".[75] Taichang was unable to address the difficult problem of overstocking at its retail outlets and continued to suffer losses. In recent years, after the second-generation leaders took over Taishin, Taichang's finances regained an equilibrium. In 2015, its retail division provided more than 20 percent of Taishin's total revenue. As of 2016, Taichang was continuing to expand its agency rights and domestic marketing.

According to the assistant manager at Taishin, "it's hard to make 'good money' in OEM in China, but Taishin's reputation was too prominent, so it couldn't just leave when it wanted to. There were also 'political considerations,' so if the company couldn't leave, it had to transform."[76] Brand-name firms still needed high-end production bases in China, so Taishin still had a role to play as an integrator of the entire supply chain for sports shoes in the Pearl River Delta. Developing inroads into the domestic market therefore became the company's main option for transforming itself on-site.

In its corporate development, Taishin faced pursuit from behind (OEM factories in China and Vietnam) and obstacles in front (brand-name firms). It therefore had no choice but to find a niche in the GVC. Taishin's moves in recent years include buying out a ticketing system for public sporting events in Taiwan, cooperating with brand-name firms to develop new technology, and establishing an innovation and research center in central Taiwan. At the same time, it has cooperated with another international sporting goods brand on innovation and development. The

74. Interview: ALN201304.
75. Interview: HTS201310.
76. Interview: XX2016.

concept of the innovation and research center originated with the laboratory of Mizuno, a Japanese company in Osaka, which can accurately measure the posture of athletes as a basis for product innovation. This development is oriented toward a shift at the top end of the value chain: In the past, Taishin's profit model was a vertically integrated production chain and its aim was to seize value and gain profit from each link in the production chain, but this profit model had become saturated. The new trend commenced with a sports concept emphasizing horizontal integration. Overall, Taishin's strategy was to move toward the brand end of, but not to create its own brand in, the global market.

Taishin's growth trajectory over the past half-century has conformed to the movement and expansion of the GVC while the company has also climbed the chain. It started out as a family-style plastic shoe factory and then became a professional OEM manufacturer for international brands, later becoming an ODM, and integrating its production chain step by step. After establishing a manufacturing base in China, it was able to expand its output and also use China's institutional characteristics and concessionary policies to make massive profits from low wages. Over the past ten years, with increases in the costs of China's factors of production and under pressure for industrial upgrading, the company has undergone migration inland and overseas as well as upgrading and other transformation on-site, and the profitability of its vertical integration has nearly reached its limit. Figure 6.1 shows Taishin's current position on the GVC in relation to its internal organization. As a transnational corporation focused on manufacturing, Taishin has constantly pushed its way toward the top of the GVC, but the marginal costs of taking the last mile are enormous. The company has continued its attempt to reach a core position on the GVC, but it has been unable to cast off the GVC's logic of hegemonic domination, and it has encountered insurmountable limits (see Wang Jenn-hwan 2010).

4. The Changing Ecosystems of Taiwanese and Chinese Companies

During the transformation of the Guangdong model, the changing ecosystem of Chinese-owned companies has formed a key contrast to that of Taishang. The ecology of Chinese-owned companies can be divided

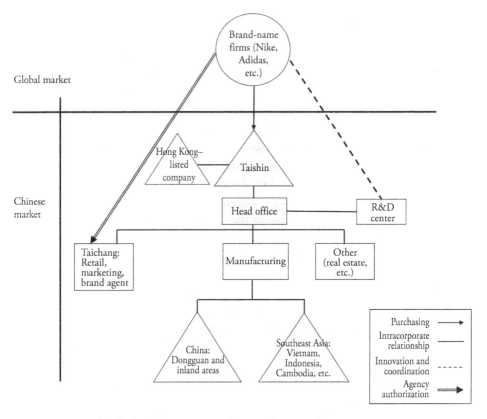

FIGURE 6.1. Taishin's GVC position in relation to its internal organization.

into two sections for the purpose of analysis: The first section is traditional manufacturing, exemplified by the rise of local supply chains in the footwear industry. The second is the emergence of ICT production chains dominated by Chinese-owned companies.

1) The Taishang Code in the Production Chain of Mainland-Owned Traditional Industries

One of the greatest changes in the transformation of traditional industries in the Pearl River Delta has been Taishang's moving one step closer to the pinnacle of the GVC—for instance, by transforming themselves into quasi-international buyers and transferring orders to mainland-owned OEM factories (with Smiles as a classic example) or by expanding their scope of business into retail marketing (with Taishin as a classic example). In both cases, mainland-owned factories have played an increasingly important role. Mainland-owned sports shoe factories began taking OEM business from second-tier brands (shoes with mid to low unit prices) in the late 2000s. In terms of first-tier brands (shoes with high unit prices), they gradually became partnering OEM factories for Taiwanese-owned companies, but in these cases shoe-making equipment and materials were still controlled by Taishang. The bifurcation between high and low unit prices indicates the spatial displacement and redeployment of the Pearl River Delta export shoe industry.

The burgeoning mainland-owned OEM factories have some obvious features: First, the factories tend to be small on average, typically with only two or three molding lines and employing only a few hundred people; and there is close interaction between factories, characterized by flexible production networks and rapid response. Second, they have relatively low production costs: mainland-owned factories have lower costs than other factories in terms of wages, social insurance, housing provident funds, and so on, and they also obtain some of their raw materials at lower prices. The differential enforcement applied to mainland-owned factories by local governments routinely gives them a way out of penalties, and local governments also subsidize privately owned enterprises (Cheng Chih-peng 2016). Third, mainland-owned OEM factories' relationships with Taiwanese-owned companies have caused Taishang technology to spread and corporate culture to penetrate the organization of rising mainland-owned factories. We therefore need to understand the technical learning capacity of mainland-owned factories, as well as the diffusion of technology from Taiwanese-owned factories in this process.

Cheng Chih-peng (2016) has observed the birth of mainland-owned factories under a Taiwanese system, or what could be called the Chinese version of *oo-tshiú piàn thâu-ke* (apprentice turned boss; for this concept, see Shieh Gwo-Shyong 1992 and 1997). In the Pearl River Delta, privately owned enterprises in export-oriented traditional industries have a strong Taiwanese flavor and style, with many new proprietors having initially been migrant workers in Taiwanese-owned factories. In the process of starting their businesses, they became vehicles of technology diffusion by Taishang in China. Even more significant in this process of technology diffusion was the importation, imitation, and appropriation of Taishang culture (Cheng Chih-peng 2016). The founders of mainland-owned factories who had once worked in Taiwanese-owned factories obtained technology from those factories, and their relationships of social trust with Taishang also deeply influenced their subsequent business development trajectories. After establishing their businesses, they took on orders that Taishang contracted to them, and Taishang also provided them with technical training to enhance their production capacity. The unintended consequence was that as Taishang initially moved their production westward, they transplanted Taiwan's original network-style organization and contracting system to China. Then, with the extension and transformation of GVCs and localization of supply chains, mainland-owned factories penetrated the original Taishang socioeconomic spatial structure and caused a reorganization of its supply chains (see Cheng Chih-peng 2014b).

From the theoretical standpoint, Martin Hess's concept of social embeddedness can help us analyze Taiwanese-owned companies as economic and cultural actors that influenced the places in China where they were located. Hess uses the biological metaphor of the genetic code to refer to the importance of the backgrounds of the actors: when they go abroad to engage in global production networks, they carry the genetic code with them, and at the same time they are exposed to the different cultures of their foreign network partners (Hess 2004, 176 and 180). Based on the same logic, we can argue that local partners have the genetic codes of their social embeddedness, which interact with those from outside. It is through the extension and expansion of GVCs in China that Taishang and Taigan have exchanged genetic codes with mainland-owned companies and Lugan. In this process of mutual social imbedding, heterogeneous as well as hybrid forms of networks may develop and may transform the structure of global production networks (Hess 2004, 180). I believe that this process of mutual embedding gave birth to mainland-owned factories under a Taiwanese system as well as to the Chinese version of apprentice turned boss.

In this historical process, localized supply chains penetrated the cluster structures of the Taishang community. Cheng Chih-peng (2014b, 54) describes the result as an enclave disorganizing, but I see it somewhat differently. My divergence from Cheng originates in our different understandings of Taishang clusters as a kind of enclave economy. Previous studies tend to hold that the enclave-type economies of Taishang migrating to China's coastal regions had introverted flexible production networks (Cheng Lu-lin 1999; Chen Ming-chi 2012), but there seems to be a contradiction here. If Taishang networks were intensely introverted, why were mainland-owned factories subsequently able to gain outsourcing opportunities from Taishang? Cheng Chih-peng's explanation points to phased differences, with introversion referring to the early phase (before the mid-2000s) and openness to outsourcing coming in later, after the restructuring of the world economy. But this explanation still doesn't go far enough. The actual reason Taiwanese-acculturated mainland-owned factories were able to so rapidly take on orders subcontracted to them by Taishang after 2008 is that the introversion of the enclave economy was not as intense as the original research held. The Taishang community was embedded in local society to a considerable degree—whether through production links, government-business relationship links, or consumer links—and this social embeddedness was the main vehicle for technical diffusion and the transmission of cultural models of behavior. Those quasi-Taishang had learned their manufacturing and management techniques during their prior work experience in Taiwanese-owned factories (Cheng Chih-peng 2016). Regardless of the motivation of the Taishang employer or Taigan, mainland employees have the opportunity to rise from ordinary worker to production or management cadre, and this process has to a great extent penetrated the introverted nature of the Taishang community. For this reason, we need to revise our views on the so-called enclave quality of Taishang. Based on the same point, the arguments in past research proposing that Taishang are disembedded or "a fortress in the air" (Chen Ming-chi 2012) in the production networks of China's coastal regions are also theoretically questionable from the current perspective (see Cheng Lu-lin 1999).

In the visualization of disembeddedness, the host country's political structure and local society lack subjectivity and resilience and therefore accept without question any conditions proposed by foreign companies. For example, during the reunification of East and West Germany, the way that West German capital entered East Germany brought about the collapse of East Germany's informal economic networks and resulted in the development of capitalism without capitalists (Grabher 1994). China had a different relationship with foreign investors, however. This book's evidence and arguments point out that China's local governments have not lacked leverage in the GVC governance structure. On the contrary, local governments have intervened in value capture and distribution. In the labor participation process, a portion of China's migrant workers have gained opportunities for advancement to the management level, learned production techniques and organizational skills, and gained opportunities to launch their own businesses. Viewed from this angle, this process of technical diffusion revises the presumption of disembeddedness and an enclave economy when considering varying degrees of local agency.

As Taishang manufacturers in the Pearl River Delta migrated inland, their production chains extended with them and interacted with the inland economy and society. Taishin's experience in Hunan is worth noting. Taishin invested in a factory that made products exclusively for a second-tier brand-name firm. After a time, however, that firm pulled its order from Taishin and transferred it to a mainland-owned factory that could produce the same quality as Taishin at a 20 percent discount to the OEM price. The reason was that the mainland-owned factory didn't supply dormitories or three meals a day for its workers, didn't pay into social insurance or the housing provident fund, and provided no kindergarten or other benefits for workers and their families. Instead, the mainland-owned factory turned a portion of what it saved on expenses into cash bonuses, a practice very popular among local workers. As a result, there was a wage discrepancy between Taishin's factory and the mainland-owned factory: A Lugan at the level of section head earned around 4,500 yuan per month, but a manager of the same rank at the mainland-owned factory took home around 6,500 yuan, including wages, a cash bonus, and an amount for home contracting (using small home-based workshops).[77] This gives an inkling of how mainland-owned factories gained a competitive edge over Taiwanese-owned factories, and it shows the process and mechanism by which the GVC's exploitation mechanism infiltrated the inland regions. Here we once again witness the Chinese version of the apprentice-turned-boss narrative in which the pure labor consciousness of workers is faintly discernible (Shieh Gwo-Shyong 1997).

77. Interview: XX2015.

The export-oriented supply chains for traditional industries that sprang up in the Pearl River Delta cannot all be traced back to the influence of Taiwanese-invested companies—an influence that depended on the type of industry. But the lasting imprint of Taiwanese investment is evident in the footwear, garment, handbag and luggage, toy, and bicycle industries. We can also see how the work experience of Lugan in Taiwanese-owned factories affected the bicycle industry in the Yangtze Delta (Chiu Chun-hung 2005). In Guangdong, this phenomenon was not limited to the so-called traditional industries but can also be seen in the Pearl River Delta's computer industry. A Taiwanese scholar quotes one interviewee as saying: "If it is said that these kinds of contacts between Taiwanese and mainland staff were very good from 1998 to 2003, it was always Taigan that guided Lugan running businesses from the start. In that atmosphere it was very easy to engage with Taiwanese managers; they were easy to talk to" (quoted in Wang Po-chi 2014, 46). Apart from their experience on the production lines of Taiwanese-owned factories, Lugan's following the business practices of Taigan was related to the diffusion of technology, standards, and orders. By around 2006, the quality of some mainland-owned component suppliers matched that of Taiwanese and Japanese manufacturers (2014, 44–46). Wang Po-chi's field research shows that of the ten suppliers for the Taiwanese-invested Tungjih Company, three were Taiwanese owned and six were mainland owned; in addition, only one of the ten was established in 1997, with the rest all established in the 2000s (2014, 10–11). This research shows that the Pearl River Delta's mainland-owned computer industry emerged during the same period that the footwear industry was transformed.

The places where Taiwanese-acculturated mainland-owned factories cut into the global-local linkage reveal the dynamics of the GVC's extension, along with the localization process and technical emulation and diffusion that came with it. As they climbed the GVC ladder of power, mainland-owned factories also strove to catch up with Taishang. As I have discussed above, Taishang were able to play the role of quasi-international buyer or GSC integrator in the traditional industrial sector because the technical quality of mainland-owned factories was still behind that of Taishang factories. But can Taishang maintain that advantage in the foreseeable future? According to the above analysis, manufacturers that were unable to bear up under the pressure for industrial transformation either shut down, ran off, or moved inland in pursuit of production conditions similar to those of mainland-owned factories. The Taishang that were able to remain in the Pearl River Delta had been tested by a round of state policy changes and labor strikes and had achieved a degree of industrial upgrading that allowed them to draw closer to the lead firm pinnacle of the value chain. The transformation of Taishin and Smiles testifies to the survival capacity of this category of Taishang. Yet we should note that as long as manufacturing Taishang continue to seek survival in the hegemonic logic of the existing GVC, they will run the risk of being overtaken by mainland-owned factories. In fact, Taiwanese-owned factories have been facing similar pressure in Southeast Asia as well, especially in Vietnam. The rules of the game for climbing the GVC power ladder were established by the lead firms of core countries, and Taishang can maintain their position as number two only by following and catching up, while keeping a step ahead of the competition.

2) The New ICT Ecosystem

The rise of Chinese-owned companies in the Pearl River Delta's ICT production chains followed a different path than that described above for companies in traditional industries.[78] Taishang also played quite an important role in ICT companies, but a new ecosystem emerged. This system relied on China's vast domestic market and gained key support from state policy while also adopting human-wave and head-hunting strategies in R&D. China's ICT industry made initial breakthroughs in certain key production links that gave the sector a jump start and enhanced its manufacturing strength and enabled it to capture a share of the global market within a relatively short time.

(A) THE NETWORK COMMUNICATIONS INDUSTRY
I first analyze the network communications industry. Observing the trajectory of the rise over the past fifteen years of China's top-tier networking companies (such as TP-Link and Digital China), which are on par

---

78. The analysis in this section benefited from the repeated advice of Lo Ming-ling, to whom I am greatly indebted. It has also benefited from discussions with Michelle Fei-yu Hsieh.

with Taiwan's main networking companies (such as Accton, Zyxel, Alpha, and Gemtek), we can divide that rise into roughly three stages.

In the first stage, mainly because at that time China's market was enormous but not focused on quality, a company first expanded, establishing economies of scale and developing the ability to keep costs extremely low. This stage began by luring talent from Taiwan, especially for the hardware portion of the industry. The pattern was as follows: The Chinese company would hire someone from a Taiwanese company at the level of associate general manager (factory manager), promote him to vice president and channel him into the company's core policy-making circle (typically composed of seven people, of whom the other six were mainland Chinese). The salary would be double or triple that at the original Taiwanese company. The Taiwanese vice president would help the Chinese company find supply chain manufacturers for printed circuit boards, plastic and metal casings (mechanical parts), and so on. Mr. Lok, a former general manager of a Taiwanese-owned networking equipment company said: "In this way, scalping [head-hunting] one factory manager was like scalping a production chain. But allowing the Taiwanese factory manager to take part in core decision making depended completely on the boss's attitude. If someday he felt he'd squeezed you dry, he'd tell you not to come to meetings anymore, and you'd be kicked out of the decision-making circle."[79] The Chinese side would chiefly look at the Taiwanese employee's abilities in manufacturing hardware. In terms of the software portion, Taiwan was originally at a disadvantage, so there was no head-hunting of staff in this area. Chinese-owned companies had capital to spend on long-term training of software professionals. Some of these had returned to China after studying or working overseas. This stage used China's domestic market to foster production capacity and technology.

In the second stage, the Chinese-owned company already had the capacity to enter the international market, but because of the sub-par quality of its goods, it could enter the market only through using a low-price strategy. As quality improved each year, the company's market expanded from India and Africa to advanced nations in Europe and elsewhere. In the early part of this stage, the Taiwanese were still important, but in the latter part, mainland-produced talent gradually matured. As a result, some

79. Interview: LM201508.

of the Taiwanese that had worked for the company began flowing back into the Taiwanese system.

In the third stage, the Chinese-owned factory matured. The product quality of these first-tier companies was at a standard that made them competitive in the mid- to high-end international markets. Taiwan's few networking brands came under immense competitive pressure from Chinese companies and even suffered setbacks in some markets. At this stage, China no longer needed Taiwanese talent.

As for Huawei and ZTE, the two Chinese networking giants are unique enterprises that receive enormous state support, which gives them an advantage in large-scale telecommunications equipment manufacturing. ZTE is a state-owned holding company, listed in Hong Kong and Shenzhen and with strong ties to the Chinese military-industrial complex (Balding, 2018). Huawei is registered as a nonstate enterprise but believed to have close relations to the Chinese military. Huawei calls itself employee-owned, but researchers have challenged this claim (Balding and Clarke 2019). In recent years, both manufacturers have gradually acquired world-class technology and production capacity and is already globally competitive with Ericsson, Nokia, Cisco, Fujitsu, and other foreign lead firms. These Chinese manufacturers have close relationships with the state, whose supporting role is especially apparent in terms of the military, network controls, finance, and monopolizing the domestic market. An analysis of the value chains of large-scale telecommunications equipment manufacture shows that China already occupies a strategic position, with service providers such as China Mobile, which relies on its monopoly of the enormous domestic market; equipment brands such as Huawei and ZTE; and application software designers such as Huawei and ZTE at the uppermost reaches of China's value chains. Huawei and ZTE have mastered the technology of IP [internet protocol] Multimedia Subsystem (IMS), which is a highly innovative software. China has an abundance of software talent (including college students and graduate students trained in the country and engineers returning from abroad), capital, state subsidies, and preferential policies that allow for investing seven to eight years in grooming talent. The above-quoted Lok said that the rise of China's telecommunications equipment industry "is not particularly the result of the technical capabilities of Taiwanese manufacturers. Early on, Taiwan's firms didn't know what to think of Huawei and ZTE and even looked down on them. Now those companies are already competing with Ericsson, Nokia, and other heavyweight companies, while Taiwan doesn't have a single network communications company that can compete with them."[80]

A key reason why "Taiwan's firms didn't know what to think of Huawei and ZTE" had to do with the political systems in and strategic differences between the two countries: Taiwanese companies weren't familiar with China's resources. Companies like Huawei and ZTE establish themselves in the China market in the early stage of their development, and the Chinese state intervenes in the domestic market to a high degree through monopoly or oligopoly. The state not only intervenes in the market but also needs to control the product design of those companies to carry out its internet surveillance. For example, telecommunications equipment can control the internet, so Huawei and ZTE inevitably have a close relationship with the Chinese government. As outsiders, Taishang do not know how to maneuver in this environment. As China began building its Great Firewall in the 1990s, it contacted European and American computer companies in an attempt to grasp internet control technology. Because Huawei and ZTE were related to China's national defense and state security sector, their attempts to capture the Western market through their low prices triggered controversies over national security, especially in the United States, Canada, and Australia and also led to a high degree of concern in Taiwan (Rogers and Ruppersberger 2012; *American Interest* 2012; Shan 2014). When first established, this kind of company focused on creating a brand and devoted itself to acquiring a key position in the GVC. In this process, the Chinese government could use the latecomer's advantage strategy through its enormous domestic market and various incentives and subsidies. Some researchers believe that companies such as Huawei, which obtain state funding but can still achieve industrial upgrading and technical innovation, are the exception in China (Fuller 2016). This argument deserves attention.

In any case, we need to evaluate the rise of China's indigenous network communications and telecommunication industry at the national level. The effort by Huawei and ZTE to expand their territory qualifies as a neomercantilist state policy (Wein, Ezell, and Atkinson 2014), and

---

80. Interview: LM201509.

the impetus behind it is economic nationalism. Based on a similar logic, the Chinese government is fostering new industries with functions similar to those of Google, YouTube, Facebook, WhatsApp, Line, and Amazon, such as Baidu, Tudou, Youku, Tencent QQ, WeChat, and Alibaba. This strategic matrix includes three mutually linked key elements: the state surveillance society, domestic market protectionism, and elimination of Western technology monopolies. If these links aren't considered as a whole, it is impossible to fully understand the rise of manufacturers such as Huawei. From a theoretical standpoint, the strategy of China's telecommunications industry is to develop an alternative route to bypass the value chain hegemony of core Western manufacturers. Here we observe the resilience and agency of the local polity toward global capital forces (see figure 1.2).

(B) THE CELL-PHONE INDUSTRY: FROM A COPY TO A
GLOBAL PRODUCT

After analyzing the prototype of the network communications ecosystem, I now turn to the Shenzhen region—an industrial spatial cluster for the ICT industry's transformation model, which can be divided into two types for analysis. I will discuss the first type in this section and the second type in the next section, where I also compare the two types. The first type is related to the localization of traditional industry supply chains. The location is mainly in the areas surrounding the Shenzhen SEZ, where many migrant workers and Lugan who originally worked in Taishang supply chain factories went out on their own to establish businesses and accepted orders from Taishang or foreign buyers. The main industrial categories, as mentioned above, were in the traditional industries. At the outset they also included lower-end ICT manufacturing, but as production capacity rapidly improved, it fostered local supply chains, accompanied by the emergence of copycat factories in the mid-2000s (Tu Hsinfei 2011; Hsu Rongrong 2011).

The critical juncture in the rise of the copycat cell-phone industry resulted from the enhanced purchasing power for China's low-end smartphones. As an emerging market, China had massively divergent spending power, which created a unique business model. The counterfeit cell-phone business model was driven by platforms, with resources provided by foreign companies and local governments. The Taiwanese-owned MediaTek, a fabless semiconductor company, provided chipsets and technical service platforms, and local governments provided land and other resources. Because the entry threshold was low, local copycat cell-phone factories were established rapidly. There were around two thousand of them, most of which were small or medium-size ventures that modified MediaTek platform. The profit margins of these businesses were very slim, but on average in 2008–15, MediaTek that provided the chipsets made a 48.4 percent gross profit. According to a Chinese scholar, "Because Chinese businesses could only manufacture 'roughed out rooms,' MediaTek provided 'furnished rooms' that were 'move-in ready,' so the gross profit was high."[81]

Chinese manufacturers entered the cell-phone market with pirated cell-phones, and then Huawei also entered the market. In just a few years, the Chinese brands Huawei, Xiaomi, and Lenovo were among the world's top five market shareholders. According to IDC, in the second quarter of 2015, Samsung had 21.4 percent of the global market; Apple had 13.9 percent; and Huawei, Xiaomi, and Lenovo together had 19.0 percent. The main market for Chinese brands was the Asia-Pacific region (especially China's domestic market), followed by the Middle East, Africa, India, and other third-world countries. Xiaomi especially relied on the Chinese market. The business model of Xiaomi cell phones was unique: the price-performance ratio of its handsets was high, and at the early stage it rose mainly by using the MediaTek platform. The handsets didn't need to be profitable, and the company even abandoned profitability as a hardware manufacturer in favor of focusing on internet sales, fostering an enormous fan base, and creating profit from the consumer and advertising markets revolving around its cell phones.[82] In the fourth quarter of 2017, Samsung had 18.9 percent of the global market for cell phones; Apple had 19.7 percent; and Huawei, Xiaomi, and OPPO combined had 24.8 percent. Chinese cell-phone brands continued to capture a growing share of the market, mainly through Xiaomi's capture of the low-price Indian and Russian markets and the newly ascendant OPPO's gaining a

81. Interview: T201402.
82. Interview: T201402.

foothold in developing Asian markets such as India, Indonesia, and Vietnam.[83]

(C) VENTURE CAPITAL FOR ICT COMES CHIEFLY
FROM OVERSEAS RETURNEES

The second type is the establishment of cutting-edge ICT industries. The location for this was primarily within the Shenzhen SEZ, and the founders were mainly professionals and graduates returning from overseas and graduates of Chinese universities. The scale was concentrated in small and medium-size industries, and there were many examples before 2000. The rise of this sector is largely unrelated to the original Taiwanese-invested networks in the Pearl River Delta: instead, the sector rose as a result of Chinese venture capital and R&D. A representative industry is drones. China manufactures drones of excellent quality at low prices that have been able to capture the international market. Drone technology involves four levels: wireless, software, manufacturing (including electronics and robotics), and engines and controls. At all four levels, Chinese manufacturers have the capacity for their own R&D.

The interaction and embedded relationships between these two types (the copycat manufacturing apparatus and the system founded by overseas returnees) deserve an in-depth look. Some of the venture capital companies in the second type that were engaged in ICT in the Shenzhen SEZ placed orders with the first type of copycat manufacturers to carry out custom manufacturing. In other words, the maturity of the first type's manufacturing technology was able to support the second type by serving as its manufacturing base. This copycat ecosystem in the manufacturing industry had three characteristics: First, quite a few of the founders of the copycat factories were originally managers of low-end production lines of Taiwanese-owned factories, who subsequently opened their own factories (which had certain characteristics of Taiwanese-acculturated

83. *AUTHOR'S POSTSCRIPT:* In the third quarter of 2021, Samsung had 20.8 percent of the global market; Apple had 15.2 percent; and the Chines brands Xiaomi, Vivo, and OPPO combined had 23.5 percent, while Huawei had been pushed out of the game due to US sanctions. For the market share figures, see IDC, October 28, 2021, https://www.idc.com/promo/smartphone-market-share/.

mainland-owned companies). Second, MediaTek provided chipsets in this ecosystem. Third, the average Taishang could not cut into this system.

Why was the average Taishang unable to enter the copycat manu-facturing system? This was mainly because of the system's great flexibility. Taishang could not obtain cheap components from the system because the Taishang purchasing system was rigid. In the ODM system domi-nated by American lead firms or international buyers, the selection, pur-chasing, and testing segments had a set of formalized procedures, and it was impossible to manage and control the high-risk characteristics intrin-sic to the copycat system (for example, the high percentage of substan-dard products). According to Lok, "The selection and purchasing staff of Taiwanese-owned companies have something like a bureaucratic men-tality, in which inaction is better than error, and they are unwilling to take risks. And the company bosses also don't encourage selection and purchasing behavior that requires new risk-management models. As a re-sult, Taiwanese-owned companies are unable to profit from purchasing from these copycat factories."[84] Yet the copycat industry's high failure rate was problematic because the ultimate markets for most Taishang were European and American countries, and if a problem occurred with prod-uct quality, the companies would have to deal with legal actions and compensation. The caution of Taishang can be seen as the behavioral out-come of following the American-dominated GVC in their production. Apart from MediaTek, it was rather hard for Taishang to cut into this emerging ecosystem, and it was also hard to capture the ICT piece of the China market (unlike the path that Taishin took, by developing its mar-keting in the Chinese footwear industry). However, since the mid-2000s, MediaTek has been attacked from behind. The rapid ascent of China's Unisoc (formerly Spreadtrum, a Shanghai-based company that was bought out by Tsinghua Unigroup in 2013 and merged with RDA Micro-electronics) has created strong competition for MediaTek. MediaTek's gross profit dropped to 35 percent in the second quarter of 2016.[85]

84. Interview: LM201509.

85. "Lianfake dierji EPS wei 1.52 yuan, chuang shangshi yilai lishi xindi jilu" (Medi-aTek Q2 EPS at $1.51, a record low since IPO), MoneyDJ, July 31, 2017, https://www .moneydj.com/kmdj/news/newsviewer.aspx?a=ee50b494-f4ab-4e4a-b3a7-9eff9fc5ffad. *Author's Postscript:* However, MediaTek had quickly rebounded from low point since then. In 2019, MediaTek introduced a 5G SoC (system on chip) for fifth-generation

In the Pearl River Delta, apart from the emerging Chinese-invested ecosystems (including the enormous production network derived from the copycat industry), Foxconn is Apple's largest systems assembly manufacturer, forming a mammoth supply chain system with a complex interweaving of Taiwanese and mainland-owned businesses. The foundation of Foxconn's development is Taiwan's outstanding technology in molding, metal components, and so on, along with the numerous technically skilled workers in this network-style production. On this foundation the company has developed into a contract manufacturing empire that has triumphed by volume. Yet Foxconn continues to play the game of surviving and catching up under the hegemony of the Apple-controlled GVC.

When Fuller compared the industrial upgrading potential for various industry types in China, he proposed a type called hybrid FIEs, which are neither the typical transnational enterprises nor the classic state-protected domestically invested enterprises. These companies have China as their strategic operational base, but their links to the global market make them very competitive and can enhance the technical standard of China's manufacturing (Fuller 2016). The innovative capacity of the abovementioned ICT venture capital dominated by overseas returnees closely resembles that of the hybrid FIEs defined by Fuller.

From the analysis above, we can observe that China's enormous market and the support of the state's focused policies and jump-starting

---

smartphones that restored its competitive edge over Unisoc. MediaTek reported a high gross profit (42.5 percent) in the fourth quarter of that year; it reported an even higher gross profit of 49.6 percent in the fourth quarter of 2021, a record high for eleven years. Amid the intense US technological war against China, Chinese cell phone manufacturers had to rely more heavily on MediaTek's chips, mainly manufactured by TSMC. The case of MediaTek has once again proved the value of high-technology Taishang to the Chinese supply chains and Taishang's critical role in the US-China technology war. For MediaTek's continually rebounding profits, see Chou Kang-yu, "Lianfake 5G danjingpian daitouchong, Q4 maolilv 42.5% chuang sannianlai xingao" (MediaTek sprints with 5G SoC, reporting a record high 42.5% profit margin for past three years), ETtoday, February 7, 2020, https://www.ettoday.net/news/20200207/1640323.htm#ixzz6d CkQ5Um1; Wei Chih-hao, "Lianfake fashuo, qunian Q4 maoli feiyue caice biaoshang 49.6%" (MediaTek corporate conference, gross profit exceeded that by financial forecast and soared to 49.6 % in last year), Anua, January 27, 2022, https://news.cnyes.com /news/id/4808884?exp=b&utm_medium=news&utm_source=fbfan.

strategy, have played key roles in the rapid growth of the Chinese ICT industry's own brands and production chains. Imai and Shiu's (2011) assessment of China's cell-phone industry, using the GVC approach, is also consistent with this observation. They found that China's indigenous companies have created domestic value chains, transformed themselves with technology brought in by foreign companies, and used the vast and diverse local markets to establish business opportunities. The authors' research shows that China's enormous scale gives it characteristics that are rarely seen in other countries: a continuously enlarging retail market, an enormous engineering talent bank, and many entrepreneurs prepared to establish their own brands at any moment. These characteristics have allowed China first to move forward without submitting to the power structure dominated by transnational corporations under the hegemony of the GVC, and then to create its own value chain system and forge ahead to industrial upgrading. The modular technology provided by China's indigenous suppliers has laid an important foundation for indigenous industries. For the cell-phone industry, the characteristics of China's indigenous value chains took shape through modular exchanges among indigenous brand manufacturers, independent design houses, and technology platform suppliers. Although their innovative capacity is still insufficient compared with that of the existing value chains of Western countries, China's indigenous enterprises have been able to respond rapidly to the demands of the enormous, diverse, and constantly changing domestic market.

Generally speaking, Guangdong's industrial upgrading policy has also been influenced by China's grand strategy for overall industrial development. In 2014, the central government established the National Integrated Circuit Industry Investment Fund to support the semiconductor industry through massive capitalization. In 2015, the central government launched Made in China 2025, the first item of which was the semiconductor industry. In response to the central government's policy initiative, various provinces submitted applications to establish wafer foundries, but because of the high cost of these foundries, not all of the provinces were able to obtain state subsidies. In 2017, Guangzhou announced a plan to create a twelve-inch wafer foundry, but it apparently encountered difficulties. Guangdong's attempt to develop its semiconductor industry was a link in China's semiconductor supply chain related to the industrial upgrading strategy under Made in China 2025 (see chapter 7, section 4, and the conclusion for further discussion).

5. Industrial and Social Upgrading

This chapter has analyzed Guangdong's transformation process over the past ten years or so, including the pressure for industrial upgrading, adjustment of state policies, rising labor costs, response methods of Taishang, and changes to the local industrial structure. Since the 1980s, the model of growth with the labor-intensive processing trade as its focus has experienced exhaustion and gradual decline. In terms of traditional industries, China's local manufacturing capacity has increased; and in terms of high technology, China's new ICT industry ecosystem has emerged. Taishang have followed a variety of paths, from factory closures to migration inland, migration overseas, and upgrading on the spot.

Pushed by the extension and migration of the GVC, Taishang in the traditional labor-intensive industries began to enter Guangdong in the late 1980s and obtained new opportunities for development. At that time, under the new global arrangements dominated by the lead firms of core countries, Taishang had little choice but to continue accepting this domination and to seek niches as semiperipheral agents. In the late 2000s (when GVCs shifted once again), many Taishang were still seeking a niche by following the GVC logic of shifts in spatial distribution—for example, by moving from Guangdong to China's inland provinces or moving out of China to Southeast Asian countries. This restructuring strategy merely continued the existing GVC internal power structure relations and shifted along with the GVC in continued pursuit of lower costs for labor and other factors of production. Yet the case studies in this book show that some Taishang, although locked into their existing value chains, still attempted to climb up the ladder from their fixed positions—for example, by adopting integrated production and engaging in brand development or marketing. There were also manufacturers that changed their position in the value chain, including those that turned into trading companies.

In contrast, Chinese manufacturers of certain products in the ICT industry adopted a strategy of bypassing the existing GVC hegemony. Relying on China's vast domestic market, they launched a low-cost output offensive, established basic technology and production capacity, enhanced their brand image, used low prices to capture the international market and develop their production in leapfrog fashion, and went on to enhance their position in global competition.

It may still be too early to assess the results of Guangdong's industrial upgrading, but some scholars believe that the overall achievements of China's ICT industrial upgrading are still quite limited (Fuller 2016). A preliminary comparison of two of China's coastal regions can provide some clues. The early investment by Taishang export processing industries was concentrated in the Pearl River Delta and Yangtze Delta regions. The Yangtze Delta had a later start than the Pearl River Delta. In the 1990s, Taishang formed industrial clusters in places such as Suzhou, Kunshan, and Shanghai. Ling Chen (2014) compared the results of ICT industrial upgrading in the Yangtze Delta and Pearl River Delta and discovered that the strategy adopted by local governments in the former region was to form alliances with multinational companies at the pinnacle of the value chain and strengthen the stratified production structure, shrinking the upgrading space for local manufacturers and squeezing them to the bottom of the value chain. In contrast, in the Pearl River Delta local governments formed alliances with small-scale foreign-owned companies investing at the bottom of the value chain, which facilitated breaking through the stratified segmented structure and opened up more potential for manufacturers to learn and innovate in place. The results of industrial upgrading were therefore more striking than in the Yangtze Delta.

My research found that network relationships between Taishang and local manufacturers were stronger in the Pearl River Delta than in the Yangtze Delta, and that an enclave economy character was more apparent in Yangtze Delta Taishang clusters than in the Pearl River Delta. Furthermore, closer networks between foreign-owned companies and the local economy contribute to the depth and breadth of technology dissemination, and the results of the Pearl River Delta's industrial upgrading were in fact superior in this respect. Furthermore, publicly owned companies (state-owned and collective enterprises) made up a relatively high proportion of the companies in the Yangtze Delta at the outset of opening reforms. In comparison, the foundation for state-owned enterprises in the Pearl River Delta was weak, and the actual strength of collective enterprises there was much lower than in the Yangtze Delta. As a result, the small and medium-size privately owned mainland factories that participated in Taishang networks gained a chance for survival and found niches in global-local linkages that allowed them to cut into GSCs.

In terms of network relationships, the Pearl River Delta industrial clusters have a *shiji gan* (the feel of a market town)—disorderly, bustling, and vital.[86] In contrast, the industrial areas of places such as Suzhou or Kunshan in the Yangtze Delta, where Taishang are also concentrated, give the impression of being orderly, secluded, and even isolated. For example, over the long period of time when I carried out my observations and study in both regions, in the Pearl River Delta I often saw groups of migrant workers hanging around in the streets of the factory areas or strolling and shopping in busy downtown areas not far away. In the Yangtze Delta, however, the towns were very quiet at night, and I seldom saw migrant workers gather in groups. I had similar observations of interactions between Taishang (and Taigan) and local officials. In the Pearl River Delta's restaurants and karaoke lounges, Taiwanese and Chinese could be observed eating, drinking, and enjoying each other's company much more than in establishments in the Yangtze Delta. If we turn the phrase "the feel of a market town" into the terminology of economic sociology, the personal interactions between Taiwanese and Chinese manufacturers in the Pearl River Delta region have a higher density and the relationships involve stronger ties. This factor is conducive to information exchange and the diffusion of technology, and it also facilitates breaking up enclave structures—with the result that Taiwanese-acculturated mainland-owned factories in traditional industries have been able to develop. In traditional industries, we observe the Taishang community forming embedded relationships in their production, government-business relationships, and consumer links and becoming carriers for the dissemination of technology and transmission of behavioral cultural models. In the ICT industry, based on the feel of a market town and the path dependence shaped by the social structure, we can infer that this type of networking relationship also appears. For example, as described above, in the rise of China's copycat cell-phone industry, many start-up proprietors were orig-

86. Interview: LM201509.

inally employees in Taiwanese-owned factories, and the industry had the characteristics of Taiwanese-acculturated mainland-owned factories. In a word, apart from the variable of industrial upgrading strategies, the feel of a market town is an interesting cultural indicator that we observe in the process of industrial upgrading.

Butollo (2015) holds that although Guangdong has gone through industrial upgrading, it has not experienced social upgrading: even emerging industries such as ICT still rely on the labor-intensive production model, and migrant workers remain the main production contingent; and although wages have increased noticeably, the average working conditions, technical levels, and so on have not been upgraded. The empirical research in this book suggests that this statement requires two qualifications. First, after the wave of labor strikes in 2013–14, the social welfare benefits for migrant workers in the foreign business sector were adjusted upward, but this has not been evident in the sector of private mainland-owned businesses. This is the case because these local factories are positioned at the bottom of the GVC, where exploitative conditions are more serious. Second, if social upgrading includes gaining opportunities for upward mobility by establishing one's own business under the apprentice-turned-boss system, a portion of migrant workers in Guangdong have already attained social upgrading through this route. However, the majority of migrant workers do not have this opportunity. When Taiwan was in its rapid industrialization stage, it also took the apprentice-turned-boss route, which changed the social distribution of skills as well as the distribution of earnings. It is possible that a portion of the Pearl River Delta's industries are currently taking the same path that Taiwan did in the past.

The transformation process of the Guangdong growth model has a striking phenomenon: Although the processing trade became saturated by the global market and was then pursued by developing countries, it has quite a strong continuity. This is because the Pearl River Delta has had a long-term structural reliance on the export processing industry and was deeply infiltrated by the GVCs. International brand buyers still need the Pearl River Delta as a production base for high-end products, and they also need Taishang to play the role of supply chain integrators. Furthermore, the timely addition of mainland-owned factories to the production chains has caused the Pearl River Delta's export processing system to maintain a measure of integrity. And local governments are path dependent, due to their long-term drawing of financial revenue from the export processing sector.

Another striking phenomenon is the phasing out of the processing-management fee. The original growth alliances were like a stable institutional equilibrium, in which the mutual interests between local governments and foreign companies served to maintain the balance, and processing-management fees were the bearings for the system's operation. Processing-management fees became interwoven with the organizational form of factories engaged in the processing of shipped materials in what was essentially a logic of financial distribution. If the foreign company registered as a solely owned company, it had to pay taxes, and the taxes went to the state (each local government was allocated a portion of the tax revenue in accordance with the law). If the foreign company registered as a factory processing shipped materials, it didn't have to pay taxes, but most of the processing-management fees it paid went to the local government. Through this game of financial distribution, local governments could maintain a pivotal role in government-business relationships and control the agreements and concessions related to taxes and fees. China's central government was not ignorant of these loopholes: rather, it intentionally delegated authority to local governments, which in turn yielded benefit to FIEs. As a result, local officials enjoyed space for institutional rent seeking, and this gave them a strong incentive to attract investment. This was the political and economic logic built into the Guangdong growth model. The equilibrium of this model revolved around the set of formal and informal rules built on the processing-management fee, which was also the institutional foundation for the local growth alliances. It was only when the central government decided to promote a new round of industrial policies and institutional reforms that the destruction of the financial distribution model of the processing-management fee became inevitable. In turn, that upset the existing equilibrium and caused changes in the growth model and the government-business model. This was the new situation that Guangdong faced beginning in the mid-2000s.

The local growth alliances that continued from the 1980s until the mid-2000s underwent processes of reorganization at various stages over the years. Among the partners of local government alliances, some of the highly exploitative labor-intensive FIEs withdrew from the alliances, while the foreign companies that underwent industrial upgrading on-site remained in the alliances, and mainland-owned companies participating in global production chains also became members. The emerging local ICT industry became an important new partner. In these years, collective actions by migrant workers spurred improvements in wages, social welfare, and labor conditions, but migrant workers were still excluded from the growth alliance.

Finally, in traditional industry supply chains, mainland-owned factories gradually replaced the Taiwanese-owned OEM factories, and since mainland-owned factories tended to suppress costs, it can be inferred that the increasing share of mainland-owned factories resulted in local governments' drawing a lower percentage of their revenue from the export sector. Where were local governments to obtain the financial resources they required? And what role were local governments to play in the emerging new growth alliances as they groped their way toward institutional equilibrium? These questions will be the focus of future research. In recent years, many local governments have begun increasing the enforcement of the property tax, which suggests that local governments are seeking new sources of revenue under the pressure of industrial transformation.

CHAPTER SEVEN

The GVC and the Rent-Seeking
Developmental State

U sing Guangdong's experience as the starting point, this chapter presents a wide-angle analysis of China's development trajectory and the China model and states a theoretical proposition. The strategy in China's opening reforms was to create links with global capitalism through Guangdong. As the prototype for China's development, the Guangdong model used the influx of foreign manufacturing investment and technology and the international market, with Taishang playing a decisive role in the process. The rapid growth of Guangdong's economy also established the foundation for China's rise. This book critically applies the literature about four theories to explain China's case: (1) development theory, (2) government-business relations and rent-seeking theory in political economy, (3) value or commodity chain theory in economic sociology, and (4) property rights theory in new institutional economics. This chapter engages with this literature to propose that there was a reorganization of growth alliances under changes in the value chain, as well as rent seeking by institutions and the developmental state. In addition, the chapter compares what happened under the Guangdong or China model with the development experience of East Asia.

1. Changes in the GVC and Reorganization of the Growth Alliances

The story of Guangdong's forty years of development is one of following the GVC to create the world's factory. I have revised the GVC or GCC theory to propose a concept of locally embedded governance in which the state is regarded as a capturer of value. Using this framework, I have analyzed how China's local governments used the historical opportunity of the GVC shift to play an intermediary role between China's local polity and manufacturing FIEs and promote the path of labor-intensive export processing industrialization. At this stage, China then accumulated a huge foreign exchange surplus, extracted fiscal revenue, acquired manufacturing technology and industrial and organizational capabilities, and linked up with the world market. Then, after accumulating a degree of manufacturing prowess, the governments wielded China's formidable national capacity to break through the power relations in the value chain governance structure and create an indigenous value chain system controlled by Chinese manufacturers (the so-called red supply chain). China is no longer satisfied to rely on the GVC game and is anxious to develop an alternative route. To that end, it has proposed the vision of Made in China 2025 to construct an industrial system under its own control. The overall objective of Made in China 2025 is to transform the economy from the labor-intensive growth model to the technology-intensive growth model and cast off technical dependency on core Western countries.

This book's locally embedded governance perspective aims to explain the nodes where the local Chinese state participates in the GVC's distribution of benefits. This concept is used to supplement GVC theory and expand its perspective from chain activities and chain governance to cover the embedded interactions between value chains and the local polity. I have then constructed a concept of local growth alliances to analyze the role of Chinese local governments and officials in value chain activities and how they gain access to benefits such as taxes and fees and capture surplus from the value chain. The specific financial extraction methods include processing fees, management fees, land leases, social insurance fees, and other such mechanisms.

The cases of Taiyang and the Taishin Shoe Manufacturing Group demonstrate the roles that the central government, local governments, and cadres play in value capture. By suppressing migrant worker wages, China wielded the processing trade's mechanism for earning foreign exchange to allow the central government to gain a massive foreign exchange surplus and local governments to earn processing fees and other income. This facilitated the high accumulation model of state capitalism and laid the foundation for China's economic rise. I propose the use of G-D-L to observe the financial motivations of local governments, which extract economic rent and capture economic surplus by participating in the value chain's governance structure and in fictive ownership contractual arrangements. This concept also helps us analyze both the mutual embedding of the three elements in the G-D-L model and how the state's participation in the GVC influences the value chain's governance structure, especially the methods of benefit distribution.

For more than twenty years, Taiyang's business in China involved paying head taxes and management fees to its sponsoring work unit, along with a multitude of additional fees, in exchange for protection and a relatively stable economic environment. The head tax was paid through a set of complex rent-dividing formulas that used processing fees and the sharing of foreign exchange earnings to allow value capture by Chinese organs. Although there was an official formula for the payment of head tax or management fees, FIEs could use their *guanxi* with their partnering Chinese work units to gain various discounts. Likewise, the social insurance fees for factory workers (the vast majority of whom were migrant workers) could be discounted through negotiation. These discounts were then transferred to the pockets of local governments and officials through other methods. We can observe the clientelist relationships and exchange of power and money in this kind of government-business interaction (see chapters 3 and 4).

Taishin invested in a factory in Guangdong in the late 1980s at the urging of Nike, its international client. Taishin signed an agreement with the local government under the model of processing shipped materials and paid a processing fee. The status of processing shipped materials gave Taishin flexibility in its business operations, as well as many tax concessions. However, these concessions also meant that part of the surplus that the company earned was handed over to the local government. Taishin's land lease with the local government reveals the use of political power for capital gain. Taishin and officials were able to capture enormous profit, including Taishin's corporate profits, the private profits of Taishin's top managers and local officials, and the profits of the officials. But the cooperative relationship between Taishin and the local government was not always a smooth one. As the central government's policies changed—for example, under new policies for industrial upgrading and improving working conditions—Taishin experienced labor strikes, and rather than taking management's side, the local government clearly adopted the role of balancer by forcing Taishin to make good on its debts (unpaid social insurance fees and provident fund payments). The labor strike crisis during that period also made Taishin's managers aware that the past operational model of cozy government-business relationships was becoming shaky, and that Chinese officials had adopted a policy that more actively protected workers' rights and interests. As strikes pressing for back payments of social insurance and provident fund fees and addressing other issues raised costs for Taiwanese-owned processing factories, we can observe the role of the government (including public security organs) in the distribution of benefit in the value chains (see chapter 6).

In this growth alliance made up of manufacturing FIEs and local governments, the GVC-dominating lead firms (international buyers) and China's central government played the roles of invisible allies and shared in the distribution of economic surplus. The greatest beneficiaries were the lead firms, with manufacturing FIEs coming in second, and China's central and local governments were also major beneficiaries. But this growth alliance was not unchangeable. It was established on the institutional equilibrium of a series of conditions, and this equilibrium would be destroyed when these conditions changed—for example, in a saturated or sluggish international market, with reduced profits for brand buyers, under China's industrial upgrading pressure, and with the rising cost of China's labor force and the emergence of cheap labor markets in other countries. The case of Guangdong shows that this equilibrium began to change in the mid-2000s, and following the assault of the 2007–8 global financial crisis, as well as through rounds of foreign investment flight and workers' collective resistance in the 2010s, the relationship between the Chinese government and foreign-owned companies deteriorated to that of rival partners with open conflict over widely divergent interests. The growth alliance consequently faced the crisis of dissolution. With the loosening and reorganization of the original growth alliance, new cooperative models emerged. The first of these models is the birth of a new ecosystem, with Chinese capital as its foundation. For example, in the telecommunications industry, using state power and capital, China has attempted to join forces with private capital to create a value chain system controlled by China. The second model consists of mainland-owned factory supply chains (generated by the spillover effect from Taishang production networks) forming links with the GVCs. Here Taishang play an intermediary role as quasi-international buyers and GSC integrators, and continue to participate in the value capture game by entrenching their role as semiperipheral elbows of core countries, in which Taiwanese companies as agents of global capital (most of which are small and medium-size transnational Taiwanese companies) perform a controlling role in carrying out value-chain governance at Chinese manufacturing sites. Mainland-owned factories have thus achieved a degree of industrial upgrading through this supply chain reorganization.

The emergence of the second model is closely related to this book's main argument and impels us to revisit the topic of "enclave economy." Past research has often regarded export processing zones as enclave economies (Warr 1989). The transnational corporation-dominated industrial clusters of developing countries are often assumed to be enclaves both spatially and in terms of their social relations (an enclave economy has only minimal social interaction with the local society and economy). The sociospatial model of this type of industrial cluster is therefore not conducive to industrial upgrading in developing countries (Narula and Dunning 2000; Whittaker et al. 2010). The linking of China's export processing sector with global capital has been considered a "shallow integration" that is not beneficial to local economic development (Steinfeld 2004). Taiwanese scholars also tend to regard the relationship between the export processing Taishang community and local Chinese communities as one of an enclave economy (Cheng Chih-peng 2014b) or disembeddedness (Cheng Lu-lin 1999) or portray the organizational model of Taiwanese-invested companies as "fortresses in the air" (Chen Ming-chi 2012). In the latter case, the Taishang community is seen as inclined to maintain dense internal networks but as having only minimal links with local society to avoid losing its competitive advantage. This literature can help us understand the operation model of FIEs in China at the early stage, but reviewing historical developments reveals two analytical weaknesses in these propositions. First, the theoretical preconception of minimal links between an enclave economy and local society leads researchers to over-look the interactive relationship between global capitalism and global manufacturing, on the one hand, and the local polity, on the other hand. The empirical research in this book shows that FIEs must engage in a high degree of interaction with the local polity to gain a stable operational environment. Second, that theoretical preconception assumes that highly trust-bound and internally cohesive networks, and a wariness against a draining of technology and market relationships, result in Taiwanese-invested companies having only loose ties with local production net-works. The inference here is that local mainland-invested systems can-not easily join the GVC and gain opportunities for industrial upgrading. However, the technological diffusion that Taiwanese-invested companies have brought to China over the years has facilitated the rise of Taiwanese-acculturated mainland-owned factories (Cheng Chih-peng 2016), and at the same time it has hastened the emergence of China's local export-oriented labor-intensive production chains. For this reason, local manu-facturing clusters that were initially launched by FIEs have undergone obvious structural changes.

Although Taishang entering China's coastal regions in the 1980s ini-tially used an entry model that was close to helicoptered industrial im-plantation and established spatial structures similar to FIE enclaves, that implantation didn't mean that they didn't need to form relationships with local political players and society. On the contrary, their alien relation-ship with local society and government, as well as the rampant rent seek-ing and bribe collecting in China's political and economic system, made them even more in need of the assistance and protection of local officials and gave rise to complex government-business relationships. As a result, this book argues, although the early Taishang loathed the rent-seeking behavior of local officials, they had no choice but to deal with these of-ficials and seek a clientelist relationship. Playing off the dual meaning for *guanxi*, which in different contexts can mean either connection or worry, Taishang came up with a phrase they liked to repeat that reflects this para-doxical situation: "*you guanxi jiu mei guanxi, mei guanxi jiu you guanxi*" (with *guanxi*, there are no worries [*guanxi*]; with no *guanxi*, there are worries [*guanxi*]). The embedded relationship of FIEs with the local polity was not a matter of its existence or extent, but rather the mode of embeddedness. This book's theoretical contribution is to propose the concept of locally embedded governance and to provide ample cases, interviews, and data as supporting evidence for the theoretical significance of the links between the GVC and the local polity.

With the rise of China's indigenous production chains, taking the footwear industry as an example, mainland-owned factories gradually took over the role of Taishang in some key segments of the GSC from 2008 onward, and some transformed themselves into quasi-international buyers. This change did not occur suddenly: rather, mainland-owned factories were gradually integrated into the supply chains originally controlled by Taishang. The spread of technology among mainland-owned factories had already been under way for some time, but a chain of crises prompted by the global financial crisis brought the role of mainland-owned companies to the forefront. In other words, we cannot infer that technological diffusion did not occur simply because Taishang did not initially trust mainland managers and therefore adopted an attitude of caution at the early stage. The technological advancement of mainland-owned factories and their acquisition of international orders are facts, indicating a structural transformation of the helicoptered implantation model. This is also manifested in the formation of new supply chain relationships resulting from cooperation between Taishang and mainland-owned factories. The apparently sudden change around 2008 served only as a catalyst. The indigenous Chinese supply chain system fostered by Taishang challenges the claim of dependency theory that "transnational corporations cannot become locally embedded" (Cheng Chih-peng 2016, 182). The argument made in past research that the production networks of Taishang in China's coastal regions resembled off-site organizations or were disembedded has a weak theoretical basis.

The revised global-local linkage structure that this book proposes involves multiple embedded relationships, including the interactive relationships between global capital and the local polity, the three domains in the G-D-L links, and the value chain governance domain and locally embedded governance domain (see figures 1.1, 1.2, and 1.3, respectively). This analytical framework clarifies the complex relationship between the

GVC and local embedding, and it shifts the analytical perspective toward a previously overlooked but nevertheless important point: the political and business relationships between FIEs and local governments result from the GVC's being channeled into locally embedded governance. In these government-business relationships, the governments of host countries accepting foreign investment intervene in the distribution of the GVC's economic surplus through a series of institutional arrangements. This research finding therefore helps us open a black box in the segments of the commodity chain that Hopkins and Wallerstein (1977) touched on when they first proposed the concept of the commodity chain.

The Chinese government used the embedded relationship between FIEs and the local political and economic system to capture enormous financial gain, and then it used part of that gain to promote industrial upgrading and build indigenous supply chains in an attempt to compete with the hegemonic forces of global capitalism. As a result, a new telecommunications industry ecosystem emerged in Guangdong, which caused China's telecommunications equipment, handsets, chip design, and other spheres to rapidly catch up. If the development of the first thirty years of the Guangdong model can be summarized as creating the world's factory, then the transformation of the Guangdong and China models in the most recent ten years has been fixated on bypassing the existing GVC hegemons and constructing a value chain system that Chinese capital can control.

2. A Theory of the Rent-Seeking Developmental State

China's local government used the institutional rent-seeking model to cut into GVC governance links and capture value. I therefore shift the analytical perspective to a rent-seeking model with Chinese characteristics, and I observe how this rent-seeking model joined with the development state to become a tool for harnessing economic growth. Based on this research finding, I have proposed the concept of the rent-seeking developmental state. The Chinese economy is both different from and similar to the East Asian and world economies. Although China's economic scale and particularities are sui generis, its enormous scale and influence give it a theoretical importance beyond that of the average country.

Let's start with traditional rent-seeking theory. Rent-seeking behavior is pervasive in all kinds of economic systems, but it is generally believed that rent-seeking activity is closely related to the government's regulatory policies. The similarity between rent seeking and corruption also leads to the two often being placed within the same analytical category. The mainstream view in the literature is that a rent-seeking society creates an erosion of welfare, wastes social resources, and is an impediment to economic growth (Krueger 1974; Tullock 1990 and 1993; Murphy, Shleifer, and Vishny 1993; Frye and Shleifer 1997). In some countries, however, rent seeking and corruption have not created economic stagnation, which raises quite a few doubts about this view. For example, Rodrik (2011, 93) raises a question about countries such as South Korea, Thailand, and Malaysia: "How had these countries registered such miraculous rates of economic growth if corruption was rampant?" This question is also applicable to Taiwan in its phase of rapid economic growth and especially to China. As everyone knows, China is a country in which serious rent seeking has been accompanied by rapid economic growth, a puzzle that was raised as early as the 1990s: "All of these mechanisms, including discretion in the reduction of taxes, seem subject to corruption, collusion, and rent seeking. The big question, to which we don't quite know the answer, is why these problems do not seem to be serious enough to hamper growth, as seems to be the case in many Latin American countries" (Qian and Stiglitz 1996, 192).

Curiously, China's thirty years of sustained economic growth were not obstructed by rampant corruption and rent-seeking behavior (Wedeman 2003 and 2012). In the case of Guangdong, there is an obvious coexistence of economic growth and local governments' rent-seeking behavior. Rent-seeking behavior through institutional designs such as the use of processing fees and the sharing of foreign exchange earnings (foreign exchange spread) have brought generous profits to local governments at all levels. Along with extrabudgetary income under various names, this turns grassroots cadres into a kind of rentier class. The coexistence of a pervasive rentier class with thirty years of economic growth clearly challenges traditional rent-seeking theory. At the same time, while Taishang and other FIEs have had to face the problems of official corruption and rent-seeking behavior, these problems have not seriously affected their willingness to invest. The flood of foreign investment has fueled China's long-term high growth rates as well as its rapid accumulation of foreign reserves. I proposed a preliminary explanation in my research in the 1990s (Wu Jieh-min 1998), and here I attempt to carry out a more complete interpretation: Institutional rent seeking by China's local officials during a specific historical phase spurred the mobilization of economic resources by local governments and oriented them toward labor-intensive export processing industrialization, bringing about rapid economic growth and capturing value distribution from the governance links of the GVC. This analysis calls for a new understanding of rent-seeking behavior, rent production and distribution, and the incentive structures for local officials.

1) The Traditional Definition of Rent-Seeking Behavior

Rent seeking is typically considered unproductive or counterproductive behavior. Jagdish Bhagwati (1982) relaxed the demarcation of this behavior and proposed the concept of directly unproductive profit-seeking activities (DUP), defining various types of DUP. According to Bhagwati's framework, the rent-seeking behavior that Anne Krueger (1974) explored in her classic thesis, caused mainly by trade controls and import quotas, was only a type of DUP. Similarly, Gordon Tullock (1990 and 1993) held that government interference in the market produced artificial monopolies, which then led businesses and officials to pursue rent from monopolies. However, the rent-seeking behavior defined by Tullock, in which individuals and companies are the principal participants, is likewise only a form of DUP. The DUP economic behavior defined by Bhagwati includes traditionally defined rent seeking, but it has a wider scope. Bhagwati holds that certain types of DUP are not counterproductive or wasteful of social resources but can have positive consequences for society (e.g., lobbying for the withdrawal of tariffs). For this reason, the connection between nonproductive behavior and economic growth or economic stagnation is not simply linear. Bhagwati's new conceptualization helps us better understand the economic consequences of behavior such as rent seeking, corruption, bribe seeking, and bribery. Research on the developing countries of Southeast Asia also points to a nonlinear relationship between rent-seeking behavior and economic growth or stagnation, as well as to the need to look at the type of rent and the process and outcome of rent seeking (Khan and Jomo 2000).

In the early development of the concept, Tullock and Krueger compared the rent-seeking society with an imaginary original state of market economy. According to Krueger's classic thesis, in a rent-seeking society, people devote social resources to nonproductive activities to compete for rent, resulting in social waste and the squandering of rent value and therefore harming economic growth. In discussing the political implications of limiting rent-seeking activities, Krueger (1974, 302) states: "The existence of rent seeking surely affects people's perception of the economic system. If income distribution is viewed as the outcome of a lottery where wealthy individuals are successful (or lucky) rent seekers, whereas the poor are those precluded from or unsuccessful in rent seeking, the market mechanism is bound to be suspect." The "market mechanism" here is presupposed to be some kind of original ideal state, so according to the argument, there will no be rent seeking or competition for rent without government controls. This hypothetical situation is based on the ideal type of liberal market capitalism (Khan 2000, 21), but this ideal type is not applicable to transitional economies in the stage after state socialism. For example, in China the state originally guided economic activity and controlled enormous public assets, so ubiquitous control and intervention were the norm. This normal situation is what should be the starting point of analyses. Our puzzle is not why rampant rent-seeking behavior does not bring about economic stagnation. Rather, it is: What factors in transitional economies enable rampant rent-seeking activity to coexist with economic growth, or to not impede economic growth? And under what conditions will bureaucratic rent seeking not devolve into pure financial pillage of businesses? Going a step further, from the viewpoint of private businesses, the question should be: What factors have made Taishang (FIEs) willing to accept rent-seeking behavior and continue to invest in China?

2) Defining Institutional Rent Seeking

Based on the above analytical starting point, this book proposes that the relationship between rent-seeking and economic growth must be analyzed within the context of macro political economics and historical institutions. The distinguishing feature of the Chinese-style rent-seeking society that is most worthy of attention (apart from widespread individual rent seeking) is the collective, organized, and institutional rent-seeking activities of local officials. Collective rent-seeking behavior by officials—that is, the institutional rent-seeking model proposed by this book—is closely related to industrial policies and is also linked to the incentive mechanisms that the central government grants to local officials. In China's transitional economy, institutional rent seeking emerges from one main institutional foundation: The Chinese political system endows each level of local government with highly elastic authority over control and approval. Local governments can gain extrabudgetary income and supplement local finances in the process of exercising this authority, and these governments can also cut into the GVC governance structure and capture economic surplus from it.

In traditional theory, the demarcation of rent-seeking behavior or DUP is based on the relationship between the behavior and its economic consequences. This analytical method has serious limitations, however, because it overlooks the theoretical implications of the rent seeker as a sociological actor. For this reason, I create a new typology of rent-seeking behavior from the organizational standpoint and propose a two-dimensional analysis (see table 7.1). The degree of organization of the actor is divided into two main categories (collective and corporate versus individual), and the relationship between the actor and the governmental authorities is also divided in two (state versus nonstate actors). As a result, table 7.1 produces four pure types of rent-seeking behavior, with type A being the institutional rent seeking that is the focus of our analysis. Institutional rent seeking has two characteristics. First, in the economic realm, the government and officials are not only the regulators of the rules of the game, but they are also participants in the rent-seeking activity. Second, this rent-seeking behavior is endorsed or authorized by the state and has a degree of legitimacy. However, a gray area exists. For example, gaining investment by offering companies discounts on processing fees is up to the discretion of local governments and officials, but it can also be an exchange of interests between power and capital, as when the discount is exchanged for a bribe. In another example, in the case of Nafu Village, there is an ambiguous exchange of power and money

Table 7.1. Categories of rent-seeking behavior from the organizational standpoint

	Collective or corporate	*Individual*
State actor	(A) Institutional rent seeking: processing, management, and social insurance fees; leasing property, etc.	(C) Official corruption: soliciting and accepting bribes, kickbacks, selling a position, etc.
Nonstate actor	(B) Corporate rent-seeking behavior: import quotas, franchising rights, low-interest loans, export tax rebates, etc.	(D) Individual rent-seeking behavior: bribery, buying a position, etc.

Source: Author's analysis.

between the property transaction and the special management fee. Therefore, the legitimacy of this kind of rent-seeking behavior is contingent on specific institutional conditions.[1]

Chinese officials in the transitional economic system possess quite a wide scope of discretion. For example, the profits from processing fees (a target of institutional rent seeking and one of the focuses of this book) have certain power and institutional characteristics. The central government gave the various levels of local government and state-owned enterprises the authority to engage in the processing trade. They in turn conferred this power on other actors (including government work units,

---

1. *AUTHOR'S POSTSCRIPT:* After this book's publication in Chinese in 2019, I read Yuen Yuen Ang's (2020) argument that "access money" or "efficiency wages" paid to officials in exchange for favorable policy treatment is a dominant type of corruption in China that may not harm the economy. Ang's point parallels my discovery. My analysis overlaps with but differs from hers. I emphasize not only collective corruption or rent-seeking activities, but I also propose an institutionalist logic to explain them. Furthermore, Ang states that access money operates like "the steroids of capitalism. . . . The harm of access money blows up only in the event of a crisis" (Ang 2020, 12–13). Contrary to her theory, corruption or rent seeking could threaten businesses at any time and deteriorate into financial plunder. I argue that, in addition to the logic in favor of institutional rent seeking, the structural factor of global connections helps restrain financial plunder. See the argument below.

private individuals, and FIEs). We can refer to this power that local officials gained as the right to permit the processing trade. The extrabudgetary revenue that local governments derived from processing trade authorizations alone included other types of revenue in addition to processing fees, such as foreign exchange rights, the leasing of factories and land to FIEs, labor management fees, fees for processing temporary residence permits for migrant workers (these fees have been abolished), social insurance fees, housing provident funds, and other localized types of covert revenue. Furthermore, the engagement of local governments in transactions with manufacturing FIEs concerning exports engendered other collective and personal gains, such as officials' obtaining material benefits for granting foreign businesses discounts on processing fees or export tax rebates. According to Tak-Win Ngo (2010)'s formulation, the creation, distribution, and seeking of rent constitutes a rent production chain. This book goes one step further by stating that local officials in this chain perform the roles of rent creation, distribution, and seeking, as well as performing tasks under this triple role through organized and syndicated methods.

3) The Operational Mechanism of Institutional Rent Seeking

This book regards institutional rent seeking as a kind of value-capturing behavior and argues that there may be a positive correlation between rent seeking and economic growth. This positive correlation is not universal, however, and must occur in a specific time and space. We must always bear in mind that a high degree of affinity between bureaucratic rent seeking on the one hand and corruption and bribe seeking on the other hand makes it difficult to distinguish between the two. Actions taken by rulers (including central and local governments) in pursuit of gain can very easily turn into predatory behavior (Levi 1988). In China, which institutional and structural factors and which spatiotemporal conditions confine institutional rent seeking within certain parameters and keep it from becoming pure plunder? This question is in response to the theory of harmless rent seeking. We can further ask why institutional rent seeking has been able to promote economic mobilization during China's economic transformation process and to be conducive to economic expansion and growth. This question is in response to the theory of rent seeking for growth. I next argue that in China, harmless rent seeking and rent seeking for growth became possible at a specific period in history.

First, I consider the changing economic role of China's enormous bureaucratic apparatus as that socialist country shifted toward a market economy. This role change shouldn't be taken for granted: it is a thorny political issue. With the opening reforms launched in the late 1970s, China did not develop a classic market capitalist economy but rather a so-called transitional economy. Mechanically applying Krueger's hypothetical natural market state (i.e., using market capitalism as an ideal type) to transitional Chinese society—a society permeated with political mobilization and bureaucratic organization—is a misleading analytical starting point. At that time, Chinese society had a Maoist socialist framework with a great deal of social waste (idle resources) and obstruction of economic activity. The banner of politics in command brandished by the bureaucratic class was not conducive to private commercial activity. In contrast to the situation in the former Soviet Union and countries of Eastern Europe, the historic changes that China began experiencing in 1978 were reforms, not revolutions. Eastern European countries experienced a political revolution in the 1990s, and the mission of that revolution was to thoroughly abolish the socialist system and channel those countries into market capitalism. At that time, both the market and capital had a high degree of legitimacy in those countries. But the direction of China's changes were the opposite of those in Eastern Europe: There were gradual market reforms but shelved political reforms. The official ideology still insisted on the legitimacy of socialism. The CCP upheld the Four Cardinal Principles[2] in the early stage of the reforms, which meant that it was still the ruling party and the vast state bureaucracy was still the political ruling class. How could this ruling class be turned from opposing capitalism to hankering to attract investment? This was the greatest problem when China's economic reforms were launched in the late 1970s.

Chapter 2 tracked the political crisis and the large-scale purge of corruption cases that Guangdong faced in the opening stage, which provide

---

2. TRANSLATOR'S NOTE: The Four Cardinal Principles, stated by Deng Xiaoping in 1979, were upholding the socialist path, upholding the people's democratic dictatorship, upholding the leadership of the CCP, and upholding Mao Zedong thought and Marxism-Leninism.

evidence of the doubts about capitalism harbored by the CCP's conservative leaders at that time. The party's reformist faction had to legitimize the new policies by constantly reaffirming that opening reforms were being carried out within the framework of socialism and were not taking the capitalist road as a means of removing political impediments to the opening reform policies. However, the CCP's Central Committee also had to provide incentives for the bureaucratic class. While Deng Xiaoping was in power, he changed the bureaucratic apparatus from one of politics in command to one of economics in command, and he successfully mobilized the initiative of the bureaucracy to promote economic growth. One key method was to provide the bureaucratic class with positive political and economic incentives. Local economic growth thus became a criterion in assessing cadres, and different regions had different incentive mechanisms. In the Guangdong model, the processing trade and foreign exchange income became the impetus for EOI. Vast idle resources (the labor force, land, and factory facilities) were mobilized. When provided with information and power, officials who had originally obstructed economic activity were transformed into experts on attracting investment, and the approval authority that bureaucrats grasped became a bargaining chip in transactions between government and business. Under this comprehensive economic mobilization, China approached the situation of having the entire party and nation engaged in business, and bureaucrats' institutional rent-seeking behavior became a component of this system. Consequently, during a certain phase in the post-Mao era, institutional rent seeking accelerated economic mobilization and expanded markets, which meant that rent-seeking behavior became interwoven with rapid economic growth. In this transitional economy, attracting investment offered two inducements to local officials: One inducement was extrabudgetary local fiscal revenue, such as processing fees and management fees. The other was personal benefit to officials and cadres, as when cadres became able to draw dividends and collect fees on economic earnings—that is, so-called transactive corruption (Wedeman 2012).

Second, in China, rent seeking comes in a variety of forms, but institutional rent seeking has the most distinctive characteristics and is closely bound to the economic development model. The cases in this book show that the governmental rent seeking that firms faced is that of organized, centralized actors rather than decentralized actors, and this affects firms' estimation of the transaction costs of official rent seeking. Shleifer and Vishny (1993) proposed that because economic activity involves government goods provided by different government departments, if there is a lack of organization between different bureaucrats (or agencies), and each acts as an independent monopoly, then individual bureaucrats will seek to maximize their personal bribe revenues and will not need to consider the effect of their behavior on other bureaucrats. Conversely, if the bureaucrats organize themselves into a joint monopoly, they will strive to maximize bribe revenues for the entire group and will internalize any externality. Consequently, a centralized rent-seeking network is conducive to reducing rent levels, supplying better government goods and creating a smaller scale of distortion of resource allocation (Blackburn and Forgues-Puccio 2009). This theoretical assumption has gained a certain degree of support in empirical research (Rock and Bonnet 2004), and this book's empirical findings confirm the hypothesis. Guangdong's institutional plan of imposing processing and management fees and sharing foreign exchange earnings while promoting the processing trade functioned very similarly to the abovementioned centralized rent-seeking network, allowing firms to deal with the government without constantly wasting large amounts of resources on nonproductive activities. In other words, institutional rent seeking can reduce the target's transactional costs in dealing with rent-seeking behavior. At the individual case level, this book analyzed Taiyang's cooperative partners, the Guanqiang Import-Export Company (at an early stage) and Nafu Village (at a later stage). The behavior of these two government service providers was similar to that of a cartel within the scope of a specific administrative jurisdiction, and in terms of handling the coordination and distribution of rent among all of the government agencies involved (multiple rent seekers). In the eyes of the firms, this kind of mother-in-law (official sponsor) provided one-stop service and a single window, thus offering prompt assistance in resolving difficult problems. Firms felt that they had an efficient and cooperative partner, which made the fee-collecting behavior seem more acceptable.

This book's findings and arguments approach the organized bureaucratic corruption hypothesis of Shleifer and Vishny (1993). We can further formulate China's development experience as follows: China is not a country under the rule of law, and under the currently limited property rights safeguards, institutional rent-seeking actors are like a cartel that helps firms by providing them with government goods, increasing the predictability of government policies and behavior, and reducing firms' transaction costs. From the property rights perspective, this mafia-style government provides firms with a degree of credible commitment.[3] But it must once again be emphasized that this is an analytical rather than a prescriptive proposition, and it does not apply universally across space and time but must satisfy several conditions: First, the legitimacy of institutional rent-seeking behavior is conditional legitimacy and must be occur in specific spatiotemporal conditions to be tenable. Second, the legitimacy of institutional rent-seeking behavior depends on institutional equilibrium. Third, institutional rent-seeking behavior is constrained by its ties to the international market.

Third, referring first to the third condition above, it is important to focus on the GVC dominance structure and observe how it restrains the rent-seeking behavior of local governments. The prices of products in export market-oriented industries are controlled by the ceiling effect of multiple firms competing simultaneously in the global market. The international market is different from the domestic market: China's domestic market is clogged with monopolies and protectionism, but export products face a high degree of competition in the international market, which puts a degree of constraint on rent-seeking behavior. That is, the cost of economic rent must have certain limits (a capped price) and a commonly accepted price—otherwise, firms cannot survive. In other words, export-oriented local growth alliances must link up with the world market, where the global competitiveness and prices of its end products are controlled by the set prices of the value chain lead firms. This structurally delimits the boundaries of local government rent seeking and reduces the likelihood that rent-seeking behavior will be rampant enough to make the survival of the firms impossible. Generally speaking, the profits that firms expect after from paying rent must be greater than the rent itself; and in the export markets, since commodity selling prices are constrained by the international market, firms cannot arbitrarily shift the cost of rent to commodity prices. This is an important role that the GVC plays in restraining plundering by governments.

3. For example, the Property Rights Law through which China safeguards private property rights was not promulgated until 2007. The government's inability to provide reliable property safeguards is typically considered an impediment to long-term growth. Regarding the concept of credible commitment, see North (1993).

Fourth, whether or not there is institutional equilibrium affects the legitimacy of rent-seeking behavior. From the institutional arrangements of Guangdong's processing trade, we can observe that institutional rent seeking has a certain degree of predictability, including its explicit and unspoken rules, the range and scale of the rent, the trading partner for the rent, and so on. As a result, from the standpoint of institutional economics, the rent-seeking behavior of China's local governments is accompanied by a degree of credible commitment. Another factor that constrains financial plundering is that multiple competitive patrons exist in a single locality. As we observed in the case of Taiyang, when the institutional equilibrium changed, several potential patrons vied for a sponsoring relationship, which effectively lowered the rent level. The factors of credible commitment and competitive patrons give the transactional relationship between firms and local governments a quasi-institutional stability. Whether firms regard rent-seeking behavior as legitimate or not depends on the institutional equilibrium. However, when state policies change, it may shake that equilibrium and affect the cognition and feelings of the rent payer. For example, when the Chinese government abolished the dual-track foreign exchange system in 1994, firms began to challenge the legitimacy of the rent-creation method of using foreign exchange for the payment of processing fees (Wu Jieh-min 2001). Hence, processing fees as a form of rent began gradually withdrawing from the historical stage and were replaced with items such as management fees and collaboration fees. Then new policies such as those imposing social insurance fees and implementing the housing provident fund were put on the table, and land finance also became a new way for local governments to create income. In other words, the central government's 1994 tax and foreign exchange reforms shrank the rent-seeking space of local governments and led them to search for new rent-seeking channels, while at the same time allowing the central government to capture a larger amount of economic surplus from the GVC.

In a nutshell, the coexistence of rent seeking and growth has a specific historical stage: when the window of historical opportunity closes, rent seeking will become intolerable to firms and others and will become detrimental behavior as the social psychology of economic behavior evolves. From the 2000s onward, at the same time that Guangdong faced transformation, firms' tolerance for government rent-seeking activity plummeted. In particular, the rapid increase in wages and the costs of land and other essential factors of production delegitimized official rent-seeking behavior. The creation and distribution of economic rent effectively activated the profit motives of local bureaucrats during the initial stage of opening reforms, but this incentive to attract investment has gradually lost steam since then. Assuming that China's industrial upgrading will show results, institutional rent seeking will decline in the long term. Even so, local finance and bureaucratic income remain path dependent. This model is still difficult to eradicate in Guangdong, where institutional rent seeking has been customary for decades. As recently as 2013, Dongguan issued a document titled "Implementation Opinions on the Dongguan City People's Government Further Easing the Burden of Enterprises and Optimizing the Business Environment" in an attempt to reduce the additional fees paid by firms, but in fact many village and township governments continue to collect additional fees under various other names. In the subjective experience of firms, this fee-collecting behavior has become pure financial plundering.

The above explanation of rent seeking and economic growth is not one of linear cause and effect. The methodological standpoint of this book is closer to that of a conjunctural explanation: in a historical time and space incorporating an international factor (structural reorganization of the international division of labor) and a domestic factor (the post–Mao era opening reforms), China's socialist economic system transitioned toward a capitalist market economy. The government attracted foreign investment using its plentiful labor force (exploiting migrant workers) and other factors of production (cheap land and low environmental costs) and mobilized the economic incentives of the bureaucratic class. Under a highly authoritarian political system and exploitative labor regime, it generated economic growth. The factors of this explanation are entwined and combined. This is also an explanation of historical institutionalism. Rent-seeking behavior has been a dynamic factor in China's economic development. Its effects fluctuate and are not inevitably positive or negative, but they are historical. It is both theoretically and empirically debatable to think of rent seeking as an indispensable component of economic policy and to see rent seeking and growth as having a normal and positive relationship (Wu Yongping and Wu Derong 2010).

To sum up, at a specific historical stage, institutional rent seeking with Chinese characteristics—combined with elements of developmentalism, driven by globalization, and linked to the world market—prevented the Chinese state from becoming a predatory one. Institutional rent seeking in the era of China's (specifically, Guangdong's) flourishing (from the 1980s until the 2000s) occurred at the historical stage when the rent-seeking developmental state developed its vitality.

It is easy to describe the contours of the rent-seeking developmental state by synthesizing the above discussion: The state grants local governments and officials the power and space for institutional rent seeking as an inducement for local governments to attract investment and develop the economy. This method of conferring authority includes both written and informal rules. Local governments are able to use this power and space to join in the process of economic globalization and intervene in the governance process of the GVC, which facilitates economic expansion and growth and captures value.

3. Comparing the Development Experiences of China and the Rest of East Asia

There is a consensus among scholars that China has become a developmental state since embarking on opening reforms (Evans 2010), but what distinguishing features does China have within this large category? What is the nature of China as a developmental state? First, we must place China in the context of the East Asia region to understand the theoretical significance of its development space and treat that region as a category of historical space. East Asia's trade expansion after World War II has a time gradient. Expanding from Japan and the Four Little Dragons to China, this expansion process is manifested in the dynamic of processing export industrialization driven by the GCC/GVC. Hamilton and Gereffi have called for observing the historical momentum of trade expansion under globalization from the GCC standpoint and extending the GCC analytical framework to explain the economic development of specific countries. They have also criticized the past pattern in economic sociology of centering explanations on the state and, when explaining economic development and institutional change, of laying excessive stress on endogenous variables and neglecting the dynamics of globalization (Hamilton and Gereffi 2009, 143). This book's narrative of China's development is closely aligned to their viewpoint, similarly starting with the shift and extension of the GCC or GVC to explain the dynamic of China's linking up with the global economy. Yet given China's scale and subjective agency, we must not overlook the crucial effect of China's domestic institutional structure.

The East Asia region experienced rapid and sustained economic growth after World War II, and the development performance of the Four Little Dragons, which originally had low levels of industrialization, gained world renown. The experience of each of these countries has differed, but generally speaking, their experiences (especially in the cases of Taiwan and South Korea) have some common characteristics. These include the geopolitical role of the United States, an authoritarian political structure, a strong developmentalist state, export-oriented industrial policies, and the oppression of workers. The commonalities revealed in these countries should be viewed from East Asia's overall trade expansion process. China's launch of its EOI policies in the early 1980s essentially continued the trade expansion dynamic of the East Asia region. After China joined the ranks of East Asia's developmentalist countries, the abovementioned characteristics all became apparent in China. But China's massive scale and the distinctive features of its institutional structure shaped its unique development experience. Comparing China with the northeastern Asian countries that preceded it (Japan, Taiwan, and South Korea), Boltho and Weber (2015) hold that China basically followed in the footsteps of Northeast Asia, and key economic indicators show that all of these countries belonged to the same model, which differentiated them from Latin American countries and India. But China's performance was particularly outstanding in several aspects, such as the share of the world market taken up by its manufacturing exports and its high savings rates. Yet China's distribution of its economic gains was far less equitable than in the three Northeast Asian countries, and China's reliance on foreign direct investment was also far greater. In fact, although China became one of the East Asian developmental states, the characteristics and dynamics of its development were sui generis.

Table 7.2 presents a comparison of China, Taiwan, and South Korea. The era covered for Taiwan and South Korea is the 1960s to the 1980s, and for China it is the 1980s to the 2000s: both periods occurred within the thirty years of rapid growth following the launch of EOI. The 1980s

Table 7.2. The developmental states of China (Guangdong), Taiwan, and South Korea

	China 1980s–2000s	Taiwan 1960s–1980s	South Korea 1960s–1980s
Prerequisites for development			
Geopolitical structure	United States and China align against the Soviet Union; East Asian Cold War defense line shifts	Height of the Cold War, Korean War, and Vietnam War	Height of the Cold War, Korean War, and Vietnam War
Development conditions and processes			
State-market relationship	EOI, market regulations, command-style control of SOEs, investment in infrastructure	EOI, market regulations, SOEs relatively shrunken, investment in infrastructure	EOI, market regulations, fostering large enterprise groups, investment in infrastructure
Property ownership structure	Public ownership, inadequate protection for private capital, fictive ownership relations	Private ownership, party-state capital	Private ownership, chaebols
FDI as a proportion of industrial investment	Relatively high	Relatively low	Relatively low
Exploitation and control of labor	Dual labor market, differential citizenship	State corporatist controls, constraints on autonomous labor unions	State joins with large privately owned capital to repress worker resistance movements
Official rent seeking	Extensive; institutional rent seeking	Moderate	Moderate

Results of development

Effect on industrial structure	State capitalism, support for large-scale SOEs, suppression of private sector	Network of small and medium-size privately owned enterprises	Massive privately owned chaebols
Transformation of authoritarian political structure	From limited opening of the Leninist party-state system to reconsolidation of the party-state system	From a quasi-Leninist party-state system to electoral democracy	From a bureaucratic-authoritarian system to electoral democracy
Transformation of the economic system	From state socialism to state capitalism	From party-state capitalism to market capitalism	From bureaucratic-authoritarian capitalism to market capitalism
Current position in the GVC	Rapidly climbing the GVC ladder, attempting to create an autonomous value chain system (beginning in the mid-2010s)	Minority of firms with lead firm status in the GVC (beginning in the 2010s)	Minority of brands and firms with lead firm status in the GVC (beginning in the 2010s)

Source: Author's analysis.

to the 2000s marked the flourishing of Guangdong's EOI development model, which was the prototype for the China model. Below I lay out the prerequisites for development, the development conditions and process, and the development results to highlight the distinctive features of the China model.

1) Geopolitics and the Drive for Industrialization

The extension of the GVC has often been influenced by geopolitical changes. After World War II, the economic development of Taiwan and South Korea was to a considerable extent decided by their position in the geopolitical structure. During the Cold War, adjustments to the East Asia strategy of the United States caused Taiwan and South Korea to become outposts for containing the communist world, giving those countries opportunities for rapid economic growth that were second only to Japan's. The United States opened its domestic market to these countries and provided preferential tariffs. Pressure from the United States and persuasion by international advisors (mainly in the case of Taiwan) or the pressure of economic crisis (mainly in South Korea) pushed EOI and caused the GVC to rapidly extend to these countries, bringing about thirty years of sustained and rapid growth. The critical juncture when China launched EOI in the 1980s was also related to Cold War structural changes and America's strategic shift. Beginning in the 1970s, the United States changed its policy of containing China into one of forming an alliance with it to counter the Soviet Union. As a result, East Asia's Cold War defense line shifted from the Taiwan Strait to the Sino-Soviet border. By the 1980s, the capitalist world's economic division of labor had also undergone structural changes: The 1985 Plaza Accord brought sharp appreciation to the Japanese yen, followed by the New Taiwan dollar and the Korean won. Rapid fluctuations in the costs of essential factors of production caused the GVC to extend toward China. The traditional manufacturing industries of Taiwan and South Korea inundated China's coastal regions in search of cheaper production costs. At this stage, the United States opened its domestic market to China. From the economic miracle of the Four Little Dragons to China's rise, we can observe the effect of geopolitical change. China grasped this window of opportunity by changing its Mao-era autarky and rapidly linking up with the international market to become the factory of the world. Yet unlike Taiwan and South

Korea, China was characterized by massive size and national autonomy. This meant that its economic rise was accompanied by a political ascent and enhanced military capacity that allowed China to influence geopolitical relations. Although Japan's postwar economic revival made it into a world economic power, it was unable to enjoy the kind of geopolitical status that accompanied China's rise.

In sum, geopolitical change is a premise that cannot be overlooked in the development of East Asia. Geopolitical changes have brought geoeconomic changes and at the same time have influenced the economic and trade policies of the United States, the global hegemon, toward Asia, as well as driving the shift, expansion, and extension of commodity chains. After World War II, the United States helped the Japanese economy to recover rapidly and facilitated the industrialization of Taiwan and South Korea, as well as China's industrialization and entry into the capitalist world system. When the GVC extended from other parts of East Asia to China, geographical proximity and linguistic and cultural affinity both had an effect. These two factors can explain why Hong Kong and Taiwanese capital occupied a key position in Guangdong in the first wave of China's capital shift.

2) State-Market Relations

In East Asian development, an authoritarian regime was the starting point for Taiwan, South Korea, and China in promoting EOI policies. All three qualified as strong states, and the states harnessed the markets (Wade 1990), promoted the EOI strategy, and invested in infrastructure. However, there were still differences among the three countries in terms of structural details. At the launch of rapid growth in Taiwan and South Korea, the both states had the quality of militaristic authoritarianism. In contrast, China was a state-socialist system established after a socialist revolution. Both Taiwan and China were party states. China was a typical Leninist regime, and one of the main legacies of the Mao era was the state's powerful capacity to mobilize society. However, Taiwan was a quasi-Leninist regime (Cheng Tun-Jen 1989).[4] This type of regime has

4. Prior to its democratization, Taiwan's Kuomintang was in a similar category to Mexico's Partido Revolucionario Institucional, but there were obvious differences. The main one was that Taiwan was ruled by a clan (with a familial dynastic succession from

especially strong capacity to control the economic sphere. With its state control of property rights and land ownership, China adopted gradual economic reforms, and political power was firmly in the grasp of the CCP. As a result, the state's control of the economy was not fundamentally shaken after opening reforms. The state merely granted privately owned enterprises a chance to survive and opened the country up to foreign investment. Although Taiwan also had a party-state system and a government that controlled enormous state-owned enterprises and party-owned assets, under the influence of the United States, the government gradually relaxed its control over the privately owned sector. In addition, the party-state system was challenged by an opposition movement and began showing signs of easing its grip on the society in the 1970s. In terms of relations between the state and the market (and companies), the state apparatuses of Taiwan, South Korea, and China each had a powerful capacity to control and regulate, but their operational modes and enforcement had obvious differences. The Chinese government pervasively used the tools of macroeconomic regulation and command-type control, and it continued to foster state-owned enterprises. In the 1980s and 1990s, it unleashed township and village enterprises and the private business sector, but the financial sector heavily favored the state-owned sector, and private businesses had difficulty obtaining loans. As privately owned businesses gradually became stronger, the state increased its control of the private sector, and the phenomenon of state sector advancing and the private sector retreating since the 2000s led to limitations on the development of private enterprises (Huang Yasheng 2008).

In contrast, in Taiwan's industrialization, although the state-owned sector enjoyed state support, its share of industrial output gradually shrank, causing the economic system to approach classic market capitalism and to be dominated by small and medium-size companies. Unlike Taiwan, South Korea at the launch of EOI had a privately owned economic foundation, but under the state's industrial policy, massive conglomerates produced an extremely large share of the GDP, and oligopolistic capital predominated (Amsden 1989). In terms of overall economic

---

Chiang Kai-shek to Chiang Ching-kuo), while Mexico's authoritarian regime allowed limited competition within the party. As a result, Mexico had a certain degree of stability during its seventy-one years of authoritarian rule (1929–2000).

development, China's distinguishing characteristic was that during the economy's evolution from socialism to capitalism, the state maintained a tight grasp on economic policy decisions and the management of massive state-owned enterprises (Tsai and Naughton 2015). On this foundation, the state apparatus has been able to carry out economic and political mobilization. China has transformed a portion of its economic surplus into capital for infrastructure and has invested in large-scale infrastructural projects such as urbanization, highways, and high-speed railways at an almost unprecedented rate. This gives China's capitalism unique qualities in the context of East Asia's developmental states. It is worth noting that because of the enormous scale of the Chinese economic system and the country's expansionist ambitions, these unique qualities have injected new elements into East Asian capitalism and redefined the connotations of the East Asian developmental state. These new elements include more comprehensive market controls in China than in Northeast Asian countries, the pervasive use of command-style regulation, tight control over state-owned enterprises, and more concentrated investment in designated infrastructure projects.

3) Ownership Structure

The ownership structure also highlights the differences between China, on the one hand, and Taiwan and South Korea, on the other hand. In the EOI development of both Taiwan and South Korea, privately owned business was an important element in the ownership structure. The proportion of Taiwan's party-state capital as a share of GDP gradually dropped under rapid industrialization, while South Korea developed huge chaebols on the foundation of private ownership. In contrast, the development of Chinese capitalism relied on the state's continuing to control the ownership of enterprises. The Chinese government also played a decisive role not only in the system of state-owned land but also in the distribution of resources, which confronted privately owned enterprises with developmental constraints and unstable property rights. The government's inadequate protection of private capital, financial plundering of private enterprises, and pervasive bureaucratic rent seeking led to the emergence of various types of fictive ownership. Private capital sought the sponsorship and political protection of government work units, which created even more opportunities for bureaucratic rent seeking and exacerbated rampant fictive ownership. A major finding of this book is the close affinity between fictive ownership and bureaucratic rent seeking: in Guangdong, local governments were financially motivated to use participation in the value chain's governance structure to derive rent income and capture value under the state's dual-track foreign exchange policy and through fictive ownership contractual arrangements. This kind of bureaucratic activity essentially draws economic surplus (value) from the production process, but under the packaging of fictive ownership, the directly unproductive local government work units became fictive firms and obtained legitimate profits while also concealing their financial extraction role in this process.

It is also very meaningful to compare China's development characteristics with those of Taiwan and South Korea. As former Japanese colonies, both of the latter countries inherited a huge amount of publicly owned businesses and assets after World War II. South Korea's 1948 constitution, adopted in the administration of President Syngman Rhee, emphasized economic planning and state control of heavy industry, public utilities, and foreign trade. But in 1954, under the antagonistic Cold War relationship with North Korea's communist regime and the influence of the United States, South Korea began progressively privatizing state-owned companies and banks, facilitating the formation of an indigenous capitalist class (Cheng Tun-Jen 1990). The trajectory of change in Taiwan's property ownership structure was different from that in South Korea. After the Kuomintang government moved from the mainland to Taiwan in 1949, it rapidly molded itself into a quasi-Leninist party-state system and used the enormous assets taken over from Japan to form party-state capital (a category of state capitalism). As an émigré regime from 1949 to the late 1980s, the Kuomintang was qualitatively different from the electoral democracy that the United States established in South Korea (which quickly degenerated into authoritarianism) and the totalitarian regime that emerged from the CCP's socialist revolution.

Taiwan, South Korea, and China all experienced a stage of ISI before launching their EOI policies at different points in time, and all experienced sustained periods of rapid economic growth. But two circumstances differentiated Taiwan from China. First, the EOI that began in Taiwan in the 1960s did not constrain the development of small and medium-size enterprises; and unlike in China, in Taiwan the state ideology was not fundamentally hostile to private enterprise—even though Chiang Ching-kuo stifled the development of large indigenous enterprises. Second, in the 1970s, soon after Taiwan's economic takeoff, the democracy movement was launched (although it was repeatedly suppressed). The mainstream standpoint of the democracy movement at that time held that breaking up the state-owned capital monopolies was a key prerequisite to Taiwan's democratization (Chen Shih-meng 1992). Beginning in the 1990s, the combination of these two factors led Taiwan to experience a privatization of state-owned enterprises that shifted its original state capitalistic system toward market capitalism.

4) Manufacturing FDI and the Export Economy

There has been intense debate in the development theory literature about the effect of foreign investment. Proponents of dependency theory hold that foreign investment puts backward countries into a vicious circle of underdevelopment, while modernization theory regards foreign investment as a medium for promoting economic development (Stallings 1990). Examples are Latin America in the first case and the newly industrialized countries of East Asia in the second case. Foreign investment and foreign aid (primarily from the United States) played a key role in Taiwan and South Korea in the 1950s, but beginning in the 1960s, the proportion of foreign investment sharply decreased. In other words, during the EOI stage, FDI did not stand out. The same was true in Hong Kong, but in Singapore the proportion of FDI was very high (Haggard and Cheng 1987). In comparison, China is distinguished by its reliance at the initial stage of EOI on a massive influx of manufacturing foreign investment, which brought capital, technology, and export markets. Driven by FDI, China's southeastern coastal region was rapidly transformed into an export economy. FDI played a leading role in Guangdong's development for a long time. The weight of foreign investment in China's total capital (fixed assets) reached its peak in the mid-1990s: in 1994 it reached a high of 21.6 percent in Guangdong; in 1997, during the second wave of opening reforms, it reached a high of 17.7 percent in Jiangsu; and the high point for the entire country was 11.8 percent in 1996. After the Asian financial crisis, the percentage dropped yearly, falling in 2000 to 10.5 percent in Guangdong, 9.4 percent in Jiangsu, and 5.1 percent in the country as a whole. This decrease continued after the global financial crisis: by 2013, it had fallen to 2.5 percent in Guangdong, 2.6 percent in Jiangsu, and 0.9 percent in the entire country (see chapter 2). It could be said that foreign investment was of the utmost importance in the first stage of EOI, from the Pearl River Delta region (Guangdong) to the Yangtze Delta region (Jiangsu). China relied on foreign investment to promote its export economy and capture enormous amounts of foreign exchange. For this reason, the percentage of exports' contribution to China's GDP has been higher than the average figure for other East Asian economies (Ho-fung Hung 2016, 77). For the Chinese government, this dependency model seems to have the aspect of a virtuous circle, allowing the Chinese government to extract financial resources from the export economic sector. In terms of EOI's contribution to the country's development, China clearly follows the East Asian development model. However, China's reliance on foreign investment at the initial stage of EOI is more obvious than is the case in Taiwan and South Korea, and China used its global links to promote domestic institutional reforms and push economic modernization (Gallagher 2005).

5) Labor Exploitation, Unequal Distribution, and High Accumulation

The distinctive features of China's development are unequal distribution, high accumulation, and low consumption. Rural migrant workers provided the labor force for China to develop its export-oriented economy, which was the chief means of rapid capital accumulation. In Taiwan and South Korea, during the launch stage of EOI, rural areas provided a large number of high-quality but low-cost migrant laborers, and under these countries' authoritarian systems, wages were assiduously suppressed, labor union activities were controlled by the government, the popular sector (farmers, workers, and lower middle class) was excluded from the share of political power, and government social security and welfare expenditures were also suppressed. In Taiwan, the government used state corporatism to control the workers and stifle autonomous labor unions; in South Korea, the state teamed up with private-sector capital to suppress the worker resistance movement (Deyo 1987 and 1990; Koo 2001). Most of these features of the situation in Taiwan and South Korea can also be observed in China, but China's exploitation of workers has other unique characteristics—in particular, the dual labor market and differential citizenship, the market's institutional basis. The *hukou* status of migrant workers is "peasant," but their occupation is "worker," an ambiguity that causes them to suffer dual exploitation according to status and class. The wages and social welfare benefits of China's migrant workers are greatly inferior to those of the typical "employee with an urban registration status, allowing businesses to hire cheap migrant labor at the minimum wage and pay lower social insurance fees. The minimum wage was meant to serve as a payroll floor to safeguard workers, but in practice it has become a ceiling for hourly wages. The government uses the dual labor market to maintain the stability of the low-cost labor supply and to gain opportunities for rent seeking.

Under this labor system, wages have long made up a relatively smaller percentage of GDP than those in other major economies. That percentage averaged 51.8 percent from 1994 to 2003. It dropped gradually to 40.6 percent from 2005 to 2007 and recovered to 45.5 percent from 2009 to 2012. Over the long term, China's real minimum wage (adjusted to the price index) has been nearly stagnant (1990s) or in a situation of low-level growth (2000s), and it has not kept up with GDP growth. Beginning in the 2000s, China's coastal regions experienced labor shortages and faced pressure to increase wages, but wages didn't begin rising faster until after the global financial crisis. Long-term wage suppression limited the purchasing power of China's masses as well as the development of a domestic consumer industry.

During their rapid growth phases, Taiwan and South Korea gained renown for growth with equity. However, China has experienced a serious urban-rural gap and unequal distribution with its rapid growth. China's Gini coefficient in 1978 was a relatively equitable 0.293 (Kanbur and Zhang 2005), but by 2008 it had deteriorated to 0.430.[5] In comparison, at the initial stage of EOI in 1961, Taiwan had a Gini coefficient of 0.469, which dropped to 0.277 in 1980 and was 0.303 in 1989; and South Korea's

5. World Bank, "Gini Index (World Bank Estimate)—China," accessed December 29, 2017, https://goo.gl/ubnk7k.

Gini coefficient was 0.320 in 1961, 0.386 in 1980, and 0.349 in 1992.[6] One sign of China's capital accumulation was a high savings rate, especially in the corporate sector (Selden and Wu 2011). According to Ho-fung Hung's research, China's fixed capital formation as a share of GDP from the mid-1990s onward has been much higher than the average for other East Asian economies. From around 40 percent in the mid-1990s, it increased to around 45 percent in the early 2010s. In comparison, the share was only around 36 percent for other East Asian economies at their peak in 1973. China's private consumption as a share of GDP has been lower than the average for other East Asian economies since the 1970s. From around 50 percent in the 1980s, it dropped to around 35 percent in the early 2010s (Ho-fung Hung 2016, 78). According to these data, the foundation for China's rapid capital accumulation and high savings rate was the use of rapid export expansion to obtain profit and capital, along with the stifling of individual and household consumption to achieve national capital accumulation. When China's exports became persistently depressed after the 2008 global financial crisis, the government's stimulus measure was to increase investment in fixed assets. Overaccumulation resulted in overcapacity and steeply declining returns on fixed assets. The state cut welfare expenditures, and domestic consumption remained suppressed (Ho-fung Hung 2016, 157–63).

China's institutional exploitation of migrant workers highlights its difference from other developmental states such as Taiwan and South Korea. The Chinese labor regime of differential citizenship has institutional stickiness: Although the Chinese government has promulgated new policies in an attempt to improve the treatment of migrant workers (such as the 2008 Labor Contract Law and the 2011 Social Insurance Law), the labor regime continues to exploit and discriminate against migrant workers and their families. Moreover, major cities, based on their own interests, emphatically discriminate against nonnatives (mainly migrant workers). The Beijing government's mass banishment of the low-end population in the winter of 2017 proves that the system of differential citizenship still exists and that it has become further consolidated with the despotic power of the state apparatus.

6. Areppim, "The Complete Gini Coefficients, 1960–2012," http://stats.areppim.com/listes/list_gini_1960x2012.htm.

Arrighi (2007) treats the East Asia region as a coherent historical space. He holds that since the 1880s, East Asia's development dynamic has been labor-intensive industrialization, using a high-quality labor force and markets strategically controlled by the state. His explanation is basically the same as past explanations of the East Asian developmental state, apart from emphasizing the historical redivision of labor in the capitalist world system. But his analysis overlooks the exploitation of the migrant worker class by the state and capital, and his excessively structured analytical framework is unable to explain the institutional mechanism through which China rapidly achieved capital accumulation. A major cost of promoting the EOI model—which lowered labor costs to strengthen export competitiveness and suppressed the purchasing power of the popular classes—was the bankrupting of the countryside (Ho-fung Hung 2009). As a result, Arrighi overlooks the role of the authoritarian differential citizenship system in exploiting labor and excessively praises the China model without seeing the structural imbalance and mounting social conflict created by high exploitation and accumulation.

6) EOI, Institutional Rent Seeking, and Exploitation

The rent-seeking phenomenon is pervasive and serious in developing countries. However, a rent-seeking society and economic growth do not have to be mutually exclusive, and the phenomenon is manifested differently in different countries. In their ISI stage before launching EOI, Taiwan and South Korea also experienced rent-seeking activity, mainly because foreign exchange controls, two-tier exchange rate policies, import controls, and other policies created a favorable environment for rent-seeking opportunities. But the blatancy of rent seeking is also related to the political regime. The administration of President Rhee in South Korea addressed its financing needs by engaging in exchanges of power for profit with private business groups, with the result that rent seeking became egregious. In Taiwan, in contrast, the organizational power and financial autonomy of the party-state prevented the dictatorial regime of President Chiang Kai-shek from becoming dependent on the capitalists (Cheng Tun-Jen 1990). After Taiwan and South Korea shifted toward EOI development, rent-seeking behavior eased under the increased constraints of globalized linkages.

In the process of China's rapid economic growth, rent-seeking activity proceeded apace, mainly because of the postsocialist transitional economic structure. As analyzed above, China's widespread rent-seeking activities include a special category of institutional rent seeking, and this type of rent seeking has a definite relationship with economic expansion. Comparing China with past East Asian developmental states, we see that China's institutional rent seeking has several distinguishing features: (1) the state allows local governments to create rent and rent-seeking space (or tacitly consents to their doing so); (2) rent seeking occurs not only in the ISI sector, with local governments also seeking rent in the EOI sector; and (3) local officials participate in capturing economic surplus from the value chain through locally embedded governance venues.

Generally speaking, in the EOI development process, economic surplus is mainly created through labor-intensive industries, so an abundant and low-cost labor force is essential. When the relative price of labor increases, labor-intensive industries begin to decline, and the demand for industrial upgrading gradually emerges. Assuming that other conditions remain constant, the proportion of economic surplus extracted from the labor force will drop. The space for institutional rent seeking in the export sector will therefore shrink. This is the situation that emerged in China in the late 2000s. Consequently, the question at the current stage is whether China will be able to continue using its rent-seeking developmental model. On the one hand, the industrial structure's rapid adjustment is shrinking the legitimate rent-seeking space that the state has granted to local governments. On the other hand, local governments are dependent on institutional rent seeking, so they have begun to use disguised forms of rent seeking, increasing their financial plundering. These two forces are currently engaged in an antagonistic tug-of-war.

Viewing institutional rent seeking in the long-term relationship between the state and the peasants, we see that it is a camouflaged form of exploiting the peasant labor force. What lies behind it is a disguised exploitation of the agricultural sector by the industrial sector and of the countryside by the state. This new form of exploitation can be called the "new price scissors." In fact, exploitation of rural laborers is a historical-spatial shift of the price scissors.[7] For more than thirty years, part of

---

7. Regarding the concept of the price scissors, see chapter 5, section 4.

the price scissors (the surplus from suppressed labor costs) extracted from rural migrant workers has been captured by capitalists (both foreign-owned and domestically owned companies), and another part has been drawn by the state and has become a necessary condition for the rapid accumulation of capital. The identification and analysis of China's rent-seeking developmental state enriches our understanding of developmental states and presents the potential for theoretical revision of comparative studies on developmentalism and development policies.

7) A Comparison of and the Interaction between the Results of Development

Taiwan's rapid growth from the 1960s to the 1980s fostered an industrial network of decentralized production with small and medium-size manufacturers as its leading force (Ka Chih-Ming 1993; Chen Chieh-Hsuan 1994; Michelle Hsieh 2011). The supply chains constituted by these networks were closely linked to the GVC and turned Taiwan into an economy that responded rapidly to the market demand of core countries (Hamilton and Kao 2018). This development characteristic also gave rise to a generation of apprentices turned bosses (Shieh Gwo-Shyong 1997). This historical process elevated Taiwan to the status of a semiperipheral state in the capitalist world system, and some of the bosses were also upgraded to invisible champions with global competitive power and high profitability (Hsieh Fei-yu 2017). Sustaining development on this foundation, a small number of Taiwanese manufacturers had gained lead firm status in the GVC by the beginning of the twenty-first century. For example, TSMC, which specializes in wafer fabrication for the semiconductor industry, has captured a large share of the global foundry market. In this process, Taiwan's economic system changed from party-state capitalism to market capitalism. Economic and social development also provided Taiwan with the conditions for overall transformation from a quasi-Leninist party-state system to an electoral democratic system: it launched political liberalization in 1986 and democratization in 1992. Before the 1990s, Taiwan's developmental state enjoyed great economic power and used patron-client relationships with state corporatism to govern private business. This government-business relationship changed under political democratization: With economic liberalism, controls were removed, privatization took place, and the state's role became more subtle and complicated (Wang Jenn-hwan 2010). In addition, businesses grew in scale, and privately owned conglomerates gradually emerged (Lin Thung-Hong and Hu Bo-Wei 2017). The clan quality of business groups was still strong, however (Lee Zong-Rong 2011). As a result, the developmental state gradually turned toward a neoliberal state (Hsia Chuan-Wei 2015).

In South Korea, Park Chung-hee launched a coup d'état in 1961 and seized power under a military dictatorship. After several years of chaos and fumbling about, he set up an authoritarian bureaucratic regime, and economic crisis spurred him to push an EOI policy. Korea's EOI policy had a different orientation from Taiwan's. Taiwan adopted a policy of decentralization and dispersion, while Korea adopted a policy of centralization and focused cultivation. The Korean state banks gave loans to designated industries and encouraged industries to borrow money overseas (whereas in Taiwan FDI was preferred), and industrial distribution was concentrated in the major cities of Seoul and Pusan (in contrast to the dispersed industrial areas of Taiwan). As a result, chaebols became the backbone of the South Korean economy, and exports were concentrated among the top ten major companies—demonstrating the alliance between state power and the major companies (Cheng Tun-Jen 1990; Amsden 1989). Since the end of the 1980s, bureaucratic authoritarianism began evolving into a form of electoral democracy. The overall economic system changed from authoritarian capitalism to market capitalism. It was also at this stage that Korea entered a semiperipheral position in the capitalist world system, but in terms of income distribution its performance was somewhat inferior to Taiwan's. The 1998 Asian financial crisis dealt a severe blow to South Korea, and to address its foreign debt and meet the demands of the International Monetary Fund, it carried out neoliberal structural reform. At the beginning of the twenty-first century, the South Korean economy continued developing in a way that brought it closer to the economies of core countries, and the branding strategies of the chaebols began showing results. A small number of brands gained lead firm status in the GVC, and famous international brands emerged in the automotive, consumer electronic, cell-phone, display device, and semiconductor industries. For example, Samsung has become competitive with Apple in the international market for high-end cell phones.

China's development outcomes have been very different from Taiwan's and South Korea's. The results of China's EOI development did not suppress the state-owned sector: rather, the results allowed the state to gain enormous financial strength, which it used to transform state socialism into a type of state capitalism. The state gained capital from rapid growth and was able to engage in mergers, acquisitions, and investment abroad, using its geoeconomic leverage to enhance its international political status. Internally it engaged in infrastructural development, greatly strengthening its power to penetrate society and enhancing its social controls. At one point in the early stage of China's launch of EOI, the Leninist party-state system developed a limited openness. But after the 1989 Tiananmen Incident and the political purges that followed, political reforms were stalled for a long time. After Xi Jinping rose to power in 2012, he implemented a return to totalitarianism and high-tech social surveillance that reconsolidated the party-state system and turned it into Leninist state capitalism.

Comparing Taiwan and China from the angle of transformation of the party-state system is very useful. Studies of Taiwan make extensive use of the concept of "party-state capitalism," as opposed to China's Leninist state capitalism. There are three main differences between the two countries. First, there was a different starting point in terms of the nature of the regimes: Taiwan's authoritarian Kuomintang regime combined quasi-Leninist political controls with traditional dynastic rule, while China had a classic Leninist totalitarian regime. Second, in Taiwan the Kuomintang, as the ruling party, gained enormous party assets through the "national treasury to party treasury" system, while in China, the CCP does not have assets similar to those of the Kuomintang but rather controls enormous national economic resources through its princelings (the descendants of prominent and influential senior communist leaders). And third, the Chinese economy has experienced forty years of opening reform, yet its nature continues to be one of highly centralized management (Nan Lin 2011), and the state's control of the economy is very strong, while Taiwan's party-state capitalism underwent economic liberalization and privatization in the 1980s.

After forty years of development, China has consolidated its semiperipheral position in the capitalist world system and has rapidly climbed up the GVC in some manufacturing categories. Through the state's forceful intervention, it has attempted to sidestep the value chain hegemony dominated by core countries and has established a value chain system under its own control. Behind GVC hegemony is the US-dominated neoliberal global control structure. Although China is still unable to fully contend with the United States at the global level (Ho-fung Hung 2016), it is already a regional power in terms of geopolitical and overall economic power. China has improved its status by attempting to amend the rules of the game: it has formulated technical specifications, fostered an indigenous supply chain, established the Asia Infrastructure Investment Bank, and carried out the Belt and Road Initiative to export its surplus capital.

In Guangdong's development experience, we can see the Chinese state (including both central and local governments) increase state power by intervening in GVC governance through locally embedded governance, using taxation and rent-seeking methods to extract economic surplus, and using industrial policies to forcibly impose industrial upgrading and deal with polluting industries. The local polity is developing a competitive relationship with global capitalism (core countries) through its state capital and burgeoning manufacturing capacity. China is attempting to move from the semiperiphery to the core, adopting something like an enhanced version of Korea's big-push strategy, but with the Chinese government playing a more active and commanding role than that of the South Korean government.

Returning to this book's historical survey of China's development, during China's rapid growth process, the Guangdong model was the prototype for and core component of the Chinese development model, and Taiwanese-owned companies were a key component of Guangdong's foreign investment. A counterfactual thought experiment is useful here: It is hard to imagine the Guangdong model without Taiwanese investment; and without the Guangdong model, the rise of China would not have occurred. We can therefore infer the critical status of Taiwanese investment and the Guangdong model in China's development process.

According to this book analytical framework using G-D-L, Taiwanese capital has a dual role in the interactive sphere of global capital and local polity links: On the one hand, Taiwanese companies perform a controlling role in the value chain governance in China. On the other hand, they play a coordinating role as diffusers of technology and management knowledge, fostering talent in local mainland-owned factories and promoting industrial upgrading and indigenous supply chains. This dual role can be observed from the traditional industries to the ICT industries. In terms of the latter, Taiwanese integrated circuit (IC) design firms such as MediaTek played a notable role in promoting China's cell-phone industry from earliest copycats to current global market players.

In recent years, China has vigorously promoted its semiconductor industry and built many new chip factories, pulling in many high-level Taiwanese managers and engineers. With the effort of Taiwanese talent, China's semiconductor industry has developed a complex relationship with Taiwan (in addition to core countries), as exemplified by an earlier lawsuit between TSMC and SMIC and an ongoing lawsuit in which Micron Technology is suing JHICC and United Microelectronics (UMC) for intellectual property theft.[8] Here we can see the interaction, competition, and cooperation between Taiwanese and Chinese capital.

4. A Preliminary Evaluation of the Semiconductor Industrial Upgrading Blueprint of Made in China 2025

How can industrial upgrading be promoted as economic growth goes into a downslide?[9] China's policy makers clearly intended to use the state's strong capacities to push their industrial upgrading plan. The Twelfth

---

8. *AUTHOR'S POSTSCRIPT:* In 2017, Micron accused UMC of stealing its technology and passing confidential information to China's JHICC. A US grand jury indicted UMC and JHICC in 2018 on economic espionage and other charges. In October 2020, UMC pleaded guilty and agreed to pay a US$60 million fine to settle the lawsuit. It also agreed to cooperate with the US government in the investigation and prosecution of JHICC. See Yu Nakamura, "Taiwan's UMC nears settlement on leaking Micron secrets to China," *Nikkei Asia*, October 23, 2020, https://asia.nikkei.com/Business /Technology/Taiwan-s-UMC-nears-settlement-on-leaking-Micron-secrets-to-China; Cheng Ting-Fang and Lauly Li, "Taiwan's UMC to Pay $60M Fine to Settle US Trade Secrets Case," *Nikkei Asia*, October 29, 2020, https://asia.nikkei.com/Economy/Trade -war/Taiwan-s-UMC-to-pay-60m-fine-to-settle-US-trade-secrets-case.

9. The analysis in this chapter benefited from discussions with Freedom Huang, to whom I offer special thanks.

Five-Year Plan, which began in 2011, emphasized developing the domestic market as the basis for opening up foreign markets. The expression "red supply chain" was a product of that stage. In 2014, the State Council established the Big Fund to nurture the domestic semiconductor industry, raising more than 130 billion yuan in the first stage; and in 2018, the government announced that it had raised 300 billion yuan.[10] In 2015, the State Council came out with Made in China 2025. In that same year, The Strategy Advisory Committee for National Manufacturing and Strong Nation mobilized "forty-eight academicians and more than 400 experts" to discuss and draft the "Made in China 2025 Key Sectors Technical Road Map" (2015, 2) This plan for catching up with the manufacturing technology of core Western countries demonstrates China's ambition to develop an innovative drive and achieve transformative upgrading. Using this blueprint, China widely publicized Made in China 2025 and intensified its efforts to gain technology from abroad, attracting worldwide attention. But how feasible is this grand strategy? What roadblocks is it likely to encounter?

Given the vast scope of the industries involved in Made in China 2025, I will assess only the wafer fabrication of the semiconductor industry here. After the Big Fund was established, China was reportedly planning to build twenty-six new wafer fabrication plants from 2018 to 2020,[11] some of which were sponsored by the Big Fund. But the Big Fund was meant to cover the entire semiconductor supply chain, including integrated circuit design, wafer fabrication, testing and packaging, equipment, materials, and other domains.

There are three main ownership models for the wafer fabrication plants currently in operation or being built in China. The first is wholly foreign-owned. TSMC already had an eight-inch wafer fabrication plant

---

10. Yun Chun-chieh, "Zhongguo peizhi bandaotiye ni jiama touzi 1.4 zhao yuan (taibi)" (China raises the stakes of fostering its semiconductor industry to NT$1.4 trillion), Central News Agency, May 6, 2018, http://www.cna.com.tw/news/acn/2018050 60005-1.aspx.

11. Liu Milo, "Zhongguo jingyuanchang dayuejin! Weilai sinian jiang xian 26 zuo xin chang, cheng bandaoti shebei zhichu disan daguo" (China's Great Leap Forward in chip factories! Twenty-six new plants will appear in the next four years, third ranking country in expenditure on semiconductor facilities), *Keji xinbao* (TechNews), December 14, 2016, http://technews.tw/2016/12/14/semiconductor-fab-and-equipment-forecast/.

in Shanghai. It invested US$3 billion in building a plant for twelve-inch wafers in Nanjing using sixteen-nanometer technology, which began mass production in May 2018. The second is joint venture or cooperation. Examples include a factory that GlobalFoundries built with the cooperation of the Chengdu government; Nexchip, the result of cooperation between Taiwan's Powerchip Semiconductor and the Hefei government, with the government providing the initial investment and the company providing technical cooperation through the shareholding method; and Nanjing Tacoma's cooperation with Israel's TowerJazz, in which the latter provided technical expertise and operational and integration consulting in return for 50 percent of the production capacity of a new eight-inch wafer fabrication plant to expand its China market.[12] The third is mainly Chinese-owned. One example is SMIC's Shanghai factory, for which SMIC gained Datang Telecom as a strategic investor, making a state-owned enterprise its major shareholder. The Big Fund supports SMIC as a key enterprise in domestic wafer fabrication. In June 2017, the Big Fund became the company's second-largest shareholder, with 15.91 percent of the shares.[13] In 2015, a consolidated company created by SMIC, Huawei, IMEC (a Belgian electronics research center), and Qualcomm

---

12. Tower Semiconductor, "TowerJazz and Tacoma Announce a Partnership for a New 8-Inch Fabrication Facility in Nanjing, China," GlobalNewswire, August 21, 2017, https://reurl.cc/X4ZoZR. *Author's Postscript:* Nanjing Tacoma, financially backed by the local government, raised funds with great fanfare, but it went bankrupt in July 2020. See Juo Guoping and Denise Jia, "Chinese $2.8bn Memory Chip Project Goes Bust," *Nikkei Asia*, July 14, 2020, https://asia.nikkei.com/Spotlight/Caixin /Chinese-2.8bn-memory-chip-project-goes-bust. Another local government-sponsored company, Wuhan Hongxin Semiconductor Manufacturing Company (HSMC), hired Chiang Shang-yi, the retired co–chief operating officer of TSMC, as its CEO and touted its high-end process capabilities, but it also went bust in a financial scandal in October 2020. Chiang said in an interview: "My experience with HSMC was a nightmare, unfortunately! It's really hard to describe in a few words." See Sidney Leng, "China's Semiconductor Dream Takes a Hit as Local Authority Takes Over 'Nightmare' Wuhan Factory," *South China Morning Post*, November 18, 2020, https://www.scmp .com/economy/china-economy/article/3110368/chinas-semiconductor-dream-takes-hit -local-authority-takes.

13. "Nage sanci chuangye 'Zhongguo xin' de Meiji Taiwanren huilaile" (That American Taiwanese who undertook 'Chinese wafers' three times has returned), *Wenxuecheng xinwen pindao*, April 24, 2018, https://zh.wenxuecity.com/news/2018/04/24 /7192051.html.

developed a 14-nanometer process.[14] In 2017, SMIC hired Liang Mong-Song, the previous head of research and development at TSMC, to serve as its co-CEO in charge of R&D.[15] In 2016, Tsinghua Unigroup merged with Wuhan Xinxin Semiconductor to form Yangtze Memory Technologies, which convinced the former chairman of the board of a major Taiwanese dynamic random access memory factory to serve as its chief operating officer.[16]

The abovementioned operational methods reveal several characteristics. First, the semiconductor industry is highly capital- and technology-intensive, requiring an enormous amount of investment. That's why the government and state-owned enterprises take on a vital role in a place like China that originally had no advanced semiconductor manufacturing.[17] The Big Fund's current investment in wafer fabrication includes SMIC and five other prominent manufacturers.[18] Second, trading markets for technology is the main strategy China uses to demand that foreign companies form joint ventures. China has stipulated self-sufficiency rates for the semiconductor industry and backs its demands on foreign companies

14. Chen Liang-rong, "Zhongguo za zhong ben, meng bing gou, weihe pinbuchu dierge Taijidian?" (China makes heavy investment in mergers and acquisition, why is it unable to create a second TSMC?), *Tianxia zazhi* (CommonWealth magazine), May 21, 2018, https://www.cw.com.tw/article/article.action?id=5090025.

15. Liang Mong-song previously taught at South Korea's Sungkyunkwan University, which is supported by the Samsung Group, and in July 2011 he joined Samsung Electronics as deputy CEO for R&D. During this time, he was credited with helping develop Samsung's high-end processes. At one point TSMC sued Liang for infringing on its intellectual property rights.

16. Liu Milo, "Gao Qiquan chushou, Taiwan DRAM chanye kong xian yu bai ren-cai chuzou chao" (Charles Kau steps up, Taiwan's DRAM industry faces exodus of more than 100 skilled personnel), *Keji xinbao* (TechNews), August 26, 2016, https://technews.tw/2016/08/26/charles-kau-dram/.

17. Before SMIC and Grace Semiconductor were established in Shanghai (in 2000 and 2003, respectively), China had nonadvanced wafer fabrication plants, including Shanghai's Advanced Semiconductor Manufacturing Corporation and CRC Shanghua Technology (established in 1988 and 1997, respectively).

18. "2018 nian Zhongguo jingyuan zhizao chanye jingzheng shengji, 12 cun yuechanneng bijin 70 wan pian" (In 2018, competition in China's wafer manufacturing industry will intensify, with 12-inch production capacity nearing 700,000 pieces per month), *Keji xinbao* (TechNews), January 17, 2008, https://finance.technews.tw/2018/01/17/2018-cn-wafer-factory-12-inches-700-thousand-per-month/#more-322806.

with policy document stipulations, requiring that foreign companies establish factories in China or engage in technology transfer through joint ventures or cooperation. According to Mr. Ng, a former manager of a Taiwanese-owned semiconductor factory in Shanghai, "this makes foreign companies accountable to Chinese customers and reduces the pressure when obtaining Chinese orders."[19] Third, China routinely poaches talent, usually key personnel from the United States, South Korea, Singapore, or Taiwan (see Hsung Ray-May, Chen Kuan-jung, and Guan Yi-Ren 2017). Taiwanese investment and technical personnel stand out in the examples above. Fourth, China's construction of a large number of wafer fabrication plants in the mature process segment, regardless of the quality of their future products, may affect the market structure in the future.

In fact, China has been engaged in the semiconductor sector for many years, but its technology has always lagged far behind the most advanced technology in the world. For example, SMIC was established in 2000 and is the eight-inch fabrication plant with the greatest exposure in the Chinese media. It has invested in seven plants in China and one in Italy, but its reported production yields have always been doubted in the industry. SMIC was originally established by Richard Chang's team, which originated in Taiwan, but soon after its establishment, SMIC faced a lawsuit from TSMC alleging infringement of intellectual property rights. The two sides reached a settlement in 2009 under which SMIC paid TSMC US$200 million in compensation, along with 8 percent of its shares.[20] SMIC's financial report for the first quarter of 2018 states that the 28 nanometer (nm) node made up only 3.2 percent of its total sales volume, compared to 21.7 percent for the 40–45 nm mode, 20.9 percent for the 55–65 nm mode, and 38.9 percent for the 150–180 nm node (SMIC 2018, 7). In comparison, TSMC, which is considered a global leader in wafer fabrication, began 28 nm chip production in 2011 and 7 nm in June 2018. According to Ng, "SMIC and TSMC are separated by at least three

---

19. Interview: NG201807.

20. "Press Releases: SMIC Settles All Pending Lawsuits with TSMC: Anticipates No Disruption to Customers," Shanghai, November 10, 2009, https://www.smics.com /en/site/news_read/4334.

generations, or seven to ten years, of production technology."[21] Similarly, TSMC's 2017 revenues were US$32 billion, accounting for 55.9 percent of the global pure-play foundry market, while SMIC had revenues of US$3.1 billion, or 5.4 percent of the global market. TSMC's gross profit in the first quarter of 2018 was 50 percent (TSMC 2018, 5), while SMIC's was 26.5 percent (SMIC 2018, 1), a vast difference.

China accounted for 11 percent of the global pure-play foundry market in 2015 and 12 percent in 2016. With the gradual rise of fabless semiconductor companies in China, the estimate for 2017 is 13 percent, or US$7 billion. Within this share, TSMC makes up 46 percent of the China market, and SMIC, China's semiconductor leader, makes up only 21 percent.[22] In July 2018, AMD, the major American CPU company, confirmed that it was cooperating with TSMC in trial production of the first seven-nanometer Rome server processor and would use TSMC for the processor's mass production.[23] This indicates TSMC's global lead in such production, which helped AMD surpass Intel in its technology.[24]

SMIC has been in business for nearly twenty years, but it has still not been able to close its technological gap with TSMC. In the trade, this is typically attributed to limits in manufacturing experience, technology accumulation, and intellectual property rights as well as to cultural issues. Comparing the technical competence of SMIC and TSMC, we can see China's eagerness to overtake the technology of core nations. Can China replicate in the semiconductor industry its successful experience in telecommunications and high-speed railways? China gained technology for high-speed railways through cooperation with Japan and Germany, used its vast market to rapidly construct a railway network and

21. Interview: NG201806.

22. "Pure-Play Foundries Boosting Their Presence in China," IC Insights, October 5, 2017, http://www.icinsights.com/news/bulletins/PurePlay-Foundries-Boosting -Their-Presence-In-China/.

23. Tu Chih-hao, "Taiji yongduo chaowei 7 naimi dadan" (TSMC grabs big AMD 7 nm order), *Gongshang shibao* (Commercial Times), July 31, 2018, http://www .chinatimes.com/newspapers/20180731000229-260202.

24. Atkinson, "AMD de 7 naimi zhicheng chuliqi 2018 nian jiang liangchan, zhengshi chaoche Yingte'er" (AMD's 7 nm manufactured processor will be produced in 2018, officially surpassing Intel), *Caijing xinbao*, June 27, 2018, http://finance.technews.tw /2018/06/27/amd-7nm-chip/.

industry chain, and then began exporting the products of its railway industry. However, China's semiconductor industry is fundamentally weak. Can it be built up through a similar big push to overtake the competition? The answer to this question is not promising. In spite of investing in many fabrication plants for large size wafers and purchasing high-tech equipment to increase output, China is not guaranteed to achieve advanced manufacturing processes and high product quality, even by poaching talent from advanced countries. Lok commented: "The semiconductor industry needs technological depth, which is related to 'culture.' China's current manufacturing culture encourages products with short lead times, but the IC industry has long product cycles that require stability and security. Job hopping and poaching are unsuited to the characteristics of the IC industry."[25]

When it comes to culture in manufacturing behavior, habitual differences across countries are often a key issue. Sanitation requirements in the semiconductor industry are extremely high. Ng, who used to work in a semiconductor factory in Shanghai, told me: "Our boss once toured a semiconductor plant in Beijing, and with his own eyes he saw operators move equipment and parts in pushcarts and enter clean rooms without moving the items to pushcarts inside, but just keep on going, and all the dust and dirt sticking to the cartwheels was tracked into the clean room. In Taiwan, equipment has to be moved onto special pushcarts inside the clean room—they have to switch carts—but in China the operators, whether out of negligence or laziness, don't comply with this SOP [standard operating procedure] and take it [the carts] in with them."[26]

The Taiwanese semiconductor industry has consistently challenged China's method of poaching talent to obtain technology. In the Made in China 2025 blueprint, China has set gradually higher self-sufficiency targets in the semiconductor industry. For example, self-sufficiency in the domestic market is set at 40 percent for 2020 and 70 percent for 2025. But the difficulty in obtaining the relevant technology makes reaching those milestones doubtful.[27] Furthermore, the likelihood of China's

25. Interview: LM201805.

26. Interview: NG201806.

27. "Without Technology, China's 'MIC 2025' Results for ICs Likely to Fall Woefully Short of Its Goals," IC Insights, January 31, 2017. https://goo.gl/2bYsU6.

achieving technology transfer by poaching talent from Taiwan and other advanced countries is not high, because technology transfer involves intellectual property rights and many patent issues, and it will be difficult for China to avoid patent barriers. SMIC's compensation to TSMC for infringing the latter's intellectual property rights serves as a lesson. Liang Mong-song was also sued by TSMC for assisting Samsung. Now that Liang has joined SMIC, it remains to be seen how much of a difference he will make.

In 2017, Guangzhou's Huangpu District government and the Guangzhou Open Economic Zone Management Board cooperated with Richard Chang to form Guangzhou CanSemi Technology Inc., a twelve-inch wafer fabrication plant. Chang proposed a commune integrated device manufacturer (CIDM) model, which integrates chip design, end-user enterprise customers, and a wafer foundry with joint investment by all three parties, thus resolving the issues of financing and risk sharing.[28] This model, which originated with Tech Semiconductor Singapore Pte Ltd, is new to China. CanSemi is still in the planning and fund-raising stage (it held a ceremony to begin construction on the project at the end of 2017), but joint investment brings its own operational complications, and questions have been raised about whether the CIDM model is suitable for China. According to reports in the Chinese media, "after signing a contract with the Guangzhou side, there has been no further word [of CanSemi], and it is possible that the project has fallen through."[29]

Spurred by the ZTE Incident, public discussion about "chip shortage pain" surged in China. Not long after the incident, while Xi Jinping was inspecting a factory run by the Wuhan Fiberhome Technology Group, he emphasized "establishing self-reliance in core technology, key technology, and key national industries. . . . In the past when we were externally blocked, we reconstructed ourselves, tightened our belts and grit-

28. Huang Jia-qing, "'Zhongguo xinpian jiaofu,' Zhang Rujing huo jiang pojie Guangzhou 'que xin zhi tong'" ("The godfather of Chinese wafers," Richard Chang, may break through Guangzhou's "chip shortage pain"), *Jinyangwang*, November 4, 2017, https://baijiahao.baidu.com/s?id=1583007371456073038.

29. Jiweiwang, "Touzi 150 yi Zhang Rujing Xin'en qianyue Qingdao, Guangzhou xiangmu huoyi liuchan" (Richard Chang and SiEn's 15 billion contract for Qingdao and Guangzhou project may have been aborted), EEWorld, March 31, 2018, http://news.eeworld.com.cn/manufacture/article_2018033123861.html.

ted our teeth to create the 'two bombs and one satellite,' because we brought the advantages of the socialist system into play and concentrated our strength to accomplish great things."[30] While inspecting Wuhan's Xinxin Semiconductor Manufacturing Corp., he pointed to the need to implement the struggle objectives of the Two Centenaries:[31] the difficulties in some major core technologies have to be overcome through China's own efforts and home-grown R&D to make more rapid breakthroughs in chip technology.[32] Rumors have circulated in Taiwan's semiconductor industry that the mainland government has pushed BOE Technology, a Chinese leader in display panel production, to use mainland-produced products in at least 50 percent of its driver ICs, and handed down the directive: "Poor quality is of no consequence; use it first and then deal with it."[33]

The ZTE Incident accelerated the already relentless push in China's semiconductor industry. Based on the historical propensity of Chinese officials to "launch satellites,"[34] the current method of promoting the construction of wafer fabrication plants is packed with risk. The competition

30. Quoted in "Xi Jinping zongshuji hubei zhixing disantian" (Day Three of General Secretary Xi Jinping's Visit to Hubei), Xinhuawang, April 27, 2018, http://big5 .www.gov.cn/gate/big5/www.gov.cn/xinwen/2018-04/27/content_5286249.htm.

31. *Translator's Note:* The Two Centenaries are a set of goals advanced by Xi Jinping in 2012 as the basic foundation for achieving the Chinese dream. The name refers the 2021 centenary of the founding of the CCP, and one goal is to achieve a comfortably middle-class society with the doubling of 2010 per capita income levels. The name also refers to the 2049 centenary of the founding of the PRC, and another goal is to become a strong, democratic, civilized, harmonious, and modern socialist country.

32. Yun Di, "Xi Jinping: Xinpian dengtong xinzang, yao jiakuai xinpian jishu tupo!" (The chip is the heart, to speed up the chip technology breakthrough!), *Business-Focus*, April 30, 2018, https://reurl.cc/OpmıQ9.

33. "Lu jiasu bandaoti zizhi, chongji Taichang" (Mainland accelerates production of its own semiconductors in an assault on Taiwanese factories), *Jingji ribao*, June 19, 2018, reposted on the Regional Industry Integrated Development Project, Industrial Development Bureau, Ministry of Economic Affairs, https://www.siido.org.tw/News/Detail /8f8ce14f-abdf-4b9b-9472-5405de7feacd?ModuelID=N3.

34. During China's Great Leap Forward, various regions competed to report the highest grain yields and sent inflated figures to the upper-level governments. For example, local cadres in Henan reported yields of ten thousand catties per *mu*, a practice known as "launching satellites." The result of these inflated reports was the Great Famine. In 1957, the Soviet Union launched the world's first man-made satellite, Sputnik 1, a technological feat that shook the world and spurred China's plan to surpass the

to invest in and build plants invariably involves disregarding technological standards in favor of speeding construction and launching production. The costly equipment for the plants requires enormous investments. The machinery rapidly burns through money, with state-of-the-art lithography machines (using extreme ultraviolet lithography technology) costing around 120 million euros each. Based on the habitual rent-seeking behavior of Chinese officials and industries, I predict that purchasing such expensive machinery will leave considerable latitude for speculation and profiteering. Furthermore, driven by the collective "satellite launching" attitude, an approach of "whatever the leader says goes, regardless of the cost or quality" in the context of surpassing other countries in the semiconductor industry is extremely irrational. In a technology war with the West, it would be impossible to rapidly acquire the manufacturing culture needed in the semiconductor industry.

Guided by Made in China 2025, China is attempting to overtake the rest of the world in terms of advanced manufacturing technology and jump to the top of the GVC, using this model to propel sustained economic growth. Is this grand industrial upgrading strategy feasible? That remains the big question for now.

Author's Postscript

By 2019, the fanfare of Made in China 2025 had vanished from the public scene amid the heightened technology war. Many wafer fabrication factories planned or constructed during the Made in China 2025 campaign became failures, rent-seeking scandals, or scams, such as Nanjing Tacoma and Wuhan Hongxin mentioned above.

Over the years, China has strived for advancement in semiconductor manufacturing and has made substantial progress. For instance, SMIC, China's largest chipmaker, ranks in the top fifth with an estimated total revenue of US$5.08 billion or 4.9 percent of the global pure-play foundry market share in 2021. But overall, China's technology and ca-

---

United Kingdom and catch up with the United States. This is the source of the term "launching satellites."

pacity still lag far behind Intel (global leader in integrated device manufacturing), TSMC (taking 54.5 percent of the global pure-play foundry market), and Samsung (17.3 percent of global pure-play foundry market). China produced 15.9 percent of its US$143.4 billion IC market in 2020; it produced merely 10.2 percent in 2012 and it is forecast to increase to 19.4 percent in 2025. Yet, the pace falls short of its Made in China 2025 self-sufficiency goal of 70 percent (IC Insights 2021, 1).

A brief comparison between SMIC and TSMC can shed some light. Regarding technology, TSMC obtained 50 percent of its net revenue from 7 nm and 5 nm process nodes combined in 2021, while SMIC wholly relied on the mature process of 28 nm node or above. TSMC's 3 nm fabrication plant is on schedule for mass production in 2022. Apple, Intel, AMD, Qualcomm, MediaTek, and Broadcom will be customers of this state-of-the-art technology. TSMC reported net revenue of US$15.74 billion with a 52.7 percent gross margin in the fourth quarter of 2021 (TSMC 2022, 2); SMIC reported net revenue of US$1.58 billion with a 35 percent gross margin in the same period (SMIC 2022, 5). TSMC played a predominant role in China's semiconductor supply chain, more critical than Chinese-owned SMIC. TSMC's pure-play foundries' China sales increased from US$2.12 billion (taking 44 percent of China foundry market) in 2015 to 9.05 billion (61 percent of China foundry market) in 2020. By contrast, SMIC's pure-play foundries' China sales increased from US$ 1.08 (taking 22 percent of China's foundry market) to 2.45 billion (16 percent of China's foundry market). Consequently, China took 21 percent of TSMC's global sales, second only to the United States in 2020 (IC Insights 2017, 1; 2021, 2).

TSMC was crucial for Huawei's mobile phone sector. Hit by the US sanctions, HiSilicon, the IC design arm of Huawei, could not place its advanced-chip orders with TSMC for production. As a result, the Chinese market dropped to about 15 percent of TSMC's global sales. Still, it didn't affect its overall strong growth because, as its former chief financial officer put it, "We're everybody's foundry" (quoted in Chen Liangrong 2019); the company has been nimble at adapting to geopolitical and GSC shifts.

Under pressure from the United States, TSMC announced the establishment of an advanced chip fabrication plant in Arizona in 2020. In the previous year, its founder Morris Chang said, "In peacetime, TSMC just quietly plays its part in the supply chain. But when the world gets restless, which is now, TSMC becomes a battleground for geo-strategists" (quoted in Lin Yi-ju 2019). Chang accurately diagnosed a problem facing TSMC. But the battleground defined as such applies not only to TSMC, but to the entirety of Taishang, Taiwan, China, and the whole world.

In December 2020, SMIC and its related companies were added to the US entity list "as a result of China's military-civil fusion (MCF) doctrine and evidence of activities between SMIC and entities of concern in the Chinese military industrial complex" (Department of Commerce Bureau of Industry and Security 2020, 83416). The US sanctions have created further challenges to China's semiconductor upgrading plans.

Pitfalls and Challenges

It has been forty years since China's return to capitalism, and the results have attracted the full attention of the world. Globalization has remolded China's economy, and China has introduced new factors to the world's political economy. Many people worry about China's changing the rules of the globalization game, but many others question China's ability and will to do so. In this conclusion, I respond to three questions: Will China fall into the pitfalls of development? Why is the United States resisting China's Made in China 2025 industrial upgrading plan? And what theoretical challenges are posed by China's return to the capitalist world?

1. The Pitfalls of China's Development

After World War II, East Asian countries experienced forty years of development during which Japan and the Four Little Dragons underwent a relatively smooth upgrading of their industrial structure, greatly enhanced social welfare, and saw growth in the middle class and reductions in social disparities. Then China joined the ranks of East Asian developmental states and also experienced a period of rapid growth. Over the past forty years, its gross national income has increased rapidly, and its economy has become the second largest in the world. However, the enormous surplus extracted from migrant workers in the labor-intensive industrialization model has been divided between the state and capital, and this model of surplus distribution and capital accumulation has created extreme inequality in the distribution of gross national income, as well as resulting in serious damage to the environment, highly leveraged financial operations, and serious asset bubbles. Although long-fermenting socioeconomic contradictions have been suppressed and concealed by the regime, they frequently erupt in social discontent. Can China sustain its development momentum and avoid the pitfall of dramatically slowing growth? An even more fundamental question is can China implement systemic reforms that will surmount the limitations of the existing development model?

In this conclusion, I first look back at this book's key findings. The Guangdong model was the starting point for China's rejoining the capitalist world. The labor-intensive export industrialization model suppressed workers' wages and labor costs, helping China obtain large amounts of foreign exchange and economic surplus—with the state and capital (including foreign-owned companies, state-owned capital, and private companies) being the greatest beneficiaries. China's ruling elites, skilled at linking the local and the global, have captured rich profits on the links of the GVC. Part of the enormous economic surplus extracted by the state sector has entered the pockets of cadres and officials (in the form of dividends, bribes, rent, etc.), while another portion has funded national construction. This development model established the foundation for China's economic rise. We should not therefore underestimate the enormous contribution of labor-intensive industries during the period from the 1980s until 2008. Especially in the 1990s, much of the funding for China's development still came from overseas Chinese capital, of which Taiwanese investment and Taishang were major sources. In the Guangdong model (and the China model), the tools the state used to suppress the labor cost of migrant workers were differential citizenship and the dual labor market. Suppressing the labor costs of migrant workers and stifling consumption by the wider public were the distinguishing features of China's exploitation and accumulation model and defined the China model. Even today, the elements and effects of the Guangdong model have left their mark on the trajectory of China's overall development.

Paradoxically, the development achievements of China's previous stage created a pitfall for the next stage. China's development model of the past forty years has been for the state to create a migrant worker class and then extract massive surplus through migrant workers to achieve high accumulation, thus facilitating the rent-seeking developmental state. In the previous phase, this institutional structure helped China attain rapid growth and create large-scale infrastructure. However, it also brought about a distorted distribution of national income and is the fundamental reason for persistent socioeconomic inequity. In 2016, China's per capita GDP was US$8,123, equivalent to purchasing power parity of US$15,529.[1] According to World Bank data, from 1978 to 2016, China's real per capita GDP grew at an average rate of 8.6 percent. China's economy went into a downslide after the 2008 global financial crisis, and although it stabilized, the growth rate began easing in 2012: from 2012 to 2016 it was 6.8 percent.[2] China's sustained growth in the long term is full of uncertainties—for example, whether it can enhance productivity and innovation and establish an open competitive market and educational environment, a society based on the rule of law, and property rights protections. Collectively, these tough problems, along with the abovementioned socioeconomic contradictions, constitute a major challenge. After China passed through its first stage of rapid growth, the high-growth model of the labor-intensive processing trade was gone forever, and China has encountered bottlenecks in developing self-sufficient technology and domestic markets. As a result, the growth momentum has eased, and if the growth rate continues to slide, China may well descend into developmental slowdown or stagnation.

Many scholars and policy advisors point out the need for China's economy to undergo restructuring, in particular changing its accumulation model, substantially enhancing wages and social welfare, granting the broader population more purchasing power, and developing the domestic market. The country's rebalancing policy inevitably involves reorganizing local growth alliances and has had a serious effect on vested interest groups. Furthermore, China needs to carry out political reforms and introduce a system that is more accountable to the public and expands the Chinese people's political participation rights. However, since

---

1. World Bank, "GDP Per Capita Growth (Annual %)—China," accessed June 28, 2019, https://data.worldbank.org/indicator/NY.GDP.PCAP.KD.ZG?locations=CN.
2. Calculated from World Bank, "GDP Per Capita Growth (Annual %)—China."

Xi Jinping came to power in 2012, he has employed a model of anticorruption campaigns and greater centralization of political power, using enhanced party-state discipline to rectify the behavior of officials while skirting systemic issues. The Chinese government clearly has no intention of changing the control and resource allocation methods of the party-state apparatus, and its political policies have not mitigated the abovementioned socioeconomic contradictions. Not only has there not been political liberalization, but the government has harshly repressed social resistance forces, handing down a "seven unmentionables" policy[3] and carrying out high-tech surveillance in what a German scholar has referred to as "digital Leninism."[4] This represents a decrease in the legitimacy of the Chinese Communist regime, which uses ever more exacting methods to control society. This suffocating political system, lacking freedom of thought and space for innovation, is antithetical to the development of a market economy. If the current state-capitalism pattern continues to emphasize state investment in infrastructure, the massive state-run capital monopolies will become even more entrenched, while privately owned capital will need to seek out alliances and protection from state capital or red second-generation capital, and it will have to join the rent-seeking game in the domestic market. Genuine private capital will have difficulty surviving, let alone thriving, under this structure. These trends will discourage sustained growth and make more equitable distribution of income even more difficult.

A key factor in the past accelerated growth stage and the feasibility of the rent-seeking developmental state was its extroversion, including the close links between the processing export sector and world markets and the constraining effect of international competition on rent-seeking behavior. At that stage, the embeddedness of global capitalism in the local polity brought about positive institutional diffusion. But with the Xi Jinping regime's intensified promotion of deepening import substitution

3. *Translator's Note:* The "seven unmentionables" are universal values, freedom of the press, civil society, citizens' rights, the party's historical errors, the capitalist elite, and judicial independence.

4. Andrew Browne, "China Uses 'Digital Leninism' to Manage Economy and Monitor Citizens," *The Wall Street Journal*, https://www.wsj.com/articles/xi-jinping-leads-china-into-big-data-dictatorship-1508237820. Oct. 17, 2017.

industrialization and the party-state capital group's continued expansion, the phenomenon of the state sector advancing and the private sector retreating has become more pronounced, leading to ever intensifying social controls and the construction of a closed political and economic apparatus. This direction runs counter to the past development model. If it continues, the rent-seeking developmental state will encounter obstacles that are even harder to surmount than those faced in the past ten years, and it will face extinction. The institutional rent seeking that once coexisted with development will also rapidly devolve into financial plundering.

In March 2018, the National People's Congress amended China's constitution by eliminating term limits for the state president, which would give Xi Jinping supreme power as leader for life. Lifetime tenure for the state leader postpones power succession. In the short term it mitigates competition for succession among the party elite and ostensibly allows the Xi regime to focus on the issues it considers most pressing. In the long term, however, it would destroy the two-term succession rule of the previous twenty years, and an even more fundamental problem is that while the lifetime tenure system freezes time pressures on political decision making, it also delays China's opportunity to carry out a rebalancing of the economic structure. If China's economic growth continues to slow, reducing the financial revenues that the state extracts, this will intensify infighting among the rent-seeking forces within the ruling clique and will put pressure on the state's financial capacity to preserve stability. If these problems continue to ferment and are not resolved, they are certain to erupt in a post-Xi succession struggle and become a political hurdle that will be difficult for China to surmount. But who can accurately predict when the post-Xi moment will arrive?

2. The United States Challenges Made in China 2025

Since China's economic rise, there have been two contrasting readings of the possible effects on the American-dominated world order. One viewpoint holds that given China's vested interest in neoliberal globalization and its symbiotic relationship with the United States, it has neither the motivation nor the ability to challenge US power (Johnston 2003; Ho-fung Hung 2016). The other viewpoint holds that China is rapidly narrowing its power gap with the United States and has a strong motivation to challenge the American-dominated world order. According to this viewpoint, China has already become a revisionist power, and the Western camp must guard against a hegemonic shift. China and the United States have fallen into the so-called Thucydides trap, and if the situation is not handled well, a war of the hegemons will be hard to avoid (Friedberg 2011; Mearsheimer 2014; Allison 2017; Shambaugh 2018).

These competing viewpoints have spread beyond the American academic community and are debated in the wider public sphere because the future existence of American hegemony and China's international standing are at stake. In the debate about whether or not China is changing the rules of the global game, the focus is on China's ability and will. The typical belief is that China's national strength is not yet sufficient to challenge American hegemony, but the extreme rapidity of China's rise and America's corresponding decline has empowered China to strive for supremacy. As to China's desire and motivation, in Graham Allison's view, the fundamental problem is the antagonistic tension between rising and ruling powers. Fear and interests dominate the behavior of the powerful: "In particular, ruling powers' fears often fuel misperceptions and exaggerate dangers, as rising powers' self-confidence stimulates unrealistic expectations about what is possible and encourages risk-taking" (Allison 2017, 39). Allison's comment essentially depicts the psychological interaction of antagonists as based on structural tensions. The Chinese government understands this rationale, as Xi Jinping made clear in remarks in Seattle in 2015: "There is no such thing as the so-called Thucydides trap in the world. But should major countries time and again make the mistakes of strategic miscalculation, they might create such traps for themselves."[5] Xi intended to convince the United States that China hoped to cooperate and was maintaining a nonconfrontational attitude.

---

5. "Full text of Xi's Speech on China-US Relations in Seattle," China.org.cn, September 24, 2015, http://www.china.org.cn/xivisitus2015/2015-09/24/content_36666620 .htm.

One school of international relations theory emphasizes the importance of perception. In the history of foreign affairs, erroneous perceptions often occur, leading to strategic misjudgment or unintended consequences (Jervis 1976). Whether or not China will challenge or is challenging American hegemony is not only an objective assessment of China's capacity and voluntary motives. Rather, it also involves a subjective cognitive orientation: the current strategic interaction between the United States and China is closely related to their assessments and perceptions of each other's strategic intentions. The current situation is that the majority of the American political and economic elite believes that China wants to change the existing global power structure. As a result, America's strategic assessment of China has targeted China's grand plan of industrial upgrading.

Over the past ten years or so, China's central and local governments have been forcefully promoting industrial upgrading. To do so, China's policy makers clearly intend to reinforce core political leadership, break free of the existing economic base, and facilitate industrial leapfrogging through the country's capabilities as a powerful state. The grand plan of showcasing innovative drive and transformative upgrading through the red supply chain, Big Fund, and Made in China 2025 is a product of this mind-set.

China's industrial upgrading plan does not necessarily threaten the technological hegemony of core Western countries, or at least it is unlikely to do so in the short term. However, the development of China's domestic situation and, even more critically, China's pattern of behavior toward the outside world is causing an increasing number of Western political and economic elites to believe that China plans to challenge the existing global rules of the game and threaten the West's technological hegemony. This perception is the result of several simultaneous trends. First, China's expansionism in the geopolitical sphere, from the East China Sea and the Taiwan Strait to the South China Sea, is seen as changing the existing order. Likewise, in the geoeconomic sphere, China's growing influence in Africa and Latin America over the past ten years or so has been criticized for colonialist intentions. China's recent Belt and Road Initiative for exporting its surplus infrastructural capacity has given it a strategic advantage in South and Southeast Asia. For example, Sri

Lanka recently turned over its southern port of Hambantota to China on a ninety-nine-year lease as repayment of a debt.

Second, China's exercise of sharp power around the globe is drawing scrutiny (Cardenal et al. 2017). For example, Confucius Institutes used to be considered a display of China's soft power, but today's conceptual framework regards them as an important example of sharp power: the institutes have turned from sources of benign cultural and academic exchange into cultural infiltration with malevolent intent.[6] Over the past year or two, Australia discovered that Beijing was using "local collaborators"[7] in the overseas Chinese community to carry out political fund-raising to interfere in domestic politics and manipulate the news media. Similar instances have occurred in New Zealand. Over the past ten years, an increasing amount of academic research has pointed to China's export of authoritarianism to other parts of the world (Diamond, Plattner, and Walker 2016). The Australian incident sounded a warning bell in the Western world that nightmares of China's export of authoritarianism were coming true (Garnaut 2018). The greatest worry of Western countries is sharp power's erosion of democracy. Criticism of China's sharp power shows a transformation in the way Western countries view China. Placing this transformation in a larger perspective, it reflects an upsurge in Western countries' awareness of the global effect of China's rise, triggering a wariness of China's quest for hegemony and calls to adopt new policies of shielding or containing China.

Third, China has sparked a high degree of concern in Western countries because of its highly centralized political power, suppression of civil society, digital surveillance of its citizens, persistent repression of Tibet and Xinjiang, assault on Hong Kong's democracy movement, and interference in Taiwan's elections. Xi Jinping's elimination of term limits for

6. From the outset, Confucius Institutes (and Confucius classrooms) were important tools for China to extend its ideological apparatus abroad. Their mission was in fact very clear, but Western countries initially did not regard them with suspicion and considered them organizations for disseminating Chinese language classes and Chinese culture. By the time the West discovered that the institutes were carrying out information control and ideological propaganda, these organizations had already penetrated universities and communities all over the world, and many leading Western universities had already signed cooperation agreements with them.

7. Regarding the concept of "local collaborators," see Wu Jieh-min 2016 and 2017b.

the Chinese president has only confirmed misgivings that China's Communist regime is returning to totalitarianism.

Fourth, in this political context, China's vigorous promotion of Made in China 2025, its massive international corporate buying spree, and constant reports in Western media about intellectual property violations by Chinese companies have raised even greater misgivings in Western countries.[8] For example, the Chinese manufacturer Midea Group in 2016 merged with the German industrial robotics manufacturer KUKA Robotics. Soon afterward, Fujian's Grand Chip Investment Fund was reported to be acquiring the German chip equipment maker Aixtron, but the German authorities refused to allow the acquisition.[9] In 2017, a report commissioned by the US-China Economic and Security Review Commission warned of the vulnerability of the US government's purchases of information and communications products that relied on Chinese supply chains.[10] China has always traded markets for technology, requiring foreign investors to use the joint-venture model and transfer technology. A report by the Office of the United States Trade Representative in March 2018 particularly targeted technology transfer by foreign investors and the ownership structure for investing in China,[11] specifically criticizing controls on the percentage of ownership, the use of administrative discretion, informal administrative directives, and other conditions that China imposes on foreign investors in its technology transfer

---

8. President Donald Trump explicitly accused China of stealing large amounts of intellectual property from American companies. See Donald Trump, "National Security Strategy of the United States of America," White House, December 2017, 21, https://trumpwhitehouse.archives.gov/wp-content/uploads/2017/12/NSS-Final-12-18 -2017-0905.pdf.

9. Paul Mozur, "Germany Withdraws Approval for Chinese Takeover of Aixtron," *New York Times*, October 24, 2016, https://www.nytimes.com/2016/10/25/business /dealbook/germany-china-technology-takeover.html.

10. Tara Beeny, "Supply Chain Vulnerabilities from China in U.S. Federal Information and Communications Technology," U.S.-China Economic and Security Review Commission, April 2018, https://www.uscc.gov/sites/default/files/Research/Interos _Supply%20Chain%20Vulnerabilities%20from%20China%20in%20U.S.%20Federal %20ICT_final.pdf.

11. Office of the United States Trade Representative, "Findings of the Investigation into China's Acts, Policies, and Practices Related to Technology Transfer, Intellectual Property, and Innovation under Section 301 of the Trade Act of 1974," March 22, 2018, https://www.hsdl.org/?view&did=809992.

system.[12] In the same month, the Trump administration rejected a buy-out of Qualcomm by Broadcom on security concerns, the main worry being potential influence by Huawei.[13] In 2012, an investigative report by the US House of Representatives' Permanent Select Committee on Intelligence had accused Huawei and ZTE of constituting a threat to American national security because both companies were believed to be closely associated with the Chinese government (Rogers and Ruppersberger 2012).

In spring 2018, the United States and China embarked on a trade war. The United States threatened to impose tariffs on Chinese imports to force China to address its unfair trading practices and theft of American intellectual property. In April, the US Department of Commerce announced that it was fining ZTE for illegally shipping US-origin items to Iran, and it banned American companies from selling key components to ZTE. This measure effectively prevented ZTE from obtaining IC chips from Qualcomm. The technology embargo on ZTE was generally considered the first salvo in America's technology war with China, imperiling China's development of 5G communication networks. It was just the tip of the iceberg. Would this battle affect Huawei, which was even more important to China's technology development strategy, as well as China's entire industrial chain?[14] Lok observed: "If ZTE is a little fox, Huawei is a big bad wolf. If the United States isn't well prepared, it won't have

12. According to Chinese regulations, in specific industries such as automotive manufacturing and value-added telecommunications services, foreign investors have to use the joint-venture method, and they cannot hold more than 50 percent of the shares in a given company; in the banking industry, the maximum cannot exceed 20 percent or 25 percent. See Office of the United States Trade Representative, Findings of the Investigation into China's Acts, Policies, and Practices Related to Technology Transfer, Intellectual Property, and Innovation under Section 301 of the Trade Act of 1974."

13. Michael Leiter, Ivan Schlager, and Donald Vieira, "Broadcom's Blocked Acquisition of Qualcomm," Harvard Law School Forum on Corporate Governance, April 3, 2018, https://corpgov.law.harvard.edu/2018/04/03/broadcoms-blocked-acquisition-of-qualcomm/.

14. At the same time, the US Department of Commerce began investigating Huawei. In June 2018, ZTE and the department reached an agreement under which ZTE would pay a large fine. In early July the department partially lifted the sanctions on ZTE, but the US Congress still relentlessly pursued the case. ZTE spent an enormous amount of money lobbying members of Congress, and in early August the Senate passed a bill that allowed ZTE to escape tough penalties. See Ana Swanson and Ken-

an easy time dealing with Huawei. Technology embargos will seriously effect China's telecommunications industry, but it has been building strength over the years and may be stronger than some media believe. Even if there's a negative effect, it won't be a death blow."[15] Furthermore, Huawei has never been able to enter the US market, and the enormous amounts of money it has spent on political lobbying has not eased the US government's suspicions of Huawei's relationship with the Chinese government and military. In April 2018, soon after the United States declared sanctions on ZTE, Huawei announced that it was laying off five American lobbyists in Washington, which suggested that Huawei had given up on capturing the US market for the time being.[16]

In June 2018, the US government announced that it was imposing tariffs on trade with China totaling hundreds of billions of dollars, and China declared that it would retaliate. By putting pressure on the Chinese government to change its economic behavior, the US government was using a trade war to fight a technology war and defend property rights. The main US concerns were the Chinese side's infringement on the intellectual property rights of US businesses, limits on the ownership shares of foreign investors, and stipulations on self-sufficiency. At the end of June, China announced a new version of its Foreign Investment Admission Negative List, but its commitments to compromise were limited.[17]

---

neth P. Vogel, "Faced with Crippling Sanctions, ZTE Loaded Up on Lobbyists," *New York Times*, August 1, 2018, https://goo.gl/8vKn8d.

15. Interview: LM201804.

16. Raymond Zhong and Paul Mozur, "Huawei, Failing to Crack U.S. Market, Signals a Change in Tactics," *New York Times*, April 17, 2018. https://www.nytimes.com/2018/04/17/technology/china-huawei-washington.html.

17. During negotiations between the two sides, the Chinese government promised to further open its financial markets and agreed that by May 2018 it would decide on new regulations to open the finance industry, allow foreign financial groups to hold more than half of the shares in Chinese banks, and reduce tariffs on imported American cars, among other matters. At the end of June, China promised that in 2020 limitations on shareholdings by foreign firms in the manufacturing of commercial vehicles would be eliminated. It also promised that limitations on foreign shareholdings in passenger car manufacturing, as well as limitations on the same foreign company establishing joint ventures in China to produce two or fewer of the same type of whole car products, would be eliminated in 2022. See National Development and Reform Commission, "Waishang touzi zhunru tebie guanli cuoshi (fumian qingdan) (2018 nian ban)" (Special management measures for investment access of foreign firms [negative

On July 6, the Sino-US trade war was officially launched. In the first round, the tariff lists announced by both sides and the scope of trade covered was quite small, but in September the United States upped the ante, and the Chinese side followed suit, raising concerns that the escalating trade war might seriously affect the GSC.

News of the heavy-handed US tactics against Huawei began circulating soon after that. On December 1, 2018, Huawei's deputy chairman of the board, Meng Wanzhou (the daughter of Huawei's founder and CEO, Ren Zhengfei), was arrested by the Canadian authorities, on the request of the United States, while changing planes in Vancouver. The grounds for her arrest were violating US export controls by selling sensitive technology to Iran and using false accounting to cover it up. The incident created a furor throughout China, triggering campaigns in support of Huawei and denunciations of the United States and its allies, while the Chinese government retaliated by arresting two Canadians. A *Global Times* online editorial titled "Let Countries That Abuse Their Power to Harm China's Interests Pay the Price" is indicative of the collective indignation accompanying setbacks to realizing the ambition to restore the Chinese empire.[18] The United States has nevertheless continued to lobby allied countries to boycott Huawei's 5G networking equipment, and it announced formal charges against Meng on January 28, 2019. The incident has posed an enormous challenge to Huawei's creating a global 5G network and is on the front line of the American-led counterattack against China in the technology war.[19]

---

account] [2018 version]), June 28, 2018, https://www.ndrc.gov.cn/xxgk/zcfb/fzggwl/201806/W020190905495140644002.pdf.

18. "Sheping: rang zhangshi qinhai zhongguo liyi de guojia fuchu daijia" (Editorial: Let countries that abuse their power to harm China's interests pay the price), Global Times Online, December 16, 2018, https://opinion.huanqiu.com/article/9CaKrnKfZqc.

19. AUTHOR'S POSTSCRIPT: In 2019, Huawei and its numerous subsidiaries were added to the US government's entity list and the company has been losing its 5G market in western countries under the US sanctions. In September 2021, Meng Wanzhou was released by Canada after she reached an agreement with US prosecutors, and two Canadians being held in Chinese jails were freed immediately and flew back home. See Karen Freifeld, Kenneth Li, Moira Warburton, and David Ljunggren, "Huawei CFO Leaves Canada after U.S. Agreement on Fraud Charges, Detained Canadians Head Home," Reuters, September 24, 2021, https://www.reuters.com/technology/huawei-cfo-meng-appear-court-expected-reach-agreement-with-us-source-2021-09-24/.

The United States set its sights on Made in China 2025 with accusa-tions of technology theft, intending to thwart China's leapfrogging tech-nological modernization strategy, but China refused to compromise on its industrial upgrading. The method of the past Guangdong development model was to climb the GVC following conventional procedures. Local governments and foreign investors collectively formed growth alliances, and the central government was an invisible member of those alliances (see figure 1.4). Now, according to the guidance framework of Made in China 2025, the central government was forcibly intervening in government-business relations. State-owned enterprises were granted a key role that substantially changed the original alliance relationship, and party-state capital was given a more prominent role in an attempt to rap-idly obtain advanced manufacturing technology and leap to the top of the GVC.

According to this book's analytical framework of G-D-L, Made in China 2025 switches China's development focus from a locally embed-ded governance playing field (emphasizing the interaction between the local polity and domestic industrial clusters) to a hegemonic control and competition playing field (emphasizing the competitive relationship be-tween the local polity and global capital). On the topics of industrial up-grading and nurturing indigenous supply chains, Made in China 2025 has come into even greater conflict with global capital hegemons (see fig-ure 1.2). The reason is that this new development strategy seeks to cast off the logic of the previous stage of following along with the GVC to create the factory of the world, and it no longer follows conventional pro-cedures to climb up the GVC. Instead, it attempts to circumvent the value chains dominated by Western countries (in an approach called pass-ing on the curve) by constructing a self-controlled supply chain ecology and allowing the state to forcibly distribute the surplus in this new sys-tem and seize a greater amount of value. The Chinese government has repeatedly emphasized that the amount of chips imported each year must be greater than the amount of petroleum imported. China is anxious to leap from its semiperipheral status in the world system to core status. This is what really terrifies core Western countries about the China model. Na-tional desires and aspirations are not necessarily the same as national capacity and development results, but the way that Western nations regard China's grand development plan has caused the narrative of

Western nations' containment of China to take on the quality of a self-fulfilling prophecy.[20]

The Chinese side's efforts to establish indigenous industrial chains sometimes quickly come up against competition from lead firms in the GVC, as in the 5G telecommunications sector. Moreover, China has invested a great deal of research and human resources to gradually achieve results in the domain of artificial intelligence, where military applications have raised concern (Kania 2017). However, in many other domains (such as the semiconductor industry), China continues to tag along in the GVC. Some of the objectives of Made in China 2025 are clearly hard to achieve, while achieving others will still not bring China up to Western technological levels. Furthermore, the current resistance by and alarm from the United States and other Western countries has made this grand plan's vision even more difficult to attain. Taking the semiconductor industry as an example, the Big Fund has sparked the construction of wafer plants all over China, but without breakthroughs in technology and quality yield ratios, they may easily become "satellite launching" competitions that replicate the disastrous overcapacity in iron and steel, solar panels, and liquid crystal panels.

In China's development over the past four decades, we can see the formation, transformation, and predicaments of the rent-seeking developmental state. China's enhanced national capacity and determination to carry out its policy objectives are evident. The rent-seeking developmental state and the forces of global capital encounter each other in this process both in cooperation and in antagonism. Made in China 2025 is extremely ambitious, but China's domestic technological innovation is not yet mature, and its excessively aggressive behavior toward the outside world has brought it up against boycotting by Western countries. At present, it seems unlikely that this grand plan will allow China to break through the technological hegemony of core countries.

---

20. Curiously, under the pressure of the US-China trade war, China appears to be silencing itself, and there are rumors that the government has ordered the media not to mention Made in China 2025. See Raymond Zhong and Li Yuan, "As Trade Fight Looms, China Turns Censors on Its Own Policies," *New York Times*, June 26, 2018, https://www.nytimes.com/2018/06/26/business/china-trade-censorship.html.

Finally, observing China's current industrial upgrading behavior as that of a rent-seeking developmental state, this book finds that in that state's interaction with foreign investment, it is adept at cutting into the foreign investment value chain governance structure and extracting value (economic surplus). In other words, the state plays a prominent role in capturing value. But does this kind of state have the capacity to catch up in industrial upgrading while competing with foreign capital? This is the problem that is testing China's state capacity.

3. China and Globalization Theory

In 1989, when the Berlin Wall fell, Francis Fukuyama wrote:

> What we may be witnessing is not just the end of the Cold War, or the passing of a particular period of postwar history, but the end of history as such: that is, the end point of mankind's ideological evolution and the universalization of Western liberal democracy as the final form of human government. This is not to say that there will no longer be events to fill the pages of *Foreign Affairs'* yearly summaries of international relations, for the victory of liberalism has occurred primarily in the realm of ideas or consciousness and is as yet incomplete in the real or material world. But there are powerful reasons for believing that it is the ideal that will govern the material world *in the long run*. (Fukuyama 1989, 4)

The trends in China and the world at that time led Maoism to lose its revolutionary charisma: "What is important about China from the standpoint of world history is not the present state of the reform or even its future prospects. The central issue is the fact that the People's Republic of China can no longer act as a beacon for illiberal forces around the world, whether they be guerrillas in some Asian jungle or middle class students in Paris. Maoism, rather than being the pattern for Asia's future, became an anachronism, and it was the mainland Chinese who in fact were decisively influenced by the prosperity and dynamism of their overseas co-ethnics—the ironic ultimate victory of Taiwan" (Fukuyama 1989, 12). In Fukuyama's view of world history, Taiwan represented the new territory in the liberal democracy camp, pointing the way for China. In

1991, the Soviet Union disintegrated and the Cold War ended. At that time, many people believed that liberalism had thoroughly dismantled communism, and that liberal democracy and market capitalism had won the ultimate victory. A full stop had been placed at the end of ideological disputes between the left and the right, and history had ended: The ideological allure of Marxism-Leninism as a rival of liberal democracy had withered away (Fukuyama 1992).

However, twenty years later, Russia's electoral authoritarian system was firmly entrenched, and China's party-state capitalism was developing on a massive scale under the name of socialism with Chinese characteristics, compelling Western theoreticians to reexamine the proposition that human society had evolved toward liberal democracy. The retreat of democracy and the expansion of authoritarianism was occurring on a global scale, the democratic governance of Western countries was showing signs of exhaustion or crisis, and criticism of neoliberalism by various camps was becoming increasingly strident. Given the speed and efficiency of China's authoritarian development, many people in the Western camp were beginning to regard the China model with envy or infatuation. However, China's recent outward expansionism has alerted an increasing number of Western countries to the China threat. Whether the China model is viewed with approval (by what is called the Beijing consensus) or as a warning (by the Washington consensus), it is being held up as an alternative or challenge to market capitalism, respectively, which shows that "end of history" theory has lost currency in the market of political thought. Yet in the 1990s, there was still considerable optimism about the victory of liberal democracy and market capitalism, and this optimism influenced judgments of China's prospects. We can now see that China did in fact return to the capitalist world, but with a Chinese-style capitalism created on its own terms. In other words, China took part in globalization without following the theoretical script of the West. This time, the attraction or threat that China presented to the world was not a reversion to Marxism-Leninism but rather authoritarian development as a rival of liberal democracy.

At the beginning of the 1970s, neoliberal globalization emerged on the world stage. Neoliberalism is a version of economic liberalism. In addition, the neoliberal institutionalism that became all the rage from the 1980s to the 1990s was the application of liberal democratic theory to the international relations sphere. According to neoliberal institutionalism, when two parties engage in trade, their commercial exchanges incline both parties toward harmony and peace. This "doux commerce thesis" of political philosophy was proposed by Montesquieu, Kant, and other pioneers of modern democratic theory, and it was further refined and elaborated on by Albert Hirschman (1977): Two parties engaged in trade will constrain (harmful) passion for the sake of self-interest and develop peaceful, honest, and nonviolent relations. According to this theoretical standpoint, in bilateral relations between modern countries, economically advanced and politically democratic countries reinforce the value of peace and maintain peaceful and democratic coexistence. In addition, an economically advanced and politically democratic country exports the value of liberal democracy to an economically developing and politically authoritarian country, gradually changing the other side's authoritarian tendencies in a process known as peaceful evolution and achieving the democratization of that country through nonviolent and noncoercive means (using so-called soft power).

Relations between the West and China were considerably strained for a time following the violent Tiananmen crackdown in 1989. In 1992, China launched a new round of opening, and foreign capital (including Taiwanese capital) began pouring in, accelerating and promoting export-oriented growth. At this stage, the US Congress instituted an annual vetting process to grant China most favored nation status, which spurred the sale of cheap Chinese goods in the American market. At the end of the 1990s, during the administration of President Bill Clinton, debate commenced over whether or not to support China's accession to the WTO (which would give it permanent status as a most favored nation). Setting aside the calculation of economic interests, the main theoretical underpinning was based on the engagement policy derived from the doux commerce thesis: one side recommended carrying out constructive engagement with China to keep it from being isolated, in the hope of gradually softening the oppressiveness of its regime and steering it toward liberalization. Following China's economic rise, however, the outcome of its globalization was dramatically different from that anticipated by Western neoliberal institutionalists. Not only did China not move toward liberalization, but it consolidated its new form of authoritarianism.

The strategic trust of the United States in China had dramatically decreased by the end of President Barack Obama's term of office (2009–16). The "National Security Strategy of the United States of America" that

President Trump issued at the end of 2017 stated that the assumption that engagement with rivals "would turn them into benign actors and trustworthy partners" had been proven wrong.[21] In 2018, Kurt Campbell, formerly assistant secretary of state for East Asian and Pacific affairs, coauthored an essay looking back at the past half-century of US contact with China, which included this passage: "Greater commercial interaction with China was supposed to bring gradual but steady liberalization of the Chinese economy. . . . [This argument] drove U.S. decisions to grant China most-favored-nation trading status in the 1990s, to support its accession to the WTO in 2001, to establish a high-level economic dialogue in 2006, and to negotiate a bilateral investment treaty under U.S. President Barack Obama" (Campbell and Ratner 2018, 62). Twenty years later, the United States and other Western countries evidently suddenly discovered that their engagement policy was badly miscalculated: by joining the WTO, China has been able to participate in the world economy at an even deeper level, has captured enormous foreign exchange reserves, and has accumulated state capital and obtained Western technology. The enormous economic resources controlled by China's state apparatus have consolidated a new form of party-state capitalism. Close trade relations with the West have not made China freer and more democratic. Rather, its economic rise has enabled China to consolidate its authoritarian rule and use advanced technology to become a surveillance state. China used the rule book of Western neoliberal institutionalism but now shows dissatisfaction with those rules. The democratization that Western countries envisioned for China has become a remote prospect, replaced with worries about China's splitting and manipulation of Western democratic society. Containment of and resistance to China have nearly become the main goals of American policy toward that country.

Although the leapfrogging industrial upgrading planned in Made in China 2025 may not be achieved as hoped in the face of Western resistance, that doesn't mean that China's economy is doomed to fail. In fact, even if China has no intention of challenging the global hegemony of the United States or cannot do so, as long as China's government doesn't collapse and its social control doesn't disintegrate, Beijing will continue its

21. Trump, "National Security Strategy of the United States of America," 3.

geopolitical expansion into neighboring countries through its growing regional strength. The result of China's integration with the industrial and trade structure of the region enables China to exert its political influence on neighboring countries and display its strength as a geopolitical power (Blackwill and Harris 2016; Norris 2016; Wu Jieh-min 2016 and 2018). This is not only the reason why many neighboring countries have become wary of China, but it is also the root cause of John Mearsheimer's nightmare for Taiwan (2014).

This book used Taishang as the starting point to tell the story of the Guangdong model and China's rise. Starting from the global-local links that are the core concern of this book, it analyzed the historical interaction between globalization and China's modern capitalistic development, expanding our understanding of the development of world capitalism and the developmentalist state. I end the book by summarizing several extended theoretical issues to highlight the challenge that China's development experience and development model pose to theoretical innovation.

The first issue is globalization and sovereign states. The case of China challenges the theory of retreat from nation-state sovereignty. Globalization channeled China's return to the capitalist world and led China to abide by the rules of the game of global trade to a certain extent, with the effect of diffusing the rules into China's domestic institutional system. Even so, we must not overlook the fact that China has also to a certain degree shown the will and ability to change the rules, even if its changes remain marginal and have not overturned existing US hegemony. The rise of China requires reexamining the thesis that transnational companies cause a decline in nation-state sovereignty (Vernon 1971; Strange 1996; Holton 1998; Sklair 2001). In particular, state agency—including national scope, state volition, and state capacity—has been excessively underestimated as a key variable. This book has shown that China's local polity has a high degree of agency and is able to compete with global capital in the arena of hegemonic control and competition. Globalization has given China access to even more abundant capital, enabling it to use geoeconomic methods to expand national sovereignty and extend its political influence throughout the world. This state capacity is closely related to China's party-state capital, but the vitality of this party-state system and the categorical imperative of the regime's existence are also constrained by time and space. Therefore, more in-depth research is needed on the nature of the Chinese state, and it should delve into the state's strong points and structural weaknesses. The conceptual tools that this book proposes—the embeddedness of the local polity in the GVC and the rent-seeking developmental state—can provide keys for solving the puzzle.

The second issue is globalization and citizenship. Classical citizenship theory holds that with the progress of capitalism, citizen rights expand and become universal (Marshall 1994). The empirical evidence provided by this book reveals that capitalist globalization has not facilitated a liberalization of China's citizenship system: rather, it has consolidated the system of differential citizenship within the nation-state. In his analysis of the historical evolution of modern citizen rights, Mann (1987) points out that without external intervention and war (e.g., the Allied occupation and regime change in Germany and Japan after World War II), a modern form of authoritarian citizenship might continue to exist over the long term. The institutionalization and consolidation of China's stratified and unequal differential citizenship is the most important case since Nazi Germany and militaristic Japan. China's citizenship system is closely interwoven with its household registration and social welfare systems. The former came about through the influence of the Soviet Union's system, Chinese tradition, and modern governance techniques, among which the urban-rural dualism established during Maoism's socialist stage played a key historical role. Here we can observe the powerful influence of institutional stickiness and path dependence that developed in the post-state-socialist stage. Why did the development of capitalism in China engender such a high degree of affinity with the system of differential citizenship? This book provides an explanation.

The third issue is globalization and state capitalism. After China was incorporated into the global production system, the country's non-state-owned sector grew significantly at one point. However, at the beginning of the twenty-first century, state-owned enterprises were reenergized, with the result that the development of export-oriented capitalism facilitated the rejuvenation and consolidation of state-owned capital. The role played by the Chinese state was of utmost importance in the globalization process. As China transitioned from state socialism to state capitalism, the Leninist party-state system did not loosen its grip on the economy. The state also absorbed a large amount of tax revenue and foreign exchange from export-oriented development, built infrastructure, and channeled funds to the state sector, accelerating its capital accumulation and using that capital to execute the tasks of economic security and innovation (Tsai and Naughton 2015). Yet from the standpoint of this book, China's capitalist development is even more closely linked with the country's narratives of national survival or extinction and political stability. The political problems that Guangdong faced at the outset of opening reforms show that economic reform was inextricably connected with the ruling elite's understanding of regime survival and stability. Forty years of economic development, after a brief period of political reform and the prospect of economic liberalization, included a series of political suppression and purges and then returned to the main theme of strengthening state capital, echoing China's century-long grand narrative of national survival. Wei Yuan's call for a "rich, strong country" in the late Qing, Mao Zedong's call for the "Chinese people to stand up," and Xi Jinping's "great rejuvenation of the Chinese nation" are all inseparable from the development of the national economy and a strong and prosperous state. The Chinese Communist regime is even more reliant on state capital for its survival. China's traditional empire disintegrated under Western imperial invasion, but the goal of rebuilding the Chinese empire is deeply imprinted in the emotional structure of countless ruling elites and intellectuals (see Ge Zhaoguang 2017). This imperial mind-set is in symbiotic opposition to America's growing determination to defend its existing imperial hegemony. It could be said that the rise of China's state capitalism has promoted a fervent longing for a return to a Chinese empire and an attempt to rewrite the script of globalization.

Glossary

Pinyin	Chinese (complex/simplified)	English
cha'e hexiao	差額核銷/差额核销	Balance write-off.
cha'e huiru	差額匯入/差额汇入	Customs spread or differential remittance.
changzhang	廠長/厂长	Factory head, posted by the administrative district.
changzhu renkou	常住人口/常住人口	Long-term resident population.
chao guomin daiyu	超國民待遇/超国民待遇	National treatment plus benefits.
chaxu geju	差序格局/差序格局	Differential mode of association, a concept developed by Fei Xiaotong.
chengbao	城保/城保	Urban social insurance.
chukou jiagong qu	出口加工區/出口加工区	Export processing zone, a concept appropriated from Taiwan, where it was called "processing export zone" (*jiagong chukou qu*).
da cabianqiu	打擦邊球/打擦边球	Play edge ball; exploit legal loopholes to gain profit.
Gangshang	港商/港商	Hong Kong businesspeople; Hong Kong-invested enterprises.

(*continued*)

Pinyin	Chinese (complex/simplified)	English
gongjiao fei	工繳費/工缴费	Processing-management fee.
gongjiao fei huicha	工繳費匯差/工缴费汇差	Processing fee remittance differential (or spread).
gongmin shenfen chaxu	公民身分差序/公民身分差序	Differential citizenship.
guakao danwei	掛靠單位/挂靠单位	Sponsoring unit.
guanli fei	管理費/管理費	Management fee charged by local government.
guanxi	關係/关系	Personal connections, especially with officials.
guojin mintui	國進民退/国进民退	State sector advancing and private sector retreating.
he huajiu	喝花酒/喝花酒	To wine and dine.
hong bao	紅包/红包	Bribes.
huicha	匯差/汇差	Exchange-rate differential (or spread).
hukou	戶口/户口	Household registration status.
jiagong fei	加工費/加工費	Processing fee.
jieji yongren	戒急用忍/戒急用忍	Go-slow policy.
jigouhua xunzu	機構化尋租/机构化寻租	Institutional rent seeking.
jinliao jiagong	進料加工/进料加工	Processing of imported materials.
kau-puê	交陪/交陪	Taiwanese Hokkien: cultivating people to foster a deeper friendship and trust.
kuai	塊/块	Colloquial for yuan.
laodong guanxi	勞動關係/劳动关系	Labor relations with the work unit.
lailiao jiagong	來料加工/来料加工	Processing of shipped materials.
luan	亂/乱	Chaos.
Lugan	陸幹/陆干	Mainlander managers and staff members employed in Taiwanese-invested enterprises or mainland-owned factories.
luohu	落戶/落户	Settling down (for local household registration status).

Pinyin	Chinese (complex/simplified)	English
mingfen	名分/名分	A traditional concept for emphasizing name and title to denote one's status or position.
mingong	民工/民工	Migrant worker, short for *nongmingong*.
mu	畝/亩	Chinese unit of measurement for land, equivalent to 7,176 square feet or 666.7 square meters.
nongbao	農保/农保	Rural social insurance.
nongmingong	農民工/农民工	Rural migrant worker.
oo-tshiú, (or *heishou* in Chinese)	黑手/黑手	Taiwanese Hokkien: black hand, referring to technicians and mechanics.
oo-tshiú piàn thâu-ke	黑手變頭家/黑手变头家	Taiwanese Hokkien: apprentice turned boss.
putong gongmin shenfen	普同公民身分/普同公民身分	Universal citizenship.
quan'e hexiao	全額核銷/全额核销	Full write-off.
renhu fenli	人戶分離/人户分离	Separation of people's actual and registered domicile.
rentou shui	人頭稅/人头税	Head tax.
sanlai yibu	三來一補/三来一补	Three-plus-one trading mix system.
sanzi qiye	三資企業/三资企业	Sino-foreign joint ventures, cooperative businesses, and wholly foreign-owned enterprises.
shedui qiye	社隊企業/社队企业	Commune and brigade-managed enterprise.
shenfen chaxu	身分差序/身分差序	Differential status.
shiji gan	市集感/市集感	The feel of a market town, giving the impression of being disorderly, bustling, and vital.
shudi guanli	屬地管理/属地管理	Territorial jurisdiction.
Taigan	台幹/台干	Taiwanese managers and staff.

(continued)

Pinyin	Chinese (complex/simplified)	English
Taishang	台商/台商	Taiwanese-invested enterprises; Taiwanese proprietors.
taizixi luzichang	台資系陸資廠/台资系陆资厂	Mainland-owned factory under a Taiwanese system or Taiwanese-acculturated mainland-owned factories.
tenglong huanniao	騰籠換鳥/腾笼换鸟	Emptying cages and changing birds; eliminating traditional industries and promoting industrial upgrading.
tuanti geju	團體格局/团体格局	Organizational mode of association.
wailai renkou	外來人口/外来人口	Nonnative population with no local *hukou*.
xiezuofuwu fei	協作服務費/协作服务费	Collaboration fee (a form of management fee) charged by a local government.
xunzu fazhanxing guojia	尋租發展型國家/寻租发展型国家	Rent-seeking developmental state.
yuan	元/元	Unit of the Chinese currency renminbi.
zaigang zhigong	在崗職工/在岗职工	On-the-job employee.
zhenbao	鎮保/镇保	Small-town social insurance.
zhigong	職工/职工	Permanent worker with local, urban *hukou* status.
zonghe baoxian	綜合保險/综合保险	Nonnative employee comprehensive insurance.

Index of Interview Codes
(by order of persons cited)

Interview code	Interviewee's background	Date of interview
ZJC200701 ZJC201211	Taigan, general manager of a Taiwanese-owned bicycle factory in Shenzhen	January 2007 November 2012
Leegm199401 Leegm199404 Leegm199508 Leegm201510 Leegm201511	Mr. Lee, Taishang, general manager of Taiyang Company	January 1994 April 1994 August 1995 October 2015 November 2015
BL201506	European scholar carrying out a field survey in Guangdong	June 2015
LTM201510	Manager Lin, manager of Nan Ya Plastics	October 2015
Su199405 Su199508	Assistant manager Su, Taigan, Taiyang's Dongguan factory	May 1994 August 1995
ZJY200603	A migrant worker and section chief at Taiyang's Dongguan factory	March 2006
GQ_Cheng199405	Deputy director Zheng, Guanqiang Import and Export Co.	May 1994
Chang199405	Manager Chang, Taigan, Taiyang's Dongguan factory	May 1994
Yen199405	Manager Yen, Taigan, Taiwanese-owned shoe factory in Dongguan	May 1994

(*continued*)

Interview code	Interviewee's background	Date of interview
Chen199506	Assistant manager Chen, Taigan, Taiwanese-owned luggage factory in Dongguan	June 1995
CY199506	Taigan, special assistant to the assistant manager at a Taiwanese-owned luggage factory in Dongguan	June 1995
Chiu200404	General manager Chiu, Taishang, established factories in Dongguan and Kunshan	April 2004
Jerry200902 Jerry200909	Jerry, Taigan, financial affairs manager for Taiyang's Dongguan factory	February 2009 September 2009
Ben200406 Ben200504 Ben200701	Ben, Taishang, second-generation manager at Taiyang	June 2004 April 2005 January 2007
Lin200701	Manager Lin, Taigan, Taiyang's Dongguan factory	January 2007
Ah-Xiu200701	Ah-Xiu, resident of Nafu Village and factory head stationed at Taiyang's Dongguan factory	January 2007
XFL200410	Taigan, deputy manager at a Taiwanese-owned wooden furniture factory	October 2004
XZS200410	Hsu, Taigan, manager of a Taiwanese-owned furniture factory	October 2004
ZJQ200707	Taigan, section head at a Taiwanese-owned semiconductor testing and packaging plant in Shanghai	July 2007
TY_Zhu200504	Migrant worker (section head) at Taiyang's Dongguan factory	April 2005
TY_Cheng200701	Migrant worker at Taiyang's Dongguan factory	January 2007
L201504	Taigan, manager of a Taiwanese-owned footwear factory in Dongguan	April 2015
SHPD_LB_200701	Local government official, Shanghai Municipal Labor Bureau	January 2007

Interview code	Interviewee's background	Date of interview
SH-Y-ks2007	Taigan, Taiwanese-owned leisure equipment factory in Shanghai	July 2007
SH-Yeh200707	Taigan at Taiwanese-owned factories in Shanghai and northern Jiangsu; self-employed business consultant	July 2007
KS-KY2007	Taishang, general manager of a Taiwanese-owned packaging plant in Kunshan	January 2007
KS-HG2007	Taishang, general manager at a Taiwanese-owned electronics factory in Kunshan	July 2007
Xu201504	Taishang, established a vocational school in Dongguan	April 2015
KL201507	Taishang, established an electronics components plant in Dongguan	July 2015
HG200707	Taigan, general manager of a Taiwanese-owned printing plant in Kunshan	July 2007
KS_RT200810	Taigan, manager of a machinery factory in Kunshan	October 2008
XM200406	Party secretary of a Chinese village party committee, Xiamen suburbs	June 2004
TW201504	Taiwanese graduate student carrying out a field survey in Shenzhen	April 2015
CCP201507	Taiwanese scholar carrying out a field survey in Guangdong	July 2015
SP199405	Younger sister of migrant worker Xiaoqin, born in village of Zhumadian City, Henan Province; worked in Dongguan	May 1994
DD2015	Dadong, head of a labor NGO in the Pearl River Delta region	August 2015
YYPL2015	Taigan, manager of Taishin Shoe Manufacturing Group	April 2015

(continued)

Interview code	Interviewee's background	Date of interview
ZZR2015	Zhang Zhiru, head of a labor NGO in the Pearl River Delta region	May 2015
HTS200704 HTS201212 HTS201310	Taigan, veteran manager, Taishin Shoe Manufacturing Group	April 2007 December 2012 October 2013
TX3-2015 TX3-201609 TX3-201703 XX2015 XX2016 XX2016-b	Taigan, assistant manager, Taishin Shoe Manufacturing Group	May 2015 September 2016 March 2017 September 2015 March 2016 September 2016
TR201212	Mr. Hu, Taigan, deputy general manager, Smiles Shoe Company in Dongguan	December 2012
SMR200710	Ms. Chen, CEO and chair of the board of Smiles Shoe Company	October 2007
TH199405	Taigan, manager, Taishin Shoe Manufacturing Group	May 1994
ALN201304	Taigan, deputy general manager of a Taiwanese-owned footwear factory in Dongguan	April 2013
LM201508 LM201509 LM201804 LM201805	Mr. Lok, Taigan, former general manager of a Taiwanese-owned networking equipment company	August 2015 September 2015 April 2018 May 2018
T201402	Chinese scholar conducting a field survey in Guangdong	February 2014
NG201806 NG201807	Mr. Ng, Taigan, former manager of a Taiwanese-owned semiconductor factory in Shanghai	June 2018 July 2018

Works Cited

Allison, Graham. 2017. *Destined for War: Can America and China Escape Thucydides's Trap?* Boston: Houghton Mifflin Harcourt.

American Interest. 2012. "Australia, US, Canada Agree: Huawei is a Security Threat," October 10, http://goo.gl/xp64wn.

Amsden, Alice H. 1989. *Asia's Next Giant: South Korea and Late Industrialization.* New York: Oxford University Press.

Amsden, Alice H., and Wan-wen Chu. 2003. *Beyond Late Development: Taiwan's Upgrading Policies.* Cambridge, MA: MIT Press.

Ang, Yuen Yuen. 2020. *China's Gilded Age: The Paradox of Economic Boom and Vast Corruption.* New York: Cambridge University Press.

Applebaum, Richard P., David Smith, and Brad Christerson. 1994. "Commodity Chains and Industrial Restructuring in the Pacific Rim: Garment Trade and Manufacturing." In Gereffi and Korzeniewicz, *Commodity Chains and Global Capitalism,* 187–204.

Arrighi, Giovanni. 2007. *Adam Smith in Beijing: Lineages of the Twenty-First Century.* London: Verso.

Baek, Seung-Wook. 2005. "Does China Follow 'the East Asian Development Model'?" *Journal of Contemporary Asia* 35 (4): 485–98.

Bair, Jennifer, ed. 2009a. *Frontiers of Commodity Chain Research.* Stanford, CA: Stanford University Press.

Bair, Jennifer. 2009b. "Global Commodity Chains: Genealogy and Review." In Bair, *Frontiers of Commodity Chain Research,* 1–34. Bair, Jennifer, and Gary Gereffi. 2001. "Local Clusters in Global Chains: The Causes and Consequences of Export Dynamism in Torreon's Blue Jeans Industry." *World Development* 29 (11): 1885–903.

Balding, Christopher. 2018. "ZTE's Ties to China's Military-Industrial Complex Run Deep," *Foreign Policy,* July 19, 2018, https://foreignpolicy.com/2018/07/19/ztes-ties-to-chinas-military-industrial complex-run-deep/.

Balding, Christopher, and Clarke, Donald C. 2019. "Who Owns Huawei?" Social Science Research Network, April 17, https://ssrn.com/abstract=3372669.

Bhagwati, Jagdish. 1982. "Directly Unproductive, Profit-Seeking (DUP) Activities." *Journal of Political Economy* 90 (5): 988–1002.

Bin, Hongxia. 2021. "Shoutiao chukou meiguo de niuzaiku 'dansheng ji'" ("Birth story" of the first export of jeans to the United States), *Nanfang ribao* (Nanfang daily), October 9, 2021, https://news.southcn.com/node_48e4ce5277/829e4d2381.shtml.

Blackburn, Keith, and Gonzalo F. Forgues-Pucciob. 2009. "Why Is Corruption Less Harmful in Some Countries than in Others?" *Journal of Economic Behavior and Organization* 72 (3): 797–810.

Blackwill, Robert D., and Jennifer M. Harris. 2016. *War by Other Means: Geoeconomics and Statecraft*. Cambridge, MA: Belknap Press of Harvard University Press.

Blecher, Marc. 1991. "Development State, Entrepreneurial State: The Political Economy of Socialist Reform in Xinju Municipality and Guanghan County." In *The Chinese State in the Era of Economic Reform: The Road to Crisis*, edited by Gordon White, 265–91. Armonk, NY: M. E. Sharpe.

Block, Fred, and Peter Evans. 2005. "The State and the Economy." In *The Handbook of Economic Sociology*, 2nd ed., edited by Neil Smelser and Richard Swedberg, 505–26. Princeton, NJ: Princeton University Press.

Boltho, Andrea, and Maria Weber. 2015. "Did China Follow the East Asian Developmental Model?" In Naughton and Tsai, *State Capitalism, Institutional Adaptation, and the Chinese Miracle*, 240–64.

Borrus, Michael, Dieter Ernst, and Stephan Haggard, eds. 2000. *International Production Networks in Asia*. London: Routledge.

Burawoy, Michael. 1976. "The Functions and Reproduction of Migrant Labor: Comparative Material from Southern Africa and the United States." *American Journal of Sociology* 81 (5): 1050–87.

———. 1979. *Manufacturing Consent: Changes in the Labor Process under Monopoly Capitalism*. Chicago: University of Chicago Press.

———. 2009. *The Extended Case Method: Four Countries, Four Decades, Four Great Transformations, and One Theoretical Tradition*. Berkeley: University of California Press.

Butollo, Florian. 2014. *The End of Cheap Labour? Industrial Transformation and "Social Upgrading" in China*. Frankfurt, Germany: Campus Verlag.

———. 2015. "Industrial Upgrading and Work: The Impact of Industrial Transformation on Labor in Guangdong's Garment and IT Industries." In Chan, *Chinese Workers in Comparative Perspective*, 85–104.

Campbell, Kurt M., and Ely Ratner. 2018. "The China Reckoning: How Beijing Defied American Expectations." *Foreign Affairs* 97, no. 2 (March–April): 60–70.

Cardenal, Juan Pablo, Jacek Kucharczyk, Grigorij Mesežnikov, and Gabriela Pleschová. 2017. "Sharp Power: Rising Authoritarian Influence." National Endowment for Democracy, https://www.ned.org/wp-content/uploads/2017/12/Sharp-Power-Rising -Authoritarian-Influence-Full-Report.pdf.

CCP Central Committee, 1979, "Zhonggong Zhongyang, Guowuyuan pizhuan Guangdong shengwei, Fujian shengwei guangyu duiwai jingji huodong shixing teshu zhengce he linghuo cuoshi de liangge baogao" (Authorized transmission by the CCP Central Committee and State Council of the Two Reports by the Guangdong Provincial Party Committee and Fujian Provincial Party Committee regarding the implementation of special policies and flexible measures for foreign economic activity) (Central Committee Document No. 50 [1979]), Beijing.

CCP Guangdong Party Committee (CCP Guangdong Provincial Party Committee Party History Research Office), ed. 2008. *Guangdong gaige kaifang juecezhe fangtan lu* (Record of interviews with policy makers of Guangdong's reform and opening). Guangzhou: Guangdong Renmin Chubanshe.

Chakrabarty, Dipesh. 1989. *Rethinking Working-Class History: Bengal, 1890–1940*. Princeton, NJ: Princeton University Press.

Chan, Anita. 2001. *China's Workers under Assault: The Exploitation of Labor in a Globalizing Economy*. Armonk, NY: M. E. Sharpe.

———. 2011. "Strikes in China's Export Industries in Comparative Perspective." *China Journal* 65 (January): 27–51.

———, ed. 2015. *Chinese Workers in Comparative Perspective*. Ithaca, NY: ILR Press of Cornell University Press.

Chan, Jenny, Ngai Pun, and Mark Selden. 2013. "The Politics of Global Production: Apple, Foxconn and China's New Working Class." *Asia-Pacific Journal* 11 (32): 1–12.

Chan, Kam Wing. 2010a. "A China Paradox: Migrant Labor Shortage amidst Rural Labor Supply Abundance." *Eurasian Geography and Economics* 51 (4): 513–30.

———. 2010b. "Zhongguo yao zou zhengchang chengzhenhua daolu" (China must follow the normal path of urbanization). Caixinwang, December 8, http://m.china .caixin.com/m/2010-12-08/100205422.html.

———. 2014. "Jianjin de, pobing de quanmian huji gaige" (Gradual, ice-breaking comprehensive hukou reform), Paulson Institute, http://www.paulsoninstitute.org /wp-content/uploads/2017/01/PPM_Hukou_Chan_Chinese_R.pdf.

Chang, Kuei-min. 2007. "Guojia, yimin, shenti: Zhongguo chengshi wailai renkou shengyu zhengzhi" (The state, migrants, and bodies: The reproductive politics of China's urban migrant population). Master's thesis, National Tsing Hua University.

Chang, Tsung-teh. 2004. "Lailiao jiagongchang zhuanwei duzi qiye zhi duoshao" (How much do you know about transforming factories processing shipped materials into single-venture enterprises). Jinghua Consultant Co., https://goo.gl/L7Pf09.

Chen, Chieh-Hsuan. 1994. *Xieli wangluo yu shenghuo jiegou—Taiwan zhongxiao qiye de shehui jingji fenxi* (Collaborative networks and living structure—A socioeconomic analysis of Taiwan's small and medium-size companies). Taipei: Lianjing.

Chen, Chih-Jou Jay. 2015. "Zhongguo weiquan zhengti xia de jiti kangyi: Taizicang da bagong de anli fenxi" (Collective protest under China's authoritarian system: A case analysis of major strikes at Taiwanese-owned factories). *Taiwan shehuixue* (Taiwanese sociology), (no. 30): 1–53.

Chen, Hewu. 2011. "Bang yangqi zhi feng zu'ai Zhongguo jingji zhuanxing" (The trend toward central enterprises is hindering China's economic transformation). Tengxun

Caijing (Tencent finance), April 7, 2011, https://finance.qq.com/a/20110407/001222 .htm.

Chen, Huirong. 2006. "'Mingong huang' de zhengzhi jingji fenxi" (A political-economic analysis of the "migrant worker famine"). *Xianggang shehui kexue xuebao* (Hong Kong journal of social sciences), (no. 31): 27–56.

Chen, Ling. 2014. "Varieties of Global Capital and the Paradox of Local Upgrading in China." *Politics and Society* 42 (2): 223–52.

Chen, Liang-rong. 2019. "Zhongmei huzhan, weisheme taijidian yidian doubu danxin?" (Why is TSMC not worried at all when China and the US are at war with each other?), *Tianxia zazhi* (Commonwealth magazine), June 24, https://futurecity.cw .com.tw/article/720?rec=i2i&from_id=1560&from_index=8.

Chen, Ming-chi. 2012. "Fortress in the Air: The Organizational Model of Taiwanese Export-Manufacturing Transplants in China." *Issues and Studies* 48 (4): 73–112.

Chen, Shih-meng. 1992. *Jiagou dangguo zibenzhuyi: Lun Taiwan guanying shiye zhi minyinghua* (Deconstructing party-state capitalism: On the privatization of Taiwan's official enterprises). Taipei: Chiu Hei-yuan.

Chen, Xiangming. 1994. "The New Spatial Division of Labor and Commodity Chains in the Greater South China Economic Region." In Gereffi and Korzeniewicz, *Commodity Chains and Global Capitalism*, 165–86.

Chen, Yingfang. 2005. "'Nongmingong': Zhidu anpai shenfen rentong" ("Rural migrant workers": Institutional arrangements and status identification). *Shehuixue yanjiu* (Sociology research), (no. 3): 119–32.

———. 2014. "Quanli gonglizhuyi luoji xia de shenfen zhidu zhi bi" (The maladies of an identity system under the logic of rights utilitarianism). *Renmin luntan* (People's forum), (no. 2): 62–72.

Chen, Yung-fa. 2001. *Zhongguo gongchan geming qishi nian (xiudingban) shang ce* (Seventy years of China's Communist revolution [rev. ed.], vol. 1). Taipei: Lianjing.

Cheng, Chih-peng. 2014a. "Chaxu yazhixing laodong tizhi: Zhongguo liangci laodong fa zai Taizi qiye zhili jieguo de zhengzhi jinjixue fenxi" (Discriminatory and inhibiting labor regime: A political economic analysis of the governance consequences of China's two labor laws on Taiwanese-invested businesses). *Taiwan shehuixue kan* (Taiwanese journal of sociology), (no. 54): 75–129.

———. 2014b. "Embedded Trust and Beyond: The Organizational Network Transformation of Taishang's Shoe Industry in China." In *Border Crossing in Greater China: Production, Community and Identity*, edited by Jenn-Hwan Wang, 40–60. New York: Routledge.

———. 2015. "Cong Taiwan zhongxiao qiye dao Taishang: Yige jingji shehuixue shi de kaocha" (From Taiwanese small- and medium-size business to Taishang: An economic sociological study). Paper presented at the Symposium on Taiwanese Economic Sociology in the New Century, Institute of Sociology, Academia Sinica, Taipei, April 18, 2015.

———. 2016. "Waisheng de Zhongguo zibenzhuyi xingcheng: Yi Zhujiang sanjiaozhou siying qiyezhu chuangye guocheng weili" (The formation of foreign-born Chinese capitalism: The example of the undertaking of private business proprietors in the Pearl River Delta). *Taiwan shehuixue* (Taiwanese sociology), (no. 31): 141–91.

Cheng, Chih-peng, and Lin Thung-Hong. 2017. "Xiangqian de jixian: Zhongguo Tai-shang de 'kuaguo ziben jilei changyu' fenxi" (The limits of embeddedness: An analysis of the "transnational capital accumulation sites" of China Taishang). In Lee, Zong-Rong, and Lin, *Weijing de qiji*, 612–44.

Cheng, Lu-lin. 1999. "Yige banbianchui de fuxian yu yinchang: Guoji xielei shichang wangluo chongzu xia de shengchan waiy" (The emergence and concealment of a semiperiphery: The external migration of production under the reorganization of international footwear market networks). *Taiwan shehui yanjiu jikan* (Taiwan: A radical quarterly in social studies), (no. 35): 1–46.

Cheng, Tun-Jen. 1989. "Democratizing the Quasi-Leninist Regime in Taiwan." *World Politics* 41 (4): 471–99.

———. 1990. "Political Regimes and Development Strategies: South Korea and Taiwan." In Gereffi and Wyman, *Manufacturing Miracles*, 139–78.

Chinese Rural Migrant Worker Issues Research Report Drafting Committee. 2006. "Zhongguo nongmingong wenti yanjiu zongbaogao" (Research report on Chinese rural migrant worker issues). *Gaige* (Reform), http://rdbk1.ynlib.cn:6251/qw/Paper/311037.

Chiu, Chun-hung. 2005. "Xinren de bianjie: Zixingche Taishang kuajie xieli wangluo yanjiu" (Boundaries of trust: Research on bicycle Taishang cross-border collaborative networks). Master's thesis, National Taipei University.

Chiu, Mingtze. 2007. "Guojia zhengce zhixing de difang zhengzhi jingjixue: Kunshan he Wenzhou zhixing yanglao baoxian zhengce de bijiao" (The local political economy of executing state policies: A comparison of the implementation of pension insurance policies in Kunshan and Wenzhou). Master's thesis, National Tsing Hua University.

Chiu, Stephen, and Tai-lok Lui. 2009. *Hong Kong: Becoming a Chinese Global City*. London: Routledge.

Chu, Yintzu. 2011. "Shiyu de shangtong: Zhongguo Dongguan nongmingong de jiankang yu yiliao" (Wordless pain: The health and healing of migrant workers in Dongguan, China). Master's thesis, National Tsing Hua University.

Coase, R. H. 1988. *The Firm, the Market, and the Law*. Chicago: University of Chicago Press.

Coe, Neil M., Peter Dicken, and Martin Hess. 2008. "Global Production Networks: Realizing the Potential." *Journal of Economic Geography* 8 (3): 271–95.

Coe, Neil M., and Henry Wai-chung Yeung. 2015. *Global Production Networks: Theorizing Economic Development in an Interconnected World*. Oxford: Oxford University Press.

Cumings, Bruce. 1999a. "Asian Crisis, Democracy, and the End of 'Late' Development." In *The Politics of the Asian Economic Crisis*, edited by T. J. Pempel, 17–44. Ithaca, NY: Cornell University Press.

———. 1999b. "Webs with No Spiders, Spiders with No Webs." In Woo-Cumings, *The Developmental State*, 61–92.

De Propris, Lisa, Stefano Menghinello, and Roger Sugden. 2008. "The Internationalisation of Production Systems: Embeddedness, Openness and Governance." *Entrepreneurship and Regional Development* 20 (6): 493–515.

Deng, Jian-bang. 2017. "Shou difang xianding de gongchang: Zhongguo dalu neiqian Taizi zhizaoye laodong tizhi zhi bianqian" (Geographically restricted factories: Changes in the labor regime of the Taiwanese-invested manufacturing industry in mainland China). *Taiwan shehuixue* (Taiwanese sociology), (no. 33): 63–112.

Department of Commerce Bureau of Industry and Security. 2020. "Addition of Entities to The Entity List, Revision of Entry on the Entity List, and Removal of Entities from the Entity List," *Federal Register* 85 (246): 83416–83432, https://www.govinfo.gov/content/pkg/FR-2020-12-22/pdf/2020-28031.pdf.

Deyo, Frederic C., ed. 1987. *The Political Economy of the New Asian Industrialism.* Ithaca, NY: Cornell University Press.

———. 1990. "Economic Policy and the Public Sector." In Gereffi and Wyman, *Manufacturing Miracles*, 179–204.

Diamond, Larry, Marc F. Plattner, and Christopher Walker. 2016. *Authoritarianism Goes Global: The Challenge to Democracy.* Baltimore, MD: Johns Hopkins University Press.

Dickson, Bruce J. 2003. *Red Capitalists in China: The Party, Private Entrepreneurs, and Prospects for Political Change.* New York: Cambridge University Press.

Dikötter, Frank. 2013. *The Tragedy of Liberation: A History of the Chinese Revolution.* New York: Bloomsbury Press.

Ding, Xueliang. 2014. *Zhongguo moshi: Zancheng yu fandui* (The China model: Pros and cons). Hong Kong: Oxford University Press.

Dongguan Municipal Statistics Bureau, ed. 1990. *Dongguan tongji nianjian 1978–1990* (Dongguan statistical yearbook 1978–1990). Beijing: Zhongguo Tongji Chubanshe.

———, ed. 1993. *Dongguan tongji nianjian 1993* (Dongguan statistical yearbook 1993). Beijing: Zhongguo Tongji Chubanshe.

———, ed. 1995. *Dongguan tongji nianjian 1995* (Dongguan statistical yearbook 1995). Beijing: Zhongguo Tongji Chubanshe.

———, ed. 1997. *Dongguan tongji nianjian 1997* (Dongguan statistical yearbook 1997). Beijing: Zhongguo Tongji Chubanshe.

———, ed. 1998. *Dongguan tongji nianjian 1998* (Dongguan statistical yearbook 1998). Beijing: Zhongguo Tongji Chubanshe.

———, ed. 2000–2014. *Dongguan tongji nianjian 2000* to *Dongguan tongji nianjian 2014* (Dongguan statistical yearbook 2000 to 2014). Beijing: Zhongguo Tongji Chubanshe.

Duckett, Jane. 2001. "Bureaucrats in Business, Chinese-Style: The Lessons of Market Reform and State Entrepreneurialism in the People's Republic of China." *World Development* 29 (1): 23–37.

Ernst, Dieter, and Paolo Guerrieri. 1998. "International Production Networks and Changing Trade Patterns in East Asia: The Case of the Electronics Industry." *Oxford Development Studies* 26 (2): 191–212.

Evans, Peter. 1995. *Embedded Autonomy: States and Industrial Transformation.* Princeton, NJ: Princeton University Press.

———. 2010. "Constructing the 21st Century Developmental State Potentialities and Pitfalls." In *Constructing a Democratic Developmental State in South Africa*, edited by Omano Edigheji, 37–58. Cape Town, South Africa: HSRC Press.

Evans, Peter B., Dietrich Rueschemeyer, and Theda Skocpol, eds. 1985. *Bringing the State Back*. New York: Cambridge University Press.

Fan, C. Cindy. 2005. "Interprovincial Migration, Population Redistribution, and Regional Development in China: 1990 and 2000 Census Comparisons." *Professional Geographer* 57 (2): 295–311.

Fang, Zhicao, and Ho-fung Hung. 2019. "Historicizing Embedded Autonomy: The Rise and Fall of a Local Developmental State in Dongguan, China, 1978–2015." *Sociology of Development* 5 (2): 147–13.

Feenstra, Robert C., and Gary G. Hamilton. 2006. *Emergent Economies, Divergent Paths: Economic Organization and International Trade in South Korea and Taiwan*. New York: Cambridge University Press.

Fei, Xiaotong. 1957. *Chongfang jiangcun* (Jiangcun revisited). Hong Kong: Fenghuang Chubanshe.

———. 1991. *Xiangtu Zhongguo* (From the soil: The foundations of Chinese society). Hong Kong: Sanlian.

Friedberg, Aaron L. 2011. *A Contest for Supremacy: China, America, and the Struggle for Mastery in Asia*. New York: W. W. Norton.

Frye, Timothy, and Andrei Shleifer. 1997. "The Invisible Hand and the Grabbing Hand." *American Economic Review* 87 (2): 354–58.

Fukuyama, Francis. 1989. "The End of History?" *National Interest* (no. 16): 3–18.

———. 1992. *The End of History and the Last Man*. New York: Free Press.

Fuller, Douglas B. 2016. *Paper Tigers, Hidden Dragons: Firms and the Political Economy of China's Technological Development*. Oxford: Oxford University Press.

Gallagher, Mary Elizabeth. 2005. *Contagious Capitalism: Globalization and the Politics of Labor in China*. Princeton, NJ: Princeton University Press.

Garnaut, John. 2018. "How China Interferes in Australia and How Democracies Can Push Back." *Foreign Affairs*, March 9, https://www.foreignaffairs.com/articles/china/2018-03-09/how-china-interferes-australia.

Ge, Zhaoguang. 2017. *Lishi Zhongguo de nei yu wai: Youguan "Zhongguo" yu "zhoubian" gainian de zai chengqing* (Inside and outside of historical China: A reclarification of the concepts of "China" and the "periphery"). Hong Kong: Chinese University of Hong Kong Press.

Gereffi, Gary. 1994. "The Organization of Buyer-Driven Global Commodity Chains: How U.S. Retailers Shape Overseas Production Networks." In Gereffi and Korzeniewicz, *Commodity Chains and Global Capitalism*, 95–122.

———. 1995. "Global Production Systems and Third World Development." In *Global Change, Regional Response: The New International Context of Development*, edited by Barbara Stallings, 100–142. New York: Cambridge University Press.

Gereffi, Gary, John Humphrey, and Timothy Sturgeon. 2005. "The Governance of Global Value Chains." *Review of International Political Economy* 12 (1): 78–104.

Gereffi, Gary, and Miguel Korzeniewicz. 1990. "Commodity Chains and Footwear Exports in the Semiperiphery." pp. 45–68 in *Semiperipheral States in the World-Economy*, edited by William G. Martin. New York: Greenwood Press.

————, eds. 1994. *Commodity Chains and Global Capitalism*. Westport, CT: Greenwood Press.

Gereffi, Gary, Miguel Korzeniewicz, and Roberto Korzeniewicz. 1994. "Introduction: Global Commodity Chains." In Gereffi and Korzeniewicz, *Commodity Chains and Global Capitalism*, 1–14.

Gereffi, Gary, and Joonkoo Lee. 2012. "Why the World Suddenly Cares about Global Supply Chains." *Journal of Supply Chain Management* 48 (3): 24–32.

Gereffi, Gary, and Mei-Ling Pan. 1994. "The Globalization of Taiwan's Apparel Industry." In *Global Production: The Apparel Industry in the Pacific Rim*, edited by Edna Bonacich, Lucie Cheng, Norma Chinchilla, Nora Hamilton, and Paul Ong, 126–46. Philadelphia: Temple University Press.

Gereffi, Gary, and Donald L. Wyman, eds. 1990. *Manufacturing Miracles: Paths of Industrialization in Latin America and East Asia*. Princeton, NJ: Princeton University Press.

Goffman, Erving, 1961. *Asylums: Essays on the Social Situation of Mental Patients and Other Inmates*. Garden City, NY: Anchor Books.

Gold, Thomas B. 1986. *State and Society in the Taiwan Miracle*. New York: M. E. Sharpe.

Grabher, Gernot. 2004. "The Disembedded Regional Economy: The Transformation of East German Industrial Complexes into Western Enclaves." In *Globalization, Institutions, and Regional Development in Europe*, edited by Ash Amin and Nigel Thrift, 177–95. New York: Oxford University Press.

Guangdong Province Regional Historical Gazetteer Compilation Committee. 1999. *Guangdong sheng zhi: Jinrong zhi* (Guangdong province gazetteer: Financial gazetteer). Guangzhou: Guangdong Renmin Chubanshe.

————. 2006. *Guangdong sheng zhi: Xiang-zhen qiye zhi* (Guangdong province gazetteer: Township and village enterprise gazetteer). Guangzhou: Guangdong Renmin Chubanshe.

Guangdong Provincial Statistics Bureau, ed. 1993. *Guangdong tongji nianjian 1993* (Guangdong statistical yearbook 1993). Beijing: Zhongguo Tongji Chubanshe.

————, ed. 1995. *Guangdong tongji nianjian 1995* (Guangdong statistical yearbook 1995). Beijing: Zhongguo Tongji Chubanshe.

————, ed. 1997. *Guangdong tongji nianjian 1997* (Guangdong statistical yearbook 1997). Beijing: Zhongguo Tongji Chubanshe.

————, ed. 1999. *Guangdong tongji nianjian 1999* (Guangdong statistical yearbook 1999). Beijing: Zhongguo Tongji Chubanshe.

————, ed. 2001–2. *Guangdong tongji nianjian 2001* to *Guangdong tongji nianjian 2002* (Guangdong statistical yearbook, 2001 and 2002). Beijing: Zhongguo Tongji Chubanshe.

————, ed. 2004. *Guangdong tongji nianjian 2004* (Guangdong statistical yearbook 2004). Beijing: Zhongguo Tongji Chubanshe.

————, ed. 2006. *Guangdong tongji nianjian 2006* (Guangdong statistical yearbook 2006). Beijing: Zhongguo Tongji Chubanshe.

————, ed. 2008. *Guangdong tongji nianjian 2008* (Guangdong statistical yearbook 2008). Beijing: Zhongguo Tongji Chubanshe.

————, ed. 2010. *Guangdong tongji nianjian 2010* (Guangdong statistical yearbook 2010). Beijing: Zhongguo Tongji Chubanshe.

————, ed. 2012–2014. *Guangdong tongji nianjian 2012* to *Guangdong tongji nianjian 2014* (Guangdong statistical yearbook, 2012 and 2014). Beijing: Zhongguo Tongji Chubanshe.

————, ed. 2015. *Guangdong tongji nianjian 2015* (Guangdong statistical yearbook 2015). Beijing: Zhongguo Tongji Chubanshe.

Guo, Jian. 2012. "Binggui 'chongjibo'" (Merged-track "shock wave"). Zhongguo shehui baozhang (China Social Security online edition), no. 1, http://www.zgshbz.com.cn /Article7963.html. Accessed April 25, 2014.

Haggard, Stephan, and Tun-jen Cheng. 1987. "State and Foreign Capital in the East Asian NICs." In Deyo, *The Political Economy of the New Asian Industrialism*, 84–135.

Halper, Stefan. 2010. *The Beijing Consensus: How China's Authoritarian Model Will Dominate the Twenty-First Century*. New York: Basic Books.

Hamilton, Gary G., and Gary Gereffi. 2009. "Global Commodity Chains, Market Makers, and the Rise of Demand-Responsive Economies." In Bair, *Frontiers of Commodity Chain Research*, 136–61.

Hamilton, Gary G., and Cheng-shu Kao. 2018. *Making Money: How Taiwanese Industrialists Embraced the Global Economy*. Stanford, CA: Stanford University Press.

Hamilton, Gary G., Misha Petrovic, and Benjamin Senauer, eds. 2011. *The Market Makers: How Retailers Are Reshaping the Global Economy*. New York: Oxford University Press.

Hamilton, Gary G., and Wang Zheng. 1992. Introduction to Fei Xiaotong, *From the Soil: The Foundations of Chinese Society, A Translation of Fei Xiaotong's* Xiangtu Zhongguo, translated by Gary G. Hamilton and Wang Zheng, 1–36. Berkeley: University of California Press.

Hamlin, Kevin. 2010. "China Reaches Lewis Turning Point as Labor Costs Rise." Bloomberg News, https://www.bloomberg.com/news/articles/2010-06-10/china-reaching -a-lewis-turning-point-as-inflation-overtakes-low-cost-labor.

Hammar, Tomas. 1989. *"State, Nation, and Dual Citizenship."* In *Immigration and Politics of Citizenship in Europe and North America*, edited by Rogers Brubaker, 81–96. Lanham, MD: University Press of America.

Havice, Elizabeth, and John Pickels. 2019. In Ponte, Gereffi, and Raj-Reichert, *Handbook on Global Value Chains*, 169–82.

Hess, Martin. 2004. "Spatial Relationships? Towards a Reconceptualization of Embeddedness." *Progress in Human Geography* 28 (2): 165–86.

Hirschman, Albert O. 1977. *The Passions and the Interests: Political Arguments for Capitalism before Its Triumph*. Princeton, NJ: Princeton University Press.

Holton, Robert. 1998. *Globalization and the Nation-State*. Hampshire, UK: Macmillan Press.

Hopkins, Terrence, and Immanuel Wallerstein. 1977. "Patterns of Development of the Modern World-System." *Review: A Journal of the Fernand Braudel Center for the Study of Economies, Historical Systems and Civilizations* 1 (2): 111–45.

Horner, Rory, and Mathew Alford. 2019. In Ponte, Gereffi, and Raj-Reichert, *Handbook on Global Value Chains*, 555–69.

Hsia, Chuan-Wei. 2015. "Taiwan de xin ziyouzhuyi zhuangxiang: Fazhanxing guojia de bianyi yu tiaozhan" (Taiwan's neoliberalism changes direction: Changes and challenges in the developmental state). Master's thesis, National Tsing Hua University.

Hsiao, H. H. Michael. 2003. "Social Transformation, Civil Society, and Taiwanese Business in Fujian." In So, *China's Developmental Miracle*, 136–60.

Hsieh, Michelle F. 2017. "Cong Toujiadao dao yinxing guanjun: Taiwan zhongxiao qiye de zhuanxing, 1996–2011" (From island of bosses to invisible champion: The transformation of Taiwan's small and medium-size businesses, 1996–2011). In Lee, Zong-Rong, and Lin, *Weijing de qiji*, 346–82.

———. 2011. "Similar Opportunities, Different Responses: Explaining Divergent Patterns of Development between Taiwan and South Korea." *International Sociology* 26 (3): 364–91.

———. 2015. "The Creative Role of the State and Entrepreneurship: A Case from Taiwan." In *Government-Linked Companies and Sustainable, Equitable Development*, edited by Edmund Terence Gomez, François Bafoil, and Kee-Cheok Cheong, 60–81. New York: Routledge.

Hsing, You-tien. 1998. *Making Capitalism in China: The Taiwan Connection*. New York: Oxford University Press.

Hsu, He-jung. 2005. *Guoji maoyi shiwu caozuo (jinjiepian)* (International trade practices [advanced]). Taipei: Wunan.

Hsu, Rongrong. 2011. "Jia OBM, zhen OEM? Zhongguo shanzhaiji de pinpai zhi lu" (Fake OBM, genuine OEM? The branding of China's knock-off cell phones). Master's thesis, National Tsing Hua University.

Hsung, Ray-May, Chen Kuan-jung, and Guan Yi-Ren. 2017. "Hongse kuajie chuangxin wanluo de jizhi: Yi Zhongguo dalu bandaoti gongsi zhuanli famingren wangluo weili" (Mechanism of the red cross-border innovative network: The case of mainland China's semiconductor companies' patent inventor network). In Lee, Zong-Rong, and Lin, *Weijing de qiji*, 495–539.

Hu, Wu. 2006. *Wailai gong (nongmin gong) zonghe shehui baoxian touxi* (Comprehensive social insurance for migrant workers). Chengdu, China: Sichuan Daxue Chubanshe.

Huang, Philip C. C. 2017. "China's Informal Economy, Reconsidered: An Introduction in Light of Social-Economic and Legal History." *Rural China* 14 (1): 1–17.

Huang, Te-pei. 2006. "Ziben yuanshi jilei yu Zhongguo dalu de nongmingong" (The primitive accumulation of capital and mainland China's migrant workers). *Taiwan shehui yanjiu jikan* (Taiwan: A radical quarterly in social studies), no. 61: 109–47.

Huang, Yaonan. 1994. "Shenzhenshi Taiwan gongzuo huigu yu zhanwang" (Review and prospects of Shenzhen Taiwan work). In *Huihuang shiwu nian: Zhujiang sanjiaozhou juan* (Glorious fifteen years: Pearl River Delta volume), edited by Liang Lingguang, 210–16. Beijing: Guangming Ribao Chubanshe.

Huang, Yasheng. 2003. *Selling China: Foreign Direct Investment during the Reform Era*. New York: Cambridge University Press.

———. 2008. *Capitalism with Chinese Characteristics: Entrepreneurship and the State*. Cambridge: Cambridge University Press.

Hung, Ho-fung. 2009. "America's Head Servant?" *New Left Review* 60 (Nov/Dec): 2–25.
———. 2016. *The China Boom: Why China Will Not Rule the World.* New York: Columbia University Press.

IC Insights. 2017. "Pure-Play Foundries Boosting Their Presence in China." Research Bulletin, October 5, https://www.icinsights.com/data/articles/documents/1013.pdf.
———. 2021. "China Forecast to Fall Far Short of its 'Made in China 2025' Goals for ICs." Research Bulletin, January 6, https://www.icinsights.com/data/articles/documents /1330.pdf.
Imai, Ken, and Jing Ming Shiu. 2011. "Value Chain Creation and Reorganization: The Growth Path of China's Mobile Phone Handset Industry." In Kawakami and Sturgeon, *The Dynamics of Local Learning in Global Value Chains*, 43–67.
Ip, Iam-chong. 2007. "Bei yayi de huigui—Zhujiang sanjiaozhou nongmin yu chengshi kongjian" (Suppressed return—The Pearl River Delta's peasants and urban space). PhD diss., National Taiwan University.

Jervis, Robert. 1976. *Perception and Misperception in International Politics.* Princeton, NJ: Princeton University Press.
Jiangsu Provincial Statistics Bureau, ed. 2014. *Jiangsu tongji nianjian 2014* (Jiangsu statistical yearbook 2014). Beijing: Zhongguo Tongji Chubanshe.
Johnson, Chalmers. 1982. *MITI and the Japanese Miracle: The Growth of Industrial Policy: 1925–1975.* Stanford, CA: Stanford University Press.
———. 1987. "Political Institutions and Economic Performance: The Government-Business Relationship in Japan, South Korea, and Taiwan." In Deyo, *The Political Economy of the New Asian Industrialism*, 136–64.
———. 1999. "The Developmental State: Odyssey of a Concept." In Woo-Cumings, *The Developmental State*, 32–60.
Johnston, Alastair Iain. 2003. "Is China a Status Quo Power?" *International Security* 27 (4): 5–56.

Ka, Chih-Ming. 1993. *Taiwan dushi xiaoxing zhizaoye de chuangye, jingying yu shenchan zuzhi—yi Wufenpu chengyi zhizaoye wei anli de fenxi* (The founding, management, and production organization of Taiwan's urban small-scale manufacturing—An analysis using the Wufenpu garment industry as an example). Taipei: Institute of Ethnology, Academia Sinica.
Ka, Chih-Ming, and Mark Selden. 1986. "Original Accumulation, Equity and Late Industrialization: The Cases of Socialist China and Capitalist Taiwan." *World Development* 14 (10–11): 1293–1310.
Kanbur, Ravi, and Xiaobo Zhang. 2005. "Fifty Years of Regional Inequality in China: A Journey through Central Planning, Reform, and Openness." *Review of Development Economics* 9 (1): 87–106.
Kania, Elsa B. 2017. "Artificial Intelligence and Chinese Power: Beijing's Push for a Smart Military—and How to Respond," *Foreign Affairs*, December 5, https://www .foreignaffairs.com/articles/china/2017-12-05/artificial-intelligence-and-chinese-power.

Kaplinsky, Raphael. 2019. "Rents and Inequality in Global Value Chains." In Ponte, Gereffi, and Raj-Reichert, *Handbook on Global Value Chains*, 153–68.

Kawakami, Momoko, and Timothy J. Sturgeon, eds. 2011. *The Dynamics of Local Learning in Global Value Chains: Experiences from East Asia.* New York: Palgrave Macmillan.

Khan, Mushtaq H. 2000. "Rents, Efficiency and Growth." In Khan and Jomo, *Rents, Rent-Seeking and Economic Development*, 21–69.

Khan, Mushtaq H., and Jomo Kwame Sundaram, eds. 2000. *Rents, Rent-Seeking and Economic Development: Theory and Evidence in Asia.* New York: Cambridge University Press.

Koo, Hagen. 2001. *Korean Workers: The Culture and Politics of Class Formation.* Ithaca, NY: Cornell University Press.

Kornai, Janos. 1986. "The Soft Budget Constraint." *Kyklos* 39 (1): 3–30.

———. 1992. *The Socialist System: The Political Economy of Communism.* Oxford: Oxford University Press.

Korzeniewicz, Miguel. 1994. "Commodity Chains and Marketing Strategies: Nike and the Global Athletic Footwear Industry." In Gereffi and Korzeniewicz, *Commodity Chains and Global Capitalism*, 247–65.

Krueger, Anne O. 1974. "The Political Economy of the Rent-Seeking Society." *American Economic Review* 64 (3): 291–303.

Kung, Ming-hsin. 2014. *Taishang zai dalu touzi xiankuang diaocha ji dalu Tashang dui liang'an jingji gongxian zhi yanjiu* (A survey of the current situation of Taishang investment in the mainland and research on the economic contribution of mainland Taishang on both sides of the strait). Taipei: Taiwan Institute of Economic Research.

Lan, Pei-chia. 2014. "Segmented Incorporation: The Second Generation of Rural Migrants in Shanghai." *China Quarterly* 217: 243–65

Lardy, Nicholas R. 1992. "China's Foreign Trade." *China Quarterly* 131: 691–720.

Lee, Ching Kwan. 1998. *Gender and the South China Miracle: Two Worlds of Factory Women.* Berkeley: University of California Press.

Lee, Joonkoo. 2010. "Global Commodity Chains and Global Value Chains." In *The International Studies Encyclopedia*, edited by Robert A. Denemark, 2987–3006. Malden, MA: Wiley-Blackwell.

Lee, Shang-lin. 2008. "Cong zili jiuji dao shangye jingying: Beijing dagong zidi xuexiao de dansheng he fazhan" (From self-help to commercial operations: The rise and development of the Beijing School for Children of Workers). Master's thesis, National Tsing Hua University.

Lee, Yu-Jung. 2012. "Yangtan bu yangming: ziben jingji zhuanxing guochengzhong de zhengshang guanxi yu Shanghai shebao jijin" (The bare life eroded by corruptions: The social security fund in Shanghai), *Prospect and Exploration* 10 (6): 66–80.

Lee, Zong-Rong. 2011. "Taiwan qiye jituan jian qinshu wangluo de yingxiang yinsu" (The influence of kinship networks among Taiwanese enterprise groups). *Taiwan shehuixue kan* (Taiwanese journal of sociology), (no. 46): 115–66.

Lee, Zong-Rong, and Lin Thung-Hong, eds. 2017. *Weijing de qiji: Zhuanxing zhong de Taiwan jinji yu shehui* (Unfinished miracle: The economy and society of Taiwan in transition). Taipei: Institute of Sociology, Academia Sinica.

Levi, Margaret. 1988. *Of Rule and Revenue*. Berkeley: University of California Press.

Lewis, W. Arthur. 1954. "Economic Development with Unlimited Supplies of Labour." *The Manchester School* 22 (2): 139–91.

Li, Boping, and Tian Yanping. 2011. "Liang lun 'mingong huang' de bijiao fenxi yu qi-shi" (Comparative analysis and revelations from two rounds of "migrant worker famines"). *Nongye jingji wenti* (Agricultural economic issues), (no. 1): 88–94.

Li, Kwoh-ting. 1999. *Taiwan de duiwai jingji hezuo yu jiagong chukouqu* (Taiwan's for-eign economic cooperation and export-processing zone). Taipei: K. T. Li Foundation for Development of Science and Technology.

———. 2005. *Li Guoting: Wo de Taiwan jingyan—Li Guoting tan Taiwan caijing juece de zhiding yu sikou* (Li Kwoh-ting: My Taiwan experience—Li Kwoh-ting talks about the formulation and consideration of Taiwan's financial and economic poli-cies), edited by Liu Su-fen. Taipei: Yuanliu Chubanshe.

Li, Kwoh-ting, and Chen Mu-tsai. 1987. *Woguo jingji fazhan celüe zonglun* (Introduc-tion to our country's economic development strategy). Taipei: Lianjing.

Lim, Kean Fan and Niv Horesh. 2017 "The Chongqing vs. Guangdong Developmental 'Models' in Post-Mao China: Regional and Historical Perspectives on the Dynamics of Socioeconomic Change." *Journal of the Asia Pacific Economy* 22 (3): 372–95.

Lin, Nan. 1995. "Local Market Socialism: Local Corporatism in Action in Rural China." *Theory and Society* 24 (3): 301–54.

———. 2011. "Capitalism in China: A Centrally Managed Capitalism (CMC) and Its Future." *Management and Organization Review* 7 (1): 63–96.

Lin, Thung-Hong. 2007. "Chengshi Zhongguo de wuchanhua: Zhongguo chengzhen gumin jieji jiegou de zhuanxing yu shehui bupingdeng, 1979–2003" (Urban China's proletarianization: The transformation of China's urban resident class structure and social inequality, 1979–2003). *Taiwan shehuixue* (Taiwanese sociology), (no. 14): 101–53.

Lin, Thung-Hong, and Hu Bo-wei. 2017. "Jinji de juren: Taiwan qiye guimo xunsu chengzhang de yuanyin yu houguo" (The advancing colossus: The causes and effects of the rapid growth in scale of Taiwanese enterprises." In Lee, Zong-Rong, and Lin, *Weijing de qiji*, 230–66.

Lin, Thung-hong, Yi-ling Lin, and Wei-ling Tseng. 2016. "Manufacturing Suicide: The Politics of a World Factory." *Chinese Sociological Review* 48 (1): 1–32.

Liu, Kaiming. 2004. *Shenti de jiage: Zhongguo gongshang suopei yanjiu* (The price of the body: Research into China's occupational injury compensation). Shenzhen: Renmin Ribao Chubanshe.

Liu, Ya-Ling. 1992. "Reform from Below: The Private Economy and Local Politics in the Rural Industrialization of Wenzhou." *China Quarterly* 130: 293–316.

———. 2003. "Jingji zhuanxing de waizai dongli: Sunan Wujiang cong bentu jinkou tidai dao weizi chukou daoxiang" (The external dynamic of economic transforma-tion: Southern Jiangsu's Wujiang from local import substitution to foreign-invested export-orientation). *Taiwan shehuixue kan* (Taiwanese journal of sociology), (no. 30): 89–113.

———. 2009. "Zhongguo dushihua guocheng zhong xinxing de 'nongmin shouzu jieji': Wenzhou yu Wuxi 'cheng zhong cun' de zhuanxing lujing, jiti kangzheng yu fuli zhengce" (The rising "peasant rentier class" in China's urbanization process: The transformation route, collective resistance, and welfare policies of Wenzhou and Wuxi's "urban villages"). *Taiwan shehuixue* (Taiwanese sociology), (no. 18): 1–41.

Lin, Yi-ju. 2019. "Zhang Zhong-mou: shijie fenluan, taijidian cheng diyuan celuejia bizhegn zhidi" (Morris Chang: The world gets restless; TSMC becomes a battleground for geo-strategists), *Anue*, November 2, https://www.inside.com.tw/article/17988-Morris-Chang-TSMC-position-of-the-world.

Liu, Ying-feng. 2008. "Zhongguo lanyin huji zhidu de qiyuan yu bianqian: Yigong, guojia yu shichang" (The rise of and changes in China's blue stamp household registration system: Migrant workers, the state and the market). Master's thesis, National Tsing Hua University.

Lo, Chao-Kuang. 2014. "Zhongguo gongren jiti kangzheng de jihui yu juxian: Jiceng zhengfu yu caogen zuzhi de yingxiang" (The opportunities and limitations of Chinese workers' collective resistance: The influence of primary-level governments and grassroots organizations). Master's thesis, National Tsing Hua University.

Mann, Michael. 1986. *The Sources of Social Power*. New York: Cambridge University Press.
———. 1987. "Ruling Class Strategies and Citizenship." *Sociology* 21 (3): 339–54.

Mao, Zedong. 1956. *Lun shi da guanxi* (On the ten major relationships). Speech delivered on April 25, 1956, https://www.marxists.org/chinese/maozedong/marxist.org-chinese-mao-19560425.htm.

Marshall, T. H. 1994. "Citizenship and Social Class." In *Citizenship: Critical Concepts*, edited by Bryan S. Turner and Peter Hamilton, 5–44. London: Routledge.

Mearsheimer, John J. 2014. "Say Goodbye to Taiwan." *National Interest*, February 25, http://nationalinterest.org/article/say-goodbye-taiwan-9931.

Moore, Barrington. 1966. *Social Origins of Dictatorship and Democracy: Lord and Peasant in the Making of the Modern World*. Boston: Beacon Press.

Mulvad, Andreas. 2015. "Competing Hegemonic Projects within China's Variegated Capitalism: 'Liberal' Guangdong vs. 'Statist' Chongqing." *New Political Economy* 20 (2): 199–227.

Murphy, Kevin M., Andrei Shleifer, and Robert W. Vishny. 1993. "Why Is Rent-seeking So Costly to Growth?" *American Economic Review* 83 (2): 409–14.

Nanfang zhoumo (Southern Weekend). 2010. "Nanfang zhoumo jizhe wodi 28 tian jie Fushikang tiaolou zhenxiang" (*Southern Weekend* reporter goes underground for 28 days to uncover the truth behind the Foxconn suicides). China News and Commentary, May 17, https://goo.gl/BJ9k98.

Narula, Rajneesh, and John Dunning. 2000. "Industrial Development, Globalization and Multinational Enterprises: New Realities for Developing Countries." *Oxford Development Studies* 28 (2): 141–67.

National Bureau of Statistics Industrial and Transportation Statistics Division, ed. 2007. *Zhongguo gongyi jingji tongji nianjian 2007* (China industrial and economic statistical yearbook 2007). Beijing: Zhongguo Tongji Chubanshe.

———, ed. 2012. *Zhongguo gongyi jingji tongji nianjian 2012* (China industrial and economic statistical yearbook 2012). Beijing: Zhongguo Tongji Chubanshe.

National Bureau of Statistics of the People's Republic of China, ed. 1990. *Zhongguo renkou tongji nianjian 1990* (China population statistical yearbook 1990). Beijing: Zhongguo Tongji Chubanshe.

——, ed. 1991–1993. *Zhongguo tongji nianjian 1991, 1992, 1993* (China statistical yearbook, 1991, 1992, 1993). Beijing: Zhongguo Tongji Chubanshe.

——, ed. 1995–2015. *Zhongguo tongji nianjian, 1995–2014* (China statistical yearbook, 1995–2015). Beijing: Zhongguo Tongji Chubanshe.

National Bureau of Statistics of the People's Republic of China. 2017. *Laodong gongzi tongji baobiao zhidu* (The system of labor wage statistical reporting system). Concise ed. Beijing: National Bureau of Statistics.

National Bureau of Statistics Population and Employment Statistics Division, ed. 2013. *Zhongguo renkou he jiuye tongji nianjian 2013* (China population and employment statistical yearbook 2013). Beijing: Zhongguo Tongji Chubanshe.

National Bureau of Statistics Population and Employment Statistics Division. 2009. "Guanyu shangbannian chengzhen danwei zhigong pingjun gongzi de shuoming" (Notes on the average urban employees' wage in the first half of the year), August 7, http://www.gov.cn/gzdt/2009-08/07/content_1385719.htm.

National Bureau of Statistics Population and Employment Statistics Division and Ministry of Labor and Social Security Planning and Finance Division, eds. 2007. *Zhongguo laodong tongji nianjian 2007* (China labor statistical yearbook 2007). Beijing: Zhongguo Tongji Chubanshe.

National Development and Reform Commission. 2008. "Zhujiang sanjiaozhou diqu gaige fazhan guihua gangyao (2008–2020 nian)" (Pearl River Delta Region reform development plan outline [2008–20]), December 2008, https://www.dsec.gov.mo/BayArea/data/s1_001.pdf.

Naughton, Barry. 1995. *Growing out of the Plan: Chinese Economic Reform, 1978–1993.* Cambridge: Cambridge University Press.

Naughton, Barry M., and Kellee S. Tsai, eds. 2015. *State Capitalism, Institutional Adaptation, and the Chinese Miracle.* New York: Cambridge University Press.

Nee, Victor. 1989. "A Theory of Market Transition: From Redistribution to Markets in State Socialism." *American Sociological Review* 54 (5): 663–81.

——. 1992. "Organizational Dynamics of Market Transition: Hybrid Forms, Property Rights, and Mixed Economy in China." *Administrative Science Quarterly* 37 (1): 1–27.

Nee, Victor, and Sonja Opper. 2012. *Capitalism from Below: Markets and Institutional Change in China.* Cambridge, MA: Harvard University Press.

Ngo, Tak-Wing. 2010. "Zujin de shengchan yu Zhongguo de chanye fazhan" (The production of rent and China's industrial development). In Wu and Ngo, *Xunzu yu Zhongguo chanye fazhan,* 7–36.

Norris, William. 2016. *Chinese Economic Statecraft: Commercial Actors, Grand Strategy, and State Control.* Ithaca, NY: Cornell University Press.

North, Douglass. 1993. "Institutions and Credible Commitment." *Journal of Institutional and Theoretical Economics* 149 (1): 11–23.

Office of the United States Trade Representative, Executive Office of the President. 2018. "Update Concerning China's Acts, Policies and Practices Related to Technology Transfer, Intellectual Property, and Innovation," November 20, https://ustr.gov/sites/default/files/enforcement/301Investigations/301%20Report%20Update.pdf.

Oi, Jean C. 1992. "Fiscal Reform and the Economic Foundations of Local State Corporatism in China." *World Politics* 45 (1): 99–126.

———. 1996. "The Role of the Local State in China's Transitional Economy." In *China's Transitional Economy*, edited by Andrew Walder, 170–87. Oxford: Oxford University Press.

———. 1999. *Rural China Takes Off: Institutional Foundations of Economic Reform*. Berkeley: University of California Press.

Öniş, Ziya. 1991. "The Logic of the Developmental State." *Comparative Politics* 24 (1): 109–26.

Parris, Kristen. 1993. "Local Initiative and National Reform: The Wenzhou Model of Development." *China Quarterly* 134: 242–63.

Peng, Fang. 2007a. "Sushe, shitang, gongzuo xianchang: Zhu sanjiao gongren de richang shenguo yu shengchan zhengzhi" (Dormitory, canteen, worksite: The daily life and production politics of workers in the Pearl River Delta). Master's thesis, National Tsing Hua University.

———. 2007b. "Jishi gangong de baquan tizhi: Dui Huanan yijia jiagong chukou Taizichang de ludong tizhi yanjiu" (The hegemonic system of clocked rush work: A study of the labor regime of a South China Taiwanese processing export factory). *Taiwan shehuixue* (Taiwanese sociology), (no. 14): 51–100.

Po, Lan-chih, and Pun Ngai. 2003. "Kuajie zhili: Taizi canyu Kunshan zhidu chuangxin de ge'an yanjiu" (Cross-border governance: The case study of Taiwanese investment participating in Kunshan's institutional innovation). *Chengshi yu sheji xuebao* (Cities and design), (nos. 15–16): 59–91.

Ponte, Stefano, Gray Gereffi, and Gale Raj-Reichert. 2019. *Handbook on Global Value Chains*. Cheltenham, UK: Edward Elgar.

Pun, Ngai. 2006. *Zhongguo nügong—Xinxing dagong jieji de huhuan* (China's female workers—Summoning the burgeoning worker class). Hong Kong: Mingbao Chubanshe.

Pun, Ngai, and Lu Huilin. 2010. "Unfinished Proletarianization: Self, Anger, and Class Action among the Second Generation of Peasant-Workers in Present-Day China." *Modern China* 36 (5): 493–519.

Qian, Yingyi, and Joseph Stiglitz. 1996. "Institutional Innovations and the Role of Local Government in Transition Economies: The Case of Guangdong Province of China." In *Reforming Asian Socialism: The Growth of Market Institutions*, edited by John McMillan and Barry Naughton, 175–93. Ann Arbor: University of Michigan Press.

Qin, Hui. 2007. "Zhongguo jingji fazhan de direnquan youshi" (The advantage of deficient human rights in China's economic development). Ai Sixiang, November 2, 2007, http://www.aisixiang.com/data/16401.html.

Ramo, Joshua Cooper. 2004. *The Beijing Consensus*. London: Foreign Policy Centre.

Ren, Yan, and Pun Ngai. 2006. "Kuaguo laodong guocheng de kongjian zhengzhi: Quanqiuhua shidai de sushe laodong tizhi" (The spatial politics of the transnational labor process: The dormitory labor regime in the globalization era). *Shehuixue yanjiu* (Sociology research), (no. 4): 21–33.

Rock, Michael, and Heidi Bonnet. 2004. "The Comparative Politics of Corruption: Accounting for the East Asian Paradox in Empirical Studies of Corruption, Growth and Investment." *World Development* 32 (6): 999–1017.

Rodrik, Dani. 2011. *The Globalization Paradox: Democracy and the Future of the World Economy*. New York: W. W. Norton.

———. 2013. "The New Mercantilist Challenge." *Project Syndicate*, January 9, http://www.project-syndicate.org/commentary/the-return-of-mercantilism-by-dani-rodrik.

Rogers, Mike, and C. A. Dutch Ruppersberger. 2012. *Investigative Report on the U.S. National Security Issues Posed by Chinese Telecommunications Companies Huawei and ZTE*. Washington: U.S. House of Representatives.

Sabel, Charles F. 1994. "Learning by Monitoring: The Institutions of Economic Development." In *The Handbook of Economic Sociology*, edited by Neil Smelser and Richard Swedberg, 137–65. Princeton, NJ: Princeton University Press.

Sachs, Jeffrey, and Wing Thye Woo. 1994. "Structural Factors in the Economic Reforms of China, Eastern Europe, and the Former Soviet Union." *Economic Policy* 18 (1): 102–45.

Schubert, Gunter, and Thomas Heberer. 2015. "Continuity and Change in China's 'Local State Developmentalism.'" *Issues and Studies* 51 (2): 1–38.

Scott, James. 1985. *Weapons of the Weak: Everyday Forms of Peasant Resistance*. New Haven, CT: Yale University Press.

Scott, W. Richard, and Gerald F. Davis. 2007. *Organizations and Organizing: Rational, Natural, and Open Systems Perspectives*. Upper Saddle River, NJ: Pearson.

Selden, Mark, and Wu Jieh-min. 2011. "The Chinese State, Incomplete Proletarianization and Structures of Inequality in Two Epochs." *Asia-Pacific Journal* 9 (5): 1–35.

Shambaugh, David. 2018. "U.S.-China Rivalry in Southeast Asia: Power Shift or Competitive Coexistence?" *International Security* 42 (4): 85–127.

Shan, Shelley. 2014. "Ambit Corp Must Submit 4G Wiretap Report: NCC." *Taipei Times*, June 12, http://www.taipeitimes.com/News/taiwan/archives/2014/06/12/2003592576.

Shanghai Department of Human Resources and Social Security. 2013. "Guanyu dui 'yiyuan wailai hugong' deng silei lai Hu congye renyuan shixing kaizhan linghuo jiuye dengji de tongzhi, hurenshejiufa (2013) shisan hao" (Notice of trial launch of flexible employment registration for "nonnative nursing personnel in hospitals, hurenshejiufa [2013] no. 13" and for three types of people coming to Shanghai to work), March 1, Shuiwu, https://www.shui5.cn/article/fo/45814.html.

Shanghai Financial Gazetteer Compilation Committee, ed. 2003. *Shanghai jinrong zhi* (Shanghai financial gazetteer). Shanghai: Shanghai Shehui Kexueyuan Chubanshe.

Shanghai Municipal Statistics Bureau, ed. 2014. *Shanghai tongji nianjian 2014* (Shanghai statistical yearbook 2014). Beijing: Zhongguo Tongji Chubanshe.

Shao, Mingjun. 1992. *Tequ shuishou gailun* (Introduction to special zone taxation). Beijing: Zhongguo Jingji Chubanshe.

Shenzhen Municipal Statistics Bureau, ed. 2009. *Shenzhen tongji nianjian 2009* (Shenzhen statistical yearbook 2009). Beijing: Zhongguo Tongji Chubanshe.

———, ed. 2013. *Shenzhen tongji nianjian 2013* (Shenzhen statistical yearbook 2013). Beijing: Zhongguo Tongji Chubanshe.

———, ed. 2014. *Shenzhen tongji nianjian 2014* (Shenzhen statistical yearbook 20014). Beijing: Zhongguo Tongji Chubanshe.

Shieh, Gwo-Shyong. 1989. "Weibao zhidu: Bijiao lishi de huigu" (The outsourcing system: A comparative historical review). *Taiwan shehui yanjiu jikan* (Taiwan: A radical quarterly in social studies), (no. 21): 29–69.

———. 1992. *"Boss" Island: The Subcontracting Network and Micro-Entrepreneurship in Taiwan's Development*. New York: Peter Lang.

———. 1997. *Chun laodong: Taiwan laodong tizhi zhu lun* (Pure labor: On Taiwan's labor regime). Taipei: Preparatory Office of the Institute of Sociology, Academia Sinica.

Shirk, Susan. 1993. *The Political Logic of Economic Reform in China*. Berkeley: University of California Press.

Shleifer, Andrei, and Robert W. Vishny. 1993. "Corruption." *Quarterly Journal of Economics* 108 (3): 599–617.

Siu, Kaxton. 2015. "Continuity and Change in the Everyday Lives of Chinese Migrant Factory Workers." *China Journal* 74: 43–65.

Sklair, Leslie. 2001. *The Transnational Capitalist Class*. Oxford: Blackwell.

SMIC (Semiconductor Manufacturing International Corporation). 2018. "Xinwengao: Zhongxin Guoji erlingyiba nian diyi jidu yeji gongbu" (Press release: SMIC reports 2018 first quarter results), May 9, Shanghai.

———. 2022. "SMIC reports unaudited results for the three months ended December 31, 2021," February 10, 2022, https://smic.shwebspace.com/uploads/2021%20Q4%20Earnings%20Release_ENG%20final.pdf.

So, Alvin Y. 2003a. "Introduction: Rethinking the Chinese Development Miracle." In So, *China's Developmental Miracle*, 3–26.

———, ed. 2003b. *China's Developmental Miracle: Origins, Transformations, and Challenges*. Armonk, NY: M. E. Sharpe.

So, Alvin Y., and Stephen W. K. Chiu. 1995. *East Asia and the World Economy*. Thousand Oaks, CA: Sage.

Solinger, Dorothy J. 1999. *Contesting Citizenship in Urban China: Peasant Migrants, the State, and the Logic of the Market*. Berkeley: University of California Press.

———. 2006. "The Creation of a New Underclass in China and Its Implications." *Environment and Urbanization* 18 (1): 177–93.

Somers, Margaret. 2008. *Genealogies of Citizenship: Markets, Statelessness, and the Right to Have Rights*. New York: Cambridge University Press.

Stallings, Barbara. 1990. "The Role of Foreign Capital in Economic Development." In Gereffi and Wyman, *Manufacturing Miracles*, 55–89.

State Council of the People's Republic of China. 2015. "Guowuyuan guanyu yinfa 'Zhongguo zhizao 2025' de tongzhi (guofa [2015] 28 hao)" (State Council on the issuance of "Made in China 2025" notice, State Council Document [2015] no. 28), May 8, http://www.gov.cn/zhengce/content/2015-05/19/content_9784.htm.

Steinfeld, Edward. 2004. "China's Shallow Integration: Networked Production and the New Challenges for Late Industrialization." *World Development* 32 (11): 1971–87.

Strange, Susan. 1996. *The Retreat of the State: The Diffusion of Power in the World Economy*. New York: Cambridge University Press.

Strategy Advisory Committee for National Manufacturing and Strong Nation. 2015. "'Zhongguo zhizao 2025' zhongdian lingyu jishu luxiantu" ("Made in China 2025" key sectors technical road map), October, http://www.cm2025.org/uploadfile/2016 /0321/20160321015412313.pdf.

Sturgeon, Timothy. 2009. "From Commodity Chains to Value Chains: Interdisciplinary Theory Building in an Age of Globalization." In Bair, *Frontiers of Commodity Chain Research*, 100–35.

Sturgeon, Timothy J., and Richard K. Lester. 2004. "The New Global Supply-Base: New Challenges for Local Suppliers in East Asia." In *Global Production Networking and Technological Change in East Asia*, edited by Shahid Yusuf, Anjum Altaf, and Kaoru Nabeshima, 35–87. Washington: World Bank.

Suzhou Municipal Statistics Bureau, ed. 2014. *Suzhou tongji nianjian 2014* (Suzhou statistical yearbook 2014). Beijing: Zhongguo Tongji Chubanshe.

Tan, Shen. 2004. "Weilai gong de zhuyao wenti" (The main problems of migrant workers). *Zhongguo shehuixue wang* (China sociology online), reposted in Universities Service Centre for China Studies, The Chinese University of Hong Kong, http://paper .usc.cuhk.edu.hk/Details.aspx?id=3506.

Taplin, Ian M. 1994. "Strategic Reorientation of U.S. Apparel Films." In Gereffi and Korzeniewicz, *Commodity Chains and Global Capitalism*, 205–22.

Thun, Eric. 2006. *Changing Lanes in China: Foreign Direct Investment, Local Governments, and Auto Sector Development*. New York: Cambridge University Press.

Tilly, Charles. 1998. *Durable Inequality*. Berkeley: University of California Press.

Tsai, Kellee S. 2007. *Capitalism without Democracy: The Private Sector in Contemporary China*. Ithaca, NY: Cornell University Press.

Tsai, Kellee S., and Barry M. Naughton. 2015. "Introduction: State Capitalism and the Chinese Economic Miracle." In Naughton and Tsai, *State Capitalism, Institutional Adaptation, and the Chinese Miracle*, 1–24.

Tseng, Wei-ling. 2012. "Zhili shijie gonchang—yi Fushikang weili" (Governing the factory of the world—The case of Foxconn). Master's thesis, National Taipei University.

Tseng, Wei-ling, and Lin Thung-Hong. 2012. "Jiegou shijie gongchang: Taishang Fushikang jituan de quanqiu suiliehua zhuanshi shengchan tizhi" (Deconstructing the factory of the world: Foxconn's global fragmented authoritarian production regime). Paper presented at the Annual Meeting of Taiwanese Sociological Association, Taichung, Taiwan, November 24–25, 2012.

TSMC (Taiwan Semiconductor Manufacturing Company). 2018. "Taiwan Jiti Dianlu Zhizao Gufen Youxian Gongsi ji zigongsi hebing caiwu baogao ji kuaijishi heyue baogao, minguo 107 ji 106 nian diyiji" (Taiwan Semiconductor Manufacturing Company, Limited and subsidiaries consolidated financial report and auditor's report, Minguo 107 and 106 [2018 and 2017] first quarter). Hsinchu, Taiwan.

———. 2022. "Financial Results—2021Q4." January 13, https://investor.tsmc.com /english/encrypt/files/encrypt_file/reports/2022-01/485990ef5a2f4d7746b9dcb7731d5 05e62202fa7/FS.pdf.

Tu, Hsin-fei. 2011. "Shanzhaiji de jishu yu zhengzhi" (The techniques and politics of knock-off cell phones). Master's thesis, National Tsing Hua University.

Tullock, Gordon. 1990. "The Costs of Special Privilege." In *Perspectives on Positive Political Economy*, edited by James E. Alt and Kenneth A. Shepsle, 195–211. New York: Cambridge University Press.

———. 1993. *Rent Seeking*. Brookfield, VT: Edward Elgar.

Unger, Jonathan, and Anita Chan. 1995. "China, Corporatism, and the East Asian Model." *Australian Journal of Chinese Affairs* 33: 29–53.

Vernon, Raymond. 1971. *Sovereignty at Bay*. New York: Basic Books.

Vogel, Ezra F. 1989. *One Step Ahead in China: Guangdong under Reform*. Cambridge, MA: Harvard University Press.

Wade, Robert. 1990. *Governing the Market: Economic Theory and the Role of Government in East Asian Industrialization*. Princeton, NJ: Princeton University Press.

Walder, Andrew G. 1995. "Local Governments as Industrial Firms: An Organizational Analysis of China's Transitional Economy." *American Journal of Sociology* 101 (2): 263–301.

Wang, Chunyu, Jingzhong Ye, and Jennifer C. Franco. 2014. "Local State Corporatism or Neo-Guanxilism? Observations from the County Level of Government in China." *Journal of Contemporary China* 23 (87): 418–515.

Wang, Fei-ling. 2005. *Organizing through Division and Exclusion: China's Hukou System*. Stanford, CA: Stanford University Press.

Wang, Jenn-hwan. 2010. *Zhuigan de jixian: Taiwan de jingji zhuanxing yu chuangxi* (Chasing the limits: Taiwan's economic transformation and innovation). Kaohsiung, Taiwan: Chuliu.

Wang, Po-chi. 2014. "Chongfang Taishang shengchan xieli wangluo: Yi Zhu Sanjiao yijia Taizi dianzichang weili" (Revisiting the Taishang Production Networks: The example of a Taiwanese-owned electronics factory in the Pearl River Delta). Master's thesis, National Tsing Hua University.

Wang, Tso-jung. 2014. *Kanjian naxienian women chuangzao de Taiwan jingji qiji* (See the Taiwan economic miracle we created in those years). Taipei: China Times Publishing Company.

Wang, Yang. 2008. "Jinrong weiji gei Guangdong shangle shengdong yike" (Financial crisis gives Guangdong a vivid lesson). *Renmin ribao haiwaiban* (*People's Daily* overseas edition), December 10, 2008, https://news.ifeng.com/opinion/200812/1210_23_915697.shtml.

Wank, David. 1996. "The Institutional Process of Market Clientelism: Guanxi and Private Business in a South China City." *China Quarterly* 147: 820–38.

Warr, Peter G. 1989. "Export Processing Zones: The Economics of Enclave Manufacturing." *World Bank Research Observer* 4 (1): 65–88.

Wedeman, Andrew H. 2003. *From Mao to Market: Rent Seeking, Local Protectionism, and Marketization in China*. Cambridge: Cambridge University Press

———. 2012. *Double Paradox: Rapid Growth and Rising Corruption in China*. Ithaca, NY: Cornell University Press.

Wei, Cheng. 2007. *Zhongguo nongmingong diaocha* (A survey of Chinese rural migrant workers). Beijing: Falü chubanshe.

Wein, Michelle A., Stephen J. Ezell, and Robert D. Atkinson. 2014. "The Global Mercantilist Index: A New Approach to Ranking Nations' Trade Policies." Information Technology and Innovation Foundation, October, https://reurl.cc/Nr9iL6.

Weiss, Linda, ed. 2003. *States in the Global Economy: Bringing Domestic Institutions Back In*. Cambridge: Cambridge University Press.

Wen, Hsien-shen. 1984. "Jingjianhui de guoqu, xianzai yu weilai" (The past, present, and future of the Council for Economic Planning and Development). *Tianxia zazhi* (Commonwealth magazine), (no. 42): 12–25.

White House. 2017. "The National Security Strategy of the United States of America." Issued by President Donald Trump, December, https://trumpwhitehouse.archives.gov/wp-content/uploads/2017/12/NSS-Final-12-18-2017-0905.pdf.

Whittaker, D. Hugh, Tianbiao Zhu, Timothy Sturgeon, Mon Han Tsai, and Toshie Okita. 2010. "Compressed Development." *Studies in Comparative International Development* 45 (4): 439–67.

Woo-Cumings, Meredith, ed. 1999. *The Developmental State*. Ithaca, NY: Cornell University Press.

Wu, Jieh-min. 1997. "Strange Bedfellows: Dynamics of Government-Business Relations between Chinese Local Authorities and Taiwanese Investors." *Journal of Contemporary China* 6 (15): 319–46.

———. 1998. "Zhongguo xiangcun kuaisu gongyehua de zhidu dongli: Difang changquan tizhi yu feizhengshi siyouhua" (The institutional dynamics of the rapid industrialization of the Chinese countryside: The local property rights system and unofficial privatization). *Taiwan zhengzhixue kan* (Taiwan political science journal), (no. 3): 3–63.

———. 2000. "Yazha renxing kongjian: Shenfen chaxu yu Zhongguoshi duochong boxue" (Squeezing out humanity: Differential status and Chinese-style multiple exploitation). *Taiwan shehui yanjiu jikan* (Taiwan: A radical quarterly in social studies), no. 39: 1–44.

———. 2001. "State Policy and Guanxi Network Adaptation: A Case Study of Local Bureaucratic Rent-Seeking in China." *Issues and Studies* 37 (1): 20–48.

———. 2010. "Rural Migrant Workers and China's Differential Citizenship: A Comparative-Institutional Analysis." In *One Country, Two Societies: Rural-Urban Inequality in Contemporary China*, edited by Martin King Whyte, 55–81. Cambridge, MA: Harvard University Press.

———. 2011. "Yongyuan de yixiangke? Gongmin shenfen chaxu yu Zhongguo nongmingong jieji" (Forever alien? Differential citizenship and China's migrant worker class). *Taiwan shehuixue* (Taiwanese sociology), (no. 21): 51–99.

———. 2016. "The China Factor in Taiwan: Impact and Response." In *Handbook of Modern Taiwan Politics and Society*, edited by Gunter Schubert, 425–45. London: Routledge.

———. 2017a. "Migrant Citizenship Regimes in Globalized China: A Historical-Institutional Comparison." *Rural China* 14 (1): 128–54.

———. 2017b. "Yi shangye moshi zuo tongzhan: Kuaihaixia zheng-shang guanxi zhong de zaidi xielizhe jizhi" (Business model as united front: Local collaborative mechanism in cross-strait government-business relations). In Lee, Zong-Rong, and Lin Thung-Hong, *Weijing de qiji*, 676–719.

————. 2018. "Zhongguo rui shili, liang'an guanxi, quanqiu xiaoying: Yige bijiao fenxi jiagou" (China's sharp power, cross-strait relations, global effects: A comparative analytical framework). Paper presented at a seminar hosted by the Taiwan Research Institute of Waseda University and the Japan Society of Taiwan Studies, Waseda University, Tokyo, June 8, 2018.

————. 2019. *Xunzu Zhongguo: Taishang, Guangdong moshi yu quanqiu zibenzhuyi* (Rent-seeking developmental state in China: Taishang, Guangdong model and global capitalism). Taipei: National Taiwan University Press.

Wu, Jieh-min, Chen Chih-Jou Jay, Liu Ching-geng, et al. 2007. *Zhongguo yanjiu— Zhongguo shehui zhengzhi yanjiu shequn zhenghe yu yiti shenhua* (China research— Integrated and deeper discussion of Chinese social and political research groups). Taipei: National Science Council.

Wu, Jinglian. 2005. *Dangdai Zhongguo jinji gaige* (Modern China's economic reforms). Taipei: McGraw Hill.

Wu, Yongping, and Tak-Wing Ngo, eds. 2010. *Xunzu yu Zhongguo chanye fazhan* (Rent seeking and China's industrial development). Beijing: Shangwu yinshuguan.

Wu, Zhe. 2008. "Zhongguo shoujia hezi qiye Taiping shoudaichang luocheng" (Completion of China's first joint venture enterprise, Taiping Handbags Factory). *Nanfangwang*, November 19, 2008, http://news.163.com/08/1119/10/4R3V9FNH00011124J.html. Accessed August 20, 2010.

Xinhuanet. 2012. "Xin Jinping: Chengqian qihou, jiwang kailai, jixu chaozhe zhonghua minzu weida fuxing mubiao fenyong qianjin" (Xin Jinping: Inherit the past and open up the future, continue to march towards the goal of the great rejuvenation of the Chinese nation), November 29, http://www.xinhuanet.com//politics/2012-11/29/c_113852724.htm.

Yang, Kuisong. 2006. "Mao Zedong yu 'zhenya fangeming' yundong" (Mao Zedong and the campaign to "suppress counterrevolutionaries"). In *Liang'an fentu: Lengzhen chuqi de zhengji fazhan* (Divergence of two sides of the strait: Political economic development in the early Cold War), edited by Chen Yung-fa, 31–76. Taipei: Academia Sinica Institute of Modern History.

Yang, Ming. 1994. "Zhujiang moshi" (Pearl River model). In *Zhongguo chengxiang xietiao fazhan yanjiu* (Research in the coordinated development of China's cities and countryside), edited by Zhou Erliu and Zhang Yulin, 68–93. Hong Kong: Oxford University Press.

Yeung, Henry Wai-chung, Weidong Liu, and Peter Dicken. 2006. "Transnational Corporations and Network Effects of a Local Manufacturing Cluster in Mobile Telecommunications Equipment in China." *World Development* 34 (3): 520–40.

Yin, Yanlin. 1993. *Huilü: Duogui hebing yu shidu guanzhi* (Exchange rates: Multitrack merger and appropriate control). Beijing: Zhongguo Caizheng Jingji Chubanshe.

Yu, Yi-wen, Ko-chia Yu, and Tse-chun Lin. 2016. "Political Economy of Cross-Strait Relations: Is Beijing's Patronage Policy on Taiwanese Business Sustainable?" *Journal of Contemporary China* 25 (99): 372–88.

Yusuf, Shahid. 1994. "China's Macroeconomic Performance and Management during Transition." *Journal of Economic Perspectives* 8 (2): 71–92.

Zhang, Jieping. 2016. "Wukang shijian" (The Wukang Incident). Unpublished manuscript, Microsoft Word file.

Zhang, Xiaobo, Jin Yang, and Shenglin Wang. 2010. "China Has Reached the Lewis Turning Point." IFPRI Discussion Paper 000977. Washington: International Food and Policy Research Institute.

Zhang, Xuguang. 2001. "Qiantan jiaru WTO dui wo qu lailiao jiagong qiye de yingxiang" (A brief talk on how joining the WTO affected enterprises processing shipped materials in my zone). *Tequ jingji* (Special zone economics), (no. 1): 47–48.

Zhou, Hong. 2003. "Cong 'shudi guanli' dao 'pujixing tizhi'" (From "local management" to a "universal system"). *Zhongguo shehui baozhang* (Chinese social insurance), (no. 8): 22.

Zhou, Hualei. 2016. "Beijing shi 'bentu youxian': Yong ganzou haizi, lai ganzou jiazhang" (Beijing-style "local priority": Used to drive out children and parents). Duanchuanmei (Initium), August 29, https://theinitium.com/article/20160829-mainland-beijingimmigrants/.

Zhu, Weiping. 2008. "Zhujiang sanjiaozhou chanye zhuanxing wenti yanjiu" (Research on the issue of industrial transformation in the Pearl River Delta). *Xueshu yanjiu* (Academic research), (no. 10): 38–44.

Index

Accton company, 359
Adidas, 337–39, 341
Aixtron, 433
Akira, Hayami, 52
Alibaba company, 9, 362
Allison, Graham, 430
Alpha company, 359
AMD company, 418
Ang, Yuen Yuen, 386n1
Apple, 41, 297, 363, 366. *See also* Foxconn Technology Group
apprentice-turned-boss system, 195–96, 345, 371, 409
Arrighi, Giovanni, 52–53, 407
Asian financial crisis (1998), 106, 107, 403–4, 410
authoritarianism, xx–xxi, 9–10, 312, 428–29, 432–33, 440, 441, 442, 444

Baidu company, 9, 362
Bair, Jennifer, 38, 59
Bao'an County Shiyan Commune Shangwu Brigade Processing Factory, 92
BDCCs (buyer-driven commodity chains), 54, 61, 62, 63, 73
Beijing, 230, 269, 406
Beijing consensus, 75, 440

Belt and Road Initiative, 12, 44, 412, 431
Bhagwati, Jagdish, 383
Biden, Joe, xxiii
Big Fund (China National Integrated Circuit Industry Investment Fund), 10, 367–68, 414, 416, 438
Blecher, Marc, 49–50
BOE Technology, 421
brand names. *See* lead firms
British Virgin Islands, 110, 111
Broadcom, 434
Burawoy, Michael, 23–24, 295, 296, 298, 299
bureaucratic protection. *See* clientelism
Butollo, Florian, 371
buyer-driven commodity chains (BDCCs), 54, 61, 62, 63, 73

cadres: broker role, 130; and flexible measures, 86–88, 176–77, 299; and head tax, 186; and land use certification, 188, 191; local state theory on, 46–47; need for incentives, 80; and processing of shipped materials, 100, 331–32; and recollectivization, 45; regional variations, 47–48; as rentier class, xviii, 193, 382; and socialism vs. capitalism debate, 85, 389; Taiyang

cadres (*continued*)
   company case study, 188, 189; and
   villages, 32n2, 191–92. See also *guanxi*;
   institutional rent seeking; local growth
   alliances
Cambodia, 339
Campbell, Kurt, 442
Carter, Jimmy, 36
case selection, 71–77
caste system (South India), 262
CCP. *See* Chinese state
cell-phone industry, 9, 41, 362–64, 367.
   See also information and communication technology (ICT) industry
central government: and flexible
   measures, 87–88, 170, 173–74, 176–77;
   and institutional rent seeking, 47, 67,
   87–88, 173–74; local government
   authority delegation, 87, 133, 177, 385,
   386–87, 443; in local growth alliances,
   31, 40, 67, 68, 97, 264; strength of, 8;
   and tax reform (1994), 48, 133, 187. *See
   also* Chinese economic policy; Chinese
   state; labor regulations
cha'e huiru (customs spread), 134, 199–200
Chan, Anita, 47, 296, 297
Chang Kuei-min, 292, 294
Chang, Morris, 19–20, 423–24
Chang, Richard, 417, 420
changzhang (factory heads), 191, 192–93,
   204–6
chaxu geju (differential mode of associa-
   tion), 259. *See also* differential
   citizenship
Chen, Ling, 369
Chen Shui-bian, 162
Chen Yun, 84
Cheng Chih-peng, 42n5, 66, 353, 355
Chengdu model, 74
Cheng Lu-lin, 73
Cheung Tzi-mei, 91–92
Chiang Ching-kuo, 37n3, 400n4, 403
Chiang Kai-shek, 36, 400n4, 407
Chiang Shang-yi, 415n12
Chi Mei company, 1

China Mobile, 360
China model, xx, xxiv, 5, 6, 71n12, 74–75,
   398, 407, 426. *See also* Guangdong
   model
China National Cereals, Oils, and
   Foodstuffs Import and Export
   Company, 96
China National Integrated Circuit
   Industry Investment Fund (Big Fund),
   10, 367–68, 414, 416, 438
China Resources Group, 94–97
Chinese economic growth: "China
   model" on, 71n12, 74–75; developmental state theory on, 49–51, 56; and
   economic structure, 102–4; export-
   oriented development theory on, 28,
   52–57; and foreign exchange reserves,
   3–4, 30, 41, 73, 90; Guangdong model
   benefits for, 40–42; Guangdong
   model as intrinsic to, 4–5, 72–74;
   GVC/GCC theory on, 28, 30–31, 33,
   54–57, 58, 73, 394–95; and infrastructure, 41; local state theory on, 46–49;
   market transition theory on, 27,
   45–46; phases of, 28–29, 30, 37;
   slowing of, 76, 102; state-centered
   theory on, 27–28, 46–52, 56, 97; and
   tax revenues, 30, 41; world-systems
   theory on, 52–53, 54, 55; and WTO
   membership, 4, 5, 41–42, 74–75, 116,
   441. *See also* Chinese economic
   growth in East Asian context
Chinese economic growth in East Asian
   context, 394–95, *396–97*, 398–413; and
   development results, 409–13; and
   foreign direct investment, 7, 403–4;
   and geopolitics, 398–99; and institutional rent seeking, 402, 407–9; and
   migrant worker exploitation, xviii, 51,
   404–7; and ownership structure,
   401–3; and rent-seeking developmental
   state, 10, 381–82; and state-market
   relations, 399–401, 402, 411
Chinese economic policy: dual labor
   market, 7, 69–70, 264, 266, 299; and

economic crimes, 84–86; Eleventh Five-Year Plan, 313; and environmental protection standards, 135, 315, 333; Great Leap Forward (1958–60), 14, 223n1, 261n32, 421n34; Great Western Development Policy, 135; migrant workers as official class, 7, 223–26; and neomercantilism, 9, 361–62; "New Twenty-Two Articles," 97–98; pitfalls of, 425–29; Social Insurance Law (2011), 135, 194, 210, 217, 271, 274, 304–5; socialism vs. capitalism debate, 9, 81–84, 90, 91, 388–89; special economic zones, 14, 80, 81–84, 88, 91, 123, *124*, 125; tax incentives for processing of shipped materials, 99, 122, 133, 154, 174, 180; tax incentive standardization, 318–21; Twelfth Five-Year Plan, 44, 313, 317, 413–14; Two Centenaries, 421. *See also* Guangdong model; labor regulations; macroeconomic reforms (1994); migrant worker exploitation; minimum wages; transitional economy

Chinese-owned companies. *See* mainland-owned companies

Chinese state: administrative strata in, 31–32; authoritarianism, xx–xxi, 9–10, 312, 428–29, 432–33, 440, 441, 442, 444; Custody and Repatriation Methods for Urban Vagrants and Beggars, 227, 294; East Asian context, 399–401, 402, 411; economic nationalism, 9, 12–13, 20, 361–62, 445; expansionism, 2, 3, 12–13, 431–32, 440, 442–43; Four Cardinal Principles, 388; Great Firewall, 361; nature of, 300, 411, 443–44; nonhomogenous nature of, 40n4; Property Rights Law, 391n3; rural-urban dualism, 223, 232, 258–59, 260, 261, 262, 265–66, 268–70, 444; "seven unmentionables" policy, 428; size of, 49; surveillance by, 9, 292, 306, 361, 362, 411, 428, 432, 442; territorial jurisdiction doctrine (*shudi guanli*), 258, 259, 261–62. *See also* differential citizenship; foreign exchange; rent-seeking developmental state

Chinese-Taiwanese relations, xxviii–xxix, 2–3, 18–19; "31 Preferential Measures for Taiwan," 16n11, 18, 19; trade, 11–12, 17, 113–14

Chongqing, 109

Chongqing model, 74

citizenship. *See* differential citizenship

clientelism: and fictive ownership arrangements, 165–66, 169; and institutional rent seeking, 34; in local growth alliances, 34, 39–40, 67, 379–80; Taiyang company case study, 165–66, 169

Clinton, Bill, 441

Coase, Ronald, 55

Cold War, 14, 35–36, 398, 402, 439–40

collaboration fees, 333–35

commodity chain analysis, 52–53, 57, 61, 63–64

Confucius Institutes, 432

copycat industry, 362–65, 370–71

core plant business model, 323–25, 327

corporate social responsibility (CSR), 202, 250, 255, 297, 327, 336–37

corruption, 47, 382, 387, 389. *See also* institutional rent seeking

cross-strait relations. *See* Chinese-Taiwanese relations

Cross-Strait Service Trade Agreement, 3

Cultural Revolution, 82, 95, 223n1

Cumings, Bruce, 35–36

Custody and Repatriation Methods for Urban Vagrants and Beggars, 227, 294

customs spread (*cha'e huiru*), 134, 199–200

Dajin Garment Factory, 91–92

Datang Telecom, 415

Delta Electronics, 161

Deng Xiaoping: accession to power, 35; and economic crimes, 86; and foreign exchange reform, 177; and Four Cardinal Principles, 388n2; and

Deng Xiaoping (*continued*)
Guangdong model launch stage, 83, 84; and socialism vs. capitalism debate, 389; on special economic zones, 80, 91
dependency theory, 7–8, 380, 403
developmental state theory, 49–51, 56
differential citizenship, xviii, xx, 6–7, 67, 70, 257–63; and authoritarianism, xx, 444; concept origins, 257–58, 259–60; defined, 259; and dual exploitation, 34, 263–66; and educational discrimination, 267–68, 269, 289; and globalization, 444; and *hukou* system, 258–59, 261, 262–63, 265–66; institutional characteristics of, 261–63; and rent-seeking developmental state, 300; and residential permit systems, 229; and rural-urban dualism, 258–59, 260, 261, 262, 265–66, 268–69; and social insurance fee enforcement, 194; Taiyang company case study, 189–90, *190*, 194; and theoretical nature of labor regime, 299, 300; and urban protectionism, 268–70, 271, 274, 406; vs. Western citizenship ideal, 258–59. *See also* social insurance discrimination
Digital China, 358–59
Ding Xueliang, 71n12
directly unproductive profit-seeking activities (DUP), 383, 385
domestic markets: and ICT industry, 8, 9, 358, 361, 365, 366–67, 368–69, 381; and industrial upgrading policy, 8–9, 367; and lead firms, 349–50; protection of, 8, 9, 362. *See also* red supply chain
Dongguan: industrial upgrading policy, 75; social insurance discrimination, 278–79, *280*, 281. *See also* Guangdong model; Pearl River Delta region
dormitory labor regime, 286–95; and *hukou* system, 264; and informal economy participation, 290–91; and migrant worker resistance, 290, 291–93; origins of, 287–88; regional variations, 286–87, 288; and security, 293–95; and social control, 288–89; and social segregation, 289–90; and theoretical nature of labor regime, 298
doux commerce thesis, 441
drone industry, 364
dual labor market, 7, 69–70, 264, 266, 299. *See also* differential citizenship
dual-track exchange rate. *See* exchange-rate spread
Duan Yun, 96
Duckett, Jane, 50
DUP (directly unproductive profit-seeking activities), 383, 385

East Asian development model, 10, 46, 49, 51, 52, 53. *See also* Chinese economic growth in East Asian context
e-commerce, 9
economic crimes, 84–86
economic nationalism, 9, 12–13, 20, 361–62, 445
economic rent, 30n1. *See also* institutional rent seeking; rent-seeking developmental state
Eleventh Five-Year Plan, 313
embedded autonomy, 64
"empty the cage and change birds." *See* industrial upgrading policy
enclave economy, 33, 38, 288, 354–55, 369–70, 378–79
environmental protection standards, 135, 315, 333
EOM. *See* processing of shipped materials
EP/T ratio, 138–40, *139*
Evans, Peter, 64
exchange-rate spread (*huicha*): defined, 118n35; in Guangdong model, 118–19; and head tax, 183–84, 216; and institutional rent seeking, 65, 171; and 1994 reforms, 130, 132–33, 134, 176, 177, 187
exit strategies. *See* FIE response strategies (2000s)

export-oriented development theory, 28, 52–57. *See also* GVC/GCC theory

export-oriented industrialization (EOI): and import-substitution industrialization, 49; and Taiwanese economy, 36. *See also* Chinese economic growth; Guangdong model; processing of shipped materials

export processing. *See* processing of shipped materials

factory heads (*changzhang*), 191, 192–93, 204–6

Fang, Zhicao, 75

Fei Xiaotong, 259, 260

Feng Tay company, 340

fictive ownership arrangements: East Asian context, 401–2; and head tax, 184–85, 216; and Hong Kong as intermediary, 164–65; and institutional rent seeking, 65, 165–66; and processing of shipped materials, 101, 169–70; and recollectivization, 45; Taishin Shoe Manufacturing Group case study, 332; Taiyang company case study, 163–66, 169–72

FIE responses (post-2008), and social insurance fee enforcement, 218

FIE response strategies (2000s), 5; and core plant business model, 323–25, 327; factory closures, 135, 212, 213–16, 218, 302, 311; and GVC positions, 350–51; inland factories, 41, 316–17, 341–44, 356–57; and migrant worker resistance, 66, 311, 312–13; and migrant worker shortages, 241; and path dependence, 314–15; Pearl River Delta on-site transformation, 19, 348, 349–51, 358; reshoring to Taiwan, 111n32; and social insurance fee enforcement, 218; Southeast Asia factory relocations, 337–41, 348; strategy choices, 17, 43, 142, 303, 315, 318, 322, 358; Taishin Shoe Manufacturing Group case study, 337–44, 348. *See also* Guang-

dong model transformation (late 2000s)

flexible measures, 86–88, 129–30, 170, 173–74, 176–77, 300, 301

floating population. *See* migrant workers

foreign capital. *See* foreign direct investment; Taishang; Taiwanese direct investment in China

foreign direct investment (FDI): and Asian financial crisis, 106, 107, 403–4; and capital formation, 106–7, *107*; and Chinese economic growth phases, 28, 30, 37; developmental state theory on, 50–51; and domestic market protectionism, 8; East Asian context, 7, 403–4; export-oriented development theory on, 52; and global value chains, 33; and local growth alliances, 33, 38, 58–59; and migrant worker exploitation, 34; source countries for, 109–11; trends in, 107–9, *108*. *See also* foreign-invested enterprises

foreign exchange: and black market, 168, 170; and Chinese WTO membership, 41–42; customs spread (*cha'e huiru*), 134, 199–200; and Guangdong model, 41, 99, 116–19, *118*, *119*, 138–40, *139*; and ownership sectors, *141*, *142*; and processing management fees, 94n9, 170–71; and processing of shipped materials, 99, 138–40, *139*; reform (1994), 130, 132–33, 176–79, 180, 187–88; remittance spread, 120, 166–69, *167*, 170–71, 178, 200, 204, 332–33; reserves as growth resource, 3–4, 30, 41, 73, 90; swap centers, 171n23; and Taiwanese economy, 3. *See also* exchange-rate spread

foreign-invested enterprises (FIEs) (*sanzi qiye*): cadre roles, 48; defined, 100n15; enclave appearance of, 33, 38, 288, 378–79; increased contribution of, 140–41, *141*; migrant worker employment numbers, 241, *242*, *243*, 244; and processing of shipped materials, foreign-invested enterprises (FIEs) (*sanzi qiye*) (*continued*) 98–99, 100, 119–20, 121–22; reregistration of, 121–22, 133–34, 331. *See also* fictive ownership arrangements; FIE response strategies (2000s); local growth alliances

Four Cardinal Principles, 388

Four Little Dragons: industrial relocation to China, 37, 76; influence on Guangdong model, 14–15, 89–91; labor exploitation in, 51

Foxconn Technology Group (Hon Hai Precision Industry Co., Ltd.), 1, 41; dormitory labor regime, 288; excessive overtime, 6, 253–57, *256*; expansion of, 159; inland factories, 318; and lead firms, 366; paternalism, 294–95; second-generation Taigan, 346; suicides at, 6, 254, 296, 297, 304; and triangular trade, 160, 161

Franco, Jennifer, 48

Fujian Jinhua Integrated Circuit Company, 11n8

Fujian Province, 76n15, 81

Fukuyama, Francis, 439

Fuller, Douglas B., 366

Gangshang, 31

GCC theory. *See* GVC/GCC theory

G-D-L (global capital–domestic industrial district–local polity) linkages, *32*, 59–61, *60*, *62*, 64, 65–66, 312, 380. *See also* local growth alliances

Gemtek company, 359

Gereffi, Gary, 38, 53–54, 55, 56, 58, 59, 64, 73, 394

Giant company, 20n17

global financial crisis (2008), 102, 134, 135, 136, 138, 147, 212, 313–14. *See also* FIE response strategies (2000s)

GlobalFoundries, 415

globalization: and differential citizenship, 444; GVC/GCC theory on, 54, 56; and institutional rent seeking, 29;

and migrant worker exploitation, 7; and migrant workers as official class, 223; and nation-state sovereignty, 443; and state-centered theory, 51, 56; and state-owned enterprises, 444–45; and Taiwanese direct investment in China, 17. *See also* global value chains

globalization theory, 439–41

global production network theory, 70

global value chains (GVCs): capitalistic exploitation as intrinsic to, 5–6; defined, 54–55; and FIE on-site transformation, 350–51; and foreign direct investment, 33; and Guangdong model continuity, 371–72; lead firm hegemony in, 44, 70–71, 158–59, 341, 349, 391; and "Made in China 2025" strategy, 15, 437–38; and mainland-owned companies, 329, 357–58, 378, 380; and restraints on institutional rent seeking, 40, 391, 407; and retail revolution, 157–58; and Taiwanese economy, 16; Taiyang company case study, 153–54, 156–57, *158*. *See also* GVC/GCC theory; GVC shifts; lead firms; local growth alliances

governance structure in local growth alliances, 33–34, 58–59, *62*, 64–65

Grand Chip Investment Fund, 433

Great Leap Forward (1958–60), 14, 223n1, 261n32, 421n34

Great Western Development Policy, 135

guakao danwei, 146

Guangdong model, 80–143; benefits of, 40–42; and capital formation, 106–7, *107*; and case selection, 71–73, *74*; and economic structure, 102–3; embedded production chains, 315–16; and FDI trends, 107–9, *108*; and flexible measures, 86–88, 129–30, 170, 173–74, 176–77, 300, 301; and foreign exchange, 41, 99, 116–19, *118*, *119*, 138–40, *139*; and foreign trade dependence, 114–16, *115*; and GVC/GCC theory, 73; as intrinsic to

Chinese economic growth, 4–5, 72–74; and local state theory, 47; management localization, 206–8, 325; overview, 375–78; and per capita income, 104–5; and regional variations, 74, 75, 76–77; and security, 293–95; simple narrative of, 3–4; source countries for FDI in, 109–11; Taishin Shoe Manufacturing Group case study, 330–37; terminology for, 91; theoretical nature of labor regime, 296–98; and urban-rural divide, 105; weakening of, 76, 140. *See also* dormitory labor regime; fictive ownership arrangements; foreign-invested enterprises; Guangdong model launch stage; head tax; Hong Kong direct investment in China; Hong Kong as intermediary for Taishang; institutional rent seeking; migrant worker exploitation; processing management fees; processing of shipped materials; Taishang; Taiyang company case study

Guangdong model launch stage, 130, *131*, 132; bottom-up origins, 97; and economic crimes, 84–86; and enclave appearance, 33, 38, 288, 354–55, 378–79; Four Little Dragons influence, 14–15, 89–91; and geopolitics, 398–99; and GVC shifts, 153–54, 156–58, 375; and Hong Kong direct investment, 89, 91–92, *93*, 94, 100, 110; and socialism vs. capitalism debate, 81–84, 90, 91, 388–89; Taiyang company case study, 152–54, 156–57, 158; and US-Chinese relations, 441. *See also* Hong Kong as intermediary for Taishang

Guangdong model transformation (1994): and continued institutional rent seeking, 200; FIE reregistration, 121–22, 133–34, 331; and local growth alliances, 200–201; overview, 121–22, *131*, 132–34; Taishin Shoe Manufacturing Group case study, 331; and Taiyang

company case study, 144–45. *See also* macroeconomic reforms (1994)

Guangdong model transformation (late 2000s): and continued institutional rent seeking, 333–34, 392–93; and continuity, 371–72; and GVC shifts, 322, 323, 325–26, 350–51, *352*; and local growth alliances reorganization, 42–43, 69–70, 216, 219–20, 318, 321, 369–70, 377–78; and migrant worker resistance, 176, 304, 305, 312–13; and migrant worker shortages, 135, 208, 241, 304; overviews, 42–43, *131*, 134–35, 136, 138, 302–3, 377–78; and ownership sectors, 140–41, *141*; and processing management fee decreases, 204; shift to processing of imported materials, 101, 133, 134, 136, *137*, 216, 331; Smiles Shoes Company case study, 322–27, 353, 358; and tax incentive standardization, 318–21. *See also* FIE response strategies (2000s); industrial upgrading policy; mainland-owned companies; social insurance fee enforcement; Taishin Shoe Manufacturing Group case study

Guangzhou CanSemi Technology Inc., 420

Guanqiang Import and Export Company. *See* Taiyang company case study

guanxi: in local growth alliances, 122, 200–202, 203, 379–80; weakening of, 321, 348

Gu Mu, 84, 86, 87, 89–90, 97

GVC/GCC theory, 28, 30–31, 33, 54–57, 58, 73, 394–95. *See also* global value chains

GVC shifts: and government-business relationships, 67–68; and Guangdong model launch stage, 153–54, 156–58, 375; and Guangdong model transformation (late 2000s), 322, 323, 325–26, 350–51, *352*; and Hong Kong as bridge, 161–63; impacts on exporters, 159–61; Smiles Shoes Company case study, 322, 323, 325–26; and triangular trade, 113–14

Hamilton, Gary G., 37n3, 56, 158, 259n28, 394

head tax (*rentou shui*), 183–86; and customs spread, 134; disappearance of, 216–17, *217*; and exchange-rate spread, 183–84, 216; and fictive ownership arrangements, 184–85, 216; floating significance of, *185*; as institutional rent seeking, 166–69, 174–75, 176; origins of, 183–84, *184*; and processing of shipped materials, 185–86, 216; Taishin Shoe Manufacturing Group case study, 332–33, 334–35; Taiyang company case study, 168–69, 170, 172, 174–75, 182, *217*

Heberer, Thomas, 48–49

Henan Province, 109

Hess, Martin, 354

Hirschman, Albert, 441

historical institutionalism, 31

Hong Kong: and FIE response strategies (2000s), 302, 314. *See also* Four Little Dragons; Gangshang; Hong Kong direct investment in China; Hong Kong as intermediary for Taishang

Hong Kong direct investment in China: and early cadre cooperation, 100; extent of, 109–10, 163; and Guangdong model, 89, 91–92, *93*, 94, 100, 110; state-centered theory on, 51; Taiping Handbag Factory case, 91–92; world-systems theory on, 52

Hong Kong Eagle Industrial Ltd., 92

Hong Kong entrepreneurs. *See* Gangshang

Hong Kong as intermediary for Taishang, 4, 73, 399; Gu Mu on, 90; and information sharing, 161–62; and processing management fees, 92, *93*, 94; Taiyang company case study, 151–52, 162n14, 164–65; and triangular trade, 154, 160–61, 162

Hon Hai Precision Industry Co., Ltd. *See* Foxconn Technology Group

Hopkins, Terrence, 53, 55, 381

household registration system. *See hukou* (household registration) system

housing provident fund fees. *See* social insurance system

HSMC (Wuhan Hongxin Semiconductor Manufacturing Company), 415n12, 422

Hu Yaobang, 84, 85, 86

Huawei company: and cell-phone industry, 363; and Chinese state, 360–61; and domestic markets, 361; and industrial upgrading policy, 8–9; and "Made in China 2025" strategy, 415–16, 423; and neomercantilism, 361–62; and red supply chain, 43; and regional variations, 75; and US-Chinese hegemonic competition, xxiii, 13, 434–35, 436

Hua Yuan company, 96

huicha. See exchange-rate spread

hukou (household registration) system, 34; and differential citizenship, xviii, 258–59, 261, 262–63, 265–66; and dormitory labor regime, 264; and institutional rent seeking, 263; and migrant workers as official class, 224, 225–26; and residential permit systems, 228–32; and rural-urban dualism, 223

human wave strategy, 8, 358

Humphrey, John, 55

Hung, Ho-fung, 75, 406

hybrid FIEs, 366

ICT industry. *See* information and communication technology (ICT) industry

Imai, Ken, 367

IMEC, 415–16

import-substitution industrialization (ISI), 29, 36, 49

indigenous supply chains. *See* red supply chain

industrial espionage. *See* intellectual property violations

industrial upgrading policy ("empty the cage and change birds"; *tenglong*

huanniao), 135–36, 313–18; Big Fund, 10, 367–68, 414, 416, 438; and domestic markets, 8–9, 367; and economic nationalism, 12–13; and GVC shifts, 68; hybrid FIEs, 366; and inland factories, 316–17; and labor regulations, 313–14; and local growth alliances reorganization, 42–43, 369–70; results of, 369–70; and social insurance fee enforcement, 219, 316; and social upgrading, 8, 371; Taiyang company case study, 147, 215, 315; and US-Chinese hegemonic competition, 431. *See also* FIE response strategies (2000s); "Made in China 2025" strategy
industrious revolution theory, 52
information and communication technology (ICT) industry: Big Fund, 10, 367–68, 414, 416, 438; cell-phone industry, 41, 362–64, 367, 370–71; Chinese weakness of, 419; cutting-edge technologies, 364–68; and domestic markets, 8–9, 358, 361, 365, 366–67, 368–69, 381; and industrial upgrading policy, 316, 318; inland factories, 41; and intellectual property violations, 11, 413, 417; and neomercantilism, 9, 361–62; network communications industry, 358–62; state investment in, 8–9; and talent poaching, 8, 16, 358, 359–60; transnationalization, 161; Yangtze Delta region, 5, 41. *See also* Foxconn Technology Group; industrial upgrading policy; "Made in China 2025" strategy; red supply chain
inland factories, 41, 316–17, 341–44, 356–57
institutional rent seeking, 29; and access money, 386n1; ambiguity in, 385–86; and central government, 47, 67, 87–88, 173–74; and clientelism, 34, 39–40; collaboration fees, 333–35; East Asian context, 402, 407–9; and environmental protection standards, 333; and exchange-rate spread, 65, 171; and fictive ownership arrangements, 65,

165–66; and flexible measures, 87–88, 173–74, 177; and Guangdong model transformation (late 2000s), 333–34, 392–93; and *guanxi*, 200–201, 202, 203; GVC/GCC theory on, 30–31, 57; and handicapped employee quotas, 203; head tax as, 166–69, 174–75, 176; and *hukou* system, 263; and labor regulations, 251; and land use certification, 191, 333; and local government authority delegation, 385, 386–87; and local state theory, 47; and macroeconomic reforms (1994), 177–78, 200; and mainland-owned companies, 373; and migrant worker exploitation, 264–65; operational mechanism of, 387–94; and organized bureaucratic corruption hypothesis, 390–91; and path dependence, 371–72; and processing of shipped vs. imported materials, 101, 216; and rentier class, xviii, 193, 382; restraints on, 40, 391–92, 407; and security services, 175; and social insurance fee diversion, 265; specific conditions for legitimacy of, 384–85, 387, 391–94; Taishin Shoe Manufacturing Group case study, 333–34; Taiyang company case study, 171, 174–76, 191; and tax incentive standardization, 318–20; and transitional economy, 384–85, 388–89, 393, 408; variations in, 186. *See also* local growth alliances; social insurance fee avoidance
Intel, 423
intellectual property violations, 11, 16, 413, 417, 435–36, 437
international buyers. *See* lead firms
Inventec company, 161
ISI (import-substitution industrialization), 29, 36, 49

Japan: economic growth, 36, 49; Plaza Accord, 36–37, 73, 145–46, 398–99; US relations with, 36
JHICC, 413

Jiang Zemin, 348
Jiangsu Province, 103, 109, 116, 132
jinliao jiagong (processing of imported
    materials), 101, 133, 134, 136, *137*, 199,
    216, 331
joint-venture companies. *See* fictive
    ownership arrangements

Kant, Immanuel, 441
Kao Cheng-shu, 37n3, 158
Kinpo company, 161
Kissinger, Henry, 13–14
Korean War, 35–36
Kornai, Janos, 46
Krueger, Anne, 383, 384, 388
KUKA Robotics, 433
Kunshan model. *See* Suzhou (Kunshan)
    model

Labor Contract Law (2008), 135, 147, 194,
    211, 212, 217, 271, 313–14, 324
labor regulations: and excessive overtime,
    250–51, 253, 255, 257; and industrial
    upgrading policy, 313–14; Labor
    Contract Law (2008), 135, 147, 194, 211,
    212, 217, 271, 313–14, 324; and
    overtime, 253, 255, 257; Taishin Shoe
    Manufacturing Group case study, 348;
    and theoretical nature of labor regime,
    298, 299. *See also* social insurance fee
    enforcement
labor strikes. *See* migrant worker
    resistance
labor unrest. *See* migrant worker
    resistance
lailiao jiagong. See processing of shipped
    materials
lead firms: corporate social responsibility
    demands, 202, 250, 297, 336–37; and
    domestic markets, 349–50; and FIE
    response strategies, 337–38, 340–41;
    GVC/GCC theory on, 33, 55–56;
    hegemony of, 44, 70–71, 158–59, 341,
    349, 391; and ICT industry, 366; in
    local growth alliances, 31, 33, 40, 68;

and mainland-owned companies, 329;
    Taishin Shoe Manufacturing Group
    case study, 349; Taiwanese, 16, 409;
    Taiyang company case study, 156,
    158–59; and theoretical nature of labor
    regime, 297. *See also* global value
    chains
lean inventory technique, 158
Lee, Ching Kwan, 295, 297
Lee, Joonkoo, 59
Lenovo company, 363
Lewis, Arthur, xxviii
Li Hao, 171n23
Liang Mong-Song, 416, 420
Lin, Nan, 46, 47
Lin Thung-Hong, 297
Lite-On, 161
little coffers, 87–88
Liu Tianfu, 85, 87, 90, 94
local government: authority delegation
    to, 87, 133, 177, 385, 386–87, 443;
    defined, 31–33; and flexible measures,
    86–88, 129–30, 170, 176–77, 300, 301;
    and industrial upgrading policy, 317;
    and labor NGOs, 309; and migrant
    worker resistance, 308, 309–10, 312–13;
    and tax incentive standardization,
    319–20. *See also* cadres; local growth
    alliances
local growth alliances, 58–71; analytical
    framework for, 68–69, *69*, 380–81;
    central government roles in, 31, 40, 68,
    264; clientelism in, 34, 39–40, 67,
    379–80; and embedded production
    chains, 315–16; factory heads, 191,
    192–93, 204–6; and foreign direct
    investment, 33, 38, 58–59; foreign-
    invested enterprises in, 33, 34, 38;
    G-D-L linkages in, *32*, 59–61, *60*, *62*,
    64, 65–66, 312, 380; and governance
    structure, 33–34, 58–59, *62*, 64–65;
    government-business relationship
    overview, 66–68; and Guangdong
    model transformation (1994), 200–201;
    guanxi in, 122, 200–202, 203, 379–80;

and land use certification, 188, 191, 199, 215, 333; lead firms in, 31, 33, 40, 68; and migrant worker exploitation, 66–67, 69–70, 222–23, 264; and migrant worker wage suppression, 220; rentier class in, xviii, 193, 382; rent-seeking developmental state in, 61, *62*, 63; reorganization of (late 2000s), 42–43, 69–70, 216, 219–20, 318, 321, 369–70, 377–78; and social insurance fees, 218; and Taiwanese-acculturated mainland-owned factories, 42, 355–56; Taiyang company case study, 32–33; and tax incentives, 319; village level, 188–92. *See also* institutional rent seeking; local growth alliances

local officials. *See* cadres

local state theory, 46–49

Lou Jiwei, 320

Lu Tianfu, 90

Lugan, 310–11, 342, 356, 357

Macau, 109–10

macroeconomic reforms (1994): foreign exchange reform, 130, 132–33, 176–79, 180, 187–88; Taiyang company case study, 147, 180, 198–99; tax reform, 48, 121, 133, 180, 187. *See also* Guangdong model transformation (1994)

"Made in China 2025" strategy, 136, 367–68, 375, 413–22; and global value chains, 15, 437–38; overview, 43–44; prospects for, xix, xxiv, 14, 15–16, 419–24, 438; scope of, 10n7; and talent poaching, 417, 419–20; and US-Chinese hegemonic competition, xxiv, 10–11, 44, 433, 437, 438; and US economic sanctions, 423, 424. *See also* industrial upgrading policy

mainland-owned companies, 351–68; advantages of, 324, 327–29; competition with FIEs, 42, 321, 327–29, 339, 356; and core plant business model, 323, 324, 327; dormitory labor regime,

290; and GVC positions, 329, 357–58, 378, 380; and institutional rent seeking, 373; and local growth alliances, 369–70; and local growth alliances reorganization, 318; Smiles Shoes Company case study, 323; social insurance fee avoidance, 270, 324; and Taishang technology diffusion, 353; and talent poaching, 359–60, 417; and venture capital, 364–68. *See also* information and communication technology (ICT) industry; Taiwanese-acculturated mainland-owned factories

Mann, Michael, 444

Mao Zedong. *See* Mao era

Mao era: Cultural Revolution, 82, 95, 223n1; and economic nationalism, 445; Great Leap Forward, 14, 223n1, 261n32, 421n34; high-quality labor force, 4, 52; political persecution during, 259n27; processing of shipped materials, 94–96; purging methods, 86n4; rural-urban dualism, 223, 258, 261; self-sufficiency policy, 266; state mobilization power during, 399; US-Chinese relations, 13–14, 35

market transition theory, 27, 45–46

Marshall, T. H., 257–58, 259, 260

Mearsheimer, John, 3, 443

MediaTek company, 19, 41, 363, 365, 365–66n85

Meng Wanzhou, xxiii, 436

methodology, 71–79; case selection, 71–77; data structure, 78–79; research methods, xvii, 77–78

Mexico, 38, 399–400n4

Micron Technology, 11n8, 413

Midea Group, 433

migrant worker exploitation, xvii–xviii, 29–30; developmental state theory on, 51; and development pitfalls, 426–27; dual nature of, 7, 34, 70, 193–94, 263–66; East Asian context, xviii, 51, 404–7; and fictive labor unions, 193;

migrant worker exploitation (*continued*)
and Guangdong model launch stage,
132; and Guangdong model origins,
88–89; and Guangdong model second
transformation, 135; and head count,
172–74; and *hukou* system, 34, 224,
225–26, 258, 263; and institutional rent
seeking, 264–65; invisibility of, 5–6;
late 1990s continuation of, 227–28; and
local growth alliances, 66–67, 69–70,
222–23, 264; and price scissors, 266,
408; public attention to, 227, 265,
296–97; reforms (mid-2000s), 135, 147;
and reproductive rights, 292–93; and
residential permit systems, 228–29,
230, 231, 232; social control, 39, 289;
social segregation, 289–90; state role
in, 51, 299, 300; Taiyang company case
study, 189–91; and theoretical nature
of labor regime, 295–99, 300. *See also*
differential citizenship; dormitory
labor regime; *hukou* (household
registration) system; migrant worker
resistance; migrant worker wage
suppression; overtime, excessive; social
insurance discrimination; social
insurance fee avoidance
migrant worker resistance, 306–13; and
CSR, 337; and domestic security,
307–8; and dormitory labor regime,
290, 291–93; and FIE response
strategies (2000s), 66, 311, 312–13; and
Guangdong model transformation
(late 2000s), 176, 304, 305, 312–13; and
labor NGOs, 305–6, 309, 312; labor
unions, 309; and labor unions, 309;
and local government, 308, 309–10,
312–13; and local growth alliances
reorganization, 70; and Lugan, 310–11;
and pseudo-contractual relations, 301;
and social insurance fee avoidance,
218, 219, 304, 305, 306–7, 311–12; and
social insurance fee enforcement, 219,
304, 308–9, 335–36; Taishin Shoe
Manufacturing Group case study, 309,

310–11, 336, 347, 348; Taiyang company
case study, 147, 212–13, 292, 377;
Vietnam, 339, 340; and wage increases,
304, 310
migrant workers: demographics, 232–38,
234, 236; FIE employment numbers,
241, *242, 243*, 244; and *hukou* system,
224, 225–26, 262; and informal
economy, 290–91; militarized management of, 196–97; occupational injury
insurance, 211–12, 271; as official class,
7, 223–26; and paternalism, 294–95;
residential permit systems, 228–32; rise
in wages, 208, 304, 310; and rural-urban
dualism, 223, 232, 258–59, 260, 261, 262,
265–66; severance pay, 213–14, *213*;
shortages of, 135, 208, 241, 244, 304;
and social upgrading, 371; southeastern coastal concentration of, 238–41,
239, 240; state management of (late
1990s), 227–28; suicides among, 254,
296, 297, 304; uprooted existence,
221–22. *See also* labor regulations;
migrant worker exploitation; migrant
worker resistance; migrant worker
wage suppression
migrant worker wage suppression: and
excessive overtime, 123n37, 254; and
GDP, 128–29, *128*; and Guangdong
model transformation (late 2000s), 133,
135, 304, 310; and local growth
alliances, 220; and minimum wages,
122–23, *124, 125, 126*, 127, *127*, 245–48,
246, 247; shifts in, 208, 304, 310;
Taiyang company case study, 190–91
mingong. See migrant workers
minimum wages: increases in, 208, 212,
304; and migrant worker wage
suppression, 122–23, *124, 125, 126*, 127,
127, 245–48, *246, 247*
Mizuno company, 351
modernization theory, xx–xxi, 403
Montesquieu, 441
Moore, Barrington, xx
Myanmar, 339, 341

Nanjing Tacoma, 415, 422
"National New Urbanization Plan," 231
"National Security Strategy of the United States of America, The" (The White House), 11
Naughton, Barry M., 50
Nee, Victor, 45
neoclassical theory, 29
neo-guanxilism, 48–49
neoliberal institutionalism, 440–42
neoliberalism, 9, 52–53, 440–41
neomercantilism, 9, 361–62
network communications industry, 358–62. *See also* information and communication technology (ICT) industry
network relationships. *See* local growth alliances
new-institutional economics, 47
"New Twenty-Two Articles," 97–98
Nexchip, 415
Ng Fung Hong company, 95–96
Ngo, Tak-Win, 387
Nike, 73, 330, 337–39, 340–41, 376. *See also* Taiyang company case study

Obama, Barack, 441–42
occupational injury insurance, 211–12, 271. *See also* social insurance
ODM (original design manufacturing) production, 73, 148–49, 150, 330, 349, 351, 365
OEM (original equipment manufacturing). *See* processing of shipped materials
Oi, Jean C., 46, 47, 48
One Step ahead in China: Guangdong under Reform (Vogel), xvii
opening reform. *See* Chinese economic policy; Guangdong model launch stage
"Opinions Regarding Further Moving Forward Reform of the Household Registration System," 231
Opper, Sonja, 45

OPPO company, 9, 43, 363–64
original design manufacturing (ODM) production, 73, 148–49, 150, 330, 349, 351, 365
overtime, excessive, 248–57; and dormitory labor regime, 289; Foxconn case, 6, 253–57, *256*; and labor regulations, 250–51, 253, 255, 257; and making out game, 298–99; and migrant worker wage suppression, 123n37, 254; and pseudo-contractual relations, 301

Park Chung-hee, 410
path dependence: and factory closures, 215; and FIE response strategies, 314–15; and Guangdong model transformation (late 2000s), 303; and head tax, 216; and institutional rent seeking, 371–72; and migrant worker exploitation, 51; and migrant workers, 228; and processing of imported materials, 200; and rural-urban dualism, 259; and social insurance system, 220, 276
PDCCs (producer-driven commodity chains), 54
Pearl River Delta region: economic structure, 103; local growth alliances reorganization, 369–70; scope of, 88n5; social insurance discrimination, 283, *284*, 285. *See also* FIE responses (post-2008); Guangdong model; special economic zones
Pearl's Light Import and Export Company. *See* Taiyang company case study
Peng Fang, 291, 294, 296, 297
Plaza Accord (1985), 36–37, 73, 145–46, 398–99
Pou Chen Corporation, 155, 159, 160, 161. *See also* Yue Yuen Industrial Limited
price scissors, 266, 408–9
processing of imported materials (*jinliao jiagong*), 101, 133, 134, 136, *137*, 199, 216, 331

processing management fees, 88; customs spread, 134, 199–200; decreases in, 203–4; and fictive ownership arrangements, 170; and foreign exchange, 94n9, 170–71; and foreign exchange reform, 94, 177–79; and Guangdong model transformation (1994), 133–34, 200; and *guanxi,* 202; and head count, 172–74, 200; and Hong Kong as intermediary for Taishang, 92, *93,* 94; and processing of imported materials, 199–200, 216; remittance spread, 120, 166–69, *167,* 170–71, 178, 200, 204, 332–33; and research methods, 78; statistics on, 119–22, *121;* Taiyang company case study, 172–74, *172,* 173, *181,* 182–83, 203–4; twenty-first century income decline, 121–22, 372. *See also* head tax; institutional rent seeking
processing of shipped materials (*lailiao jiagong*), 14–15, 94–101; and China Resources Group, 94–97; and factory heads, 192; and fictive ownership arrangements, 101, 169–70; and foreign exchange, 99, 138–40, *139;* and Guangdong model launch stage, 130, 132; and head tax, 185–86, 216; and Hong Kong direct investment, 91–92; "New Twenty-Two Articles" on, 97–98; and research methods, 78; and Taiyang company case study, 152, 154; tax incentives for, 99, 122, 133, 154, 174, 180. *See also* head tax; processing management fees
producer-driven commodity chains (PDCCs), 54
Property Rights Law, 391n3
"Provisional Regulations on Residential Permits," 232
pseudo-contractual relations, 300–301
public order. *See* security
Pun Ngai, 286, 289

Qin Hui, 6, 71n12
Qualcomm, 19, 415–16, 434

Quanta company, 161
quasi-state capital, 45–46

red aristocracy, xx–xxi
redcap affiliations, 48
red supply chain, 8–9; emergence of, 43, 135–36, 375, 378; and semiconductor self-sufficiency goal, 14–15; and Twelfth Five-Year Plan, 44, 413–14. *See also* "Made in China 2025" strategy
regional variations: cadre roles, 47–48; and developmental state theory, 50; dormitory labor regime, 286–87, 288; and Guangdong model, 74, *75,* 76–77; social insurance discrimination, 283, *284,* 285
remittance spread, 120, 166–69, *167,* 170–71, 178, 200, 204, 332–33
rentou shui. See head tax
rent-seeking developmental state (*xunzu fazhanxing guojia*), xxviii, 30–31, 264; defined, 394; and development pitfalls, 427, 428–29; and differential citizenship, 300; East Asian context, 10, 381–82; and local growth alliances, 61, *62,* 63; prospects for, 14; specific conditions for legitimacy of, 384–85, 387, 391–94; and traditional rent-seeking theory, 382–84, 385. *See also* institutional rent seeking
rent-seeking theory: new typology, 385–86, *386;* traditional, 382–84, 385
Ren Yan, 286, 289
Ren Zhengfei, xxiii, 436
Ren Zhongyi, 81–82, 83, 84, 85, 87
"Residential Permit Management Methods (Draft for Soliciting Opinions)," 230–31
Rhee, Syngman, 402, 407
Rodrik, Dani, 9, 382
Ruentex company, 161n13
rural-urban dualism, 223, 232, 258–59, 260, 261, 262, 265–66, 268–70, 444

Samsung, 363, 416n15, 420
sanlai yibu (three-plus-one trading mix), 77–78, 88, 91–92, 94, 96–97, 100, 133, 174. *See also* processing of shipped materials
sanzi qiye. See foreign-invested enterprises
"Say Goodbye to Taiwan" (Mearsheimer), 3
Schubert, Gunter, 48–49
Scott, James, 292
security, 175, 293–94
severance pay, 213–14, *213*
SEZs. *See* special economic zones
Shanghai: FDI trends, 109, 132; minimum wages, 127, *127*; processing of shipped materials, 100, 101; residential permit system, 230; social insurance discrimination, 271–78, *272, 275, 277, 279, 280,* 281
Shangwu Production Brigade Thermal Coil Factory, 92, *93*
Shenzhen: cell-phone industry, 362–64; Hong Kong as intermediary for Taishang, 92, *93,* 94; minimum wages, 123; residential permit system, 228–29; social insurance discrimination, 279, *280. See also* Guangdong model; Pearl River Delta region
Shenzhen Light Industry Handicrafts Import and Export Branch Company, 92, *93*
Shieh Gwo-Shyong, 301
Shiu, Jing Ming, 367
Shleifer, Andrei, 390
shudi guanli (territorial jurisdiction doctrine), 258, 259, 261–62
Shyang Ho Shoes incident (2012), 336
Sichuan Province, 109
Singapore, 403
SMIC, 11n8, 413, 415–16, 417–18, 420, 422, 423, 424
Smiles Shoes Company case study, 77, 322–27, 353, 358
smuggling, 84. *See also* economic crimes

social insurance discrimination, 7, 34, 270–85; coastal city comparison, 278–82, *280;* and dual exploitation, 263; and fee avoidance, 270–71; reforms, 274, 276, *277;* regional variations, 283, *284,* 285; Shanghai, 271–78, *272, 275, 277,* 279, *280,* 281; and urban protectionism, 271, 274
social insurance fee avoidance: coastal city comparison, 278–79; and discrimination, 270–71; and flexible measures, 129–30; and *guanxi,* 202; and local government authority delegation, 133; mainland-owned companies, 270, 324; and migrant worker resistance, 218, 219, 304, 305, 306–7, 311–12; occupational injury insurance, 211–12; Smiles Shoes Company case study, 327; Taiyang company case study, 176, 209, 210, *210,* 217
social insurance fee enforcement, 135, 216–20; and differential citizenship, 194; and FIE response strategies (2000s), 218; and industrial upgrading policy, 219, 316; and local growth alliances reorganization, 219–20; and migrant worker resistance, 219, 304, 308–9, 335–36; pressures for, *219,* 271; Taiyang company case study, 210–11, *211,* 217–18, *217*
Social Insurance Law (2011), 135, 194, 210, 217, 271, 274, 304–5
social insurance system: coverage components, 209n23; fee diversion, 265; occupational injury insurance, 211–12, 271; participation rates, 209, 210–11, *211;* Social Insurance Law (2011), 135, 194, 210, 217, 271, 274, 304–5; and theoretical nature of labor regime, 299. *See also* social insurance discrimination; social insurance fee avoidance
socialism vs. capitalism debate, 9, 81–84, 90, 91, 388–89

Social Origins of Dictatorship and Democracy (Moore), xx
soft budget constraint, 46
Somers, Margaret, 299
South Africa, 262
Southeast Asia factory relocations, 337–41, 348
South Korea: development results, 410; economic equity, 405–6; economic growth, 49; migrant worker exploitation, 404; ownership structure, 401, 402; rent-seeking activities, 407; state-market relations, 399, 400; US relations with, 36, 398, 402. *See also* Chinese economic growth in East Asian context; Four Little Dragons
Soviet Union, 260
special economic zones (SEZs): creation of, 14, 80, 88; and minimum wages, 123, *124*, 125; and socialism vs. capitalism debate, 81–84; term for, 91
state-centered theory, 27–28, 46–52, 56, 97
"State Council Opinions Regarding Solving the Problem of Rural Migrant Workers," 224–25
state-owned enterprises (SOEs): and dual labor market, 299; East Asian context, 400, 401; and foreign exchange reform, 179; and globalization, 444–45; and Guangdong model transformation (late 2000s), 140–41; ICT industry, 360, 415, 416; and industrial upgrading policy, 317; and "Made in China 2025" strategy, 415, 416; market transition theory on, 46; migrant worker employment numbers, 244; and processing of shipped materials, 99
state-surveillance society, 9, 292, 306, 361, 362, 411, 428, 432, 442
state value capture. *See* rent-seeking developmental state
Sturgeon, Timothy, 55
Sugihara, Kaoru, 52
Sun Tzu, 12

Sun Zhigang Incident, 227, 294
Sunflower Movement, 3
Suzhou (Kunshan) model, 4, 28, 74

Taigan: apprentice-turned-boss system, 195–96, 345, 371, 409; cost of, 206; defined, 72; and migrant worker resistance, 213; and militarized management, 196–97; second-generation, 194–95, 197–98, 201–2, 213, 344–48, 350; socializing culture, 197, 201–2; "warlords," 341, 344, 345–46
Taiping Handbag Factory, 91–92
Taishang: and Chinese-Taiwanese relations, 18–19; defined, 1n1, 72; and developmental state theory, 51; diversity within, 1–2; and Four Little Dragons investment in China, 76; and *guakao danwei*, 146; holding companies, 72; and ICT industry, 358, 361, 365; importance to Chinese economy of, 1, 2–3, 4–5, 15; and migrant worker resistance, 66; and Plaza Accord, 36–37, 73; Xi Jinping on, 2, 17, 18. *See also* FIE response strategies (2000s); Hong Kong as intermediary for Taishang; institutional rent seeking; Taigan; Taiwanese-acculturated mainland-owned factories; Taiwanese direct investment in China; Taiyang company case study
Taishin Shoe Manufacturing Group case study, 77, 330–51; collaboration fees, 333–35; head tax, 332–33, 334–35; inland factories, 341–44, 356; institutional rent seeking, 333–34; and mainland-owned companies, 356; migrant worker resistance, 309, 310–11, 336, 347, 348; on-site transformation, 349–51, *352*, 353, 358; overview, 330–31; processing of shipped materials, 331–37; second-generation Taigan, 344–48, 350; Southeast Asia factory relocations, 337–41, 348
Taiwan Compatriots (Taibao) (film), xxvii

Taiwanese-acculturated mainland-owned factories (*taizixi luzichang*), 42, 290, 353–54, 355–56, 357, 364–65, 370–71, 379

Taiwanese democracy movement, 18, 403

Taiwanese direct investment in China: ban on, 111n31, 162; Chinese statistical underestimation of, 111–14, *112, 114*; extent of, xix, 109, 110; recent decrease in, 17; world-systems theory on, 52. *See also* Guangdong model; Taishang

Taiwanese economy: business models, 148–51, *151*; and Chinese talent poaching, 19; development results, 409–10; and economic equity, 405; and foreign exchange, 3; and global value chains, 16; and migrant worker exploitation, 404; ownership structure, 401; and Plaza Accord, 145–46, 398–99; reform program (1960), 36; and regime type, 399–400, 402, 411; rent-seeking activities, 407; state-centered theory on, 49; and state-market relations, 399–400; transnationalization, 160–61; and TSMC, 19–20; and US policies, 36, 398, 400; and Vertical Line, 145. *See also* Chinese economic growth in East Asian context; Four Little Dragons

Taiwan-invested manufacturers. *See* Taishang

Taiwan Merchants' Associations, 201–2

Taiwan Semiconductor Manufacturing Company. *See* TSMC

Taiwan Strait Crisis (1995–96), 18

Taiyang company case study, 77; clientelism, 165–66, 169; excessive overtime, 252; factory closure, 212, 213–14, 216, 218; factory heads, 192–93, 204–6; fictive ownership arrangements, 163–66, 169–72; foreign exchange reform, 178–79, 180, 188; global financial crisis (2008), 147, 212; global value chains, 153–54, 156–57, *158*; Guangdong model launch stage, 152–54, 156–57, 158; and Guangdong

model transformation (1994), 144–45; head tax, 168–69, 170, 172, 174–75, 182, *217*; high-unit-price products, 156, 197–98; Hong Kong as intermediary, 151–52, 162n14, 164–65; industrial upgrading policy, 147, 315; institutional rent seeking, 171, 174–76, 191; land use certificate, 188, 199, 215; local growth alliances, 32–33; macroeconomic reforms (1994), 147, 180, 198–99; management localization, 207–8, 325; migrant worker exploitation, 189–91; migrant worker resistance, 147, 212–13, 292, 377; militarized management, 196–97; Nafu Village factory, 179–83, *181*, 188–94, 198–99, 212; overview (1979–94), 145–48, 376–77; processing of imported materials, 199; processing management fees, 172–74, *172, 173, 181*, 182–83, 203–4; processing of shipped materials, 152, 154; raw materials procurement changes (1995), 154–56; second-generation Taigan, 194–95, 197–98, 201–2, 213, 347; social insurance system, 176, 209, 210–12, *210, 211*, 217–18, *217*, 281; Taigan in China, 153; Taiwan business model, 148–51, *151*; triangular trade, 154

taizixi luzichang. See mainland-owned companies

talent poaching, 8, 16, 19, 358, 359–60, 417, 419–20

Tencent, 9, 362

tenglong huanniao. See industrial upgrading policy

territorial jurisdiction doctrine (*shudi guanli*), 258, 259, 261–62

theoretical nature of labor regime, 295–301

"31 Preferential Measures for Taiwan," 16n11, 18, 19

three-plus-one trading mix (*sanlai yibu*), 77–78, 88, 91–92, 94, 96–97, 100, 133, 174. *See also* processing of shipped materials

Thucydides trap, 430

Thun, Eric, 50
Tiananmen Incident (1989), 5, 441
Ting Hsin company, 1
Torreon company, 38
TowerJazz company, 415
township and village enterprises (TVEs), 48
TP-Link, 358–59
trade surplus. *See* foreign exchange
transitional economy: and developmental
   state theory, 49–50; and institutional
   rent seeking, 384–85, 388–89, 393, 408
transnationalization, 160–61
triangular trade, 113–14, 154, 160–61, 162
Truman, Harry, 35
Trump, Donald, xxiii, 11, 433n8, 434, 442
Tsai, Kellee S., 50
Tseng Wei-ling, 297
Tsinghua Unigroup, 416
TSMC (Taiwan Semiconductor
   Manufacturing Company), 1; and
   intellectual property violations, 11n8,
   413, 417, 420; lead firm status, 16, 409;
   and "Made in China 2025" strategy,
   414–15, 416, 417–18, 423–24; and
   Taiwanese economy, 19–20
Tudou company, 9, 362
Tullock, Gordon, 383, 384
Twelfth Five-Year Plan, 44, 313, 317, 413–14
Two Centenaries, 421

Unger, Jonathan, 47
Unisoc company, 365
United Microelectronics Corporation
   (UMC), 1, 11n8, 413
urban protectionism, 268–70, 271, 274, 406
U.S.-China Economic and Security
   Review Commission, 433
US-Chinese hegemonic competition,
   429–39; and Chinese authoritarianism,
   11–12; and Chinese expansionism, 13,
   14, 431–32, 440; and Chinese industrial
   upgrading policies, 431; and export
   controls, xxiii; and FIE response
   strategies, 17; and intellectual property
   violations, 435–36, 437; and "Made in

China 2025" strategy, xxiv, 10–13, 44,
   433, 437, 438; and Taishang investment,
   19; and US-Chinese trade war, 13, 434–35
US-Chinese relations: Confucius Institutes,
   432; and Guangdong model launch
   stage, 441; and neoliberal institutionalism, 440–42; as symbiotic, 429–30;
   and Tiananmen Incident, 441; warming
   (1970s), 13–14, 35, 36, 441
US-Chinese trade: and Cold War, 13–14;
   export controls, xxiii; trade war, xxiii,
   13–14, 17, 19, 434–35, 438n20; and US-
   Chinese warming, 36, 441; ZTE Incident (2018), 13, 19, 420, 421–22, 434–35
US policies: and Cold War, 35–36, 398;
   economic sanctions, 5, 13, 423, 424;
   and intellectual property violations,
   413n8; and Taiwanese economy, 36, 398,
   400. *See also* US-Chinese hegemonic
   competition
US-Taiwan relations, 36

Vietnam, 36, 338–40
Vietnam War, 36
Vishny, Robert W., 390
Vogel, Ezra, xvii

Walder, Andrew G., 47
Wallerstein, Immanuel, 53, 55, 381
Walmart, 158–59
Walsin Lihwa company, 161
Wang, Chunyu, 48
Wang Po-chi, 357
Wang Yang, 314, 315, 316
Wang Zheng, 259n28
Want Want company, 1
WeChat, 9, 362
Wei Yuan, 445
Wenzhou model, 48, 74
Western policies, and network communi-
   cations industry, 361
world-systems theory, 52–53, 54, 55
World Trade Organization (WTO),
   Chinese membership (2001), 4, 5, 41–42,
   74–75, 116, 441

Wu Nansheng, 89
Wuhan Hongxin Semiconductor
  Manufacturing Company (HSMC),
  415n12, 422
Wuhan Xinxin Semiconductor, 416
Wukan Incident (2011), 191

Xi Jinping: Belt and Road Initiative, 12,
  44, 412, 431; and economic nationalism,
  9, 445; and *guanxi,* 348; lifetime tenure,
  429, 432–33; and "Made in China 2025"
  strategy, xix, 420–21; and migrant
  worker resistance, 308; and social control, 428–29; on Taishang, 2, 17, 18; on
  US-Chinese hegemonic competition,
  430
Xi Zhongxun, 83
Xiaomi company, 9, 43, 363
xunzu fazhanxing guojia. See rent-seeking
  developmental state

Yangtze Delta region: cadre roles, 48;
  economic structure, 103; foreign direct
  investment, 101; ICT industry, 5, 41; and
  macroeconomic reforms (1994), 188;

post-2008 local growth alliances, 369–70;
  processing of imported materials, 101;
  social insurance avoidance, 279; Suzhou
  (Kunshan) model, 4, 28, 74
Yangtze Memory Technologies, 416
Ye, Jingzhong, 48
Youku company, 9, 362
You-tien Hsing, 51
Yue Yuen Industrial Limited, 159, 327
Yue Yuen strikes (2014 and 2015), 219,
  305, 306–13

Zhang Yun, 86
Zhang Zhiru, 307, 310, 312
Zhao Ziyang, 82, 84, 87
Zhejiang Province, 103, 104, 105; and
  local state theory, 47
Zhengzhou model, 74
Zhu Rongji, 180, 331–32
Zhuhai. *See* Pearl River Delta region
ZTE company, 8–9, 43, 360–62. *See also*
  ZTE Incident
ZTE Incident (2018), 13, 19, 420, 421–22,
  434–35
Zyxel company, 359

Harvard-Yenching Institute Monograph Series
(most recent titles now in print)

83. *Courtesans, Concubines, and the Cult of Female Fidelity*, by Beverly Bossler
84. *Chinese History: A New Manual, Third Edition*, by Endymion Wilkinson
85. *A Comprehensive Manchu-English Dictionary*, by Jerry Norman
86. *Drifting among Rivers and Lakes: Southern Song Dynasty Poetry and the Problem of Literary History*, by Michael Fuller
87. *Martial Spectacles of the Ming Court*, by David M. Robinson
88. *Modern Archaics: Continuity and Innovation in the Chinese Lyric Tradition, 1900–1937*, by Shengqing Wu
89. *Cherishing Antiquity: The Cultural Construction of an Ancient Chinese Kingdom*, by Olivia Milburn
90. *The Burden of Female Talent: The Poet Li Qingzhao and Her History in China*, by Ronald Egan
91. *Public Memory in Early China*, by K. E. Brashier
92. *Women and National Trauma in Late Imperial Chinese Literature*, by Wai-yee Li
93. *The Destruction of the Medieval Chinese Aristocracy*, by Nicolas Tackett
94. *Savage Exchange: Han Imperialism, Chinese Literary Style, and the Economic Imagination*, by Tamara T. Chin
95. *Shifting Stories: History, Gossip, and Lore in Narratives from Tang Dynasty China*, by Sarah M. Allen
96. *One Who Knows Me: Friendship and Literary Culture in Mid-Tang China*, by Anna Shields
97. *Materializing Magic Power: Chinese Popular Religion in Villages and Cities*, by Wei-Ping Lin
98. *Traces of Grand Peace: Classics and State Activism in Imperial China*, by Jaeyoon Song
99. *Fiction's Family: Zhan Xi, Zhan Kai, and the Business of Women in Late-Qing China*, by Ellen Widmer
100. *Chinese History: A New Manual, Fourth Edition*, by Endymion Wilkinson
101. *After the Prosperous Age: State and Elites in Early Nineteenth-Century Suzhou*, by Seunghyun Han
102. *Celestial Masters: History and Ritual in Early Daoist Communities*, by Terry F. Kleeman
103. *Transgressive Typologies: Constructions of Gender and Power in Early Tang China*, by Rebecca Doran
104. *Li Mengyang, the North-South Divide, and Literati Learning in Ming China*, by Chang Woei Ong

105. *Bannermen Tales (Zidishu): Manchu Storytelling and Cultural Hybridity in the Qing Dynasty*, by Elena Suet-Ying Chiu

106. *Upriver Journeys: Diaspora and Empire in Southern China, 1570–1850*, by Steven B. Miles

107. *Ancestors, Kings, and the Dao*, by Constance A. Cook

108. *The Halberd at Red Cliff: Jian'an and the Three Kingdoms*, by Xiaofei Tian

109. *Speaking of Profit: Bao Shichen and Reform in Nineteenth-Century China*, by William T. Rowe

110. *Building for Oil: Daqing and the Formation of the Chinese Socialist State*, by Hou Li

111. *Reading Philosophy, Writing Poetry: Intertextual Modes of Making Meaning in Early Medieval China*, by Wendy Swartz

112. *Writing for Print: Publishing and the Making of Textual Authority in Late Imperial China*, by Suyoung Son

113. *Shen Gua's Empiricism*, by Ya Zuo

114. *Just a Song: Chinese Lyrics from the Eleventh and Early Twelfth Centuries*, by Stephen Owen

115. *Shrines to Living Men in the Ming Political Cosmos*, by Sarah Schneewind

116. *In the Wake of the Mongols: The Making of a New Social Order in North China, 1200–1600*, by Jinping Wang

117. *Opera, Society, and Politics in Modern China*, by Hsiao-t'i Li

118. *Imperiled Destinies: The Daoist Quest for Deliverance in Medieval China*, by Franciscus Verellen

119. *Ethnic Chrysalis: China's Orochen People and the Legacy of Qing Borderland Administration*, by Loretta Kim

120. *The Paradox of Being: Truth, Identity, and Images in Daoism*, by Poul Andersen

121. *Feeling the Past in Seventeenth-Century China*, by Xiaoqiao Ling

122. *The Chinese Dreamscape, 300 BCE–800 CE*, by Robert Ford Campany

123. *Structures of the Earth: Metageographies of Early Medieval China*, by D. Jonathan Felt

124. *Anecdote, Network, Gossip, Performance: Essays on the* Shishuo xinyu, by Jack W. Chen

125. *Testing the Literary: Prose and the Aesthetic in Early Modern China*, by Alexander Des Forges

126. *Du Fu Transforms: Tradition and Ethics amid Societal Collapse*, by Lucas Rambo Bender

127. *Chinese History: A New Manual (Enlarged Sixth Edition)*, Vol. 1, by Endymion Wilkinson

128. *Chinese History: A New Manual (Enlarged Sixth Edition)*, Vol. 2, by Endymion Wilkinson

129. *Wang Anshi and Song Poetic Culture*, by Xiaoshan Yang

130. *Localizing Learning: The Literati Enterprise in Wuzhou, 1100–1600*, by Peter K. Bol

131. *Making the Gods Speak: The Ritual Production of Revelation in Chinese Religious History*, by Vincent Goossaert

132. *Lineages Embedded in Temple Networks: Daoism and Local Society in Ming China*, by Richard G. Wang

133. *Rival Partners: How Taiwanese Entrepreneurs and Guangdong Officials Forged the China Development Model*, by Wu Jieh-min; translated by Stacy Mosher